The Letter to the Romans

The Earth Bible Commentary Series, 7

Series Editor
Norman C. Habel

The Letter to the Romans

Paul among the Ecologists

Sigve K. Tonstad

Sheffield Phoenix Press

2016

Published by Sheffield Phoenix Press
Department of Biblical Studies, University of Sheffield
Sheffield S3 7QB

www.sheffieldphoenix.com

A CIP catalogue record for this book
is available from the British Library

Typeset by CA Typesetting Ltd
Printed on acid-free paper by Lightning Source

ISBN-13 978-1-910928-02-8

To Serena

CONTENTS

Preface

My first steps onto the path of ecology came early. I had a rural upbringing in Norway, tending sheep and working on a small farm using methods that were manual and largely outdated. The non-motorized methods were concessions to a father who firmly believed that the past was better than the present. Our sheep were few in number, each one having a name and all groomed for the annual sheep fair in our village. We, the sheep and I, brought home many prizes. While we had meat on our table, we rarely or never slaughtered our own sheep. One of the proudest pictures of my childhood captures me, at that time ten or eleven years old, holding a prize sheep in a pose meant to show off its well-proportioned body. It did not bother me that the picture was taken for the sake of the sheep and that I was no more than supporting cast. Like my father, I was convinced that the sheep deserved to be photographed.

The year I graduated from medical school in the United States I came into possession of Wendell Berry's book *The Unsettling of America: Culture and Agriculture*. The book put into words latent sentiments that were in search of clarification and strengthening. One such sentiment has to do with the materiality of creaturely existence and the conviction that the notion of an immaterial soul that lives separately from the body has been a disruptive concept in the history of ideas. Another is the bond of interdependence between humans, non-humans and the earth. A third highlights how health and wholeness are inseparable: the body cannot be whole alone. According to Berry, physicians should be interested in the health of the land and farmers in the health of people. From an ideological and inspirational point of view, the book was a great send-off to my professional life.

My exposure to the apostle Paul began before medical school, but it took on new intensity and rose to a different level at Duke University where I had the privilege of studying Paul's faith-language under Richard B. Hays and the message of Galatians under E.P. Sanders. I came away persuaded that Paul is the apostle of the faithfulness of God even more than he is the go-to spokesperson for the importance of faith. 'Faith alone', I now believe, risks becoming a disembodied concept unless it retains its connection to God's faithfulness. The ecological implications of a theology that puts the faithfulness of God at the center are incalculable, a factor that will show in much of this commentary.

When I began attending the annual meeting of the Society of Biblical Literature, at that time still a doctoral student in New Testament studies at the University of St. Andrews, I discovered the ecological hermeneutics group, and I met Norman Habel and Peter Trudinger for the first time. I attended because of an intuitive sense of belonging and also with the intention of making a contribution to the subject. The next year I gave my first SBL presentation to this group on the groaning of creation in Romans. I am grateful for what the members of the group have taught me, for opportunities given me to present papers in that forum, and now to Norman and Peter for entrusting to me to write the Romans volume in the Earth Bible Commentary. I am equally grateful for the help and guidance I have received from David J.A. Clines and Ailsa Parkin at Sheffield Phoenix Press. The manuscript could not have come into better hands.

I have approached the task with three goals in mind. First, it has been my aim to write a genuine commentary that is respectful of Paul's concern and primary errand. I am aware that authorial intent is said to be elusive and possibly out of reach, but I have nevertheless sought to discern the purpose of the actual writer of the letter and to make this count as much as I know how. This view of the task, on the one hand showing respect for the text and on the other hand seeking results that seem relevant, will not be a loss to the ecological perspective in Romans. I cannot make Paul into an apostle who speaks of the yearnings of creation if he turns out to be a complete stranger to such concerns. Conversely, if Paul knows and feels the pain and plight of creation, there is no need to turn him into anything other than what he is. Given that the latter of these options describes him best, the ecological yield of what seeks to be an open-minded commentary on Romans will be authentic even as I expect my endeavor to be subject to criticism.

The state of scholarly opinion regarding Paul and Romans has complicated the task, but it also brings the promise of new discovery. There is no short-cut to the study of Paul at this stage in the history of interpretation. Consensus among interpreters, if it ever existed (it did), has been shattered in what is now an avalanche of competing and complementary emphases. It is fool's errand to interpret Romans without paying attention to these currents, weighing their respective merits, and then make commitments on the basis of the weight of evidence one way or another. In this array of proposals and options, at once confusing and enriching, I am indebted to J. Christiaan Beker, J. Louis Martyn and Beverly Roberts Gaventa for their perception of Paul as the bearer of an apocalyptic message; to E.P. Sanders, James Dunn and N.T. Wright for their work on what is now called the New Perspective; to Richard B. Hays, Douglas A. Campbell and N.T. Wright for mapping out a new path to Paul's faith-language; to these along with Bruce Longenecker, Stanley Stowers and others for creating awareness of rhetorical and narratival dynamics in Paul's letters; and to Richard Hays, again and in particular, for showing that we cannot read Paul in isolation from the Old Testament voices that echo in his thought and message. I have come away from my study convinced that scholarship on Romans has yet to give the Old Testament the requisite billing. If other commentaries can do this without diminishing their impact, an ecological reading cannot. These—the Old Testament voices—have not been hushed in this commentary.

Unnamed but not overlooked are the many contributors to a better understanding of the Roman Empire and the relationship between the empire and the community of believers in Jesus. Among the long list of full-length commentaries on Romans, the ones that have been most helpful to me are recent, and the commentaries of C.E.B. Cranfield, James D.G. Dunn and Robert Jewett top the list.

Second, I set out to write a commentary for readers who are already interested in Paul. Readers in this category do not need an introduction to Paul or to Romans, and some readers that fit this description may feel that I have put the bar too low for their liking. This has not been done to offend, as I will explain below. I hope to make it up to readers in this category by offering an interpretation that is theologically ambitious while restoring to Paul the ecological given-ness that traditional interpretations have ignored or taken away. I explore in depth why Paul wrote the letter to begin with, my conviction on this point centering on a need sufficiently urgent for him to make the effort—and more urgent than the reasons that are usually offered. This is directly related to the rhetorical dynamics of the letter, especially the emphatic and rude smack down of a person or point of view that happens in what is figuratively the letter's first lap (Rom. 2.1-3). Other distinctives relate to Paul's account of sin and the remedy prescribed in Romans. Romans 3 (3.10-18) is usually said to give an account of individual sins while my interpretation sees it as an account of human society collectively, particularly as societies and nations are prone to debasement of language and violence. For a reader of Romans in the twenty-first century this has more than historical interest. In Romans 7, Paul is usually thought to be excruciatingly introspective. I am not denying introspection in this chapter, but what if scholars have now cut the Gordian knot not by wringing a few extra drops from an introspective Paul but by turning the gaze outward, to the biblical narrative, and particularly to the story of Eve in Genesis? Such an account of sin will have far-reaching consequences for how Paul conceives the remedy. If sin is misrepresentation of the divine command and not only violation (Rom. 7.7-12)—and if the sinner is a person deceived and not only a violator—God's remedial action will be quite different from what traditional conceptions make it out to be.

My reading has uncovered more than three ecological horizons in Romans, but I will mention just three in this foreword. First, it shall be difficult to deny that Paul speaks of non-human creation in a way that is ethically and ecologically meaningful even by criteria that are current in our time (Rom. 8.19-22). What is more, the widescreen reading I have pursued will show that Paul's theology is profoundly and genuinely an eco-theology, and his concern for non-human creation is innocent of the charge that we are exploiting the letter for purposes he never intended. Second, Paul's appeal to the Romans to live by—and to live out—'the mercies of God' (Rom. 12.1) cannot in the twenty-first century be cut off from the cry for mercy that is rising at increasing decibel from non-human creatures and the earth. Third, Paul's adjudication between 'the weak' and 'the strong', in Romans represented as differences of opinion and practice with regard to food and observance of days, invites an ecological perspective that may—retroactively—lead to a more nuanced understanding of the problem in the Roman house churches.

Third—now back to the list of items guiding my work—this commentary goes in search of readers who are interested in ecology but have little or no prior knowledge of Paul. For the benefit of readers in this category, I offer background that Paul connoisseurs may find redundant but that will be essential to the novice. Chapter 1 provides an introduction to Paul in light of the massive contemporary interest in him. Chapter 2 traces the history of Romans through the work of its most influential readers. The historical perspective frames the task for an ecologically aware reading of Romans, and it also provides a window to Western intellectual history within which Romans has been more than a marginal player. For the benefit of readers who are not accustomed to reading a text as layered as Romans, I have in each chapter provided boxes to help clarify key concepts and issues.

Perhaps I should include a fourth reason for this project, a reason subliminal and unarticulated until now. This refers to people who are interested neither in Paul nor in ecology. At the institution where I teach, we have all three categories of students, some who have significant prior knowledge of Paul but not of ecology, some who know ecology but not Paul, and many who are in the 'neither' category. With regard to both topics at hand, Paul and ecology, my students are largely non-specialists, training to become physicians, dentists, pharmacists, psychologists, nurses, or practitioners of some other health profession, interspersed with a smattering of students who specialize in physical or earth sciences. Given my background in medicine and New Testament interpretation—and now my teaching portfolio—I see the medical students the most. Much of the material in this book has been developed in a teaching context, and I am happy to report that I have seen Romans and ecology made meaningful to students in all three categories, including students who initially draw a blank with regard to Paul or ecology. It is my hope that this book will resonate with readers who are mindful of Paul, readers who are concerned about ecology, and readers not yet interested in any of them.

My aspirations for the commentary should be viewed in light of what I believe to be common ground between the message of Romans and ecology. What common ground can there be, however? What common ground can there be between a very old letter that has God as its subject and an ecosystem hurtling at high speed closer and closer to the breaking point? The common ground, I suggest, and the common *word*—is *compassion*. Compassion is an important term among contemporary ecologists and a deeply held sentiment—meaning compassion for non-human creation and for relationships seen and unseen that are threatening to unravel. But compassion is also an important word in the vocabulary of Romans. A reader who comes away from this letter thinking that he or she has read a message of compassion will not have missed the most important theological theme by much, and the moral vision of Romans is well brought together under the heading 'compassion in action'. Ecologists who cry out for compassion will in Romans encounter a message of compassion for human beings, non-human creatures, and the earth. Indeed, the way Romans defines and empowers compassion will not easily be surpassed by anything found on the subject otherwise. Moreover—and easily overlooked—the ecological yearning for compassion may spot in Romans emphases that traditional readings have failed to see. If this turns out to be the case, ecology is not coming empty-handed to the table. Conversely, theology is poised to return to ecology a message of resilient hope no matter the pressure brought to bear on it. Romans and ecology are in it together, surprising though it may seem, united under the theme of compassion.

This project has come to fruition in large part due to encouragement and support from my colleagues at Loma Linda University, with special thanks to Isabel Leon, David Larson, Ivan Blazen and the late Roy Branson at the School of Religion, to Henry Lamberton, Stephen Dunbar and William Hayes at the School of Medicine, to Farzaneh Alemozaffar at the Interlibrary Loan service and to Bud Racine for creating a much appreciated publishing fund. I am grateful for the input I have received from Douglas A. Campbell at Duke University and Steven Thompson at Avondale College. My wife, Serena, is a physician and a leading practitioner, researcher, and educator in the field of preventive medicine, a field where ecological concerns increasingly loom large. She has been an untiring supporter, and she is also the embodiment of life commitments that run *from* faithfulness *for* faithfulness, as we shall hear Paul say in what many regard as the programmatic text in Romans (Rom. 1.16-17). Faithful as person, professional, explorer, spouse, mother, homemaker, host and friend, I dedicate this book to her.

ABBREVIATIONS

AB	Anchor Bible
ABR	*Australian Biblical Review*
ASE	*Annali di storia dell'esegesi*
AUSS	*Andrews University Seminary Studies*
BBR	*Bulletin for Biblical Research*
Bib Int	*Biblical Interpretation*
BNTC	Black New Testament Commentaries
BSac	*Bibliotheca Sacra*
BTB	*Biblical Theology Bulletin*
BZNW	Beihefte zur Zeitschrift für die neutestamentliche Wissenschaft
CBNTS	Coniectanea Biblica New Testament Series
CC	Continental Commentary Series
Cornell L. Rev.	*Cornell Law Review*
CTJ	*Calvin Theological Journal*
DTT	*Dansk Teologisk Tidsskrift*
EKKNT	Evangelisch-katholischer Kommentar zum Neuen Testament
EQ	*Evangelical Quarterly*
EvTh	*Evangelische Theologie*
ExpTim	*Expository Times*
FAO	Food and Agriculture Organization of the United Nations
FC	Fathers of the Church
FRLANT	Forschungen zur Religion und Literatur des Alten und Neuen Testaments
GNS	Good News Studies
HBT	*Horizons in Biblical Theology*
HTR	*Harvard Theological Review*
ICC	International Critical Commentary
IDF	International Diabetes Federation
IJST	*International Journal of Systematic Theology*
Int	*Interpretation*
JAMA	*Journal of the American Medical Association*
JbAC	*Jahrbuch für Antike und Christentum*
JBL	*Journal of Biblical Literature*
JPS	*Jewish Publication Society*
JSNT	*Journal for the Study of the New Testament*
JSNTSup	*Journal for the Study of the New Testament*, Supplement Series
JSOT	*Journal for the Study of the Old Testament*
JTI	*Journal of Theological Interpretation*
JTS	*Journal of Theological Studies*
KD	*Kerygma und Dogma*
KEK	Kritisch-exegetischer Kommentar über das Neue Testament
LNTS	Library of New Testament Studies
LPT	Library of Protestant Thought

MNTC	Moffatt New Testament Commentary
NICNT	New International Commentary on the New Testament
NICOT	New International Commentary on the Old Testament
NovT	*Novum Testamentum*
NovT Sup	Supplement to Novum Testamentum
NTAbh	Neutestamentliche Abhandlungen
NTL	New Testament Library
NTS	*New Testament Studies*
OBT	Overtures to Biblical Theology
OTG	Old Testament Guides
PCP	Perspectives in Continental Philosophy
PP	Philosophy and Politics
PTR	*Pacific Theological Review*
RevExp	*Review and Expositor*
RSR	*Recherches de Science Religieuse*
SBLDS	Society of Biblical Literature Dissertation Series
SBLTT	Society of Biblical Literature Texts and Translations
SBT	Studies in Biblical Theology
SE	*Studia Evangelica*
SJOT	*Scandinavian Journal of the Old Testament*
SJT	*Scottish Journal of Theology*
SNTSMS	Society of New Testament Studies Monograph Series
SP	Sacra Pagina
SPCK	Society for Promoting Christian Knowledge
SR	*Studies in Religion*
SVTQ	*St. Vladimir's Theological Quarterly*
TDNT	*Theological Dictionary of the New Testament*
TrinJ	*Trinity Journal*
TSAJ	Texts and Studies in Ancient Judaism
VT	*Vetus Testamentum*
UBS	*United Bible Societies*
WBC	Word Biblical Commentary
WCC	World Council of Churches
Wesleyan Theol J	*Wesleyan Theological Journal*
WTJ	*Westminster Theological Journal*
WUNT	Wissenschaftliche Untersuchungen zum Neuen Testament
WW	*Word & World*
ZAW	*Zeitschrift für die alttestamentliche Wissenschaft*
ZDT*Sup*	Supplement to Zeitschrift für Dialektische Theologie

Chapter 1

Paul among the Ecologists

We can best take the measure of the apostle Paul by starting a thousand years before his time, with King Saul in the Old Testament. From the way the story is told, people living at the time of Israel's first king had the ability to spot an anomaly when they saw one. We read in 1 Samuel that 'when all who knew Saul before saw how he prophesied with the prophets, the people said to one another, "What has come over the son of Kish? Is Saul also among the prophets?"' (1 Sam. 10.10-11).

The sight of Saul among the prophets was so odd that it became a proverb in Israel, a peculiarity akin to 'oxymoron' in English.[1] Those who knew Saul had not found much in his prior disposition to make them expect to find him among the prophets. Later, now at the point when the obsessed king was chasing David in order to kill him, the spirit of God came upon the king a second time. The narrator says that Saul again 'fell into a prophetic frenzy', that '[h]e too stripped off his clothes, and...lay naked all that day and all that night. Therefore it is said, "Is Saul also among the prophets?"' (1 Sam. 19.23-24).

There it is again, as the unlikeliest of associations, now driven home as a retrospective comment concerning the king's behavior in the public domain. Frenzy, undressing, and lying naked 'all that day and all that night' are not behaviors befitting a king even though the narrator implies that prophets behaved that way. According to the observant chronicler, Saul among the prophets is a misfit and an oddball: an oxymoron.

And now to the other Saul in the Bible, better known as the apostle Paul. Is that Saul among the ecologists? If the answer is yes, as my reply will be, is he among the ecologists in a cameo role and only as an oddball (Rom. 8.19-22)?

Before we opt for the easy answer, a general accounting is necessary. Like his Old Testament forebear, Paul belonged to the tribe of Benjamin (Rom. 11.1; Phil. 3.5). He mentions it twice in his letters as a fact about

1. At www.dictionary.search.yahoo.com 'oxymoron' is defined as 'a rhetorical figure in which incongruous or contradictory terms are combined'. This fits our subject well.

which he appears to take pride. Either the stigma of being named after Israel's first king had worn off or there was no stigma to begin with. If the proverb about King Saul recounts incidents for which he would be best remembered, however, we have one telling linkage to Paul. This link hangs on the preposition *among*, this word now a widely used term by scholars who try to get a handle on the apostle. Looking at him through a vast array of lenses, we find him *among*…, the sentence paused and hanging in the air before taking it to completion. Time and again we find Paul *among* someone or something, whether people, cultures, conflicts, and concerns. In his reported appearances *among*, Paul seems to have struck a credible figure across a wide spectrum. On that score he beats his Old Testament ancestor by a wide margin, the hallmark of King Saul precisely that he appeared *among* a certain group but wasn't one of them (1 Sam. 10.10-11; 19.23-24. Counting only books written over the last half century, the *among-ness* of the apostle Paul is one of the most striking findings.

Paul among

Paul was *among Jews and Gentiles*, Krister Stendahl said in a pivotal lecture in 1963.[2] He advised students to seek out the authentic Paul in the intersection between Jews and *Gentiles* and not in the accretions that have been deposited on his legacy through the centuries. This legacy has been dominated by the tendency to locate Paul *among Jews and Christians* or even to see him as the arbiter among various Christian persuasions. Before history invented the Paul of Protestant orthodoxy, however, there was a real human being whose chief objective was to raise up communities of believers in Jesus across the Roman world. This Paul was among Jews and Gentiles as a Jewish believer in Jesus and not as a former Jew crusading against Jewish legalism. In an abridged version of this story, it is a point of importance that Paul was not Martin Luther or the founding father of 'the introspective conscience of the West'.[3]

2. Krister Stendahl, *Paul among Jews and Gentiles, and Other Essays* (Philadelphia: Fortress Press, 1976). Other studies of Paul among the *Jews* or highlighting the Jewishness of Paul are Brad H. Young, *Paul the Jewish Theologian: A Pharisee among Christians, Jews, and Gentiles* (Peabody, MA: Hendrickson, 1997); Pamela Eisenbaum, *Paul Was Not a Christian: The Original Message of a Misunderstood Apostle* (New York: HarperOne, 2009); Wenxi Zhang, *Paul Among Jews: A Study of the Meaning and Significance of Paul's Inaugural Speech in the Synagogue of Antioch* (Eugene, OR: Wipf & Stock, 2011).

3. Krister Stendahl, 'The Apostle Paul and the Introspective Conscience of the West', *HTR* 56 (1963), pp. 199-215.

In the broadest conception, Sarah Ruden finds Paul *among the people*.[4] If a contrast is intended in this title, it might be that Paul was among the *people* and not primarily among theologians, scholars, or feuding religionists. *People* is here a telling term, Paul specifying to some of his fellow believers that 'not many of you were wise by human standards, not many were powerful, not many were of noble birth' (1 Cor. 1.26). Locating Paul mostly among lowly people represents him more precisely than Paul among Jews and Gentiles. This means that the man who was once among the people must be returned to the people in order to be himself. The Scripture for this Paul could be his confession in 1 Corinthians.

Paul *among* in recent scholarship

- Jews and Gentiles
- Jews, Greeks, and Romans
- people
- cultures
- philosophers
- prophets
- mystics
- friends and enemies
- postliberals

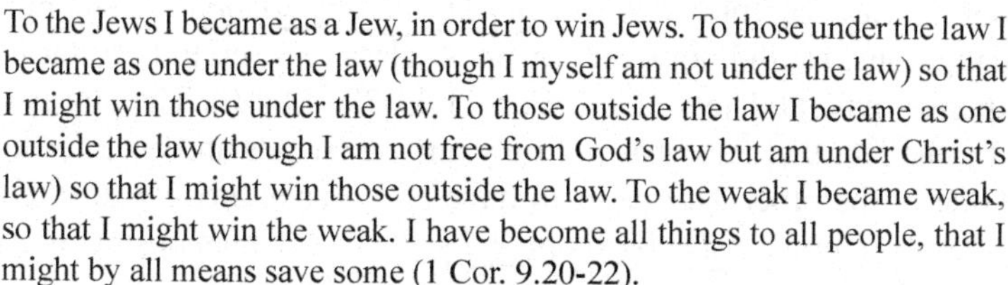

> To the Jews I became as a Jew, in order to win Jews. To those under the law I became as one under the law (though I myself am not under the law) so that I might win those under the law. To those outside the law I became as one outside the law (though I am not free from God's law but am under Christ's law) so that I might win those outside the law. To the weak I became weak, so that I might win the weak. I have become all things to all people, that I might by all means save some (1 Cor. 9.20-22).

This self-description posts a warning that Paul will not be speaking from the same notes regardless of his audience. His message is adapted to the situation, and his influence is a reflection of his adaptability. Becoming 'all things to all people' is not a task for the rigid or the fainthearted. To Paul, there seems not to have been an exclusionary zone beyond which he would not go. This aspiration carries risks. If successful, however, it also brings the prospect of influence. Readers today must strive to restore to Paul the prestige of being a face we are seeing all the time without knowing it. 'No other intellect contributed as much to making us who we are', says Ruden.[5] This Paul, moreover, is also *among the cultures*.[6] We meet him as a master anthropologist with a keen ability to discern the common humanity beneath the plethora of difference in the world (Rom. 2.11; 3.29), and as a man illuminated by an apocalyptic reordering of identities, divisions, and distinc-

4. Sarah Ruden, *Paul among the People: The Apostle Reinterpreted and Reimagined in His Own Time* (New York: Pantheon Books, 2010).

5. Ruden, *Paul among the People*, p. xix.

6. William S. Campbell, *Paul's Gospel in an Intercultural Context: Jew and Gentile in the Letter to the Romans* (Frankfurt: Peter Lang, 1991); Mark Harding and Alanna Nobs (eds.), *All Things to All Cultures: Paul among Jews, Greeks, and Romans* (Grand Rapids: Eerdmans, 2013).

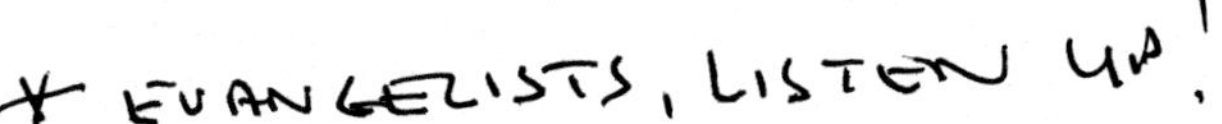

tions (Gal. 3.28; 2 Cor. 5.16).[7] This Paul, the apocalyptic anthropologist, will at the most radical point of this mission assert that '[t]here is no longer Jew or Greek, there is no longer slave or free, there is no longer male and female; for all of you are one in Christ Jesus' (Gal. 3.28; cf. Col. 3.11). A person who sees such a radical reordering in a world divided along lines of class, ethnicity, and religion 'was a go-between', says Kathy Ehrensberger.[8]

In Athens, we find Paul *among the philosophers*. It really happened, right in the Athenian Agora and hallowed cradle of ancient philosophy (Acts 17.19-31). Paul stood his ground well in the original setting, and he has struck a credible figure among philosophers right up to the 21st century.[9] Thinkers who do not believe in Paul's God do not disparage him or his writings.[10] The philosophical element in his story is not negated by statements in the letters quite disparaging of philosophy (1 Cor. 1.20; Col. 2.8). Paul is recognized as a philosopher more than the equal of his Jewish contemporary Philo without laying claim to being one.[11]

Another view captures Paul *among friends and enemies*.[12] His ministry was dangerous. He did not travel business class or sleep in five star hotels, all expenses paid (1 Thess. 2.9; 2 Cor. 11.23-39; 4.8-10). The plot is thickened by the fact that Paul was not only among friends and enemies known to be one or the other. He seems to have had special anxiety for the times when he was among '*false* brothers and sisters', enemies posing as friends (2 Cor. 11.26).

7. Daniel Boyarin (*A Radical Jew: Paul and the Politics of Identity* [Berkeley: University of California Press, 1994], p. 7) claims that 'Paul was motivated by a Hellenistic desire for the One, which among other things produced an ideal of a universal human essence'. Paul's perception of human oneness, however, should be attributed to theology and apocalyptic and not, as Boyarin does, to Hellenism. A similar criticism applies to Alain Badiou's view of Pauline universalism, cf. *Saint Paul: The Foundation of Universalism* (trans. Ray Brassier; Stanford, CA: Stanford University Press, 2003).

8. Kathy Ehrensberger, *Paul at the Crossroads of Cultures: Theologizing in the Space-Between* (New York: Bloomsbury, 2013), p. 1.

9. Linda Martin Alcoff and John D. Caputo (eds.), *St. Paul among the Philosophers* (Bloomington: Indiana University Press, 2009); David Odell-Scott (ed.), *Reading Romans with Contemporary Philosophers and Theologians* (New York: T. & T. Clark, 2007).

10. Jacob Taubes, *The Political Theology of Paul* (trans. Dana Hollander; Stanford, CA: Stanford University Press, 2004); Giorgio Agamben, *The Time That Remains: A Commentary on the Letter to the Romans* (trans. Patricia Dailey; Stanford, CA: Stanford University Press, 2005).

11. Bruce Winter, *Philo and Paul among the Sophists: Alexandrian and Corinthian Responses to a Julio-Claudian Movement* (Grand Rapids: Eerdmans, 2nd edn, 2002).

12. William E. Richardson, *Paul Among Friends & Enemies* (Boise, ID: Pacific Press, 1992).

'*Is Paul also among the Prophets*?'[13] *Also* is the key word in this book title, aligning the apostle Paul with King Saul on the strength of the same connotation of *also* with which this chapter began. King Saul and the apostle Paul have in common the unexpected association of being *among the prophets*, neither one thought to be a natural for the part. On closer look, this turns out to be much less a problem for the apostle than for the king. In 2 Corinthians, Paul provides autobiographical snippets that add up to a picture not unlike that of the prophets in the Old Testament. He was not only a commentator and exegete of ancient texts but also a first century embodiment of the unmediated access to God that marked the lives of the prophets.[14] Such a person can be said to be *among the mystics*, too, experiencing visions and revelations (2 Cor. 12.1). The mystic element was Christ-mysticism, but it was mysticism no less and in Albert Schweitzer's view the key to Paul's life and theology.[15] Schweitzer was on this point not making something out of nothing.

> I know a person in Christ who fourteen years ago was caught up to the third heaven— whether in the body or out of the body I do not know; God knows. And I know that such a person—whether in the body or out of the body I do not know; God knows—was caught up into Paradise and heard things that are not to be told, that no mortal is permitted to repeat (2 Cor. 12.2-4).

If Paul was among the prophets by the criterion of having encounters with God similar to the prophets in the Old Testament, he was also among the prophets in an indirect sense. In an exquisite study, Richard B. Hays highlights the role of Scripture in Paul's letters.[16] Romans, a letter the occasion for which is not altogether clear, can be seen as a conversation between Paul and the Old Testament. The 'conversation' implies an odd kind of contemporaneity with the original source and vocational common ground, Paul conversing with the prophets as one of them. 'Once the conversation begins, the addressees recede curiously into the background, and Paul finds himself engaged with an older and more compelling partner', says Hays.[17] This insight has far-reaching implications for the way we read Paul's letters

13. Jeffrey W. Aernie, *Is Paul also among the Prophets? An Examination of the Relationship between Paul and the Old Testament Prophetic Tradition in 2 Corinthians* (LNTS, 467; New York: T. & T. Clark, 2014).

14. Agamben (*The Time That Remains*, pp. 60-61) makes a distinction between 'prophet' and 'apostle' by the criterion of unmediated access, but this distinction is hard to sustain in the case of Paul.

15. Albert Schweitzer, *The Mysticism of Paul the Apostle* (trans. William Montgomery; Baltimore: Johns Hopkins University Press, 1998; orig. London: A. & C. Black, 1931).

16. Richard B. Hays, *Echoes of Scripture in the Letters of Paul* (New Haven: Yale University Press, 1989).

17. Hays, *Echoes of Scripture*, p. 35.

today, seeing him not only in conversation with readers and opponents but also with the Old Testament.

Time should be running out on Paul two thousand years after he criss-crossed the Roman world, but it isn't, not when a scholar begins the twenty-first century by placing Paul *among the postliberals*.[18] This Paul has staying power, having survived the ferocious critical winds that swept through New Testament scholarly circles for more than a century, beginning with F.C. Baur (1792–1860). The horizon for the surviving, post-liberal Paul is contemporary; it stretches into the future as far as the eye can see, and it comes with the curious twist of claiming to be a homecoming for and to the Paul we find in the New Testament.[19]

To get a handle on this Paul it is necessary to roll back obstacles standing in the way. The process might wisely begin by taking apart the Protestant stereotype that Judaism is an incorrigibly legalistic religion, a view now called the *New Perspective on Paul*.[20] According to this perspective, it is incorrect to say that members of the covenant (the Jews) believed that they had to earn God's favor before they could consider themselves acceptable to God.[21] Instead of working to earn God's favor, says James Dunn, the Jews '*started* from that position'.[22] Divine grace was not a novelty to Paul before his experience on the road to Damascus. What, then, was the big deal? If Paul and his Judaizing opponents had in common that a person cannot earn his or her salvation, why did Paul insist over and over—according to the traditional translation of key statements in Galatians and Romans—that 'a person is justified *not by the works of the law* but through faith in Jesus Christ' (Gal. 2.16) or that 'a person is justified by faith *apart from works prescribed by the law*' (Rom. 3.28)?[23] The material issue in Galatia, at least, centered on *works of the law* as communal barriers (Gal.

> **'New Perspective' on Paul**
> - 'Judaism' a religion of grace
> - 'Participation' more important than 'justification'
> - Controversy over boundary markers such as circumcision

18. Douglas Harink, *Paul among the Postliberals: Pauline Theology Beyond Christendom and Modernity* (Grand Rapids: Brazos Press, 2002).

19. Harink, *Paul among the Postliberals*, pp. 13-24.

20. E.P. Sanders, *Paul and Palestinian Judaism: A Comparison of Patterns of Religion* (Minneapolis: Fortress Press, 1979); cf. James Dunn, *The New Perspective on Paul* (Grand Rapids: Eerdmans, rev. edn, 2005).

21. For examples, see Dunn, *The New Perspective*, pp. 1-41.

22. Dunn, *The New Perspective*, p. 6.

23. An alternative translation, now increasingly accepted, will say that 'a person is set right not by works of law but by the faithfulness of Jesus Christ' (Gal. 2.16, translation mine).

2.11.14)—'the refusal of one group of Christians fully to accept another group of Christians!' says Dunn.[24]

The idea that communal barriers and not salvation by works were the issue in some of Paul's missionary churches has not satisfied everyone.[25] At the very least, however, the New Perspective provides an alternative to the *Judaism-as-legalism* typecast. E.P Sanders, who in one context says that Paul's only criticism of Judaism is that '*it is not Christianity*',[26] strikes a more sober note when he argues that Paul's ire focused on preferential treatment of the Jews. Preferential treatment of one group over another implies that God is arbitrary. When Paul criticizes Judaism, therefore, 'he does so in a sweeping manner, and the criticism has two focuses: the lack of faith in Christ and the lack of equality for the Gentiles'.[27]

Inclusion and equal treatment are not trivial matters if the tradition held to inequality and exclusion, distorted the terms for inclusion, or misrepresented God by implying that equality for the Gentiles was out of the question by divine decree. This emphasis may be a *New* Perspective in our time, but it is not new to the letters of Paul. 'Or is God the God of Jews only? Is he not the God of Gentiles also?' Paul asks with the force of self-evidence in Romans (Rom. 3.29). To people previously seen as outsiders he writes that 'if you belong to Christ, then you are Abraham's offspring, heirs according to the promise' (Gal. 3.29; cf. Rom. 9.9). In Ephesians, the movement from exclusion to inclusion is even more striking. 'But now in Christ Jesus you who once were far off have been brought near by the blood of Christ. For he is our peace; in his flesh he has made both groups into one and has broken down the dividing wall' (Eph. 2.13-14). No one can deny that entrenched barriers are here coming down.

Yet another new perspective holds that Paul's concept of salvation is more at home in participatory than in legal categories. Paul is above all a man *in Christ*. This view was argued forcefully by Albert Schweitzer, who held that the doctrine of righteousness by faith is a polemical doctrine generated by the conflict between Paul and his Judaizing opponents. Polemics gave birth to the doctrine—it is not the core of Paul's concern. Schweitzer wrote memorably that '[t]he doctrine of righteousness by faith is…a subsidiary crater, which has formed within the rim of the main crater—the mystical doctrine

24. Dunn, *The New Perspective*, p. 32.

25. For a defense of the 'old' perspective on Paul, see Stephen Westerholm, *Perspectives Old and New on Paul: The 'Lutheran' Paul and His Critics* (Grand Rapids: Eerdmans, 2004); cf. also Francis Watson, *Paul and the Hermeneutics of Faith* (London: T. & T. Clark, 2004).

26. Sanders, *Paul and Palestinian Judaism*, p. 552.

27. E.P. Sanders, *Paul, the Law and the Jewish People* (Minneapolis: Fortress Press, 1983), p. 155.

of redemption through being-in-Christ'.[28] This claim means that 'justification by faith' is not the most representative term for Paul's message. Proponents of *inclusion* and *participation* have provided a valuable service. There is new awareness that the concerns in Paul's letters vary—it is not all about legalism. *Participation* has as much merit as the traditional emphasis on *justification.*

In the context of ecological concerns, participation shines a more caring light on non-human beings and the earth than a legal view of salvation. The latter concerns itself almost exclusively with human beings and the afterlife. Precisely in Romans, however, and precisely in the passage that is acknowledged to have undisputed relevance to an ecological hermeneutic (Rom. 8.18-23), Paul speaks in participatory terms. God is at work in the world through the Spirit, and the Spirit enables hope (8.16). Participation in hope extends to non-human creation. Indeed, non-human creation and human beings are at the present time groaning together, hoping together, and *together* waiting for deliverance (8.22, 23).

Revelation

To these two emphases, *participation* and *justification*, we must add a third horizon. The key word for this item is *revelation* (*apokalypsis*). This word is broadly relevant to any reading of Romans, and it is relevant to ecology because it looms large in what many readers take to be the most ecological passage in the letter.

> I consider that the sufferings of this present time are not worth comparing with the glory about to be *revealed* to us (*apokalypthēnai eis hēmas*). For the creation waits with eager longing for the *revealing* of the children of God (*tēn apokalypsin tōn huiōn tou theou*) (Rom. 8.18-19).

Twice in these two verses Paul invokes the notion of *apokalypsis*, either as a verb or as a noun. Something or someone is about to be *revealed* (8.18-19). The *apokalypsis* in view denotes curtains pulled aside so as to make a hidden reality visible. As in Galatians, the apocalyptic reality must also be understood in terms of a *movement* from beyond, described by J. Louis Martyn as an *invasion*.[29] The same idea applies to Paul's terminology in Romans. Paul describes a movement from concealment to disclosure, to be sure, but he also has in mind that a battle is being fought. Powerful forces

> **Theme of Romans**
> - Justification (usual view)
> - Participation (Schweitzer, Sanders)
> - Revelation (overlooked theme)

28. Schweitzer, *The Mysticism of Paul the Apostle*, pp. 224-25.

29. J. Louis Martyn, 'The Apocalyptic Gospel in Galatians', *Int* 54 (2000), p. 254. His comment relates to Gal. 3.23-25.

are ranged against God's intervention, intent on preventing it from succeeding either as revelation *to* human beings or as the revelation *of* human beings in a sense that gives hope to non-human creation. It is not without risk to call this an *invasive* movement, but it is certainly *revelatory* (Rom. 8.18-19).

Given that God is the primary subject of Paul's apocalyptic message, we cannot take lightly that revelation *of God* is his greatest concern.

> Paul, a servant of Jesus Christ, called to be an apostle, set apart for *the gospel of God* (*eis euangelion theou*) (1.1).
>
> For I tell you that Christ has become a servant of the circumcised on behalf of *the truth of God* (*hyper alētheias theou*) in order that he might confirm the promises given to the patriarchs (15.8).
>
> Because of the grace given me by God to be a minister of Christ Jesus to the Gentiles in the priestly service of *the gospel of God* (*to euangelion tou theou*) (15.15-16).

These texts signify that God is the *source* of the good news on behalf of which Paul is God's hand-picked apostle,[30] but God is equally the *subject*. 'The gospel of God' (1.1; 15.16) is also 'the truth of God' (15.8), the phrases lining up to declare that Paul is an apostle bearing 'the good news about God' and telling 'the truth about God'.[31] Romans is proof that doubts in regard to God's righteousness (1.16-17; 3.21), God's impartiality (2.11), God's faithfulness (3.3), and God's fairness (9.1-11.36) have been addressed. 'Good news' is not primarily the counterpoint to absence of news, whether in a biblical or modernist conception. The 'good news' is also a God-ordained corrective to entrenched misconceptions. In Romans, 'the truth about God' confronts its opposite, 'lies about God', sometimes explicitly. Human beings 'exchanged the truth about God (*tēn alētheian tou theou*) for the lie (*en tō pseudei*)', Romans says in one passage (1.25, translation mine). The need for revelation is lifted even higher on the scale of priorities when we come face to face with the 'Eve story' that Paul reviews in Romans 7 in his depiction of human plight (Rom. 7.7-12).[32] The gospel corrects misperception and falsehood alike, an *apocalypse* that justifies the ringing conclusion in Romans.

> Now to God who is able to strengthen you according to my gospel (*kata to euangelion mou*) and the proclamation of Jesus Christ, according to the

30. Robert Jewett (*Romans: A Commentary on the Book of Romans* [Hermeneia; Minneapolis: Fortress Press, 2006], p. 102) and James Dunn (*Romans 1–8* [WBC; Dallas: Word, 2002], p. 10) emphasize God as *source*.

31. N.T. Wright, *Paul and the Faithfulness of God* (2 vols.; London: SPCK, 2013), pp. 410-11, 619-773.

32. The 'Eve story' will be explored at length in Chapter 10.

> revelation of the mystery (*kata apokalypsin mysteriou*) that was kept secret for long ages but is now disclosed (*fanerōthentos*), and through the prophetic writings is made known (*gnōristhentos*) to all the Gentiles, according to the command of the eternal God, to bring about obedience of faith (Rom. 16.25-26).

Revelation caps the message of Romans, as this passage shows (16.25-26), the apocalyptic errand reinforced by the verbs *disclose* and *make known*. God is the source and the subject of the revelation, and the result is 'obedience of faith' (to be explored later). Further confirmation of the revelatory intent is found precisely in the texts that are usually mined in support of the traditional message of justification by faith. Paul refers to 'the righteousness of God' in a series of exhibits that all speak of revelation, disclosure, and demonstration.

> the righteousness of God *is revealed* (*apokalyptetai*) (1.17).
>
> the righteousness of God *has been disclosed* (*pefanerōtai*) (3.21).
>
> to show his righteousness (*eis endeiksin dikaiosynē autou*) (3.25)[33]

These texts prove that we must be mindful of the apocalyptic texture of Paul's outlook and take seriously J. Christiaan Beker's claim that '[t]he apocalyptic world view is the fundamental carrier of Paul's thought'.[34] The apocalyptic perception of reality includes angels (Rom. 8.38; 1 Cor. 4.9), cosmic conflict (Rom. 8.38; Eph. 6.12), resurrection (Rom. 1.4; 2 Cor. 13.4), the notion that time is contracting (1 Cor. 7.29-31; 15.23-26), and the coming of the Son of Man at the end of the age (1 Thess. 4.16-17; 1 Cor. 15.51-55). This world view is not 'a husk or discardable frame; …it belongs to the inalienable core of the gospel', Beker notes.[35]

But what is the main concern? What do we see when we reach the top of the mountain in Paul's apocalyptic gospel?[36] In Galatians and Romans, this the sight that greets us.

33. The entry for *endeiksis* in the *UBS Greek Dictionary* has 'to demonstrate, to show'; 'the means by which one knows that something is a fact'; 'proof, evidence, verification, indication'.

34. J. Christiaan Beker, *Paul the Apostle: The Triumph of God in Life and Thought* (Philadelphia: Fortress Press, 1980), p. 181. J. Louis Martyn ('Apocalyptic Antinomies in Paul's Letter to the Galatians', *NTS* 31 [1985], pp. 410-24) finds the apocalyptic texture of Paul's message no less marked in Galatians than in other letters. See also Klaus Koch, *The Rediscovery of Apocalyptic* (trans. Margaret Kohl; London: SCM Press, 1972); John J. Collins, *The Apocalyptic Imagination* (Grand Rapids: Eerdmans, 2nd edn, 1998).

35. Beker, *Paul the Apostle*, p. 171.

36. Sigve K. Tonstad, 'The Revisionary Potential of "Abba, Father" in the Letters of Paul', *AUSS* 45 (2007), p. 12.

> For you did not receive a spirit of slavery to fall back into fear, but you received a spirit of adoption in whom we cry out, 'Abba! Father!' (Rom. 8.15, translation mine; cf. Gal. 4.6).

With this image Paul calls to mind a scene drawn from the baptismal experience of new believers, familiar in Rome and in Asia Minor alike (Gal. 4.6; Rom. 8.15). The scene captures the transition from slavery to adoption, from distance to intimacy, from subjugation to deliverance, and from fear to trust. Most importantly, the structure rests on a transforming *theological* insight. The confidence that echoes in the cry 'Abba! Father!' brings to mind the trust of Isaac in the Old Testament (Gen. 22.7-8) and the trust of Jesus in his hour of crisis (Mk 14.36). This is a relational, participatory conception and not a technical or formulaic approach to salvation. Paul's God is not the tyrant before whom the human response must be the terror of the slave or an impersonal power before which the human response must be fear in the face of a capricious reality. The fear that is common to both, in the former the fear of an angry god and in the latter the fear of a god that is impersonal or absent, has vanished. *Transformation* at the level of experience is anchored in *revelation*.[37] This revelation is of one piece with the vision God gave to Abraham on the mountain in Genesis at the conclusion of his journey of faith in what is easily the most excruciating story in the Old Testament (Gen. 22.1-18). In the wake of the revelation, says the narrator, 'Abraham named that site Yahweh-yireh, hence the present saying, "On Yahweh's mountain there is a vision"'.[38]

There is a vision in Paul's message, too. He and the believers to whom he writes claim to have seen the divine reality. *Revelation* throws the door open to *participation*, and participation is whole cloth with revelation in the cry, 'Abba! Father!' (Rom. 8.15; Gal. 4.6). Believers signify by this exclamation that they stand in the same relation to God as Jesus, and they have adopted Jesus' view of the Father. The Spirit-enabled cry is apocalyptic to the core (Rom. 8.15-16). Heard as a pent-up exclamation, revelation also means *proclamation* to the world.

Does the transformation in the divine-human relationship bring any benefit to non-human creation? In Romans, we move without pause from revelation, participation, and exclamation in the human realm (8.15-17) to revelation, participation, and exclamation on the part of non-human creation

37. Tonstad, 'Abba! Father!', pp. 5-8; Douglas J. Moo, *The Epistle to the Romans* (NICNT; Grand Rapids: Eerdmans, 1996), p. 502.

38. Ephraim A. Speiser, *Genesis* (AB; Garden City, NJ: Doubleday, 1964), p. 162; see also Claus Westermann, *Genesis 12–36* (trans. John J. Scullion; Minneapolis: Augsburg, 1985), p. 353; Nahum Sarna, *The JPS Torah Commentary on Genesis* (Philadelphia: The Jewish Publication Society, 1989), pp. 153-54.

(8.18-23). The Spirit that mediates insight in the human realm extends its sphere of operation to non-human reality (8.15-27). The benefit to non-human creation is a primary matter and not an accidental trickle down benefit. Humans, shown to be neither orphans nor slaves (8.15), are giving expression to a hope and an experience that will be shared in the non-human realm (8.21).

The Faithfulness of Jesus Christ

God's righteousness has been revealed in the gospel, says Paul (1.17). This verse will be my last entry in an attempt to establish new ground rules for a reading of Romans that is valid in general terms but also sets the stage for an eco-sensitive interpretation of the letter. For how has God's 'righteousness' been revealed? Paul answers that the righteousness of God has been revealed '*by the faithfulness of Jesus Christ* (*dia pisteōs Iēsou Christou*)' (Rom. 3.22, translation mine). My translation reflects the view now held by many scholars that the phrase *pistis Iēsou Christou* should be translated 'the *faithfulness of* Jesus Christ' and not '*faith in* Jesus Christ' (Gal. 2.16, 3.22; Rom. 3.22, 25, 26; Phil. 3.9).[39] The contested phrase 'encapsulates a *story about God's faithfulness in relation to Jesus' faithfulness*', says Douglas Harink.[40]

> ***Pistis Iēsou Christou:***
> **Paul's Faith Language**
> - faith *in* Jesus Christ (usual view)
> - the faithfulness of Jesus Christ (new view)

Two broad contextual items favor this reading. The first item, argued by Richard Hays, stresses the connection between the prophet Habakkuk and Paul's keynote text in Romans. Paul is figuratively in conversation with the Old Testament prophet, respectful of his complaint that God is guilty of dereliction of duty.

> O LORD, how long shall I cry for help,
> and you will not listen?
> Or cry to you 'Violence!'
> and you will not save?

39. Richard B. Hays, *The Faith of Jesus Christ: An Investigation of the Narrative Substructure of Galatians 3.1–4.11* (SBLDS, 56; Chico, CA: Scholars Press, 1983; repr. Grand Rapids: Eerdmans, 2002); Douglas A. Campbell, *The Rhetoric of Righteousness in Romans 3.21-26* (JSNTSup, 65; Sheffield: Sheffield Academic Press, 1992); Wright, *Paul and the Faithfulness of God*, pp. 836-51; Sigve K. Tonstad, '*πίστις Χριστοῦ*: Reading Paul in A New Paradigm', *AUSS* 40 (2002), pp. 37-59; Michael Bird and Preston M. Sprinkle (eds.), *The Faith of Jesus Christ: Exegetical, Biblical, and Theological Studies* (Peabody, MA: Hendrickson, 2009). In *Paul and the Hermeneutics of Faith*, Watson ends up with a conclusion that is close to the traditional view.

40. Harink, *Paul among the Postliberals*, p. 41.

> Why do you make me see wrongdoing
>   and look at trouble?
> Destruction and violence are before me;
>   strife and contention arise (Hab. 1.2-3).

Habakkuk's outcry is 'the passionate prayer of a desperate man', a person who is anguished by 'moral outrage and perplexity'.[41] The source of his bewilderment is God's apparent *un*-faithfulness. The moral order is coming unglued for lack of the requisite action on God's part. Covenantal expectations are in shambles. When the prophet takes up his position at his watch post, eagerly awaiting what God 'will say to me, and what he will answer concerning my complaint' (Hab. 2.1), the backdrop is God's seeming failure to hold things on course in the world.

At the height of his complaint, God responds to Habakkuk, telling him to wait for something to happen.

> Then the Lord answered me and said.
> Write the *vision* (Hebr. *ḥazo*n, Gr. *horasis*);
>   make *it* [the vision] plain on tablets,
>   so that a runner may read *it* [the vision].
> For there is still a *vision* (Hebr. *ḥazo*n, Gr. *horasis*) for the appointed time;
>   *it* [the vision] speaks of the end,
>   and [*it*] does not lie.
> If *it* [the vision] seems to tarry,
>   wait for *it* [the vision];
>   *it* [the vision] will surely come,
>   *it* [the vision] will not delay (Hab. 2.2-3).

God's answer uses the word 'vision' (*ḥazo*n) twice in these two verses, and it refers to the 'vision' pronominally eight times, creating the effect of a drumbeat. And what is the vision? What is the texture of the '*it*' that will surely come at 'the appointed time'? *It* cannot be understood as anything other than God's action in the world. *It* points to something that will happen; *it* denotes the in-breaking of a singular event; *it* will bring into view a reality that offers proof of God's faithfulness.

The punch line in God's answer to the man standing 'on the ramparts' (NIV), whether we read it in Hebrew or in Greek, projects 'faithfulness' in bold letters on the screen.

Translation of Hebrew text:	'the righteous one (adj. masc. sing.) by *his* faithfulness (third pers. masc. sing.) shall live' (Hab. 2.4, BHS)
Translation of Greek text:	'but the righteous one (adj. masc. sing.) by *my* faithfulness (first pers. sing.) shall live' (Hab. 2.4, LXX)

41. Francis I. Andersen, *Habakkuk: A New Translation with Introduction and Commentary* (AB, 25; New York: Doubleday, 2001), pp. 123, 125.

Neither the Hebrew Bible nor the Septuagint supports the translation 'the righteous live by their faith' (Hab. 2.4) or the wording of the mainstream Bible translations into English.[42] Indeed, the choice of wording in most translations of Habakkuk betrays the translators' desire to put words in Habakkuk's mouth that will fit what the same translators assume Paul to be saying when he quotes the Old Testament prophet in Romans. Rather than allowing Habakkuk to influence our understanding of Paul, we have the Paul of Protestant orthodoxy retroactively influencing translations of Habakkuk.

To ears attuned to the Protestant tradition, the Hebrew text of Habakkuk is disconcerting because it seems to endorse righteousness by works: 'the righteous shall live by his faithfulness' (Hab. 2.4, BHS). This problem is eliminated by the messianic connotation of the expression, 'The Righteous One shall live by his faithfulness'.[43] A Christologic reading excludes righteousness by works. Whether in Hebrew or Greek, the Person whose faithfulness is in view in God's answer to Habakkuk must be the faithfulness of the Person who is speaking to him in answer to his concern, that is, it must refer to the faithfulness of God.

By way of summary, the *problem* for Habakkuk is the apparent absence of God's faithfulness. The *promise* to Habakkuk is that something is to happen that will put God's faithfulness on display. The *summons* to Habakkuk, in a non-Messianic translation of the LXX, is that 'the righteous will live by my faithfulness'.

Reading Rom. 1.17 under the influence of Habakkuk's question leads to different results than the view that has been in vogue since Luther. 'The righteousness of God' in this text is precisely the attribute of God that seems to be in doubt, viewing human reality through the eyes of Habakkuk. The remainder of the text has the character of a story outlined by the movement from *problem* to *promise* to *summons* in Habakkuk.

42. Thus, 'the just shall live by his faith' (KJV); 'the righteous will live by his faith' (NASB); 'the righteous will live by his faith' (NIV); 'the upright will live through faithfulness' (NJB); 'the just shall live by his faith' (NKJV).

43. Richard B. Hays, '"The Righteous One" as Eschatological Deliverer: A Case Study in Paul's Apocalyptic Hermeneutics', in *Apocalyptic and the New Testament: Essays in Honor of J. Louis Martyn* (ed. Joel Marcus and Marion L. Soards; JSNTSup, 24; Sheffield: Sheffield Academic Press, 1989), pp. 191-215; Desta Heliso, *Pistis and the Righteous One: A Study of Romans 1.17 against the Background of Scripture and Second Temple Jewish Literature* (WUNT, 2; Tübingen: Mohr Siebeck, 2007); Stephen L. Young, 'Romans 1.1-5 and Paul's Christological Use of Hab. 2.4 in Rom. 1.17: An Underutilized Consideration in the Debate', *JSNT* 34 (2012), pp. 277-85. Other OT texts that are relevant for this question are Pss. 2.7; 89.3, 20; Isa. 53.11; see also Heb. 10.38.

For the righteousness of God (*dikaiosynē theou*)
is revealed (*apokalyptetai*) in it
from faithfulness *for* faithfulness (*ek pisteōs eis pistin*)
as it is written,
The righteous shall live by (my) faithfulness.[44]
Rom. 1.16-17 (translation mine).

With Habakkuk's concern uppermost in our minds, Romans sounds a note quite different from the one that has dominated Protestant readings. Hays asserts that 'parties on all sides of the debate have been surprisingly content to assume that Paul employs the passage (in Habakkuk) as a proof-text for his doctrine of justification by faith with complete disregard for its original setting in Habakkuk's prophecy.'[45] Habakkuk, we recall, received the answer that God's righteousness would be revealed, telling him that 'it awaits an appointed time…it will certainly come and will not delay', and then, 'the righteous one will live by my faithfulness' (Hab. 2.4, translation mine). This is the statement quoted by Paul. We should be reluctant to assume that Paul applies this answer to a completely different question than Habakkuk. 'Thus, when Paul quotes Hab. 2.4, we cannot help hearing the echoes—unless we are tone-deaf—of Habakkuk's theodicy question', says Hays.[46]

N.T. Wright takes a similar view of the faith-language in Romans, but he gets there by a different route. His perspective is less concerned with the Old Testament background, focusing instead on Paul's argument as it unfolds in Romans. 'What advantage has the Jew?' Paul asks, the question implying that perhaps there is no advantage (Rom. 3.1). But that is not Paul's view. He admits to having charged that 'all, both Jews and Greeks, are under the power of sin' (3.9). The alleged Jewish advantage is that 'the Jews were entrusted (*episteuthēsan*) with the oracles of God' (3.2). The key word here has *pistis* in its root. Wright argues that '[t]he word "entrusted" is always used by Paul in the same sense that it bears in secular Greek: to entrust someone with something is to give them something they must take care of *and pass on to the appropriate person*'.[47]

This leads straight to a key concern in Romans. If 'entrusted' means that the Jews were expected to be faithful stewards of the treasure entrusted to them, Paul produces evidence that they *weren't*. Instead of demonstrating *pistis*, here plainly in the sense of 'faithfulness', they were *un*faithful.

44. A Messianic implication would read 'the Righteous One shall live by faithfulness'.

45. Hays, *Echoes of Scripture*, p. 39.

46. Hays, *Echoes of Scripture*, p. 40. He also points to supporting evidence in Ps. 98.2, the Psalmist claiming that God 'has made known (*egnōrizen*) his salvation (*sōtērion*), in the sight of the nations he has revealed (*apekalypsen*) his righteousness (*dikaiosynēn*)' (Ps. 97.2, LXX, translation mine; cf. Hays, *Echoes*, pp. 36-37).

47. Wright, *Paul and the Faithfulness of God*, p. 837.

In Rom. 3.2, says Wright, 'the whole sentence, and the whole drift of the passage ever since 2.17, is not primarily about "Israel's guilt", but about *God's purpose, through Israel, for the world*'.[48] Israel failed to make good on what God had entrusted to them. Thus Paul's next question, 'What then? If some were unfaithful (*ei ēpistēsan tines*), will their faithlessness (*apistia*) nullify the faithfulness of God (*tēn pistin tou theou*)?' (Rom. 3.3, translation mine). Israel's unfaithfulness to her vocation is in these questions a foregone conclusion. But where does that leave God? Does Israel's failure 'nullify the faithfulness of God'? The concern is centered squarely on faithfulness vs. lack of faithfulness in the human realm. According to Wright, therefore, when Paul speaks of Israel's unfaithfulness, 'this sense is still required: does *their failure to do what their Abrahamic and Isaianic vocation demanded* mean that somehow God himself is now going to prove unfaithful?'[49]

'By no means!' Paul answers emphatically (3.4).

> The covenant God, however, is faithful, and he will provide a faithful Israelite, *the* 'faithful Israelite,' the Messiah. It is the tight coherence of this train of thought, rather than any verbal arguments about subjects and objects, prepositions and case-endings on the one hand, or preferential theological positions on the other, that persuaded me many years ago that Romans 3.22 speaks of the Messiah's faithfulness. It persuades me still.[50]

This view persuades me, too. Whether we arrive to this point by way of Habakkuk's theodicy concern that Paul picks up at the beginning of Romans (Hab. 1.2-4; 2.3-4; Rom. 1.16-17) or by way Paul's demonstration that Israel's unfaithfulness to the covenant commission creates a problem for God (Rom. 3.2-3), we have compelling contextual and textual reasons for the conclusion that 'the right-making of God has been revealed *by the faithfulness* of Jesus Christ (*dia pisteōs Iēsou Christou*)' and not by the believer's faith in Christ (3.22).[51]

Paul among the Ecologists

The world *from* which Paul is speaking on terms outlined above mirrors the world *to* which he is speaking today, only that the plight of the latter world is acutely intensified. This world, the world *to* which he now speaks, might well be described as *postliberal*, but it fits biblical and contemporary

48. Wright, *Paul and the Faithfulness of God*, p. 838.
49. Wright, *Paul and the Faithfulness of God*, p. 838.
50. Wright, *Paul and the Faithfulness of God*, p. 839.
51. Thus also the view of Douglas Campbell ('The Faithfulness of Jesus Christ in Romans 3.2', p. 69) that the conventional reading cannot explain 'a "faith" that discloses or reveals the "righteousness of God" in instrumental terms'.

concerns better to call it post-Holocaust and post-Hiroshima. Now, in the twenty-first century, we must admit that it is a world teetering on a precipice that is as much ecological as it is nuclear. In this world, God's absence is felt even more acutely than in the days of Habakkuk. Paul's indictment of people originally called to mediate God's blessing to the world now carry over to the way God has been represented in the Christian tradition.

To a world experiencing ecological dissolution and a sense of existential abandonment, Paul still speaks in the key of which he has exquisite mastery: of the instability and unsustainability of the current order (Gal. 1.4; Rom. 12.2); of the groaning of creation (Rom. 8.19-22); and of the stupendous ignorance of the rulers of this world (1 Cor. 2.7-8). Above all, he speaks of the faithfulness of God, displayed against the background of apparent abandonment, as in Habakkuk (Hab. 1.2-4; 2.1-4; Rom. 1.16-17), and fully aware of Israel's unfaithfulness (Rom. 3.2). Habakkuk, the minor Old Testament prophet to whom Paul grants the honor of striking the key note in Romans, is in that sense a post-Holocaust voice heard in pre-Holocaust times. It is in awareness of apparent god-forsakenness that Paul in Romans broadcasts the message of God's faithfulness.

Paul, we have seen, is among the people as well as among Jews and Gentiles; he is among the philosophers as well as among patriarchs and prophets; he is among friends and enemies as well as among the rich and the poor (Phil. 4.11-12; 2 Cor. 6.4-10)—among the poor to the point of taking on the nitty-gritty of a collection that he personally plans to take all the way to Jerusalem (Rom. 15.25-27; 1 Cor. 16.1-3). He has mystical experiences, claiming to speak in tongues more than any of his charismatic friends in Corinth, and yet he is grounded in the real world: in the company of others he would rather speak five words with his mind than ten thousand with tongues (1 Cor. 14.18-19). He is Jewish but also through and through human (Rom. 3.9), saying that God is not only the God of the Jews but also of the Gentiles (Rom. 3.29; 9.6-7). Indeed, it is part of his theological bottom line that God does not play favorites: there is no face-factor with God (Rom. 2.11; Col. 3.25; Eph. 6.9).

And now, posing the question again: Is Paul also among the ecologists? Will readers who are familiar with Paul object that an ecological Paul can at best make a coerced appearance, showing up only because he is forced to do it by the agendas of opportunistic and contriving interpreters?

The six Ecojustice Principles of the Earth Bible Series would be a case in point if it were shown that notions of worth, interconnectedness, voice, purpose, mutual custodianship, and resistance do not belong naturally in the Pauline vocabulary.[52] But this cannot be shown. Readings of Romans will

52. Norman C. Habel (ed.), *Readings from the Perspective of the Earth* (Sheffield: Sheffield Academic Press, 2000), pp. 24-37.

not be compromised by looking to the Ecojustice Principles for direction, but these principles should not be seen as alien impositions on an ancient text.

Paul *is* among ecologists in the Bible. His ecological guild is made up of the patriarchs, priests, and prophets among whom we have located him already and of whom he is said to be one. In the Genesis story of creation, a text that is both explicit and implicit in Romans (Rom. 5.12-21; 8.19-22), God creates the world with striking intentionality (Gen. 1.3, 6, 9, 11, 14, 20, 24, 26). God pronounces everything good (Gen. 1.4, 10, 12, 18, 21, 25, 31). On the fifth day, God endows non-human creation with a bill of rights, empowering non-human beings to flourish (Gen. 1.20-22). This is a weighty ecological perspective, and it is doubly significant because it establishes ecological concerns on a platform of rights and not only within a utilitarian framework where ecology matters mainly because of threats to human existence.

The scope of the creation account reaches beyond the human family.[53] In ecological terms, the story begins with the earth, not the land of Israel. The reach is inclusive and universal, affirming the value of the earth and all its inhabitants (Gen. 1.20-22, 28-30). Universality is the premise from which the biblical narrative proceeds and the goal to which it leads. In Paul's vision, the Creator of all must in the end be Lord of all (1 Cor. 15.24-28).

For this intent to succeed, God cannot be a bystander. When the creation account in Genesis is capped by God's rest on the seventh day, all creation is again in view (Gen. 2.1-3). God occupies the center in the account. '*God* finished the work that he had done, and (God) rested on the seventh day from all the work that he had done' (Gen. 2.2). God's activity suggests the opposite of detachment and disengagement, *cessation* better understood as *commitment* and *presence* than as absence of activity. Presence, in turn, captures a crucial theological motif in the Old Testament.[54] In this conception, the hallowing of the seventh day denotes divine commitment, a synonym for the *pistis* (faithfulness) of God. In this lies the hope for all creation.[55] The sabbath rest is in this construct 'the uncreated grace of God's presence for the whole creation', Jürgen Moltmann notes.[56] Within this conception

53. Terence E. Fretheim, *God and the World in the Old Testament: A Relational Theology of Creation* (Nashville: Abingdon Press, 2005), p. xiv.

54. Samuel Terrien, *The Elusive Presence: Toward A New Biblical Theology* (New York: Harper & Row, 1978; repr. Eugene, OR: Wipf and Stock, 2000), p. xxvii.

55. Kathryn Greene-McCreight, 'Restless Until We Rest in God: The Fourth Commandment as Test Case in Christian "Plain Sense" Interpretation', in *The Ten Commandments: The Reciprocity of Faithfulness* (ed. William P. Brown; Louisville, KY: Westminster/John Knox Press, 2004), pp. 234-35.

56. Jürgen Moltmann, *God in Creation: An Ecological Doctrine of Creation* (trans. Margaret Kohl; London: SCM Press, 1985), pp. 281-82.

of ecology, *theology* is not incidental. We encounter the same idea in Paul's Christ-centered view that 'in him all things in heaven and on earth were created, things visible and invisible, whether thrones or dominions or rulers or powers—all things have been created through him and for him. He himself is before all things, and in him all things hold together' (Col. 1.16-17). We cannot read this affirmation without noticing that it is *commitment* writ large.

Priests are not given much exposure in Paul's letters, but by the testimony of Acts he met several. He went to the high priest for a letter of authorization when he decided to pursue believers in Jesus all the way to Damascus (Acts 9.1), and he apologized to the high priest Ananias for not showing him due reverence at a later point (Acts 23.2-5). In Romans, the Jewish religious system is reviewed with respect: 'to them belong the adoption, the glory, the covenants, the giving of the law, the worship, and the promises' (Rom. 9.4; cf. 15.4). We do not know to what extent Paul reflected on the ecological ramifications of Israel's religious calendar ('the worship' in Rom. 9.4), but the ecological tenets of these ordinances are real and easily seen.

With reference to the Sabbath Year, Norman Habel says that in Leviticus (Lev. 25.2-4) the 'land, not the tenants, seems to be the primary subject of the Sabbath requirement'.[57] The text says literally that 'the land shall cease' or that 'the land shall rest', treating the land as subject. In the Jubilee ordinance, a dramatic economic reset comes to the rescue of ecology by ensuring permanently decentralized ownership of land (Lev. 25.8-28). The reset provides relief from debt and restoration of property lost during the preceding forty-nine years (Lev. 25.10). Habel aptly calls this 'economic amnesty',[58] a land economy that helps those who dwell on the land from forgetting their dependency and limitations. 'The land shall not be sold in perpetuity, for the land is mine; with me you are but aliens and tenants', says the priestly voice in Leviticus (Lev. 25.23). Jacob Milgrom sees here a socio-economic mechanism to prevent 'the ever-widening gap between the rich and the poor which Israel's prophets can only condemn, but which Israel's priests attempt to rectify in Leviticus 25'.[59] Such holistic thinking is characteristic of what Paul in Romans calls 'the worship' even if he only refers to it fleetingly (Rom. 9.4).

57. Norman C. Habel, *The Land Is Mine: Six Biblical Land Ideologies* (OBT; Minneapolis: Fortress Press, 1995), p. 103.

58. Habel, *The Land Is Mine*, p. 104.

59. Jacob Milgrom, 'Leviticus 25 and Some Postulates of the Jubilee', in *The Jubilee Challenge: Utopia or Possibility?* (ed. Hans Ucko; Geneva: WCC Publications, 1997), p. 32; idem, *Leviticus: A New Translation with Introduction and Commentary* (3 vols.; AB; New York: Doubleday), pp. 2145-2212; cf. also Robert Gnuse, 'Jubilee Legislation in Leviticus: Israel's Vision of Social Reform', *BTB* 15 (1985), p. 47.

The prophets are Paul's preferred Old Testament companions more than priests, but the ecological vision of the prophets is not drawn to a lesser scale. In Romans, the favored prophets are Habakkuk and Isaiah. Habakkuk, we have seen, speaks programmatically at the beginning of the letter (Rom. 1.16-17; cf. Hab. 2.4). Isaiah delivers the punch line at the end (Rom. 15.8-12; cf. Isa. 11.1-10). These Old Testament voices are virtual bookends in Romans. Both are aware of turmoil and dissolution in the world, and both mediate a vision of redemption for all creation. Paul's quote from Isaiah is especially pertinent, presenting a vision of healing that reverberates throughout the book. 'And again Isaiah says, "The root of Jesse shall come, the one who rises to rule the Gentiles; in him the Gentiles shall hope"' (Rom. 15.12; cf. Isa. 11.1, 10).

This vision gives the 'root of Jesse' universal significance to all levels of the created order (Isa. 11.1-10). Inclusion and redemption extend to non-human creation and the earth and is not limited to the human realm. The 'root of Jesse' that will come on the wings of revelation (Isa. 10.9), is the ultimate right-maker.

> The wolf shall live with the lamb, the leopard shall lie down with the kid, the calf and the lion and the fatling together, and a little child shall lead them. The cow and the bear shall graze, their young shall lie down together; and the lion shall eat straw like the ox. The nursing child shall play over the hole of the asp, and the weaned child shall put its hand on the adder's den (Isa. 11.6-8).

If this text proves that theology brings a benefit to ecology, the latter is happy to reciprocate. Isaiah's eco-sensitive vision yields a rich return by showing that God's faithfulness compasses all creation. The biblical ecotopia depends on God and is achievable only because of God's presence (Isa. 11.1, 10). As in the creation story, the resting-place of God is within creation, and God's healing presence is for the benefit of humans and non-humans alike (Gen. 2.1-3; Isa. 11.6-10; cf. Ezek. 47.1-12). As noted above, the eco-theological alignment is picked up by Paul in Romans, perhaps the most seminal and far-reaching of all the ecological exhibits in this letter. 'And again Isaiah says, "The root of Jesse shall come, the one who rises to rule the Gentiles; in him the Gentiles shall hope"' (Rom. 15.12).

Ecological Paul

- Embrace of materiality
- Old Testament echoes and quotations, especially Habakkuk and Isaiah
- Vision of inclusion, non-human creation not left out
- God's faithfulness to *all* creation
- Repeated appeals to *mercy*
- *Paul*, with P, as servant, not *Saul*, with S, as king
- 'Paul, a servant of *Jesus Christ*'

Theology and ecology are woven as whole cloth all the way to the end in Isaiah, God's faithfulness rebounding to all creation until all that mars the earth is removed (Isa. 65.16-17). Knowledge of God and ecological healing are linked, the former seen as the prerequisite for the latter. Isaiah and Habakkuk, the prophetic voices that bookend Romans, speak with one voice on this point.

> They will not hurt or destroy on all my holy mountain; for the earth will be full of the knowledge of the LORD as the waters cover the sea' (Isa. 11.9).
>
> They shall not hurt or destroy on all my holy mountain, says the LORD (Isa. 65.25).
>
> But the earth will be filled with the knowledge of the glory of the LORD, as the waters cover the sea (Hab. 2.14).

Like the Old Testament prophets, Paul's vision of redemption includes all creation. This is recognizable in a surface appraisal of the texts, and it now comes with an additional depth perspective that has only recently been pointed out. The prophets and narrators in the Old Testament are to some extent *agrarians* of one kind or another.[60] When we recognize the agrarian texture of biblical literature, we might even find Paul *among the agrarians*, a hitherto unnamed category in the *among*-ness of Paul. Agrarians, in turn, biblical and contemporary, have in common the conviction that 'land comes first' in a sense that is ecological more than geological or historical.[61] To the extent that agrarians have in common an 'exacting concern with the *materiality* of human existence',[62] Paul's ecological and agrarian *bona fides* are not in doubt. Precisely where he is most ecological, the voices of human and non-human creation joined in groaning, the hope for which they groan is '*the redemption of our body*' (Rom. 8.23). On these two points, materiality and the redemption of the body, Paul is an agrarian in a primary sense even if he bears the credentials of a working man only secondarily (Acts 18.2-3; 20.34-35; 1 Thess. 2.9; 2 Thess. 3.8). A person who understands the materiality of existence, perceives the groaning of creation, and makes God's faithfulness the cornerstone of his theology belongs among ecologists on substantive merits.

I have saved the most important criterion for last. Paul is among ecologists for reasons that have to do with the most noticeable traits of his character. Where Israel's first king increasingly comes across as an insecure, self-absorbed, and self-pitying person,[63] the traits that define Paul are humility and compassion. In Romans, he is 'Paul, the slave of Jesus Christ'

60. Ellen F. Davis, *Scripture, Culture, and Agriculture: An Agrarian Reading of the Bible* (New York: Cambridge University Press, 2009); idem, 'Learning Our Place: The Agrarian Perspective of the Bible', *WW* 29 (2009), pp. 109-20.

61. Davis, *Scripture, Culture, and Agriculture*, p. 28.

62. Davis, *Scripture, Culture, and Agriculture*, p. 36.

63. 1 Sam. 15.11-31; 18.5-15; 19.9-18; 26.17-25; 28.5-25.

(Rom. 1.1), the ‘P’ in Paul suggesting a telling difference from the ‘S’ in Saul. Giorgio Agamben says that ‘the substitution of *sigma* by *pi*…signifies no less than the passage from the regal to the insignificant, from grandeur to smallness—*Paulus* in Latin means “small, of little significance”’.[64] The New Testament ‘slave of Jesus Christ’ is on this score very different from the Old Testament king. Paul’s ecological credentials and aspiration cannot be measured by what he, Paul, is up to. It must be measured by what Jesus Christ, the one whose slave Paul professes to be, is up to. Compassion, awareness of the world, and sensitivity to the plight of others are ecological and not only theological conceptions. ‘Paul, a servant of Jesus Christ’ (Rom. 1.1), thus understood, was among ecologists before the vocabulary now in use existed, a luminous charter member second to none.

64. Agamben, *The Time That Remains*, p. 9.

Chapter 2

Romans and Its Most Famous Readers

Romans deserves to be read with reverence if for no other reason than that it is one of the most influential pieces of literature of all time. This claim is defensible in absolute terms, and the influence of Romans relative to its size lies beyond computation. Individuals who exerted a decisive influence in history have traced their moment of illumination to Romans, turning around to make Paul's letter the launching pad for *their* mission. Having spoken *to* them on a personal level, Romans has spoken *through* them to the world in their own time and beyond. Among the most famous individuals in this category are Origen (185–254), Augustine (354–430), Martin Luther (1483–1546), John Wesley (1703–1791), and Karl Barth (1886–1968). A review of the impact history of Romans is warranted for reasons of perspective but also with an eye to ecological concerns, explicit, implied, or absent that bear on this commentary.

Origen

From the point of view of ecological hermeneutics, Romans was off to a dismal start in the Christian tradition. The first complete commentary still extant was written by Origen (185–254). He ranks as the most learned and influential interpreter of Scripture prior to the time of the emperor Constantine, and he remains to this day the most important theologian in the Orthodox tradition.[1] His commentary on Romans was written late in his career, in 246 CE, at a time when he had been forced to relocate from Alexandria to Caesarea.[2] While his Romans commentary wielded significant influence on posterity, Origen's theological idiom is more at home in the Gospel and Epistles of John, and his preference for Johannine terminology shows in

1. Henri Crouzel, *Origen* (trans. A.S. Worrall; Edinburgh: T. & T. Clark, 1989), p. xi.

2. Origen, *Commentary on the Epistle to the Romans, Books 1–5* (trans. Thomas P. Scheck; FC, 103; Baltimore: Catholic University of America Press, 2001); idem, *Commentary on the Epistle to the Romans, Books 6–10* (trans. Thomas P. Scheck; FC, 104; Baltimore: Catholic University of America Press, 2002).

many of his books, including his *Commentary on Romans*. By the time readers had access to the Romans commentary, they had been primed by Origen's prolific output on other subjects, especially in his two great apologetic works, *First Principles* (ca. 225 CE) and *Contra Celsum* (ca. 244 CE).[3] While Johannine influences loom large in these books, too, they are of interest in the present context mostly as exhibits of the texture of Origen's thought. They show that his conceptual world was in crucial respects shaped by the philosophy of Plato and the way Plato's outlook found expression in the writings of the Jewish philosopher Philo.[4] Throughout, Origen hammers home an unrelenting disparagement of the material world. *Materiality* and *corporeality* are to him alien elements in the divine plan, at best a temporary diversion from what God had originally intended. The existence of the body is to be understood as divine punishment rather than as the Creator's actual purpose. These sentiments appear again and again in *First Principles*.

> God therefore made the present world and bound the soul to the body as a punishment.[5]

> For if all things can exist without bodies, doubtless bodily substance will cease to exist when there is no use for it.[6]

> If therefore these conclusions appear logical, it follows that we must believe that our condition will be at some future time incorporeal; and if this is admitted, and it is said that all must be subjected to Christ, it is necessary that this incorporeal condition shall be the privilege of all who come within the scope of this subjection to Christ.[7]

> Thus, it appears that even the use of bodies will cease; and if this happens, bodily nature returns to non-existence, just as formerly it did not exist.[8]

The outlook expressed in these samples is neither Johannine nor Pauline, reflecting instead the thought world of Plato and Philo, as noted above. Conspicuously and emphatically, we are not hearing the voice of Paul and

3. *Origen on First Principles* (trans. G.W. Butterworth; London: SPCK, 1936; repr. Gloucester, MA: Peter Smith, 1973); idem, *Contra Celsum* (trans. Henry Chadwick; Cambridge. Cambridge University Press, 1965). A new critical edition of the complete Greek text has been published as *Origenes: Contra Celsum libri VIII* (ed. M. Marcovich; Leiden. Brill, 2001).

4. David T. Runia, 'Philo and Origen: A Preliminary Survey', *Origeniana Quinta: Papers of the 5th International Origen Congress* (ed. R.J. Daly; Leuven: Leuven University Press, 1992), pp. 333-39; see also W.H.C. Frend, *The Rise of Christianity* (Philadelphia: Fortress Press, 1984), pp. 374-77.

5. *First Principles*, I.8.1.

6. *First Principles*, II.3.2.

7. *First Principles*, II.3.3.

8. *First Principles*, II.3.3.

certainly not the hope that 'we wait for...the *redemption of our bodies*' (Rom. 8.23; actually 'our body' [*somatos*, sing.]).

When Origen turns his attention to Romans, he gives the letter high marks. 'The Apostle seems to have been more perfect in this letter than in the others',[9] he says, and his summary of the letter is competent and confident.

> This letter yields no small difficulties in interpretation because many things are woven into this epistle concerning the law of Moses, about the calling of the Gentiles, about Israel according to the flesh and about Israel which is not according to the flesh, about the circumcision of the flesh and of the heart, about the spiritual law and the law of the letter, about the law of the flesh and the law of the members, about the law of the mind and the law of sin, about the inner and the outer man. It is enough to have mentioned these individual themes since in these it seems the contents of the letter are contained.[10]

Origen's synopsis does not mention the doctrine of justification by faith that Augustine and Luther later made to be the hallmark of Romans, but he cannot therefore be said to have missed the point.[11] As Karen Jo Torjesen notes, Origen sees the problem of sin in medical and not primarily in legal terms. 'The primary issue of sin is not that of past sin understood as a legal offence requiring forgiveness, but that those forms of existence which destroy the soul's growth toward perfection must be changed. It is not forgiveness, but transformation which solves the problem of sin,' says Torjesen.[12] Origen's preoccupation in this regard seems well within the range of Paul's description of the transformative power of the Spirit in Romans 8.

In his comments on Rom. 8.19-23, Origen does not hear Paul describing the plight of the earth or of non-human creation. It is 'the *rational* creation' that looks expectantly 'for that time when the glory of the sons of God is going to be revealed'.[13] *Rational* creation, in turn, refers only to human beings. Importantly, human beings should not hope or expect bodily existence in the life to come. The glory that Paul has in mind will be evident when humans are delivered from the burden of the body.

> To me it appears that these things are being said concerning that physical and corruptible substance of our bodies. For corruption exercises dominion over nothing else than the body. For the inner man, who has been created

9. Origen, *Commentary on Romans, Books 1–5*, p. 53.

10. Origen, *Commentary on Romans, Books 1–5*, p. 57.

11. Thomas P. Scheck, *Origen and the History of Justification: The Legacy of Origen's Commentary on Romans* (Notre Dame, IN: University of Notre Dame Press, 2008).

12. Karen Jo Torjesen, *Hermeneutical Procedure and Theological Method in Origen's Exegesis* (Berlin: W. de Gruyter, 1986), p. 77.

13. Origen, *Commentary on Romans, Books 6–10*, p. 68.

> according to God and made in the image of God, is incorruptible and invisible and can even be said to be incorporeal according to its own special nature.[14]

In this conception, the 'physical and corruptible substance of our bodies' holds hostage the *inner man* that is *incorruptible* and *invisible* and *incorporeal*, all of them favored terms in Origen's vocabulary. Later in the same exposition, Origen heightens the negative connotation of anything physical and bodily. The soul, he notes,

> was subjected to servitude to the corruptible body and was overcome by its futility. For, consider the needs of the body: the appetite for food, the embarrassing process of digestion, the sense of shame associated with procuring offspring, how children are conceived, born, and raised. And behold, what great futility is contained in these things, what great corruption to which the creation of the soul, noble and rational, has been subjected, although unwillingly.[15]

To say that ecology is absent in this perspective is a moot point. Origen's concern is purely anthropological, and his anthropology denigrates the body and material reality with no holds barred. With regard to ecology, the entire material world is dispensable, a mere interim stage on the soul's journey from a state of pure immateriality at the beginning to a state of untainted immateriality at the end. Hope means 'one day to be at rest from these bodily and corruptible matters'.[16] Origen takes his stand on this supposition with no questions or qualifications, so completely a captive of the Platonic conception as to make it virtually the complete opposite of Paul's.

Augustine

The world within which Augustine (354–430) lived and worked nearly two hundred years later is different in ways that are too numerous to count.[17] The Roman Emperor is now a Christian; the seat of executive power has in 332 CE relocated to Constantinople; the Empire frays under the pressure of

14. Origen, *Commentary on Romans, Books 6–10*, p. 69.
15. Origen, *Commentary on Romans, Books 6–10*, pp. 69-70.
16. Origen, *Commentary on Romans, Books 6–10*, pp. 71-72.
17. For excellent background reading, see Peter Brown, *Augustine of Hippo: New Edition with an Epilogue* (Berkeley: University of California Press, 2000 [orig. 1967]); idem, *The Body and Society: Men, Women and Sexual Renunciation in Early Christianity* (New York: Columbia University Press, repr. with new introduction, 2008); idem, *Through the Eye of a Needle: Wealth, the Fall of Rome, and the Making of Christianity in the West, 350–550 AD* (Princeton, NJ: Princeton University Press, 2012); Paula Fredriksen, *Augustine and the Jews: A Christian Defense of Jews and Judaism* (New Haven: Yale University Press, 2010); idem, *Sin: The Early History of an Idea* (Princeton, NJ: Princeton University Press, 2012).

the barbarian migrations; Rome itself sacked in the year 410, an event duly noted by Augustine.[18] Paganism is in retreat. The upwardly mobile citizen will be foolish not to hitch his or her wagon to the new religious reality. In the course of the third century, 'Christianity had become a church prepared to absorb a whole society', says Peter Brown.[19] The group that in the days of Origen was a persecuted minority had by Augustine's time become a power-conscious and sometimes persecuting majority. Once Augustine assumed the office of bishop of Hippo in North Africa, he would not be a passive bystander to the new dynamic. In the year 399, he started writing enthusiastically in support of militant suppression of pagan practices.[20]

With regard to persecution of Christian dissidents, Augustine was prepared to go even further. Perhaps nothing takes the measure of the change in Christian ideals better than the fact that he became the first person to write a full justification 'of the right of the state to suppress non-Catholics'.[21] Paula Fredriksen affirms that 'Augustine is even harder on nonconforming Christians than on pagans... To rebuke religiously errant Christians, if necessary by force, was a clear and sacred duty.'[22]

I have jumped ahead in the story, putting at risk the suspense and excitement that are evident in Augustine's discovery of Paul and Romans. Where Origen's theological idiom is Johannine—whether or not he represents fairly the writings attributed to John—Augustine puts himself squarely in Paul's corner. Paul 'was in the air' already in the run-up to Augustine's conversion in Milan in Italy in 386. There he had been exposed to Paul under the determined tutelage of Ambrose.[23] His life-changing encounter with Romans deserves retelling.

> As I was saying this and weeping in the bitter agony of my heart, suddenly I heard a voice from the nearby house chanting as if it might be a boy or a girl (I do not know which), saying and repeating over and over again 'Pick up and read, pick up and read'.[24] At once my countenance changed, and I began to think intently whether there might be some sort of children's game

18. The sack of Rome was a seminal incentive to Augustine's *magnum opus*, *The City of God* (trans. Henry Bettenson; London: Penguin, 2003).

19. Peter Brown, *The World of Late Antiquity,* AD *150–750* (London: Thames and Hudson, 1971), p. 82.

20. Fredriksen, *Augustine and the Jews*, p. 354.

21. Brown, *Augustine of Hippo* (1967 edn), p. 235. For the primary source, see *The Political Writings of St. Augustine* (ed. Henry Paolucci; Washington, DC: Regnery Publishing, 1996), pp. 190-240 (excerpts from Letters XCIII and CLXXXV), where Augustine carefully explains the factors that made him change from being opposed to coercion to approving it.

22. Fredriksen, *Augustine and the Jews*, p. 356.

23. Brown, *Augustine of Hippo*, p. 105.

24. In Latin, '*tolle, lege*'.

> in which such a chant is used. But I could not remember having heard of one. I checked the flood of tears and stood up. I interpreted it solely as a divine command to me to open the book and read the first chapter I might find... So I hurried back to the place where Alypius was sitting. There I had put down the book of the apostle (Paul) when I got up. I seized it, opened it and in silence read the first passage on which my eyes lit: 'Not in riots and drunken parties, not in eroticism and indecencies, not in strife and rivalry, but put on the Lord Jesus Christ and make no provision for the flesh in its lusts' (Rom. 13.12-14). I neither wished nor needed to read further. At once, with the words of this sentence, it was as if a light of relief from all anxiety flooded my heart. All shadows of doubt were dispelled.[25]

Augustine is a master of rhetoric, blending biography with theological meditation for the purpose of persuading the reader to a certain point of view. Nevertheless, there is no reason to disbelieve the account of his emotional encounter with Romans. Nor should we miss that the passage that mediates Augustine's conversion comes from a rather obscure part in Paul's letter, the part that is preoccupied with ethical and behavioral matters and not with 'theology'. On that occasion, at least, Augustine meets Paul in an arena that Origen would have applauded: The most urgent need is spiritual formation. In Augustine's narrative, the carnal inclinations that have held him back are suddenly rendered manageable. From there onwards, he embarks on a journey that takes him to sexual continence and celibacy in the personal sphere, back to North Africa in geographical terms, and forward to the vocation of bishop and teacher that will make him the most influential thinker in the Christian Church in the post-apostolic era.

Paul and Romans will remain in the foreground, the core of a complex legacy that is both theological and political. With regard to the latter, Augustine finds support for the use of coercion by claiming that Paul was at the receiving end of coercive measures at God's hand.

> And yet, after calling Peter and the other apostles by His words alone, when He came to summon Paul, who was before called Saul, subsequently the powerful builder of His Church, but originally its cruel persecutor, He not only constrained him with His voice, but even dashed him to the earth with His power; and that He might forcibly bring one who was raging amid the darkness of infidelity to desire the light of the heart, He first struck him with physical blindness of the eyes.[26]

This is less an example of stellar exegesis than an attempt to furnish theological justification for a dubious policy, parlayed into a winning argument by a master rhetorician.[27] And yet Augustine will not be deterred.

25. Saint Augustine, *Confessions* (trans. Henry Chadwick; Oxford: Oxford University Press, 1991), pp. 152-53.

26. Augustine, *Letter* 185.6.22, in *The Political Writings of St. Augustine*, p. 216.

27. Brown, *Augustine of Hippo*, p. 236.

> Where is what the Donatists were wont to cry: Man is at liberty to believe or not believe? Towards whom did Christ use violence? Whom did He compel? Here they have the Apostle Paul. Let them recognize in his case Christ first compelling, and afterwards teaching; first striking, and afterwards consoling. For it is wonderful how he who entered the service of the gospel in the first instance under the compulsion of bodily punishment, afterwards labored more in the gospel than all they who were called by word only.[28]

Peter Brown calls this 'profound and ominous changes' in Augustine's attitude,[29] but the change is in crucial respects woven into whole cloth in his mature thought.[30] Taking his cue from Paul's letter to the Romans (Rom. 9.7-29), Augustine argues that the sovereign will of God overrules the choice of created beings. The ones whom God has predestined to be saved cannot, in the Augustinian account, refuse God's decision and, by implication, those whom God has not predestined to be saved do not have the option of choosing it.[31] God's sovereignty and inscrutability have a corollary in human incapacity, all elements deriving from Augustine's reading of Romans and all combining to justify coercion at the level of policy. In this regard, as Fredriksen notes, Augustine framed 'a theological justification for the use of force that intimately linked his long-held views on sin and vitiated human will to the pastoral obligations of the church'.[32]

The contrast between Origen and Augustine is dramatic. In Origen's theological universe, God's fairness is perceptible to humans, and there is no arbitrary doctrine of predestination. God's method is persuasive and never coercive. To Augustine, human reason must yield to the reality of divine inscrutability and, as we have seen, coercion is sometimes warranted for people's own good. 'For both biblical theologians', says Fredriksen,

> God's two great attributes are justice and mercy. But Origen's god expresses these attributes simultaneously and universally. To each soul he is both just and merciful. Augustine's god expresses these attributes serially and

28. Augustine, *Letter* 185.6.23. The Donatists were dissident Catholics who insisted that Christians who had compromised their faith during the great persecution needed to be rebaptized in order to be allowed back into full fellowship.

29. Brown, *Augustine of Hippo*, p. 235; see also Fredriksen, *Augustine and the Jews*, p. 343.

30. Carol Harrison (*Rethinking Augustine's Early Theology: An Argument for Continuity* [Oxford: Oxford University Press, 2006], pp. 15-19) dissents from the traditional view of 'two Augustines', an early and a later one, where only the later Augustine embraced authority and faith over reason.

31. Eleonore Stump, 'Augustine on Free Will', in *The Cambridge Companion to Augustine* (ed. Eleonore Stump and Norman Kretzmann; New York: Cambridge University Press, 2001), pp. 134-47.

32. Fredriksen, *Augustine and the Jews*, p. 354.

> selectively. To each soul, God is *either* just *or* merciful, and those who receive mercy are in the minority. For Augustine, even babies, if unbaptized, go to hell, and the greater part of humanity is justly predestined to damnation.[33]

Augustine scales back the substance dualism that is conspicuous in Origen's anthropology. Whereas the body is undesirable and dispensable to human existence in Origen's thought, it is less so to Augustine. 'Flesh was not-self, simply the soul's inconvenient vehicle while it sojourned in time', Fredriksen says of Origen's view.[34] To Augustine, by contrast, it is the human will and not materiality as such that is the problem. 'The problem with sexual activity, for instance, was not that it engaged fleshly bodies but that it involved both soul and body in that great index of the sinful state, pleasure. Pleasure was sin's bait. It anesthetized the will.'[35]

Augustine does not repudiate material existence. In biographical terms, Augustine had a common-law wife for thirteen years until he came under the influence of Ambrose in Milan. One year into the relationship, they had a son together. When the relationship ended, his live-in companion accepted the fate prescribed by custom, returning to Africa to a life of chastity. Already before coming to Italy, in Carthage, Augustine had been exposed to sexual renunciation in the Manichean community. During the critical years in Milan, he heard Ambrose waxing eloquent on sexual abstinence and the perpetual virginity of Mary. Ambrose's idealization of sexual continence was bolstered by Augustine's reading of Neo-Platonic works by Plotinus and Porphyry, and he was exposed for the first time to Christian ascetic groups.[36] Once back in North Africa and now the leader of an all-male Christian commune (391 CE), the social context within which Augustine were to expound on the body and sexuality was set in stone.

> Augustine moved in a monochrome, all-male world. He imposed strict codes of sexual avoidance on himself and his own clergy. He would never visit a woman unchaperoned, and did not allow even his own female relatives to enter the bishop's palace. He expelled a young clergyman who had been found speaking with a nun 'at an inappropriate hour of the day'.[37]

This arrangement reflected theological convictions that had been carefully worked out. But if bodily existence as such was not the problem, what was the problem? Augustine does not disdain bodily existence nor does he argue that sexual desire only emerged after the sin of Adam and Eve, as other exegetes were prone to do. Sexual desire was a problem, as noted,

33. Fredriksen, *Augustine and the Jews*, p. 334.
34. Fredriksen, *Augustine and the Jews*, p. 334.
35. Fredriksen, *Augustine and the Jews*, p. 335.
36. Brown, *The Body and Society*, pp. 387-95.
37. Brown, *The Body and Society*, p. 396.

because it represented the most readily available proof that elements in the human constitution had become unhinged from the will. 'The twisted human will, not marriage, not even the sexual drive, was what was new in the human condition after Adam's Fall', says Brown.[38] In the personal realm, the remedy was the love of God rather than human companionship, the comfort and discipline of an all-male and tightly knit Christian community, and the hope that the *discordiosum malum*, described by Brown as 'a primal dislocation',[39] would be made right in the world to come.

> The *concupiscentia carnis* ('desire of the flesh'), indeed, was such a peculiarly tragic affliction to Augustine precisely because if had so little to do with the body. It originated in a lasting distortion of the soul itself. With Adam's Fall, the soul lost the ability to summon up all of itself, in an undivided act of will, to love and praise God in all created things. Concupiscence was a dark drive to control, to appropriate, and to turn to one's private ends, all the good things that had been created by God to be accepted with gratitude and shared with others. It lay at the root of the inescapable misery that afflicted mankind.[40]

Resilient Platonic influences remain in this outlook, bequeathed to Augustine by way of a Christian tradition within which Origen looms large, but there were other tributaries, too. The reprieve Augustine offers to the material world is real, but it is partial, and it does not suffice for an ecological hermeneutic. When Augustine began work on Romans during the last decade of the fourth century,[41] he had not yet adopted the radical view of divine foreknowledge and predestination that marked his final take on Romans. His exposition of the difficult passages in Romans 9–11 argues a point of view that seems quite reasonable: a divine course of action that can be understood.[42]

His exposition of the 'ecological' passage in Rom. 8.19-23 is human-centered almost as much as Origen's, though without the latter's resolute denigration of materiality. The groaning of creation does not imply 'a sorrowing and sighing of trees and vegetables and stones and other suchlike creatures—for this is the error of the Manichees… Rather and without any false interpretation we take "every creature" to mean man himself,' he writes.[43] Non-human creation is not in view, only 'whatever now labors in man and is subject to

38. Brown, *The Body and Society*, p. 404.

39. Brown, *The Body and Society*, p. 408.

40. Brown, *The Body and Society*, p. 418.

41. *Augustine on Romans: Propositions from the Epistle to the Romans; Unfinished Commentary on the Epistle to the Romans* (text and trans. Paula Fredriksen Landes; SBLTT, 23; Chico, CA: Scholars Press, 1982).

42. Augustine, *Propositions*, pp. 31-41.

43. Augustine, *Propositions*, p. 23.

corruption'.[44] Augustine speaks of creation being 'subject to futility as long as it is given over to temporal things, which pass like a shadow', but this refers to a misguided focus on the part of human beings and is not an indictment of material existence.[45] The creature, conceived as humans in his or her natural state, is in dire straits because he or she 'was not yet joined through faith to the number of the sons of God…who would believe'.[46] 'Creation' is in this conception a cipher for human beings and is so called 'since faith was not yet in it'. Only humans will experience freedom from decay and attain 'the glorious liberty of the sons of God through faith'.[47] Augustine's reading of Romans remains an ecological no man's land because redemption is circumscribed to include human beings only. Unlike Origen's interpretation, however, material existence will not come to an end.

Martin Luther

Martin Luther (1483–1546) began his religious vocation as an Augustinian monk, and his spiritual journey replicates Augustine's in many respects. His path, too, runs to Paul and to Romans, and he adopts many of Augustine's tenets in his reading of the apostle's longest letter. With regard to institutional loyalty and the prospect of precipitating a schism, however, Luther at first did not follow in Augustine's footsteps. In Worms in 1521 and pushed against the wall, his response to the emperor, Charles V, and the German princes was not submission for the sake of institutional unity.

> Your most serene Majesty and your lordships demand a simple reply. I am going to give it to you straight from the horse's mouth, without beating about the bush: Here it is: unless I am convinced by the evidence of Scripture or by plain reason—for I accept neither the Pope nor the councils by themselves, since it is clear that they have often been mistaken and contradictory—I am bound by the Scriptural texts I have quoted and my conscience belongs to the Word of God. I cannot and I will not retract anything, for to act against one's conscience is neither safe nor honest.[48]

I have taken this version of events from the French Roman Catholic scholar Daniel Olivier. He adds that at that stage in the proceedings, 'Luther suddenly abandoned Latin to cry out in his mother tongue, "I cannot. Do with me what you will. God help me!"'

44. Augustine, *Propositions*, p. 25.

45. Augustine, *Propositions*, p. 25. His scriptural references suggest that his focus is misguided orientation (Pss. 4.3; 143.4; Eccl. 1.2-3).

46. Augustine, *Propositions*, p. 25.

47. Augustine, *Propositions*, p. 25.

48. Daniel Olivier, *The Trial of Luther* (trans. John Tonkin; St. Louis: Concordia, 1978), p. 166.

This scene lays bare the considerable distance between Augustine and Luther with respect to church authority at that stage in Luther's career. Luther appeals to Scripture and to conscience, the latter no less important than the former. In a sermon preached in Wittenberg on March 10, 1522, a year after the confrontation in Worms, Luther expresses a point of view that explicitly repudiates coercion. The Word is the believer's sole legitimate weapon.

> For the Word created heaven and earth and all things [Ps. 33.6]; the Word must do this thing, and not we poor sinners. In short, I will preach it, teach it, write it, but I will constrain no man by force, for faith must come freely without compulsion. Take myself as an example. I opposed indulgences and all the papists, but never with force. I simply taught, preached, and wrote God's Word; otherwise I did nothing. And while I slept [cf. Mk 4.26-29], or drank Wittenberg beer with my friends Philip and Amsdorf, the Word so greatly weakened the papacy that no prince or emperor ever inflicted such losses upon it. I did nothing; the Word did everything. Had I desired to foment trouble, I could have brought great bloodshed upon Germany; indeed, I could have started such a game that even the emperor would not have been safe. But what would it have been? Mere fool's play. I did nothing; I let the Word do its work… For it is almighty, and takes captive the hearts, and when the hearts are captured the work will fall of itself.[49]

'I will constrain no man by force', says Luther, as though with one stroke intending to sweep away the rationale for coercion that originated with Augustine. Luther's mastery of language has been noted and is second to none even in comparison with geniuses like Origen and Augustine.[50] His sermon in 1522 is a case in point, worthy to be numbered among the most memorable speeches of all time.

But Luther's commitment to the non-use of coercion turned out to be short-lived. Freedom of conscience is easier to promote with respect to one's own convictions than on behalf of convictions with which we disagree. Paraphrasing Luther, Lord (Sir John) Acton takes note of the early Luther to the effect that 'heretics must be converted by the Scriptures, and not by fire, otherwise the hangman would be the greatest doctor'.[51] But Luther soon found reason to relent, denying to others the privilege he had claimed for himself. In 1531, he sided with Melanchthon that the death

49. Martin Luther, Sermon preached on March 10, 1522, in *Luther's Works* 51 (ed. J.J. Pelikan, H.C. Oswald and H.T. Lehmann; Philadelphia: Fortress Press, 1959), pp. 77-78.

50. See Gerhard Ebeling, *Luther: An Introduction to His Thought* (trans. R.A. Wilson; London: Collins, 1970), pp. 27-58.

51. Lord (Sir John) Acton, 'The Protestant Theory of Persecution', in *Lord Acton: Essays on Freedom and Power* (ed. Gertrude Himmelfarb; Boston: Beacon Press, 1949), pp. 92-93.

penalty was warranted for the Anabaptists,[52] and in one of his famed table talks he endorsed coercion with the flair of a true believer. 'Heretics are not to be disputed with, but to be condemned unheard, and whilst they perish by fire, the faithful ought to pursue the evil to its source, and bathe their hands in the blood of the Catholic bishops, and of the Pope, who is a devil in disguise.'[53]

> In thus taking refuge in the arms of the civil power, purchasing the safety of his doctrine by the sacrifice of its freedom, and conferring on the State, together with the right of control, the duty of imposing it at the point of the sword, Luther in reality reverted to his original teaching. The notion of liberty, whether civil or religious, was hateful to his despotic nature and contrary to his interpretation of Scripture.[54]

There is more than a grain of truth in Lord Acton's crass assessment. Where Augustine embraced coercion for the sake of truth and institutional unity, Luther made truth the overriding criterion, that is, *his* definition of the truth. This view, in turn, would be as supportive of coercion and institutional hegemony in Protestantism as in the Roman Catholic tradition.

In his spiritual self-understanding, Luther travels the road of Paul much like Augustine before him, drawing solace and direction from Romans. Luther's recollection in this regard is as compelling as his stance in Worms while also recapitulating Augustine's encounter with Paul. Late in life, in 1545 and thus shortly before his death, he looked back on what Gerhard Ebeling describes as 'the fundamental theological perception of the Reformation'.[55]

> A strange burning desire had seized me to understand Paul in the Epistle to the Romans; it was not coldness of heart which had stood in my way until then, but a single phrase in chapter 1: 'For in it the righteousness of God is revealed' (Rom. 1.17). For I hated this phrase, 'the righteousness of God', which I had been taught to understand philosophically, from its normal usage by all who teach doctrine, as referring to the so-called formal or active righteousness, by means of which God is righteous and punishes sinners and the unrighteous. But I, who, however blamelessly I lived as a monk, felt myself to be a sinner before God, with a deeply troubled conscience, and could not rely on being reconciled through the satisfaction I could carry out myself, did not love—no, hated—the just God who punishes sinners; and I silently rebelled against God, if not with blasphemy, at

52. Bernard Lohse, 'Conscience and Authority in Luther', in *Luther and the Dawn of the Modern Era: Papers for the Fourth International Congress for Luther Research* (trans. Herbert J.A. Bouman; ed. H.A. Oberman; Leiden: E.J. Brill, 1974), pp. 158-83.

53. From Table Talk III, quoted in Lord Acton, *Essays on Freedom and Power*, p. 103.

54. Lord Acton, *Essays on Freedom and Power*, p. 94.

55. Ebeling, *Luther*, p. 39.

> least with dreadful murmuring: Was it not enough that poor sinners, eternally lost as the result of original sin, should be cast down in pure wickedness through the law of the Decalogue, but that God should add one torment to the other through the gospel, and even through the gospel should threaten us with his righteousness and his anger? So I returned time and again to this very passage in Paul, burning with thirst to know what St. Paul meant. Finally, thanks to the mercy of God, and thinking ceaselessly of this matter one night, I recalled the context in which the words occur, namely: 'In it the righteousness of God is revealed...as it is written, 'The righteous shall live by faith'. Then I began to understand that this is the meaning of the passage: through the gospel the righteousness of God is revealed, that is, passive righteousness through faith, as it is written: 'The righteous shall live by faith'. Then I had the feeling that straight away I was born again, and had entered through open doors into paradise itself.[56]

Many questions have been raised regarding Luther's recollection. Exactly when did he have the experience to which he refers?[57] Why does he start talking about it only after 1530, more than ten years after it ostensibly happened? How does his experience relate to his exposition of Romans, the book he singles out as the source of his concern, given that he lectured on Romans as early as 1515–16? Does the exposition he gave at that time include the great light of the so-called *tower experience*?[58]

What, too, of questions that arise in light of recent scholarship on Paul and of questions that have not yet been asked? Luther makes a great discovery, undergoing a transformative experience that he attributes to Romans, but did he understand what Paul actually says? Does Luther in his state of need hear in Romans a message that to Paul had a different ring? How, indeed, could Luther be in such a predicament by reading Romans in the first place? Did Paul suffer pangs of conscience of the kind Luther reports? As for the 'conversion stories' that go with these accounts, from Paul on the Damascus Road to Augustine in the garden in Milan to Luther in his tower experience, is there a common theme? We can at least say that the latter two conversions, of Augustine and Luther, are by their first-hand testimony directly traceable to Romans. We are also on solid ground to note the experiential quality of these accounts: they do not happen in towers of ivory; they originate in existential needs and have existential consequences; and they are unmistakably of the participatory kind.

In Luther's exposition of Romans, references to Augustine abound, but already at an early stage in his written work Luther shows independence

56. Martin Luther, from Preface to *Complete Edition of Luther's Latin Writings*, here as quoted in Ebeling's translation, *Luther*, pp. 39-40.

57. Many scholars date it as early as 1514, some as late as 1519.

58. Ebeling, *Luther*, pp. 39-42; see also William M. Landeen, *Martin Luther's Religious Thought* (Mountain View, CA: Pacific Press, 1971), pp. 42-51.

of mind and is not overly awed by his predecessors. He speaks disparaging of the church fathers, making an exception only for Augustine, but even this dependence diminished with time. 'At first I did not just read Augustine, I devoured him', he says, 'but when the door to Paul opened to me and I understood the meaning of justification by faith, then I was done with him'.[59]

In his preface to Romans, published in the year of his death in 1546, Luther did much to lift Romans to a position of pre-eminence in the Protestant tradition.

> This letter is truly the most important piece in the New Testament. It is purest Gospel. It is well worth a Christian's while not only to memorize it word for word but also to occupy himself with it daily, as though it were the daily bread of the soul. It is impossible to read or to meditate on this letter too much or too well.[60]

In the same context Luther addresses fears that faith is a mere chimera with no content or consequences in the lives of believers. 'Faith', he explains,

> is a work of God in us, which changes us and brings us to birth anew from God (cf. John 1). It kills the old Adam, makes us completely different people in heart, mind, senses, and all our powers, and brings the Holy Spirit with it. What a living, creative, active powerful thing is faith! It is impossible that faith ever stop doing good. Faith doesn't ask whether good works are to be done, but, before it is asked, it has done them.[61]

In the original exposition from 1515-16, Luther identifies human pride and self-conceit as Paul's main concern in Romans.

> The chief purpose of this letter is to break down, to pluck up, and to destroy all wisdom and righteousness of the flesh. This includes all the works which in the eyes of people or even in our own eyes may be great works. No matter whether these works are done with a sincere heart and mind, this letter is to affirm and state and magnify sin, no matter how much someone insists that it does not exist, or that it was believed not to exist.[62]

Luther's take on Rom. 8.19-23 marks a genuine return to the real world in comparison to the expositions of Origen and Augustine. He notes that 'the apostle speaks of the (non-human) creature as if it were alive and capable of feeling sorrow, because it is forced to serve the wicked despite their misuse

59. From a Table Talk in 1532, quoted in Landeen, *Luther*, p. 49.

60. Martin Luther, *Commentary on the Epistle to the Romans* (trans. J. Theodore Mueller; Grand Rapids: Kregel Publications, 1976), p. xiii.

61. Luther, *Commentary on the Epistle to the Romans*, p. xvii.

62. Martin Luther, *Luther's Works* 25. *Lectures on Romans* (ed. Jaroslav Pelikan; St. Louis: Concordia, 1972), p. 135.

(*of the creature*) and their ingratitude to God; for it exists that through and in it God may be glorified by His saints (Rom. 8.19)'.[63] Philosophers' lack of interest in the particularities of existence, human and otherwise, confronts a resounding corrective in Romans, as Luther reads it.

> The Apostle thinks and argues quite differently of these matters than do the philosophers. They view the present state of things so exclusively that they speculate only about the essence and attributes (*of created things*). But the Apostle turns our attention from the consideration of the creature in its present condition and directs us to its future state. Speaking of the earnest expectation of the creature, he urges us to explore not what the creature is, but what it expects. But oh, how many foolish opinions befog our philosophy! When shall we become reasonable and perceive that we are wasting precious time by such worthless studies, putting aside things that are of so much greater value.[64]

Where Origen's view of the future state has no material world at all and no bodies, and where Augustine has a redemptive vision that includes humans only, Luther sees other creatures called to share in God's redemptive purpose. '*The creature itself also shall be delivered* (Rom. 8.21)... I take it to mean not that the creature will cease to exist absolutely, but that it will no longer be subject to vanity, for it will appear in glory,' he says.[65] Paul is in Luther's reading aware of the pain of non-human creation, its subjection to abuse and vanity, and of its God-empowered yearning. The body, the earth, and non-human creation are in Luther's reading resurfacing to more than a walk-on appearance.

Perhaps the contrast between Luther and his most notable predecessors is best appreciated in the realm of biography. We see the single and celibate Origen yearn for deliverance from bodily existence and the single and eventually celibate Augustine achieve sexual continence (after more than a decade of an active sex life). And then we see Martin Luther, the former Augustinian monk but now happily married, the father of six children (two died young), quite at home in the world as we know it and quite reconciled to the demands and blessings of married life. Katharine von Bora wrote this to her sister-in-law Christina upon Luther's passing in 1546, a rare fragment of domestic bliss and human ecology.

> For who would not be fittingly saddened and concerned for such a worthy man as my dear master was, who served so well not just a town or a single country but the whole world. I am in truth so very saddened that I cannot express my great heartache to any person and do not know how I am and feel. I can neither eat nor drink. Nor again sleep. If I had owned a

63. Luther, *Romans* (Kregel edn), p. 123.
64. Luther, *Romans* (Kregel edn), p. 124.
65. Luther, *Romans* (Kregel edn), p. 125.

> principality or empire I would not have felt as bad had I lost it, as I did when our dear Lord God took from me—and not only from me but from the whole world—this dear and worthy man.[66]

John Wesley

The link that runs from Augustine to Luther and then from Luther to John Wesley (1703–1791) is beyond doubt. For all three Paul and Romans are at the center. In the evening of May 24, 1738, Wesley reluctantly decided to attend a meeting from which he did not expect much benefit. By his own account he was in for a surprise.

> In the evening I went very unwillingly to a society in Aldersgate Street, where one was reading Luther's preface to the Epistle to the Romans. About a quarter before nine, while he was describing the change which God works in the heart through faith in Christ, I felt my heart strangely warmed. I felt I did trust in Christ, Christ alone, for salvation; and an assurance was given me that He had taken away my sins, even mine, and saved me from the law of sin and death.[67]

It is not difficult to know who is who in this account or to ascertain what is there. Luther is there, to be sure, and behind Luther, the apostle Paul. The text at hand is Romans, its message conveyed to Wesley by way of Luther. At the level of biography, Augustine, Martin Luther, and John Wesley are linked to Paul by a Damascus Road-like experience. For the three who read Romans but did not write it, the moment of illumination resembles the experience of Paul but it is mediated by Romans. In biographical and experiential terms, they encounter the letter in ways that are strikingly participatory even though their understanding of Romans makes justification by faith paramount. Augustine finds in Romans the pivot point that resolves the behavioral impasse in his life; Luther a view of God that delivers him from existential terror; Wesley an experience that transports him from an intellectual grasp of the unseen to an experiential understanding.

With important differences of nuance, Wesley will teach justification by faith in much the same way as Augustine and Luther and do it by means of the same texts.[68] His 'commentary' on Romans is too cursory to be of much use, but he preached many sermons based on Romans, publishing a number of them. *Sermons on Several Occasions*, also known as *John*

66. Katherine von Bora, Letter written in 1546, quoted in Kirsi Stjerna, *Women and the Reformation* (Hoboken, NJ: Wiley-Blackwell, 2009), p. 64.

67. John Wesley, *John Wesley's Journal*, Abridged Edition (London: Charles H. Kelly, 1903), p. 51.

68. Albert C. Outler (ed.), *John Wesley* (LPT; New York: Oxford University Press, 1964).

Wesley's Forty-four Sermons, was published in four volumes between 1746 and 1760. Nine sermons in these books are based on texts from Romans and an additional six on texts from other Pauline letters. Two sermons feature scenes from the life of Paul in Acts, adding up to seventeen 'Pauline perspectives'.[69] Of the sermons based on Romans, the first bears the title 'Justification by Faith' and the second 'The Righteousness of Faith'. Being-in-Christ is clearly the theme of sermons VIII, IX and X, bolstered by two more entitled 'The Law Established through Faith'.

Against those who claim Pauline paternity for the doctrine of predestination, Wesley issues a pointed rebuttal by means of biblical exegesis and arguments grounded in common sense.[70] On this point, too, Romans is contested territory, but Wesley will not concede that the Calvinist teaching on divine sovereignty puts the question of divine justice off limits to humans. Where is the justice, he asks, if God consigns humans to eternal damnation for lacking the grace God decided not to give them? 'O strange justice!' he exclaims. 'What a picture do you draw of the Judge of all the earth'.[71]

Wesley had an impressive Oxford education, and he was originally slated to become a minister in the Church of England. But his quest took him in new directions—to convictions at odds with the staid ways of the established church and to arenas largely untouched by conventional preaching.[72] His all-out debut in this regard happened in Bristol on April 2, 1739, duly recorded in his *Journal*. 'At four in the afternoon, I submitted to be more vile, and proclaimed in the highways the glad tidings, speaking from a little eminence in the ground adjoining the city, to about three thousand people', he writes.[73] Roy Hattersley notes that on this occasion Wesley preached in the open air for the first time.[74] He thereby joined forces with others who were taking the message to the lower classes apart from the scaffolding of the institutional church, preaching out-of-doors to the coal miners at Kingswood and Moorfields in Wales, and treating the working class as though it was as important in the sight of God as people who were more well off and far more likely to set foot in a cathedral.[75] In the course of his life as an itin-

69. John Wesley, *Sermons on Several Occasions* (London: Epworth Press, 1944). Thirteen texts based on the Sermon on the Mount.

70. John Wesley, 'Predestination Calmly Considered', in *John Wesley*, pp. 427-72.

71. Wesley, 'Predestination Calmly Considered', p. 439.

72. Albert C. Outler ('John Wesley: Folk-Theologian', *TT* 34 [1977], pp. 150-60) shows that Wesley's commitment to ordinary, uneducated people was deliberate and a labor of genuine love.

73. Stephen Tomkins, *John Wesley: A Biography* (Oxford: Lion Publishing, 2003), p. 69.

74. Roy Hattersley, *John Wesley: A Brand from the Burning* (London: Little, Brown, 2002), p. 148.

75. Richard P. Heitzenrater, *Wesley and the People Called Methodists* (Nashville:

erant preacher, it is estimated that Wesley rode 250,000 miles on horseback, gave away 30,000 pounds, wrote books, letters, and tracts that filled some fifty volumes, and preached more than 40,000 sermons, an average of fifteen sermons a week.[76] He was a tireless nurturer of the *societies*, as companies of believers were known in the fledgling Methodist movement, an abolitionist,[77] a public educator,[78] a lay physician and health reformer,[79] capping his concern for the poor by going door to door in inclement weather in order to raise money till the year of his death at the ripe age of 88. The single pitiful and pitiable blight on this Paul-like biography, while not amounting to a moral indictment, was Wesley's emotional ineptitude in the personal sphere and his spectacularly unhappy marriage to a woman he should not have married in the first place.

With the dawning of medical science, Wesley grappled with the implications of the discoveries of William Harvey (1578–1657), Thomas Willis (1621–75), and David Hartley (1705–57) with regard to the body-soul connection. The drift in the science of that time clearly went in the direction of an increasingly brain-based view of personhood. Wesley acknowledges as much, even observing the effect on mental states of coffee, alcohol, and meat. In this regard he turns the page on the radical dualism that had prevailed in one form or another since the days of Origen, but he does not accept a view of personhood that is entirely brain-based. 'The soul is an immaterial spirit—Wesley's writings consistently make that point; it perceives physical sensations, governs bodily motions, thinking, and the will, and it survives the death of the body,' says Laura Bartels Felleman.[80]

Abingdon, 2nd edn, 2013), pp. 107-109.

76. Tomkins, *John Wesley*, p. 199.

77. Ronald H. Stone, *John Wesley's Life and Ethics* (Nashville: Abingdon Press, 2001), pp. 187-98.

78. John Wesley, *A Survey of the Wisdom of God in Creation: A Compendium of Natural Philosophy* (London: J. Paramore Upper Moorfields, 4th edn, 1784). Initially published in 1763, the book went through seven editions in Great Britain; see Marc Otto and Michael Lodahl, '"We Cannot Know Much, But We May Love Much": Mystery and Humility in John Wesley's Narrative Theology', *Wesleyan Theol J* 44 (2009), pp. 118-40.

79. John Wesley, *Primitive Physic: Or, An Easy and Natural Method of Curing Most Diseases* (London: G. Paramore, 24th edn, 1792). The book was reprinted many times long after his death and is regarded as his most widely read book, the 24th edition the last 'authentic' version. See also Deborah Madden, 'Pastor and Physician: John Wesley's Cures for Consumption', in Deborah Madden (ed.), *'Inward and Outward Health': John Wesley's Holistic Concept of Medical Science, the Environment and Holy Living* (Eugene, OR: Wipf & Stock, 2008), pp. 94-139.

80. Laura Bartels Felleman, 'A Necessary Relationship: John Wesley and the Body-Soul Connection', in *'Inward and Outward Health'*, p. 154.

The shift in emphasis toward a more material view of personhood runs on parallel tracks with an interest in the well-being of non-human creation that certainly qualifies as an ecological hermeneutic.[81] In Wesley's large collection of sermons, one breaks so decisively in this direction that there is nothing like it between the days of Paul and our time. The sermon is listed as Sermon 60 and bears the title 'The General Deliverance'. Wesley's text is Rom. 8.19-22. He begins by adducing evidence from the Old Testament of God's care for non-human creatures.

> Nothing is more sure, than that as 'the Lord is loving to every man', so 'his mercy is over all his works'; all that have sense, all that are capable of pleasure or pain, of happiness or misery. In consequence of this, 'He openeth his hand, and filleth all things living with plenteousness. He prepareth food for cattle,' as well as 'herbs for the children of men'. He provideth for the fowls of the air, 'feeding the young ravens when they cry unto him'. 'He sendeth the springs into the rivers, that run among the hills, to give drink to every beast of the field', and that even 'the wild asses may quench their thirst'. And, suitably to this, he directs us to be tender of even the meaner creatures; to show mercy to these also.[82]

The sermon shows an openness toward the world and to non-human creation that is not found, even remotely, in the expositions we have considered so far. Wesley reviews Old Testament texts on the assumption that they would be familiar to Paul. He argues that non-human creatures are meant to be recipients of God's mercy. God has made provision for human and non-human creatures alike. Importantly, it is a God-ordained obligation for humans to act toward non-human creatures in a posture of mercy.

The sermon works from the premise that the present state of affairs in the world is different from the original divine intent. Referring to the plight of non-human creatures, Wesley asks how it comes to pass 'that such a complication of evils oppresses, yea, overwhelms them. How is it that misery of all kinds overspreads the face of the earth?' His answer, not unexpectedly, invokes the disruption in the divine-human relationship in the Genesis story of the fall. 'Man was the channel of conveyance between his Creator and the whole brute creation', he writes. Once that relationship was broken, the ripple effect was felt throughout the created order.

Wesley has thus established the primacy of the divine-human relationship ontologically, but he is careful not to denigrate the status of non-human creatures. In fact, this part of his sermon goes considerably beyond what might be expected, given that the topic is itself a departure from human-centered readings of Romans. With regard to ontological distinctions between humans and

81. Margaret Flowers, 'A Wesleyan Theology of Environmental Stewardship', in '*Inward and Outward Health*', pp. 51-93.

82. John Wesley, 'The General Deliverance', Sermon 60.

animals, he asks, 'What then is the barrier between men and brutes and the line which they cannot pass?' 'It was not reason', he answers. That is to say, animals are sentient beings with a reasoning capacity. What, then, is the distinction if it is not reason? 'Man is capable of God; the inferior creatures are not', he writes. 'We have no ground to believe that they are, in any degree, capable of knowing, loving, or obeying God. This is the specific difference between man and brute; the great gulf which they cannot pass over.'

Wesley finds proof of disruption and fallen-ness in the non-human realm in the 'savage fierceness' and 'unrelenting cruelty' observed in many creatures. Disruption is evident even in their appearance.

> And is not the very form, the outward appearance, of many of the creatures, as horrid as their dispositions? Where is the beauty which was stamped upon them when they came first out of the hands of their Creator? There is not the least trace of it left: So far from it, they are shocking to behold! Nay, they are not only terrible and grisly to look upon, but deformed, and that to a high degree.

Despite this alleged defect, Wesley is primarily concerned about non-human creatures as victims. Worst in this regard, non-human creatures are 'exposed to the violence and cruelty of him that is now their common enemy,—man'. At this point he deploys poignant adjectives to describe the plight of domestic animals at the hand of uncaring owners, a contrast not only between animals and humans but also between animal faithfulness and human callousness.

> Is the *generous* horse that serves his master's necessity or pleasure with *unwearied* diligence,—is the *faithful* dog that waits the motion of his hand, or his eye, exempt from this? What returns for their *long and faithful* service do many of these poor creatures find? And what a dreadful difference is there, between what they suffer from their fellow-brutes, and what they suffer from the *tyrant* man! (italics added).

Having described the plight of non-human creatures by constant reference to Romans, Wesley turns to the prospect of hope.

> But will 'the creature', will even the brute creation, always remain in this deplorable condition? God forbid that we should affirm this; yea, or even entertain such a thought! While 'the whole creation groaneth together' (whether men attend or not), their groans are not dispersed in idle air, but enter into the ears of Him that made them. While his creatures 'travail together in pain', he knoweth all their pain, and is bringing them nearer and nearer to the birth, which shall be accomplished in its season.

We may think that Wesley will be content to elicit empathy on the part of humans toward non-human creatures, but his emphasis goes further. There is empathy already—divine empathy—so as to ensure that the groans of non-human creatures 'are not dispensed in idle air, but enter into the ears of Him that made them'. While there is not complete parity between human and non-human creatures, Wesley's reading of Romans finds common ground. The hope that beckons non-human beings is similar to the one humans have.

> Nothing can be more express: Away with vulgar prejudices, and let the plain word of God take place. They 'shall be delivered from the bondage of corruption, into glorious liberty', —even a measure, according as they are capable, —of 'the liberty of the children of God'.

Throughout, the tenor in Wesley's exposition is restoration. Non-human creatures, too, will be

> restored to the vigor, strength, and swiftness… Restored to that measure of understanding which they had in paradise…affections they had in the garden of God, will be restored with vast increase… The liberty they then had will be completely restored…delivered from all irregular appetites… from all unruly passions… No rage will be found in any creature, no fierceness, no cruelty, or thirst for blood (Isa. 11.6-8).

The sermon ends on a note that calls to mind Francis of Assisi's preaching to the birds. While Wesley's actual audience are humans, his closing words suggest that non-human creatures are also in view, addressed in direct speech with the implication that there is hope and higher ground for them, too. 'Rest not till you enjoy the privilege of humanity—the knowledge and love of God. Lift up your heads, ye creatures capable of God! Lift up your hearts to the Source of your being!'

Karl Barth

Karl Barth (1886–1968) had already shown his promise as a theologian by the time the first edition of his commentary on Romans appeared in 1919, but it was Romans that set him on a track to become the most influential theologian of the twentieth century. Thomas F. Torrance, one of Barth's most enthusiastic promoters in the English-speaking world, says of Barth that he 'was unquestionably the greatest theologian that has appeared for several hundred years. His stature rivalled that of the real giants of the Church, not only those of the Reformation epoch, Luther and Calvin, but those of the ancient Catholic Church, Athanasius and Augustine.'[83] John Webster is only slightly less effusive, calling Barth 'the most important Protestant theologian since Schleiermacher, and the extraordinary descriptive depth of his depiction of the Christian faith puts him in the company of a handful of thinkers in the classical Christian tradition'.[84]

83. Thomas F. Torrance, *Karl Barth, Biblical and Evangelical Theologian* (Edinburgh: T. & T. Clark, 1990), p. 1.

84. John Webster, 'Introducing Barth', in *The Cambridge Companion to Karl Barth* (ed. John Webster; Cambridge: Cambridge University Press, 2000), p. 1.

Again, it was Barth's study of Paul in general and of Romans in particular that catapulted him into a position of prominence. His study of Paul's letter began in earnest in 1916, in the middle of World War I, and it took on the character of a conversion experience. 'I read and read and wrote and wrote', Barth confides in a later recollection.[85] His vocational context was at that time pastor of a Swiss congregation; this, too, serving as an incentive for his quest. In the wider context, the sense of disillusionment brought on by the war and the inadequacy of liberal theology to address the crisis cannot be ignored. Webster says that 'one of the most fruitful ways of reading Barth is to look at his thought in the more general context of the breakdown of 'modernity'—the decline...of idealist metaphysics and of the philosophical, moral, and religious culture of subjectivity'.[86] Bruce McCormack sounds a similar note, writing that 'Barth's new theology represented an assault on a central feature of late nineteenth-century bourgeois culture: the understanding of the human individual as the creative subject of culture and history'.[87]

God was in this culture diminished and well-nigh irrelevant: transcendence was out. With his commentary on Romans, Barth reached for means with which to address the crisis. In the first edition, he 'called upon the Church to let God be God, and let man learn again how to be man, instead of trying to be as God'.[88] The last part of the sentence is crucial because Barth worked under the conviction that humans were encroaching high-handedly on God's turf. His exposition of Romans aimed 'to make room again for the holy and transcendent God of the Bible'.[89] Whether or not he succeeded in this regard, the commentary 'exploded like a bomb among the theologians of Europe'.[90]

Rather than conceding that Christianity runs on parallel tracks with human culture and widely held notions of progress, Barth urged to the contrary that Christianity is eschatological and transcendent.[91] In the second edition, a rewriting of the entire book accomplished in the course of eleven months of intense work in 1920, Barth changed many things, but he strengthened the eschatological emphasis. To understand Barth, says McCormack, we need to hear him make the sigh in Romans 8 his own, expectation joining

85. Karl Barth, 'Concluding Unscientific Postscript on Schleiermacher', in *The Theology of Schleiermacher* (Edinburgh: T. & T. Clark, 1982), p. 265, quoted in Webster, 'Introducing Barth', p. 3.

86. Webster, 'Introducing Barth', p. 11.

87. Bruce L. McCormack, *Karl Barth's Critically Realistic Dialectical Theology: Its Genesis and Development 1909–1936* (Oxford: Clarendon Press, 1995), p. 141.

88. Torrance, *Karl Barth*, p. 7.

89. Torrance, *Karl Barth*, p. 7.

90. Torrance, *Karl Barth*, p. 7.

91. Webster, 'Introducing Barth', p. 4.

an eschatologically conditioned longing. This focus in Barth's theology lingers all the way to his final lectures in 1962. Promise, not present fulfillment, is the watchword, 'longing and hope for the coming of God, a new world, and a new humanity, and at the same time...a decisive protest against all human attainments and possessions, everything which now exists and lies ready to hand'.[92]

Perhaps this reveals and gives priority to the personal and existential element in Barth's theology. If so, the personal element is more important than his dialectical method,[93] and more important than the epistemological challenge that in the second edition of the Romans commentary (1921) unfolds relentlessly under 'the long shadow cast by Immanuel Kant'.[94] Perhaps it is in the realm of longing and hope that Barth's humanity shows most clearly. If so, again, it mutes the impression that his primary aim is to restore lost dignity to God, a tall order even for Barth's exceptional rhetorical firepower.

The polemic tone in his Romans commentary cannot be denied. Barth, even to admirers, 'was at heart a polemicist (and a rude one at that)'.[95] When critics of the first edition of his commentary argued that his exegesis seemed driven by a 'system' and not by Paul's text, Barth answers that

> if I have a system, it is limited to a recognition of what Kierkegaard called the 'infinite qualitative distinction' between time and eternity, and to my regarding this as possessing negative as well as positive significance: 'God is in heaven, and thou art on earth'. The relation between such a God and such a man, and the relation between such a man and such a God, is for me the theme of the Bible and the essence of philosophy.[96]

Whether Paul felt the epistemological crisis to which Barth gives voice is a question that must be deferred to another time and context. With regard to the overtly 'ecological' text in Romans (8.18-23), Barth seems to sense that humans and non-humans are suffering *together*. 'Whither can men turn their eyes', he asks—'men, disconsolate in what they are and longing restlessly to be what they are not—without encountering the eyes of others equally disconsolate and filled with longing equally restless'. 'Men suffer', he continues, 'in a world which suffers with them'.

92. McCormack, *Karl Barth's Critically Realistic Dialectical Theology*, p. 32.

93. McCormack (*Karl Barth's Critically Realistic Dialectical Theology*, p. 11) defines Barth's dialectical method as 'a method which calls for every theological statement to be placed over against a counter-statement, without allowing the dialectical tension between the two to be resolved in a higher synthesis'.

94. McCormack, *Karl Barth's Critically Realistic Dialectical Theology*, p. 245.

95. Webster, 'Introducing Barth', p. 6.

96. Karl Barth, *The Epistle to the Romans* (trans. Edwyn C. Hoskyns; London: Oxford University Press, 6th edn, 1968), p. 10.

There is undeniable empathy in this statement. Barth's preoccupation, nevertheless, is not with the particularity of animal and non-human suffering. Instead, he finds fault with the human orientation toward the world and the quest for understanding the world for another reason: it will not set hearts and minds at peace.

> Not for long can we suppose the peace of our direct union with God to lie in the harmony of the external world. For it is itself a COSMOS of things, themselves limited, indirect, and questionable. The more men are aware of their own insecurity and find themselves, under the poignant influence of Christianity, unable to kick against the pricks and forget that they are men, the more their attention is fixed upon the world by which they are encompassed, the more certainly they recognize their own solidarity with it, and the more passionately they seek to penetrate its secrets.[97]

The world, no matter how thoroughly investigated or how well understood, cannot be the solution because it is finite, flawed, and fractured.

> What is it which men perceive and discover, find and apprehend, in their research and in their experience? They know the COSMOS to be theirs: they seek to find their rest in Nature and in History. But instead, with fatal necessity, they discover everywhere—their own unquiet. The language of creatures and elements, of worlds above and beyond, of times both near and far, turns out to be, when once it is deciphered, a strangely human tongue. It speaks of beauty and disgust, of peace and war, of life and death, of finiteness and infinity, of good and evil. It seems as though the contradictions, so well-known to us, were also theirs, the very ground of their existence too; as though our sufferings were theirs, and our diseases also theirs.[98]

Empathy is not absent in this meditation. There is solidarity between the human and non-human realm, solidarity in the discovery of shared inadequacy and existential need. But the thrust in Barth's approach is chiefly the epistemological plight of *human* existence—*that* more than actual non-human suffering. The human turning to nature and to scientific inquiry cannot in any sense be redemptive; it is existentially and epistemologically a dead end. At best it will only intensify further the unquiet that is already there. Non-human suffering is in this scenario a secondary concern if not an incidental discovery within a misguided quest.

Conclusion

Paul is to all these expositors the original writer and Romans the pivotal text. We can only marvel at how widely his interpreters differ and how much concerns contemporary to the respective interpreter influence his reading. In the

97. Barth, *Romans*, p. 306.
98. Barth, *Romans*, p. 307.

personal sphere, Origen finds in Romans medicine for his spiritual need; Augustine the key that solves the moral impasse in his experience; Luther the door to a new view of God; Wesley the gateway to experiential knowledge of the Unseen; Barth the voice to let God speak authoritatively and from on high in the twentieth century. In the realm of eco-theology, Origen denigrates the material world within and without his reading of Romans. Augustine accepts materiality but embraces a radical notion of divine caprice. Luther lets divine grace extend to non-human reality even as he, like Augustine, finds in Romans reasons to deny grace to the majority of humans. Barth's binocular perception includes empathy with non-human creation even though the eye that triggers the empathy is less sharply focused than the eye that looks for epistemological solace in the era of scientific inquiry. Augustine, Luther, and Barth—these three together—find in Romans the mighty fortress for a theology of divine sovereignty.

Romans and Its Most Influential Readers		
	Main Emphasis	**Ecological Yield**
Origen	Participation (spiritual formation)	None direct
Augustine	Justification	Slight
Luther	Justification	Some
Wesley	Justification and participation	Significant
Barth	Justification	Some

From the standpoint of ecological hermeneutics, one reader stands apart after nearly two millennia of interpretations of Romans. That reader, hands down, is John Wesley.[99] And yet he, too, brings a cracked plate to the table of ecological hermeneutics with his affirmation of the immateriality of the human soul. All the most influential readings of Romans look away or hesitate at the doorway to ecology, lending credence to Ludwig Feuerbach's (1804–1872) contention that God in the Christian account would rather that 'there were no world', the world for that reason 'hovering between existence and non-existence, always awaiting annihilation'.[100]

99. Some might argue that Karl Barth is more deserving than Wesley, finding him to affirm a holistic anthropology, but this claim seems doubtful and is at the very least weighed down by Barth's unrelenting ambiguity; cf. *Church Dogmatics* III.2 (trans. Harold Knight, G.W. Bromiley, J.K.S. Reid and R.H. Fuller; Edinburgh. T. & T. Clark, 1986), §46, pp. 325-436; Marc Cortez, 'Body, Soul, and (Holy) Spirit: Karl Barth's Theological Framework for Understanding Human Ontology', *IJST* 10 (2008), pp. 328-45. Jürgen Moltmann (*God in Creation*, pp. 252-55) finds in Barth a rather traditional view of sovereignty, hierarchy, and domination of soul over body: the soul 'rules', the body 'serves'; the soul 'precedes', the body 'follows'; the soul is 'higher', the body 'lower'; the soul 'first', the body 'second'; the soul 'dominates', the body is 'dominated'. The notion that 'the doctrine of creation means anthropology' is evident in *CD* III.3.

100. Ludwig Feuerbach, *The Essence of Christianity* (trans. George Eliot; New York: Harper & Row, 1957), p. 110.

If the disappearance of non-human creation and the earth were a minor and accidental sin of omission in the tradition, the ecological task would be limited to reinserting the missing piece into an otherwise healthy edifice. As it is, the ecological omission is as much theological as it is ecological, meaning that an ecological reading requires careful exegetical and theological groundwork. This outlines the magnitude of the task and sets the tone for the present interpretation. The theological assignment will take precedence over the ecological in the belief that when the theological message is on key, the ecological notes in the symphony that is Romans will not be missing. In this sense the result of looking at Romans through the eyes of its most influential readers boils down to a call to read the entire letter anew.

Chapter 3

The Human Ecology of Romans (Rom. 16.1-27; 1.1-7)

Paul wrote Romans for the benefit of believers in Rome in his own time, but why did he write to them? What was the need or occasion for him to take the trouble of dictating the letter, then send it by personal courier from somewhere in Greece all the way to Rome? Romans is the only letter written to a church that Paul had not been instrumental in establishing, making it an exception in that regard in Paul's surviving correspondence. Given that the legitimacy of speaking as a 'founding father' will not apply to Romans, we might suspect that many of the clues of prior contact that abound in other letters will here be lacking. This and the next chapter will review time, place, people, and issues that are relevant to understanding what Romans was intended to accomplish among believers in Jesus in Rome at the time of its writing. I am calling it the 'human ecology' of Romans because ecology has been described as 'the science of relationships'.[1] The relational elements in Romans are often treated as an afterthought or left unexplored as though these matters are unimportant to the message of the letter. Here, by contrast, the human ecology comes first. We shall see that Paul's network of friends and fellow-workers has explanatory power for the letter as a whole.

Place and Time

'I commend to you our sister Phoebe, a deacon of the church at Cenchreae', Paul writes in the 'greeting' section of the letter (Rom. 16.1). Cenchreae was the port city of Corinth, located slightly less than ten kilometers to the east. By this apparently trivial tidbit Paul gives a hint of where he is at the time of writing Romans while also introducing the likely carrier of the letter. The spatial element moves Corinth to the top of the list of candidate cities for Romans' site of origin. 'Gaius, who is host to me and to the whole church, greets you', he says at a later point (Rom. 16.23). Scholars are widely agreed that this must be Gaius Titius Justus, one of the few

1. Aldo Leopold, 'Natural History', in *A Sand County Almanac: With Essays on Conservation from Round River* (New York: Ballantine Books, 1970), pp. 209-10.

people Paul admits to having baptized (1 Cor. 1.14), his house located next door to the synagogue in Corinth (Acts 18.7) and now, in the context of writing Romans, Paul's host (Rom. 16.23). These strands have led scholars to conclude with a high degree of confidence that Paul wrote Romans from Corinth.[2]

The temporal axis is closely related to the spatial. 'Greet Prisca and Aquila, who work with me in Christ Jesus, and who risked their necks for my life', Paul writes (Rom. 16.3-4). According to Acts, Paul had met Aquila and Prisca for the first time on his initial trip to Corinth. Upon his arrival there, 'he found a Jew named Aquila, a native of Pontus, who had recently come from Italy with his wife Priscilla, because Claudius had ordered all Jews to leave Rome. Paul went to see them, and, because he was of the same trade, he stayed with them, and they worked together— by trade they were tentmakers' (Acts 18.1-3). This important couple appear in 1 Corinthians, too, written later from Ephesus (1 Cor. 16.8). 'The churches of Asia send greetings', Paul says in that letter, adding that 'Aquila and Prisca, together with the church in their house, greet you warmly in the Lord' (1 Cor. 16.19).

Three stations are now evident on the spatio-temporal axis. At the first station, Paul meets Prisca and Aquila *in* Corinth, staying with them and working alongside them as a fellow tentmaker (Acts 18.1-3). This point has coordinates in time by the disclosure that Prisca and Aquila at that moment were recent arrivals in Corinth, having come there from Rome in connection with Claudius' expulsion of Jews. The expulsion can be confirmed from other sources. 'Since the Jews constantly made disturbances at the instigation of Chrestus, he expelled them from Rome', says Suetonius.[3] Claudius' Edict is likely to have been triggered by disturbances in one or more of the Roman synagogues over the new teaching about Jesus ('Chrestus'). At the time when this happened the Jewish population of Rome comprised perhaps as many as 50,000 people by responsible estimates.[4] We have strong reasons to believe that Prisca and Aquila were believers in Jesus when they met Paul in Corinth and already a couple of influence. The first encounter in Corinth most likely happened in 50 CE, shortly after the Edict of Claudius in 49 CE.[5]

The second station on our timeline coincides with the writing of 1 Corinthians. At that time Paul is in Ephesus in Asia Minor (1 Cor. 16.8).[6] Prisca

2. Jewett, *Romans*, p. 21.
3. Suetonius, *Claudius* 25.4.
4. Jewett, *Romans*, p. 55. Jewett has a range from 15,000-60,000.
5. James Dunn, *Romans 1–8* (WBC; Dallas: Word, 2002), p. xlix.
6. Hans Conzelmann, *1 Corinthians: A Commentary on the First Epistle to the Corinthians* (trans. James W. Leitch; Hermeneia; Philadelphia: Fortress Press, 1975), pp. 2-3.

and Aquila are with him, now joining Paul in sending greetings back to Corinth where they had first met (1 Cor. 16.19). From 1 Corinthians we have confirmation that this couple served in leadership roles, hosting a house church in Ephesus just as they seem to have done in Corinth. Paul's stay in Ephesus has been dated from August 52 until October 54 CE (Acts 19.8-9; 20.3).[7]

This leads to the third station, corresponding with the time of writing Romans. Prisca and Aquila are now back in Rome, a conclusion resting on the fact that Paul sends greetings to them in Romans (16.3-4). By sound computations of the evidence, the year is now 56 CE.[8]

By way of summary, we have Paul meeting Prisca and Aquila in Corinth no later than 50 CE. They unite with Paul in ministry, and they are with him in Ephesus, the city from which Paul writes 1 Corinthians between 52 and 54 CE. At the point when Paul returns to Corinth, Prisca and Aquila are back in Rome (16.3-4). The Claudius Edict lapsed upon the death of the emperor in 54 CE; it was in fact officially revoked. Jews were trickling back to Rome and with them Prisca and Aquila. They were sending greetings to Corinth when Paul wrote 1 Corinthians from Ephesus, and now Paul is sending greetings to them from Corinth upon their return to Rome (16.3-4). Paul is himself intent on going to Rome, he confides in Romans (1.8-15; 15.23-24), but only for a stopover on his way to Spain (15.23-24, 28). First, however, he must make a detour all the way to Jerusalem for the purpose of delivering in person the collection he has taken among the Gentiles for the benefit of Jewish believers in Jerusalem (15.25-28, 30-31). The policy of prioritizing pioneer work is the reason why his intention to visit Rome has not yet materialized (15.15-21). His work now brought to a successful completion all the way from Jerusalem to 'as far around as Illyricum' (15.18-19), he is ready to take on the pioneer work in Spain (15.24, 28). He expresses the hope that believers in Rome will sponsor the mission (15.24).[9]

7. Jeremy Murphy-O'Connor, *Paul: A Critical Life* (Oxford: Oxford University Press, 1996), pp. 29-31.

8. Udo Schnelle, *Apostle Paul: His Life and Theology* (trans. M. Eugene Boring; Grand Rapids: Baker Academic, 2005), p. 305; Murphy-O'Connor, *Paul*, p. 332; Jewett, *Romans*, pp. 18-21. Douglas A. Campbell (*Framing Paul: An Epistolary Biography* [Grand Rapids: Eerdmans, 2014]) develops a tightly argued alternative chronology for Paul's life and letters, the premise for which is to rely on the letters only and to avoid unwanted 'cross-contamination' from Acts. He ends up with much earlier dates than in the usual scheme. As for Romans, his proposed date is 52 CE, with Galatians written one year earlier.

9. For a discussion of the background of the churches in Rome and their *Jewish* origin, see Reidar Hvalvik, 'Jewish Believers and Jewish Influence in the Roman Church until the Early Second Century', in *Jewish Believers in Jesus: The Early Centuries* (ed. Oskar Skarsaune and Reidar Hvalvik; Peabody, MA: Hendrickson, 2007), pp. 179-216.

The points on the map that emerge from this background survey are mind-boggling. By our standard of awareness of the world it may not qualify as a 'global mission', but there is enough here to believe that Paul understood himself to be spearheading a message and a movement that were to go 'to the ends of the earth' (Isa. 52.10). We have Jerusalem at the far east of the Mediterranean and Spain to the far west. In between, we have key cities like Ephesus, Athens, Corinth, and Rome. We have constant travel back and forth, arduous and time-consuming, to be sure, but to all appearances undertaken by a man who is undeterred by difficulties and distance. The entire Mediterranean basin is home field, as it were, Paul's movements motivated by anxiety about the state of affairs in Jerusalem (Rom. 15.25-26, 30-31), the well-being of the church at Rome (1.11-12; 15.24), and the mission to the as yet unreached people in Spain (15.24, 28).

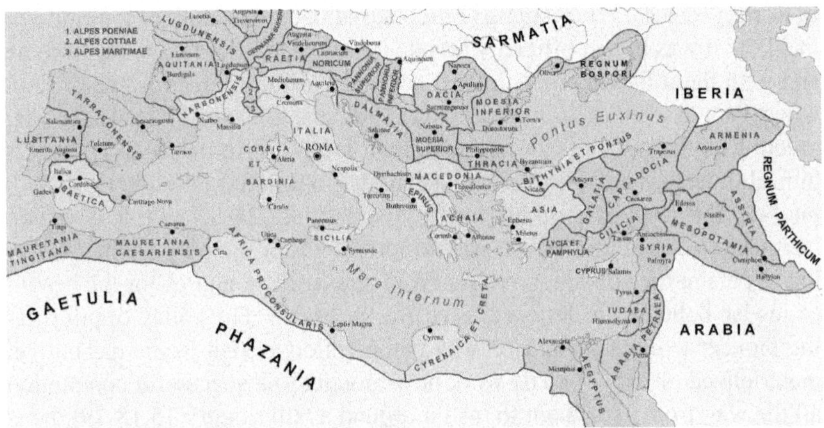

The web of relationships that comes to light in Paul's letters, and in Romans in particular, is no less impressive than the geographical range. Phoebe, the deacon in Cenchrea whom Paul commends to the congregations in Rome (16.1-2), is the strongest candidate as to who brought the letter and read it out loud to the Romans. Arland Hultgren counts it 'all but certain that she was the bearer of the letter from Paul to the Christians at Rome as attested in early sources and widely affirmed in modern scholarship'.[10] Prisca and Aquila, originally residents of Rome and now back in Rome, having spent a number of years in close collaboration with Paul in Corinth and in Asia Minor, will not see their prestige in Rome diminished by Paul's greeting and favorable mention (16.3-4). Significantly, in Rome

10. Arland J. Hultgren, *Paul's Letter to the Romans* (Grand Rapids: Eerdmans, 2011), p. 569; Schnelle, *Apostle Paul*, p. 305; see also Bruce W. Longenecker and Todd D. Still, *Thinking Through Paul: An Introduction to His Life, Letters and Theology* (Grand Rapids: Zondervan, 2014), p. 167.

as in Ephesus, a church is meeting at their house (Rom. 16.5; 1 Cor. 16.19). Epaenetus, Paul's first convert in Asia is on the list of people singled out for special mention (Rom. 16.5). 'Greet Andronicus and Junia, my relatives (or 'kindred') who were in prison with me; they are prominent among the apostles, and they were in Christ before I was', Paul continues (16.7). These individuals are significant for a point that is not made often enough in connection with reconstructions of Paul's message: they are noteworthy and highly competent witnesses in Rome to the kind of person Paul was and the message he preached. The long list of additional names is also important, but the names mentioned above have their credentials spelled out, one of them Paul's first convert in Asia (16.5), Prisca and Aquila fellow laborers with Paul (16.3-4), Andronicus and Junia former fellow prisoners and designated as 'outstanding among the apostles' (16.7, NASB).[11] Their shared history with Paul, having been exposed to him 24/7 for extended periods of time, has wide ramifications.

Some of Paul's Friends in Rome

- Phoebe, deacon, likely carrier of the letter to Rome
- Prisca and Aquila, hosts to house churches in Corinth, Ephesus, and Rome; close fellow-workers with Paul
- Epaenetus, Paul's first convert in Asia

Richard Hays contends that a responsible interpretation of Paul's letters must take into account the narrative substructure as an important means by which to ascertain meaning.[12] In most of his letters, Paul writes to people with whom he has had extensive prior contact. The prior contact appears in the letters as allusions—words, images, and flashbacks—that take up little space in the letters but makes it possible for the writer to sharpen his focus and to cover large topics with few words (cf. Gal. 3.1; 4.6; 1 Cor. 15.1-3; 2 Thess. 2.5). When we read the letters today, we lack the prior contact of the original recipients, and yet we are not absolved of the requirement to explore the allusions and unearth the underlying narrative if we want to get it right. As we have seen, Hays also argues that Paul's use of the Old Testament is a key to interpretation.[13] Again, however, the Old Testament often appears in the form of allusions, requiring the reader to engage with Paul's letter *and* the Old Testament voices upon which he draws. The believers in Rome as a whole lacked the prior experience that constitutes the 'narrative substructure' in Paul's other letters, but the disadvantage is muted by the array of *living* witnesses in the Roman house churches, Epaenetus, Prisca, Aquila, Junia, and Andronicus among them. These individuals are important in Paul's biographical narrative, and they count as channels to knowledge

11. Cf. Eldon Jay Epp, *Junia: The First Woman Apostle* (Minneapolis: Fortress Press, 2005).

12. Hays, *Faith of Jesus Christ*, pp. 33-162.

13. Hays, *Echoes of Scripture*, pp. 1-33.

of Paul and well informed second-hand mediators of Paul's preaching.[14] As Jerome Murphy-O'Connor suggests, it is not implausible that Prisca and Aquila returned to Rome in a move that was coordinated with Paul in order to assess the situation and lay the groundwork for his subsequent arrival.[15] If so, Paul's greeting to them in Romans is more than a friendly wave of the hand to old friends now at a distance. They represent an important and living element in the narrative backbone of Romans.[16]

The Roman Contingency

'Letters are words on target because of their contingency', says J. Christiaan Beker.[17] The occasion for the statement is not letters in general but specifically the letters of Paul. It is meant as a corrective to the tendency to read Paul's letters without regard for the context and situation that the letter was meant to address. In a further comment, now taking aim at the decontextualized commentaries on Romans of Karl Barth and Anders Nygren, Beker calls it

> a methodological error to view Romans as a theological structure developed in a vacuum—a view that portrays Paul as engaged with himself in thought, wrestling with the perennial truth of the gospel. The hermeneutical advantage of 'timelessness' cannot silence the historical illegitimacy and impossibility of this procedure. It is illegitimate to turn a lack of historical evidence to theological-hermeneutical advantage and to conceive of any Pauline letter as an exercise in thought without concrete historical mooring.[18]

I intend to heed this injunction in this commentary without denying the difficulties that go with it. The churches in Rome are assumed to have an early beginning in the Jewish synagogues in the city with gradual expansion to include increasing numbers of Gentile believers. The Edict of Claudius in 49 CE suggests controversy in the wake of Jews accepting Jesus as the Messiah while also serving as evidence that the message came to Rome at an early date and had a significant impact. Estimates vary as to how much

14. Peter Lampe, 'The Roman Christians of Romans 16', in *The Romans Debate* (ed. Karl P. Donfried; Grand Rapids: Baker Academic, rev. edn, 2011), pp. 216-30.

15. Murphy-O'Connor, *Paul*, pp. 331-32.

16. Jewett (*Romans*, p. 12) expands the narrative elements to include (1) the narrative of each congregation's origin prior to Paul; (2) the narrative of Paul's previous ministry; (3) Paul's situation now, meaning his plan to go to Jerusalem and then embark on the Spanish mission; and (4) 'the reading of the letter to each of the congregations in Rome'. See also Bruce W. Longenecker (ed.), *Narrative Dynamics in Paul: A Critical Assessment* (Louisville, KY: Westminster/John Knox Press, 2002).

17. Beker, *Paul the Apostle*, p. 62.

18. Beker, *Paul the Apostle*, p. 66.

Claudius' Edict influenced the make-up of the churches in Rome. Some hold that it left the Christian community depleted of Jewish influences[19] while others believe that the Edict only affected a few synagogues and that the notion of a Jewish vacuum is a myth.[20] Aside from numerical considerations, internal evidence in Romans suggests at least some communal tensions that Paul's letter makes it a point to address (14.1-17).

While the requirement that Romans must be understood against a background of situational contingency cannot be bypassed, it has proved exceedingly difficult to nail down precisely what the need was. Frank J. Matera captures the most widely held options, finding all to be legitimate. Romans can in his view be seen as (1) a summary of Paul's gospel; (2) a defense speech with Paul's upcoming visit to Jerusalem in view; (3) a letter of introduction in view of Paul's mission to Spain in the hope of eliciting support from the Roman churches; and (4) an attempt on the part of Paul to mediate matters regarding 'the weak' and 'the strong' in the Roman congregations.[21] Matera stops short of adjudicating in favor of any of these views, a decision that seems prudent in the short run, but it carries the risk of being a survey of *what* Paul wrote rather than an answer to *why*.

Udo Schnelle finds more than a single reason, but he assigns priority to one. 'In order to carry out his planned mission to Spain, the apostle needs the support of the Roman church both financially and in terms of personnel. Thus he introduces himself to the Roman Christians, most of whom he does not know personally, by means of an extensive presentation of his own theology,' says Schnelle.[22] He adds that Paul also had Jerusalem on his mind, 'clearly not sure that the Jerusalem church will accept the offering he is bringing, for only on this presupposition can we understand his request for the prayers of the Roman church and the doubts that continue to plague him (cf. 15.30, 31)'.[23] A third factor is the aftershock of the crisis in Galatia and Paul's letter to the Galatians, 'for Paul's line of argument is still visibly shaped by the disputes with the Galatians in the immediate past, and the church in Rome will also have already heard reports about Paul and his gospel from the mouths of his opponents (cf. Rom. 3.8, 31a; 6.1, 15; 7.7;

19. Schnelle (*Apostle Paul*, p. 303) attributes huge significance to the Edict, saying that it (1) effected the final separation of Christians from the synagogue; (2) made Jewish believers in Jesus (Schnelle calls them 'Christians') a minority after 49 CE; (3) prevented Paul from coming to Rome earlier; (4) made it necessary for the Christian community to find its own way with regard to the Roman authorities, apart from the synagogue. Variants of this view are held by a majority of interpreters.

20. Murphy-O'Connor, *Paul*, p. 333.

21. Frank J. Matera, *Romans* (Paideia; Grand Rapids: Baker Academic, 2010), pp. 8-10.

22. Schnelle, *Apostle Paul*, p. 305.

23. Schnelle, *Apostle Paul*, p. 305.

16.17-18)'.[24] All these reasons are certainly possible, but they do not distil easily into one sharply focused reason, ranging as they do from the planned mission to Spain to Paul's upcoming trip to Jerusalem, and then, further back, to the conflict in Galatia and the prospect that a 'Galatian' problem may be in the making in Rome.

James Dunn uses different terminology, but the gist of his proposal is quite similar to Matera's. According to Dunn, we have the options of (1) a *missionary* purpose anchored in Paul's self-understanding as the apostle to the Gentiles; (2) an *apologetic* purpose meant to establish a bond with believers in Rome *and* a practice run in preparation for what he intends to say in Jerusalem in order to allay fears among Jewish believers 'at home' concerning his theology; and (3) a *pastoral* purpose, seeking to counter potential divisions in the Roman house churches relative to friction between 'liberated' Gentile believers and less 'liberated' believers with Jewish backgrounds.[25] These options are plausible and have explanatory power, but they do not provide a single focus, certainly nothing by way of what has Murphy-O'Connor speak of Paul *learning* in the context of the Thessalonians, addressing a *crisis* in Galatia, adding his voice to *contemplation* at Colossae, seeking *partnership* in Philippi, or helping resolve *confusion* in Corinth. While these terms carry risks relative to the issues in these letters, no one has come up with the single word that captures Romans. Murphy-O'Connor is a case in point, his heading for Romans a wistful *looking westward.*

Robert Jewett's magisterial commentary commits to a decision with regard to the Roman contingency that at first sight, at least, gives the impression that Paul had a single reason after all.

> The basic idea in the interpretation of each verse and paragraph is that Paul wishes to gain support for a mission to the barbarians in Spain, which requires that the gospel of impartial, divine righteousness revealed in Christ be clarified to rid it of prejudicial elements that are currently dividing the congregations in Rome.[26]

This suggestion makes the Spanish mission count 'in the interpretation of each verse and paragraph', indicating that Paul throughout writes with that purpose in mind. But the sharp focus of this assertion is attenuated by the qualifying reasons, Jewett's sentence bending over backwards and sideways to make the theological content of the letter and the perceived pastoral problems in the Roman churches link organically with the Spanish mission. Was the mission to Spain so imminent and urgent that it required a letter like Romans to get it started? Were conditions in Rome a make-it-or-break-it deal

24. Schnelle, *Apostle Paul*, pp. 305-306.
25. Dunn, *Romans 1–8*, p. lv.
26. Jewett, *Romans*, p. 1.

with respect to the mission? Can one imagine a Pauline mission to Spain that had the support of believers in Rome in the absence of Paul's letter? Paul is indeed announcing his plan for a mission to Spain (15.24, 28), but does the announcement amount to the actual reason for writing the letter? The body of Jewett's commentary exposes the relentless drive for honor and dignity in the Roman value system and the fallacy of imperial genuflection to power and conquest. It casts Romans as Paul's effort to break the stranglehold of the anxiety-ridden and communally divisive way of life engendered by these values, replacing them with the honor code made manifest in the paradox of Christ crucified and a life dedicated to the good of others. 'Each of us must please our neighbor for the good purpose of building up the neighbor', is in that sense Paul's bottom line for communal living (15.2). This adds up to a compelling and in many ways groundbreaking account of the contrast between Roman imperial 'theology' and the Roman social reality on the one hand, and the shame-defying, shame-shattering theology of the cross and the Christian social alternative on the other.

And yet we must ask whether Jewett makes the case that Paul had to succeed in this regard in order for the Spanish mission to proceed. Rather than showing how the Spanish mission bears on 'the interpretation of each verse and paragraph', Paul's counter-value message to the Romans seems quite enough in and of itself, the Spanish mission still important but not necessarily the generative force that the paragraph quoted above makes it out to be.

Douglas A. Campbell attempts a complete reset for Paul's theology in general and for Romans in particular. He commendably takes on the task of identifying the contingency in Romans that others have explored with mixed success and probably less determination.[27] He approaches the topic broadly, paying attention to the text, prior scholarship, and the need for defining criteria for assessing the merits of a given proposal. He ends up with a total of eleven possible 'contingencies', his own proposal the last of the eleven and the most unique.[28] It lies beyond the scope of this commentary to review each option and its merits in detail. Suffice it to say that the strongest candidates are found among the ones that have been considered above. Campbell's preferred alternative stands sufficiently apart to warrant more extensive treatment. In short, he sees Romans as 'an attempt to negate the influence of hostile countermissionaries at Rome'.[29]

> Fundamentally, Romans was written for the same reasons that Galatians was written—to defend Paul's gospel against the depredations of certain

27. Douglas A. Campbell, *The Deliverance of God: An Apocalyptic Rereading of Justification in Paul* (Grand Rapids: Eerdmans, 2009), pp. 469-600.
28. Campbell, *Deliverance of God*, pp. 470-518.
29. Campbell, *Deliverance of God*, p. 495.

> hostile countermissionaries. Moreover, the significant differences between these two letters are more apparent than real—the similarities are well known—and all are explicable in terms of the different relationship Paul had with the Roman Christians, most of whom did not know him or his gospel (or this debate).[30]

Campbell admits that this theory builds largely—but not exclusively—on a feature in the frame section—'Paul's caustic warnings in the letter closing against false teachers (16.17-20)'. He regards this as 'the only feature in the data that seems self-sufficient or independently valid *and* capable of expansion in a way that can plausibly explain all the other issues'.[31] In these verses Paul issues a strongly worded exhortation to be wary of troublemakers (16.17-20). 'If Paul thought that teachers preaching a gospel opposed to many of his own most important concerns were approaching Rome, he would surely have seen this as a dire threat', says Campbell.[32] Instead of being able to count on the support of believers in Rome for his mission, he would be facing 'a nightmare scenario…in evangelistic terms'.[33] Paul's concern in this regard is encoded in the letter, as well. Implicit awareness of competing influences may be inferred from Paul's mention that he is preaching only where Christ has not been named (15.20). Why aren't the countermissionaries doing pioneer missionary work? Why, and here, too, are they piggy-backing on his labor? The similarity between Romans and Galatians that has been noted by many is not explained by taking Romans to be a decontextualized and sanitized presentation of themes found in Galatians—a full six years have intervened between these two letters—but because the Roman churches are facing the same kind of false teachers, if not the very same Teacher.[34] In a further expansion on this scenario, Campbell argues that 'Paul will turn out to focus on a single Teacher—presumably, a particular figure who led the small group that was hostile to Paul'.[35] Given that the emerging scenario and confrontation have an antecedent, Paul and the Teacher aware of each other from previous rounds, we expect the familiarity to show in the letter. As to the specific

30. Campbell, *Deliverance of God*, p. 495.

31. Campbell, *Deliverance of God*, p. 495.

32. Campbell, *Deliverance of God*, p. 501.

33. Campbell, *Deliverance of God*, p. 501.

34. Campbell, *Deliverance of God*, pp. 504-505. In *Framing Paul*, as noted, Campbell proposes a personal and epistolary chronology within which Paul writes Romans a few months after writing Galatians in 52 CE, shortly thereafter departing for Jerusalem. Neither the counter-missionary hypothesis nor the similarity between Galatians and Romans requires acceptance of Campbell's proposed chronology.

35. Campbell, *Deliverance of God*, p. 506. The notion of 'a *single* Teacher' is unnecessary and goes beyond the evidence in Romans. 'Those who cause dissensions' in Rom. 16.17-20 certainly refer to more than one.

identity of Paul's implied opponent, he is 'a Jewish Christian, so the entire debate unfolds 'in-house', between different Jewish Christian understandings of the pagan mission and its implication'.[36] Jewish *Christian*, or Jewish believer in Jesus, is here a key term. In this conception, the 'Jewish' elements in Romans cannot be read as a dress down of Judaism.

This leads to the boldest and most risky aspect in Campbell's construct, the dialogical character of Romans, the sense of an ongoing give-and-take, and to instances of *prosōpopoiia*, irony, and 'speech-in-character'. This is part of the rhetorical and persuasive strategy in Romans, the technical terms for which is *diatribe*. Jewett says that the diatribe was not only 'a combative argumentative technique' as scholars earlier have thought; its main arena was actually the classroom. In the diatribe, the teacher 'created imaginary interlocutors to voice the questions and misconceptions that push the discussion forward'.[37] The teaching analogy is a useful category, but we must still take into account the actual situation Paul was addressing. Was his main purpose *clarification* and *demonstration*, these terms reflecting the need to enable grasp of a complex subject, or was it also *refutation*, dialogical speech driven by the need to defeat a real opponent and an opposing point of view? By either reckoning Romans is a dialogical text. Stanley Stowers says that 'Paul wrote in dialogical exchanges, ring compositions, transitional false conclusions and rejections, various rhetorical figures, speech-in-character, and so on'.[38] In awareness of such features, it will be necessary to ascertain whether some of the 'characters' in Romans are real and also when they are speaking, whether real or made up.

If we follow Campbell's lead, we hear at various points in Romans voices other than Paul's.[39] Campbell is not alone in claiming that some passages in Romans must be read as mimicry and speech-in-character,[40] but this feature looms larger in his analysis than in other interpretations. His investment in 'hearing' the voices in Romans promises significant gains, but the gains are matched by commensurate risk. Campbell's reading of Rom. 1.18-32 is the most important case in point. In order to capture the feature of speech-in-character in this passage, we are expected to discern *who* is talking when it is not Paul and *how* this person is talking: we must strive to *hear* the voice. I shall put this to the test in greater detail in Chapter 5.

36. Campbell, *Deliverance of God*, p. 506.

37. Jewett, *Romans*, p. 25.

38. Stanley K. Stowers, *A Rereading of Romans: Justice, Jews, and Gentiles* (New Haven: Yale University Press, 1994), p. 11.

39. Campbell, *Deliverance of God*, pp. 528-29.

40. Stowers (*Rereading of Romans*, pp. 16-21) argues at length for speech-in-character in Romans, as does Jewett (*Romans*, pp. 25-28, 71).

Why Paul Wrote Romans: Ranking the Options according to Explanatory Power		
Reason	Proponent(s)	Explanatory Power
Contain hostile countermissionaries	Campbell	High
Preparation for Spanish mission	Jewett, Schnelle, Dunn	Fair
Theological testament or defense of gospel	Bornkamm, Käsemann, Dunn	Fair
Mediate between 'the weak' and 'the strong'	Donfried, Minear, Wright, Reasoner	Fair

So far, we have a plausible reconstruction for time and place, and we have a short list of plausible reasons why Paul wrote the letter. A commitment with regard to what is the most persuasive reason should still be on hold although I will admit at this early stage that the explanatory power of the 'countermissionary hypothesis' appears strong. To this we must add that the threshold for writing a letter would be high. The letter had to be hand carried by a courier at a time when travel meant a lot of hardship, time, and expense, the distance between Corinth and Rome in itself a huge deterrent. To put this in perspective, there was no wireless messaging, internet, or even an organized mail service available to Paul.

The Contingency of Romans: the Key Texts

Most of the texts that hold explicit promise in a search for the reason that led Paul to write to the Romans are found in the letter frame at the beginning and the end of the letter (1.1-17; 15.14–16.20). I will now take a closer look at the key texts, beginning with Rom. 1.1-7. This passage conforms to customary epistolary practice in Paul's day and to how Paul's other letters begin except for two distinctives. In Romans, the greeting is longer and more elaborate, one sentence stretching to a full seven verses and in the process reading like a carefully worded summary of the entire letter. While in other letters Paul usually includes the name(s) of his fellow worker(s) with him at the time of writing, in Romans Paul stands alone at the beginning of the letter. If the long and topically loaded greeting tends toward the impersonal, this is counterbalanced by the fact that there is only one face and one hand at the point of origin.

> Paul, a servant of Jesus Christ, called to be an apostle, set apart for the gospel of God, which he promised beforehand through his prophets in the holy scriptures, the gospel concerning his Son, who was descended from David according to the flesh and was declared to be Son of God with power according to the spirit of holiness by resurrection from the dead, Jesus

> Christ our Lord, through whom we have received grace and apostleship to bring about the obedience of faith (*eis hypakoēn pisteōs*) among all the Gentiles for the sake of his name, including yourselves who are called to belong to Jesus Christ, To all God's beloved in Rome, who are called to be saints. Grace to you and peace from God our Father and the Lord Jesus Christ (Rom. 1.1-7).

Caveats apply from the very beginning. Paul has never been to Rome or seen the Roman congregations in person. This might tempt the first-time reader to believe that the letter will be the Romans' first awareness of him. With the letter he is, as it were, parachuting into their lives from afar, counting on the claims made in the opening sentence to establish his importance. If this should be our impression, we have already reviewed evidence to the contrary. Like letters and books otherwise, Romans is best understood by the *re-reader*. Re-readers know that Prisca, Aquila, Epaenetus, Julia, Andronicus and a host of Paul's friends live in Rome, having made their acquaintance in the closing section of the letter (16.1-16). Have these individuals not told their fellow congregants about Paul? Has Epaenetus not shared his testimony of how he became a believer in the Jewish Messiah and Paul's first convert in Asia Minor (16.5)? Have Prisca and Aquila not related to the Roman believers how they met Paul in Corinth, then went with him to Ephesus or joined him there, witnessing first-hand what Paul thought and said and wrote in a host of other contexts (16.3-4)? Did Paul leave them in the dark about *his* story or his missionary activities, including the crisis in Galatia that most likely occurred around the time when they first met? Had he failed to tell them about the trials and triumphs preceding their encounter in Corinth, or they about theirs in Rome? It is not only safe but necessary to assume that Junia and Andronicus passed on to their fellow-believers in Rome what Paul shared with them when they at some point were fellow-prisoners with him (16.7). Extensive prior knowledge of Paul on the part of the Roman believers must be taken as an established fact.[41] What Paul is becoming to the Roman believers by means of the letter he already is to Phoebe, Prisca, Aquila, Epaenetus, and many others. The letter is not the bridgehead to Paul's subsequent arrival in person; the bridgehead is already there.[42]

Conversely, the list of names and details at the end of the letter is proof that Paul is well informed about the Roman house churches. How would he otherwise be able to write with such confidence, 'Greet Mary, *who has*

41. Simon Gathercole, 'Romans 1–5 and the "Weak" and the "Strong"', *RevExp*, 100 (2003), pp. 36-38.

42. *Contra* Campbell (*Deliverance of God*, pp. 148-51), the notion of 'biographical silence' in Romans has limited use whichever way it is turned in view of the numerous living connections between Paul and the Christian community in Rome.

worked very hard among you' (16.6, italics added)? Prisca and Aquila were likely his primary source of information, but they need not be the only ones or the most recent. Moreover, it is possible that the individuals named in the closing section of the letter correspond to select members in various house churches across Rome. Paul, pre-eminently a pastor, is in that regard a master of detail and of the personal touch.

In the long opening sentence Paul sets forth his apostolic credentials, his calling echoing the calling of Old Testament prophets before him (Rom. 1.1; cf. Jer. 1.4-5). Pedigree at the level of calling is corroborated by lineage with respect to message: 'the gospel of God' is precisely what God 'promised beforehand through his prophets in the holy scriptures' (Rom. 1.2). 'Here it is claimed that the prophets articulated the gospel of God in the period before Christ', says Jewett.[43] Paul would be well aware that the claim of continuity with regard to message and purpose will be contested by other interpreters of the Jewish scriptures, but this is the claim he is committed to defending. Some scholars contend that the introduction contains the rudiments of an early Christian creed that precedes Paul and in that sense a statement that might be known to the Romans:[44] his gospel is anchored in the Jewish scriptures; it is centered on God's Son, 'who was descended from David according to the flesh' and certified as the long-awaited Jewish Messiah (1.3); its ramifications and veracity are confirmed 'by resurrection from the dead' (1.4). This is certainly God-centered, and it is also Jewish. If the letter is written to congregations having a Gentile majority, there is no downplaying Jewishness. Paul may not qualify as a 'Judaizer' in other regards and is rarely thought of as one, but in this respect he is 'Judaizing'. God is the God of the Jewish Scriptures, and Jesus Christ is the Jewish Messiah, now reaching out to the Gentiles (1.3-4).

Paula Fredriksen has captured the magnitude of this change with commensurate verve. Noting that 'ancient gods traveled in the blood; ethnicity anchored piety', she emphasizes that Paul's message imposed on the Gentiles the same requirement that Judaism made in the pre-Christian period. This was no small step. '*But to make a commitment to a foreign god to the point of forsaking the gods of one's own people*—a condition unique to Judaism in the pre-Christian period—*was to behave with alarming and insulting disloyalty*', says Fredriksen.[45] Paul the Jewish believer in Jesus was not offering Gentiles a more congenial option in that regard.[46]

43. Jewett, *Romans*, p. 103.

44. Jewett, *Romans*, p. 103.

45. Fredriksen, *Augustine and the Jews*, p. 27.

46. 'Israel's god was famously demanding of his people, insisting that he be the sole recipient of their worship'; cf. Paula Fredriksen, 'Judaizing the Nations: The Ritual Demands of Paul's Gospel', *NTS* 56 (2010), p. 236.

Paul claims that he is uniquely called and commissioned by God to tell this story in the Gentile world in order 'to bring about [the] obedience of faith (*eis hypakoēn pisteōs*) among all the Gentiles for the sake of his name' (1.5; cf. 15;18; 16.26). What does he mean by 'obedience of faith', the expression occurring here and again at the very end of the letter (16.26)? Our decision as to the meaning of this expression is important because the phrase reads as a statement of purpose for Paul's mission among the Gentiles.[47]

C.E.B. Cranfield presents a list of seven options.[48]

(i) 'obedience to the faith' (obedience to the body of doctrine)
(ii) 'obedience to faith' (the authority of faith)
(iii) 'obedience to God's faithfulness attested in the gospel'
(iv) 'the obedience which faith works'
(v) 'the obedience required by faith'
(vi) 'believing obedience'
(vii) 'the faith which consists in obedience'

He concludes in favor of the last of these options (vii), arguing that to Paul faith *in* God and obedience *to* God are equivalent and interchangeable. 'Paul's preaching is aimed at obtaining from his hearers true obedience to God, the essence of which is a responding to His message of good news and faith'.[49] In this construal, faith *is* obedience, and *obedience* is to have faith.

This view is favored by the majority of scholars, but it has not won unanimous support. Jewett deems it problematic to make faith and obedience interchangeable terms. 'Since the expression "obedience of faith" is found only in 1.5 and 16.26 in the entirety of ancient literature, it was most likely coined by Paul to fit the rhetorical exigency of this letter', he says.[50] As to content, he argues that 'Paul speaks here of the special sort of obedience produced by the gospel'.[51] He locates the need for making this point in the respective leanings of Jewish and Gentile Christians in Rome. 'Since "obedience" was a favored concept for Jewish theology and "faith" was a favorite shibboleth for Gentile believers in Rome (14.1, 22, 23), the combi-

47. Jewett, *Romans*, p. 110.

48. C.E.B. Cranfield, *A Critical and Exegetical Commentary on the Epistle to the Romans* (2 vols.; ICC; Edinburgh: T. & T. Clark, 1975–79), I, p. 66.

49. Cranfield, *Romans*, p. 1.66; cf. John Murray, *Romans* (2 vols.; NICNT; Grand Rapids: Eerdmans, 1974), p. 13; Brendan Byrne, *Romans* (SP; Collegeville, MN: Liturgical Press, 1996), p. 46; Ernst Käsemann, *Commentary on Romans* (trans. Geoffrey W. Bromiley; Grand Rapids: Eerdmans, 1994), pp. 14-15. Scriptures cited in support for this view are Rom. 1.8; 10.16; 15.18; 16.19; cf. 2 Cor. 9.13.

50. Jewett, *Romans*, p. 110.

51. Jewett, *Romans*, p. 110. This is option (iv) on Cranfield's list, 'the obedience which faith works'.

nation of these two terms conveys an interest in finding common ground', he writes.[52] Don B. Garlington has in an in-depth study sought to bring the two options together, Paul coining 'an ambiguous phrase which expresses two ideas at the same time: the obedience which consists in faith and the obedience which is the product of faith'.[53] Obedience in the ordinary sense of the word must not be left out. He proposes 'faith's obedience' or 'believing obedience' as viable translations in English that preserve the intention and ambiguity in Romans.[54]

These options share the omission of leaving out a discussion of *pistis* in Romans, either because most of the discussion belongs to the era before the meaning of *pistis* became an important topic or because other options are felt to be undeserving.[55] How will the phrase *eis hypakoēn pisteōs* ('for the obedience of faith') in Rom. 1.5 read if *pistis* carries the connotation *faithfulness*? We recall from chapter 1 that this option commends itself in Romans on the strength of the connection between Romans and Habakkuk. When Habakkuk complains about God's absence and apparent unfaithfulness (Hab. 1.2-4), he is assured that God will intervene and bring to light what is missing (Hab. 2.2-4). What is missing in Habakkuk's despairing outlook is not resilient faith but proof of divine faithfulness. Thus God's prescription, 'The Righteous (One) shall live by my faithfulness (*pisteōs mou*)' (Hab. 2.4, LXX; cf. Rom. 1.17). By an alternative route, *faithfulness* is also the meaning of *pistis* in the contrast between human *unfaithfulness* and divine *faithfulness* in the story of Israel (Rom. 3.2-3). 'Will their faithlessness (*apistia*) nullify the faithfulness (*pistis*) of God?' Paul asks (3.3).

Is Paul's specially coined phrase—if that is what it is—captured adequately in a translation that centers on the human *response*, whether in the form of faith *as* obedience or as faith that leads to obedience? This view, if accepted, will largely cement the stereotype that Paul is striving to iron out the relationship between faith and works and the proper definition of the two. If, on the other hand, Paul's horizon is wider for the *pistis* that qualifies 'obedience',[56] how wide is the horizon? Has Paul coined a phrase that will not leave out the divine *initiative* that undergirds obedience in the human realm, obedience now rising on the foundation of divine faithfulness?

52. Jewett, *Romans*, p. 110; cf. also Moo, *Romans*, p. 52.

53. D.B. Garlington, 'The Obedience of Faith in the Letter to the Romans', *WTJ* 52 (1990), p. 224.

54. Garlington, 'The Obedience of Faith', p. 224.

55. Cranfield (*Romans*, p. 1.66) includes an alternative that nuances the meaning of *pistis*, 'obedience to God's faithfulness attested in the gospel' (alt. iii), but he does not dignify this option with a discussion.

56. Note, as Jewett does (*Romans*, p. 110) that 'a substantive in the genitive limits the meaning of a substantive on which it depends'. By this rule *pistis* limits the meaning of *hypakoē*.

An argument in favor of such a reading is found in the immediate context of the phrase. Paul is set apart for

> the gospel of God
> which [God] promised beforehand
> through his prophets
> in the holy scriptures,
> the gospel concerning his Son,
> who was descended from David
> according to the flesh
> declared to be Son of God
> with power
> according to the spirit of holiness
> by resurrection from the dead,
> Jesus Christ our Lord (1.1-4).

This statement captures the most important elements in the story concerning which Paul is the foremost ambassador among the Gentiles. And what is it—if not the story of God's faithfulness? What is it, as he notes at the very end of Romans—if not 'the revelation of the mystery that was kept secret for long ages' (16.25)? Even if Paul is telling the story 'to bring about the obedience of faith among all the Gentiles' (1.5), faith understood as the human response to the story, the response will not allow daylight between faith and the faithfulness of God that anchors faith. Taking this a step further, we have to open up to seeing *pistis* as *divine faithfulness* not only as a permissible inference but as the intended meaning of Paul's unique phrase. All of the foregoing happened 'for the sake of his *name*', says Paul (16.5). *Name* stands for the character of the Person in question. As Ernst Käsemann notes, 'the name, as elsewhere in antiquity, is the nature of the bearer becoming manifest, and it can thus be personified'.[57] For this reason 'the obedience of faith relates to the revelation of Christ'.[58] The range of meanings now possible for the phrase *eis hypakoēn pisteōs* compasses *revelation* and *participation*, the former embedded in *pistis*, the latter in *hypakoē*.

Galatians supplies two strands of evidence in support of this line of thought. First, in Galatians Paul speaks of *pistis* as an event, even depicting an action in motion. 'Now before *pistis came*, we were imprisoned and guarded under the law until *pistis* would *be revealed* (*eis tēn mellousan pistin apokalyphtēnai*)', Paul says (Gal. 3.23). He proceeds to press the case that *pistis* '*has come*' (Gal. 3.25, italics mine). Translations that convey Paul's intent might be 'before the message came', 'before Christ came', or even, grasping that *pistis* is shorthand for a larger story, 'before (God's) faithfulness was demonstrated', especially when the last part of the

57. Käsemann, *Romans*, pp. 14-15.
58. Käsemann, *Romans*, p. 15.

verse says that *pistis* 'would be *revealed*' (Gal. 3.23).[59] Hans Dieter Betz, in a break with precedent, notes that *pistis* in Gal. 3.23 and 3.25 'describes the occurrence of a historical phenomenon, not the act of believing of an individual'.[60]

Second, in Galatians Paul describes the parties in the conflict as 'those of faith' or 'those of faithfulness' (*hoi ek pisteōs*) at one side (Gal. 3.7, 9), and 'those of works of law' (*hosoi ex ergōv nomou*) on the other side (Gal. 3.10), the latter group also referred to as 'those of circumcision' (*hoi ek peritomēs*) (Gal. 2.12). J. Louis Martyn regards these terms as phrases coined for the occasion and thus analogous to Paul's phrase in Rom. 1.5: they are short-hand expressions adapted to the needs in the conflict at hand. In Galatians, the phrases are best seen as markers of identity.[61] Those who are *ek pisteōs* (Gal. 3.7, 9) refer to believers whose identity is built on *pistis*; the other phrases to believers whose identity is built on '*works of law*' or '*circumcision*' (Gal. 3.10; 2.12).

Crucially, *pistis* in the argument is more than *faith* posing as the counter-point to *works*, as though one group derives its identity from the stance of believing and the other from the works they do. As Martinus C. de Boer notes, the phrase *ek pisteōs* 'is an abbreviation of the phrase *ek pisteōs* (*Iēsou*) *Christou*', and the *pistis* of Jesus Christ refers to his faithfulness.[62] Paul uses succinct rhetorical tools in order to draw a contrast between those whose spiritual identity are centered on the faithfulness of Jesus Christ and those whose identity has a competing focus. In Galatians, notably, the competing focus is circumcision (Gal. 3.1-3). If the countermissionary agents that caused such trouble in Galatians are closing in on believers in Rome, as Campbell argues, the struggle in Rome will also relate to competing points of reference for the community's sense of identity.

Emphases in the Letter Opening (Rom. 1.1-7)

- Paul's divine calling (prophet-like)
- 'Judaizing' message: bringing the God of the Old Testament to the Gentiles
- 'Gospel of God', i.e. good news about God
- Materiality and physicality
- Obedience grounded in the faithfulness of God

Focus on divine action is at the heart of Paul's message in Romans. The righteousness of God has been revealed '*by the faithfulness of Jesus Christ*

59. Martyn, 'The Apocalyptic Gospel in Galatians', p. 254.

60. Hans Dieter Betz, *Galatians* (Hermeneia; Philadelphia: Fortress Press, 1979), p. 176 n. 120.

61. Martyn, *Galatians*, p. 299.

62. Martinus C. de Boer, *Galatians* (NTL; Louisville, KY: Westminster/John Knox Press, 2011), p. 204.

(*dia pisteōs Iēsou Christou*)' (Rom. 3.22, translation mine). Likewise, 'for what the law was unable to do, rendered powerless by the flesh, *God* (*did*) by sending his Son in the likeness of sinful flesh' (8.3, translation mine). And again, 'Out of Zion will come the Deliverer' (11.26). Paul is over and over again telling the story of what *God* did. Much as he craves acceptance of the story in the form of faith, his focus in the introduction of Romans rehearses what God did: the prophets are vindicated; the Davidic kingship is no longer in shambles; the presence and power of God have been manifested in the world by the resurrection of Jesus from the dead (1.1-4).

Pistis thus understood is therefore more than 'faith' in a doctrine or a Person even if the Person in question is God. It is more than anything shorthand for the story Paul is telling in the Gentile world, a story that has God as its main subject. This takes us back to the phrase Paul uses to explain his mission among the Gentiles—'to bring about obedience grounded in the faithfulness of God (*eis hypakoēn pisteōs*) among all the Gentiles' (1.5; cf. 16.26, translation mine).

When the polemic context for this phrase is recognized, it is evident that the other side in the controversy seeks to upstage Paul by claiming to bring about a superior brand of obedience (*hypakoē*) among the Gentiles, circumcision and all (2.25-29). Paul, however, will not be upstaged. It is precisely on the point that what the other side brandishes as its foremost distinctive that Paul's message delivers—and the other side does not.

Ecological Fallout

The 'human ecology' of Romans is distinctive for bringing to light an extensive web of relationships exceeding what we find in other letters. But the ecological fallout of the introductory passage in Romans is also major, 'ecological' now in the usual sense of the word. Paul has anchored 'the gospel of God' to the promises given beforehand 'through his prophets in the holy scriptures' (1.2). As we saw in chapter 1, the prophetic horizon is inclusive, offering hope to the earth and to non-human creation. Placing Jesus as the true heir to David's throne brings up the revealer and restorer in the prophets (Isa. 11.1-10; Jer. 23.5; 33.15; cf. Acts 13.22-23). As it is written, Paul could well say, 'On that day the branch of the LORD shall be beautiful and glorious, and the fruit of the land shall be the pride and glory of the survivors of Israel' (Isa. 4.2).

Above all, there is unapologetic and irreducible materiality in the story. Jesus is 'descended from David *according to the flesh* (*kata sarka*)' (Rom. 1.3). God is in Jesus embracing the world and humanity, taking on the expectations and obligations invested in David. Materiality is not an embarrassing feature or a transitory stage on the way to a higher state of existence. *Flesh* is redeemed by the resurrection and not abolished by it (1.4).

When we bring the competency of re-readership to bear on the opening passage in Romans, we discover extensive contact between Paul and Rome, mediated through a large network of people well known to Paul and Paul to them. The web of relationships and the cities dotting the routes of travel depict an earthy apostle. Paul does not chafe at the world and its needs as he moves unstoppably from Jerusalem to Corinth, then from Corinth to Ephesus and back to Corinth, writing from there of his intention to go to Rome and on to Spain—but not before he has tended to the material needs of brothers and sisters in Jerusalem (15.25-33).

If we allow the phrase *eis hypakoēn pisteōs* to be 'obedience grounded in divine faithfulness' (1.5), the commitment and self-sacrifice implied in the divine action sets the pattern for human obedience. An obedience thus construed cannot dissociate itself from the rights and needs of other creatures or of the earth. Divine faithfulness structures and empowers faithfulness in the human realm even though nothing in the human realm can match it. For this reason the most hopeful ecological configuration in the opening sentence in Romans is divine action and the faithfulness of God.

Chapter 4

'Not Ashamed of the Good News' (Rom. 1.16)

The opening passage of Romans (Rom. 1.1-7) is well served by an earthy hermeneutic for its errand to appear in force. We find in it an announcement of 'the gospel of God' (1.1), its content outlined by Paul's affirmation of the message of the prophets in the Jewish scriptures (1.2); the embrace of materiality and humanity in the Davidic descendant 'according to the flesh' (1.3); hope confirmed by the resurrection of the body (1.4); and obedience in the human realm reflecting the faithfulness of God to all creation (1.5; cf. 8.19). Although Paul's apostolic mandate, pastoral concerns, and missionary intent so far are too general to explain fully his purpose in writing to the Romans, the opening passage touches on key elements in the letter as a whole. As we shall see, Paul follows through with more clues in the letter frame (1.8-15; 1.16-17; 15.22-33; 16.17-20). In light of evidence we have looked at so far, we can shorten the list of likely reasons why Paul wrote the letter to three main options that are specific enough to be testable. Paul wrote in order to (1) prepare and solicit support for the Spanish mission;[1] (2) mediate in matters regarding 'the weak' and 'the strong' in the Roman congregations;[2] or (3) defend the message of God's faithfulness against the program of divisive counter-missionaries, one tenet of which is that Gentile believers need to be circumcised.[3]

Rome on his Mind

The next passage in Romans follows established letter conventions in form but not in content.[4]

1. Schnelle, *Apostle Paul*, p. 305; Jewett, *Romans*, p. 1.
2. Paul S. Minear, *The Obedience of Faith: The Purposes of Paul in the Epistle to the Romans* (SBT; London: SCM Press, 1971), pp. 1-35; Campbell, *Paul's Gospel in an Intercultural Context*, pp. 21-22; Philip Esler, *Conflict and Identity in Romans: The Social Setting of Paul's Letter* (Minneapolis: Fortress Press, 2003), pp. 111-34, 339-56.
3. Campbell, *Deliverance of God*, p. 495.
4. Cranfield, *Romans*, p. 73; Käsemann, *Romans*, p. 17.

> First, I thank my God through Jesus Christ for all of you, because your faith is proclaimed throughout the world. For God, whom I serve with my spirit by announcing the gospel of his Son, is my witness that without ceasing I remember you always in my prayers, asking that by God's will I may somehow at last succeed in coming to you. For I am longing to see you so that I may share with you some spiritual gift to strengthen you—or rather so that we may be mutually encouraged by each other's faith, both yours and mine. I want you to know, brothers and sisters, that I have often intended to come to you (but thus far have been prevented), in order that I may reap some harvest among you as I have among the rest of the Gentiles. I am a debtor both to Greeks and to barbarians, both to the wise and to the foolish—hence my eagerness to proclaim the gospel to you also who are in Rome (Rom. 1.8-15).

Paul commends the Roman believers for their *pistis* (1.8). We can translate this as 'faith' or 'faithfulness'.[5] Here the commendation is best viewed broadly as praise for their acceptance of the message about Jesus. Their commitment is worthy of note in the Roman world, perhaps to the effect of facilitating Paul's work. Paul and the Romans are allies because the message concerning which he is an apostle is identical to the message in which they have put their trust. Endorsements matter. A Roman validation of Paul's ministry and message would not be inconsequential even though there is an element of hyperbole in the claim that their 'faith' is proclaimed '*in all the world*' (1.8).[6] If corroboration for this claim were needed, we might think of the Edict of Claudius in 49 CE on account of 'Chrestus', the ensuing expulsion of Jews sufficient to be noted in the Roman Empire.[7]

The depth of the alliance between Paul and the Roman believers appears in Paul's claim that he has been praying for them, this glimpse into the private sphere conveyed in language that suggests authenticity and warmth (1.9). Paul's spiritual engagement with the Romans is not an interest that

5. Rudolf Bultmann (art. πίστις, *TDNT* 6, pp. 174-82) demonstrates that πίστις in classical Greek on the one hand carries the meaning 'reliability', 'trustworthiness', 'proof', and even the 'means of proof', and on the other hand represents the stance toward one whose trustworthiness is above question, that is, 'confidence' or 'trust'. The Old Testament conditioning of πίστις in the New Testament is undeniable and crucial, but Old Testament and Hellenistic usage merely expands the scope and direction of meanings that are already intrinsic to the Greek term. According to Ian G. Wallis (*The Faith of Jesus Christ in Early Christian Traditions* [SNTSMS, 84; Cambridge: Cambridge University Press, 1995], pp. 1-23), lexical evidence for pre-New Testament use of πίστις in the Septuagint and in Hellenistic Jewish Literature favors the notion 'faithfulness' rather than 'faith'. If, 'as the OT understands it, faith is always man's reaction to God's primary action' (Weiser, art. πίστις *TDNT* 6, p. 182), the premise of the term is God's faithfulness. See also Douglas A. Campbell, 'The Meaning of ΠΙΣΤΙΣ and ΝΟΜΟΣ in Paul: A Linguistic and Structural Perspective', *JBL* 111 (1992), pp. 91-103.

6. Murray, *Romans*, p. 57.

7. Suetonius, *Claudius* 25.4.

came on the spur of the moment. While he cannot claim paternity for the house churches in Rome, his unceasing prayers on their behalf count as genuine pastoral involvement, placing the Roman congregations within the sphere of his apostolic mission and pastoral jurisdiction.

This leads naturally to the repeated statement of intent to visit Rome in person.

> that... I may somehow at last succeed in coming to you (1.10).
>
> I am longing to see you (1.11).
>
> I have often intended to come to you (1.13).
>
> hence my eagerness to proclaim the gospel to you also who are in Rome (1.15).
>
> I desire, as I have for many years, to come to you (15.23).

Is there a hidden agenda in these claims, or an agenda yet to be disclosed, the long delayed visit to Rome a mere pretext for other items tucked away in Paul's sleeve? This possibility certainly exists in his admission 'that I may reap some harvest among you' (1.13), reading this statement as a preview of his declared aim to undertake a mission to Spain and his need of Roman support for the mission (15.23-24). But such a utilitarian reading is insufficiently mindful of the terms of endearment in the opening passages of the letter. On the strength of this passage (1.8-15), the eventual Roman visit is best seen as an end and not only as the means to an end. The twice-repeated, in more or less the same words, 'I am longing to see you' (1.11) and 'I have often intended to come to you' (1.13; cf. 15.23) cannot be reduced to a mercenary relationship. Paul writes in the diction of legitimacy, familiarity, and fondness that we find in his letters otherwise, virtually obliterating the difference between congregations that are 'his' by virtue of being their founder and the church in Rome. His hope to 'reap some harvest among you' (1.13) does not necessarily mean that 'harvest' has a monetary referent. A better option is to take at face value his wish to 'share with you some spiritual gift to strengthen you' (1.11) and the more modest objective that 'we may be mutually encouraged by each other's faith, both yours and mine' (1.12).

Notions of mutual benefit are unpretentious and soft-spoken, to say the least. John Murray says that 'Paul is eager that the Romans know of his heartfelt concerns for them and desire to see them. Perhaps there were some in the church who felt slighted that the "Apostle to the Gentiles" had not yet deigned to visit the capital of the Gentile world.'[8] These are plausible inferences, but they leave a '*so what*' impression. What is shaping up so far in the letter, instead, suggests that Paul is motivated by a

8. Murray, *Romans*, p. 58.

combination of *his* love and *their* need and not *his* love and *his* need, the latter referring to his need for their support for the westward mission. His expressions of intent and affection imply that Paul writes to the Romans because he has a sense of who they are and what they need. The *need* aspect could be fully as acute as the occasions that gave rise to Pauline letters to believers in Thessalonica, Galatia, or Corinth. Within the broad context of Paul's affection for them, we need to identify the situational warrant that carries enough weight for Paul to make the effort despite the unremitting demands on his time.

Not Ashamed

This leads into the statement that is widely regarded as the theme or thesis statement in Romans.[9]

> For I am not ashamed of the gospel; it is the power of God for salvation to everyone who has faith, to the Jew first and also to the Greek. For in it the righteousness of God is revealed from faithfulness for faithfulness; as it is written, 'The Righteous One will live by [my] faithfulness' (1.16-17, translation mine).

Paul introduces the subject with a reference to shame, or rather, absence of shame. Three main options need to be considered for the shame-aspect, one relating to Roman culture, a second relating to opposition to Paul's message, and a third to realities that are partly existential and partly biblical.

Shame, as Robert Jewett notes over and over in his commentary, is the one thing all Romans wish to avoid. Conversely, honor ranks highest on the Roman scale of values, the pursuit of honor and of things deemed to promote honor sought without embarrassment. Against the assumed background of Roman preoccupation with honor and avoidance of shame, Paul embraces Jesus, a figure recognized to be shameful through and through. 'A divine self-revelation on an obscene cross seemed to demean God and overlook the honor and propriety of established religious traditions, both Jewish and Greco-Roman', says Jewett.[10] Within this framework, the apostle confronts the Roman value system head-on by the statement, 'I am not ashamed (*epaischynomai*)' (1.16). Jewett follows through on the Roman backdrop to Paul's contention, writing that the thesis of Rom. 1.16-17 at its center 'is the paradox of power, that in this shameful gospel that would seem to lack the capacity to prevail, the power of God is in fact revealed in a compelling manner'.[11]

9. Jewett, *Romans*, p. 135.
10. Jewett, *Romans*, p. 137.
11. Jewett, *Romans*, p. 137.

The polemical horizon emerging in this scenario becomes more evident when it is recognized that Paul claims on behalf of his gospel what the Roman emperor and the imperial cult celebrate as the hallmark of the Roman system.[12] That system, bursting at the seams with symbols of conquest and military power, a 'national security state' in all senses of the term, is a source of pride and is advertised in prideful ways with abandon. By contrast, the Roman religion and value system are in Paul's message exposed and undone by a figure that does not play the power card. Crucially, it is part of the gospel *exposé* that the Roman imperial 'savior' (*sotēr*) does not deliver the life, salvation, and plenitude that are tirelessly and tiringly advertised in the imperial propaganda, whether in the person of Augustus as 'the savior of the universe' or Nero as 'the savior and benefactor of the universe'.[13] The imperial propaganda, its fallacies at times apparent to the Romans as an emperor without clothes apart from Paul's exposé, faces censure for being an idolatrous constellation and for failing the test of truth-in-advertising. Reading Paul's 'thesis statement' with awareness of the anti-imperial message makes seemingly innocuous phrases in the statement ring with prosecutorial significance: it is '*in it* (*en autō*)', that is, in the *gospel* (*to euangelion*) that the righteousness of God is revealed; it is '*in it*' and not in the preposterous claims of the Roman imperial cult that life, dignity, and healing are found (1.16-17). Words that recur like a mantra in the imperial propaganda are taken over by Paul as though they can have no other referent than Jesus, *power* (*dynamis*) and *salvation* (*sōteria*) now drawn to a different scale and untarnished by deception and the predatory ways of the imperial system (1.16).[14]

Honor and shame will not fully disappear, only that they are now defined by a different standard and conceived in a setting within which even Roman emperors will be called to account (2.5). In Jewett's conception,

> All who place their faith in this gospel will be set right, that is, be placed in the right relation to the most significant arena in which honor is dispensed: divine judgment. Thus the triumph of divine righteousness through the gospel of Christ crucified and resurrected is achieved by transforming the system in which shame and honor are dispensed. The thesis of Romans therefore effectively turns the social value system of the Romans upside down.[15]

12. Jewett, *Romans*, pp. 137-40.

13. Jewett, *Romans*, p. 139.

14. The predatory character of *Pax Romana* has been well documented; e.g. Klaus Wengst, *Pax Romana and the Peace of Jesus Christ* (trans. John Bowden; London: SCM Press, 1987), pp. 7-54; J. Nelson Kraybill, *Apocalypse and Allegiance: Worship, Politics, and Devotion in the Book of Revelation* (Grand Rapids: Brazos Press, 2010). Thus Kraybill, 'Caesar's peace depended on violence' (p. 59).

15. Jewett, *Romans*, p. 139.

Whether Paul made it his primary goal to take on the Roman value system of honor and shame, as Jewett implies, or whether the criticism is incidental and unintentional, it cannot be doubted that Gentiles in the Roman Empire perceived the contrasts in the story Paul told and in the communities that formed in the wake of his telling the story. Paul's sense of obligation is certainly conditioned by a different way of seeing the world, declaring himself to be 'a debtor both to Greeks and to barbarians, both to the wise and to the foolish' (1.14), the barbarian now counting as much in God's eyes as privileged Roman citizens and cultured Greeks.

'I am *not ashamed*' in Romans

- Contrast to Roman value system of honor and shame
- Contrast to opponents' wish to mute the '*shame* factor'
- Affirmation of Old Testament conviction that God will not—and has not—put the believer to shame

Nevertheless, it is premature to conclude that the imperial horizon is the main referent for Paul's engagement with the subject of shame early on in the letter (1.16). The presumed setting for a second, alternative option will be intra-communal, reviving the possibility that Paul seeks to stem the influence of counter-missionaries in the fledgling churches along lines similar to his struggle in Galatians. When the subject of circumcision pops up with no apparent prior warning in Romans (2.25-29), the letter clearly addresses a conflict within which circumcision is a specific point of dispute. Why, suddenly and as if out of the blue, does Paul bring up this question, speaking in second person as though he is addressing a genuine, opposing point of view? 'Circumcision indeed is of value if you obey the law', he says without explicit prodding in the lead-up, 'but if you break the law, your circumcision has become uncircumcision' (2.25).

The dialogical and combative character of the argument is inescapable. Paul addresses the subject of circumcision because someone has brought it up and is promoting it in the Roman congregations. That 'someone' attributes value to circumcision that in Paul's eyes is overrated and misplaced. The controversy bears on Paul's contention that he is 'not ashamed of the gospel' (1.16), recalling that a shame-factor is very much at issue in the dispute over circumcision in Galatians. 'But my friends, why am I still being persecuted if I am still preaching circumcision?' Paul asks in that letter. 'In that case the offense of the cross has been removed', he claims (Gal. 5.11). In Martyn's translation we read that 'my preaching circumcision would amount to wiping out the scandalous character of the cross'.[16] The people said to be persecuting Paul in Galatians are not Roman Gentiles but believers in God who profess faith in Jesus. Their faith commitment blends with the rite of circumcision and the persistence of communal barriers betokened

16. Martyn, *Galatians*, p. 467.

by it. Circumcision is in Galatians so much a counterpoint to the gospel as to make Paul exclaim, 'Listen! I, Paul, am telling you that if you let yourselves be circumcised, Christ will be of no benefit to you' (Gal. 5.2). He turns the problem into an either-or proposition, impugning the motives and the agenda of his opponents. 'It is those who want to make a good showing in the flesh that try to compel you to be circumcised—only that they may not be persecuted for the cross of Christ', he says of the teachers stirring up trouble (Gal. 6.12). In Paul's view there is no advantage in circumcision because 'the circumcised do not themselves obey the law, but they want you to be circumcised so that they may boast about your flesh' (Gal. 6.13).

The honor-shame polarity of the dispute over circumcision is undeniable. On the one hand, circumcision is billed as a cause for boasting (Gal. 6.13; Rom. 2.17). On the other hand, the cross is a signifier of scandal and shame. Circumcision mutes the shame-factor of the cross by representing a competing and not merely a complementary point of reference. On a symbolic and spiritual level, the dispute captures the concern of the entire letter 'by the antinomy between God's act in the cross of Christ and the human act of circumcising the flesh', as Martyn notes.[17] Indeed, if Paul were to 'advocate the circumcision of Gentile converts, he would become the propagator of an acceptable religion, and the persecutory opposition to his work would cease. That move on his part would also terminate his proclamation of God's gracious—and scandalous—invasion of the world in the hideous event of Christ's crucifixion (Gal. 2.21; 3.1; 1 Cor. 1.23).'[18] We may grasp the thrust of this argument intuitively: the cross signifies an unimaginable, unrepeatable singularity, circumcision business as usual. In what way, for instance, can a surgical procedure on the male genitals convey the reality of the cross, either by way of preparation or by way of consequence?

On a communal level, circumcision preserves the old order, at least the old order of gender distinction (only males are circumcised) while also preserving a residue of ethnic difference (cf. Gal. 3.28). As Paula Fredriksen notes, circumcision is 'singled out in Hellenistic, pagan, Jewish, and Christian literature as the premier mark of the Jew, and especially of the convert to Judaism'.[19] In Galatians, Paul's opponents insist on circumcision as a condition for table fellowship between Jewish and Gentile believers in Jesus and thus as a requirement for inclusion in the community (Gal. 2.1-14). Important texts in the New Testament represent this as a problem that challenged the original in-group (Jewish believers) on a visceral level (Acts 10.1-48; cf. Gal. 2.11-14). Were Paul to 'preach circumcision', therefore,

17. Martyn, *Galatians*, p. 476.

18. Martyn, *Galatians*, p. 476.

19. Paula Fredriksen, 'Judaism, the Circumcision of the Gentiles, and Apocalyptic Hope: Another Look at Galatians 1 and 2', *JTS* 42 (1991), p. 537.

he would be reinforcing 'the distinction and barrier between covenant Jew and outlaw Gentile, and thus removing or abolishing the offence which his gospel of the cross caused for the more traditional Jewish understanding of God's covenant promise and purpose' (Gal. 2.11).[20] There is more merit to the first part of this claim than to the second because the so-called 'traditional Jewish understanding' was far less insistent that Gentiles be circumcised as a requirement for communal participation than what is evident in the heated disagreement regarding Jews and Gentiles in Paul's experience.[21] To the extent that elements of honor and shame prevail in the social economy of circumcision, the community brought into existence by the cross terminated the most basic polarities of the old order (Gal. 3.28).

Jewish communities in the Diaspora enjoyed hard-won exemption from Roman cultic participation.[22] Gentile affiliation with the synagogue could take many forms, in some cases including circumcision. Of the novelties impacting the synagogue in the wake of the message about Jesus, the circumcised Gentile had the prospect of benefiting from the exemption clause that the empire granted to Jews. While this aspect of the circumcision debate cannot be ignored, by itself it lacks explanatory power. Fredriksen points to factors that seem more important. 'But the enthusiastic proclamation of a Messiah executed very recently by Rome as a political troublemaker—a *crucified* Messiah—combined with a vision of the approaching End preached also to the Gentiles—this was dangerous', she says.[23] Paul's gospel, highlighting precisely the *crucified* Messiah, the inclusion of the Gentiles, and the end of the age *without* the attendant, stabilizing requirement of circumcision, represented a riskier, more combustible mix. Paul's conflict with the advocates of circumcision in Galatia and Rome plays out in an environment where conflicting theological perceptions are muted or magnified by real existential and social hazard. 'The open dissemination of a Messianic message put the entire Jewish community at risk', says Fredriksen.[24]

When we take this scenario into account, the confession, 'I am not ashamed of the gospel', contrasts with the stance of his opponents. His opponents, rather than or more than, Roman imperial reality are a primary

20. James D.G. Dunn, *The Epistle to the Galatians* (BNTC; London: A. & C. Black, 1993), p. 281.

21. Fredriksen, 'Judaism, the Circumcision of the Gentiles, and Apocalyptic Hope', pp. 532-48.

22. Menahem Stern, 'The Jewish Diaspora in the Second Temple Era', in *A History of the Jewish People* (ed. H.H. Ben-Sasson; Cambridge, MA: Harvard University Press, 1976), p. 280.

23. Fredriksen, 'Judaism, the Circumcision of the Gentiles, and Apocalyptic Hope', p. 556.

24. Fredriksen, 'Judaism, the Circumcision of the Gentiles, and Apocalyptic Hope', p. 556.

concern (Rom. 1.16). '*I* am not ashamed', he writes, knowing full well that *they* are, their approach designed to diminish the shame and mute the risk. The conflict over circumcision later in the letter will not come as a surprise when we include the perspective of his opponents in the thesis statement.

A third horizon for Paul's assertion (1.16) looks to the Old Testament, to texts in the Psalms and the prophetic literature dealing with the discrepancy between reality and expectations—and specifically to the believer's sense that he or she *has been put to shame*. This perspective is existential as much as it is biblical. From the point of view of the Jewish believer,

> the prophetic promise of God's righteousness comes precisely as the answer to this question, that is, as an answer to the problem of theodicy. In Scripture the theodicy problem is occasioned not by the general question of how a just God can allow suffering in the world but rather by the particular problem of how Yahweh can abandon Israel.[25]

The notion of shame is again in play—not as a counterpoint to the imperial value system or as determination to stick to the less traveled road of the cross against incentives to seek a more congenial path—but in the sense of being let down by God. 'Fear of embarrassment that one's expectations may prove false', is how the Friberg Lexicon explains Paul's key word (1.16). The choice of words suggests that the apostle is resolutely headed into the conceptual and scriptural turf of psalmists and prophets.

> *Paul*: I am not ashamed (*epaischynomai*) of the gospel (Rom. 1.16).
>
> *Old Testament:* You have made us the taunt of our neighbors, the derision and scorn of those around us. You have made us a byword among the nations, a laughingstock among the peoples. All day long my disgrace is before me, and shame (*aischynē*) has covered my face at the words of the taunters and revilers, at the sight of the enemy and the avenger. All this has come upon us, yet we have not forgotten you, or been false to your covenant (Ps. 44.13-17; 43.14-18, LXX).
>
> Now you have rejected (us) and put us to shame (*katēschynas*) (Ps. 44.9; 43.10, LXX).
>
> O my God, in you I trust; do not let me be put to shame (*kataischyntheiēn*) (Ps. 25.2; 24.2, LXX).

In the Old Testament, 'shame' works both ends of the field, first as the plight of the disgraced believer, the distress of whom is intensified by his or her failure to understand (Ps. 44.9, 13-17). The plight is further aggravated by the scorn and derision that rain down on him or her, the subjective corollary of which is shame. The psalmist's plea not to be put to shame seeks redress for the intolerable situation (Ps. 24.2, LXX). At that point 'shame'

25. Hays, *Echoes of Scripture*, p. 38.

appears—or *dis*-appears—at the other end of the field in the form of assurance that God will in no way abandon the believer to shame.

> See, I am laying in Zion a foundation stone, a tested stone, a precious cornerstone, a sure foundation, and the one who trusts will not be put to shame (*kataischynthē*) (Isa. 28.16, LXX, translation mine; cf. Rom. 10.11).

> The Lord GOD helps me; therefore I have not been disgraced (or 'put to shame); therefore I have set my face like flint, and I know that I shall not be put to shame (*aischynthō*) (Isa. 50.7, LXX).

It will not be easy to discount Hays' argument that Paul's vocabulary in Romans is conditioned by notions of shame and vindication along Old Testament lines,[26] especially since the perspective occurs more than once in Romans (1.16; cf. 9.32; 10.11). God has in Christ delivered on God's promise. In Romans, Paul adds his voice to the chorus of Old Testament voices, affirming that God has not put the believer to shame. Romans, like Psalm 40, is testimony to God's faithfulness on the subject that existentially counts the most.

> I have told the glad news of deliverance (*ṣedeq*)
> in the great congregation;
> see, I have not restrained my lips,
> as you know, O LORD.
> I have not hidden your saving help (*ṣᵉdāqâ*)
> within my heart,
> I have spoken of your faithfulness (*'ĕmunâ*)
> and your salvation;
> I have not concealed your steadfast love
> and your faithfulness (*'ĕmunâ*)
> from the great congregation (Ps. 40.9-10).

When we read the same text in the Septuagint, the vocabulary is even more striking on two counts that matter in Romans: *Righteousness* (*dikaiosynē*) is on the lips of the person speaking, and righteousness must be understood as *right-making*.

> I have proclaimed (your) *right-making* (*dikaiosynēn*)
> in the great congregation;
> see, I have not held back my lips,
> as you know, O LORD.
> Your *right-making* (*tēn dikaiosynēn sou*)
> I have not hidden in my heart,
> and your salvation I have declared.
> I have not hidden your mercy (*eleos*)
> and your faithfulness (*tēn alētheian sou*)
> from (the) great congregation (Ps. 39.10-11, LXX, translation mine).

26. Hays, *Echoes of Scripture*, pp. 36-41.

Of the three options we have assessed with the aim of coming to terms with the 'shame' factor in Paul's thesis statement (1.16-17), the third option is the most existential and scriptural. While this option shows Paul to be in conversation with the Old Testament and the deep existential concerns often expressed in the Old Testament, as seen in the texts above,[27] it does not remove the possibility of counter-influences or counter-missionaries from the equation. Paul's 'mission statement' speaks to the existential predicament of believers who are at a loss explaining the discrepancy between God's promises and *their* reality. Something is missing, and the missing element is something *God* has failed to do. Paul's message amounts to an announcement that the missing element is no longer missing. This interpretation puts the content of what God has done squarely at the center. God has addressed the problem of God's apparent absence and non-performance in the message of the life, death, and resurrection of Jesus. Note, too, that God's intervention is described in terms of 'mercy'—a world seen with eyes of compassion. All of this projects divine right-making in bold colors and is a message that in its entirety speaks of what God does.

Contrast this to the implications of counter-missionary influences that have circumcision as part of its agenda. Paul's affirmation is in no way muted if we read it against a background of conflict. The competing program will, first, frame the requirement of circumcision against a different idea as to what is missing, its focus on something humans have failed to do. Second, the content of what is missing represents a contrasting and competing focus to the content of Paul's gospel message. Just as Paul anchors his central affirmation in the Old Testament, the other side does, too. As we shall see, they begin with the problem of human sin and not with the problem of God's apparent absence. Paul's 'thesis statement' may well represent his deepest conviction, but he does not express his conviction in neutral territory. If this captures the situation that forms the background of Romans, the 'thesis statement' stakes out a position against a different and—to Paul—menacing and damaging view.

The affirmation of God's faithfulness that began in the letter opening (1.1-7) continues here and is now raised to be the thesis of the letter (1.8-17). This is the most ecological of the options considered above, more ecological than shame in light of Roman notions of honor and shame, and also more ecological than the shame that Paul's opponents

27. Hays (*Echoes of Scripture*, pp. 36-7) has shown that Ps. 98.2-3 (97.2-3, LXX) sounds the same theme of revelation, right-making, and vindication; cf. also Douglas A. Campbell, 'An Echo of Scripture in Paul, and Its Implications', in *The Word Leaps the Gap: Essays on Scripture and Theology in Honor of Richard B. Hays* (ed. J. Ross Wagner, C. Kavin Rowe and A. Katherine Grieb; Grand Rapids: Eerdmans, 2008), pp. 367-91.

seek to avoid. Concern for the well-being of the earth and non-human creation is not an afterthought in the Old Testament books that underlie the affirmation in Romans (Pss. 96.10-13; 104.5-28; 147.8-9; Isa. 11.7-9; 65.17; Ezek. 47.1-12). In this scenario, non-human creation will not be put to shame any more than believers, as Paul will say explicitly at a later point (Rom. 8.19-23).

When we add this perspective to the exposition of Paul's faith-language, Paul's thesis statement is firmly grounded in the Old Testament affirmation of God's faithfulness.

> For I am not ashamed of the gospel,
> for it is the power of God
> for salvation
> to every one who has faith,
> to the Jews first and also to the Greek.
> For God's right-making
> is revealed in it
> *from* faithfulness *for* faithfulness,
> as it is written,
> The righteous shall live by [my] faithfulness.
> (Rom. 1.16-17, translation mine).

Rome, Spain and Jerusalem

Paul's claim in the letter introduction that he has been praying for the believers in Rome and plans to visit Rome in person (1.9-15) moves concern for the believers in Rome to the top of the list of conceivable reasons for writing to them. The letter substitutes for presence until presence is possible. On this logic, as noted, the Roman believers are more than the means to an end. While it is true that Paul intends to pass through Rome en route to Spain (15.24, 28), he does not consider the believers in Rome to be mostly of instrumental interest. The priority of Rome and the wish to pay the church in Rome a visit return in force in the closing part of the letter (15.14–16.27), albeit in somewhat oblique ways. 'In addition to its length', says Matera, 'one of the most distinctive characteristics of the letter closing of Romans is the way in which it echoes the letter opening'.[28] The twin emphases in the letter opening of Paul's love for them and their need recur in the closing section. Once more, Paul delineates his apostolic mandate and the unrestricted reach of his pastoral jurisdiction.

> I myself feel confident about you, my brothers and sisters, that you yourselves are full of goodness, filled with all knowledge, and able to instruct

28. Matera, *Romans*, p. 329.

> one another. Nevertheless on some points I have written to you rather boldly by way of reminder, because of the grace given me by God to be a minister (*leitourgon*) of Christ Jesus to the Gentiles in the priestly service (*hierourgounta*) of the gospel of God, so that the offering of the Gentiles may be acceptable, sanctified by the Holy Spirit. In Christ Jesus, then, I have reason to boast of my work for God (Rom. 15.14-17).

Paul adheres to the wise policy that 'it is courteous to assume that one's fellow-Christians are moderately mature until they have given positive evidence of their immaturity'.[29] His statement to this effect (15.14) has nevertheless been preceded by a detailed account of what maturity in faith entails in practice (12.1–14.23). If the lengthy exhortation mutes the commendation somewhat, it suggests that he believes that good is better advanced by commendation than by censure.[30] His rather formal assertion 'to be a minister (*leitourgon*) of Christ Jesus to the Gentiles in the priestly service (*hierourgounta*) of the gospel of God' (15.16) adds luster to the apostolic calling and mandate claimed in the letter opening (1.1, 5). Brendan Byrne comments appropriately that Paul's description of his calling here 'is one of the most solemn to be found in his writings', amounting to 'a forceful claim to unique status in the entire Christian movement'.[31] Together, these verses and the careful terminology show Paul claiming to be the undisputed standard-bearer and norm-setting executor of the Gentile mission. If this is said in the context of conflict, as seems likely, Paul is more than gingerly positioning himself above his opponents (15.16-17).

> For I will not venture to speak of anything except what Christ has accomplished through me to win obedience from the Gentiles, by word and deed, by the power of signs and wonders, by the power of the Spirit of God, so that from Jerusalem and as far around as Illyricum I have fully proclaimed the good news of Christ. Thus I make it my ambition to proclaim the good news, not where Christ has already been named, so that I do not build on someone else's foundation, but as it is written, 'Those who have never been told of him shall see, and those who have never heard of him shall understand'. This is the reason that I have so often been hindered from coming to you (Rom. 15.18-22).

Nothing speaks more persuasively for Paul than what he has done, and he has accomplished a lot (15.18). In fact, 'he offers his record to the Roman church as part of his credentials'.[32] While he does not say that he has finished

29. Cranfield, *Romans*, p. 752.

30. Cf. Dunn, *Romans 9–16*, p. 866. Moo (*Romans*, p. 887) says that 'Paul walks on eggshells in his desire not to offend Christians in Rome by assuming an authority over them that they would not recognize'.

31. Byrne, *Romans*, p. 435.

32. C.H. Dodd, *The Epistle of Paul to the Romans* (MNTC; London: Hodder and Stoughton, 1932), p. 227.

all that there is to do from Jerusalem to the region of present-day Croatia in an absolute sense (15.19),[33] he has 'brought to completion in the regions designated his own special apostolic task of planting strategic churches'.[34] The visit to Rome has been delayed 'so often' because of the overriding priority of the Gentile mission (15.22). Here, too, a contrast is implied between Paul and other claimants vying for influence. Paul has led the way in the work 'to win obedience from the Gentiles' (15.18), setting him apart from lesser lights who prefer to show up after the hard work has been done. He does not go 'where Christ has already been named' (15.20) while that is precisely his critics' favored venue. He does not 'build on someone else's foundation' (15.20), a rhetorical contrast aimed to expose the *modus operandi* of his opponents but not to deny Paul the right to get involved with the churches in Rome or be guilty of inconsistency—whether in his letter or in the announcement that he is eager to go to Rome for the purpose of preaching the gospel there (1.15).

> But now, with no further place for me in these regions, I desire, as I have for many years, to come to you when I go to Spain. For I do hope to see you on my journey and to be sent on by you, once I have enjoyed your company for a little while. At present, however, I am going to Jerusalem in a ministry to the saints; for Macedonia and Achaia have been pleased to share their resources with the poor among the saints at Jerusalem. They were pleased to do this, and indeed they owe it to them; for if the Gentiles have come to share in their spiritual blessings, they ought also to be of service to them in material things. So, when I have completed this, and have delivered to them what has been collected, I will set out by way of you to Spain; and I know that when I come to you, I will come in the fullness of the blessing of Christ. I appeal to you, brothers and sisters, by our Lord Jesus Christ and by the love of the Spirit, to join me in earnest prayer to God on my behalf, that I may be rescued from the unbelievers in Judea, and that my ministry to Jerusalem may be acceptable to the saints, so that by God's will I may come to you with joy and be refreshed in your company (Rom. 15.23-32).

Of the three most prominent places in this survey of impending travel plans—Rome, Spain, and Jerusalem—Rome tops the list. A dream long held is at last coming to fruition in Paul's mind (15.23). While he says that he will visit Rome 'when I go to Spain' (15.24), the plan to go to Spain need not be the reason for going to Rome. Jewett's idea that the Spanish mission should be 'the basic idea in the interpretation of each verse and paragraph' in Romans puts too heavy a load on a theory that has slender shoulders relative to other options,[35] and it does not have sufficient explanatory power for the

33. C.K. Barrett, *The Epistle to the Romans* (BNCT; Peabody, MA: Hendrickson, 1991), p. 276; Murray, *Romans*, pp. 214-15.

34. Moo, *Romans*, p. 896.

35. Jewett, *Romans*, p. 1.

letter as a whole.[36] Looking toward Jerusalem at the other end of the Mediterranean, Jacob Jervell postulates that the Roman addressees are merely a foil for the *actual* primary readers, these being believers and critics in Jerusalem.[37] While Paul clearly has anxiety about the upcoming visit to Jerusalem, the first stop on his pan-Mediterranean itinerary (15.25-27, 30-31), the view that a letter sent to Rome—and that a letter abounding in details about matters *Roman*—is meant for the Jerusalem community, fails the plausibility test. A key element in Jervell's 'Jerusalem theory', however, has to do with the rhetorical characteristics of Romans. He finds 'the characteristics of a speech with marked apologetic, and to a lesser degree, polemic tendencies'.[38] These are features of speech suitable for situations of conflict, but the conflict in question need not be the one in Jerusalem. Instead, with awareness of the polemical character of Romans, the conflict is brewing in Rome.[39]

In the passage noted above (15.23-32), Paul adopts a tone of familiarity and intimacy, writing as though the believers in Rome are in his confidence and he in theirs. A high level of bonding and burden-sharing is assumed when he calls on them to participate in the Spanish mission (15.24, 28) and to pray for a happy outcome with respect to his visit to Jerusalem (15.25-31). Dunn notes that his request for their prayers is no light request, 'for what he calls for is a hard discipline of prayer, an earnest striving: an agonizing'.[40] All in all, Paul's wide-ranging plans and wall-to-wall concerns in this passage are astounding, the plan spanning the outer bounds of the Mediterranean with priority for the imperial capital in the middle, the concerns extending from the collection of means for needy believers in Jerusalem,[41] to the unique challenges of the mission to barbarian Spain,[42] and last but not least his anxiety

Jerusalem vs. Rome in Romans

- To Jerusalem with anxiety, to Rome with joy
- Network of friends seems greater in Rome
- Rome, not Jerusalem, as the implied 'home church'

36. 'Why is Romans So Long?' J. Paul Sampley asks ('Romans in a Different Light: A Response to Robert Jewett', in *Pauline Theology*, vol. III [ed. David Hay and E. Elizabeth Johnson; Minneapolis: Fortress Press, 1995], pp. 109-129). He answers that the length and complexity of Romans exceed what the Spanish mission hypothesis can account for.

37. Jacob Jervell, 'Romans 14:1–15:13 and the Occasion of Romans', in *The Romans Debate* (ed. Karl P. Donfried; Peabody, MA: Hendrickson, 1991), pp. 53-64.

38. Jervell, 'Romans 14:1–15:13 and the Occasion of Romans', p. 61.

39. Campbell, *Deliverance of God*, p. 503.

40. Dunn, *Romans 9–16*, p. 883.

41. For this neglected feature of Paul's ministry, see Bruce W. Longenecker, *Remember the Poor: Paul, Poverty, and the Greco-Roman World* (Grand Rapids: Eerdmans, 2010).

42. Jewett, *Romans*, pp. 74-79, 87-91.

about troublemakers encroaching on the believers in Rome (16.17-20). The mention of Macedonia and Achaia (15.26) is a reminder of Paul's approximate location at the time of writing Romans, and the whole passage shows him to be more than the self-declared apostle to the Gentiles (Rom. 1.5; 15.16, 18; cf. Gal. 2.7-8). He is concerned for the well-being and prosperity of the church universal, from the mother church in Jerusalem to the as yet unreached barbarians of Spain, and for the unity of the church, Jew and Gentile, to make good on its unique calling in Rome (Rom. 12.1-21). At the conclusion of the passage describing his travel plans, Paul writes as though his yearning to make it to Rome brings with it the prospect of respite from the troubles of travel in general and the specific difficulties in Jerusalem, 'so that by God's will I may come to you with joy and be refreshed in your company' (15.32). Rome, not Jerusalem, is in this scenario the 'mother' church and the destination where he most expects a genuine homecoming. The believers in Rome, not Jerusalem, will be the church sending him to Spain (15.24), and, as the closing chapter has shown (16.1-23), it is in Rome that Paul has the greatest number of friends and soul-mates.

Hostile Countermissionaries

It is now time to take a closer look at Douglas Campbell's contention that Romans is best understood as a pre-emptive attempt 'to defend Paul's gospel against the depredations of certain hostile countermissionaries'.[43] This view makes the health and well-being of the churches in Rome Paul's reason for writing the letter without the need to deny that Paul was at liberty to bring up other important matters, among these his journey to Jerusalem and the plans to extend his mission to 'barbarians' living in Spain. Evidence for such a purpose is in Campbell's view inscribed into the body of the letter at many junctures, but it is most explicit in the letter closing (16.17-20).

> I urge you, brothers and sisters, to keep an eye on those who cause dissensions (*dichostasias*) and offenses (*skandala*), in opposition to the teaching that you have learned; avoid them. For such people do not serve our Lord Christ, but their own appetites, and by smooth talk (*chrēstologias*) and flattery (*eulogias*) they deceive the hearts of the simple-minded. For while your obedience is known to all, so that I rejoice over you, I want you to be wise in what is good and guileless in what is evil. The God of peace will shortly crush Satan under your feet. The grace of our Lord Jesus Christ be with you (Rom. 16.17-20).

Troublemakers do exist on the Roman horizon, and they count as more than a fleeting concern. Paul's admonition 'to keep an eye on those who

43. Campbell, *Deliverance of God*, p. 495.

cause dissensions (*dichostasias*) and offenses (*skandala*)' (16.17) amounts to a 'strong exhortation'.[44] Moreover, Paul describes the troublemakers with great care. In particular, they are good at 'smooth talk (*chrēstologias*) and flattery (*eulogias*)' (16.18). Campbell justifiably takes this to mean that 'they are eloquent'.[45] The terms used, *chrēstologia* and *eulogia*, denote persuasive speech and well-spokenness, in Paul's perception deployed with the aim of stirring up trouble and not for the purpose of building up. Given that *eulogia* is the etymological root for the word 'eulogy' in modern English, it is probable that the troublemakers' eloquence has a flattering bent. Paul's disparaging characterization that the agitators 'do not serve our Lord Christ, but their own appetites' (16.18) is a derogatory way of describing an essentially self-serving agenda and not a depiction of licentious food preferences on the part of the troublemakers. It could even mean that the troublemakers are in it for the sake of material gain. While it might normally be polite and sometimes even beneficial to listen to a different opinion, Paul is unwilling to extend this courtesy to the people in question. His prescription is curt and uncompromising: 'avoid them' or 'steer clear of them' (16.17). There is enough detail in the characterization of these people and the measure taken against them to suggest that Paul knows who they are from personal experience. That the people causing trouble are an ominous threat and not a minor nuisance is more than suggested by his declaration that 'the God of peace will shortly crush *Satan* under your feet' (16.20).

Now that troublemakers are in view in Romans, in Campbell's estimation 'hostile countermissionaries', is it warranted to regard this threat as Paul's main reason for writing the letter? Supporting indicators for this view in the letter body are suggestive. Among such indicators are (1) his declaration that he is not 'ashamed of the gospel', combining in this assertion that God has not let the world down and that he is faced with opponents who are eager to mute the shame factor (1.16-17); (2) the evident similarity to Galatians, this linkage not incidental but evidence of a similar kind of problem and, as in Galatians, of actual opponents;[46] (3) the polemical character of Romans, a charged give-and-take that implies a fraught dispute with much at stake and not simply a teaching device;[47] (4) the sharply focused probe into the subject of virtue, Paul exposing illusions on the part of his interlocutors in this regard (and on this point providing substantial warrant for Martin Luther's contention that the purpose of Romans is 'to break down, to pluck up, and to destroy all wisdom and righteousness of the flesh');[48] (5) the strong and

44. Campbell, *Deliverance of God*, p. 497.
45. Campbell, *Deliverance of God*, p. 498.
46. Campbell, *Deliverance of God*, pp. 504-505.
47. Jervell, 'Romans 14:1–15:13 and the Occasion of Romans', p. 61.
48. I am referring to the indictment of Gentile depravity in Romans 1.18-32 and

pointed emphasis on his apostolic mandate and credentials (1.1, 5; 15.16); (6) the designation of Paul as the undisputed steward of the Gentile mission (1.5; 15.16); (7) his commitment to pioneering outreach and the attestation of God's blessing on his work (15.18-21); (8) the sudden entry of the subject of circumcision into the argument (2.25-29), although sudden only for the reader who could not have prior awareness of the contestants and their respective points of view; (9) the overall explanatory power of this view.[49] With regard to the last point, the sense that Paul engages opponents with a different point of view—or prepares the Roman churches for the arrival of such individuals—has greater explanatory power than proposals seeing Romans as a generic summary of Paul's gospel, a preparatory initiative for the Spanish mission, or an attempt to mediate matters regarding 'the weak' and 'the strong' in the Roman congregations.

Counter-missionaries as Subtext
- Explicit mention (16.17-20)
- Implicit factors
  - Circumcision controversy
  - '*Shame*-factor'
  - Polemical tone
  - Apostolic credentials
  - Pioneering mission
  - Similarity to Galatians
  - God's right-making
  - Vision of inclusion

The foregoing add up to weighty reasons for taking seriously the view that Romans was written for the benefit of believers in Rome in the context of a need not altogether different from the crisis Paul confronted in Galatia. The need presented Paul with an opportunity to give the most extensive account of the faithfulness of God found in his entire correspondence and to spell out the implications of the Gentile mission. Given that the precipitating danger occurred on his turf (the Gentile mission) and within his area of expertise (a gospel without circumcision), there was no need to beat about the bush or be self-conscious about getting involved. Romans shows Paul's keen reading of the radar screen of mission and his determination to pre-empt the influence of teachers insisting on the circumcision of the Gentiles in Rome.

If we look for specific images to represent the difference between Paul and the troublemakers in ecological terms, Paul's vision will be apocalyptic, inclusive, and exquisitely world aware (8.18-23) while his opponents, by contrast, are invested in circumcision and business as usual even though the right-making potential of business as usual has been exposed as a fallacy (2.17-29). Above all, Paul's message centers on God's faithfulness, promised by God 'beforehand through his prophets in the holy scriptures' (1.2) and now, in this letter, made to be the theme and the reason why Paul, as believer and apostle, is not ashamed (1.16-17).

the unexpected and harsh corrective to this representation in 2.1-29, see next chapter. Luther's statement is taken from his *Lectures on Romans*, p. 135.

49. Campbell, *Deliverance of God*, pp. 501-11.

Chapter 5

ROMANS BY WAY OF THE FIRST QUESTION (ROM. 1.18-2.29)

The dialogical character of the first eleven chapters in Romans is conspicuous, distinctive, and widely recognized.[1] How should readers today weigh the two competing views regarding this feature? Does the dialogical character imply a conflict with a real opponent pushing an opposing view, including a view that represents a threat to Paul's mission? Or, as a second option, is the back-and-forth manner of the letter mostly a teaching strategy by a masterful pedagogue? Of these options, scholars have largely embraced the second. Stanley Stowers concludes his work on the subject by saying that Paul's technique in Romans is similar to discourse employed in the philosophical schools of his day. On this logic, the rhetorical features in Romans assume a setting not unlike a school. 'In the letter Paul presents himself to the Romans as a teacher', says Stowers.[2] He adds pointedly that the dialogical elements are '*not* an expression of polemic or an attack on the enemies or opponents of philosophy'.[3]

Dialogue in Romans—Two Options

- Does Paul resort to dialogue because he is confronting real people and opposing points of view that threaten his mission?
- Is the dialogical character of Romans—the animated questions and answers—a teaching technique in the hands of a clever pedagogue?

But the first of the two main alternatives will not easily go away, and it should not. In significant ways it is the stronger alternative, better mirroring the challenges faced by Paul. He did not need to construct fictitious opponents to make a point because there were actual opponents aplenty. His arena was not the classroom or the controlled environment of the philosophical schools but the battlefield of mission and counter-mission, the latter so evident in Galatians that it threatened to wipe out his pioneering

1. For an in-depth exposition of the subject, see Stanley K. Stowers, *The Diatribe and Paul's Letter to the Romans* (SBLDS, 57; Chico, CA: Scholars Press, 1981).
2. Stowers, *Diatribe*, p. 175.
3. Stowers, *Diatribe*, p. 175 (italics added).

work and its carefully laid foundation. Moreover, as Edwin A. Judge notes and Stowers acknowledges, the *diatribe*,[4] the teaching style thought to be on display in Romans, 'deals in commonplaces, delivered as a literary creation against stock targets. It lacks altogether the engagement with actual people, circumstances and disputed ideas that is characteristic of Paul.'[5] 'Actual people' could well be the feature that best captures Paul's distinctive cause and context.

In Romans, the dialogical back-and-forth is driven by a virtual hailstorm of questions. These questions offer advantages to the reader whether or not we think that the 'partner' in the dialogue is real or made up. While the arguments in Romans often get convoluted, the questions are straightforward and to the point. Above all, they are many, by my count a full 75.[6] Sometimes the questions are like stepping stones to help move the argument forward (Rom. 3.1, 27, 29), often they are the means to prevent the reader from drawing unwarranted conclusions (3.8, 31; 6.1, 15),[7] and sometimes they are formulated sharply, almost as though they aim to corner an opponent and show him or her up for the fallacy of their position (2.3, 21-23). The very first question in Romans is a case in point, a 'sudden turning', Stowers calls it understatedly.[8] In my view, it is a 'turning-point' question that holds the key to much of what follows.

Question Number One

The very first question in Romans has the quality of a head-on attack on an opponent or on a point of view that Paul subjects to sharp criticism (2.3). It sets the tone for much of the rest of the letter. Within the immediate context, it reads like this.

4. The key characteristic of the *diatribe*, as Rudolf Bultmann showed early in his career (*Der Stil der paulinischen Predigt und die Kynischstoische Diatribe* [FRLANT; Göttingen: Vandenhoeck & Ruprecht, 1910], pp. 10-11) is speech and 'counter-speech' rather than straightforward, flowing speech from one single point or point of view. Complementary features are tone of voice, characterizations, stereotypical representations, 'sound pictures' (like-sounding words), 'type figures', ironic or emotive imperatives, personification, and comparisons (pp. 10-46). Most of these are pertinent to Romans but not necessarily as elements of interaction with a *fictitious* opponent.

5. E.A. Judge, 'St. Paul and Classical Society', *JbAC* 15 (1972), p. 33; Stowers, *Diatribe*, p. 42. Judge attributes Bultmann's perception of the *diatribe* to the History of Religions School that was hugely influential in biblical scholarship at the beginning of the twentieth century. This 'school' sought explanations in generalizing features at the expense of particular, situational features in a text.

6. The statistical outlier is chapter 3, with seventeen questions.

7. Stowers (*Diatribe*, pp. 119-54) deals with this feature under the heading 'Objections and False Conclusions'.

8. Stowers, *Diatribe*, pp. 86, 93.

> Therefore you have no excuse, O 'virtuous' person (*ō anthrōpe*), you and all who judge others; for in passing judgment on another you condemn yourself, because you, the judge, are doing the very same things. You say, 'We know that God's judgment on those who do such things is in accordance with truth'. *Do you imagine, O 'virtuous' person* (*ō anthrōpe*), *that when you judge those who do such things and yet do them yourself, you will escape the judgment of God?* (Rom. 2.1-3, translation mine).

Whichever way we read these verses, a harsh smack down is evident. Note that I have translated the vocative and exclamatory *ō anthrōpe* with the phrase 'O "virtuous" person' and not as 'whoever you are' (2.1, 3), as in the NRSV.[9] 'Whoever you are' is far too generic and polite, failing to convey the harshness of the address. Placing 'virtuous' in inverted commas is meant to capture the moral tenor of Paul's address and to compensate for our inability to do tone of voice in print (see box). 'O paragon of virtue' in a sarcastic sense might work, too, the qualifying adjectives highlighting the need to make explicit what is done by tone of voice when the letter is read out loud. Rudolf Bultmann took the phrase to denote the shallowness or foolishness of the person at the receiving end of the rebuke, a form of condescending 'address to the hearer in the tone of a teacher to his silly student'.[10] Stowers is broadly in agreement with this view, stressing that Paul is addressing 'someone' who is 'pretentious and arrogant'.[11] He suggests 'hey, mister', as a translation that conveys the implied pretension and arrogance.[12]

Characterizing the 'Person' Addressed in Romans 2.1-3

'virtuous'	sanctimonious
'upright'	self-satisfied
'righteous'	holier-than-thou
pompous	judgmental
puffed up	superficial
vainglorious	bigoted
pretentious	arrogant

What on earth did he or she say, however, the person or persons at the receiving end of this verbal ambush in Romans? Why the need for such a severe smack down, occurring at a point when the reader is barely in his or her seat? The notion of an actual opponent, the view advanced by Douglas Campbell, does not mean that Paul is addressing a person directly in real life, but it means that a figure akin to the one addressed in this passage

9. Other translations have 'O man' (KJV, NKJV, ESV), 'everyone' (NASB), or simply 'you' (NIV). 'Mere human being' has been suggested as a viable option, but this term, too, loses the moral tenor of Paul's smack down.

10. Bultmann, *Der Stil der paulinischen Predigt*, p. 66; cf. Stowers, *Diatribe*, p. 81. Note that tone of voice is part of the communicative arsenal. To Bultmann, *ō anthrōpe* in Rom. 2.1, 3 has the same tenor as 'fool' (*afrōn*) in 1 Cor. 15.36. In polite address, Paul's usual term is 'brothers and sisters' (*adelfoi*). The notion of a mere 'silly student', however, falls short of the matter at stake in Romans and the gravity of Paul's errand.

11. Stowers, *Diatribe*, p. 110.

12. Stowers, *Diatribe*, p. 85; cf. idem, *A Rereading of Romans*, pp. 11-12.

really existed in an approximation of what Romans makes that figure out to be.[13] The alternative view, as noted, and the view more widely held, does not see an actual opponent or 'countermissionary'. Paul is instead 'addressing' a fictitious character that he has invented in order to make a point. The *diatribe*, or appearance of a dialogue, is in this scenario a teaching device. While each of these options are possible with regard to the first question in Romans, they are not equal with respect to what was at stake in the Roman churches, and they differ in their portrayal of Paul. If an actual opponent is in view, Paul is mostly in dead earnest. If, on the other hand, he resorts to the diatribe as a teaching technique, he is mostly extremely clever.

Paul's question in Rom. 2.3 is by most scholars put in the 'clever' category; Jewett calls it 'a brilliant rhetorical trap'.[14] The question follows the massive indictment in Rom. 1.18-32, a passage that argues for a causal link between idolatry and sexual promiscuity and is at the same time the opening salvo in the body of the letter. I will reproduce the passage with the structural divisions suggested by Alec J. Lucas.[15]

> *Introduction: Suppression of the knowledge of God:*
> For the wrath of God is revealed (*apokalyptetai*) from heaven against all ungodliness and wickedness of those who by their wickedness suppress the truth. For what can be known about God is plain to them, because God has shown it to them. Ever since the creation of the world his eternal power and divine nature, invisible though they are, have been understood and seen through the things he has made. So they are without excuse (*anapologētous*); for though they knew God, they did not honor him as God or give thanks to him, but they became futile in their thinking, and their senseless minds were darkened (1.18-21).
>
> *Indictment 1:*
> A1. Claiming to be wise, they became fools; and they *exchanged* (*ēllaxan*) the glory of the immortal God for images resembling a mortal human being or birds or four-footed animals or reptiles (1.22-23).
>
> B1. Therefore God *gave them up* (*paredōken*) in the lusts of their hearts to impurity, to the degrading of their bodies among themselves (1.24).
>
> *Indictment 2:*
> A2. because they *exchanged* (*metēllaxan*) the truth about God for a lie and worshiped and served the creature rather than the Creator, who is blessed forever! Amen (1.25).
>
> B2. For this reason God *gave them up* (*paredōken*) to degrading passions (1.26a).

13. Campbell, *Deliverance of God*, pp. 495-518.

14. Jewett, *Romans*, p. 200.

15. Alec J. Lucas, 'Reorienting the Structural Paradigm and Social Significance of Romans 1:18-32', *JBL* 131 (2012), pp. 121-41.

> *Indictment 3:*
> A3. Their women *exchanged* (*metēllaxan*) natural intercourse for unnatural, and in the same way also the men, giving up natural intercourse with women, were consumed with passion for one another. Men committed shameless acts with men and received in their own persons the due penalty for their error (1.26b-27).
>
> B3. And since they did not see fit to acknowledge God, God *gave them up* (*paredōken*) to a debased mind and to things that should not be done. They were filled with every kind of wickedness, evil, covetousness, malice. Full of envy, murder, strife, deceit, craftiness, they are gossips, slanderers, God-haters, insolent, haughty, boastful, inventors of evil, rebellious toward parents, foolish, faithless, heartless, ruthless. They know God's decree (*dikaiōma tou theou*), that those who practice such things deserve to die—yet they not only do them but even applaud others who practice them (1.28-32).

We will return shortly to details in this passage—its diction, careful word play, theology, and ecology—but for now it must suffice to take a bird's eye view for the purpose of making sense of the first question in Romans. 'Do you imagine, O "virtuous" person, that when you judge those who do such things and yet do them yourself, you will escape the judgment of God?' (2.3, translation mine).

Those who think that Paul suddenly turns to the diatribe form for teaching purposes generally believe that the imaginary person who has been speaking in Rom. 1.18-32 is a generic Jew.[16] Paul is thought to be in wholehearted agreement with the views puts forward by this person and no less intent on making the indictment stick than the Jewish interlocutor. But that is only half the story. Once Paul has read the Gentile world the riot act with regard to God's wrath upon idolatry and sexual promiscuity—in agreement with the Jewish view of Gentiles—he unexpectedly turns around to incriminate the Jewish position more severely than the Gentiles (2.1-3). They are worse off for their judgmental stance *and* for being hypocritical with regard to their true condition. By way of recapitulation, 'you have no excuse…for in passing judgment on another you condemn yourself, because you…are doing the very same things' (2.1).

Commentators are in awe over the assumed rhetorical masterstroke at this turn in Romans. In the words of Richard Hays,

> Romans 1.18-32 sets up a homiletical sting operation. The passage builds a crescendo of condemnation, declaring God's wrath upon human

16. Moo, *Romans*, pp. 125-76; Byrne, *Romans*, pp. 63-106; Dunn, *Romans 1–8*, pp. 54-128. Runar M. Thorsteinsson (*Paul's Interlocutor in Romans 2: Function and Identity in the Context of Ancient Epistolography* [CBNTS, 40; Stockholm: Almquist & Wiksell, 2003], pp. 151-242), by contrast, argues that the interlocutor is a Gentile convert and that Romans addresses a predominantly Gentile audience.

> unrighteousness, using rhetoric characteristic of Jewish polemic against Gentile immorality. It whips the reader into a frenzy of indignation against others: those unbelievers, those idol-worshipers, those immoral enemies of God. But then, in Romans 2.1, the sting strikes. 'Therefore, you have no excuse, whoever you are, when you judge others; for in passing judgment on another you condemn yourself, because you, the judge, are doing the very same things'.[17]

Likewise, now in the words of Brendan Byrne, 'Paul's tactic at first has been to lull this audience (1.18-32) into a complacent, conventional judgment upon the Gentile world. Now (2.1) it is time to spring the rhetorical trap.'[18] It follows from this, he says, that 'the principal target from the start is the Jewish audience, seen as sitting in habitual judgment upon the behavior of the surrounding Gentile world'.[19] Dunn concurs, writing that 'Paul's attack is aimed most directly at what he sees to be a *typically* Jewish attitude'.[20] And Moo agrees with only a slight qualification. 'Although some application to self-righteous Gentiles cannot be entirely removed from what Paul says in 2.1-11, it is clear that Paul's main target is the Jew'.[21] In Byrne's version of Paul's rhetorical feat, the tactic after springing the trap (2.1-3) 'is to erode Jewish confidence of being preserved from God's eschatological wrath on the basis of a privileged position with respect to judgment'.[22] The bottom line in this construct is unambiguous: the Gentile world is under indictment for the sins delineated in Rom. 1.18-32, but the Jews—and possibly 'Judaism'—are in greater trouble because of the sins of bigotry, hypocrisy, and, to top it off, 'for doing the very same things' as the Gentiles (2.1).[23]

Even if the figure addressed by the first question in Romans is seen as a rhetorical creation, therefore, it sets striking priorities. While it is possible that Paul is as committed to denouncing Gentile sins in Rom. 1.18-32 as the interlocutor that he subjects to his withering attack (2.1-3), he is more concerned to unmask the implied 'Jewish' conceit. It is not unimportant whether the inventory of Gentile sins represents Paul's view, but we are

17. Richard B. Hays, *The Moral Vision of the New Testament: Community, Cross, New Creation* (Edinburgh: T. & T. Clark, 1996), p. 389.

18. Byrne, *Romans*, p. 80.

19. Byrne, *Romans*, p. 80.

20. Dunn, *Romans 1–8*, p. 89 (italics added).

21. Moo, *Romans*, p. 126.

22. Byrne, *Romans*, p. 80. See also Käsemann, *Romans*, p. 54.

23. Jewett, *Romans*, p. 199. For the notion of Jewish hypocrisy, see Alec J. Lucas, 'Unearthing an Intra-Jewish Interpretive Debate? Romans 1,18-2,4; Wisdom of Solomon 11-19; and Psalms 105 (104)-107(106)', *ASE* 27 (2010), p. 71. Thorsteinsson (*Paul's Interlocutor in Romans 2*, pp. 151-242) agrees that hypocrisy is the problem but is convinced, as noted, that the interlocutor is a Gentile.

expected to understand that the Gentile sins are a lesser concern. Alleged 'Jewish' sanctimony and sense of moral superiority represent a harder nut to crack. When Paul takes on his interlocutor with the question, 'Do you imagine that...*you* will escape the judgment of God?' his agreement with the views expressed may actually be in doubt.

As we have seen already, Douglas Campbell does not think that the voice we hear in Rom. 1.18-32 belongs to Paul. In his view there is more to the speaker whom Paul deftly corners with the first question in the letter. He or they represent(s) a real person and a familiar point of view, but *he does not represent 'Judaism'*. Speech-in-character and mimicry are meant to do justice to the views of a real-life character and the means with which to counter an influence soon to be felt in the churches in Rome. The implied adversary is a believer in Jesus who, from the vantage point of smug self-assessment, seeks to make Jewish forms and traditions more prominent among Gentile converts. 'If', as Campbell notes, 'Paul is beginning to trap the Jews from 2.1 onward, then his argument works only if hypocrisy is *intrinsic* to his definition of Judaism! Otherwise, Jews simply reject this description and in effect walk away from his contentions—doubtless either puzzled or offended, and certainly unmoved.'[24] The sin of 'doing the very same things' (2.1) will in that case not apply across the board to 'Judaism', but it may pertain to issues in the life of Paul's pro-circumcision speaker.

The character that emerges in this scenario, then, is not a staple Jew in the first century, and his theological platform is not that of 'Judaism'. Even more important, the views expressed in Rom. 1.18-32 represents the views and convictions of this character *but not necessarily the views of Paul*. Uncertainty as to whether Paul agrees with the interlocutor in Rom. 1.18-32 in the traditional reading of Romans is in this scenario turning into the likelihood that he does not.[25]

Does this view, at once more situational and radical with respect to the first instance of dialogue in Romans, have merit? It is relatively easy to accept that there are genuine, nonverbal elements in Paul's letters.[26] By this is meant that the letters were *performed* in the presence of the recipient audience and not read out in monochrome and monotone.[27] The *aural* aspect

24. Campbell, *Deliverance of God*, p. 364.

25. Even if Rom. 2.1-3 is mainly 'a homiletical sting operation', the message takes precedence over the indictment in Rom. 1.18-32. Stanley Stowers ('Paul's Four Discourses about Sin', in *Celebrating Paul: Festschrift in Honor of Jerome Murphy-O'Connor and Joseph A. Fitzmeyer* [ed. Peter Spitaler; Washington, DC: Catholic Biblical Association of America, 2011], pp. 100-27) finds Rom. 1.18-32 depicting 'the sinfulness of the non-Judean peoples', a sub-category of 'the degeneration of humanity'.

26. Campbell, *Deliverance of God*, p. 531.

27. Thus Neil Elliott ('The Apostle Paul's Self-Presentation as Anti-imperial Performance', in *Paul and the Roman Imperial Order* [ed. Richard A. Horsley; London:

was conspicuous; what we call *reading* was in the ancient world—and for the Romans—'an experience of *hearing* the text'.[28] If we apply this to the reading of Rom. 1.18-32, we run into features that are supportive of a voice other than Paul's. To put this possibility to the test, we now turn to the diction, word play, theology, and—eventually—ecological outlook of this passage (1.18-32).

First, we note that there are pivots in the letter between the personal statement about the gospel in 1.16-17, expressed in first person singular, the impersonal litany about sin in 1.18-32, all recounted in third person plural, and the sharp and sudden turn in 2.1-3, all stated in second person singular.

Rom. 1.16-17	Rom. 1.18-32	Rom. 2.1-3
I	they	you

With regard to the latter (2.1-3), 'Paul now switches from third person plural to second person singular, swinging around, as it were, in good diatribe style, to confront an imaginary onlooker', says Dunn. 'Who is this hidden interlocutor who provides a foil for Paul's argument but seems to say nothing?' he adds.[29] The tone Paul adopts in addressing the 'hidden interlocutor' is even sharper than we have hinted in the foregoing. 'Therefore you have no excuse, O pretentious person!' (2.1, translation mine), Paul adopting 'the haranguing style of the popular preacher', as Dunn notes.[30] To this we must add two crucial correctives to Dunn's representation. He says that the interlocutor is hidden and that he or she 'seems to say nothing'.[31] But this is definitely not the case. The speaker is not hidden at all; he or she has shown his or her hand clearly in the foregoing, and it is not as if the person had nothing to say given that we have just heard him or her say it (1.18-32). Indeed, the haranguing tone that Dunn hears in Paul's counter-address has an immediate antecedent: *'haranguing' is precisely the speaker's diction and tone of voice*.

Jewett is more generic but no less aware of the dramatic shift. 'The pericope opens with an abrupt shift in style to that of direct, second person diatribe that is typical for Greco-Roman addresses to imaginary interlocutors',

Trinity Press, 2004], p. 72), 'The effect of Paul's message *performed orally* would have been to create an atmosphere of effectual energy, an orbit of power. We expect the creation of this "acoustic space" to have been the responsibility of the associate to whom Paul entrusted the letter; thus, Paul would presumably have taken care to prepare this messenger to *perform* the letter as part of his apostolic strategy, for the letter had only done its work once it was performed.'

28. Campbell, *Deliverance of God*, p. 531.
29. Dunn, *Romans 1–8*, p. 89.
30. Dunn, *Romans 1–8*, p. 79.
31. Dunn, *Romans 1–8*, p. 89.

he says.[32] Cranfield notes that Paul in 2.1-3 shifts the address to the second person singular, but he says rather lamely that this is done 'for the sake of vividness'.[33]

Second, there is more than a change in style. Campbell draws attention to five features in Rom. 1.18-32.

(i) its self-contained structure, with an opening thesis statement;
(ii) an astonishing incidence of scathing 'alpha-privatives'—seventeen in all;
(iii) a dense concentration of third person plural verbs—thirteen—along with an equally dense incidence of third person pronouns—the vile 'they';
(iv) the presence of various puns and wordplays;
(v) a long and distinctive vice list.[34]

The traditional reading of Romans expects the reader to accept that Paul launches the body of the letter—in his own voice—with the statement, 'For the wrath of God is revealed from heaven against all ungodliness and wickedness...' (1.18). His point of departure for the gospel proper begins with the problem of human wickedness and divine wrath. Further, the long list of so-called 'alpha-privatives' in the passage can, depending on how it is read, sound pompous and almost shrill, a god-awful catalogue of how terrible things are in the world, counting on visceral revulsion to establish the connection between idolatry and sexual excess. 'Their women (even) exchanged natural intercourse for unnatural,[35] and in the

32. Jewett, *Romans*, p. 196.

33. Cranfield, *Romans*, p. 142.

34. Campbell, *Deliverance of God*, p. 534. The vice list in Rom. 1.29-32 has similarities to the list in 2 Tim. 3.2-4, but distinctives of context and content are significant; cf. Anton Vögtle, *Die Tugend- und Lasterkataloge im Neuen Testament* (NTAbh; Münster: Verlag der Aschendorffschen Verlagsbuchhandlung, 1936), pp. 16-21.

35. Jeramy Townsley ('Paul, the Goddess Religions and Queer Sects: Romans 1.23-28', *JBL* 130 [2011], pp. 707-28) documents the complexity of Roman goddess religions and the wide range of temple-based sexual practices. Specifically, the notion of females exchanging 'the natural use for what is contrary to nature (*para physin*)' (1.26b) could refer to orgiastic male-female relations with the female in a dominant and 'contrary-to-nature' role. 1 Cor. 11.14 argues that having long hair for a male is contrary to 'nature' (*physis*). Dale Martin ('Heterosexism and the Interpretation of Romans 1.18-32', *BI* 3 [1995], pp. 332-55), following Victor Paul Furnish, notes that for ancient moralists, homosexual behavior was 'the most extreme expression of heterosexual lust'. Kathy Gaca ('Paul's Uncommon Declaration in Romans 1:18-32 and Its Problematic Legacy for Pagan and Christian Relations', *HTR* 92 [1999], pp. 165-98) shows quite plausibly, at least in light of the reception history of Romans, how the 'uncommon' indictment of pagan idolatry in Rom. 1.18-32 became the go-to warrant for biblically motivated intolerance.

same way also the men, giving up natural intercourse with women, were consumed with passion for one another!' (1.26-27, exclamation mark added). 'Alpha-privatives' are words that begin with the letter a-, the a-denoting the absence of the quality that the word otherwise conveys. The list of words beginning with a- does not exhaust the catalogue of vices in the opening indictment in Romans, but they give the feeling of a mantra, a virtual Oxford Dictionary of Vice assembled by a first century expert on the subject.

senseless (*asynetos*)
shameless (acts) (*aschēmosynē*)
worthless (*adokimos*)
faithless (*asynthetos*)
heartless (*astorgos*)
ruthless (*aneleēmōn*)
disobedient (*apeithēs*)
inexcusable (*anapologētos*)
ungodliness (*asebeia*)
wickedness (*adikia*)
impurity (*akatharsia*)
degrade (*atimazō*)
degrading passions (*pathē atimias*)

Moreover, the import of the repetitive third person plural in the indictment is to unleash a flood of utterly negative associations concerning the people who are subject to prosecution.

'they are without excuse' (1.20).

'they did not honor him as God' (1.21)

'they became futile in their thinking' (1.21).

'their senseless minds were darkened' (1.21).

'they became fools' (1.22).

'they exchanged the glory of the immortal God' (1.23).

'they exchanged the truth about God for a lie' (1.25).

'their women exchanged natural intercourse for unnatural' (1.26).

'the men...were consumed with passion for one another' (1.27).

'they did not see fit to acknowledge God' (1.28).

'they were filled with every kind of wickedness' (1.29).

'they know...that those who practice such things deserve to die' (1.32).

'they not only do them but even applaud others who practice them' (1.32).

Whatever there is to say about the people depicted in this passage, putting together the vice list of alpha-privatives and the drumbeat diction of the third person plural, the speaker's point is by now abundantly clear. These people are really, really bad, and they surely deserve to be punished! Revulsion, not compassion, is the implied emotional tenor. Not to stop there, the threesome of idolatry, depravity, and coming retribution pack still greater punch if, as Philip Esler argues at length, the entire passage deploys allusions to Sodom in the Old Testament.[36] The speaker will then be implying that *conditions are now just as bad as in Sodom, and look what God did to Sodom*!

It has long been recognized that the indictment proper makes effective use of a striking word play, and it also has a logic that leads surefootedly from the basic premise to the manifold and dire consequences.[37] The text is prose, but when the link between the theological premise and the behavioral consequences is stripped to its essence, it creates the impression that the message could be conveyed in verse.

> *Indictment 1:*
> A1. they *exchanged* (*ēllaxan*) the glory of the immortal God for images resembling a mortal human being or birds or four-footed animals or reptiles (1.22-23).
>
> B1. therefore God *gave them up* (*paredōken*) in the lusts of their hearts to impurity (1.24).
>
> *Indictment 2:*
> A2. they *exchanged* (*metēllaxan*) the truth about God for a lie (1.25).
>
> B2. for this reason God *gave them up* (*paredōken*) to degrading passions (1.26a).
>
> *Indictment 3:*
> A3. their women *exchanged* (*metēllaxan*) natural intercourse for unnatural (1.26b).
>
> B3. since they did not see fit to acknowledge God, God *gave them up* (*paredōken*) to a debased mind (1.28).

Three times in this passage we hear that the people in question *exchanged* the truth for a lie in their belief system, and three times the fateful exchange has the consequence that *God gave them up* (1.22, 24; 1.25-26; 1.26, 28). The pattern is broken slightly in the third cycle, where the exchange and

36. Philip F. Esler, 'The Sodom Tradition in Romans 1.18-32', *BTB* 34 (2004), pp. 4-16.

37. Erich Klostermann, 'Die adäquate Vergeltung im Rm 1.22-31', *ZNW* 32 (1933), pp. 1-6; Joachim Jeremias, 'Zu Rm 1.22-32', *ZNW* 45 (1954), pp. 119-21; Jewett, *Romans*, p. 165.

the consequence are virtually synonymous (1.26b, 28), but the causal nexus of idolatry is retained in the statement that 'they did not see fit to acknowledge God' (1.28). The indictment reads as a staple of Jewish monotheistic theology, reflecting the causal connection between polytheism and moral nihilism with regard to sexual conduct.[38] The structure of the passage and the evident word play amount to a skillful composition. If the passage represents the theological and literary handiwork of someone other than Paul, notably the troublemakers that are mentioned explicitly in the letter ending (16.17-20), it offers proof that these people are persuasive and well-spoken (16.18).

Beyond the surface features noted above, less obvious questions arise.

First, the passage begins with a ringing missive centered on 'the wrath of God (*orgē theou*)' (1.18).[39] For Romans as a whole, by contrast, the dominant concept is 'the righteousness of God (*dikaiosynē theou*)'.[40] While one can readily set up a scenario where 'the wrath of God' is complementary and compatible with 'the righteousness of God', one can also, imagining an adversarial contrast between the message of Romans and the speaker in Rom. 1.18-32, detect competing emphases. One side emphasizes wrath and retribution, the other side righteousness that is primarily understood as right-making. In this scenario, 'the wrath of God' is programmatic for the accompanying emphasis on retribution.

'So as to render them without excuse (*anapologētous*)', the speaker says emphatically in the initial indictment (1.20, translation mine). Is that a fair and coherent representation? Our interpretation of Romans will be off on the wrong foot unless we take seriously the connection between Paul's statement in Romans (1.16-17) and the problem voiced by Habakkuk in the Old Testament (See Chapter 1). Habakkuk is not unaware of human sin, but his complaint is directed at God and not against human beings (Hab. 1.2-4). In fact, Habakkuk's concern makes God seem at fault. In his paradigm, trust in God is neither a given nor a duty simply by the fact of God's existence and power, as the speaker in Rom. 1.18-32 implies. Instead, as Habakkuk expects (Hab. 1.2-4) and as God affirms (Hab. 2.2-4), it is on the evidence of God's faithfulness and not by claims of God's mere existence that trust will rise. On the logic of Paul's programmatic statement in Romans (Rom. 1.16-17), Paul will travel to Rome and then to Spain to make known what

38. Lucas, 'Romans 1,18-2,4; Wisdom of Solomon 11-19; and Psalms 105 (104)-107(106)', pp. 69-91; see also Gathercole, 'Romans 1–5 and the "Weak" and the "Strong"', pp. 41-42.

39. See also Rom. 1.18; 2.5, 8; 3.5; 4.15; 5.9; 9.22; 12.19; 13.4, 5.

40. See Rom. 1.17; 3.5, 21, 22, 25, 26; 4.3, 5, 6, 9, 11, 13, 22; 5.17, 21; 6.16, 18, 19, 20; 8.10; 9.30, 31; 10.3, 4, 5, 6, 10; 14.17; cf. Sam K. Williams, 'The "Righteousness of God" in Romans', *JBL* 99 (1980), pp. 241-90.

God has done to set things right—this rather than the implied logic of sin and retribution in Rom. 1.18-32.

Second, therefore, Romans 1.18-32 implies that there is a punitive logic at work in history that anticipates the ultimate punitive horizon awaiting at the eschaton (1.32). Human beings sin by willfully turning to false gods (1.23, 25, 28), reaping in return spiritual, relational, and sexual chaos (1.24, 26, 28). A.T. Hanson has in his exposition of divine wrath in Romans given this a benevolent twist. 'Paul describes the wrath as it is working itself out in the contemporary Graeco-Roman world'.[41] This is said as a comment on what in his view comes close to 'a handbook on the working of the wrath' (i.e. Rom. 1.18-32).[42] In Hanson's conception of the passage, wrath is not to be seen 'as something directly inflicted by God, but as something which men bring upon themselves'.[43] This is a reasonable interpretation, but it is threatened by the prospect that the passage also envisions retribution on the Day of Judgment (1.32; cf. 2.5).[44] The punitive paradigm is not only that idolatry and polytheism are punished by sexual anarchy in this life but that the perpetrators 'deserve to die' (1.32). In Campbell's reading, by contrast, Paul is not speaking in his own voice; he mimics his opponents 'fiery rhetorical entrance, which is lit—like that of so many preachers—by the flickering backdrop of hell'.[45] All in all, therefore, wrath and retribution loom large in the world view and theology of the speaker in Rom. 1.18-32.[46]

Third, the wordplay and structure in the passage are certainly adept, but the basic proposition seems formulaic, and the threefold repetition accentuates the formulaic construct. Does the indictment represent Gentile reality fairly? Is the causal linkage between idolatry and sexual misconduct as ironclad as the passage makes it seem? Is *sexual* profligacy the most adequate measure of human sin, the homoerotic images serving as poster pictures of what ails humanity at its worst?[47] In the presence of certain audiences, an indictment that is heavy-handed toward the sins of others and insufficiently self-aware is easy to do,[48] and the speaker in question speaks

41. A.T. Hanson, *The Wrath of the Lamb* (London: SPCK, 1957), p. 83.

42. Hanson, *The Wrath of the Lamb*, p. 83.

43. Hanson, *The Wrath of the Lamb*, p. 85.

44. Käsemann (*Romans*, p. 37) argues *contra* Hanson that the phrase 'God gave them up' pictures God at work in what otherwise looks like an 'immanent causal connection' so as to rule out 'an impersonal nemesis' or 'a human condition'.

45. Campbell, *Deliverance of God*, p. 530.

46. Campbell, *Deliverance of God*, p. 543; cf. Wright, *Paul and the Faithfulness of God*, p. 767.

47. Thus Stowers ('Paul's Four Discourses about Sin', p. 118), the wrath of God called forth 'by human sinfulness having reached epic proportions, the fullness of sin, the apex of sin'.

48. Sanders (*Paul, the Law, and the Jewish People*, pp. 123-35) devotes an appendix

with the confidence of someone preaching to the choir whether or not Paul agrees with the point of view that is expressed.

The possibility that there is a flaw at the core of the formula, a threat to its most basic premise, is suggested by the contrast between the bleak portrayal of the Gentiles in Rom. 1.18-32 and the far more congenial description of Gentile conduct in Rom. 2.14-16.

> When Gentiles, who do not possess the law, do instinctively what the law requires, these, though not having the law, are a law to themselves. They show that what the law requires is written on their hearts, to which their own conscience also bears witness; and their conflicting thoughts will accuse or perhaps excuse them on the day when, according to my gospel, God, through Jesus Christ, will judge the secret thoughts of all (Rom. 2.14-16).

In this passage the Gentiles, though at a disadvantage because they 'do not possess the law' (2.14), are doing well morally because they abide by the dictates of the law that is written on their hearts. Indeed, they do better than those who have the law, a group that by implication will be innocent of polytheism, idolatry, and the moral turpitude that go with it. It follows, at least hypothetically, that Paul is not merely nuancing the negative portrayal of Gentile reality in Rom. 1.18-32 but is actually pursuing an opposite representation. The Gentile stereotype in the opening missive must now, like Job's friends in the Book of Job, deal with potentially deal-breaking evidence that scrambles the formula (cf. Job 21.29-30).

Fourth, the introduction to the indictment says that 'the wrath of God is *revealed* (*apokalyptetai*) from heaven' (Rom. 1.18). The verbal action is described in the currency of the verb *apokalyptein*, 'to reveal'. The same verb is used in the preceding verse, there with reference to 'the righteousness of God' (1.17).

> 'for in it (the gospel) the righteousness of God is revealed (*apokalyptetai*)' (1.17).
>
> 'for the wrath of God is *revealed* (*apokalyptetai*) from heaven' (1.18).

These might be complementary exhibits of God's revelatory activity in the world, but if so, they differ greatly. What is said to be revealed in the gospel (1.17) refers to God's singular revelation in Jesus Christ. The alleged revelation of God's wrath (1.18), on the other hand, has as its topic the ongoing, ho-hum reality of idolatry and debauchery of Roman everyday life. In the context of Paul's letters, the deployment of *apokalyptein* for the subject described in 1.18 is in that case unique: everywhere else in Paul's

to idiosyncrasies in Rom. 1.18–2.29, objecting to flat, credulous readings of 1.18-32. He notes instances of slashing, exaggerated rhetoric, concluding that the passage is consistent with a synagogue sermon.

letters *apokalyptein* and the corresponding noun *apokalypsis* refer to revelatory action that is in the category 'special revelation'.[49] While this could be legitimate and appropriate uses of the same verb for realities playing out on different stages, a reading that perceives a hostile voice in Rom. 1.18-32 will be tempted to find the speaker guilty of debasing the currency of special revelation for an undeserving purpose.[50]

Fifth, even though the speaker in the passage says repeatedly that 'God *gave them up*' (1.24, 26, 28), God's removal from the lives of those who are given up has the connotation of God's presence.[51] In other words, God is doing something in the world; the Judge of the world is on the throne, and the divine judgment is not idle.[52] But this depiction confronts another contrast in Romans when, at a critical point in the argument, Paul alleges that God 'in his divine forbearance...had *passed over* the sins previously committed' (3.25). This verse suggests *absence* of divine action, God having fallen behind on doing what God is expected to do. To make up for the implied delinquency on God's part, God put forth Jesus 'as a means of reconciliation through the faithfulness of his bloody death', and God did this '*to show his righteousness*' (3.25, translation mine).[53] The premise of the divine action in the latter passage (3.21-26) is the problem of divine inac-

49. For Paul's use of *apokalyptein* as unique, 'special revelation', see Rom. 1.17; 8.18; 1 Cor. 2.10; 3.13; 14.30; Gal. 1.16; 3.23; Eph. 3.5; Phil. 3.15; 2 Thess. 2.3, 6, 8. For Paul's use of *apokalypsis*, see Rom. 2.5; 8.19; 16.25; 1 Cor. 1.7, 14.6, 26; 2 Cor. 12.1, 7; Gal. 1;12; 2.2; Eph. 1.17; 3.3; 2 Thess. 1.7.

50. Christopher Rowland ('The Visions of God in Apocalyptic Literature', *JSJ* 10 [1979], p. 138) says that conceptions of apocalyptic often miss that the main emphasis is 'on the revelation of things *as they actually are* in the heavenly world'. In *The Open Heaven: A Study of Apocalyptic in Judaism and Early Christianity* (London: SPCK, 1982; repr. Eugene, OR: Wipf & Stock, 2002), pp. 9-10, Rowland shows that the emphasis is on revelation of divine secrets in a way that 'differs markedly from other ways of ascertaining the divine will which tend to rely on more indirect modes of discernment, like the interpretation of scripture'.

51. Beverly Roberts Gaventa ('God Handed Them Over: Reading Romans 1:18-32 Apocalyptically', *ABR* 53 [2005], pp. 42-53) develops the notion of 'handing over' as a term reflective of conflict; indeed, a cosmic conflict. The person who is 'given up' or 'handed over', is not simply abandoned but turned over 'to a third party'. This reflects the view that humans always live 'in the grasp of some power'. To Gaventa, the notion of God being absent from the process does not fit Paul's thought.

52. Thus Gathercole ('Romans 1–5 and the "Weak" and the "Strong"', p. 42), 'the consequences are the product of divine actions'. See also Käsemann, *Romans*, p. 37.

53. Campbell, *The Rhetoric of Righteousness*, pp. 156-60; 177-91. Stowers ('Paul's Four Discourses about Sin', p. 120) takes the view that punishment 'by bondage to passion (Rom. 1.22-26) does not satisfy God's judgment that they deserve death (1.32) and God has allowed their sins to accumulate'. The double jeopardy of this scenario is divine punishment by being given up to passion in this life and more direct punishment in the eschaton.

tion, a problem that is less acute in Rom. 1.18-32, where divine action finds expression in the working of God's wrath in the present and in the anticipated future action of God's wrath toward people who 'deserve to die' (1.32). Receiving their 'just desert' is also the import earlier in the passage when men 'committing shameless acts with men are by necessity receiving the due reward for their error' (1.27, translation mine), that is to say, 'they had it coming, and they richly deserve it'.

Sixth, while it is possible to take the statement that 'God gave them up' (1.24, 26, 28) at face value, this assessment gives at best only a limited picture of God's action toward the Gentiles. Later in Romans, the assessment comes in for major revision. *God did not give them up at all*; indeed, the entire letter is dedicated to the proposition that God has not given up human beings, Jew or Gentile (5.6-10), and God has not given up the world (8.19-22). In the main, again, God's intervention in the world is described in terms of a right-making initiative and not in terms of wrath.

Seventh, the juncture at which we encounter the first question in Romans raises questions about psychology and persuasive strategy. The letter will be read aloud before (presumably small) audiences consisting of Jewish and Gentiles believers in Jesus. How should Paul talk to people he has never met, Jew and Gentile, if it is his aim being to bring them together and eventually to win their support for the Spanish mission? How should he insert himself in matters far away, his mandate for intervention arguably quite weak despite his apostolic credentials?[54] How should he begin if, in Rome, too, he will deal with sentiments and actual people who have a proven track record for disruption in general and disregard for him in particular, as the Galatian struggle shows? If the missive concerning Gentile reality in Romans 1.18-32 and the ensuing turning of the tables aimed at Jewish reality in Rom. 2.1-3 are primarily rhetorical constructs, they are bold in the extreme. If, however, Rom. 1.18-32 represents the views and diction of well-spoken troublemakers, and Rom. 2.1-3 represents Paul's determination to take them to task, the fairness in the representation is greater than the boldness, and there can be no offense. Just as important, this would be a matter concerning which Paul would be the undisputed expert and where the need to intervene would not be in doubt. In the former, traditional view, too, the invented person has to be credible, and the persuasive strategy has to serve its intended purpose. In the second scenario, the person who comes under attack in the first question in Romans is not invented. Paul's representation of that person's view is to the point, and the rhetorical weaponry he uses to neutralize and counter the view expressed is well matched to the need.

54. Patricia M. McDonald ('Romans 5.1-11 as a Rhetorical Bridge', *JSNT* 40 [1990], pp. 81-96) shows awareness of this challenge. She points to features in the letter (1.1-17; 5.1-11) that are personable and 'bonding', the intervening passages (1.18-4.27) less so.

Getting Off on the Right Foot: Options for the First Question in Romans (2.3)		
Scenario	**Fictitious opponent**	**Real opponent**
Who?	No one in particular in real life	Believer in Jesus, possibly Jewish, pushing the need for circumcision
Speech	Rhetorical construct	Speech tailored to actual problem and real danger
Issue	Gentile sin (1.18-32) and 'Jewish' hypocrisy (2.1-29)	Blunt rejoinder to the implied speaker in 1.18-32
Theology	Line running from sin to wrath to retribution—and only then to right-making	Line running from need to right-making, the need not defined in the currency of wrath and retribution

This does not prove that the voice we hear in Rom. 1.18-32 is the voice of a hostile countermissionary,[55] but it burdens that voice with a number of elements that are problematic for a straight Pauline attribution. N.T. Wright's objection that the use of 'for' (*gar*) four times in Rom. 1.16-18 is proof of one voice and a seamless argument must be taken seriously,[56] but it is not sufficient to put to rest the impression that another diction and line of thought begin in Rom. 1.18.[57] Most attempts to impose a structure on Romans envision a suture line at 1.18, 'for' or no 'for'.[58] By contrast, a *performed* mes-

55. Campbell, *Deliverance of God*, p. 534; idem, 'An Apocalyptic Rereading of "Justification" in Paul: Or, an Overview of the Argument of Douglas Campbell's *The Deliverance of God*', *ExpTim* 123 (2012), pp. 382-93.

56. Wright, *Paul and the Faithfulness of God*, pp. 764-65; see also Leander Keck, 'What Makes Romans Tick?', in *Pauline Theology*, vol. III (ed. David M. Hay and E. Elizabeth Johnson; Minneapolis: Fortress Press, 1995), p. 4.

57. While *gar* usually has a causal or explanatory force, Maximilian Zerwick (*Biblical Greek: Illustrated by Examples* [trans. Joseph Smith; Rome: Biblical Institute Press, 1963], p. 159) singles out Rom. 1.18 as one of several exceptions. Here, *gar* is closer to *de*, he notes, and a causal relation to the foregoing sentence (1.17) is not apparent. A.T. Robertson (*A Grammar of the Greek New Testament in the Light of Historical Research* [London: Hodder and Stoughton, 3rd edn, 1919], p. 1191) notes that *gar* in biblical Greek generally conforms to its usage in classical Greek. Herbert Weir Smyth (*Greek Grammar* [Cambridge, MA: Harvard University Press, 1966], p. 639) notes the *anticipatory* use of *gar*, where *gar* 'states the cause, justifies the utterance, or gives the explanation, of something set forth in the main clause which *follows*'. A causal or explanatory function of *gar* in an anticipatory sense must in that case be sought in Romans 1.18 and following. J.D. Denniston (*The Greek Particles* [London: Oxford University Press, 2nd edn, 1950], pp. 56-108) notes the anticipatory use of *gar* and that *gar* on occasion implies dissent, not assent. A corrective and even contrastive sense of *gar* is evident in Rom. 5.7b.

58. Stowers, *A Rereading of Romans*, p. 83; Byrne, *Romans*, pp. vi, 62; Moo, *Romans*, pp. 90-93; Dunn, *Romans 1–8*, p. 51; Jewett, *Romans*, p. 148. Otto Michel (*Der Brief an die Römer* [KEK; Göttingen: Vandenhoeck & Ruprecht, 1978], pp. 95-111) gives

sage could easily capture the break. It is the viewpoint expressed in Rom. 1.18-32, if not also the person(s) saying it that meets the sharp rejoinder of the first question in Romans (2.3). It is the implied sanctimony of *that* view *and not the sentiment expressed in Romans 1.16-17—unmistakably Paul's voice*—that comes under attack.[59] This is in my view the most important and puzzling aspect of the smack down because it is not difficult to conjure up an imperial horizon that would make the indictment work—and more. James Romm catalogues crimes of any hue in the Eternal City just before and while Romans was written: sadism, madness, and debauchery during the reign of Caligula (37–41 CE); frightful assassinations and imperial incest sanctioned by the Roman Senate during the reign of Claudius (41–54 CE); then on to Nero (54–68 CE), the chapter headings for whose reign are *regicide*, *fratricide*, *matricide*, *maritocide*, *Holocaust*, and *suicide*.[60] The catalogue of crime and vice add to the merit of the indictment in Rom. 1.18-32, but it mostly makes the pushback we have in the first question in Romans all the more mystifying. Why the need to say *that*—and so rudely (2.1-3)?[61]

preferential weight to the redemptive message of Rom. 1.17 over the 'wrath' in Rom. 1.18. Käsemann (*Romans*, p. 35) notes a *thematic* disjunction: wrath 'is not the content of the gospel, nor part of the divine righteousness, nor its function. Justifying righteousness and condemning righteousness do not run in parallel.'

59. Thorsteinsson (*Paul's Interlocutor in Romans 2*, pp. 151-242) misses the crucial pivot point by assigning Rom. 1.16-32 to Paul with the interlocutor entering at 2.1. Robin Griffith-Jones ('Beyond Reasonable Hope of Recognition? Prosōpopoeia *in Romans 1:18-38*', in *Beyond Old and New Perspectives in Paul: Reflections on the Work of Douglas Campbell* [ed. Chris Tilling and Edward Adams; Eugene, OR; Cascade Books, 2014], pp. 161-81) argues that a speaker switching scenario at Rom. 1.18 is implausible because there is at that point no explicit hint or indicator in the text of a switch. This is a valid point, *but it does not block the retroactive influence of Rom. 2.1-5 on 1.18-32*. Theologically speaking, there should be no need to find fault with the content of Rom. 1.18-32, and yet Paul's rebuttal makes the sin of judging the actual concern, not the sins catalogued in the initial indictment. The surprise of this turn has been muted and downplayed in the history of interpretation and still is. *Prosōpopoeia* and speaker switching have greater explanatory power for the harsh and unexpected rebuttal in Rom. 2.1-5.

60. James Romm, *Dying Every Day: Seneca at the Court of Nero* (New York: Vintage Books, 2014). The headings refer to the poisoning of Claudius in 54 CE, the murder of Claudius' son Britannicus shortly thereafter, the orchestrated murder of Nero's mother Agrippina, the murder of his wife Octavia, Claudius' daughter, the burning of Rome and the savage persecution of Christians that followed ['Holocaust'], and finally the suicide of Nero. The notion of a 'Golden Age' during the first five years of Nero, ostensibly owing to Seneca's responsible tutelage, is not sustained in Romm's account. Seneca, willingly or not, comes across as Nero's enabler. See also Edward Champlin, *Nero* (Cambridge: Belknap Press, 2003).

61. The notion that the interlocutor is 'doing the very same thing' (2.1), that is to say, practicing idolatry and sexual promiscuity is not easily sustained in a generalizing, all-inclusive scenario but other sins are (Rom. 1.29).

Yet another objection to a scenario of actual conflict in the letter concerns apparent thematic continuity with regard to wrath in Rom. 1.18-32 and 2.1-11. To the person under attack (2.1-3), now said to be impenitent in addition to being a hypocrite, Paul warns that by 'your hard and impenitent heart you are storing up wrath for yourself on the day of wrath, when God's righteous judgment will be revealed' (2.5). Likewise, he says that there 'will be anguish and distress for everyone who does evil, the Jew first and also the Greek, but glory and honor and peace for everyone who does good, the Jew first and also the Greek' (2.9-10). These verses indicate continuity, but they work from the premise established by the person who is under attack. Paul later puts distance between himself and the way humans ordinarily speak about 'wrath' (3.5), opening for the possibility that he is here attempting to persuade the person by the logic of his or her own argument without the need or the time to nuance the underlying premise (i.e. in 2.5).[62]

In a careful study of the transition from divine right-making (1.16-17) to divine wrath (1.18), Daniel Rodriguez puts forward evidence that the particle *gar* ('for') can occur in contexts that do not denote a single speaker or a single point of view. He provides examples from Euripides' *Bacchae* and from the Septuagint translation of Isaiah to that effect. Even though *gar* commonly signifies explanatory material that strengthens or supports the information that precedes it, it can in the context of a dialogue also accommodate 'speaker switching scenarios'.[63] Assertions are in this scenario logically connected, or at least they have the appearance of a logical connection, but one assertion *comes from the mouth of another speaker*. Rodriguez has the following representation of a 'speaker switch' in Romans 1.[64]

> **Paul:** That's why I want so much to tell the Good News to you there in Rome. For me (*gar*) there is no shame in telling the Good News. No, because (*gar*) it is the power God uses to save everyone who believes—the Jews first, and now also the Greek. Yes (*gar*), the Good News shows how good and faithful God is to do what he has promised. It shows how the faithfulness of one leads to the faith of many. As the Scriptures say, 'The one who is accepted by God will live by faithfulness' (Rom. 1.16-17).
>
> **Interlocutor:** Well (*gar*), we also see how God shows his anger against all the bad things wicked people do. They show no respect for him, and they do wrong to each other. Their evil lives keep the truth about God from being known. God is angry with them because they should know better, right? They can see what can be known about him. Yes (*gar*), God has made it clear to them (Rom. 1.18-19).

62. See Appendix I, 'Wrath in Romans'.

63. Daniel Rodriguez, 'On *Gar'd*: Dialogue in LXX Isaiah and Romans', paper presented to the Biblical Lexicography section, San Diego, November 22, 2014, p. 4.

64. Rodriguez, 'On *Gar'd*', p. 10.

In this representation, *gar* mediates logical connections, but the connection is not simply explanatory or causal. Sometimes 'well' and 'yes' capture the meaning better than 'for'. In other words, *gar* can also indicate caveats and a new direction in the argument, and there may be speaker switching. Rodriguez' study shows that the steady use of *gar* does not guarantee a single speaker and an unbroken line of argument. When one looks more closely at the content, the possibility emerges that Rom. 1.18-32 'is about some other news and some other delivery system for the news', the missing element now the story of divine wrath.[65] 'The last *gar* of the series that starts in v. 16 is finished in v. 18 in the mouth of another speaker. Paul strategically crafts a switch in speaker *and in fact a switch in gospel*,' Rodriguez says.[66] In such a perception of the situation, the smack down in 2.1-3 will no longer be a surprise.

The questions appearing downside from the first question in Romans (2.1-3) fit this scenario because they all seem aimed at dislodging the speaker in Rom. 1.18-32 from his or her high perch of orthodoxy and moral superiority.

> You, then, that teach others, will you not teach yourself? (2.21).
>
> While you preach against stealing, do you steal? (2.21).
>
> You that forbid adultery, do you commit adultery? (2.22).
>
> You that abhor idols, do you rob temples? (2.22).
>
> You that boast in the law, do you dishonor God by breaking the law? (2.23).
>
> So, if those who are uncircumcised keep the requirements of the law, will not their uncircumcision be regarded as circumcision? (2.26).

And there it is, as question number 7 in Romans, a reference to circumcision virtually out of the blue, 'will not their uncircumcision be regarded as circumcision?' This is henceforth—and *explicitly*—a contested issue in Romans. However, the contested issue has been *implicit* up to this point, Paul's comment and question made necessary by the fact that someone is pushing for the Gentile believers in Rome to be circumcised as one element in a continuum that includes the indictment of the Gentiles in Rom. 1.18-32. We recall that circumcision was the material point of conflict in the Galatian controversy while insistence on circumcision was not seen as a problem in the wide range of Gentiles affiliations with the synagogue in the Jewish Diaspora.[67] *Someone is making circumcision a problem in*

65. Rodriguez, 'On *Gar'd*', p. 11.

66. Rodriguez, 'On *Gar'd*', p. 11 (italics added).

67. Fredriksen, 'Judaism, the Circumcision of the Gentiles, and Apocalyptic Hope', pp. 539-43.

Rome. Paul counters that the uncircumcised Gentile who heeds the dictates of the moral law has nothing to gain by being circumcised (2.26). He denies the necessity of circumcision by continued positive mention of the Gentiles that we were led to loathe for their beliefs and behavior in the initial indictment (1.18-32). In the rejoinder, Paul finds Gentile reality less bleak: it is self-evident that 'their uncircumcision (will) be regarded as circumcision' (2.26).[68]

Ecological Perspective

We are now ready to look for raw material that has ecological potential in the first flurry of give and take in the body of the letter. The interlocutor in Rom. 1.18-32 says that 'what can be known about God is plain to them (the Gentiles), because God has shown it to them. Ever since the creation of the world (*apo ktiseōs kosmou*) his eternal power and divine nature, invisible though they are, have been understood and seen through the things he has made' (1.19-20). Nature and non-human creation are here making their first appearance in Romans, but we must not oversell the ecological significance. To be sure, the created, visible world should to the unbiased observer be seen as proof of God's existence and power (1.20), and it should lead to a sense of indebtedness and gratitude (1.21). But it is not the natural world as such that interests the speaker. He or she has an epistemological interest in the subject, using nature as leverage for the indictment of Gentile idolatry. In slightly anachronistic terms, the speaker is more interested in the origin of the world than in its care; the latter does not become an explicit subject in Romans until a later point when we can be certain that Paul is speaking in his own voice (8.19-22).

In a further elaboration, the Gentiles have made 'images resembling a mortal human being or birds or four-footed animals or reptiles' into objects of worship (1.23), thereby serving 'the creature rather than the Creator' (1.25). Such use of non-human creatures has not served human society well, badly eclipsing transcendent reality and substituting unworthy creatures in place of God and transcendence. There is no evidence that the elevation of the animals that are quite unlovingly named has brought any benefit to these animals and their respective species.

68. John Barclay ('Paul and Philo on Circumcision: Romans 2.25-29 in Social and Cultural Context', in John Barclay, *Pauline Churches and Diaspora Jews* [Tübingen: Mohr Siebeck, 2011], pp. 61-79) deems it 'an astonishing claim' that Paul equates keeping the law with circumcision, negating the need for the latter.

Reeling from the Decisive Pivot

In sum, the first question in Romans is a rebuttal to a speech intended as a diagnostic of the offensive ways of Gentile reality. Paul's response suggests that the outlook of the speaker is a greater concern than the problems catalogued in Rom. 1.18-32. He will later say by way of review that 'we have already charged that all, both Jews and Greeks, are under the power of sin' (3.9). The scales in this comparison nevertheless tilt negatively toward the 'Jewish' side and the accompanying insistence on circumcision, but the 'Jewish' side is not identical with 'Judaism'. As we have seen, the first seven questions in Romans are of one piece and do not let up in this regard, whether the addressee is a countermissionary of the same kind Paul combatted in Galatia or a rhetorical construct aiming to defeat a certain point of view. Parallels to the Galatian controversy are so striking as to have explanatory power for the occasion for Romans. If, as keen readers of Galatians believe, Paul in that letter seems to despair of winning the argument and countering the hostile influence (Gal. 4.12-20),[69] he will take no chances when similar influences are encroaching on the churches in Rome, and he cannot afford to lose time getting down to business (Rom. 2.1-3). The most urgent business, here as in Galatia, is to confront the condescension, condemnation, and contempt that go along with his adversaries' chauvinism of virtue and the visceral means by which they express it (1.18-32). Paul's apocalyptic gospel perceives the implied 'virtue' of the initial indictment to be a more recalcitrant and obnoxious problem than Gentile vice. The smack down at the beginning of the letter effectively brings to light the theme and even the reason for writing the letter in the first place. As J. Louis Martyn does with assistance from Flannery O'Connor with respect to Galatians, Paul sets up an apocalyptic trajectory that moves from grace to sin and not, as in the adversarial depiction, in the other direction.[70]

Accessing Romans by way of the questions dissolves the division many commentaries make between the 'theological' section that compasses Rom. 1.16–8.39 and the 'Jewish' section that dominates chaps. 9–11. In the history of interpretation, the latter section has often been seen as an afterthought, the real meat of Romans concentrated in the section that is regarded as Paul's most accomplished theological treatise (1.16–8.39). That this view is

69. Betz, *Galatians*, pp. 236-37. J. Louis Martyn ('Romans as One of the Earliest Interpretations of Galatians' in J. Louis Martyn, *Theological Issues in the Letters of Paul* [Nashville: Abingdon Press, 1997], p. 39) imagines that 'the Teachers' success was less than total'. This may indeed be the case, but Romans suggests that there were 'teachers' in Rome, too.

70. Martyn, 'The Apocalyptic Gospel in Galatians', pp. 246-66; Flannery O'Connor, 'Revelation', in *Flannery O-Connor: The Complete Stories* (New York: Noonday, 1996), pp. 488-509.

a mistake is increasingly recognized, the better view easily corroborated by the way certain questions are distributed throughout Romans.

In light of the foregoing, I will take two things to be evident that will bear on the interpretation of the rest of the letter. First, the letter is situational, and Paul does not keep for last the primary problem addressed in the letter, such as in constructs that take mediation between the 'weak' and the 'strong' or the Spanish mission to be the letter's 'situation'. The main problem comes up immediately, captured in the first back-and-forth movement between the indictment in Rom. 1.18-32 and the rebuttal in 2.1-29. This exchange sets the stage and the tone for the rest of the letter, replete with evidence that Paul attempts to contain negative outside influences.

Second, in the remainder of the letter we must not lose sight of Paul's audience, including the unwanted and undesirable element. This element does not have control of the content of the letter throughout, but it controls the stage-setting and is never completely absent. Paul may in sections of the letter expound on things that are on his mind or elaborate beyond the call of necessity on matters that have come up in the adversarial parts of the letter, but his opponents retain a rhetorical presence that shows throughout in the form of correctives (3.8; 6.1, 15; 7.7) and sharp, even harsh, put-downs (2.1, 3; 9.20). For this reason, Romans is best understood as a series of 'pivots', some more drastic than others, but all perfectly reasonable in light of the problem he faces and the arguments he makes.

The decisive initial push-back and the subject matter of the first seven questions in Romans (2.1-29) so upend the balance that the next questions read like a rescue operation directed at the 'Jewish' side. If, as Campbell believes, the 'Jewish' side is represented by believers in Jesus who are pressing for the Gentiles to be circumcised with more ardor than Jewish proselytizers were otherwise known to do, the case for circumcision faces an uphill struggle. But an 'opponent' now seems less clearly in view because the subject of the first round has been so portentous that it will take a lot of hard work to put things in their place. For that reason the confrontational posture of the opening round gives way to a more reflective stance in the questions that now arise.

> 'Then what advantage has the Jew? Or what is the value of circumcision?' (3.1).

Paul will give a convincing answer to the first question but not do much to help the second. The Jewish advantage amounts to 'much in every way for in the first place the Jews were entrusted (*episteuthēsan*) with the oracles of God' (3.2). The advantage of circumcision, whatever it might be, is not specified, and the Jewish advantage crumbles into nothing and worse than nothing by the next question, 'What if some were unfaithful (*ēpistēsan*)?' (3.3). 'Some' are here a modest estimate, as the letter soon will show, and

Pivots in Romans

I. Introduction: 1.1-17

Synopsis of message: 1.1-7
Desire to come to Rome: 1.8-15
Thesis statement: God's right-making revealed: 1.16-17

II: First Pivot: 1:18:32

Indictment of Gentiles by unnamed interlocutor: 1.18-32

III: **Second and Decisive Pivot**: 2.1-29

Harsh push-back and put-down of unnamed interlocutor: 2.1-3
Alternative representation of Gentile reality: 2.4-29

IV: Third Pivot: 3.1–4.25

Jewish unfaithfulness vs: divine faithfulness: 3.1-8
Alternative representation of sin: 3.9-19
God's right-making by the faithfulness of Jesus: 3.20-31
Abraham as believing Gentile: 4.1-25

V: Fourth Pivot: 5.1–8.39

Paradox of peace and suffering: 5.1-5
Love of God and death of Jesus: 5.6-11
Problem of sin and death—Adam's story: 5.12-21
Problem of death-in-life: 6.1–7.6
Alternative representation of sin—Eve's story: 7.7-25
The law of the Spirit of life in the hands of Jesus: 8.1-17
The threefold groaning: 8.18-30
Love of God and death of Jesus: 8.31-39

VI: Fifth Pivot: 9.1–11.36

God's faithfulness and Israel's alienation: 9.1–10.21
Has God rejected Israel? 11.1-12
Redeemer will come from Zion: 11.13-36

VII: Sixth Pivot: 12.1–15.7

Alternative community: 12.1-21
Relation to governing authorities and society: 13.1-14
The 'weak' and the 'strong': 14.1–15.7

VIII: Seventh Pivot: 15.8-33

Summary of message: 15.8-21
Desire to go to Rome—and to Spain: 15.22-33

IX: Final Pivot: 16.1-27

Paul and his friends in Rome: 16.1-16
Beware of the troublemakers—avoid them: 16.17-20

the answer to the question is implied in the question itself. The assumed Jewish advantage is dwindling to the point of placing God's reputation in jeopardy. 'Will their faithlessness (*apistia*) nullify the faithfulness (*pistin*) of God?' (3.3). In answer to this question, we will for the first time hear Paul say, 'By no means! (*mē genoito*)' (3.4). He will say *mē genoito* a full ten times in Romans, always at points when there is a risk that the audience is about to draw the wrong conclusion. Here, the wrong conclusion is that human unfaithfulness—and especially Jewish unfaithfulness—means that God has proved unfaithful. Paul turns the problem around to make human unfaithfulness serve to *establish* God's faithfulness. In fact, the questions imply that when God drew the boundary of God's faithfulness, human unfaithfulness was factored in and did not come as a surprise.

Matters 'Jewish' and theology are again intertwined when Paul asks, 'Or is God the God of Jews only? Is he not the God of Gentiles also?' (3.29). Equality for the Gentiles is in part assumed and in part proven, but how? It is proven by the *Shema*, the most Jewish of all Jewish affirmations about the oneness of God.[71] 'Yes', Paul answers, '*since God is one*; and he will justify (set right) the circumcised on the ground of faith (*ek pisteōs*) and the uncircumcised through that same faith (*dia tēs pisteōs*)' (3.29-30). The use of the *Shema* in Paul's argument becomes more striking when the Jewish ownership of the confession is acknowledged. 'The recitation of the Shema marked the line between the practicing Jew and idolators', says Jewett.[72] The Jewish advantage, it now emerges, turns out to be possession of the Scriptures and knowledge of the one God, a God whose oneness is to the advantage of Gentiles and Jews. The oneness of God grounds the inclusion of the Gentiles at the most basic level because it is as much a statement about God's character as about ontology, and the means by which God effects the inclusion of Jews and Gentiles is the same.[73] But the means, as the faith-language in Paul shows, is broad. Faith (*pistis*) on the human level is grounded in God's faithfulness (*pistis*), and the bivalence of *pistis* must not be compromised.[74] Paul's answer could therefore just as well be translated '*since God is one*, [he] will set right (*dikaiōsei*) uncircumcised on the ground of faithfulness (*ek pisteōs*) and uncircumcised through that same faithfulness (*dia tēs pisteōs*)' (3.30, translation mine). In the latter instance, it will also be appropriate to represent *pistis* with the

71. Cranfield, *Romans*, I, p. 222.

72. Jewett, *Romans*, p. 300.

73. Mark D. Nanos, *The Mystery of Romans: The Jewish Context of Paul's Letter* (Minneapolis: Fortress Press, 1996), pp. 179-82; Christopher Bruno, '*God Is One': The Function of Eis Ho Theos as a Ground for Gentile Inclusion in Paul's Letters* (LNTS; London; Bloomsbury, 2013), pp. 114-61.

74. Morna D. Hooker, *'Pistis Christou'*, *NTS* 35 (1989), pp. 321-42.

broader word 'message'. Inclusion of the Gentiles is not an afterthought in the divine plan.[75] Thus the next question, 'Do we then overthrow the law by this faith?' (3.31), that is, 'Do we now overthrow the Torah in its broadest configuration, not only as law code but also as story, by the message of God's faithfulness (*dia tēs pisteōs*)?' (3.31, translation mine). The question is necessitated by the innuendo that has been stirred up in the wake of Paul's ministry and now making itself felt in Rome. The answer, as Paul's argument already has demonstrated, will again be an emphatic, 'By no means! (*mē genoito*). On the contrary, we uphold the law' (3.31). Throughout, the emphasis on equal access and equal treatment for the Gentiles is conspicuous, and it is repeated later in Romans. 'For there is no distinction between Jew and Greek; the same Lord is Lord of all and is generous to all who call on him' (10.12).

'Then what becomes of boasting?' Paul asks (3.27), returning to the attitude-problem he has spotted earlier (2.17-23). 'It is excluded', he answers (3.27). 'By what law?' he wants to know, proceeding to offer an option that is self-evidently no good, 'By that of works?' 'No', he counters, 'but by the law of faith (*nomou pisteōs*)' (3.27). Concepts like a 'law of works' and even more a 'law of faith' need not have the sense of codified law. Paul may instead be comparing two paradigms, 'the logic of works' vs. 'the logic of *pistis*'. The boasting that is excluded must be understood against the background of the earlier attack on the speaker in Rom. 1.18-32. Paul has taken this 'person' to task for boasting in his or her 'relation to God' (2.17; cf. 2.23). 'Boasting' must now be excluded on at least two counts: by evidence of inconsistency in the life of the person who 'relies on the law' and by 'the logic of *pistis*', a logic that brings unexpected benefits to a person who has done nothing to deserve it (3.27). The specter of 'boasting' in the Galatian controversy also hovers over the subject, the false teachers in that context wanting the Galatians to be circumcised 'so that they may boast about your flesh' (Gal. 6.13). The ensuing question in Romans, 'Do we then overthrow law (*nomon*) by this message?' (Rom. 3.31, translation mine) is so broad as to invite three scenarios, (1) 'No, we do not overthrow law as code because it was never in the power of the code to bring about the conduct it prescribes'; (2) 'No, we do not overthrow the law as Torah because the story of the Old Testament is confirmed by the message we preach'; and (3) 'No, we do not prescribe lawlessness and anarchy because it is only the message that we preach that contains the essential right-making remedy'. Or, in the words of Paul, 'By no means! (*mē genoito*). On the contrary, we uphold the law' (3.31).

75. Thus Sanders (*Paul, the Law and the Jewish People*, p. 162), 'God always intended this—he proclaimed it in advance to Abraham—and his will is uniform and stated in Holy Writ'.

Are false teachers also in view here? I have entertained that possibility on several occasions, and another hint to that effect is implied in the confrontational statement, 'But if you call yourself a Jew (2.17)?' 'Jew' is here best marked with inverted commas so as to ensure that the 'Jew' in question is specific to the discussion in Romans. Controversy with a real and not merely an imaginary opponent is confirmed by direct reference to people who claim that Paul's message provides license for loose living. 'And why not say (*as some people slander us by saying that we say*), 'Let us do evil so that good may come'?' (3.8) Again, the wrong-headed inference is not rejected by Paul in order to show off his masterful teaching technique. Real people are in view, people who misrepresent Paul while working to promote an alternative message and mission agenda.

Then and Now

Virtually all interpreters agree that there are at least two groups in the Roman house churches, a majority Gentile group and a minority consisting of Jewish believers in Jesus. When we access the message of Romans by way of the questions, as I have done here, the very first question strengthens the probability that Paul is addressing a *third* group or entity that was not part of the Roman churches as such (2.3). In Romans, Paul confronts this party and the problem they are creating in Rome. Their presence has explanatory power for much of the letter. When Paul addresses them, whether this group consists of one or many, his tone is recognizably 'altogether different' from that of the letter opening (1.1-15) and from what can be inferred when the irenic, personable tone found in the introduction resumes (5.1-11).[76] The activity and influence of this entity should be seen as an important—in my view the most important—generative factor for Paul's letter. The 'out-of-the-blue' mention of circumcision in Paul's argument (2.25) owes to the role of this entity, Paul countering early and decisively in order to negate its influence (2.1-4.27). When Paul addresses them, as the present interpretation sees it, or as a point of view that he is determined to combat, as other interpreters see it, 'there is no direct appeal to the good will of the Roman believers, who are in fact all but lost sight of'.[77] In this perception of the situation, the thunderous indictment of Gentile reality in Rom. 1.18-32 belongs to the theological and rhetorical program of this entity. Whether or not Paul agrees with the content of the initial indictment (1.18-32), he takes issue with the package to which it belongs, the material element of circumcision (2.25-29), and the attitude that goes with it (2.1-5). That was then.

76. McDonald, 'Romans 5.1-11 as a Rhetorical Bridge', p. 85.
77. McDonald, 'Romans 5.1-11 as a Rhetorical Bridge', p. 85.

What is now? For Romans to speak authentically now, the receiving audience must be rethought and relabeled. Who, now, is represented in Paul's alleged 'homiletical sting operation' in the initial indictment (1.18-32), whether or not Paul agrees with the view expressed? Who, now, is at the receiving end of the crushing corrective that marks Paul's first question in Romans (2.3)? Who, now, are the people who 'do instinctively what the law requires' (2.14) even though they are ethnically, nationally, and ideologically at a disadvantage because they do not have the law? Because of whom, now, is the name of God blasphemed (2.24), and who, now, are the ones among whom God for that reason is held in low esteem? Who, now, within an ecological hermeneutic of Romans, has the least reason to boast when, now as much as then, 'all have sinned and fall short of the glory of God'? (3.23)[78]

78. Falling short of 'the glory of God' should not be seen only as defective conduct but also as a flawed perception of God.

Chapter 6

'Their Throats Are Opened Graves' (Rom. 3.13)

'What then? Are we any better off?' Paul asks (Rom. 3.9). The translation is at this point uncertain, the alternative reading—and probably to be preferred—saying, 'What then? Are we *at a disadvantage*',[1] that is, *worse off*? The question is posed at the conclusion of Paul's claim that God's faithfulness is not invalidated by human, and particularly *Jewish*, unfaithfulness (3.1-8). The notion that Jews could actually be *worse off* is more logical. Jews cannot be *better off* for the evident unfaithfulness that Paul has driven home, but they are not worse off because the impartiality that prevails in God's treatment of Jews and Gentiles reckons with equality in sin (2.12). 'No, not at all', Paul answers, 'for we have already made the case that all, both Jews and Greeks, are *under sin*' (3.9, translation mine).

But then, in a move that takes command of the argument, Paul proceeds to say that while Jews are not worse off than Gentiles, both groups are far worse off than they imagine (3.10-18). They are worse off with reference to a bird's eye view of human reality that cannot be seriously contested; worse off, too, for the specific features of human reality that Paul singles out for special mention.

'Under sin' (*hypo hamartian*) (Rom. 3.9; cf. Gal. 3.22) is a sweeping, undifferentiated summary of the human condition that conforms to the root notion of *hamartia*, all humans '*failing to hit the mark*'.[2] '*Under*' describes humanity's captivity to a condition or power from which it is unable to extricate itself. It is therefore the powerlessness and not only illicit actions that are depicted. '"Sin" is presented as an external power which can and does dominate all humankind', says Dunn,[3] and the expression '*under sin*' is 'unparalleled either in Paul's other letters or in other early Christian literature'.[4]

Despite Paul's claim that the case has been made that all, both Jews and Greeks, are 'under sin', he will give 'sin' a different representation than the

1. Jewett, *Romans*, pp. 253-57.
2. *Thayer's Greek Lexicon*, entry 277.
3. Dunn, *Romans 1–8*, p. 156. Note that Gal. 3.22 has the same expression.
4. Cranfield, *Romans*, p. 195.

indictment laid out earlier in Romans (1.18–2.29). This representation will set the stage for his amazing exposition of the right-making of God by the faithfulness of Jesus Christ (3.21-26).

'As it is Written'

The Old Testament is Paul's main ally when he now spells out more fully the meaning of being 'under sin' (Rom. 3.10-18). 'As it is written', he says,

> There is no one who is righteous (*dikaios*),
> not even one (*oude heis*);
> there is no one who has understanding (*ho syniōv*),
> there is no one who seeks God.
> All have turned aside,
> together (*hama*) they have become worthless;
> there is no one who shows kindness,
> there is not even one (vv. 10-12).
>
> Their throats are opened graves;
> they use their tongues to deceive.
> The venom of vipers is under their lips.
> Their mouths are full of cursing and bitterness (vv. 13-14).
>
> Their feet are swift to shed blood;
> ruin (*syntrimma*) and misery (*talaipōria*) are in their paths,
> and the way of peace (*hodon eirēnēs*) they have not known (vv. 15-17).
>
> There is no fear of God before their eyes (v. 18).

I have reproduced the passage with the divisions that are generally recognized in this representation of sin.[5] Three broad categories of 'sin' are specified, (1) humanity's estrangement from God (vv. 10-12); (2) humanity's embrace of untruthful speech (vv. 13-14); and (3) humanity's penchant for violence (vv. 15-18). All the categories of 'sin' and each item within the three categories are modified quotations from the Old Testament. The phrase 'there is not' or 'there is no one' (*ouk estin*) occurs a full six times in the indictment (3.10-12, 18). Twice, with slightly different wording, comes the assertion, 'not even one' (*oude heis; heōs henos*) (3.10, 12). The universal scope is reinforced by the claim that '*all* (*pantes*) have turned aside' (3.12). If *all* are included in the indictment, no one excluded, and if the entire argument aims to prove that Jews and Greeks are in the same boat, there is less reason to single out 'Jews' as the primary target. While the flow of argument seems to run from the one to the many, that is, from reality as it appears in the lives of individuals, to collective, societal reality, the named categories of sin are descriptive

5. Cranfield, *Romans*, pp. 191-92.

of societal reality more than a moral inventory of individual lives. For this reason the logic of the indictment is best seen to run in the opposite direction, from a collective reality to the individual life or at least with reciprocity between the two. Participation in the collective reality is all-inclusive, 'not even one' therefore more than hyperbole. The momentum for the 'not-even-one' assertion derives in part from the way things are and from the way they are said to be in the Old Testament. The introductory statement, '*as it is written*' (3.10a), is therefore important. It gives the statement a declarative and authoritative flavor, no counter-argument possible, and the content of what is written points to observable facts that are intended to discourage disagreement further.[6] Lack of voices to the contrary, that is, of voices that can *legitimately* paint a rosier picture of human reality is so much an element in the argument that Paul concludes it with the expectation that 'every mouth may be silenced, and the whole world may be held accountable to God' (3.19).

While most of the Old Testament quotations are taken from the Psalms, Dunn is probably correct that the first comes from Ecclesiastes.[7]

> Surely there is no one righteous (*ouk estin dikaios*) on earth
> who will do good and will not [ever] sin (Eccl. 7.20, LXX, translation mine).

The text in Ecclesiastes is ambiguous because the context oscillates between counsel not to be 'too righteous' or 'too wicked' (Eccl. 7.16, 17) and thus pointing away from the absolutist claim that 'there is no one righteous' (Eccl. 7.20). In the original context, the discovery that 'there is no one righteous' will be less worrisome if the wise counsel is not to try too hard.[8]

Similar sentiments are expressed in the Psalms, containing the fuller charge that humanity is oriented *away* from God along the lines depicted in Romans.

6. Hays (*Echoes of Scripture*, p. 50) refers to the scriptural catena in Rom. 3.10-18 as a 'jackhammer indictment'. Beverly Roberts Gaventa ('From Toxic Speech to the Redemption of Doxology', in *The Word Leaps the Gap*, pp. 392-408) laments the lack of serious scholarly engagement with the passage and its Old Testament background texts. Her suggestion that there is a movement in Romans from 'toxic speech' to praise and doxology (as in Rom. 15.6-13) is well argued. 'Toxic speech' is indeed at the center of the indictment in Rom. 3.10-18. However, Paul's smack down in Rom. 2.1-3 of the preceding speech in 1.18-32 suggests a movement from 'toxic speech' to doxology that is broader and deeper than Gaventa envisions.

7. Dunn, *Romans 1–8*, p. 150.

8. Roland E. Murphy (*Ecclesiastes* [WBC, 23A, Dallas: Word, 1998], pp. 69-72) notes the ambiguity, one solution to which is that the counsel not to be 'too righteous' is ironic and is meant for the person who pretends to be righteous but is not.

Fools say in their hearts,
'There is no God'.
They are corrupt,
they commit abominable acts;
there is no one (*ouk estin*) who does good.
God looks down from heaven on humankind
to see if there are any who are wise,
who seek after God.
They have all (*pantes*) fallen away,
they are all alike perverse;
there is no one (*ouk estin*) who does good,
no, not one (*ouk estin heōs henos*) (Ps. 53.1-3; 52.2-4, LXX; cf. 14.1-3, LXX).

What I describe above as 'estrangement from God' is not denial of God's existence (as in a philosophically oriented atheism) but better understood as 'false thinking about God'.[9] Divine non-involvement and detachment are central tenets of the 'false thinking'. The erroneous ideas manifest themselves in conduct that to the writer of the psalm make individuals and society into whole cloth. Frank-Lothar Hossfeld and Erich Zenger capture the psalmist's perception well: 'those who act *in this way* do so always as individuals...and at the same time they do so as part of a collective, structural evil power'.[10] Evil holds sway because no one struggles against it, evil therefore taking the form of a monolithic, systemic reality.

Paul's visit to Athens is in Acts portrayed as a systemic failure in the Graeco-Roman world, his description there centered on what broadly conforms to 'false thinking about God' (Acts 17.15-33). While waiting for his companions to catch up with him in Athens, says Acts, Paul 'was deeply distressed to see that the city was full of idols' (Acts 17.16). To cover all bases, the Athenians had taken care to build a temple to a god they did not know, an implicit admission that the gods they know need to be complemented by something yet unknown. According to Acts, Paul has the opening he needs.

Three Categories of Sin in Romans 3
- 'false thinking about God'
- debasement of language
- resort to violence

Then Paul stood in front of the Areopagus and said, 'Athenians, I see how extremely religious you are in every way. For as I went through the city and looked carefully at the objects of your worship, I found among them an altar with the inscription, "To an unknown god". What therefore you worship as unknown, this I proclaim to you' (Acts 17.22-23).

9. Frank-Lothar Hossfeld and Erich Zenger, *Psalms 2: A Commentary on Psalms 51–100* (trans. Linda M. Maloney; Hermeneia; Minneapolis: Fortress Press, 2005), p. 41.

10. Hossfeld and Zenger, *Psalms 2*, p. 42.

This would be an unproblematic representation with respect to Gentiles, but what of the Jews, who had only one Temple and one God? Can Paul claim that the Jews, too, are guilty of not seeking God (Rom. 3.11)? Let the Jews be guilty of everything else in the indictment (3.13-17), but let them not be guilty of *that*. Paul cannot possibly mean that strict Jewish monotheists of the Second Temple period are guilty of not seeking God in a sense that takes away their advantage over Gentiles? Such a claim can only stand if we factor in Paul's later argument. 'No one seeks after God' in the sense that humans never makes the first move: 'it depends not on human will or exertion, but on God who shows mercy' (9.16).

In Romans 3.10-18, however, Paul does not engage in such subtlety. He lumps everyone together, hammering away that 'there is no one' six times (3.10-12, 18) and 'no, *not even one*' twice (3.10, 12), with no allowance for special pleading or exception with regard to the subject matter or the people whom it may concern.[11] Here, too, Paul remembers from where he has come (1.16-17), and he anticipates where he is going (3.21-26). If, as he will shortly say, 'the righteousness of God has been disclosed...*by the faithfulness of Jesus Christ*' (3.21-22), then God and Jesus must be so intimately aligned that failure to see God in Jesus amounts to missing the mark. If Gentiles are 'under sin' for seeking all the gods that can be named except God, Jews are equally 'under sin' for repudiating the God revealed in Jesus and—by repudiating Jesus—failing to hit the target as much as the Gentiles.[12] E.P. Sanders' suggestion that 'Paul's thought did not run from plight to solution, but rather from solution to plight' is not without merit,[13] but it must be nuanced with respect to the plight that comes to view in this passage. Paul does not only describe human plight in order to expose needs that will drive a person to Jesus. Not seeing Jesus is at part of the human plight, perhaps capturing the human predicament at its most acute point. For this version of human plight, Paul more than once offers his own life story as proof (Gal. 1.11-12; Phil. 3.3-11; Rom. 1.16-17). The contention that 'there is no one who seeks God' (Rom. 3.11) is not the weakest part of the indictment but the one most certain to stand. The God revealed in Jesus is the world's unknown God.

The second part (3.13-14) turns on human speech, again with recourse to the Old Testament. 'The strophe concentrates on men's speech, and the amount devoted to this subject in relation to the whole cento is striking', says Cranfield.[14]

11. Dunn, *Romans 1–8*, p. 157.

12. This view of the Jewish problem is explicit in Rom. 10.3-4.

13. Sanders, *Paul and Palestinian Judaism*, p. 443.

14. Cranfield, *Romans*, p. 194; Käsemann (*Romans*, p. 86) also notes that 'sins of the word are especially stressed'.

Their throats are opened graves;
  they use their tongues to deceive.
The venom of vipers is under their lips.
  Their mouths are full of cursing and bitterness (Rom. 3.13-14).

This is colorful language, to say the least, a death-driven and death-making discourse that has no redemptive features. For this part, too, the Old Testament background is striking, depicting dishonesty in speech that runs deep and wide.

There is nothing reliable in what they say;
  Their inward part is destruction (*mataia*) itself;
Their throat is an open grave;
  They flatter with their tongue (Ps. 5.9).
His mouth is full of curses and deceit and oppression;
  Under his tongue is mischief and wickedness (Ps. 10.7).

They make their tongue sharp as a snake's (Hebr. *nāḥāsh*; Gr. *ofis*),
  and under their lips is the venom of vipers (Ps. 140.3; 139.4, LXX).

Speech that is like the speech of the serpent is more than a toxic form of lying (Ps. 140.3). The speech in question also has a theological and narratival connotation, conjuring up the image of the serpent's speech in Genesis (Gen. 3.1). In Psalms, the context of the indictment is persecution of the righteous (Ps. 5), oppression of the poor (Ps. 10), and violent evildoing accompanied by speech that does not represent reality truthfully (Ps. 140). When we factor in the serpent's speech in Genesis, the speech pouring forth from throats that seem like open graves abounds in misrepresentation of God (Gen. 3.1).[15]

The third part of the indictment centers directly on violence.

Their feet are swift to shed blood;
  ruin and misery are in their paths,
  and the way of peace they have not known (Rom. 3.15-17).

For this part of the indictment, the background text is Isaiah. This is noteworthy because Israel is the target of the original Old Testament indictment.

Their feet run to evil,
  and they rush to shed innocent blood;
  their thoughts are thoughts of iniquity,
  desolation and destruction are in their highways.

15. Whether in Hebrew or Greek, the word for the 'snake' in question is the same as in Genesis (Ps. 140.3; Gen. 3.1). Given that 'false thinking about God' looms large in the Old Testament background texts, as noted above, this theme is present throughout. In Ps. 140, 'speech' is depicted as a continuum, from planning, to execution, to 'deathly effect', the entire cascade conceived as 'speech'; cf. Frank-Lothar Hossfeld and Erich Zenger, *Psalms 3: A Commentary on Psalms 101–150* (trans. Linda M. Maloney; Hermeneia; Minneapolis: Fortress Press, 2011), p. 551.

The way of peace they do not know,
 and there is no justice in their paths.
Their roads they have made crooked;
 no one who walks in them knows peace (Isa. 59.7-8).

If Paul is targeting Gentile depravity in Rom. 1.18-32 before turning around to corner the 'Jews' in 2.1-29, as the traditional view sees it, the indictment in 3.10-18 represents a change of tone and content that amounts to an alternative representation of 'sin'. While the tenor of the former passage is accusatory (1.18-32), the tone of Romans 3.10-18 is closer to a lament, and its inventory of 'sin' transcends ethnic and religious labels. If, too, sexual promiscuity is the named sin in Rom. 1.18-32, not telling the truth and violence are the named sins here (3.10-18). As noted already, there is a shift from sins that are clearly not applicable to all (1.24-28) to sins that have a systemic, structural character—a reality that knows no exceptions (3.10-18). The fact that the entirety of the indictment consists of scriptural quotations gives it an aura of objectivity, in medical terms having the import and certainty of a pathologist's report after the autopsy has been performed. Romans 3.10-18 invites a response at the level of emotions and not merely a grudging acknowledgment that Paul has made his case in factual terms. No part of the indictment elicits assent more than the twice-repeated lament, 'No, *not even one*' (3.10, 12). This statement makes it certain that a solution will not arise from the reality thus described. Help from without will be needed.

Idolatry, Debasement of Language, and Violence

Could the inhabitants of the Roman Empire see the connection between 'false thinking about God', debasement of language, and propensity to violence that Paul puts forward as basic features of human reality in Rom. 3.10-18? The propagandists of the empire were hard at work trying to keep citizens from seeing it. It has been shown that the propagandists harnessed the same vocabulary as Paul, including words like 'good news' (*euangelion*), 'lord' (*kyrios*), 'son of god' (*huios theou*), 'savior' (*sōtēr*), 'salvation' (*sōtēria*), 'faithfulness' (*pistis*), 'righteousness' (*dikaiosynē*), 'peace' (*eirēnē*), and 'wrath' (*orgē*),[16] but the rhetorical clothing provided to imperial reality struggled to cover the most hideous parts of the Roman body politic.[17] By the time of Paul the clothing had worn very thin.[18] An analysis of the subject in the mid-first century, says L.L. Welborn,

16. Dieter Giorgi, *Theocracy in Paul's Praxis and Theology* (ET; Minneapolis: Fortress Press, 1991), pp. 79-104.

17. A. Wallace-Hadrill, 'The Golden Age and Sin in Augustan Ideology', *Past & Present* 95 (1982), pp. 19-36.

18. Ekkehard W. Stegemann, 'Coexistence and Transformation: Reading the Politics

> would demonstrate that the figure of death-in-life, which makes its appearance in Ovid, Philo, and Seneca, was by no means idiosyncratic, but was endemic, at least in the literature of persons of a certain social class. In the writings of those who were most self-conscious and articulate, we glimpse a subject cringing around a void, simultaneously registering and repressing knowledge of the death-driven situation by which his existence was constrained. The ground of this experience of disillusionment was not personal, despite Philo's fixation upon the wickedness of Caligula, but structural: the geopolitical expansion of the Roman Empire, and the emergence of sole sovereignty, exercised through an ongoing 'state of exception', ensured that 'the actions of one man, the emperor could indeed affect the known world'.[19]

The diagnostic terms used in this description are telling for a reality of ill health: 'death-in-life', 'cringing around a void', 'death-driven', all represented as pervasive structural phenomena. While the selection criteria for Paul's catena of Old Testament quotations in Rom. 3.10-18 cannot be determined with certainty, the texts capture Roman imperial reality well. The illusory *Golden Age* was built by 'feet swift to shed blood' (Rom. 3.15), or, in the words of Nicholas Purcell, 'peace was the product of victory won by the soldier'.[20] While the government of the Roman Empire cast itself as a benefactor and caring father, it was government by conquest and military rule.[21]

What else, beyond the military horizon? Welborn locates the elephant in the room, hidden in plain sight in the sense that upper class writers will not even name it. 'Death-in-life' and the void around which civilization cringes do not refer to the anxieties of the well-bred and well-fed. The death in question is actual death, in huge numbers, and the people marked for death in the Roman Empire are the slaves. Moreover, the *cross* is the instrument of death that no one will name. On two specific counts, not telling the truth and feet that are rushing to shed blood, Roman imperial reality confirms that Paul was not exaggerating or making things up (3.13, 15). For Roman slaves, death on the cross was an ever-present possibility. Crosses set up for that purpose were not a rarity.

of Identity in Romans in an Imperial Context', in *Reading Paul in Context: Explorations in Identity Formation: Essays in Honour of William S. Campbell* (ed. Kathy Ehrensberger and J. Brian Tucker; London: T. & T. Clark, 2010), pp. 3-23.

19. L.L. Welborn, '"Extraction from the Mortal Site": Badiou on the Resurrection in Paul', *NTS* 55 (2009), p. 303.

20. Nicholas Purcell, 'The Arts of Government', in *The Roman World* (ed. John Boardman, Jasper Griffin and Oswyn Murray; New York: Oxford University Press, 1986), p. 163.

21. Purcell, 'The Arts of Government', p. 165.

> In speaking about the ubiquity of the cross, I do not have in mind the occasional use of crucifixion as the 'supreme penalty' in notorious cases of high treason, nor the more frequent use of crucifixion as a means of suppressing rebellious subjects in the provinces, but rather *the regular employment of the cross* as a punishment for slaves in cities throughout the Roman Empire. Just outside the Esquiline Gate at Rome, on the road to Tibur, was a horrific place where crosses were routinely set up for the punishment of slaves. There a torture and execution service was operated by a group of funeral contractors who were open to business from private citizens and public authorities alike. There slaves were flogged and crucified at a charge to their masters of 4 *sesterces* per person.[22]

This depiction of Roman life dispels the fog, making it possible to see plainly Roman imperial reality with respect to the people at the bottom of the ladder. In the big picture of things, they were the raw material from which the prosperity of the few was built: their subjugation and misery made possible the upward mobility of the upper class. This helps us understand why Paul's preaching of the cross, a symbol etched into the life stories of the slave population of the empire, would be transforming news. Just imagine a private business, like an automobile repair shop or a tire store, taking away a wealthy patron's slave to have him crucified on a Monday or Tuesday morning, in one case for the offense of having finished off a half-eaten plate of fish which he had been told to remove from the table untouched and uneaten.[23] Imagine a cross going up for another trivial offense with no access to due process for the victim. Welborn calls this the 'situated void' of imperial reality, 'the specific, *material density* within the situated void around which Roman power was constructed'.[24]

> Indeed, the cross was not only the ominous specter around which the consciousness of the slave cringed, but because the cross was the evil instrument by which the legal institution of slavery was maintained, that extracted the surplus upon which the power of the ruling class depended, the cross may be regarded as the dark, gravitational center which, whether recognized or repressed, allotted places to all those who lived within the socio-symbolic edifice of the Roman Empire, and compelled thought to consent to those places.[25]

22. Welborn, 'Extraction from the Mortal Site', pp. 308-309 (italics added).
23. Welborn, 'Extraction from the Mortal Site', p. 307.
24. Welborn, 'Extraction from the Mortal Site', p. 309.
25. Welborn, 'Extraction from the Mortal Site', pp. 308-309. Edward E. Baptist (*The Half Has Never Been Told: Slavery and the Making of American Capitalism* [New York: Basic Books, 2014]) documents how slavery was a hugely significant factor in the economic growth and prosperity of the American colonies, extracting a surplus for the ruling few at the expense of the oppressed many in ways similar to Roman imperial reality.

What emerges in this depiction is a cross-centered reality, the cross now serving as an instrument of terror to some, an object of fear and loathing to others, and a fact of life so unnamable that good and decent writers will not stoop to mention it. That is, they leave unmentioned what captures the essential ideological and practical power base of the empire better than images of the Roman legions. Why, then, was not such a government held in contempt? Why would the imperial system not be the object of disgust? Perhaps it was, its complex make-up only imperfectly concealed by the pandering of the provincial governors toward the central government and by imperial patronage in the other direction. S.R.F. Price has documented the role of the imperial cult in this power construct,[26] the cult itself a celebration of qualities the emperors did not have and of benefits they could not and did not provide. The imperial economy of death was aided and abetted by relentless propaganda, an attempt to create a narrative of beneficence, peace, and prosperity that had little or no basis in reality. Paul's indictment is appropriate for the matter at hand: 'they use their tongues to deceive' (3.13). Concealment of the underlying cruel and coercive reality was achieved by careful orchestration of the public discourse in the panegyric utterances of writers and, above all, by the omnipresent imperial cult. It is not uncharitable to say that the imperial cult represented the deceitful reality of predation, violence, and repression at its most subtle by taking command of the imagery and the discourse in the public square. If this system offered proof of a culture that 'worshiped and served the creature rather than the Creator' (1.25), it was also an immensely effective political tool. Stability, or at least the appearance of stability, was achieved in a system that was carefully structured; 'the symbolism evoked a picture of the relationship between the emperor and the gods. The ritual was also structuring; it imposed a definition of the world,' says Price.[27]

Nevertheless, some saw the rot underneath the veneer, like the Jewish nationalist writer who wrote, 'Just as a pig lies down and sticks out his trotters as though to say, "I am clean" [because they are cloven], so the evil empire robs and oppresses while pretending to execute justice'.[28]

26. S.R.F. Price, *Rituals and Power: The Roman Imperial Cult in Asia Minor* (New York: Cambridge University Press, 1986), p. 248. It is far easier to document the formal and rhetorical role of the imperial cult than to assess its actual function in the thought world of citizens and slaves.

27. Price, *Rituals and Power*, p. 248. Romm (*Dying Every Day*, pp. 62-65) describes how Seneca, in a moment of unusual and daring candor, heaps scorn on the deceased emperor Claudius in a text known as 'the Pumpkinification of the Deified Claudius [*Apocolocyntosis Divi Claudii*]'. The alleged post-mortem *divinization* of the emperor is held up to unrelenting scorn.

28. Purcell, 'The Arts of Government', p. 172.

Paul's indictment is universal, applying to Jew and Gentile, because the Jewish side does not play a stronger hand in this equation of debasement of language and violence. Militarism had by Paul's time become an integral feature of Jewish messianism. As Paul had experienced by direct participation, this included the willingness to shed the blood of dissenters (Acts 7.58; 8.1; 22.20; Gal. 1.13; 1 Cor. 15.9; Phil. 3.6; 1 Tim. 1.13).[29] At the root of this mindset lay the Jewish revolt against the forced Hellenization of Antiochus Epiphanes in the second century BCE. This conflict, as described in the Maccabean chronicles, was not solely a conflict of Israel against the world or of Jewish faith against Hellenization. It was also a conflict internal to the Jewish community (1 Macc. 1.11-15; 2 Macc. 4.12-20; 6.1-6). Elias Bickerman has shown that the Maccabean resistance was an uprising by force of arms against Antiochus Epiphanes and also against those in the Jewish community who actively promoted Hellenization at the expense of Jewish distinctives.[30]

When the Maccabees fought, therefore, they did not fight only against the Seleucids. They also fought against fellow Jews. When they killed, they did not only kill Seleucids. They also killed their own apostate kin. Thus, says Bickerman, 'the Maccabees of whom Scripture speaks were not merely martyrs. They were also militants for their faith who, sword in hand, fought for what is God's. Thus they became the model for every "crusade".'[31] Creation of a narrative favorable to this undertaking was as important to the Maccabees on the smaller stage in Palestine as it was to the Roman Empire on the larger world stage. As soon as Mattathias had won over his group to

29. According to Romm (*Dying Every Day*, pp. 46-47), Gallio, the governor of Achaia and Seneca's older brother, stood idly by when Jewish plaintiff's seized Sosthenes 'and beat him to death'. The assailants were angered at Sosthenes for allowing Paul a hearing in the synagogue in Corinth. Acts (18.7) says that 'they beat him', not that they beat him to death, but the main point is the role of violence in the defense of faith.

30. Thus Elias Bickerman (*The God of the Maccabees: Studies in the Meaning and Origin of the Maccabean Revolt* [Leiden: E.J. Brill, 1979], p. 90), '[t]he Maccabean movement was, above all, a civil war, a religious struggle between reformers and orthodox'. Victor Tcherikover (*Hellenistic Civilization and the Jews* [Peabody, MA: Hendrickson, 1999 (orig. 1959)], pp. 183-200) agrees with Bickerman that the Hellenistic reform arose as a Jewish initiative but not with the idea that the persecution under Antiochus was initiated by the Jewish reformers. See also William R. Farmer, *Maccabees, Zealots, and Josephus: An Inquiry into Jewish Nationalism in the Greco-Roman Period* (Westport, CT: Greenwood Press, 1956), p. 50; János Bolyki, '"As soon as the Signal Was Given" (2 Macc. 4.14): Gymnasia in the Service of Hellenism', in *The Books of the Maccabees: History, Theology, Ideology. Papers of the Second International Conference on the Deuterocanonical Books* (ed. Géza G. Xeravits and Jósef Zsengellér; Leiden: Brill, 2007), pp. 131-39.

31. Bickerman, *The God of the Maccabees*, p. 24.

a stance of combatancy in the early days of the resistance, they set off on their two-fold mission against Antiochus Epiphanes *and* against their own.

> They organized an army, and struck down sinners in their anger and renegades in their wrath; the survivors fled to the Gentiles for safety. And Mattathias and his friends went around and tore down the altars; they forcibly circumcised all the uncircumcised boys that they found within the borders of Israel... They rescued the law out of the hands of the Gentiles and kings, and they never let the sinner gain the upper hand (1 Macc. 2.44-48).

What we see in the Maccabean 'corpus', therefore, is not only war as a means of defense against an outside enemy but violence in the service of revival and reformation. Israel will be purged, if need be by the sword. The historiography of 1 and 2 Maccabees borrows luster from the exodus narrative, conferring legitimacy on violence by showing that its heroes were merely emulating the founding fathers.[32] The revolt needed a narrative of nobility in support of bloodshed in order to proceed. Salvation and violence are the two sides of the same coin, the union hallowed by those who tell the story.

> But Judas and his men, calling against the great Sovereign of the world, who without battering-rams or engines of war overthrew Jericho in the days of Joshua, rushed furiously upon the walls. They took the town *by the will of God*, and slaughtered untold numbers, so that the adjoining lake, a quarter of a mile wide, appeared to be running over with blood (2 Macc. 12.15-16).

> But the Jews *called upon the Sovereign* who with power shatters the might of his enemies, and they got the town into their hands, and killed as many as twenty-five thousand of those who were in it (2 Macc. 12.28).

> So, fighting with their hands *and praying to God in their hearts*, they laid low at least thirty-five thousand, and were greatly gladdened by God's manifestation (2 Macc. 15.27).

Judas and his men did not prevail quite the way Joshua did against Jericho, but his mandate, source of inspiration, and the final outcome run on parallel tracks with the earlier story. The bloodshed does not trouble the Maccabean chronicler, to whom piety and military prowess are a seamless garment. The narrator is careful to provide continuous ideological cover although it is not entirely convincing. What does victory in a war fought by such means do to the self-understanding of the faith? What does violence do to the perpetrator of carnage? The Maccabean victors' treatment of the wicked Nicanor, now slain, is to these questions a case in point.

32. Katell Berthelot, 'The Biblical Conquest of the Promised Land and the Hasmonean Wars according to 1 and 2 Maccabees', in *The Books of the Maccabees* (above), pp. 45-60.

> When the action was over and they were returning with joy, they recognized Nicanor, lying dead, in full armor. Then there was shouting and tumult, and they blessed the Sovereign Lord in the language of their ancestors. Then the man who was ever in body and soul the defender of his people, the man who maintained his youthful goodwill toward his compatriots (Judas Maccabeus), ordered them to cut off Nicanor's head and arm and carry them to Jerusalem. When he arrived there and had called his compatriots together and stationed the priests before the altar, he sent for those who were in the citadel. He showed them the vile Nicanor's head and that profane man's arm, which had been boastfully stretched out against the holy house of the Almighty. He cut out the tongue of the ungodly Nicanor and said that he would feed it piecemeal to the birds and would hang up these rewards of his folly opposite the sanctuary. And they all, looking to heaven, blessed the Lord who had manifested himself, saying, 'Blessed is he who has kept his own place undefiled!' (2 Macc. 15.28-34).

The crude violence in this depiction may offend sensibilities even in our time. Had God manifested himself in this manner? Was this the way to keep God's place undefiled? The writer of 2 Maccabees has no compunctions; he or she seems oblivious to the possibility that victory by such means might do damage to the victor and to the character of faith. In the Maccabean power project there is early on evidence of the corrupting effect of power and the gradual dimming of the spiritual luster of the Hasmoneans. We see it in the early concession to *Realpolitik* as the Maccabees negotiate treaties with Rome (1 Macc. 8.1-2, 21-30; 12.1); we see it in the embrace of imperial patronage (1 Macc. 10.18-21; 11.23-27; 14.38-39); we see it in the evident relish of court ceremonial with 'a purple robe and a golden crown' (1 Macc. 10.62-66); we see it in the early hint of dynastic aspirations (1 Macc. 13.27-30); and we see it, or we ought to see it, in the uncritical embrace of Simon and Jonathan as warrior priests (1 Macc. 14.29-43). Beyond the horizon of 1 Maccabees, we also see it in the biography of John Hyrcanus (135–104 BCE), the son of Simon Maccabeus and the grandson of Mattathias. 'No longer was it with him merely a question of religious freedom or political independence. He dreamt of a kingdom, an empire. He began to wage aggressive war on all sides,' says Isidore Epstein.[33] This was the relatively recent and celebrated reality in the Jewish paradigm when Paul wrote Romans.

Maccabean militarism influenced Jewish messianism, the Hasmonean uprising given an institutional memory in the annual festival of Hanukkah, albeit without an explicit messianic connotation.[34] Josephus commends

33. Isidore Epstein, *Judaism: A Historical Presentation* (Baltimore: Penguin, 1959), p. 95. Josephus (*Ant.* XIII.10.7) says of John Hyrcanus that he was 'accounted by God worthy of three of the greates privileges—the government of his nation, the dignity of the high priesthood, and prophecy'.

34. Farmer, *Maccabees*, pp. 132-5.

Judas Maccabeus without reserve even though he is constrained by his context, his abandonment of the Jewish cause, and his Roman patrons.[35] He can praise the Maccabean uprising because the Maccabees were on friendly terms with Rome, but he cannot praise their stance on principle even though the war against Rome in 66–73 CE broke out in response to a similar provocation.[36] For Josephus, the task of dissuading his fellow countrymen from taking up arms against the Romans could not succeed by recalling the triumph of the divinely inspired Maccabean revolt. *That* story could only serve to empower and embolden the case for armed resistance. Josephus was not ready to concede that the pro-war party were the true spiritual heirs of the Maccabees.[37] A pro-war stance *and* a messianic connotation are undeniable with respect to the Second Jewish-Roman War (132–135). Even the great Rabbi Akiba (c. 50–135 CE), foremost among the Mishna teachers, believed that Shimon Bar-Kokhba was the Messiah.[38]

When Paul in his indictment seizes on debasement of language (propaganda) and disposition to violence (Rom. 3.13-17), he captures a reality held in common by Gentiles and Jews. What many in the Jewish reality see as the way to make things right is actually an account of what is wrong. What is held to be salvation is not salvation but *sin*![39] In both camps, and thus for human reality in general, there is a God-deficit best described as 'false thinking about God' (3.10-11, 18), a deficit with regard to truth-telling (3.13-14), and a peace-deficit (3.15-17) sufficient to silence every mouth and make the whole world 'accountable to God' (3.19).

More 'Opened Graves'

The applicability of Paul's diagnostic in Rom. 3.10-18 has not been bleached by the passage of time. Indeed, the connection between debasement of language and violence persists into the Christian era, rising to unimaginable levels of devastation in the 20th century. When we allow Romans to speak to realities that from the vantage point of Paul belong to the future, the target audience no longer fits the label Jew or Gentile. It applies to humanity

35. Josephus, *Ant.* XII.11.2.

36. Thomas A. Idinopulos, 'Religious and National Factors in Israel's War with Rome', in *Jewish Civilization in the Hellenistic-Roman Period* (ed. Shemaryahu Talmon; Philadelphia: Trinity Press, 1991), pp. 50-63.

37. Farmer, *Maccabees*, pp. 126-29.

38. Epstein, *Judaism*, pp. 117-18.

39. Vincent M. Smiles ('The Concept of 'Zeal' in Second-Temple Judaism and Paul's Critique of It in Romans 10:2', *CBQ* 64 [2002], pp. 283, 289) shows that 'zeal' in Second Temple Judaism 'had to do with an impassioned defense of the covenant by observance of that Law' that could include the use of force against others. See also James D.G. Dunn, *The Theology of Paul the Apostle* (Grand Rapids: Eerdmans, 1998), pp. 346-54.

in general and particularly to the Christian world that is celebrating two thousand years of devotion to Paul and centuries of careful study of his letter to the Romans. For this problem, we need the hermeneutic of retrieval that ecological readings of the Bible seek to empower.[40]

A hermeneutic of retrieval will factor in Eusebius' tribute to the emperor Constantine in the fourth century. His accolade reads much like the adulation of the imperial propagandists in the first century, hitting the same notes for the same partisan reasons. To the delight of Eusebius, Constantine and his sons show their nobility by making it their very first action 'to wipe the world clean from hatred of God'.[41] The rhetoric of 'wiping clean' is noteworthy for the implied violence and evident imperial connotation. Dissenters have reasons to fear because they will 'pay the penalty which their mad and reckless obstinacy deserves'.[42] Like the Maccabean narrators and the imperial apologists, the Christian bishop went to work 'as the emperor's mythmaker'.[43]

Christian myth-making and bloodshed rise to a new high during the Crusades. Steven Runciman shows that the Crusades started with propaganda as the essential prelude to the military campaign. 'God wills it! God wills it!' the audience that heard pope Urban's speech at Clermont in France are reported to have said, on this point exceeding the pope's expectations.[44] Runciman writes that when the crusaders reached their God-ordained goal of liberating Jerusalem in 1099, Raymond of Aguilers had to 'pick his way through corpses and blood that reached up to his knees' on his way to the Temple area.[45] The crusaders had emptied the Holy City of Jews and Muslims—men, women, and children—with a degree of savagery that is more than a footnote to Paul's message in Romans: 'ruin and misery are in their paths' (Rom. 3.16).[46]

40. 'Ecojustice Hermeneutics: Reflections and Challenges', by the Earth Bible Team, in *The Earth Story in the New Testament* (ed. Norman C. Habel and Vicky Balabanski; London: Sheffield Academic Press, 2002), pp. 1-2.

41. Eusebius, *The History of the Church,* X.9.9 (trans. G.A. Williamson; London: Penguin, 1989), p. 333.

42. A.H.M. Jones, *Constantine and the Conversion of Europe* (Toronto: University of Toronto Press, 1978), p. 103.

43. James Carroll, *Constantine's Sword: The Church and the Jews* (New York: Mariner Books, 2002), p. 178.

44. Steven Runciman, *A History of the Crusades*. I. *The First Crusade and the Foundation of the Kingdom of Jerusalem* (Harmondsworth: Penguin, 1971), p. 108.

45. Runciman, *A History of the Crusades*, p. 287.

46. Cranfield (*Romans*, p. 194) comments aptly on Rom. 3.16, 'After this concentration on words the last strophe directs attention to deeds—to the fratricidal character of men's conduct'.

Debasement of language and proclivity for violence are two sides of the same coin in the two greatest wars of devastation known to humanity. I cannot leave this out, writing as I do close to the centennial of the outbreak of World War I and preparing for the task by traveling to what remains of the trenches near the Belgian city Ypres. Christopher Clark writes of the plot to assassinate Archduke Franz Ferdinand and his wife in Sarajevo in 1914 that the plotters were motivated by a nationalist narrative that had 'assassinations, martyrdom, victimhood and the thirst for revenge on behalf of the dead' as its central themes.[47] When the war was about to begin it was certain that it would start, but it was not altogether clear why or against whom. So Clark asks, 'But who was the enemy?' He answers as evidence dictates it to him, 'Nobody knew'.[48] Obfuscation and propaganda followed, proving that Paul was not barking up the wrong tree when he forged a link between false speech and war (3.13-17). The problem for the decision-makers at the outbreak of the war was so acute that Clark reaches independently for imagery that E.P. Sanders uses in his view of Paul: 'we need to nuance the argument and distinguish between the reasons for decisions and the arguments chosen to advertise and justify them'.[49] When the decision-makers on the Austrian-Hungarian side in Vienna formulated the necessity of going to war, they could do it only by brazen debasement of language. 'What strikes the present-day reader about these communications is their panicky lack of focus, the preference for swollen metaphors over clear formulations, the employment of histrionic devices to achieve an emotional effect, the juxtaposition of different perspectives in the absence of a unifying meta-narrative', says Clark.[50]

The other side, meanwhile, also had its work cut out. Great Britain intended to play the role of the Knight in the white armor in a war billed as though it was forced upon the British Empire against its will. Adam Hochschild writes that key British officials had from the beginning 'grasped that this war would require propaganda of unprecedented sophistication and scope—something all the more important in a country where, without conscription, attracting the necessary millions of army recruits depended on public enthusiasm'.[51] Propagandists rose to the occasion, the government mobilizing to mislead its citizens about the necessity of sending their sons off to die. The Church of England was second to none among

47. Christopher Clark, *The Sleepwalkers: How Europe Went to War in 1914* (London: Penguin, 2013), p. 23.

48. Clark, *The Sleepwalkers*, p. 554.

49. Clark, *The Sleepwalkers*, p. 545; cf. Sanders, *Paul, the Law, and the Jewish People*, p. 4.

50. Clark, *The Sleepwalkers*, p. 401.

51. Adam Hochschild, *To End All Wars: A Story of Loyalty and Rebellion, 1914–1918* (New York: Houghton Mifflin Harcourt, 2011), pp. 147-48.

the entities willing to help the government, here in the words of the Bishop of London, Arthur Winnington-Ingram, in a sermon preached in September 1914.

> But when we have said all that, this is a Holy War. We are on the side of Christianity against anti-Christ. We are on the side of the New Testament which respects the weak, and honours treaties, and dies for its friends, and looks upon war as a regrettable necessity…it is a Holy War, and to fight in a Holy War is an honour… Already I have seen the light in men's eyes which I have never seen before.[52]

In another sermon preached about a year later, now with the armies dug in on both sides in a gruesome war of attrition, the Bishop stood in the pulpit to cheer the people and the brave soldiers on.

> Kill Germans! Kill them! … Not for the sake of killing, but to save the world… Kill the good as well as the bad… Kill the young as well as the old… Kill those who have shown kindness to our wounded as well as those fiends who crucified the Canadian sergeant [a story then circulating]… I look upon it as a war for purity, I look upon everybody who dies in it as a martyr.[53]

Many were indeed killed, nearly ten million in all—and all reckoned as valiant martyrs by its side, everyone claiming God and destiny to be their source of inspiration.[54] In the Somme offensive alone, 'of the 120,000 British troops who went to battle on July 1, 1916, more than 57,000 were dead or wounded before the day was over, nearly two casualties for every yard of front'.[55] Paul did not go by numbers in his indictment in Romans, but he knew that the numbers were there, if proof were needed.

> Their feet are swift to shed blood;
> ruin and misery are in their paths,
> and the way of peace they have not known (Rom. 3.15-17).

When the war was over, the side claiming victory imposed such harsh terms on the side deemed to be the aggressor that George F. Kennan called the Treaty of Versailles 'a piece which had the tragedies of the future written

52. Michael Burleigh, *Earthly Powers: Religion and Politics in Europe from the French Revolution to the Great War* (London: HarperCollins, 2005), p. 450.

53. Hochschild, *To End All Wars*, p. 151.

54. Philip Jenkins (*The Great and Holy War: How World War I Changed Religion For Ever* [Oxford: Lion, 2014], p. 5) documents that World War I was a thoroughly religious and *Christian* war, 'a holy war, a spiritual conflict'. His depiction of the war conforms in every way to (1) eagerness to resort to violent means and (2) extreme debasement of language, the propaganda exploiting the most hallowed Christian symbols with the church as full participant.

55. Hochschild, *To End All Wars*, p. 206.

into it as by the devil's own hand'.[56] Within seven years of the precarious peace, Hitler would write in *Mein Kamp* 'how each one of the points of that Treaty could be branded in minds and hearts of the German people until sixty million men and women find their souls aflame with a feeling of rage and shame; and a torrent of fire bursts forth as from a furnace, and a will of steel is formed from it, with the common cry, "We will have arms again!"'[57]

Paul's indictment does not need the churning resentment of Adolf Hitler and the propaganda machinery of the Third Reich to ring true, but his description can hardly be surpassed for the way it applies to key events in world history, more relevant with the passage of time.

> Their throats are opened graves;
> they use their tongues to deceive.
> The venom of vipers is under their lips.
> Their mouths are full of cursing and bitterness (Rom. 3.13-15).

In hindsight, the Bible's designation of the *throat* as a *grave* seems particularly prescient, speech serving as the instrument of murder and the line of demarcation between deceptive words and violent deeds made invisible. In search for a colloquial term that captures the triumph of false speech, the word *bullshit* is serviceable to a point. Harry G. Frankfort, the Princeton moral philosopher, pays his respects to the offensive term by a small treatise on the subject.[58] Included in the term but not exhausting it are '*deceptive misrepresentation*', especially misrepresentation '*of somebody's own thoughts, feelings, or attitudes*'.[59] Misrepresenting the other side, in other words, is a key feature. This perspective will be extremely useful when we get to Paul's widescreen representation of sin in Romans 7 (7.7-13), but it is helpful here, too. Frankfurt specifies that the bullshitter need not be an outright liar for his or her business to succeed: 'his only indispensably distinctive characteristic is that in a certain way he misrepresents what he is up to'.[60] Indeed, he says, the bullshitter 'is neither on the side of the true nor on the side of the false. His eye is not on the facts at all, as the eyes of the honest man and of the liar are, except insofar as they may be pertinent to his interest in getting away with what he says.'[61] These comments would

56. George Kennan, *American Diplomacy, 1900–1950* (Chicago: University of Chicago Press, 1951), p. 69.

57. From Hitler's *Mein Kampf*, quoted in Hochschild, *To End All Wars*, p. 358.

58. Harry G. Frankfurt, *On Bullshit* (Princeton, NJ: Princeton University Press, 2005). Humor aside, Frankfurt dignifies his subject by serious and pertinent references to St. Augustine, Pascal, and Wittgenstein, all of whom made significant contributions to the topic.

59. Frankfurt, *On Bullshit*, pp. 6-7, 12-23.

60. Frankfurt, *On Bullshit*, p. 54.

61. Frankfurt, *On Bullshit*, p. 56.

amount to good exegesis of Paul's perspective even if not intended as such. We should not take it for granted that Paul would object to the terminology or that history has the right to be offended by it. Do we not see the triumph of *bullshit* in the propaganda of the Roman Empire, whether from the point of view of those who wrote the propaganda or with respect to the millions who went along with it? Does not the same term apply to the Maccabean chroniclers and to the myth-making of Eusebius that created the foundation for the Christian state? Did not the initiators of the Crusades innocently count on *bullshit* to create the momentum for its savagery, raising at the outset the cry, 'God wills it, God wills it'?[62] It may seem irreverent to use the word in a commentary on a revered book of the New Testament, but this is essentially what Paul describes in his sweeping diagnostic of human reality—the use of misrepresentation and *bullshit* to enable violence and war (3.12-17), taken to heights in the twentieth century of which Paul could only dream.

In Hitler's debasement of language, the Nazis adopted the terminology of disease, contagion, and cleansing as the conceptual and ideological foundation on which to launch the 'Final Solution'. Hitler was in this regard the master diagnostician and the only person having the will and courage to apply the requisite treatment. Saul Friedländer calls this '*redemptive* anti-Semitism', a contrast to ordinary anti-Semitism in that 'the struggle against the Jews is the dominant aspect of a worldview in which other racist themes are but secondary appendages'.[63] In this struggle, 'the outcome could only be envisioned in religious terms: perdition or redemption'.[64] Counting the religious element, therefore, means that the threefold aspects of Paul's indictment all apply: 'false thinking about God', debasement of language, and violence (3.10-18).

> **Sins of Romans 3**
> **in Light of World History**
>
> - **'their throats are opened graves'** Myth-making and propaganda in favor of violence as in the Maccabean revolt, the Crusades, and the global wars of the twentieth century.
> - **'their feet are swift to shed blood'** Execution of sacralized myths of violence so as to make religion in general and Christianity in particular aid and abet the invention of ever more terrifying arms and ever more devastating wars, for now culminating in the creation and use of nuclear weapons.

When World War II ended with the decision to drop nuclear bombs on Hiroshima and Nagasaki, even the descriptive power of Rom. 3.10-18 is

62. Runciman, *A History of the Crusades*, p. 108.

63. Saul Friedländer, *The Years of Persecution: Nazi Germany and the Jews 1933–1939* (London: Phoenix, 1999), p. 87.

64. Friedländer, *The Years of Persecution*, p. 100.

stymied. Nuclear war is the ecological fast track to extinction. At the peak of the Cold War, there were about fifty thousand nuclear warheads in the world possessing the equivalent of one million six hundred thousand times the yield of the bomb that was dropped on Hiroshima.[65] Jonathan Schell likens this to 'a pit into which the whole world can fall', a devouring monster the measure of which is life itself.[66] Given that the nuclear predicament lies 'in scientific knowledge rather than in social circumstances',[67] the prospect of extinction is an entrenched, irreversible fact of human existence. As Schell notes, 'there will never again be a time when self-extinction is beyond the reach or our species'.[68] In comparison to the 'death-in-life' imagery that applies to the Roman Empire and its 'death-driven' foundation,[69] human civilization in the twenty-first century has embraced death with risks and prospects exceeding those of the Roman Empire by orders of magnitude. 'Seen as a planetary event, the rising tide of human mastery over nature has brought about a categorical increase in the power of death on earth', says Schell.[70]

Discourse needs enormous resources of verbal engineering to make this reality seem innocuous. Not for nothing has the speech-aspect of modern civilization become emblematic, 'Orwellian' serving as the in-the-know word for feats of rhetorical engineering that make words mean the exact opposite of what the word under normal circumstances suggests. George Orwell imagined a Ministry of Truth in Oceania designed as 'an enormous pyramidal structure of glittering white concrete, soaring up, terrace after terrace, 300 meters into the air', its task to convince people that 'war is peace, freedom is slavery, and ignorance is strength'.[71] 'Political language', he said on another occasion, 'is designed to make lies sound truthful and murder respectable, and to give an appearance of solidity to pure wind'.[72] Paul's picture of human reality in the first century breaks along the same lines.

Roman civilization devised rituals and rhetoric that enabled a positive self-evaluation even if revolting things happened in full view, as the crosses near the Esquiline Gate prove. 'There is no fear of God before their eyes', says Paul of the reality he saw in his time (3.18), 'a figurative way of saying that the fear of God has no part in directing his life, that God is left out of his

65. Jonathan Schell, *The Fate of the Earth* (London: Picador, 1982), p. 3.
66. Schell, *The Fate of the Earth*, p. 3.
67. Schell, *The Fate of the Earth*, p. 100.
68. Schell, *The Fate of the Earth*, p. 109.
69. Welborn, 'Extraction from the Mortal Site', p. 303.
70. Schell, *The Fate of the Earth*, p. 111.
71. George Orwell, *1984* (New York: Signet Classics, 1950), p. 4.
72. George Orwell, 'Politics and the English Language', *Horizon* (April, 1946); also in *Shooting an Elephant and Other Essays* (London: Secker and Warburg, 1950).

reckoning, that he is a practical, whether or not he is a theoretical, atheist'.[73] Similarly, in the words of Karl Barth, 'the whole course of history pronounces this indictment against itself (3.10-18). How can a man be called "historically minded", if he persistently overlooks it?'[74]

An Alternative Reality—and the Right-Making of God

An alternative reality is implied in Rom. 3.10-18. It is brought to view by the reminder that the ancient Church, as Henry Chadwick notes, 'deeply disapproved of capital punishment and judicial torture'. The Christian magistrate was forbidden 'to order an execution on pain of excommunication'.[75] Torture had many reasons against it, one of which was that it forced 'innocent people to confess to crimes they had never committed'.[76] In this regard the Early Church adopted practices that were at odds with imperial tradition. An alternative reality is also evident if we include the ideology and the visions of Daniel in the Maccabean equation of armed struggle. In Daniel's apocalyptic perspective, divine intervention takes precedence over human action. Human action, in turn, is construed as faithfulness to God without recourse to arms. In contrast to 1 Maccabees, 'the book of Daniel does not espouse a militant ideology', says Rainer Albertz.[77] John Collins, likewise, draws a contrast between the Maccabean militant stance and 'Daniel's ethic of quietism'.[78] Deliverance by divine intervention, not militant struggle, is the bottom line of this book (Dan. 12.1). Collins is on solid ground when he writes that there is 'an ideological gulf between the militant ethos of 1 Maccabees and the apocalyptic quietism of Daniel'.[79] The same gulf must apply to what is essentially a militant, 'Maccabean' view of right-making, widely diffused under many names in history, and the message of Paul in Romans.

But there is no gulf between Daniel and Paul's solution to the predicament of Gentiles and Jews. I have previously surveyed the background for a

73. Cranfield, *Romans*, p. 195.

74. Barth, *Romans*, p. 85.

75. Henry Chadwick, 'Envoi: On Taking Leave of Antiquity', in *The Roman World*, p. 418.

76. Chadwick, 'On Taking Leave of Antiquity', p. 418.

77. Rainer Albertz, 'The Social Setting of the Aramaic and Hebrew Book of Daniel', in *The Book of Daniel: Composition and Reception*, 2 vols. (ed. John J. Collins and Peter W. Flint; Leiden: Brill, 2002), p. 171.

78. John J. Collins, 'Daniel and His Social World', *Int* 39 (1985), p. 142.

79. John J. Collins, *Daniel: A Commentary on the Book of Daniel* (Hermeneia; Minneapolis: Fortress Press, 1993), p. 72. Thus also Anathea E. Portier-Young (*Apocalypse against Empire: Theologies of Resistance in Early Judaism* [Grand Rapids: Eerdmans, 2011], p. 223), 'No book of the Hebrew Bible so plainly engages and opposes the project of empire as Daniel'.

different translation of Rom. 3.21-26 (chap. 3). Here, I offer the result with the short comment that Paul's depiction of the right-making of God highlights the *way* God makes right what is wrong in the world, this element conspicuously left out in traditional translations and in the theology based on these translations.

But now apart from law
the right-making of God[80] has been disclosed,
witnessed by the law and (by) the prophets,
the right-making of God
through the faithfulness of Jesus Christ (*dia pisteōs Iēsou Christou*)
to all who believe.

For there is no difference,[81]
for all have missed the mark
and lack the glory of God.[82]

They have been set right freely by his grace
through the liberation (which is) in Christ Jesus.

God set him forth publicly[83]
as a means of reconciliation[84]
through the faithfulness of his bloody death (*dia (tēs) pisteōs en tō autou haimati*).
(He did this) in order to show his right-making
(in view of the fact that) he had passed over
the sins previously committed
in the forbearance of God;

80. 'The righteousness of God' should not only be thought of as righteousness sufficient to meet a certain standard. It is better understood as *God's way of being righteous*, better yet as God's *right-making*.

81. 'no difference', that is, between Jews and Gentiles with respect to coming up short.

82. Campbell (*Righteousness*, p. 203) has 'everyone sinned and lacks the glorious image of God'. Lacking 'the glory of God' is usually thought of in purely ethical terms: knowing what is right, but failing to do it. But the term may be seen as an amplification of 'the righteousness of God'. Lacking 'the glory of God' then means ignorance of God, failing to see God for what God is.

83. This reading is preferred by the context, but also because it resonates with the narrative background that is assumed in Galatians. 'You foolish Galatians! Who has bewitched you? It was before your eyes that Jesus Christ was *publicly exhibited* as crucified!' (Gal. 3.1) The 'public display' referred to Paul's previous *preaching* of the crucified Jesus and stands as the programmatic point of reference for the entire letter; the public display (*proetheto*) in Rom. 3.25 referring to the event itself. This rendering is preferred by Christian Maurer in *TDNT* VIII, p. 166.

84. *Hilastērion* lacks the article and should not be seen as a definite entity, such as 'the mercy seat'. Adolf Deissmann (*Bible Studies* [trans. Alexander Grieve; Edinburgh: T. & T. Clark, 1901], pp. 124-35) worked out the case for the present translation.

(that is,) in order to demonstrate
his right-making at the present time,
that he (God) may be right
in the very act of setting right
the one who (lives on the basis of) the faithfulness of Jesus (*ton ek pisteōs Iēsou*).

(Rom. 3.21-26, translation mine)

This is God's remedy for a reality that in Paul's eyes is trapped 'under sin' (3.9). The predicament is driven home yet again in the statement that 'all have missed the mark and lack (*hysterountai*) the glory of God' (3.22). Powerlessness is in view, and guilt, too, as this text usually is read, but humanity's lack with respect to 'the glory of God' is not only that humans are at fault for failing to live up to God's requirements.[85] Paul's verb (*hystereō*) is in the passive voice, the distinctive of which is that it softens the blame that goes with the active voice, and it has the connotation of need.[86] The lack and need in view extend to a defective perception of God and not only to flawed performance. This lack with respect to 'the glory of God' echoes the beginning of Paul's indictment, humans falling victim to 'false thinking about God' (Rom. 3.10; Ps. 52.2-4, LXX).[87]

'And lack the glory of God'	
Traditional view	**Alternative view**
Defective performance	Defective perception

It remains to make two final observations. First, the exegesis of Rom. 3.10-18 that I have pursued above, stressing plight manifested in the most irredentist manner by a discourse of deception and penchant for violence (3.13-17), adds greatly to the reasons for seeing in Paul's remedy 'the faithfulness of Jesus Christ' and not only, as the traditional reading has it, 'faith in Christ' (3.22, 25, 26). The 'personal' or individual view of sin to which Romans has been held captive does not do justice to the indictment in this chapter (3.10-18): it fails conspicuously with respect to the big sins in world, the mountain of sin that nobody owns. Who owns systemic sins like the Crusades, or World War I, or Hiroshima, or the current war? Who writes and owns the script that enables and justifies the violence? Where did the 'false thinking about God' come from? We shall find ourselves in these sins

85. Thus the notion that they 'are not good enough' (ICB, ERV) or 'fall short' (ASV, CEB).

86. *Friberg Greek Lexicon*, entry 27697 ὑστερέω; BDAG, entry 7659 ὑστερέω.

87. Hossfeld and Zenger, *Psalms 2*, p. 41. In Gal. 3.22, Paul writes that 'scripture has locked up all things under sin (*hypo hamartian*) in order that the promise anchored in the faithfulness of Jesus Christ may be given to those who believe' (translation mine). This line of thought (1) mutes the doom aspect of sin because (2) it makes the solution outshine the plight by (3) leading straight from sin to God's right-making by the faithfulness of Christ.

if we acknowledge (1) that Paul's understanding of sin belongs to a larger story, (2) that we are bound together in a 'matrix of responsibility' for the sins no one individual owns,[88] and (3) that debasing language and resorting to violence register high on the Richter Scale of sin in the accounting we find in Romans.[89]

Second, it cannot be stressed too much that for Paul, 'the continuing and present significance of the Christ, even after his death and resurrection, consists of nothing other than the fact that he *is the crucified*'.[90] Welborn exaggerates when he says 'nothing other', but he captures the essential element in the expression *pistis Iēsou Christou*—'the faithfulness of Jesus Christ'. He adds that 'the purpose of God's intervention in history was not the liberation of the universal subject from the path of death, but rather the redemption of the many oppressed, whose identities are submerged in shame, and whose lives are in danger of disappearing, on account of the annihilating power of the cross'.[91] Again, his *either-or* proposition is exaggerated, but awareness of the cross-centered and death-bound features of Roman life enable us to understand 'how the *crucified rather than the resurrected* Messiah could be a vital rupture in the death-constrained existence of the oppressed'.[92] As Welborn notes, 'we infer that the proclamation of the crucified Messiah summoned the weak and the low-born into the material density of the cross, where Christ's willingness to suffer the very death that threatened their existence became the resource for living-on in righteousness, sanctification, and redemption'.[93] Christ, says Paul,

88. I am indebted to John Silber for the concept 'matrix of responsibility'; cf. 'Kant at Auschwitz', Appendix 1 in *Kant's Ethics: The Good, Freedom, and the Will* (Berlin: W. de Gruyter, 2012), pp. 335-42.

89. Helpful in this regard, although not adequate, are Walter Wink's attempt to capture systemic aspect of sin in human reality; cf. *Naming the Powers: The Language of Power in the New Testament* (Philadelphia: Fortress Press, 1984); idem, *Unmasking the Powers: The Invisible Forces that Determine Human Existence* (Philadelphia: Fortress Press, 1986).

90. Welborn, 'Extraction from the Mortal Site', p. 310. J. Daniel Kirk (*Unlocking Romans: Resurrection and the Justification of God* [Grand Rapids: Eerdmans, 2008]) argues that the resurrection, not the crucifixion, is the key to 'the justification of God' in Romans. By commonsense logic this seems a wise choice because the right-making potential of the resurrection can readily be appreciated, and Paul has much to say about the resurrection. In Rom. 3.21-26, however, perhaps the most sustained exposition of God's right-making in the letter, the focus is cross-centered, and the dominant image is the public display of the bloody death of Jesus. Welborn's choice of this image rather than the resurrection captures better the counter-intuitive aspect of Paul's right-making vision.

91. Welborn, 'Extraction from the Mortal Site', p. 310.

92. Welborn, 'Extraction from the Mortal Site', p. 310 (italics added).

93. Welborn, 'Extraction from the Mortal Site', p. 311.

> had shared the fate of a piece of human garbage, one of those whom life had demolished, and who had touched bottom...even if they lived in the shadow of the cross and died a bit every day, and even if the cross should be their tomb, as it was of their fathers and grandfathers, its power over them was broken and undone, so that they could live-on with value and meaning and love and hope, because the one who had died in this contemptible way was the anointed one of God.[94]

In Romans, God's right-making happens against a human and societal background of 'false thinking about God', debasement of speech, and rampant us of violence (3.10-18). The view of sin that comes to light in this passage stands in need of a determined hermeneutic of retrieval in order to represent the message of Romans faithfully to the world while also representing honestly to itself a world that in our time is kept safe by thousands of nuclear warheads. If the unnamable void in the twenty-first century differs from the void in Roman society, the difference is chiefly that our hole is bigger. Violence by means of nuclear weapons exposes a death-driven reality in the present that needs an ecological perspective in order to capture fully the 'ruin and misery' that looms in its path (3.16). Paul's right-making counterpoint to this reality, in our time more distinctive than ever, is the cross and the faithfulness of Jesus Christ (3.21-26).

94. Welborn, 'Extraction from the Mortal Site', p. 312.

Chapter 7

'He Is the Father of All of Us' (Rom. 4.16): Abraham as Ecological Role Model

Why is Abraham such a conspicuous figure in Romans, big enough for Paul to claim that 'he is the father of all of us' (Rom. 4.16)? And why is he a towering figure in Galatians and Romans *only*, mentioned just once outside these letters and then merely in passing (2 Cor. 11.22)? In Galatians, Abraham is contested theological territory, featuring a pitched verbal battle so crucial that whoever wins it is likely to be the victor in the conflict between Paul and the pro-circumcision agitators (Gal. 3.1-29). Given that the believers in Galatia had a Gentile background, we do right to wonder who brought Abraham to their attention in the first place. Whose idea was it to introduce Gentiles in the remote reaches of Asia Minor to the founding father of another religion and the ancestor of the ethnic lineage of another people? How, five hundred miles from home, so to speak, and eighteen centuries removed, could Abraham become a subject of intense interest and debate? Did Paul bring him up in his staple presentation of the good news, or did the Galatians have to wait for the Teachers to introduce Abraham after Paul had left?

Speaking of the situation in Galatia, Gordon D. Fee answers that 'Abraham would have played no role at all had it not been for the "agitators" who had tried to disrupt Paul's churches in Galatia by insisting on the circumcision of Gentile believers'.[1] This view implies that Abraham is more serviceable to the cause of Paul's opponents than to Paul's message, the subject forced upon him by unforeseen events downstream from his pioneering ministry.

But this view cannot be correct. If Paul could leave out Abraham with no damage to his message, how could the Teachers bring him in? It is far

1. Gordon D. Fee, 'Who Are Abraham's True Children? The Role of Abraham in Pauline Argumentation', in *Perspectives on Our Father Abraham: Essays in Honor of Marvin R. Wilson* (ed. Steven A. Hunt; Grand Rapids: Eerdmans, 2010), p. 126. de Boer (*Galatians*, pp. 186-87) does not say outright that the Teachers brought Abraham into the equation, but he seems to attribute the role of Abraham in the argument in Galatians to the influence of the Teachers.

On Abraham

- Abraham models a way of life and is not only foil for a certain doctrine.
- Abraham's faith is important, but God's faithfulness—the object of his faith—is more important than his faith.
- Abraham's relation to land, possession, and people has far-reaching ecological significance.

more likely that the Teachers in Galatia found an opening because Paul gave it to them. Abraham was a pivotal person in Paul's presentation of the good news; he was not a dispensable figure that could just as well be left out.[2] The patriarch looms large in the faith-construct of Gentile believers in Jesus because he was and is large. Paul's advantage was to recognize this and teach accordingly (Gal. 3.5-29; Rom. 4.1-25; cf. Acts 13.13-39). While both sides agree that Abraham is important, the meaning and legacy of Abraham give rise to controversy.

What, then, is the meaning of Abraham in Romans? As many as six years may have elapsed between Galatians and Romans,[3] a long time in Paul's event-packed ministry, and yet Romans reads as a recapitulation of the issues in Galatia. The rhetoric is less charged, and there are variations in the argumentation, but the similarities are greater than the differences. Udo Schnelle, as noted earlier, says that Paul's line of argument in Romans 'is still visibly shaped by the disputes with the Galatians in the immediate past, and the church in Rome will also have already heard reports about Paul and his gospel from the mouths of his opponents (cf. Rom. 3.8, 31a; 6.1, 15; 7.7; 16.17-18)'.[4] But Romans is more than a mental debriefing after Galatians, more than an attempt on the part of Paul to steady the theological ship for the church universal after the fraught controversy in the Galatian churches. If troublemakers similar to the ones Paul battled in the Galatian churches are making their influence felt in Rome, the similarities between the two letters are due to similar situations and not merely to aftershocks from the earlier controversy.

Getting down to specifics, it is noteworthy that Paul does not need to explain to the Romans who Abraham was. The mostly Gentile church in Rome know of Abraham already, and they know him not only because the Jewish minority in these churches made sure to teach them. The route to Abraham does not only run through Paul or through the Jewish community

2. Thus N.T. Wright (*The Letter to the Romans*, in the *New Interpreter's Bible* [ed. Leander Keck; Nashville: Abingdon Press, 1994–2004], p. 488), 'Paul's whole theme in Romans is the faithfulness of God to the covenant, the divine saving justice by which the world is both condemned and rescued'. If this was Paul's story in general, leaving Abraham out would be impossible.

3. Campbell (*Framing Paul*, pp. 404-14) adopts a different time line. Using evidence from the letters alone, he puts Galatians and Romans less than one year apart with Romans written in the spring of 52 CE.

4. Schnelle, *Apostle Paul*, pp. 305-306.

in Rome but through the gospel message itself. Perhaps the most telling evidence in this regard is the 'Abba! Father!' memory that Paul invokes in Galatians and Romans alike (Gal. 4.6; Rom. 8.15). This was a treasured piece of common ground in the baptismal experience of new believers in in Rome and in Asia Minor whether or not they owed their conversion to Paul.[5] Abraham is part of the common ground because it is widely acknowledged that echoes of the *Akedah*, the story of the binding of Isaac, resound in the cry, 'Abba! Father!'[6]

At the point where Abraham enters the argument in Romans, circumcision has already come up—as if from nowhere (Rom. 2.25-29). From 'nowhere', that is—only to the unsuspecting reader. When Paul mentions it for the first time in the letter (2.25), he is joining a conversation in progress, and there is no surprise. The sequence in Romans suggests that circumcision and Abraham are as closely linked as in the Galatian controversy (Rom. 4.9-11; Gal. 3.1-10). In Romans, too, circumcision is so much the material concern that it must be seen as the engine that pulls the other wagons in the train of thought along.

> Circumcision (*peritomē*) indeed is of value if you obey the law; but if you break the law, your circumcision has become uncircumcision (*akrobustia*) (2.25).

> Rather, a person is a Jew who is one inwardly, and real circumcision is a matter of the heart—it is spiritual (*pneumati*) and not literal (*grammati*) (2.29).

In these texts, Paul takes the moral and rhetorical high ground in the debate before he gets to Abraham. He denigrates circumcision that is not accompanied by a transformed life (2.25), and he argues that the transformed life is proof of the only circumcision that matters (2.29). But he cannot consider the case closed before he has positioned Abraham on his—the correct side—of the argument. The opposing side will argue from a text that, taken at face value, makes circumcision irrevocable and mandatory. 'This is my covenant, which you shall keep, between me and you and your offspring after you', God says to Abraham.

> Every male among you shall be circumcised. You shall circumcise the flesh of your foreskins, and it shall be a sign of the covenant between me and

5. E.A. Obeng, '"Abba, Father": The Prayer of the Sons of God', *ExpTim* 99 (1988), p. 364; John A.T. Robinson, 'The One Baptism', *SJT* 6 (1953), pp. 262-63; Betz, *Galatians*, p. 210; Martyn, *Galatians*, p. 391.

6. Sigve K. Tonstad, 'The Revisionary Potential of "Abba, Father" in the Letters of Paul', *AUSS* 45 (2007), pp. 5-18; idem, 'Inscribing Abraham: Apocalyptic, the Akedah, and "Abba! Father!" in Galatians', in *Galatians as Examined by Diverse Academics* (ed. Heerak Christian Kim; Newark, NJ: Hermit Kingdom Press, 2013), pp. 15-27.

> you. Throughout your generations every male among you shall be circumcised when he is eight days old, including the slave born in your house and the one bought with your money from any foreigner who is not of your offspring... So shall my covenant be in your flesh an everlasting covenant. Any uncircumcised male who is not circumcised in the flesh of his foreskin shall be cut off from his people; he has broken my covenant (Gen. 17.10-14).

Does Paul have an answer for this?

Abraham in Romans

Paul's first explicit comment on Abraham is phrased as a question that takes awareness of him and of circumcision for granted. Richard Hays notes that Abraham 'is introduced into the discussion rather abruptly',[7] but it is abrupt for the same reason that there is no prior warning in the letter that circumcision is a controverted topic. We can be certain that neither circumcision nor Abraham came as a surprise to the original audience. When Abraham does come up, as noted, Paul has drained circumcision of much of its appeal by faulting its advocates for hypocrisy (2.25) and by stressing that true circumcision is an inward matter to which a surgical procedure on the genitals of males adds nothing (2.29). Somewhat different translations are possible at the point when Paul introduces Abraham (4.1), but they have in common that both address the question of legacy. 'What then are we to say was gained by Abraham, our ancestor according to the flesh?' formulates an open-ended question (4.1, NRSV). 'Have we found Abraham to be our forefather according to the flesh?' in Richard Hays' translation,[8] makes the answer implicit in the question. 'No, of course not, Abraham is not our forefather according to the flesh only'. What is he then? Again, implicitly, Abraham defines a spiritual paradigm, not physical ancestry. Given that the proponents of circumcision deploy Abraham as the torch bearer for their cause, Paul will not make it easy for them. The contest over Abraham is therefore a contest of hermeneutics. Who is the better reader of Genesis? Who has found Abraham to be what God intended him to be? Will Paul be able to put distance between Abraham and circumcision, given that circumcision begins with the patriarch?

'For if Abraham was set right by works, he has something to boast about', Paul continues (4.2, translation mine). This rhetorical constellation is damaging to the cause of circumcision because the 'works' to which Paul refers are a cipher for circumcision.[9] Paul's linkage between circum-

7. Hays, 'Our Forefather according to the Flesh', p. 86.
8. Hays, 'Our Forefather according to the Flesh', pp. 77-98.
9. Terence L. Donaldson, ('The Juridical, the Participatory and the "New Perspec-

cision and boasting might nevertheless elicit a howl of foul play by the circumcision-advocates. 'Why', they can object, 'we have never thought of circumcision as a cause for *boasting*. That is not our theology. Circumcision has nothing to do with boasting now or in Genesis. You, Paul, are making things up, accusing us of promoting opinions we do not hold.'

And sure enough—*boasting* is nowhere to be seen in Genesis, whether in the context of Abraham's faith or when Abraham and the male members of his household are circumcised. Nowhere in these texts is there a hint that the procedure puts the person at risk of becoming boastful. Boasting, however, is a subject in Galatians and Romans. Paul says to the Galatians that even though 'the circumcised do not themselves obey the law...they want you to be circumcised so that they may *boast* about your flesh' (Gal. 6.13). In this accounting, circumcision is cast as a tangible, quantifiable measure of achievement that counts in part as a substitute for real transformation and in part as the means by which the Teachers in Galatia count their sheep. When Paul senses a similar discordant melody about to be played by promoters of circumcision in Rome, he casts the opponent as someone who *boasts* in the law while at the same time dishonoring God by breaking it (Rom. 2.17, 23). The pothole of *boasting* continues to blight the road that the circumcision party invites Gentile converts to travel. 'Then what becomes of *boasting*?' Paul asks after making it clear that humans are set right by the faithfulness of God and not by the remedial powers of the law (3.22-26). 'It is excluded', he answers, not by the logic of law but by the law and logic of God's faithfulness (3.27).

Still, however, the proponents of circumcision have reason to feel offended. 'Why', they object again, '*boasting* is not a feature of our theology. You are misrepresenting our position. While we do advocate circumcision, you are barking up the wrong tree by harping on *boasting*.'

For Paul's argument to work, therefore, whether in Galatia or Rome, it is necessary to look beyond what his opponents are *saying*. *Boasting* is Paul's word, not theirs.[10] Paul posits a connection between circumcision and boasting to which no self-respecting proponent will admit at the level of proposition and profession. If there is a connection—and Paul has no doubt that there is—it operates at the level of psychology and communal consequences. Less subtly, the boasting is certified by the behavior and manners

tive" on Paul', in *Reading Paul in Context*, p. 233), in line with a New Perspective reading of this text, says that 'the only kind of "works" that Paul ever objects to are those things that identify the Jews as Jews, and therefore the things that Gentiles need to do in order to become Jews'.

10. While the legitimacy of boasting has a basis in Jewish texts (*Jub.* 21.1-3; Sir. 34.4-9), Paul's argument—and the debate assumed by his argument—takes command of the word so as to make boasting an unmitigated negative.

of his opponents. In Paul's representation, they reek with inconsistency and misguided priorities. Paul saddles the cause of circumcision with the stigma of boasting not only because it is psychologically true but also because he confronts opponents who are guilty as charged. *Boasting* is not the stuff of malicious slander.

The polemical character of the argument is increasingly evident. When Paul says that 'if Abraham was set right by works, he has something to boast about' (4.2, translation mine), he cannot hang the cowbell of boasting around the neck of Abraham. The connection between Abraham and boasting is precisely that there is no connection, and the lack of connection unravels the case for circumcision. The bell hangs around the neck of Paul's opponents who insist that Gentile believers in Jesus are at risk of forfeiting their salvation unless they are circumcised. Protestant readings see in this argument a theology that teaches 'salvation by works' from the ground up: people must earn God's favor by good behavior and thereby put God in their debt. Such a view misreads and over-reads the problem Paul is addressing at this stage in Romans.[11] Paul's wording, says Dunn, is 'part of the analogy drawn from the world of contract and employment. He does *not* say, "If you think of Abraham's faith as a work, you must think of his righteousness as a reward". The contrast is solely between working and believing, between what the worker is due and what is given as a complete favor.'[12]

Paul contends for the integrity of God's gift as *gift*. For the *gift* to be that and nothing else, the notion of deserving it must be completely excluded. Abraham's trust, as we shall soon see in greater detail, is a response to what God is and does. For trusting that he is reckoned to be in a right relationship with God (Rom. 4.3; Gen. 15.6).

> For what does the scripture say? 'Abraham believed God, and it was reckoned to him as righteousness.' Now to one who works, wages are not reckoned as a gift but as something due. But to one who without works trusts him who justifies the ungodly, such faith is reckoned as righteousness. So also David speaks of the blessedness of those to whom God reckons righteousness apart from works. 'Blessed are those whose iniquities are forgiven, and whose sins are covered; blessed is the one against whom the Lord will not reckon sin' (Rom. 4.3-8).

Paul momentarily broadens the horizon from a narrow focus on Abraham and circumcision to take in the human condition, speaking of the person 'who without works trusts him who sets right the ungodly' (Rom.

11. According to Cranfield (*Romans*, p. 227), '[t]hat Abraham was justified on the ground of his works was indeed what Paul's Jewish contemporaries were accustomed to assume'. It is precisely this stereotyping of 'Judaism' as a legalistic, works-based religion that has been challenged and largely debunked by the 'New Perspective'.

12. Dunn, *Romans 1–8*, p. 204.

4.5, translation mine). He calls David to the witness stand to make the same argument in favor of those who do not have 'works' to show for themselves (4.6-8). But circumcision remains a dominant concern. Paul readies for the kill by putting forward Abraham in the dimension of *oneness*—as the head of the one family of faith (4.1).[13] Abraham is pronounced 'blessed' for trusting God (4.4-5): 'Abraham *believed* (*episteusen*) God, and it was reckoned to him as righteousness' (Rom. 4.3; Gen. 15.6). For Paul's argument to work, however, it is necessary to nail down the timing of Abraham's trust. 'Is this blessedness, then, pronounced only on the circumcised, or also on the uncircumcised?' (Rom. 4.9), that is, did the blessing have anything to do with the fact that Abraham was circumcised? If circumcision is the physical expression of Abraham's 'Jewish' character, what happens if it can be established that Abraham was counted blessed in a state of uncircumcision, that is, as a *Gentile*? With timing now the crucial point Paul pinpoints it like a lawyer who knows that he has a strong case. 'How then was it reckoned to him? Was it *before* or *after* he had been circumcised?' (4.10) This is a key point, and we should imagine a pause in a performed version of the letter. Once the pause has done its work, Paul will deliver the *coup de grâce* to the cause of circumcision. 'It was not *after*, but *before* he was circumcised' (4.10, emphasis added).

> He received the sign of circumcision as a seal of the righteousness that he had by faith (*sfragida tēs dikaiosynēs tēs pisteōs*) while he was still uncircumcised. The purpose was to make him the ancestor of all who believe without being circumcised and who thus have righteousness reckoned to them, and likewise the ancestor of the circumcised who are not only circumcised but who also follow the example of the faith that our ancestor Abraham had before he was circumcised (Rom. 4.11-12).

Paul has milked the timing aspect for all that it is worth, cutting off the argument for circumcision by uniting believing Gentiles and believing Jews at the ancestral source in the person of Abraham. Abraham is no longer the forefather mostly according to the flesh (4.1). The oneness of Jews and Gentiles is now twofold, held together by the oneness of God and the oneness of Abraham. Paul universalizes the promise to Abraham to its original all-inclusive measure. 'For the promise that he would inherit the world did not come to Abraham or to his descendants through the law but through the righteousness of faith (*dia dikaiosynēs pisteōs*)' (Rom. 4.13; cf. Gen. 12.3; 17.4-5; 22.17-18), that is, it is an inheritance no longer limited to the borders of Canaan (Gen. 12.5-7; 13.14-17; 15.7; 17.8), a claim that, if understood in political terms, would set the alarm bells ringing in Rome.[14] Paul, however, is not launching a political movement with his vision of inclusion.

13. Hays, 'Our Forefather according to the Flesh', pp. 76-98.

14. Jewett, *Romans*, p. 325.

Abraham was reckoned to be righteous *before* he was circumcised, that is, *before* he acquired the physical insignia that denote a Jewish identity. Blessedness is in the divine economy also extended to the uncircumcised Gentile.

> Is this blessedness, then, pronounced only on the circumcised, or also on the uncircumcised? We say, 'Faith was reckoned to Abraham as righteousness.' How then was it reckoned to him? Was it before or after he had been circumcised? It was not after, but before he was circumcised. He received the sign of circumcision as a seal of the righteousness that he had by faith while he was still uncircumcised. The purpose was to make him the ancestor of all who believe without being circumcised and who thus have righteousness reckoned to them, and likewise the ancestor of the circumcised who are not only circumcised but who also follow the example of the faith that our ancestor Abraham had before he was circumcised (Rom. 4.9-12).

Nevertheless, Abraham *was* circumcised, as Paul must acknowledge and, in Genesis, circumcision is not optional (Gen. 17.14). The movement from uncircumcision to circumcision is precisely the opposite of what Paul aims to achieve with his argument. A literal reading of the text in Genesis will not resolve this dilemma in Paul's favor. He has to infer that God's higher purpose in Genesis has only now, in connection with Paul's Gentile mission, risen into full view. Abraham is the model believer for the uncircumcised and the circumcised, for the former only if they remain uncircumcised and for the latter only if they are in a state of trusting God. Circumcision is not obsolete for the latter group, but it can no longer be a defining matter. The spiritual import of Paul's argument marginalizes circumcision for either group, but the communal significance of the argument in the context of Romans is huge. Circumcised Jewish believers and uncircumcised Gentile believers are both united in a common spiritual origin. Either group can look to Abraham and call him 'our ancestor' (Rom. 4.12). This is in agreement with Hays, who argues that the crucial issue here 'is not how Abraham got himself justified but rather whose father he is and in what way his children are related to him'.[15]

Oneness and inclusivity appear again in the letter ending.

> For I tell you that Christ has become a servant of the circumcised on behalf of the truth of God in order that he might confirm the promises given to the patriarchs, and in order that the Gentiles might glorify God for his mercy. As it is written, 'Therefore I will confess you among the Gentiles, and sing praises to your name' (Rom. 15.8-9; cf. 2 Sam. 22.50; Ps. 18.49).

God-ordained inclusion defines Paul's calling, and Abraham is resolutely in *his*—Paul's—corner: he 'is the father of all of us' (Rom. 4.16).

Inclusion and universality are now firmly on the horizon, as are the means by which they will be achieved. Paul posits a conflict between promise

15. Hays, 'Our Forefather according to the Flesh', p. 97.

(*epangelia*) and law (*nomos*) (4.13). This is a novel antithesis in the context of Romans, but the disjunction is not new to Paul or to the discussion at hand. 'For the promise that he would inherit the world did not come to Abraham or to his descendants through the law but through the righteousness of faith', says Paul (4.13). The same argument is pursued doggedly in Galatians, Paul claiming priority for the promise with respect to *time* and *means* (Gal. 3.16-18): the promise is superior because it came first, and it is better because God's promise alone will set right what is wrong (Gal. 3.21-26).

Two other elements are worthy of note in this verse (Rom. 4.13). First, Paul does not say that Abraham and his descendants (*spermati*) were meant to inherit Palestine or Canaan; he makes the grandiose claim that they are to 'inherit *the earth*' (4.13). This is not what Genesis says, but 'this was how the promise to Abraham was regularly understood'.[16] Dunn adds that

> the promise thus interpreted was fundamental to Israel's self-consciousness as God's covenant people: it was the reason why God had chosen them in the first place from among all the other nations of the earth, the justification for holding themselves distinct from the other nations, and the comforting hope that made their current national humiliation endurable.[17]

Just as Abraham's paternity must be construed in spiritual terms with reference to believing Jews and Gentiles, the territorial claim must also be conceived spiritually. The earth will be given to the believer (4.13), but the means must precede and control the end. When Jewett says that 'Paul and other early Christian thinkers are really articulating a new social order, based not on force but on persuasion, not on dominance but on cooperation, with an ethic of responsibility rather than of exploitation',[18] the balance between means and ends in the statement is excellent. To the house churches in Rome, however, their social and political status would tax credulity to the breaking point if not for the eschatological horizon that is implied in Paul's claim.[19]

Second, Paul is moving closer to personifying the phrase 'righteousness by faith' (*tēs dikaiosynēs pisteōs*) (4.13) and will do so explicitly when 'the Righteousness of Faith' is represented as a talking subject (10.6).[20] This, however, is precisely what 'the Righteousness of Faith' is: he or she is not an 'it'. He or she is a talking, storytelling subject, and the story he or she tells is the story of what God has done to make right what is wrong. For that reason the Righteousness of Faith says, 'Do not say in your heart, "Who will

16. Dunn, *Romans 1–8*, p. 233.
17. Dunn, *Romans 1–8*, p. 233.
18. Jewett, *Romans*, p. 326.
19. Käsemann, *Romans*, p. 120.
20. Hays, *Echoes of Scripture*, p. 73.

ascend into heaven?" (that is, to bring Christ down) or "Who will descend into the abyss?" (that is, to bring Christ up from the dead)' (10.6-7). No one needs to say that because Christ has of his own come down from heaven, and Christ has risen from the dead. This, needless to say, is the flip side of the story told by the Righteousness of Faith.

Paul then turns to the superiority of the promise (*epangelia*) over law (*nomos*), familiar turf from the dispute in Galatians (Gal. 3.16-18).

> If it is the adherents of the law who are to be the heirs, faith (*pistis*) is null and the promise is void.[21] For the law brings wrath (*orgē*); but where there is no law, neither is there violation. For this reason it depends on faith (*ek pisteōs*), in order that the promise may rest on grace and be guaranteed to all his descendants, not only to the adherents of the law but also to those who share the faith of Abraham (for he is the father of all of us, as it is written, 'I have made you the father of many nations')— in the presence of the God in whom he believed, who gives life to the dead and calls into existence the things that do not exist (Rom. 4.14-17).

The NRSV renders *pistis* with the traditional 'faith' (4.14b), meaning that there is *promise* at the source on God's side of the equation and *faith* at the receiving end on the human side. However, it would be equally valid to project that action is happening mostly on God's side. 'If those of law (read *circumcision*) are heirs, the faithfulness (of God) is null and the promise (of God) is void' (4.14, translation mine).[22] 'For this reason', likewise, 'it hinges on faithfulness', that is, 'it hinges on the faithfulness of God' (4.16, my translation and interpretation). Abraham's paternity plays out by way of a spiritual and not a physical lineage, and in that sense he is not of interest as anyone's ancestor *according to the flesh* (4.1). God, the source of trust, looms larger than Abraham, who trusts, because God is the one 'who gives life to the dead and calls into existence the things that do not exist' (4.17). Mere sexual intercourse in Abraham's and Sarah's old age would not have led to Isaac being conceived (Gen. 21.1-7), and nothing Abraham could do would bring Isaac back to life had he been sacrificed (Gen. 22.9-10).

'Hoping against hope', Paul continues, Abraham

> believed that he would become 'the father of many nations', according to what was said, 'So numerous shall your descendants be'. He did not weaken in faith when he considered his own body, which was already as good as dead (for he was about a hundred years old), or when he considered

21. Paul writes that '*the* faith (*hē pistis*) is null, and *the* promise (*hē epangelia*) is void' (Rom. 4.14, translation mine), *pistis* and *epangelia* mutually reinforcing and both with the definite article. This legitimizes the paraphrase that 'the faithfulness of God is null and the promise of God is void'.

22. Paul's use of the definite article with *pistis* and *epangelia* give them the same valence.

> the barrenness of Sarah's womb. No distrust made him waver concerning the promise of God, but he grew strong in his faith as he gave glory to God, being fully convinced that God was able to do what he had promised. Therefore his faith 'was reckoned to him as righteousness'. Now the words, 'it was reckoned to him', were written not for his sake alone, but for ours also. It will be reckoned to us who believe in him who raised Jesus our Lord from the dead, who was handed over to death for our trespasses and was raised for our justification (Rom. 4.18-25).

Paul may here be guilty of speaking of Abraham better than he deserves because Abraham did waver (Gen. 15.1-4), and he was a willing participant to Sarah's ill-conceived remedial proposal to get an heir through Hagar (Gen. 16.1-4). This scheme seems to be concocted after 'Abraham believed the LORD and the LORD reckoned it to him as righteousness' (Gen. 15.6).[23] He even laughed his heart out when God kept on insisting that Sarah would have a child in her old age (Gen. 17.15-22). But if Paul speaks better of Abraham than Abraham deserves, he tells a more representative story than those who make Abraham the guarantor for the message of circumcision. Abraham deserves the reputation Paul gives him, and the truly important elements are better preserved in Paul's account than in the use that his opponents make of Abraham. It is not Abraham's circumcision that matters but the other elements in the story that are hinted at—the decaying bodies of Abraham and Sarah being beyond the ability to produce offspring (Gen. 17.17; 18.10-15; 21.1-7), a more important memory than circumcision and a more telling representation of the human condition. The big ticket items in Paul's selection eclipse the small ticket items in the Abraham portfolio of his opponents. Paul ends his exposition by linking the birth, death, and resurrection in Abraham's story to Jesus, 'handed over (*paredothē*) for our trespasses and...raised to set us right' (Rom. 4.25, translation mine).[24] This—but not circumcision.

Abraham as Ecological Mentor

Paul shows himself to be a better reader of Genesis than his opponents, denying to them the use of Abraham as a pillar of support for the circumcision of Gentile believers in Jesus. The theme of Abraham as *believer* recurs again and again in Paul's argument. 'Abraham *believed* (*episteusen*) God, and it was reckoned to him as righteousness' (4.3); '*faith* (*pistis*) was reckoned to Abraham as righteousness' (4.9); and again, 'it (his *faith*)

23. For a compelling account on the domestic, theological, and national turmoil engendered by Abraham's liaison with Hagar, see Pamela Tamarkin Reis, 'Hagar Requited', *JSOT* 87 (2000), pp. 75-109.

24. Here, as it must, the resurrection is part of God's right-making (Rom. 4.25), see also Louw-Nida Lexicon, entry 34.46.

was reckoned to him as righteousness' (4.22, translation mine). So much is made of Abraham's faith that it threatens to obscure the reality that anchors his commitment. Abraham's trust is important, but it is God's faithfulness, not Abraham's faith, that creates the possibilities and makes the difference. Thus, in Rolf Rendtorff's exposition of who did what when Abraham believed, and God 'reckoned it to him as righteousness' (Gen. 15.6), *God* is the truly important subject.

> The linguistic structure of the verse leaves the subject of this second half of the verse open (Gen. 15.6). According to the traditional interpretation, God counted Abraham's faith as righteousness. But in medieval Jewish interpretation we already find that view that it is Abraham who recognizes and acknowledges God's promise as an expression of God's righteousness. This finds support in Neh. 9, where, like a liturgical response to the sentence that God found Abraham's heart 'faithful', we read 'for you (God) are righteous' (*saddîq*, v. 8). God's righteousness here is his faithfulness to his promise. Abraham believed in God's faithfulness and confirmed it, as it were, by 'acknowledging' it.[25]

Abraham's trust is not a doctrinal commitment or a theoretical exercise, as his wanderings in Genesis show, and his trust does not play out only within a legal construct of sin and forgiveness. His trust is deep, relational, and comprehensive. Whenever we see Abraham's faith extolled, therefore, its grounding in God's faithfulness wears a translucent veil. This connection establishes conclusively the bivalence of the terms 'the Righteousness of Faith' (Rom. 4.11, 13; 10.6), God's right-making faithfulness counting for more than right-made faith on the human side. In another note on Genesis 15.6, Rendtorff sees the message to be that 'ultimately Abraham's faith, his confidence in the reliability of the promises and the guidance of God, will determine his image as a whole'.[26] Here, too, however, the reliability of God is the cornerstone.

Later, at a point when neither the promise of the land nor the promise of an heir have materialized, God's reliability is the big question. The prospect of an heir is in doubt by the fact that 'it had ceased to be with Sarah after the manner of women' (Gen. 18.11), but God keeps repeating the promise to Abraham. He will have land, and he will have an heir, and the heir will be born to Sarah (Gen. 18.10, 14). God's reliability is nevertheless on the line, so much that God will voice the question that is thick in the air, 'Is anything too wonderful for the LORD?' (Gen. 18.14). Walter Brueggemann calls this 'the question of the entire Bible'.

25. Rolf Rendtorff, *The Canonical Hebrew Bible: A Theology of the Old Testament* (trans. David E. Orton; Leiden: Deo Publishers, 2005), p. 27.

26. Rendtorff, *A Theology of the Old Testament*, p. 27.

> Can he (God) do the hard thing? Can he bring freedom out of slavery, life out of death, fertility out of barrenness, rivers out of desert (Isa. 41.18), cypress out of thorns (Isa. 55.13), joy out of sorrow (Jn 16.20)? Can a sojourner receive an eternal possession? The issue turns on the power and fidelity of Yahweh.[27]

God's reliability is also the cornerstone for the ecological role of Abraham. From the beginning of the story, God has plans for the earth and its many nations, and God calls Abraham to be a channel of blessing and revelation.

> Now the LORD said to Abram, 'Go from your country and your kindred and your father's house to the land that I will show you. I will make of you a great nation, and I will bless you, and make your name great, so that you will be a blessing. I will bless those who bless you, and the one who curses you I will curse; and in you all the families of the earth shall be blessed (lit. "shall bless themselves").' So Abram went, as the LORD had told him; and Lot went with him. Abram was seventy-five years old when he departed from Haran (Gen. 12.1-4).

Abraham's migration of faith would be noteworthy even in a time of air travel and the Internet; its import in the ancient world lies beyond computation. While we have in the foregoing stressed the priority of God's faithfulness over Abraham's faith, it is now time to make it up to Abraham's faith. The trust he has in God translates into actual leaving the known that is near and dear for the unknown that is far away and uncertain. Nahum Sarna says that '[t]he enormity of God's demand and the agonizing nature of the decision to be made are effectively conveyed through the cluster of terms arranged in ascending order according to the severity of the sacrifice involved: country, extended family, nuclear family'.[28] Brueggemann is similarly awed.

> The new history begins with a call to repentance, a summons to leave and go somewhere we are not, a radical breaking off and departure, to become someone we have not been. We know nothing about the place Abraham left. The text is constructed to suggest that it is also a place of coercion and hopelessness.[29]

If Brueggemann's last sentence has merit, Abraham is leaving on a journey of liberation and hope for him and for the world to which he will mediate hope.

27. Walter Brueggemann, *The Land: Place as Gift, Promise, and Challenge in Biblical Faith* (OBT; Minneapolis: Fortress Press, 2002), p. 22.

28. Sarna, *Genesis*, p. 88.

29. Brueggemann, *The Land*, p. 17.

And then land—or promise of land—the most salient aspect of ecology. Abraham's heirs will have land (Gen. 12.7; 13.12-17; 15.7, 13-21; 17.8; 24.7), a perspective so dominant in the Old Testament that 'the possession of the land plays a fundamental role', and references back to the patriarchs are 'connected with the promise of land especially often'.[30] Actual possession is deferred, however, for Abraham belonging to a distant horizon (Gen. 15.13-21). His fate is to reside 'as an alien (*gēr*) many days in the land of the Philistines' (Gen. 21.34). When possession of the land is realized, important stipulations apply. The land inheritance is described as *naḥ^alāh*, a term first used in Genesis by Rachel and Leah. It is triggered by their concern that they will leave home empty-handed (Gen. 31.14; cf. Gen. 48.6; Num. 26.52-56). This term is basic to the land economy of Israel, implying ownership that is never dissociated or detached from a theological framework. Land disposal is not autonomous because the land is held in trust. Rendtorff explains that *naḥ^alāh* is a theological legal term, expressing 'the fact that the land is given over to Israel for its disposal and use, but that it remains God's possession'.[31] The deferral of possession that is spelled out in Gen. 15.13-21 could be a case in point, certain terms of possession applying to 'the people of the land' in the days of Abraham as much as they will apply to Abraham's descendants. Indeed, Abraham's sojourn as a resident alien (*gēr*) in the Promised Land is an important respect the rule and not the exception, a permanent feature and not a transitional state. Thus, God is said to tell Israel in the days of Moses that even with Israel settled 'the land shall not be sold in perpetuity, for the land is mine; with me you are but aliens (*gērim*) and tenants' (Lev. 25.23).

The import of the land promise and qualified possession is highlighted by a second feature that is important to ecology in the Abraham narrative. When a dispute arises between his herdsmen and the herdsmen of Lot (Gen. 13.7), Abraham arbitrates the conflict in a way that seems to his economic detriment and less than he is entitled to claim. His stance and the approach taken by Lot suggest options that are paradigmatic and timeless.

> Now Abram was very rich in livestock, in silver, and in gold... Now Lot, who went with Abram, also had flocks and herds and tents, so that the land could not support both of them living together; for their possessions were so great that they could not live together, and there was strife between the herders of Abram's livestock and the herders of Lot's livestock... Then Abram said to Lot, 'Let there be no strife between you and me, and between your herders and my herders; for we are kindred. Is not the whole land before you? Separate yourself from me. If you take the left hand, then I will go to the right; or if you take the right hand, then I will go to the left.' Lot looked about him, and saw that the plain of the Jordan was well watered everywhere like the garden of the LORD, like the land of Egypt, in

30. Rendtorff, *A Theology of the Old Testament*, p. 457.
31. Rendtorff, *A Theology of the Old Testament*, p. 458; cf. Habel, *The Land*, p. 35.

> the direction of Zoar; this was before the LORD had destroyed Sodom and Gomorrah. So Lot chose for himself all the plain of the Jordan, and Lot journeyed eastward; thus they separated from each other. Abram settled in the land of Canaan, while Lot settled among the cities of the Plain and moved his tent as far as Sodom. Now the people of Sodom were wicked, great sinners against the LORD (Gen. 13.2-13).

Should not Abraham have the first choice, being the older person and the actual recipient of God's promise? Should not Lot defer to him? Would it not be legitimate to solve the conflict by an appeal to *rights*, in a statutory manner? The suggestion that the primary issue in the conflict centers on Lot as the closest, legitimate heir and Lot's decision to forgo that privilege is not persuasive.[32] One reason, as Dan Rickett notes, has to do with Abraham's remark, 'We are kindred' (Gen. 13.8). Lot is represented as a relative but not as an heir. 'The phrase literally reads, "we are men, brothers". *'āḥ* can be used for those of the same family or those of the same tribe but is never used in relation to sonship. Here the only meaning that makes sense is that Abraham and Lot are of the same family.'[33] In fact, in Rickett's construction of the story, Lot is a member of Abraham's family, but he is not a primary recipient of the blessing. 'He is at best an estranged family member. Or better, he is an outsider.'[34]

This makes Abraham's conduct toward Lot the pivotal point, highlighting his high-mindedness. When strife is evident between the two groups, Abraham 'is the first to feel the unworthiness of such strife'.[35] His peace-making is active and irenic in tone, showing from the outset willingness to be part of the solution and a determination to lower the bar for the other side in the dispute even if it should put him at a disadvantage (Gen. 13.8-9). The character of Lot is not fully evident, but there is a suggestion that Lot has a combative posture that needs to be softened. Second, although Abraham is the older man and Lot's uncle, 'he does not insist on seniority or priority of rights'.[36] The magnanimous deference to Lot invites an attitude of reciprocity on Lot's part and acknowledgement of the older man's kindness, but nothing of the sort is forthcoming. Third, therefore, with Abraham's decision to let Lot have the first choice comes the possibility that Lot will make a choice that is to Abraham's loss. If that is the risk, Abraham accepts it. Gordon Wenham notes in this regard that 'Abram's generosity toward his nephew Lot in allowing him

32. Larry R. Helyer, 'The Separation of Abram and Lot: Its Significance in the Patriarchal Narratives', *JSOT* 26 (1983), pp. 77-88.

33. Dan Rickett, 'Rethinking the Place and Purpose of Genesis 13', *JSOT* 36 (2011), p. 48.

34. Rickett, 'Rethinking the Place and Purpose of Genesis 13', pp. 40-41.

35. Gerhard von Rad, *Genesis* (trans. John H. Marks; London: SCM Press, 2nd edn, 1963), p. 166.

36. Sarna, *Genesis*, p. 98.

to pick the best of the land for himself is recognized by most commentators as being set out as a model for his descendants to imitate'.[37]

Abraham emerges as a figure of blessing. This is precisely what God promised that he would be (Gen. 12.2-3), and the promise is not slow in being fulfilled. Early on in his migrant state Abraham mediates blessing, peace, and conviviality to Lot and the surrounding community. When the narrator in Genesis says that at that time 'the Canaanites and the Perizzites lived in the land' (Gen. 13.7), the potential for rivalry and hostility is evident. Yet these peoples are witness to Abraham and his peace-making role and have a front seat to encounter in Abraham a mediator of revelation. As Habel notes, 'Abraham is portrayed an exemplar of how to share the land, overcome conflict, and mediate blessing to the inhabitants of the land'.[38] In Romans, addressing his interlocutor, Paul says that 'the name of God is blasphemed among the Gentiles because of you' (Rom. 2.24). Abraham, by contrast, earns the respect of the people he encounters, and it is implied that there will be reverence and admiration for Abraham's God (Gen. 14.22-24; 20.15; 23.6). People feel blessed by his presence in their midst.

Theology and Ecology in the Life of Abraham

- Abraham's sense of vocation has a theological foundation: the faithfulness of God.
- He lives as a wanderer in the Promised Land, leaving a small ecological footprint.
- He earns the respect and admiration of the people of the land and, indirectly, respect and admiration for God.

With Abraham, then, begins the story of restoration of the disorder created by humans that is told at the beginning of the Bible. Walter Vogels notes in an evocative study of Abraham and Lot that there is sacrifice on the part of Abraham at the beginning and ending of the narrative, different in magnitude but comparable in kind.[39] At the beginning, Abraham offers the land to Lot even though God has promised it to him (Gen. 13.8-9). At the end, he offers the child of promise to God (Gen. 22.1-18). Thus, says Vogels, there is sacrifice of the land to the brother or fellow human being and of the child to God. Abraham leans on the promise as promise not in the sense that the promise is relinquished but in the sense that it is entirely in God's hands. If the land represents security in the present and the child security and hope for the future, Abraham commits the present and the future to God. The mediating role of Abraham in Genesis finds a parallel in Paul's commitment to mediate peace and mutual respect between Jewish and Gentile believers in Rome (Rom. 14.1–15.3). Indeed, it is the wider implication of his

37. G.J. Wenham, *Genesis 1–15* (WBC; Dallas: Word, 1998), pp. 299-300.

38. Habel, *The Land*, p. 125.

39. Walter Vogels, 'Abraham et l'offrande de la terre (Gn 13)', *SR* 4 (1974–75), pp. 51-57.

ministry that Jews and Gentiles are equally the objects of God's faithfulness (Rom. 15.9-12). It is therefore not contrived to say that what Abraham is in his itinerant life, Paul will be in his itinerant ministry. Paul's promotion of Abraham in Romans happens equally by word and example.

Lot, by contrast, makes choices that on the surface seem to be wise but are actually short-sighted and harmful. Wenham invokes the notion of 'theological geography' in connection with Lot's choice,[40] Lot moving to the edge of Canaan if not beyond it. In Rickett's careful analysis of Lot's moves, God 'occupies the land of Canaan', at least figuratively, and Lot is demoting God on his list of priorities.[41] The images that come to mind to Lot, the Garden of Eden and the land of Egypt (Gen. 13.10), are 'surprisingly worldly and enlightened'.[42] The winning ticket thus ascertained (Gen. 13.10), Lot 'chooses quickly'.[43] To Rickett, Lot recapitulates Eve in the Garden of Eden by the way he sizes up his options, figuratively joining Adam and Eve and Cain on a journey 'eastward' once his mind is made up (Gen. 13.10-11).[44] Enticed by land and the prospect of prosperity, and possibly by a life of ease, Lot moves closer and closer to disaster in the land that at a distance looked to him like the lost paradise (Gen. 13.12-13). In social and relational terms, Lot comes across as self-serving and calculating, his spiritual priorities defeated by the material calculus. In ecological terms, the land has tempted him in a way that possession of land cannot tempt Abraham.[45] Later, in the prophetic body of the Old Testament, Ezekiel remembers the sins of the city where Lot took up reference not for sexual depravity but for covetousness: the cities of the plain 'had pride, excess of food, and prosperous ease, but did not aid the poor and needy' (Ezek. 16.49). Should the rapacious pursuit of real estate in the Western capitalist economy be in need of a patron saint, therefore, he will be Lot, not Abraham.

Abraham and Lot in Ecological Terms

	Abraham	**Lot**
Resident status	sojourner	settled
Priority	spiritual	material
Disposition	unselfish	self-interested
Ideology	accommodating	acquisitive
Orientation	communal	individualistic

40. Wenham, *Genesis 1–15*, p. 297.

41. Rickett, 'Rethinking the Place and Purpose of Genesis 13', p. 39.

42. Von Rad, *Genesis*, p. 167.

43. Von Rad, *Genesis*, p. 167.

44. Rickett, 'Rethinking the Place and Purpose of Genesis 13', p. 49.

45. Brueggemann, (*The Land*, p. 55) says that 'the central temptation of land is coveting', and Marvin L. Chaney ('You Shall Not Covet Your Neighbor's House', *PTR* 15 [1982], pp. 3-13) argues persuasively that the commandment regarding covetousness had a particular concern for land policy.

The extent of real estate actually in Abraham's possession as his life draws to a close does not amount to much. This takes us to the third and final exhibit that carries ecological weight in the Abraham narrative. After Sarah's death at the reported age of 127 years (Gen. 23.1-2), Abraham engages 'the people of the land' (Gen. 23.7, 12) in order to secure a burial plot. His dialogue with the Hittites is a case study of subtlety and decorum. Abraham shows humility, tact, and mastery of the art of negotiation, seeming not to wince at the hefty price that Ephron son of Zohar quotes to him while pretending that the price is a virtual giveaway (Gen. 23.7-16).[46] As the cultural premise for the transaction, Stephen C. Russell distinguishes between 'an estate of production' and 'an estate of administration', the former giving the right to use the land and the latter entailing actual ownership.[47] When offered the former (Gen. 23.6), Abraham politely declines, making it clear that he seeks ownership and a formal transfer (Gen. 23.8-9), a transaction that only the Hittites have the standing to authorize. Abraham, then, 'does not seek temporary acquisition of land for grazing, nor life-long acquisition of land for a fixed residence. Rather, he seeks a permanent site for Sarah's burial, to be accessible in perpetuity by his descendants.'[48]

Again, although the land has been promised to him, Abraham recognizes the rights and dignity of the people of the land. His theological writ has no part in the negotiations, and he does not think it his prerogative to take the land by force.

> Rather, he pays the ultimate respect to the Hittites, who are here designated as 'the people of the land' (23.7). He bows down to them (23.7, 12) and buys the field of Ephron in accordance with the legal procedures depicted as customary among the Hittites. The piece of land then becomes Abraham's permanent legal possession (*'aḥuzzah*, 23.18), a symbol of God's promised land and an example of just dealings in the appropriation of land. This legal transaction also implies that Abraham treats the Hittites as the legitimate owners of the land with the right to negotiate its sale.[49]

Habel notes that Abraham represents a land ideology that is 'accommodating rather than acquisitive', functioning 'as an ambassador of goodwill among equals'.[50] The theological and existential symbolism of the transaction is as striking as social, economic, and political aspects. Only when Abraham approaches death does he have actual ownership, 'enough turf in

46. E.A. Speiser, *Genesis: Introduction, Translation, and Notes* (AB; New Haven: Yale University Press, 2008), p. 172.

47. Stephen C. Russell, 'Abraham's Purchase of Ephron's Land in Anthropological Perspective', *Bib Int* 21 (2013), pp. 153-70.

48. Russell, 'Abraham's Purchase of Ephron's Land', p. 163.

49. Habel, *The Land*, p. 129.

50. Habel, *The Land*, pp. 126, 127.

which to be buried' (Gen. 25.9-10), and, indeed, 'only a small plot'.[51] This, in Brueggemann's interpretation (Gen. 23.4), suggests that 'for the narrative, it is the *landless sojourner* who is *God's prince*'.[52] Only in death are Abraham and Sarah no longer strangers in the land,[53] but a promise that is fulfilled in death or on the threshold of death drives home its incompletion. Paul's claim that 'Abraham *believed* God' can now be shouted at the requisite decibel (Rom. 4.3), trust manifested in the context of the impermanence of human existence, in the unsettled state, participatory,[54] to be sure, and certainly not compressible only to a juridical framework. For Abraham, experiencing possession only at death's door and at the point when faith has run its course to completion, the faithfulness of God must come to the rescue, his enduring legacy in Genesis as it is in Romans. 'For in hope we were saved', writes Abraham's leading interpreter, and 'hope that is seen is not hope. For who hopes for what is seen?' (Rom. 8.24).

The ecological implications of Abraham's faith are more than a sideshow or a detour. Transience and death are not incidental to ecological attunement because they temper acquisitiveness. We would hardly know Abraham unless this aspect of the story is factored in—his wanderings, the promise of land, the conflict with Lot, and his communal influence. Paul's claim that Abraham 'is the father of all of us' (4.16) can rightly be extended to include ecologists. His life commitments hold promise as ecological ideals, and his trustworthiness is beyond doubt precisely because his ecological footprint is so small. In the story line of Romans, Abraham's hope and God's right-making in Jesus are whole cloth (4.16-25). They set the stage for telling the story of the love of God in widescreen, as Paul will do next.

51. Brueggemann, *The Land*, p. 23.

52. Brueggemann, *The Land*, p. 196.

53. von Rad, *Genesis*, p. 243.

54. Donaldson ('The Juridical, the Participatory, and the "New Perspective"', pp. 239-40) opts for a terminology of *status* and *experienced process* as improvements upon E.P. Sanders' notions of *state* and *transfer*. *Experienced process* is the more telling image, reflecting Paul's (as Donaldson reads Paul) view of sin as a power. *Vis-à-vis* traditional salvation terminology, *experienced process* covers much of the territory previously allotted to sanctification. This term has excellent descriptive adequacy when applied to Abraham.

Chapter 8

THE LOVE OF GOD IN WIDESCREEN (ROM. 5.1-21; 8.31-39)

Paul's discussion of Abraham (Rom. 4.1-25) is the last leg of the steep, uphill climb that has been in progress from the beginning of the letter body of Romans (1.18). By 'steep' and 'uphill' I have in mind the polemics, evident disagreement, convoluted argument, and sometimes rather punchy rhetoric to which the reader has been exposed so far. ('You that abhor idols, do you rob temples?' [2.22].) Even if the climb is not over, the terrain is for the moment leveling off (5.1-11), the pace is quicker, the stride longer, and we are no longer gasping for air. In hiker's terminology, there is less need to keep an eye on the trail and more opportunity to take in the view. Circumcision of the Gentiles, a principal concern up to this point, is not brought up again. With the transition into more congenial terrain, friendliness is also evident in the tone and turn of phrase of Romans, as Patricia McDonald notes.[1] While Paul has so far been addressing issues—and probably actual people—coming from without the Roman house churches, he is now speaking directly to the members of the church.[2] Leaving polemics behind for a while, for the first time in Romans Paul 'draws repeated attention to the de facto unity that exists between himself and those to whom he is writing: along with all who believe, they constitute "we"'.[3]

Higher Ground: Romans 5.1–8.39

- Transition to friendly, intimate tone and inclusive 'we'-form.
- Section framed by the love of God revealed in the self-giving death of Jesus (5.6-11; 8.31-39).
- Abraham in view at the beginning and ending, not only as a person who is faithful to God but as a revealer of God's faithfulness (8.32).
- 'Widescreen' to be understood as *cosmic perspective*, *comprehensive narrative*, *profound existential insight*, and *exquisite emotional depth*.

1. McDonald, 'Romans 5.1-11 as a Rhetorical Bridge', pp. 81-96.
2. Circumcision and the theological package that goes with it have been the main issues so far.
3. McDonald, 'Romans 5.1-11 as a Rhetorical Bridge', p. 81.

Here (5.1-11), says McDonald, 'Paul has once more in the forefront of his mind those to whom he is writing'.[4]

On closer examination, the 'we'-form begins already at the close of Paul's discussion of Abraham (4.23-25), indicating that Abraham has not disappeared from view. He is still influencing Paul's topic well into the transition, now as a treasure and symbol of the faith Paul and the Romans hold in common.[5] As Karl Olav Sandnes points out, 'Abraham who became the friend of God is a paradigm for Paul's description of the believers in Rom. 5.1-11'.[6]

This sets the stage for two remarkable changes in Romans that I will call *expanding spheres* in the next section of letter (5.1–8.39). With respect to audience, Paul is no longer focusing only on influences he hopes to hold at bay (as in 2.1-29). While he is speaking *to* the Romans, he speaks to them as though *from within* the Roman faith community. The implied referent for the '*we*'-form now refers to a group that is assumed to be on his side, Paul adopting the mantle of spokesperson for the faith outlook *of* the Romans. From the expanding 'we-group' at the point of origin the message enters an expanding orbit at the point of reception. It is increasingly a message *to whom it may concern*.

The expanding sphere with respect to audience is reflected in the subject matter. Here, too, there is a generalizing tendency, especially in Paul's depiction of the human predicament (5.1-21; 7.7-25). Paul turns his attention to the human condition on the two points that are most fraught. The first is death itself (5.1-21). The second centers on demonstrable moral incapacity on the part of human beings, the discrepancy between what is and what ought to be, and, even worse, sin's success in turning what is good to its own advantage (7.7-25). This is not the problem of death in biological terms but the problem of death-in-life. Paul probes the problem to excruciating depth, personalizing it with the intent of generalizing. When he exclaims, 'Who will rescue me from this body of death?' (7.24) he counts on the Roman readers to feel the predicament as deeply as he does and to shout it with him with the same degree of existential despair.

There is much that is memorable, quotable, and beautiful in this section (5.1–8.39), Paul at times waxing lyrical and euphoric (8.31-39). From the point of view of ecological hermeneutics, the stakes are enormous. Now, if not before, Paul spells out terms, conceptually and existentially, that can be appreciated only within a material conception of reality. Peering into the abyss of death's horror, Paul restores to death the prestige it is owed but has

4. McDonald, 'Romans 5.1-11 as a Rhetorical Bridge', p. 85.

5. Karl Olav Sandnes, 'Abraham, the friend of God, in Rom 5', *ZNW* 99 (2008), pp. 124-28.

6. Sandnes, 'Abraham, the friend of God', p. 128.

often been denied. Death's stature is magnified by the death of Christ in particular (5.6-8) and by the universality of death (5.12-14, 21), but it is also necessary to see it the other way around. Only when death stands tall and cold and forbidding is it possible to take the correct measure of the disposition of the one who willingly accepted death (5.6-7). Death's biology is the premise for death's finality. Indeed, biology and theology may be able to avoid each other as unrelated disciplines, but they cannot avoid each other at the point of death. Because life is constituted materially, Christ accepted the lot of biological life and the prospect of biological extinction. Paul's anthropology extends the hand of respect and solidarity to the material world, acknowledging common ground in plight with non-human creation and also common ground in hope (8.19-22).

The history of ideas has raised a high bar to understanding Paul's view of death and his singular, all-eggs-in-one-basket proclamation of the end to the Reign of Death. Out of respect for the stakes involved, the exploration of this section must begin with Plato and Philo and not with Paul.

Interlude: Death as Liberation

'Do we believe that there is such a thing as death?' Socrates asks his student interlocutor in Plato's retelling in *Phaedo*, described as 'the most moving of all Plato's dialogues'[7] and one of the four books comprising a collection sold under the title *The Last Days of Socrates*.[8]

'To be sure', Simmias replies.

'And is this anything but the separation of soul and body? And being dead is the attainment of this separation when the soul exists in herself, and is parted from the body and the body is parted from the soul—that is death?' Socrates continues.

Simmias, accepting the line prescribed for him, delivers according to expectations. 'Exactly, that and nothing else', he says.[9]

This is death as Socrates defines it, the voice of Plato possibly saying more than Socrates actually may have done. Scholars note that the Socratic dialogues are often disingenuous. They affect an exchange of views as if to persuade someone to a point of view previously not held. In reality, the lines spoken by the interlocutors are as predictable as the dialogues in an American television sitcom, and the 'opposing' view is therefore easily

7. I.F. Stone, *The Trial of Socrates* (New York: Anchor Books, 1989), p. 192.

8. Plato, *Euthyphro, Apology, Crito, Phaedo* (trans. Benjamin Jowett; New York: Prometheus Books, 1988); also published as *The Last Days of Socrates* (trans. Hugh Tredennick; New York: Penguin Books, 2003).

9. *Phaedo* (Jowett translation), pp. 76-77.

demolished. Simmias, the student in this exchange, is a case in point and a telling example of the 'submissive yes-men' in the Platonic canon.[10]

Socrates (or Plato) is aware that the dismissive view of death espoused above needs more corroboration. He proceeds to provide it by prescript, example, and bold postulates, now in dialogue with Cebes. To show that the soul is immortal he invokes the 'cyclical argument', claiming that one member of a pair of opposites generates its opposite.[11] By this logic, light generates darkness, and darkness gives birth to light. Life and death are similarly related, one generating the other. Death thus conceived is no longer a negative and not something to be feared, given that it generates life. Socrates then turns to the 'argument from recollection'. Knowledge is not the acquisition and mastery of a new body of information and insight—not at all.[12] Instead, knowledge is recollection and therefore proof of the soul's prior existence. Next, Socrates brandishes the 'affinity argument', hypothesizing that while the body is visible and changing, the soul is immaterial, unseen, and unchanging.[13] This means that the soul has enduring qualities and is superior to the body. Above all, it means that the soul is immortal. In what seems intended to be the clincher in this sequence of exercises, Socrates finally invokes the 'odd principle'.[14] The even number 'two' is not the opposite of the odd number 'three', but they are mutually exclusive: 'two' cannot be 'three' and vice versa. By the same logic, the life-giving soul cannot be death or be susceptible to death any more than 'two' can be 'three'. At all steps in the argument, Cebes offers no resistance. Plato beckons the reader to acquiesce in a similar manner.

'Then the soul is immortal?' Socrates asks at the conclusion of the exchange.

'Yes', Cebes answers.

'And may we say that this is proven?' Socrates queries.

'Yes, abundantly proven, Socrates', Cebes obediently intones.[15]

Socrates fortifies his 'proofs' by postulating that the soul exists by moral necessity. The soul's immortality is an incentive to good behavior and the only way to avoid being recycled in ever new bodies. In the absence of the soul's immortality, there would be no reason for good behavior. 'If death had only been the end of all, the wicked would have had a good bargain in dying', he says.[16]

10. Stone, *The Trial of Socrates*, p. 72.
11. *Phaedo* (Jowett translation), pp. 84-85.
12. *Phaedo* (Jowett translation), pp. 87-93.
13. *Phaedo* (Jowett translation), pp. 95-9.
14. *Phaedo* (Jowett translation), pp. 122-26.
15. *Phaedo* (Jowett translation), p. 126.
16. *Phaedo* (Jowett translation), p. 128.

Above all, however, Socrates teaches the doctrine of the immortality of the soul by his serene example. 'And have you any commands for us, Socrates—anything to say about your children, or any other matter in which we can serve you?' Crito asks when the moment to drink the hemlock approaches. Socrates remains unperturbed. 'Nothing particular, Crito', he answers. 'And in what way shall we bury you?' Crito wants to know. 'In any way that you like', says Socrates, still unaffected, 'but you must get hold of me, and take care that I do not run away from you'. Burial matters are irrelevant because the real Socrates cannot be entombed. The philosopher's true self is headed for liberation and ascent at the point of death.[17] Phaedo, Plato's narrator in the dialogue, interjects that at that point Socrates 'turned to us, and added with a smile', his calm demeanor the embodiment of how death should be understood.[18] Socrates complains that Crito's dullness of comprehension stands in the way of grasping the wonderful truth he is teaching—that and not death's resistance to being explained away.

> I cannot make Crito believe that I am the same Socrates who have been talking and conducting the argument; he fancies that I am the other Socrates whom he will soon see, a dead body—and he asks, How shall he bury me? And though I have spoken many words in the endeavor to show that when I have drunk the poison I shall leave you and go to the joys of the blessed,—these words of mine, with which I was comforting you and myself, have had, as I perceive, no effect upon Crito.[19]

Poor Crito, so much a captive of material existence that he is unable to see the liberation and ascent of the soul at the moment of death. He struggles to apprehend the wonderful truth that biological realities have no bearing on the human self because the self is not materially constituted. When the jailer brings the cup of poison, Socrates takes it 'in the easiest and gentlest manner, without the least fear or change of color or feature', says Phaedo. He notes that Socrates drinks it 'cheerfully'. This is too much for his friends and students, who are now weeping uncontrollably in the mentor's presence. 'Socrates alone retained his calmness', Phaedo says admiringly. 'What is this strange outcry?' Socrates asks. In keeping with the misogyny that is typical of Socrates' all-male company, he adds that 'I sent away the women mainly in order that they might not misbehave in this way, for I have been told that a man should die in peace'. One last item of business remains, these being the last words of Socrates, 'Crito, I owe a cock to Asclepius; will you remember to pay the debt?'[20]

17. *Phaedo* (Jowett translation), p. 135-36.
18. *Phaedo* (Jowett translation), p. 136.
19. *Phaedo* (Jowett translation), p. 136.
20. *Phaedo* (Jowett translation), pp. 137-38.

By then Socrates has talked up the superiority of the soul over the body in every facet of existence, construing death not as defeat and demise but as emancipation and ascent. The statements I have assembled below are all taken from *Phaedo*, the Socratic postulates meant to be proofs of the veracity of his teaching. For this reason the implied question mark that accompanies each postulate is meant to be erased on the logic that the question carries within it the self-evident answer.

> And thought is best when the mind is gathered into herself and none of these things trouble her—neither sounds nor sights nor pain nor any pleasure,—*when she takes leave of the body, and has as little as possible to do with it*, when she has *no bodily sense or desire*, but is aspiring after true being?

> And he attains to the purest knowledge of them who goes to each with the mind alone, not introducing or intruding in the act of thought sight or any other sense together with reason, but with the very light of the mind in her own clearness searches into the very truth of each; *he who has got rid, as far as he can, of eyes and ears and, so to speak, of the whole body, these being in his opinion distracting elements which when they infect the soul hinder her from acquiring truth and knowledge*—who, if not he, is likely to attain the knowledge of true being?

> 'Have we not found', (the real philosopher) will say, 'a path of thought which seems to bring us and our argument to the conclusion, that *while we are in the body, and while the soul is infected with the evils of the body*, our desire will not be satisfied? and our desire is of the truth. *For the body is a source of endless trouble to us…the body is always breaking in upon us… we must be quit of the body*—the soul in herself must behold things in themselves, and then we shall attain the wisdom which we desire… *For then, and not till then, the soul will be parted from the body and exist in herself alone*. In this present life, I reckon that we make the nearest approach to knowledge *when we have the least possible intercourse or communion with the body*, and are not *surfeited with the bodily nature*, but keep ourselves pure until the hour when God himself is pleased to release us. And thus *having got rid of the foolishness of the body* we shall be pure and hold converse with the pure, and know of ourselves the clear light everywhere, which is no other than the light of truth.'[21]

Socrates piles on one association more negative than the previous one with respect to the body. Death, we have seen, is no more than the separation of the soul from the body: it is *that and nothing else*. Its attractiveness is enhanced by casting death as a journey upward and homeward, the soul at last liberated from *the foolishness of the body*. Biology must not be allowed to burden this vision with unbecoming doubt, and materiality is the one inadmissible deterrent. Socrates has no fear of death, joking with his

21. Excerpts from *Phaedo* (Jowett translation), pp. 77-80.

disciples when he drinks the hemlock. The absence of women is notable for many reasons, one of which is that women might allow an emotional and intuitive grasp of death to intrude on the cerebral serenity that Socrates is keen to preserve.

Does Plato's depiction of death have merit? Is it persuasive? Emily Wilson comments kindly that 'all four arguments offered by "Socrates" for the soul's immortality are riddled with logical errors and false premises'.[22] When Cebes claims that the soul's immortality has been 'abundantly proven', the truth is rather nothing of the sort. Many of the 'proofs' are patently meaningless and, as I.F. Stone says of Socrates' quest for definitions and abstractions, they amount to 'stratospheric nonsense'.[23]

And yet Plato's doctrine of the soul was destined for success in the history of ideas, and it achieved success even where one might think that its chances would be most dismal. In Alexandria, the intellectual capital of the 'Middle Platonists' (80 BCE to 220 CE), the Jewish philosopher Philo (ca. 20 BCE to 40 CE) established a bridgehead between Plato's anthropology and the Old Testament. No one can read Philo's musings without hearing Plato's whisper in the background.

> Clearly this indicates the incorruptibility (*aphtharsia*) of the Soul, which removes its habitation from the mortal body and returns as if to the mother city (*metropolis*) from which it originally removed its habitation to this place. For when it is said to a dying person, 'Thou shalt go to thy fathers', what else is this than to represent another life without the body, which only the soul of the wise man ought to live?[24]

> The death of worthy men (*spoudaioi*) is the beginning of another life. For life is twofold; one is with corruptible body; the other is without body and incorruptible. So that the evil man 'dies by death' (Gen. 2.17) even while he breathes, before he is buried, as though he preserved for himself no spark at all of the true life, which is excellence of character. The decent and worthy man, however, does not 'die by death', but, after living long, passes away to eternity, that is, he is borne to eternal life.[25]

Philo bequeathes to Christian interpreters in Alexandria a reading of the Old Testament that paves the way for the Platonic doctrine of the soul in Christian theology. Origen (185–254 CE), as we have seen earlier (Chapter 2), is the most radical Christian exponent of a thoroughgoing dualist anthropology, but his influence is decisive even though others take a less radical

22. Emily Wilson, *The Death of Socrates* (Cambridge, MA: Harvard University Press, 2007), p. 106.

23. Stone, *The Trial of Socrates*, p. 72.

24. Philo, *QG* III.2, quoted by John Dillon, *The Middle Platonists 80 B.C. to A.D. 220* (New York: Cornell University Press, 1996), p. 177.

25. Philo, *QG* I.16, in Dillon, *The Middle Platonists*, p. 177.

view. For Origen, as for Plato, disembodied existence is not only possible but desirable. The body exists only as a punitive and temporary element on the human journey toward liberation.[26] Restoration entails that the body becomes superfluous: 'we must believe that our condition will be at some future time incorporeal', he says.[27] Again, echoing Plato, 'even the use of bodies will cease...just as formerly it did not exist'.[28] Materiality is unnecessary and ultimately unworthy of God. 'For if all things can exist without bodies', says Origen, 'doubtless bodily substance will cease to exist when there is no use for it'.[29]

Roy Porter, writing as a historian of medicine, captures succinctly the hugely consequential transformation in the Christian outlook.

> The Hellenization of Christianity, with its metaphysics of the separate soul, began, perhaps ironically, with Philo the Jew, a first-century Alexandrian deeply sympathetic to Greek thinking. Drawing on the Stoic idea of *pneuma* as the divine substance breathed into man, Philo proposed a radical body-soul dualism that was foreign to Old Testament faith. He also drew on Plato's *Phaedrus* myth of the 'fall' of the soul; dwelling in the body as in a tomb, the soul was condemned to be a 'pilgrim and sojourner' while on earth.[30]

How important is this turn of events in the history of ideas, particularly with reference to the *Christian* outlook? Werner Jaeger answers that

> the most important fact in the history of Christian doctrine was that the father of Christian theology, Origen, was a Platonic philosopher at the school of Alexandria. He built into Christian doctrine the whole cosmic drama of the soul, which he took from Plato, and although later Christian Fathers decided that he took over too much, that which they kept was still the essence of Plato's philosophy of the soul.[31]

In the Platonic paradigm, death means the liberation of the soul from the mortal body and, as Jürgen Moltmann keenly notes, death becomes 'the soul's best friend'.[32] In Paul's outlook, by contrast, death is the last enemy

26. *Origen on First Principles*, I.8.1.
27. Ibid., II.3.3.
28. *On First Principles*, II.3.3.
29. *On First Principles*, II.3.2.
30. Roy Porter, *Flesh in the Age of Reason: How the Enlightenment Transformed the Way We See Our Bodies and Our Souls* (London: Penguin Books, 2003), p. 35.
31. Werner Jaeger, 'The Greek Ideas of Immortality', (Ingersoll Lecture, 1958) in *Immortality and Resurrection* (ed. Krister Stendahl; New York: Macmillan, 1965), p. 112.
32. Jürgen Moltmann, *The Coming of God: Christian Eschatology* (trans. Margaret Kohl; London: SCM Press, 1996), p. 60. Thus the importance of the resurrection: 'The immortality of the soul is an opinion—the resurrection of the dead is a hope' (p. 64). Platonizing influences are also acknowledged by J. Christiaan Beker, 'The Relationship

(1 Cor. 15.26), and death's reality mirrors death's biology.[33] Perhaps it takes an agrarian reader to see the problem, as here, in Wendell Berry's summons to a thoroughgoing reassessment.

> This separation of the soul from the body and from the world is no disease of the fringe, no aberration, but a fracture that runs through the mentality of institutional religion like a geologic fault. And this rift in the mentality of religion continues to characterize the modern mind, no matter how secular or worldly it becomes.[34]

Anthropology emerges as a relevant and revealing constituent in Berry's agrarian and ecological concern.[35] It will be no less important in theology and to theology's most acute point of contact with the material world: the death of Jesus Christ. With this excursus now complete, we are ready to return to Paul's exposition of the death of Jesus (Rom. 5.6-11).

God's Love in Widescreen (5.1-11; 8.31-39)

'Now that we have been set right by faith (*ek pisteōs*)', *pistis* now understood not only as human faith but also projecting the message of God's faithfulness, 'we have peace with God through our Lord Jesus Christ' (Rom. 5.1, translation mine).[36] Paul's mention of 'our Lord Jesus Christ'

Between Sin and Death in Romans', in *The Conversation Continues: Studies in Paul and John in Honor of J. Louis Martyn* (ed. Robert T. Fortna and Beverly R. Gaventa; Nashville: Abingdon Press, 1990), pp. 55-61. Historically, dualist sentiments received another boost when René Descartes (1596–1650) made the immortality of the soul the central tenet of his epistemology, his conceptual ingredients indistinguishable from Plato's; cf. René Descartes, 'Meditations on First Philosophy', in *The European Philosophers from Descartes to Nietzsche* (ed. Monroe C. Beardsley; New York: Random House, 1960), p. 33.

33. Thus Joel B. Green (*Body, Soul, and Human Life: The Nature of Humanity in the Bible* [Grand Rapids: Baker Academic, 2008], pp. 147, 179), who stresses that 'death is the cessation of life in all its aspects' and that 'there is no part of us, no aspect of our personhood, that survives death'. This is a good example of a 'hermeneutic of retrieval'.

34. Wendell Berry, *The Unsettling of America: Culture and Agriculture* (New York: Avon Books, 2nd edn, 1996), p. 108.

35. Norman Wirzba ('Placing the Soul: An Agrarian Philosophical Principle', in *The Essential Agrarian Reader: The Future of Culture, Community, and the Land* [ed. Norman Wirzba; Washington, DC: Shoemaker & Hoard, 2003], pp. 80-97) stresses the connection between anthropology and agrarian concerns (with credit to Wendell Berry) but seems to hold on to an idea of the soul—and self—separate from the body. At the level of metaphor, the idea that the loss of the soil equals the loss of the soul, 'soul' understood as meaning and purpose, is a conceptual and rhetorical feat worthy of note.

36. Manuscript evidence allows and may favor the subjunctive *echōmen* ('let us have peace') over the indicative *echomen* ('we have peace'), but some scholars find the

means that God's faithfulness has found concrete expression in the life and death of Jesus (cf. also 3.21-26). The sentence is bi-directional, on the one hand looking back to the story of God's faithfulness toward Abraham and to Abraham's faith, and on the other hand taking account of present privilege and promise. Thus, it is through the faithfulness of Jesus that 'we have obtained access to this grace in which we stand' (5.2a); it is on that basis that 'we boast in the hope of (participating in) the glory of God' (5.2b, translation mine). Peace with God is a privilege that belongs to the present while hope has a future horizon in view.

Paul speaks in the inclusive, congenial we-form, but situational matters and terms suggesting conflict and contrasts are still evident. Two terms hold particular interest. Paul says that 'we *boast* (*kauchōmetha*) in the hope of the *glory of God* (*tēs doxēs tou theou*)' (5.2b, translation mine). *Boasting* has been a subject of concern earlier in the letter as well as in the Galatian context. In Romans, Paul points the finger at people who boast of their relation to God and the law (2.17, 23), and in Galatians he confronts teachers who want Gentile believers 'to be circumcised so that they may boast about your flesh' (Gal. 6.13). In both contexts, circumcision is the disputed material issue (Rom. 2.25; Gal. 6.13), and the charge of boasting is meant to stigmatize the program and those who promote it. Here, however, the negative connotation that attaches to boasting is sanitized for two paradoxical reasons. *Boasting*, in fact, is turned into an opportunity for Paul to state his message in somewhat different terms. He and the believers with whom he claims common cause 'boast in the hope of participating in the glory of God' (Rom. 5.2). The reason for boasting lies in the hope and not in themselves or anything they do. While still on the subject of boasting, Paul turns apparent negatives into positives. 'And not only that, but we also boast (*kauchōmetha*) in our sufferings (*thlipsesin*), knowing that suffering produces endurance (*hypomonēn*), and endurance produces character (*dokimēn*), and character produces hope (*elpida*), and hope does not disappoint us, because God's love has been poured into our hearts through the Holy Spirit that has been given to us' (5.3-5). The theological negative of *boasting* has been transformed into an experiential positive even with regard to what by all accounts ought to be an irreducible negative: suffering (*thlipsis*). Suffering, however, is not only the experiential engine that brings a host of desirable benefits in its train, among them endurance, character, and hope. Everything Paul says about suffering may be true and heartening in a general sense, but a contrast

overall weight of evidence to be on the side of the latter; cf. Verlyn D. Verbrugge, 'The Grammatical Internal Evidence for "ECHOMEN in Romans 5.1', *JETS* 54 (2011), pp. 559-72; see also Michael Wolter, *Rechtfertigung and zukünftiges Heil: Undersuchungen zu Röm 5,1-11* (BZNW, 43; Berlin: W. de Gruyter, 1978), pp. 89-95, 135-38.

is implied. In Galatia, the pro-circumcision teachers had as part of their agenda 'that they not be persecuted for the cross of Christ' (Gal. 6.12). Avoidance of suffering is said to be one of the tenets of Paul's opponents. This makes Paul's embrace of suffering all the more striking. Galatians and Romans are on the same page with respect to how the Christ- and cross-centered faith is experienced in the world. In the context of Romans (5.1-11), there is a contrast between 'we' and 'them' on this point. Indeed, the contrast is nowhere more evident than with regard to the matters about which the two sides *boast*.

> *'They'*
> 'you...boast of your relation to God' (2.17)
> 'you boast in the law' (2.23).
>
> *'We'*
> 'we boast in our hope' (5.2)
> 'we also boast in our suffering' (5.3)

The message concerning which Paul is not ashamed (1.16) corresponds to the moral and experiential high ground concerning which Paul will boast (5.2-5). Hope has the future as its horizon, but the hope that shines its light from the future into the present cannot disappoint because God's love has in the present 'been poured into our hearts through the Holy Spirit that has been given to us' (5.5).[37] A hope of that kind is not a fiction. Moreover, the earlier admission that 'all have sinned and fall short of *the glory of God* (*tēs doxēs tou theou*)' (3.23) is now replaced with the confidence of participating 'in *the glory of God* (*tēs doxēs tou theou*)' to the point of boasting about it (5.2). The lack that was evident in the former state, whether we see it primarily as lack of fitness, lack of hope, or even as gross misapprehension of God (3.23), has been remedied. The demonstrated faithfulness of Jesus has opened the way to 'the hope of participating in the glory of God' (5.2). Better yet, the faithfulness of Jesus is itself the definitive revelation of 'the glory of God'.

If the foregoing indicates that Paul is still addressing a charged situation in the Roman churches, the generalizing tendency is also evident. Against the former challenge, Paul's letter represents an alternative and a corrective, but it also offers images and points of entry for people who may be peripheral to the conflict in Rome or even unaware of it. Romans 5.6-11 is a case

37. As Käsemann notes (*Romans*, p. 135), there is an Old Testament echo in the hope that does not 'disappoint' (5.5a): it is of one piece with Paul's programmatic assertion in Rom. 1.16. The one who hopes will not be 'put to shame' along the lines envisioned in Pss. 21.6; 24.20, LXX. The progression from suffering to endurance to character to hope (5.3-5) implies not only increasing moral fortitude or deepening conviction but also eschatological vindication.

in point, a general summary of Paul's message that is second to none while also posing a challenge to missionaries who contradict Paul.

> For while we were still weak, at just the right time Christ died for (*hyper*) the ungodly. Indeed, rarely will anyone die for a righteous person—though perhaps for a good person someone might actually dare to die. But God proves his love for us in that while we still were sinners Christ died for (*hyper*) us. Much more then, now that we have been set right by his blood, will we be saved through him from the wrath. For if while we were enemies, we were reconciled to God through the death of his Son, much more, having been reconciled, will we be saved by his life. But more than that, we even boast in God through our Lord Jesus Christ, through whom we have now received reconciliation (Rom. 5.5-11, translation mine).[38]

Plight and solution are closely linked in this passage, and yet it is still pertinent to ask. What is the problem if this is the solution?

Reading the passage as a corrective to teachers who 'boast in the law' (2.23) and who play up the necessity of circumcision (2.25), Paul's difference with them is not hard to spot. The human plight, as they see it, is drawn to a manageable scale. Indeed, the voices that Paul takes to task earlier in the letter project strength and accomplishment rather than weakness and failure (2.1-29; cf. 5.6). Above all, the view these people espouse, the self-understanding they have, and the stance they project rise from the foundation of being on impressively friendly terms with God (2.17). As such, they see themselves as 'a guide to the blind, a light to those who are in darkness, a corrector of the foolish, a teacher of children' (2.19-20).

Paul, by contrast, draws a different picture of human plight (5.1-11). Divine intervention does not take place on the behalf of people who are strong, or good, or on friendly terms with God (cf. 5.6-8, 10). On the contrary, Christ died 'while we were still weak;' he died 'for the ungodly' (5.6); he died 'while we were still sinners' (5.8), and, to top it off, 'while we were enemies' (5.10). A contrastive reading of this passage is not only workable but necessary, in part because of the contrast that Paul sets up from the very beginning (2.1-3) and more so because conflict and contrast surface again and again in passages to come even if we sense that Paul's opponents have retreated to the back of the room.

The 'we'-form is meaningful in a contrastive reading, too, Paul counting on the Romans to be in his corner. Jews or Gentiles are conceding together the plight factor to be exactly as Paul describes it. Christ died 'while we were still *weak*'; he died 'for the *ungodly*' (5.6); he died 'while we were still *sinners*' (5.8), and—of all things—'while we were *enemies*' (5.10). The

38. The translation follows the NRSV except for using 'set right' instead of 'justified' and by saying 'the wrath' instead of 'the wrath of God' (5.9), my translation more literal with respect to the latter.

parenthetical, 'perhaps for a good person someone might actually dare to die' (5.7), seems more at home in a Roman imperial context of heroic valor than in a Jewish framework, but it certainly preserves the point that 'dying for shameful, unworthy people is unprecedented'.[39]

Probing the passage apart from the contrast to teachers who complicate Paul's mission, his choice of adjectives or adjectival nouns is not haphazard. While being 'weak' and 'ungodly' and 'sinners' suggest lack of moral rectitude (5.6, 8), priority should go to the phrase '*while we were enemies* (*echthroi*)' (5.10). This is the most radical term for the plight described (5.10).[40] It rises to the top because it is the most extreme term and because it premises and captures the great reversal in the passage (5.6-11). Being 'weak' and 'ungodly' and 'sinners' point to worthlessness, or waywardness, or helplessness. Being '*enemies*', however, imply something much worse, a state of active, unfriendly, hostile relations. A plight thus understood is theological even more than it is moral. Weakness, ungodliness, and sinfulness, the initial triad of plight in the passage (5.6-8), are depictions of a defect on the human side of the relationship. Hostility and enmity are different, allowing for the possibility that the enmity could have a reason. Why such unfriendly relations? Why would human beings see God as an *enemy*?

Categories of Sin by Degree of Severity

- 'weak'
- 'ungodly'
- 'sinners'
- 'enemies'
- Question: Which of these categories is most severe and most difficult to solve?

Restoration of previously friendly relations is precisely the aim of God's action, captured by the words 'reconcile' (*katallassein*) and 'reconciliation' (*katallagē*).[41] 'We were God's enemies, but he made us his friends (*katēllagēmen*) through the death of his Son. Now that we are God's friends (*katallagentes*), how much more will we be saved by Christ's life! But that is not all; we rejoice because of what God has done through our Lord Jesus Christ, who has now made us God's friends (*katallagēn*)' (5.10, 11, GNB). Hostility is evident, to be sure, and it is all on the human side of the divide! Jewett notes that 'the theme of God's hatred is alien to this passage, which has repeatedly stressed divine grace, love, sacrifice, and salvation from wrath'.[42]

39. Jewett, *Romans*, p. 360.

40. Theodore Pulcini ('In Right Relationship with God: Present Experience and Future Fulfillment. An Exegesis of Romans 5.1-11', *SVTQ* 36 [1992], p. 78) notes the increasing severity in Paul's depiction.

41. According to Jewett (*Romans*, p. 365), the terms signify how 'warring groups, quarrelling citizens, or alienated marital partners make peace'.

42. Jewett, *Romans*, p. 364.

Three elements in the passage serve to establish further that enmity and misapprehension on the human side are the most serious obstacles. First, Paul stresses that Christ died to *demonstrate* God's love (5.8), 'not to prompt a transformation of divine wrath into love'.[43] *Revelation* is here the short hand meaning of Christ's death. Second, the verbal action combines *revelation* and *persuasion*. 'God *proves* (*synistēsin*) his love for us', as the NRSV translates it, has the meaning of *revealing* as well as *commending*, the former with the sense of causing 'something to be known by action', the latter in the sense that what is thus made known commends acceptance on the part of the party to whom it is made known.[44] If there is a point to having proof of God's love, what could the point be other than doubt in regard to God's love in the first place? God's demonstration answers the vexing question in a persuasive, definitive manner. Third, we cannot discount the variant reading at the beginning of the passage. Paul does not write in the indicative mood, 'we have peace', but in the subjunctive mood of appeal, 'let us have peace with God' (5.1).[45] This matches well a line of reasoning in the Corinthian correspondence that is similarly predicated on hostility on the human side. 'We entreat you on behalf of Christ, be reconciled (*katallagēte*) to God', Paul says to the Corinthians (2 Cor. 5.20). God and human beings are in a state of enmity with respect to each other, but the hostility is entirely on the human side. All in all, as Jewett notes in the context of Romans, 'to turn this into a drama of assuaging God's anger or counterbalancing divine justice is to impose later theories of the atonement onto a passage where they do not belong'.[46]

The timing of the divine action should also be given greater depth and sharper focus than a casual reading tends to do. While it is appropriate to say that Christ died 'at the *right* time (*kata kairon*)' (Rom. 5.6), the timing cannot be limited to time with regard to prophecy or chronology (cf. Gal. 4.4). The timing must be linked to the state of *need* Paul is exposing in the passage (Rom. 5.6-10). The *right time* is not only *promised* time but also time of *need*. By this reckoning, Christ died *in the nick of time*, at the moment of excruciating need, human beings and the world teetering on the brink.

And then to the image at the center of the passage, 'Christ died' (5.6, 8). We can now approach his death, too, in its stark physicality, biology, ecology, and finality.[47] There is no immortal soul in the death of Jesus, cheerily easing its way out of the mortal body on the wings of immaterial nothing.

43. Jewett, *Romans*, p. 364.
44. Louw-Nida Lexicon, entry 6208.
45. Jewett, *Romans*, p. 364.
46. Jewett, *Romans*, p. 364.
47. C. Clifton Black II ('Pauline Perspectives on Death in Romans 5–8', *JBL* 103

Christ died an earthling, a fact that is elaborated later when Paul compares Adam and Christ (5.12-14). In ecological terms, he participated fully in the material reality of creation. The human self of Jesus experienced biological demise in the same manner as other humans—and other creatures. As earthling, he suffered a slow and excruciatingly painful death. Socially and politically, he died publicly on the cross as a spectacle (Gal. 3.1), displayed in the unnamable, gaping void in Roman society where shame and cruelty meet.[48] Whether by the measures of physicality and biology, ecology and economy, or anthropology and theology, the all-ness and all-out-ness of his death drive home an act of stupendous self-giving, nothing held back, death's biology the premise for its all-ness. If, in anthropomorphic terms, there could be a reason for human enmity toward God, a perception of disdain, or detachment, or wrath, the death of Jesus, rightly understood, dispels the delusion in one cataclysmic blow. God does not regard human beings with disdain, detachment, or wrath. In Paul's words, reading Romans as a corrective to human misperception of God, 'God demonstrates his love for us, in currency that cannot be doubted, in that while we were sinners Christ died for the ungodly' (5.8, paraphrase mine).

The death of Jesus can now be displayed on three different screens, all of them relevant within the context of Romans but with clear priority for one over the others. The three screens provided for the projection are (1) Paul's opponents, (2) Roman imperial reality, and (3) the widescreen of the biblical narrative. With respect to Paul's opponents, the special friendship and intimacy with God of which they boast are an illusion (2.1-3, 17-24). In fact, while they imagine themselves to be on good terms with God, the God with whom they are on good terms stands in a posture of wrath toward the world (1.18-32). The greatest defect in their outlook is not only how they see themselves or how they see the world but how they see God. 'You', Paul tells them, 'boast of your relation to God' (2.17), and 'you boast in the law' (2.23), but 'we boast in our hope' (5.2) and not in something we have in our hands. The hope, in turn, consists in its innermost core of a *theological* transformation, brought to light in the fact that God's love stands revealed in the death of Jesus (5.6-11).

With respect to Roman imperial reality, the contrasts are similarly mind-boggling. Roman politics and religion revel in symbols of strength, conquest, and honor. The celebrated elements are defeat of the enemy rather than reconciliation: killing the enemy is the prestigious thing to do while dying for the benefit of the enemy would be unthinkable (5.6-8). Paul is aware of the contrast, and he presses the point of what Christ did as

[1984], pp. 413-33) has shown that death in Romans have a variety of theological meanings, but death is in all instances real biological loss of life.

48. Welborn, 'Extraction from the Mortal Site', p. 311.

compared to what someone might be willing to do (5.7). Where Romans present to the world the victor as an object for admiration and reverence, Paul's counterpoint is a victim, publicly displayed on the cross. Details aside, these are ideologically and strategically different visions of right-making. God's right-making has nothing in common with Roman religion or Roman imperial reality.

Above all, however, the Paul's message of the love of God and the death of Jesus projects on the widescreen provided by the biblical narrative. More is to come that will fill in what is lacking in Paul's narratival horizon (5.12-21; 7.7-13), but the most important element is here (5.8). The human predicament is not adequately described in terms of violation of the divine command as though this is the main problem that needs to be made right. What, then, is the other—the main—problem? The main problem is misrepresentation and misperception of God's character (Gen. 3.1-6). The death of Jesus is redemptive as *revelation* because it addresses the kind of person God is (Rom. 5.6, 8). Erstwhile enemies become friends by force of the discovery that the human perception of God was widely off target (5.10).

Before I proceed to Paul's second deep-dive into the love of God and the death of Jesus (8.31-39), a timeout is due in order to consider how the linkage between the love of God and the death of Christ (5.6-11) stands in relation to the rest of the letter. I wish to put two propositions to the test. First, Paul's linkage states the theme of Romans in the most fundamental, far-reaching, and comprehensible way. Second, the bond between the love of God and the death of Jesus is closely related to the connection between the righteousness of God and the faithfulness of Jesus so as to make the two sets virtually synonymous. To the extent that they are not synonymous, however, the former link takes command of the latter.

For proof of these propositions, Paul has already announced that 'the righteousness of God *is revealed* in (the gospel)' (1.17), elaborating that 'the righteousness of God *has been disclosed*...by the faithfulness of Jesus Christ' (3.21-22), the bloody death of Jesus the *demonstration* of God's righteousness in currency that is resistant to depreciation (3.25). Now, in the less contentious and more expansive part of the letter (5.1-8.39), Paul says that 'God *proves* his love for us in that... Christ died for us' (5.8). These verses align 'the righteousness of God' with 'God's love' and 'the faithfulness of Jesus' with the death of Jesus, the verbs highlighting the *revelatory* import of the linkage.[49] Moreover, the revelation that is common to both takes place in the context of doubt, confusion, and even enmity (5.10). Given that the

49. The alignment of 'the righteousness of God' and *pisteōs Iesou Christou* (3.21-22) with God's love and the death of Jesus (5.6-8) is more than incidental evidence in favor of reading *pisteōs Iesou Christou* (3.22) as a subjective genitive, that is, as 'the faithfulness of Jesus Christ'.

programmatic announcement in Rom. 1.16-17 echoes Habakkuk, the revelation of the righteousness of God addresses the problem of God's apparent absence (1.16-17; 3.21-26). Worse is to come, however, when Paul later describes human plight not in terms of divine *absence*, as in Habakkuk (Hab. 1.2-4), but in terms of *enmity* (Rom. 5.10). Human enmity toward God could be understood as rank unreasonableness on the part of humans, a diseased state of mind, but it is better understood in terms of incomprehension or misconception. *The God toward whom human beings are hostile, is a God thought to be hostile toward them*. Sin's triumph, thus understood, is nowhere more evident than in its success in construing God as though standing in the posture of a virtual executioner toward humans. When human enmity is not predicated on divine absence, as in Habakkuk, but on a perception of divine hostility, God's action must address the reason for the enmity. This should be taken to be the primary—and the revelatory—meaning of the statement, 'We were God's enemies, but he made us his friends (*katēllagēmen*) through the death of his Son' (5.10, GNB).

Further support for this reading is necessary, and Paul is not stingy in providing it. So as not to lose sight of the connection between the love of God and the death of Jesus and the momentum it now has in Romans, we will fast-forward to the passage that to most scholars conclude the line of thought in this portion of Romans (5.1-8.39).[50] Here, too, it has been noted, Paul uses the we-form with even greater confidence than at the beginning (5.1-11 vs. 8.31-39), 'no longer seeking to convince his audience, but now—in this peroration—he makes a final appeal which is based on the elite audience's agreement and aims at evoking a full and emotionally charged consent to the shared affirmation'.[51]

> What then are we to say in response to these things? If God is for (*hyper*) us, who is against us? He who did not withhold his own Son, but gave him up for (*hyper*) all of us, will he not with him also give us everything else? Who will bring any charge against God's elect? It is God who sets right. Who is to condemn? It is Christ Jesus, who died, yes, who was raised, who is at the right hand of God, who indeed intercedes for us. Who will separate us from the love of Christ (*tēs agapēs tou Christou*)? Will hardship, or distress, or persecution, or famine, or nakedness, or peril, or sword? As it is written, 'For your sake we are being killed all day long; we are accounted as sheep to be slaughtered'. No, in all these things we are more than conquerors (*hypernikōmen*) through him who loved (*tou agapēsantos*) us. For I am convinced that neither death, nor life, nor angels, nor rulers, nor things present, nor things to come, nor powers, nor height, nor depth, nor anything

50. Gottfried Schille, 'Die Liebe Gottes in Christus: Beobachtungen zu Rm 8.31-39', *ZNW* 59 (1968), p. 230; Leonora Tubbs Tisdale, 'Romans 8.31-39', *Int* 42 (1988), p. 69.

51. A.H. Snyman, 'Style and Rhetorical Situation of Romans 8.31-39', *NTS* 34 (1988), p. 227.

> else in all creation, will be able to separate us from the love of God (*tēs agapēs tou theou*) in Christ Jesus our Lord (8.31-39, translation mine).[52]

Fast-forwarding to this passage does not bypass important difficulties nor is it arbitrary. As Jewett notes, the passage (8.31-39) concludes what he calls 'the second proof', that is, the portion of Romans that begins in 5.1-11, and it is more closely linked to the opening passage of this section (5.1-11) than to the intervening parts.[53] The sense of conclusion, climax, and book-ending in Jewett's presentation of the evidence speaks for itself.[54]

	Beginning	*Conclusion*
set right	5.1, 9	8.33
suffering	5.3	8.35-37
God's love	5.5, 8	8.35, 39
Christ's death	5.6, 10	8.34, 39
saved from wrath	5.9	8.31-34
Christ's resurrection	5.10	8.34
rejoicing in God	5.11	8.31-39

What, here (8.31-39), is the eye-catching element? Once again, as at the beginning (5.1-11), the topic is the love of God and the death of Jesus.[55] The latter explains and gives proof of the former. And what is the problem if this is the solution? Whatever perplexity there be on the 'plight' side of the equation, Paul restates the problem with compelling clarity. 'What then are we to say in response to these things? If God is for (*hyper*) us, who is against us?' (8.31, translation mine) That is to say, if the 'plight' side of the equation has come to center on doubt as to where and how God stands toward human beings, we now know where and how God stands. Dropping the question format for a moment, Paul will say that 'God is *for* us';[56] that is to say, God is on *our* side. But the question is more than Paul's preferred rhetorical device, paving the way for two crucial sequiturs that will be missed in a mere affirmation. First, if anyone is against us, *it isn't God!* And second, someone *is* against us, as Paul's long list of human and super-human adversaries emphatically concedes (8.35-39). *God is against them!* Connecting

52. The translation largely follows the NRSV with the exception of 'in response to' instead of 'about' (8.31) and 'sets right' instead of 'justifies' (8.33).

53. Jewett, *Romans*, p. 535.

54. Jewett, *Romans*, p. 535.

55. Beverly Roberts Gaventa, 'Interpreting the Death of Jesus Apocalyptically: Reconsidering Romans 8.32', in *Jesus and Paul Reconnected: Fresh Pathways into an Old Debate*' (ed. Todd D. Still; Grand Rapids: Eerdmans, 2007), pp. 125-45.

56. Peter Fiedler, 'Röm 8.31-39 as Brennpunkt paulinischer Frohbotschaft', *ZNW* 68 (1977), p. 23.

the dots back to the beginning and to Paul's observation that Christ died 'while we were *enemies*' (5.10), we are now unequivocally reminded that *God was never the enemy*. 'We were *enemies*' by virtue of a catastrophic distortion with regard to God's disposition (5.10). God's revelation in Jesus has blown to smithereens the misconception, and Paul does human beings more than a small favor by pointing out who the real enemy is.[57]

The passage that marks the thematic zenith in Romans (8.31-39) has in common with the former passage (5.1-11) that it makes the love of God and the death of Jesus a seamless whole, but it is unique for *interpreting the death of Jesus apocalyptically*, as Beverly Roberts Gaventa shows in her exceptional exposition of Rom. 8.32. Jesus' death bears witness to the love of God, but the measure of God's love now has the cosmic conflict as its frame of reference. Paul presents the love of God in widescreen, comprehensively. To put it more bluntly, Jesus dies in the context of a cosmic war; he does not die in the temple precincts to candlelight and soothing organ music, if this at times is the connotation of the conventional understanding. When Paul now writes that God '*gave him up* (*paredōken*) for all of us' (8.32), God sent Jesus into the lion's den of conflict. God *handed him over* with the understanding that demonic powers stood at the ready to do their work. In the context of cosmic conflict God sent forth Jesus to fight—to do battle *for us*—against overwhelming cosmic forces. In Gaventa's words, 'when Paul says that God handed over his own Son, he means that God handed him over to *anti-god powers*'.[58]

> On this construal of the text, *it is not sufficient to describe God's handing over only as a loving, sacrificial act, a gracious giving up; it is also an event in the ongoing struggle between God and anti-god powers.* God brings an end to the 'handing over' of humanity to Sin and Death by means of another handing over, this time of God's Son.[59]

This notion can be extrapolated backwards to other statements connecting the love of God with the death of Jesus. These statements will now say that 'Christ died (in battle) for the ungodly' (5.6); 'Christ died (in battle) for us' (5.8); indeed, 'Christ died (in battle) while we were enemies' (5.10), as if dying under conditions when *we were found to be fighting against God on the side of the cosmic powers hostile to us!*

Suggestive verbal elements enrich and bolster this interpretation and its overriding theological and existential concerns. First, as many have noted, Paul echoes the *Akedah*, the story of the binding of Isaac.[60]

57. The depiction of hostile, cosmic powers in Rom. 8.36-39 is part of this, but the operation of the powers by force of deception and not only 'power' is generally ignored.

58. Gaventa, 'Interpreting the Death of Jesus Apocalyptically', p. 127.

59. Gaventa, 'Interpreting the Death of Jesus Apocalyptically', p. 136.

60. Dunn, *Romans 1–8*, p. 501; Nils Alstrup Dahl, 'The Atonement—an Adequate

> He who did not withhold (*ouk efeisato*) his own Son (Rom. 8.32)
>
> Because you have done this, and have not withheld (*ouk efeisō*) your son, your beloved son from me (Gen. 22.16, LXX).

Just as Abraham is the background and the bridge to the easier terrain we are now traversing (4.1-25), he reappears in force at the conclusion (8.32). Dunn says perceptively that Paul in his lengthy exposition of Abraham's story omitted any explicit mention of the offering of Isaac 'where his Jewish interlocutor would have expected it' (Rom. 4.1-25).[61] Instead, however, and now as further proof that Paul's overriding aim was always the faithfulness of God and not the faith of Abraham, he deploys an allusion to the story of the binding of Isaac at the conclusion of his argument. God is now the subject, not Abraham. 'In what must be accounted a very neat turning of the tables', says Dunn, 'Paul indicates that Abraham's offering of his son serves as a type *not of the faithfulness of the devout Jew, but rather of the faithfulness of God*'.[62]

Second, Paul keeps piling up verbs that all have *giving* in one form or another as their theme, all of them radiating from the reality of the death of Jesus. God *did not withhold* means that God *gave*; God *handed him over* also means that God *gave*, the extent of God's giving making it certain that God '*will give* us all things with him' (8.32, translation mine). If sentiments of God's absence or enmity have terrorized human beings, the accompanying feelings of hopelessness and horror are put to rest in the presence of the giving God. Thus, in the words of Karl Barth,

> [i]f we fix our eyes upon the place where the course of the world reaches its lowest point, where its vanity is unmistakable, where its groanings are most bitter and the divine incognito most impenetrable, we shall encounter there—Jesus Christ. On the frontier that is observable He stands *delivered up* and *not spared*. In place of us all He stands there, delivered up *for us all*, patently submerged in the flood.[63]

Third, we have read three times in Romans that God, responding to pagan idolatry, '*gave them up* (*paredōken*) in the lusts of their hearts to impurity' (1.24); 'God *gave them up* (*paredōken*) to degrading passions' (1.26a); and 'God *gave them up* (*paredōken*) to a debased mind' (1.28). Now, however, the object of the verbal action of *giving up* is not recalcitrant pagans but Jesus. Paul says that God 'gave *him* up (*paredōken*) for all of us' (8.32;

Reward for the Akedah (Rom. 8.32)', in *Neotestamentica et Semitica: Studies in Honour of Matthew Black* (ed. E. Earle Ellis and Max E. Wilcox; Edinburgh: T. & T. Clark, 1969), pp. 15-29; Philip Sigal, 'A Prolegomenon to Paul's Judaic Thought: The Death of Jesus and the Akedah', *Proceedings* 4 (1984), pp. 222-36.

61. Dunn, *Romans 1–8*, p. 501.

62. Dunn, *Romans 1–8*, p. 501, italics added.

63. Barth, *Romans*, p. 327.

cf. 4.25). Interpreters generally see these as parallel actions. Just as God *gave up* the pagans, he now *gives up* Jesus, in both cases with the implication that hostile powers in various guises are prepared to take command of the person given up.[64] If, however, as we have explored earlier, the outrage expressed over pagan idolatry and sexual immortality comes from the stump speech of teachers that are hostile to Paul (1.18-32), a parallel is less in evidence than a contrast. *They* say that God handed *them* over (1.24, 26, 28), but Paul says that God handed *him* over (8.32), the severe and punitive dynamic of the former vision held up to a vision of healing.

Fourth, therefore, when Paul in this passage (8.31-39) gives the death of Christ a cosmic frame of reference, he revisits and fortifies the theme of liberation that he has already put forward as a reason for Christ's death. Human beings are 'set right by his grace as a gift through the liberation (*apolytreōseōs*) that is in Christ Jesus' (3.24, translation mine). Campbell notes that the key word here 'describes a process of release from an enslaved condition'.[65] Gaventa concurs, noting that Paul in key passages in Romans (3.21-26; 8.31-39) 'depicts the death of Jesus Christ as bringing release from captivity'.[66] Sin and Death are among the powers that hold humans captive, both posing as scheming, personified entities (5.12-14; 7.8, 11, 13, 17, 20), but these are a step below powers that are not *rhetorically* personified: they are actual, personal powers—angels, rulers, and powers (8.38). In 1 Corinthians Paul places the crucifixion and death of Jesus in direct relation to God's determination to bring down 'the rulers of this age (*tōn archontōn tou aiōnas*)' (1 Cor. 2.8). The love of God designed a trap that surpassed what 'the rulers' were able to anticipate or understand. For the notion that 'love wins', it means that love outwitted the powers. 'But we speak God's wisdom, secret and hidden, which God decreed before the ages for our glory', Paul says. 'None of the rulers of this age understood this; for if they had, they would not have crucified the Lord of glory' (1 Cor. 2.7-8). In Romans, this leads to questions Paul delights to pose, confident in the implied and certain answer. 'Who will separate us from the love of Christ?' he begins (Rom. 8.35). The list of formidable forces is long, real, and present.

> Will hardship,
> or distress,
> or persecution,
> or famine,
> or nakedness,
> or peril,
> or sword? (Rom. 8.35).

64. Gaventa, 'Interpreting the Death of Jesus Apocalyptically', pp. 130-34.

65. Campbell, *Deliverance of God*, p. 657; see also, idem., *The Rhetoric of Righteousness*, pp. 116-30.

66. Gaventa, 'Interpreting the Death of Jesus Apocalyptically', p. 137.

The answer to these threats is not only that none of them amount to much but that greater threats in the form of actual, super-human powers are nullified. All along (8.31-39), *questions* serve to drive home the affirmations better than up-front *assertions* can do. In a poetic flurry that matches 1 Corinthians 13 and Phil. 2.5-12, Paul exults that

> I am convinced that
> neither death,
> nor life,
> nor angels,
> nor rulers,
> nor things present,
> nor things to come,
> nor powers,
> nor height,
> nor depth,
> nor anything else in all creation,
> will be able to separate us
> from the love of God
> in Christ Jesus our Lord (Rom. 8.38-39).

These are all affirmations about the love of God, and they are anchored in the conviction that '*God is the Right-Maker* (*theos ho dikaiōn*)' (8.33), that is, 'God is the one who sets things right'.[67] God's right-making does not happen only along the lines of time-honored formulas of salvation but in the broadest possible way.[68] In the context of the conflict within which Paul makes this affirmation, God is on our side, and 'God is *delivering* humanity'.[69] God is not the one who brings charges (8.33) nor is God the one who condemns and imprisons (8.34). Paul's emphatic clarifiers are declarations about the kind of Person God is. What God *does* must be understood in light of what God *is*, and God is the 'Right-Maker' (8.33).

In the home stretch of this section of Romans (5.1–8.39), the love of God and the death of Jesus are again seamlessly linked just as at the beginning of the section (5.6-8, 10).

Who will separate us from the love of Christ (*tēs agapēs tou Christou*)? (8.35).

> No, in all these things we are more than winners in the conflict through him who loved us (*tou agapēsantos*) (8.37, translation mine).

> For I am convinced that neither death, nor life, nor angels, nor rulers…nor powers…will be able to separate us from the love of God (*tēs agapēs tou theou*) in Christ Jesus our Lord (8.38-39).

67. Jewett, *Romans*, pp. 540-41.

68. See D.E.H. Whiteley, *The Theology of St. Paul* (Oxford: Basil Blackwell, 1974), pp. 131-51.

69. Campbell, *Deliverance of God*, p. 664.

The measure of the love of God is in Romans the death of Jesus. For the magnitude to be seen at full height, death must be delivered from the alien thought world to which it has been held captive through much of the history of Christianity. God's love is not diminished by acknowledging life's materiality and death's biology. Just as ecology is unthinkable apart from materiality, so is the death of Jesus—the measure of the love of God.

Chapter 9

'Where Sin Kept Increasing' (Rom. 5.20)

Romans soars in the passage that links the love of God and the death of Jesus (Rom. 5.6-11), then descends to slightly lower altitude for much of the next three chapters before rising again as this section of the letter closes (8.31-39). We can represent the section in the following way, the representation meant to highlight how Paul's exposition of sin, death, and the law is framed by the love of God. Readers who get lost in the thicket of Paul's demanding thoughts about the law are well advised to retreat from time to time to the high ground at the beginning (5.6-11) and at the ending (8.31-39) of this section (5.1-8.39). Whatever meanings Paul gives to the death of Jesus in Romans, the love of God comes first, and the death of Jesus takes the most expansive measure of God's love.

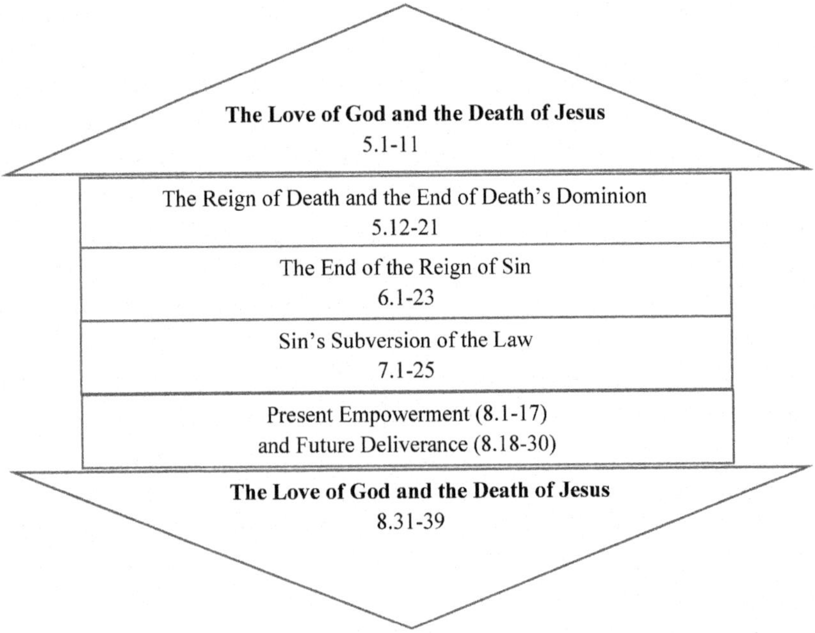

The Love of God and the Death of Jesus
5.1-11

The Reign of Death and the End of Death's Dominion
5.12-21

The End of the Reign of Sin
6.1-23

Sin's Subversion of the Law
7.1-25

Present Empowerment (8.1-17)
and Future Deliverance (8.18-30)

The Love of God and the Death of Jesus
8.31-39

The Reign of Death and the End of Death's Dominion

> Therefore, just as sin came into (*eisēlthen*) the world through one man, and death came through sin, and so death spread (*diēlthen*) to all because all have sinned—sin was indeed in the world before the law, but sin is not reckoned when there is no law. Yet death exercised dominion (*ebasileusen*) from Adam to Moses, even over those whose sins were not like the transgression of Adam, who is a type (*typos*) of the one who was to come (Rom. 5.12-14).

The first thing to notice in this passage is that Paul takes familiarity with the Old Testament for granted. Here, though certainly not only here, the letter draws on a prior narrative—a known story—known also to readers whom Paul has never met.[1] Suspense as to who the 'one man' might be (5.12) is quickly relieved when the 'one man' is identified as Adam (5.14). Genesis is therefore in view, specifically the declaration to Adam that he will return to the ground (*'adāmā*), 'for out of it you were taken; you are dust, and to dust you shall return' (Gen. 3.19). This is an important premise and point of departure for the argument Paul is pursuing, featuring a description of death that is faithful to the human experience of death—*to dust you shall return*—a statement vastly more in awe of death than Socrates' attempt to portray death as liberation and a journey upward.[2] Death's biology has ecological ramifications because human beings share a material and a linguistic connection with the earth. We are made of the same material and occupy, in the most literal sense, *common ground*.[3]

Second, death is represented as a problem, if not *the* problem (cf. 1 Cor. 15.26). In Paul's construal, death is neither nice nor natural if by *natural* is meant what God intended for creation in general and for human beings in particular. Like sin, death '*came* into (*eisēlthen*) the world' (Rom. 5.12), from the very first charged with such a momentum that it 'penetrated (*diēlthen*) to all' (5.12, translation mine). Death's *coming* is in this representation that of an intruder, and the notion that 'death exercised dominion (*ebasileusen*)' (5.14) signifies that the intruder took control.[4] Paul counts on human experience to corroborate his depiction: human anguish in the face of death is predicated on death being terrifying no matter how much one

1. Edward Adams, 'Paul's Story of God and Creation: The Story of How God Fulfils His Purposes in Creation', in *Narrative Dynamics in Paul: A Critical Assessment* (ed. Bruce W. Longenecker; Louisville, KY: Westminster/John Knox Press, 2002), pp. 19-43.

2. *Phaedo* (Jowett translation), pp. 76-77.

3. Carol Newsom, 'Common Ground: An Ecological Reading of Genesis 2–3', in *The Earth Story in Genesis* (ed. Norman C. Habel and Shirley Wurst; Sheffield: Sheffield Academic Press, 2000), pp. 60-72.

4. Beverly Roberts Gaventa, 'The Cosmic Power of Sin in Paul's Letter to the Romans: Toward a Widescreen Edition', *Int* 58 (2004), pp. 229-40; Jewett, *Romans*, p. 377.

tries to make it a matter of course. The Reign of Death with its unrelenting parade of loss and grief means that death stands front and center in any representation of the human condition.

Third, however, when death *came*, it did not come alone as though by some preordained and inevitable design. '*Sin* came into (*eisēlthen*) the world...and death (came) through *sin*' (5.12). Sin and death are linked like Siamese twins.[5] If it were possible to draw a line of demarcation between them, *sin* came first—with the implication that if not for sin there would not be death.[6] *Sin* is therefore the game changer, and death is the measure of the change. Moreover, even though 'sin came into the world through *one* man' (5.12), nothing else necessary for death to become the lot of all, Paul's argument will not separate the two either at the point of origin or at any subsequent point: 'death penetrated to all in that all sinned' (5.12, translation mine). Sin and Death are powers only a little short of being personified. Paul now defines a predicament that has cosmic ramifications. The cosmic perspective, as Beverly Roberts Gaventa notes, demands a remedy beyond the ordinary conceptions. The 'résumé of Sin's accomplishments requires something more than a generous God who forgives and forgets, and something entirely other than a Jesus who allows people to improve themselves by following the example of his godly behavior'.[7]

Fourth, Paul adds an element to his depiction of the relationship between sin and death that complicates the passage severely: the law. Should not the law belong to a threesome—the law, sin, and death—in that order and the law at least equal to the other two? And yet Paul says that 'sin was indeed (*gar*) in the world before the law' (5.13), that is to say, 'sin was most certainly in the world before the law'. Why the need to lay down a temporal marker with respect to the law—and in such a pointed manner? Sin and death, the argument goes, had it all worked out in the absence of the law. Paul casts the law as a latecomer, an addendum ordained to keep track of the score because 'sin is not reckoned when there is no law' (5.13).

Why does Paul bring the law into the picture only to marginalize it? Jewett notes that 'Paul undermines this entire construct by arguing that sin existed prior to the law's promulgation for the first time in the era of Moses'.[8] Sin takes priority over the law and has to some extent independent standing. This is the truly curious part and would seem contrived if not for the need at hand. What Paul has said about sin and death is no more than a recapitulation of the story in Genesis, but the law's appearance in the argument brings

5. Dunn (*Romans 1–8*, p. 288) calls sin and death the 'chief villains', portrayed as personified powers. See also Brian Vickers, 'Grammar and Theology in the Interpretation of Rom 5.12', *TrinJ* 27 (2006), pp. 277-88.

6. Dunn, *Romans 1–8*, pp. 288-89.

7. Gaventa, 'The Cosmic Power of Sin', p. 235.

8. Jewett, *Romans*, p. 377.

his opponents into the fray. They seek recognition of the law for its diagnostic as well as for alleged remedial powers while Paul is quite willing to dispense with both. If sin 'was...in the world before the law' (5.13), even the diagnostic function of the law is diminished. When Paul thus deprives his opponents of their chief asset, we are reminded that the polemical setting of Romans cannot be ignored. If no one reading Romans today knows quite what to do with the explanatory caveat, we can be sure that the original recipients understood it very well and knew 'to whom it may concern'. Again, therefore, we must not forget that the letter was primarily for them.

The thought that 'death reigned from Adam to Moses' (5.14, translation mine) has the same import. Just as sin and death colluded efficiently without the law, Moses is a latecomer and a cipher for the law's marginal role. The rhetoric is striking. Paul' opponents are committed to a linear understanding of salvation history while Paul is pushing a view that sees points rather than a line.[9] Now, in Paul's punctiliar reading, the two points that matter are Adam and Jesus (5.14). The movement that counts happens between these two figures. Abraham, too, and not only Moses, recedes into the background.

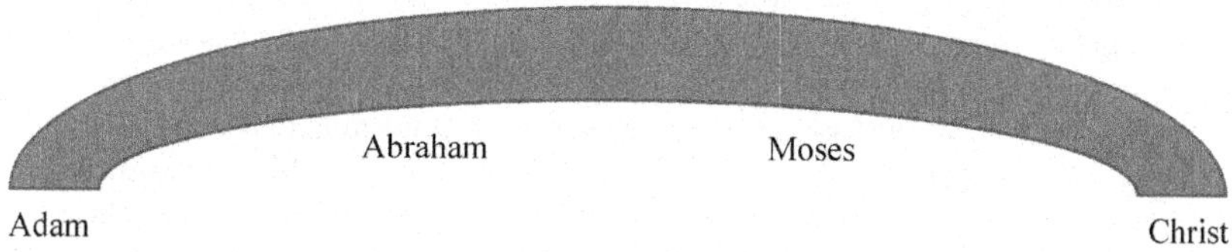

The illustration is meant to show that Adam and Christ are in the line of traffic while Abraham and Moses are not. For a Gentile mission that includes circumcision, Paul's representation of the Old Testament counters the mission by moving to bedrock essentials: we now have before us the *human* condition without anything *Jewish*, oneness and universality established in Adam at one end and in Christ at the other.

Fifth, in what way is Adam 'a type (*typos*) of the one who was to come'? Ryan Schellenberg argues that the typology is not really between Adam and Christ; it is between Adam's *sin* and '*what* was to come', that is, a willful transgression of a divine command in the era before the law heralding more of the same once the law was in place.[10] This translation is possible on grammatical and narratival grounds, but it works less well for the comparison and contrast between Adam and Christ that dominate the

9. This is similar to J. Louis Martyn's interpretation of Abraham's 'singular seed' in Galatians, where the punctiliar figures are Abraham and Christ; cf. *Galatians*, pp. 347-48.

10. Ryan S. Schellenberg, 'Does Paul Call Adam a "Type of Christ"? An Exegetical Note on Romans 5,14', *ZNW* 105 (2014), pp. 53-61.

rest of the chapter. The conventional reading should therefore be preferred even though it, too, has problems. Jewett limits the typology to figures that have in common that they 'determine the fate of their subjects', otherwise they 'are more antithetical than similar'.[11] Byrne, likewise, sees Adam as 'a figure of universal significance for the remainder of the race', this being the only similarity between Adam and Christ.[12] As to where the comparison originated and by whom, Jewett notes the absence of 'credible evidence that Jewish thinkers ever viewed the Messiah as a kind of second Adam'.[13]

That is nevertheless what Paul makes Christ out to be in his juxtaposition of the respective portfolios of 'the one' and 'the (other) one' (5.12-19).

> But the free gift (*to charisma*) is not like the trespass (*to paraptōma*). For if the many died through the one (*tō tou henos*) man's trespass, much more surely have the grace of God and the free gift in the grace of the one (*tē tou henos*) man, Jesus Christ, abounded for the many. And the free gift (*dōrēma*) is not like the effect of the one man's sin. For the judgment (*krima*) following one trespass (*hamartēsantos*) brought condemnation (*katakrima*), but the free gift (*charisma*) following many trespasses brings justification (*dikaiōma*). If, because of the one man's trespass, death exercised dominion through that one, much more surely will those who receive the abundance of grace (*tēn perisseian tou charitos*) and the free gift of righteousness (*tēs dōreas tēs dikaiosynēs*) exercise dominion in life through the one man, Jesus Christ. Therefore just as one man's trespass led to condemnation (*katakrima*) for all, so one man's act of righteousness leads to justification (*dikaiōsin*) and life (*zōē*) for all. For just as by the one man's disobedience (*parakoēs*) the many were made sinners, so by the one man's obedience (*hypakoēs*) the many will be made righteous (*dikaioi*) (Rom. 5.15-19).

As noted above, the differences are greater than the similarities except for the way 'the one' affects 'the many' (5.15). We can represent the contrast in the following way.

'(the) one man'	**'(the) one man'**
sin (*hamartia*)	righteousness (*dikaiosynē*)
sinner (*hamartōlos*)	righteous (*dikaios*)
disobedience (*parakoē*)	obedience (*hypakoē*)
trespass (*paraptōma*)	free gift (*charisma*)
transgression (*parabasis*)	free gift (*dōrēma*)
judgment (*krima*)	grace (*charis*)
condemnation (*katakrima*)	justification (*dikaiōma*)
death (*thanatos*)	justification (*dikaiōsis*)
	life (*zōē*)

11. Jewett, *Romans*, pp. 378-79.
12. Byrne, Romans, p. 178.
13. Jewett, *Romans*, p. 79.

It is possible to categorize these portfolios in a number of ways, but some features loom larger than others. First, going from top to bottom in each column, we have an overriding movement from 'sin' to 'death' in the column representing Adam. The corresponding movement in the column representing Christ runs from 'righteousness' to 'life'. These terms are the most basic constituents in the respective portfolios, in the case of Adam an economy of death, in the case of Christ an economy of life. 'Sin' is the death-maker in Adam's life and legacy, 'righteousness' the life-maker in Christ's arsenal with the added force that 'righteousness' is not a static notion but is itself a dynamic right-maker.

Second, if the problem on the left side is that Adam first and then the human family were constituted as sinners (5.12), the remedial horizon on the right cannot be less than a complete reversal, that is, it cannot be less than sinners becoming righteous. This prospect is explicit in the passage. 'For just as by the one man's disobedience (*parakoēs*) the many were made sinners (*hamartōloi*), so by the one man's obedience (*hypakoēs*) the many will be made righteous (*dikaioi*)' (5.19). We are free to infer that Paul sees the reversal brought to completion only in the eschaton, but there cannot be doubt as to the extent of the promised reversal.[14] The technical language of the theological tradition is on this point manifold, but a statement by D.E.H. Whiteley captures the essential element. 'Christ deals with sin, not by throwing a cloth over the eyes of God but by setting us, at the cost of his own life, in a relationship within which sin can be done away'.[15]

Third, some of the words in each column are almost identical in meaning even though they are different in Greek. Paul strives for variation in order to cushion repetitiousness, but it is precisely the repetitiousness that drives home the contrast. Selecting the dominant word groupings, the contrast looks like this.

'(the) one man'	**'(the) one man'**
disobedience (*parakoē*)	obedience (*hypakoē*)
trespass (*paraptōma*)	gift (*charisma*)
transgression (*parabasis*)	gift (*dōrea*)
judgment (*krima*)	gift (*dōrēma*)
condemnation (*katakrima*)	gift (*charis*)
	right-making (dikaiōma)

In this abbreviated representation, the 'disobedience' (*parakoē*) of Adam is countered by the 'obedience' (*hypakoē*) of Christ (5.19), and 'trespass' (*paraptōma*) is countered by 'right-making' (*dikaiōma*) (5.15-16).

14. Dunn, *Romans 1–8*, p. 296.
15. Whiteley, *The Theology of St. Paul*, p. 146.

The legal terms (*krima*, *katakrima*) on the left are under-matched on the right hand in at least two ways. The words that are translated 'justification' in the NRSV, *dikaiōma* (5.16) and *dikaiōsis* (5.18), do not normally mean 'justification' in a legal, declarative sense. By themselves, they are better translated 'right-doing' or 'right-making', but the notion of 'justification' or 'acquittal' is usually preferred on the logic that Paul intended these terms to match the legal terms in Adam's portfolio of death. They are, from the point of view of translators, given meanings that is more indebted to theological assumptions than to lexical usage.[16] Three of the terms in Adam's legacy are words that have the prepositional prefix *para-*, one with the sense of not hearing correctly (*parakoē*) (5.19), one with the sense of walking over or stepping over (*parabasis*) (5.14), and the last one also with the sense of mis-stepping (*paraptōma*) (5.15). These words have legal connotations, signifying actions for which the person will be held legally accountable, but they also have profound descriptive, existential, and relational significance. Adam's portfolio is in every sense *para-*; he is *off* and trapped in a losing gambit quite apart from the fact that he is in legal trouble. In everyday speech, he is *off-key* for his hearing disorder (5.19), *off course* and *off target* for his direction (5.14), and simply *off-track* (5.15). For the person thus afflicted, his or her need surpasses the legal ramifications of the condition.

Most striking, however, now in the column on the right, is Paul's repetitive reference to 'gift' by at least four different words, *charis* (5.15, 17, 20, 21), *charisma* (5.15, 16), *dōrea* (5.15, 17), and *dōrēma* (5.16). The many synonyms might seem redundant, and the apparent redundancy is magnified by phrases that are composites of 'gift', such as 'the free gift in the grace' (*hē dōrea en chariti*), or simply 'the gift in the gift' (5.15, my translation), and 'the abundance of grace' (*tēn perisseian tou charitos*) (5.17), meaning 'the overflowing of the gift'. As Dunn notes, 'Paul's piling up of language in superfluous repetition is an instinctive or deliberate attempt to mirror the superabundant quality of grace given and received'.[17]

'Gift' is not enough. It must be 'gift' head over heels, Paul's vocabulary stumbling over itself to capture and catch up with the reality it tries to describe. This means that *giving* looms large in God's disposition. God is in Paul's representation a generous, giving God, withholding nothing and stopping short of nothing that can benefit those who are trapped in the dynamic of death that holds sway on Adam's side of the equation. Even more to the point, if we pursue the Adam narrative in Genesis to its core, the problem is not simply disobedience to the divine command. I touched in this in the previous chapter, and here the problem shows up again. Before Adam's

16. Jewett, *Romans*, pp. 382-83.
17. Dunn, *Romans 1–8*, p. 281.

disobedience, the serpent caricatures the divine command by casting it as privation, hardship, and lack. 'Did God say, "You shall not eat from any tree in the garden?"' (Gen. 3.1) When Adam 'disobeys' the divine command, he acts in response to a malicious misrepresentation of the command so as to make his disobedience the violation of a command God did not give.[18] An ethical or legal account of Adam's 'disobedience' obscures the theological predicament created by the serpent's entrapment (Rom. 7.8-11).[19] Paul's purview in Romans is sweeping and general, but it captures well Adam's plight in the Garden of Eden: hearing that is *off-key* and a choice that is *off target* and profoundly *off-track*. To the extent that Adam and Eve in Genesis perceive the divine command to express privation (Gen. 3.6), the verbal excess in Paul's depiction of the reversal is to the point. While God's original economy is represented as an economy of plenitude (Gen. 2.15-17), the divine economy in Paul's account radiates abundance even more intensely.[20] Most important, of course, and now as the greatest contrast between Adam's disobedience (*parakoē*) and Christ's obedience (*hypakoē*), the obedience of Christ cannot be described in terms of something *he did not do*. Adam, we recall, would have been obedient if he had *not* eaten of the Tree of Knowledge. The measure of Christ's obedience, by contrast, is what *he did*. What he did, as Paul has told us already, refers to his death on the cross (Rom. 5.8, 19, 21; cf. Phil. 2.8).[21] This is God's supreme act of giving and the reason why Paul cleans out the verbal cupboard of all the words that mean 'gift' in order to do justice to his subject.

Returning to the essential differences, Paul writes that 'death exercised dominion' (*ebasileusen*) (Rom. 5.14), a turn of phrase that echoes God's intention in Genesis for human beings to 'have dominion' (*katakurieusate*) (Gen. 1.28, LXX) in an economy of abundance. Instead, as Paul notes with a keen eye for the irony, the plan unraveled 'because of the one man's trespass', and 'death exercised dominion (*ebasileusen*) *through that one*' (Rom. 5.17).

18. See R.W.L. Moberly, 'Did the Serpent Get It Right?', *JTS* 39 (1988), pp. 1-27; Martin Emmrich, 'The Temptation Narrative of Genesis 3:1-6: A Prelude to the Pentateuch and the History of Israel', *EQ* 73 (2001), pp. 3-20.

19. Dietrich Bonhoeffer, *Creation and Fall: A Theological Interpretation of Genesis 1–3* (trans. John C. Fletcher; London: SCM Press, 1959), p. 71.

20. Linn Marie Tonstad ('Trinity, Hierarchy, and Difference: Mapping the Christian Imaginary', PhD Dissertation, Yale University, 2009) compares 'economies of lack' and 'economies of plenitude', the former 'structured by relations of competition and ontological hierarchy', the latter 'by relations of sharing and overflow' (p. 28). I am indebted to her work for these concepts, and the definitions are broadly compatible with the alleged 'economy of lack' in Adam and the 'economy of plenty' in Christ.

21. Dunn, *Romans 1–8*, p. 284.

The ecological implications of this statement are huge, and the need for clarification is also urgent. *Dominion* and the exercise of dominion has in the story of Genesis become a loaded concept in the history of interpretation. Were humans in Genesis commissioned to 'fill the earth and subdue (Hebr. *kavash*, LXX *katakurieusate*) it; and have dominion (Hebr, *radah*, LXX *archete*)' (Gen. 1.28) in the sense that they were at liberty to oppress and exploit other creatures at will? This is the view expressed in an extremely influential essay by Lynn White, Jr., published in the journal *Science* in 1967.[22] As though cued by the passage in Genesis, White claimed, first, that '[t]he victory of Christianity over paganism was the greatest psychic revolution in the history of our culture', and, second, that 'God planned all of this explicitly for man's benefit and rule: no item in the physical creation had any purpose save to serve man's purposes'.[23]

Exercise of 'Dominion'

- 'Dominion' in Genesis is a category of trust and responsibility, not a mandate to dominate.

This opinion makes the mistake of counting on the historical reality of Christian culture to have a textual mandate in Genesis,[24] and it allows words and the connotation of words to dominate the passage at the expense of the context, a mistake that even astute exegetes are prone to make.[25] Reading Genesis in context will confirm that humans occupy a uniquely important role in creation and that humans ontologically are the deal-making and deal-breaking ecological species, but it will not for one moment support the notion that other species exist only 'to serve man's purposes'. Before the God-given commission to humans to 'subdue…and have dominion' (Gen. 1.28), non-human creation receives a bill of rights that (1) is similar to the commission to humans and (2) precedes it.

> God blessed them (sea creatures and birds), saying, 'Be fruitful and multiply and fill the waters' (Gen. 1.22).
>
> God blessed them (human beings), and God said to them, 'Be fruitful and multiply, and fill the earth' (Gen. 1.28).

The fact that non-human creation has a God-given mandate to flourish is not negated by the subsequent commission to humans 'to subdue… and have dominion' (Gen 1.22, 28). Genesis announces that there is a purpose for nature and all its inhabitants. Non-human creation, too, receives

22. Lynn White, Jr, 'The Historical Roots of Our Ecologic Crisis', *Science* 155 (1967), pp. 1203-207.

23. White, Jr, 'Historical Roots', p. 1207.

24. Richard Bauckham, *Living with Other Creatures: Green Exegesis and Theology* (Waco, TX: Baylor University Press, 2011), p. 19.

25. Jakob Wöhrle, '*dominium terrae*: Exegetische un religionsgeschichtliche Überlegungen zum Herrschaftsauftrag in Gen 1,26-28', *ZAW* 121 (2009), pp. 171-88.

the 'word of empowerment' that is intrinsic to the blessing (Gen. 1.22),[26] what Claus Westermann calls 'a silent advance of the power of life in all realms'.[27]

Human beings are ontologically unique, as noted, because 'God created humankind in his image, in the image of God he created them' (Gen. 1.27). But this does not entail liberty to dominate and exploit other species. On the contrary, it means that 'humans image God when they do the work of God in the world', as Wilma Ann Bailey notes in a tribute to Walter Harrelson.[28] That is to say, 'image and likeness reside not in our being, as in Greek thought, but in our responding to the relationship that we have with God'.[29] On this logic, the 'image of God' is a vocational obligation and not only a privilege or status. The 'image of God' confers on humans the responsibility to act toward the rest of creation according to God's character and intention.[30] 'The verb *radah* ('rule') does not itself define how this dominion is to be exercised',[31] but the context does, and the context reverberates with amicable relations, respect, abundance, and life. The story presents 'the themes of *responsibility for* as well as *commonality with* the earth and its creatures', says James Limburg.[32] There is no mandate for humans to oppress other creatures or abuse the earth.

When we read the creation story in Genesis 2 as a complementary story and not as a competing or unrelated account, the theme of responsibility is resolutely in the foreground.[33] Genesis says in this account that 'there was no one to till (*'ābad*) the ground' (Gen. 2.5) as if to suggest that humans are created for the sake of the earth and not the other way around.[34] This impression is not softened in subsequent disclosures of God's intention.

26. Fretheim, *God and the World in the Old Testament*, p. 50.

27. Claus Westermann, 'Creation and History in the Old Testament', in *The Gospel and Human Destiny* (trans. Donald Dutton; ed. Vilmos Vajta; Minneapolis: Augsburg, 1971), p. 30.

28. Wilma Ann Bailey, 'The Way the World Is Meant to Be: an Interpretation of Genesis 1.26-29', *Vision* 9 (2008), p. 47.

29. Bailey, 'The Way the World Is Meant to Be', p. 47.

30. William J. Dumbrell, 'Genesis 1–3, Ecology, and the Dominion of Man', *Crux* 21 (1985), p. 22.

31. Theodore Hiebert, 'Rethinking Dominion Theology', *Direction* 25 (1996), p. 18.

32. James Limburg, 'The Responsibility of Royalty: Genesis 1–11 and the Care of the Earth', *WW* 11 (1991), p. 128.

33. Kristin Swenson, 'Care and Keeping East of Eden: Gen 4:1-16 in Light of Gen 2–3', *Int* 60 (2006), pp. 373-84.

34. This perspective is intriguingly laid out in *Meeting the Expectations of the Land: Essays in Sustainable Agriculture and Stewardship* (ed. Wes Jackson, Wendell Berry and Bruce Colman; San Francisco: North Point Press, 1984).

> The Lord God took the man and put him in the garden of Eden to till it (*'ābad*) and keep it (*shāmar*) (Gen. 2.15).

> Therefore the Lord God sent him forth from the garden of Eden, to till (*'ābad*) the ground from which he was taken (Gen. 3.23).

> Now Abel was a keeper (*rā'â*) of sheep, and Cain a tiller (*'ābad*) of the ground (Gen. 4.2).

All these texts resound with the commission 'to till it (*'ābad*) and keep it (*shāmar*)', defining the relationship between the earth and humans in the primeval world (Gen. 2.15). Men and women will 'till' (*'ābad*), meaning that they will serve, minister to, and preserve the earth. They will 'keep' (*shāmar*), meaning that they will guard, protect, and shield the earth from harm. The narrow occupational connotation of Abel as 'a keeper of sheep, and Cain a tiller of the ground' must not be cut off from the broader vocational scope. Cain the tiller and Abel the keeper are not only engaged in useful employment in the work that is most readily at hand. They are fulfilling a God-ordained vocation.

Later, when Cain has murdered his brother and is told that he will be 'cursed from the ground', the earth that was forced to open 'its mouth to receive your brother's blood from your hand' has turned against him (Gen. 4.11). 'When you till the ground', God tells him, 'it will no longer yield to you its strength' (Gen. 4.12). The curse springs from below, from the ground up. Nature itself is against him, demonstrating its outrage by withholding the crops he has come to expect. These are terms of reciprocity and not of dominion, certainly not dominion that only takes the human point of view into account.[35] In the case of Cain, his opinion is made to matter less than the opinion of the earth.

Dominion as a mandate for exploitation is without foundation in the Genesis story of creation.[36] William Dumbrell claims against Lynn White, Jr. that '[s]o far from man's dominion over the world producing the [ecological] problems...**the very opposite is the case**. It has been the **failure** by man to exercise dominion, in the sense which this concept is understood by Genesis 1–3 which has caused the problem.'[37] Non-human creates are in Genesis given 'a right to their habitats',[38] and, as James Barr notes, the Genesis account does not even envisage the idea of human beings 'using the animals for meat and no terrifying consequences for the animal world'.[39] To this Karl Barth adds that the non-human creature along with

35. Dumbrell, 'Genesis 1–3, Ecology, and the Dominion of Man', pp. 17-18.
36. Sarna, *Genesis*, pp. 12-13.
37. Dumbrell, 'Genesis 1–3, Ecology, and the Dominion of Man', p. 24.
38. Bailey, 'The Way the World Is Meant to Be', p. 48.
39. James Barr, 'Man and Nature: The Ecological Controversy and the Old Testament',

humans 'depends on the same objective guarantee of its dwelling-place and the same light by day and by night, and has been assigned to the same table spread by God'.[40]

What, in this light, of the miscue of 'the one man' that Paul describes in Romans (Rom. 5.12-21), adding ecological breakdown and non-human misery to the trail of death? And what, in this light, of Matthew Scully's rueful admonition,

> [w]hen a quarter million birds are stuffed into a single shed, unable even to flap their wings, when more than a million pigs inhabit a single farm, never once stepping into the light of day, when every year tens of millions of creatures go to their death without knowing the least measure of human kindness, it is time to question old assumptions, to ask what we are doing and what spirit drives us on.[41]

Human beings are consequential, and humans are also ecologically consequential. Nothing less fits Paul's contrasting 'the one man' and the (other) 'one man' in Romans (Rom. 5.12-21), *dominion* and the exercise of dominion falling into the hands of death in every nook and cranny of created reality (5.14, 17, 21). In fact, when Paul narrates the loss and the reversal in the same sentence, saying that 'death *exercised dominion* through that one (Adam)', and then goes on to write that 'those who receive the abundance of grace and the free gift of righteousness (will) *exercise dominion* in life through the one man, Jesus Christ' (5.17), the circle is closed. Ecological demise is in this construct a feature of loss of dominion, and ecological healing is possible when the recipients of grace are restored to the lost dominion, bringing with them the economy of life that was lost. In closing out the passage, Paul recapitulates and expands in the horizontal plane, but he ends resoundingly in major key so as to lift the argument to crescendo heights in the vertical plane, 'sin' and 'death' defeated by 'gift' and 'life'.

> But law came in (*pareisēlthen*), with the result that (*hina*) the trespass multiplied; but where sin increased, grace abounded all the more, so that, just as sin exercised dominion (*ebasileusen*) in death, so grace might also exercise dominion (*basileusē*) through right-making (*diakiosynēs*) leading to eternal life through Jesus Christ our Lord (Rom. 5.20-21, translation modified).

In this 'summary', we note that the malignant twosome are again linked, *sin* exercising dominion in *death* (5.21), now confronted by a twosome more than their equal, *gift* (*charis*) taking the reins through massive *right-making*

in *Ecology and Religion in History* (ed. David and Eileen Spring; New York: Harper & Row, 1974), pp. 62-63.

40. Karl Barth, *Church Dogmatics* I.3: *The Doctrine of Creation* (trans. G.W. Bromiley; London and New York: T. & T. Clark, 2004), pp. 177-78.

41. Matthew Scully, *Dominion: The Power of Man, the Suffering of Animals, and the Call to Mercy* (New York: St. Martin's Press, 2002), p. x.

(*diakiosynē*) so as to restore *life* to its lost dominion. More than legal measures are in view, the hope that 'grace might exercise dominion through right-making' (5.21, translation mine) a more representative rendition than the narrower 'justification' preferred by many translations.

And yet, lest we lose sight of the situational specifics in the generalizing, universal tendency of Paul's argument, the conclusion sends another jolt to give the local concern its due. One last recognition—and insult—remains for the law, or must we not say that they are two affronts and not only one? Paul says that 'the law *sneaked in* (*pareisēlthen*)' (5.20), his first disparagement, following through with a second put-down, 'with the *result* that (*hina*) the trespass *multiplied*', or worse, 'with the *intent* (*hina*) to make the trespass *multiply*' (5.20, translation mine). The take-down of the law is shocking in either version. Paul casts the law as an intruder that sneaked in by stealth and secrecy and not by divine intention. Given the close connection between Galatians and Romans, there could easily be a spillover effect to Paul's opponents in Galatia, false brothers 'secretly brought in, who *slipped in* (*pareisēlthon*) to spy on the freedom we had in Christ' (Gal. 2.4).[42] Jewett, afraid that interpreters will be prone to undercut Paul, says that since 'this verb is so frequently employed in contexts of unwanted, illegitimate entry or of the insertion of an object into an area where it would not ordinarily belong', we should not succumb to the temptation to soften the derogatory connotation.[43]

If the *sneaking-in* of the law is a cipher for the *sneaking-in* of Paul's opponents, his rhetoric aims to expose them and their agenda and is not a context-free commentary on the law. That the law in question has no right-making powers is evident whether by the fact that sin *increased* as a result or by the stronger assertion that the law came 'in order to *increase* the trespass' (5.21).[44] Contrary to the view of his opponents, the law made sin multiply, but, and this is the main point, 'where sin increased', grace was up to the challenge by abounding 'all the more' (5.20).

The End of the Reign of Sin (6.1-23)

When Paul now turns to spelling out existential and behavioral consequences of the preceding line of reasoning, we again need awareness of outside factors for the argument to become intelligible. Recapping the prior argument, Paul has told the story of the defeat of sin and death by the divine intervention that breaks sin's dominion (5.12-21). An action that is aimed to put sin out of commission cannot be a license for sin. Such an inference is so far-fetched that it can only come from hostile opponents who misrepresent his

42. Jewett, *Romans*, p. 387.
43. Jewett, *Romans*, p. 387.
44. Jewett, *Romans*, p. 387.

position to make it say precisely what he is not saying. Misrepresentations are nevertheless a staple of human reality, and some misrepresentations are so subtle and well-aimed that they gain traction (Gen. 3.1-6; Rom. 3.8; Mt. 5.11; 10.25). While Paul writes so as to fend off misrepresentations of his message and the promoters behind it, he continues to speak in the 'we-form' of intimate discourse.[45] To the extent that hostile influences are in view, therefore, Paul's idiom ensures that they are seen as hostile not only to him but also to the Roman believers. 'What then are *we* to say?' signifies, on the one hand, the joint response of Paul and the Roman believers to the message of liberation that he has laid out in the preceding passage (5.12-21) and, on the other hand, that there is nothing in *his* and *their* response to justify the notion that Paul has written a blank check for sin.

> What then are we to say? Should we continue in sin in order that grace may abound? (Rom. 6.1).

Again, as noted above, the question does not arise naturally from the previous passage (5.12-21). But Romans has already made explicit that it confronts a threat that makes Paul out to say precisely what he is *not* saying, the misrepresentation concocted by the opponents' determination to pave the way for circumcision and alleged remedial powers of the law. 'And why not say (*as some people slander us by saying that we say*), "Let us do evil so that good may come"?' Paul has asked at an earlier juncture (3.8). This makes it certain that Paul is responding to people who misrepresent him to say that he takes sin more lightly than they do while also implying that their remedy is superior to his.

'Should we continue in sin in order that grace may abound?' (Rom. 6.1). The question, once imagined and expressed, requires an answer, and the short answer is in keeping with the quality of the question. 'By no means! How can we who died to sin go on living in it?' (6.2) 'Never!' or 'Certainly not!' or the colloquial, 'No way!' are alternative ways to 'signal the laughable quality of this diatribal exchange'.[46]

If this is all that needs to be said by way of taking apart the false inference, more must be said with respect to how Jesus brings an end to the Reign of Sin.

> Do you not know that all of us who have been baptized into Christ Jesus were baptized into his death? Therefore we have been buried with him (*synatafēmen*) by baptism into death, so that, just as Christ was raised from the dead by the glory of the Father, so we too might walk in newness of life. For if we have been united with him in a death like his, we will certainly

45. Jewett (*Romans*, p. 394) notes the 'nondenunciary style' that goes along with the rebuttal of the false inference.

46. Jewett, *Romans*, p. 395.

> be united with him in a resurrection (*anastaseōs*) like his. We know that our old self was crucified with him (*synestaurōtē*) so that the body of sin (*to sōma tēs hamartias*) might be destroyed, and we might no longer be enslaved to sin. For whoever has died is freed from sin. But if we have died with Christ, we believe that we will also live with him. We know that Christ, being raised from the dead, will never die again; death no longer has dominion (*kurieuei*) over him. The death he died, he died to sin, once for all; but the life he lives, he lives to God. So you also must consider yourselves dead to sin and alive to God in Christ Jesus. Therefore, do not let sin exercise dominion (*basileuetō*) in your mortal bodies, to make you obey their passions. No longer present your members to sin as instruments of wickedness (*hopla adikias*), but present yourselves to God as those who have been brought from death to life, and present your members to God as instruments of righteousness (*hopla diakosynēs*). For sin will have no dominion (*kurieusei*) over you, since you are not under law but under grace (Rom. 6.3-14).

Sin is not only the cause of death but also a label for the way death impacts reality at the level of lived experience. Whatever vocabulary Paul's opponents have for sin and sin's blight, it will not exceed Paul's. Luise Schottroff notes that the radicalness in Paul's notion of sin has no parallel in other relevant sources in antiquity.[47] Importantly, his view of sin-suffused reality does not primarily stem from *intro*-spection. His perception is conspicuously *extro-spective*, a view of reality where the lid has come off, in medical language akin to a dissection that brings to view hidden pathology. As Schottroff puts it, 'Paul thinks apocalyptically', having at his disposal tools of seeing that exceed those of casual or even keen observers.[48] Conversely, whatever remedy Paul's opponents propose, it will not match Paul's nor will it fix the problem. As in the previous chapter, Paul sets up the contrast between sin and death on the one hand and deliverance and life on the other, only now with the difference that here the solution is encroaching on his description of the problem, and the solution marks a new page in lived experience.

Sin-side of the Story	**Life-side if the Story**
so that the body of sin (*to sōma tēs hamartias*) might be destroyed (6.6)	so we too might walk in newness of life (6.4)
For whoever has died is freed from sin (6.7)	we will certainly be united with him in a resurrection like his (6.5)
The death he died, he died to sin, once for all (6.10)	we believe that we will also live with him (6.8)
So you also must consider yourselves dead to sin (6.11)	Christ, being raised from the dead, will never die again (6.9)
	the life he lives, he lives to God (6.10)

47. Luise Schottroff, 'Die Schreckensherrschaft der Sünde und die Befreiung durch Christus nach dem Römerbrief des Paulus', *EvTh* 39 (1979), p. 497.
48. Schottroff, 'Die Schreckensherrschaft der Sünde', p. 507.

At the level of experience, the movement from sin and death to resurrection and life is anchored in baptism.[49] Baptism, in turn, signifies reenactment of the death, burial, and resurrection of Jesus (5.3-4). But the reenactment is also an act of *participation* and not only of *representation*. Participation is brought to view by adding the prefix *syn-* to the verbs describing the most important occasions in Jesus' story (6.4, 5, 6, 8). In fact, Jesus' story is described by means of verbs in first person plural: '*we* were buried with' (6.4); '*we* have been united with' (6.5); '*we* were crucified with' (6.6); '*we* died with' (6.8); '*we* shall live with' (6.8).[50] The baptizand is play-acting the story of Jesus while also expressing a compressed version of his or her own story as participants. On the one hand, 'the cross is actualized in the act of baptism',[51] bringing Christ's entire 'career' into view. On the other hand, 'conformity to the "career" of Christ...lies at the heart of Paul's insistence, negatively, upon Christians' "death" to sin and, positively, their orientation towards a new, righteous life'.[52] Co-crucifixion with Christ does not give sin a reprieve, given that it happens 'so that the body of sin (*to sōma tēs hamartias*) might be destroyed' (6.6). Nothing is shallow in Paul's conception, rhetoric, or anticipated result. If '*body of sin*' captures human plight in its most severe conception, it also makes the plight collapse into remedial action that is definitive and complete: '*the old person of us was crucified with him*' (6.6, translation mine).

Imagery of Participation

- buried with — *synetafēmen* (6.4)
- united with — *symfytoi* (6.5)
- crucified with — *synestaurōthē* (6.6)
- died with — *apethanomen syn* (6.8)
- live with — *syzēsomen* (6.8)

Much as the movement from death to life is represented as an established fact, it also involves an active element. '*Consider* yourselves (*logizesthe heautous*) dead to sin and alive to God in Christ Jesus' is choice at the level of thought and self-representation (6.11).[53] This is to be followed by choice at the level of action: '*present* yourselves (*parastēsate heautous*) to God as those who have been brought from death to life' (6.13). While Paul in

49. Günther Bornkamm, 'Baptism and New Life in Paul', in *Early Christian Experience* (trans. Paul L. Hammer; London: SCM Press, 1969), pp. 71-86; Jewett, *Romans*, p. 396; Dunn, *Romans 1–8*, p. 308.

50. As prefix and part for the verb, *syn-* gives an intimate representation: *co*-buried or *with*-buried, *co*-crucifed, *co*-live.

51. Käsemann, *Romans*, p. 168.

52. Byrne, *Romans*, p. 190.

53. According to N.T. Wright (*Christian Origins and the Question of God*. III. *The Resurrection of the Son of God* [Minneapolis: Fortress Press, 2003], p. 252), '[w]hen I have completed the "reckoning", I have not brought about a new state of affairs in the real world outside of my mind; the only new state of affairs is that my mind is now aware of the way things actually are'.

Rom. 5.12-21 describes the triumph of life over death in 'the one', death understood as a life-ending and absolute termination of existence, in Rom. 6.1-14 he describes the triumph of life over death, death now understood as death-in-life. The expression 'as out of dead living' (*hōsei ek nekrōn zōntas*) (6.13) is therefore best understood 'as living people brought from the death of sinful existence'.[54] Paul will not spell out the ecological implications of the promised deliverance from death-in-life until later in Romans (8.19-23), but we can anticipate the only possible outcome: death-making must turn into life-making.

Commentators have observed a transition from the indicative—what *is* (6.2-10) to the imperative—what *ought to be* (6.11-14) in this section. To some, the transition has seemed either unnecessary, baffling, or contradictory. 'Does not the indicative take away the impact of the imperative, and does not the imperative limit the certainty and validity of the indicative?' Günther Bornkamm asks.[55] Can one speak meaningfully that something *ought to be* if it already *is*? Teresa Kuo-Yu Tsui answers that both emphases are held together within Paul's apocalyptic frame of thought. 'Paul in the indicative in 6.2-10 expresses his apocalyptic vision of the new life in Christ, which envisions believers as transformed people. Paul then uses the imperative, exhorting believers to get hold of this apocalyptic vision through *logizomai* ("reckoning", Rom. 6.11).'[56] *Apocalyptic* is at work not only at the level of the event Paul describes but also with regard to *perception* and *self-understanding*. Seeing or 'reckoning' entails scales coming off the eyes of the person who sees. The transformation is whole cloth with what is seen because the 'transformed mind shaped by the apocalyptic vision of the new life in Christ is prior to the ethical action and serves as the basis of it'.[57]

> For sin will have no dominion over you, since (*gar*) you are not under law but under grace (6.14).

In view of the opening question, 'Should we continue in sin in order that grace may abound?' (Rom. 6.1) we now have a conclusion that the opponents cannot have anticipated and that is certain to leave them at a loss. Recall that the premise of their critique of Paul is the allegation of license to sin, that is, a message that does not take the correct measure of sin and thus fails to prescribe the requisite remedy (3.8; 6.1). Paul turns the table on these charges one hundred and eighty degrees. Not only has he

54. Teresa Kuo-Yu Tsui, 'Reconsidering Pauline Juxtaposition of Indicative and Imperative (Romans 6:1-14) in Light of Pauline Apocalypticism', *CBQ* 75 (2013), p. 303.

55. Bornkamm, 'Baptism and New Life in Paul', p. 71.

56. Tsui, 'Indicative and Imperative', p. 304.

57. Tsui, 'Indicative and Imperative', p. 304.

demonstrated that the tentacles of sin run deeper than his opponents envision. He has also taken his readers—and by extension his opponents—on a conceptual and rhetorical *tour de force* that they will not be able to match. Paul's narrative and anatomy of sin cannot be separated from the narrative and anatomy of liberation, the former completely blended into his recounting of the story of the life, death, and resurrection of Jesus. Paul owns the copyright to this way of telling the story, as it were (1.5; 15.15-16), but there is no need to repeat the claim here because the proof of the pudding is in the eating. We can be certain that his opponents tell a story that is more atomistic and externalized with respect to sin and far less captive to the story of Jesus. Paul's implicit critique, now delivered by way of the withering conclusion (6.14), is that sin's dominion will continue in their prescription but not in his. Only within the logic of grace will sin's dominion come to an end (6.14).

> What then? Should we sin because we are not under law but under grace? (6.15).

The question seems redundant and almost ludicrous given the fact that it is almost identical to the question that has already been answered. But Paul decides to make his opponents run another lap around the track with him, not because his opponents' criticism has traction or because his first rebuttal fell short. He has another image up his sleeve, and there are pastoral reasons for sharing it, not only theological or apologetic reasons.

Once again, his short answer to the question above is the familiar, 'By no means!' (6.15) From there onward, he takes his readers into another venue of lived reality, giving it an unfamiliar twist.

> Do you not know (*ouk oidate*) that if you present yourselves to anyone as obedient slaves, you are slaves of the one whom you obey, either of sin, which leads to death, or of obedience, which leads to righteousness? (6.16).

The new image is slavery, a negative image now harnessed for a new, positive application. According to Jewett, studies of slavery in the ancient world indicate that 'somewhere between one- and two-thirds of the population were either slaves or former slaves'.[58] This number is more than sufficient to take for granted that the recipients of the letter knew what he was talking about. If the make-up of the believers in Jesus Rome was anything like the believers in Corinth, they, too, had reason to consider their call: 'not many of you were wise by human standards, not many were powerful, not many were of noble birth' (1 Cor. 1.26). The terms of slavery meant that the reins were entirely in the hands of the master and slave-owner. Western readers belonging to cultures prizing individual autonomy cannot easily

58. Jewett, *Romans*, p. 416.

fathom Paul's argument or the fact that it is grounded in a cultural reality precisely the opposite. 'It is presupposed here as elsewhere that a person belong constitutively to a world and lies under lordship', says Käsemann.[59] While this assessment is culturally true, Paul's argument is not only conditioned by culture, as we shall see shortly.

> But thanks be to God that you, having once been slaves of sin (*douloi tēs hamartias*), have become obedient from the heart (*hypēkousate ek kardias*) to the form of teaching to which you were entrusted, and that you, having been set free from sin, have become slaves of righteousness (*edoulōthēte tē dikaoisynē*) (='enslaved to righteousness'). I am speaking in human terms because of your natural limitations. For just as you once presented your members as slaves to impurity and to greater and greater iniquity, so now present (*parastēsate*) your members as slaves to righteousness (*doula tē dikaiosynē*) for sanctification. When you were slaves of sin, you were free in regard to righteousness. So what advantage did you then get from the things of which you now are ashamed? The end (*telos*) of those things is death. But now that you have been freed from sin and enslaved to God, the advantage (*karpon*) you get is sanctification. The end (*telos*) is eternal life (Rom. 6.17-22).

'Slaves of sin (*douloi tēs hamartias*)' may be a culturally conditioned figure of speech because of the prevalence of slavery (6.17), but in Paul's view it is applicable to the human condition irrespective of culture. The population of the Roman Empire can be divided into free people and slaves, or slave owners and slaves, but Paul's conception universalizes the latter condition. Schottroff says that Aristotle is careful to distinguish between sovereign and subjects, but he 'could never imagine a grown man from the upper echelons as a slave under some or other power'.[60] Paul can. Subjection and incapacity are in his conception widely diffused so as to obliterate the distance between citizens of the Roman Empire in the first century and human beings in the twenty-first. If, within the cultural logic of the first century, life without a master would be unthinkable, the theological logic of Paul's slavery-image has not moved an inch. Life's two options are slavery to sin or slavery to righteousness (6.16, 18), both options joined in the notion of slavery and yet so different that the slave to sin has nothing in common with the slave to righteousness. Indeed, the slave to sin was 'free' of sorts, 'free in regard to righteousness' (5.20), of all things. But what gain did it bring? It brought only *shame*, Paul continues (5.21), as if expecting to see heads nodding in the circle. Given that 'sin rules over all humans as over slaves',[61] and given that slaves are not in position to secure freedom by their own volition, someone must come to their rescue. That is

59. Käsemann, *Romans*, p. 179.
60. Schottroff, 'Die Schreckensherrschaft der Sünde', p. 501.
61. Schottroff, 'Die Schreckensherrschaft der Sünde', p. 502.

exactly the point in Paul's argument, and it is possible to state the proposition in slightly more palatable terms: there will not be self-mastery except under the mastery of Another. The way forward sees believers in Jesus 'enslaved to righteousness' (*edoulōthēte tē dikaoisynē*) (6.18), the whole being with all its members presented 'as slaves to righteousness (*doula tē dikaiosynē*) for sanctification' (6.19). All the negative connotations of enslavement vanish, however, because the new enslavement sets the person oppressed by sin on the road toward recovery, decency, dignity, and life. The metaphor is forced, says Dunn, 'but Paul's message is clear—that righteousness is the effect of God's lordship over his creatures and cannot be realized otherwise'.[62] Schottroff adds that the power of Christ is for Paul not 'directed against the misuse of freedom but against lack of freedom'.[63]

It is now possible to see that Paul's two exhibits promising deliverance from the death-in-life predicament follow the same pattern with regard to the question asked from without (Paul's opponents), the question asked from within (Paul's question), and the answers given.

	'Baptized into his death' Romans 6.1-14	**'Slaves of righteousness'** Romans 6.15-23
Question	Should we continue in sin in order that grace may abound?	Should we sin because we are not under law but under grace?
Response at the level of seeing	Do you not know (*agnoeîte*) that all of us who have been baptized into Christ Jesus were baptized into his death?	Do you not know (*ouk oidate*) that if you present yourselves to anyone as obedient slaves, you are slaves of the one whom you obey, either of sin, which leads to death, or of obedience, which leads to righteousness?
Response at the level of reckoning	consider yourselves dead to sin and alive to God	obedient from the heart
Response at the level of action	present your members to God as instruments of righteousness	present your members as slaves to righteousness for sanctification

The apocalyptic tenor persists in both panels. 'Do you not *know* (*agnoeîte*)?' Paul asks with regard to baptism in the first panel (6.3), indicating that the apocalyptic venue to knowing has not completely opened up. 'Do you not *know* (*ouk oidate*)?' he asks again with reference to slavery in the second panel (6.16), suggesting that here, too, the door is not fully open. Likewise, still on the topic that apocalyptic plays a role at the level of *perception*, he tells his readers in the first panel to '*consider* yourselves dead to sin and alive to God' (6.11) and then to '*present* your members to God

62. Dunn, *Romans 1–8*, p. 355.
63. Schottroff, 'Die Schreckensherrschaft der Sünde', p. 510.

as instruments of righteousness' (6.13), affirming them in the second panel for having become 'obedient from the heart' (6.17) and therefore on track to presenting 'your members as slaves to righteousness' (6.19). Reason is his medium in the realm of description and prescription, but apocalyptic must be the effective agent at the level of perception and action.

All along he colorizes sin in hues that drains away its appeal quite apart from what sin may do to a person's relationship with God. 'The end (*telos*) of those (sin) things is death', he says, in this context thinking of death not only in biological terms (6.21). Similarly on the opposite side, 'The end (*telos*) (of the God-things) is eternal life', implying a new quality as much as infinite duration (6.22).

The closing statement of this section (6.1-23) as in the previous one (5.12-21) recapitulates, specifies, and expands on his theme, succeeding so admirably that it has become one of the most quoted statements in the repository of memorable Pauline confessions.

> For the wages of sin (*ta opsōnia tēs hamartias*) is death, but the free gift of God (*to charisma tou theou*) is eternal life in Christ Jesus our Lord (6.23).

Sin and death are linked once more, 'nearly interchangeable in their role as world ruler and slave driver'.[64] Paul could have said that death is the *punishment* for sin, but he does not say that even though this is what many readers have heard him saying. Sin is in his construal doing double duty as the power that takes human beings *off course* and then extracts punishment. In this scenario the violation of the norm is not a greater concern than the warping of a life (6.21): there is death-in-life as much as there is death to bring a life to an end. Paul could also have said that death is *God's* punishment for sin, but he does not say that either. God stands in his representation at a distance to the outworking of sin in much the same way that slavery to sin and slavery to righteousness are 'free' with regard to each other (6.21). Perhaps we can say that God left it to sin to mind its own gloomy business: death is sin's territory and domain. Whatever wages were due, they were assessed by sin and paid out in sin's favored currency (6.23). Paul is here using a slang term that reinforces the negative connotation,[65] like 'loose change' or 'petty cash' paid for an inferior meal. Conversely, gift and right-making run a different and separate business, an economy of life that markets 'eternal' as a quality and as duration (6.23). And the greatest contrast—so as not to forget the message of his opponents—is that sin pays its due as a wage earned while God in Christ offers life as gift and un-earned favor (6.23; cf. 3.27; 4.2).

64. Schottroff, 'Die Schreckensherrschaft der Sünde', p. 501.

65. Jewett, *Romans*, p. 425.

Chapter 10

'I WAS ONCE ALIVE' (ROM. 7.9)

Romans 7 ranks as one of the most studied and fought-over chapters in the Pauline corpus. While there are many reasons for this, one overlooked reason is that interpreters have focused almost exclusively on Paul without paying much attention to his audience. Romans 7 has often been read as a compilation of 'stages in the life of Paul' rather than steps in the course of an argument. Given the situational character of the letter, this chapter demands attention to the '*to whom*' and '*for what reason*' question as much as any other portion.[1] Here, too, external influences and contrary points of view are evident (7.1-6). Here, too, sensitivity to the original setting breaks the subject open, enabling readers to perceive nuances otherwise lost. Here, too, the letter suggests a triangle consisting of Paul, the Roman believers in Jesus, and the dissenting voices that promote an idyllic view of the law and the circumcision of the Gentiles. In Romans 6, Paul has addressed the problem of death-in-life in by way of participation with Christ in baptism (6.1-14) and the transition from being slaves of sin to becoming slaves of righteousness (6.15-23). Why the need to say more—and *a lot more*?

The need must be sought among the issues stirring within Paul's implied audience. Paul's final blow to the law (7.1-6) is best understood as an answer to people who may be ready to concede points Paul has made so far but still cling to the conviction that unless new believers go beyond Paul's message, they have an unmet obligation on their résumé.[2] That is to say,

1. Thus Moses Stuart (*A Commentary on the Epistle to the Romans* [New York: Wiley and Halsted, 4th edn, 1859], p. 463), 'that we should understand every writer... as speaking to the purpose which he has immediately before him'. On this logic, '[t]he question concerning chap. vii.5-25 is not, whether it be true that there is a contest in the breast of Christians, which might, at least for the most part, be well described by the words there found; but, whether such a view of the subject is congruous with the present design and argument of the apostle.'

2. As Paul W. Meyer notes ('The Worm at the Core of the Apple: Exegetical Reflections on Romans 7', in *The Conversation Continues: Studies in Paul and John in Honor of J. Louis Martyn* [ed. Robert T. Fortna and Beverly R. Gaventa; Nashville: Abingdon Press, 1990], p. 71), Rom. 7.1-6 is part of the preceding larger unit running from 6.1 to 7.6 rather than belonging to 7.7-25.

even if the law turns out to be neither the diagnostician nor the balm that its proponents originally held it to be, it is still an obligation. Paul now moves to silence that argument.

Remarriage without Adultery

> Do you not know, brothers and sisters—for I am speaking to those who know the law—that the law is binding on a person only during that person's lifetime? Thus a married woman is bound by the law to her husband as long as he lives; but if her husband dies, she is discharged from the law concerning the husband (*katērgētai apo tou nomou tou andros*). Accordingly, she will be called an adulteress (*moichalis*) if she lives with another man while her husband is alive. But if her husband dies, she is free from that law (*eleuthera apo tou nomou*), and if she marries another man, she is not an adulteress (*moichalida*). In the same way, my friends, you have died to the law through the body of Christ, so that you may belong to another, to him who has been raised from the dead in order that we may bear fruit for God. While we were living in the flesh, our sinful passions, aroused by the law, were at work in our members to bear fruit for death. But now we are discharged from the law (*katērgēthēmen apo tou nomou*), dead to that which held us captive (*apothanontes en hō kateichometha*), so that we are slaves not under the old written code (*palaiotēti grammatos*) but in the new life of the Spirit (Rom. 7.1-6).

Paul's analogy makes use of the web of obligations that attach to marriage, counting on well-known legal and visceral elements to make his point. As to legal matters, marriage is regulated by law. A married woman cannot enter into a relationship with another man while the husband is still alive except to find herself in violation of the law. If the husband dies, however, nothing stands in the way of her entering into a new relationship. In fact, the new marriage is also protected by law and is perfectly appropriate. Peter Spitaler summarizes the legal aspects as follows.

> That man's death affects the woman in four interrelated ways. First, his law's authority over her ends with his death. Second, despite the fact that the man is dead, his law nevertheless continues to protect the woman, who 'becomes another man's partner', from others charging her with adultery. Third, his death is the basis that justifies her legally 'becoming another man's partner'. Fourth, discharge from the man's law affords the woman the possibility of becoming, upon remarriage, subject to another partner's law. Thus, all cases of 'becoming another man's partner' are governed by law: the law of the man to whom a woman is already married, the law of the man whose partner she might become, and either man's laws that define adultery and regulate (re)marriage or widowhood.[3]

3. Peter Spitaler, 'Analogical Reasoning in Romans 7.2-4: A Woman and the Believers in Rome', *JBL* 125 (2006), p. 726.

The visceral element in Paul's example is 'woman'. Paul's reference point is Jewish and not Roman law.[4] 'Equality before the law' for men and women with regard to divorce was a tenet of Roman law but not of the Jewish legal canon. According to Jewish law, 'a married woman is bound by the law to her husband *as long as he lives*' (Rom. 7.2; cf. Deut. 24.1). The only legal recourse for a woman to end a marriage is the death of the husband. Just as the legal strictures on the woman are more stringent in the Jewish paradigm, so are the visceral elements. Twice Paul resorts to the word 'adulteress' (Rom. 7.3), implying not only that the woman's hands are tied but also that contempt and ostracism await her should it occur to her to start another relationship while the husband is still alive. 'Illegal' and 'immoral' are blazoned over such an action, the latter more than the former. Paul's choice of the woman's side in the relationship is not sexist but designed to advance his argument more effectively. She is 'caught' and 'cornered' in the relationship because of 'the law *of her husband*' (7.2), the law standing as an unbending enforcer toward her. Society and social convention will stigmatize her more than it is in their power to stigmatize a man. Once the husband has passed away and she is free to 'tie the knot' with another man, however, she is ensconced within protections that guarantee legal rights as well as social approval.

Paul's analogy is not perfect, but it is effective for its intended purpose. That purpose, in turn, is to put to rest the notion of law as obligation that still flickers in his opponents' diminishing armamentarium. The slight flaw in the analogy, if we want to be picky, is that it describes an entrapped woman who is free to marry once her husband dies while Paul's application appears to describe the death of the believer who nevertheless lives on to marry again. But this impression places rigid and mistaken demands on how analogies work.[5] It is of little concern that the husband's death is not the same as the believer being put to death by God when the main point is that 'the wife is released from the law's obligation' (7.4, 6).[6]

Paul's analogy makes death—and the death of Christ—the means that puts the believer resolutely beyond the reach of the law. But the believer's escape will not be a cause for mourning when the law's function in actual experience is faced with honesty. While the woman is trapped in a life that promises to get better only when the husband dies, the burdensome real-life partner is the law, and the law is a harassing, sin-arousing

4. Dunn, *Romans 1–8*, p. 360.

5. Dunn, *Romans 1–8*, p. 361. Dunn (*Romans 1–8*, p. 369) identifies 'the real anomaly' in the fact that 'the only one who has really died is the new partner, Christ! The fact is that the illustration is *not* one of the believer's transition from one state to another, but of the basic principle that death liberates from the law.'

6. Jewett, *Romans*, p. 432.

entity. Paul claims that while in the flesh, 'our sinful passions, *aroused by the law* (*ta dia tou nomou enērgeito*), were at work in our members to bear fruit for death' (7.5). The law's negatives are unrelenting: it stirred up sinful passions rather than curb them; it bore fruit for death rather than lead to life; it held us captive rather than set us free; it made us to be slaves 'under the old written code' (7.6). In addition to explicit negatives, Paul blends in rhetorical contrasts that are viscerally damaging to the standing of the law. The believer is released from the oppressive relationship 'so that you may belong to another' (7.4). The desire to exchange one partner for another is an unflattering view of the original relationship, happiness and peace of mind possible only in a new marital union with 'him who has been raised from the dead' (7.4). In this final juxtaposition, 'old' lines up across from 'new', 'death' across from 'life', and 'written code' across from 'Spirit'. The rhetorical skill by which Paul drives home content that seems to be meticulously thought-through is impressive—as is the fact that his argument represents the last nail driven into the law's coffin.

Charged Contrasts

• old	new
• death	life
• written code	Spirit

What now? If his argument is the answer to his opponents' insistence that that new believers must be circumcised and brought into compliance with the law, do they have an answer for it? Is there anything else they can say once Paul puts the law in the service of sin (7.5; cf. 3.20; 4.15; 5.20; 1 Cor. 15.56) and then proceeds to announce the termination of its claims (7.1-4)? On my reading, they do not. What I call 'the last nail into the law's coffin', above, can also be seen as the final blow to his opponents' argument and aspirations. From here on in this section, at least, there is less of them and more of the concerns that are intrinsic to the new message and to matters internal to congregations consisting of Jews and Gentiles in Rome.

Paul's conceptions have brought forth a new theological universe put in place by the reality of the cross (Rom. 5.6-8; 8.31-39) and the revelation of Jesus Christ (Gal. 1.12; 6.14).[7] The conceptions of his opponents, by contrast, envision a less dramatic transition between old and new. 'The old written code' (Rom. 7.6) is a cipher for a hermeneutic that hesitates to re-center around the revelation of God in Jesus; it is communally incremental for insisting on circumcision; and it is anthropologically on a different track

7. The shift is seismic. The Gospel Paul proclaims was (1) not received from a human source 'nor was I taught it, but (2) I received it through a revelation of Jesus Christ' (Gal. 1.12). Discontinuity at the level of means is also reflected in discontinuity at the level of content, the latter highlighted in J. Louis Martyn's translation of Gal. 1.11 (*Galatians*, p. 178), 'The gospel I preach is *not* what human beings normally have in mind when they speak of "good news"'. See also Beverly Roberts Gaventa, 'Galatians 1 and 2: Autobiography as Paradigm', *NovT* 28 (1986), pp. 309-26.

(3.9; 5.12). The 'we'-terminology that dominates the letter from the beginning of chap. 5 is increasingly a sign that Paul counts on the Roman believers to be in his corner. 'Do you not know, *brothers and sisters* (*adelfoi*)', he says in a tone of friendly, intimate address (7.1; cf. 7.4).[8] The objections raised by Paul's opponents are for the time being fading from the screen, and his message is now mostly for 'brothers and sisters' within the community. This does not mean that there is no more work to do for them if they, too, along with Paul, take their stand on a platform that sees the law as a sin-arousing, sin-increasing entity. In the wake of Paul's portrayal of the law the question that now is due was surely unthinkable within the old paradigm whichever way we imagine it.

'Is the law sin?' (7.7).

Apology for the Law

'What then should we say? That the law is sin (*ho nomos hamartia*)?' (7.7) A host of questions can be imagined in the wake of Paul's put-down of the law, but this one seems far beyond the pale. More conceivable alternatives would be, 'Is the law passé?' 'Is the law unimportant?' or even 'Is the law powerless?' the latter emphasis suggesting itself in light of Paul's repeated assertion that the law is devoid of remedial powers (5.20; 7.5). Even from a purely secular point of view it is a challenge to logic to make 'the law' complicit in sin to the point of having to ask, 'Is the law sin?' Surely the law cannot be seen as the cause of the very things it is designed to prevent? In a Jewish mode of thinking, the affront to the law is worse because the law comes with the prestige of being God-given, and its ennobling powers should be even less in doubt. Dunn notes that Paul's diction is sparse, if not terse, 'the law, sin?' suggesting a turn of phrase that 'can only be given effect by inflection of the voice'.[9] An argument that counts on intonation to make the point is a reminder that the conversational, 'live' tenor of Romans gives us a text is heard rather than read.

The quick rejoinder, 'By no means (*mē genoito*)!' is not enough to mute the shock of having heard the question asked in the first place (7.7). And yet 'undoing damage' is not a fit description for what Paul will do next. Only at this point is he ready to tell the larger story.

> Yet, if it had not been for the law, I would not have known sin. I would not have known what it is to covet if the law had not said, 'You shall not covet'. But sin, seizing an opportunity in the commandment, produced in me all

8. Bultmann (*Der Stil der paulinischen Predigt*, p. 66) notes that Paul's usual term is 'brothers and sisters' (*adelfoi*) but that he sometimes resorts to harsher address, as in Rom. 2.1-3.

9. Dunn, *Romans 1–8*, p. 378.

> kinds of covetousness. Apart from the law sin lies dead. I was once alive apart from the law, but when the commandment came, sin revived and I died, and the very commandment that promised life proved to be death to me. For sin, seizing an opportunity in the commandment, deceived me and through it killed me. So the law is holy, and the commandment is holy and just and good (Rom. 7.7-12).

In defense of the view that Paul is now talking to the Roman believers to the virtual exclusion of other concerns, the subject matter in this passage requires an engaged, friendly audience. We are expecting too much of Paul's opponents if we believe them willing to be party to an argument that begins with the question, 'Is the law sin?' (7.7) Paul's rejoinder that the law is not sin does no more than pull the law back from the precipice of the most negative association. What follows, however, will give back to the law as much or more than Paul's arguments took away and is for that reason even more unexpected than the previous put-down. Scholars are in wide agreement that Paul embarks upon 'an apology for the law'.[10] When he is done, he has opened up vistas for how to think about the law that are distinctive with regard to scope and depth and only vaguely appreciated.

'Yet, if it had not been for the law, I would not have known sin', Paul begins (7.7). 'I would not have known what it is to covet if the law had not said, "You shall not covet"' (7.7). Three clarifications or caveats are in order at this point. First, we need to delineate the meaning of Paul's use of the 'I'-form that dominates the remainder of the chapter. Is he talking about himself? Or does the 'I' represent someone else or another reality? C. Leslie Mitton claims that when Paul in this paragraph speaks in the first person singular, 'the Apostle speaks of that which is very real to him in his own spiritual autobiography'.[11] In an echo of the same sentiment, J.I. Packer avers that 'Paul speaks throughout in the first person singular, and his teaching takes the form of personal reminiscence and self-analysis'.[12] This is a resilient view, but it is almost certainly mistaken.[13] Clues in the passage suggest that Paul is rehearsing a story that is already familiar to the believers in Rome; he is not primarily giving them a bird's eye view of his spiritual

10. Dunn, *Romans 1–8*, p. 377.

11. C. Leslie Mitton, 'Romans vii. Reconsidered—1', *ExpTim* 65 (1953–54), p. 78.

12. J.I. Packer, 'The "Wretched Man" in Romans 7', *SE* 2 (1964), p. 621.

13. Cranfield (*Romans*, pp. 342-43) lists six options for the identity of the speaking 'I' in Rom 7.7-13: an 'I' that is (i) strictly autobiographical (Paul telling his story); (ii) a depiction of the typical Jewish individual; (iii) Adam; (iv) the experience of the Jewish people as a whole; (v) the experience of mankind as a whole; (vi) a depiction of the situation of humanity in the absence of the law told in first person for the sake of vividness. He dismisses options (i) and (ii), expressing preference for either (iii) or (vi) and mostly for the latter, admitting, however, that the passage is laced with allusions to the Genesis story of the fall.

journey.[14] The notion that Paul is engaged in self-analysis fails to pick up allusions to the Old Testament in the passage (7.7-12), allusions that are important not only for how they illuminate the plight of the speaking 'I' but also for the way they describe the 'history of the law'.[15] Moreover, the plight of the speaking 'I' coincides with a disastrous event in the history of the law. For reasons that will become more apparent as we proceed, Paul's rhetoric and his allusions to the Old Testament feed off each other to tell a larger story than what the simplistic 'autobiographical' reading envisions.[16] Rather, the 'I' must first be located outside Paul, and we shall find him—or *her*, even—by regarding Paul as an apocalyptic seer keenly attuned to the Old Testament.[17] Paul's 'I' will on these terms be best understood as speech-in-character, Paul *speaking to believers in the house churches in Rome in the person of Eve in Genesis*.[18]

14. Stanley Stowers, 'Romans 7:7-25 as a Speech-in-Character (προσωποπεία)', in *Paul in his Hellenistic Context* (ed. T. Engberg-Pedersen; Minneapolis: Fortress Press, 1995), pp. 180-202; idem, *A Rereading of Romans*, p. 11. Stowers sees the speaking 'I' as someone who 'speaks with great personal pathos of coming under the law at some point, learning about his desire to sin and being unable to do what he wants to do because of enslavement to sin and flesh. If one asks whether Paul gives his readers any clues at all elsewhere in the letters that this might be his autobiography, the answer is clearly "no".' The speaking 'I' will by this criterion be a Gentile ('Romans 7.7-25', pp. 191-92).

15. Exceptional studies of the Old Testament background for Paul's story about the law are J. Louis Martyn, '*Nomos* Plus Genitive Noun in Paul: The History of God's Law', in *Early Christianity and Classical Culture: Comparative Studies in Honor of Abraham J. Malherbe* (ed. John T. Fitzgerald, Thomas H. Olbricht and L. Michael White; NovTSup; Atlanta: Society of Biblical Literature, 2003), pp. 575-87; Austin Busch, 'The Figure of Eve in Romans 7.5-25', *Bib Int* 12 (2004), pp. 1-36; Jan Dochhorn, 'Röm 7,7 und das zehnte Gebot: Ein Beitrag zur Schriftauslegung und zur jüdischen Vorgeschichte des Paulus', *ZNW* 100 (2009), pp. 59-77.

16. Dunn, *Romans 1–8*, p. 382. Paul's 'spiritual autobiography' must reckon with the poignant self-disclosures in Gal. 1.11–2.14 and Phil. 3.3-11.

17. Emma Wasserman ('The Death of the Soul in Romans 7: Revisiting Paul's Anthropology in Light of Hellenistic Moral Psychology', *JBL* 126 [2007], pp. 793-816) objects to apocalyptic elements in the construct of Paul's 'I' in Romans 7, but this objection fails to take Paul's 'Eve story' into account, and it also misses the apocalyptic intensity of Paul's 'I' toward the end of the argument (Rom. 7.24).

18. Stowers, 'Romans 7.7-25 as a Speech-in-Character', pp. 180-202; Busch, 'The Figure of Eve in Romans 7.5-25', pp. 13-14; Stefan Krauter, 'Eva in Röm 7', *ZNW* 99 (2008), pp. 1-17; idem, 'Röm 7: Adam oder Eva?' *ZNW* 101 (2010), pp. 145-47; Gerald J. Janzen, 'Sin and the Deception of Devout Desire: Paul and the Commandment in Romans 7', *Encounter* 70 (2009), pp. 50-51. L. Ann Jervis ('"The Commandment which is for Life" (Romans 7.10): Sin's Use of the Obedience of Faith', *JSNT* 212 [2004], pp. 193-216) rejects the link to Genesis while pursuing a somewhat distinctive 'autobiographical' reading. Recognizing that the law alone cannot do all that Paul makes out to be the problem in Rom. 7.7-25, she argues that 'the Law and (Christian) paraenesis could "incite transgressions"'. Among shortcomings in her study are

Second, while Paul appears to restore to the law the prestige of being an able diagnostician of sin—'if it had not been for the law, I would not have known sin' (7.7)—this will be too narrow if we limit it to a new view of the Ten Commandments in his personal experience. A larger and more complex plot is emerging, painted on the canvas of the human story as this story is told in the Bible.

Third, while Paul chooses the commandment that appears most probing and introspective—'You shall not covet' (7.7)—we should not rush to the conclusion that Paul smartly singles out the commandment that reveals the spiritual intent of the Ten Commandments (Exod. 20.17; Deut. 5.21), on the one hand, while exposing the inner workings of self-seeking, on the other.[19] The larger story emerges when we turn to the most crucial part of the 'biography' and the identity of 'I' will soon declare itself.

> I was once alive apart from the law (*choris nomou*), but when the commandment *came* (*elthousēs de tēs entolēs*), sin revived and I died, and the very commandment that promised life proved to be death to me. For sin, seizing an opportunity in the commandment, deceived (*exēpatēsen*) me and through it killed me (Rom. 7.10, 11).

The story of the fall that Paul has recounted in prose in the third person in Rom. 5.12-19 is now dramatized in the first person. Jan Dochhorn demonstrates persuasively that Paul is telling 'an Adam story, of an "I" that meets the law in the form of the tenth commandment and who through this encounter falls under the power of sin—with lethal consequences'.[20] Better yet, as Austin Busch argues, and better even than Dochhorn's excellent exposition, it is an 'Eve story'.[21]

(1) insufficient attention to the problem facing the churches in Rome; (2) erroneously concluding that the notion of 'coveting' is absent in Genesis; (3) lack of interest in the role of 'deception' in Genesis and Romans 7 (Gen. 3.13; Rom. 7.11); (4) lack of attention to the story line in *The Apocalypse of Moses*; and (5) a proposal regarding 'sin's use of the obedience of faith' that confuses more than it clarifies.

19. Stendahl (*Paul among Jews and Gentiles*, pp. 78-96) traces this reading to Augustine and from Augustine to Luther, arguing that Paul's experience has little in common with either one of these interpreters. Benjamin Myers ('A Tale of Two Gardens: Augustine's Narrative Interpretation of Romans 5', in *Apocalyptic Paul: Cosmos and Anthropos in Romans 5–8* [ed. Beverly Roberts Gaventa; Waco: Baylor University Press, 2013], pp. 39-58) gives a more respectful reading of Augustine's exposition of Romans, arguing that his exposition (1) is not individualistic the way Stendahl perceived it; (2) links 'the personal and corporate dimensions of the self' for reasons that are indebted to Paul; and (3) represents—in a positive sense—'an immense re-imagining of what it means to be human'.

20. Dochhorn, 'Röm 7,7 und das zehnte Gebot', p. 60.

21. Käsemann (*Romans*, p. 196) makes the hasty claim that '[t]here is nothing in the passage that does not fit Adam, and everything fits Adam alone'. Krauter ('Eva in

> In Romans 7 Paul…uses the symbolic economy associated with Eve in the scene of the primeval transgression. Paul's allusion to the Genesis episode is subtle, but it permeates almost the entire chapter and suggests a complex interpretation of Eve's temptation and sin.[22]

The parallels are striking, especially with respect to deception in Genesis and in Paul's allusion to the Genesis story.

> The woman said, 'The serpent deceived (Hebr. *hišj'ani*, Gr. *ēpatēsen*) me, and I ate' (Gen. 3.13, NIV).

> For sin, seizing an opportunity in the commandment, deceived (*exēpatēsen*) me and through it killed me (Rom. 7.11).

Deception is a key element in both accounts: it is deception that triggers the illicit desire (*epithymia*) that also constitutes a key element in Paul's dramatic retelling in Romans. The word 'desire' is not explicit in Genesis, but it is certainly implicit.

> So when the woman saw that *the tree was good for food*, and that *it was a delight to the eyes*, and that *the tree was to be desired to make one wise*, she took of its fruit and ate; and she also gave some to her husband, who was with her, and he ate (Gen. 3.6).

This description is not a simple and objective run-down of the qualities of the tree; it is a narrative that reeks with desire wholesale and retail, desire rushing headlong against a commandment that in Paul's summary simply amounts to this: 'You shall not covet' (Rom. 7.7). Moreover, the desire that is evident has come into being after deception has done its work (Gen. 3.1-5). Thus, as Dochhorn notes, we 'can assume a matching hermeneutic, extracting from the Hebrew text of Gen. 3.6 that violation of the tenth commandment preceded the eating of the fruit'.[23]

Strictly speaking, no other transmission link is necessary, assuming that Paul could singly and alone map the line that runs between Genesis and Romans 7.[24] But there is more, as Dochhorn's reconstruction demonstrates, bringing in parallels from the apocryphal story of *The Life of Adam and Eve*. This story is also known as *The Apocalypse of Moses*, and it is old enough to be of relevance to the argument in Romans.[25] First, in this retell-

Röm 7', pp. 1-17) treats the text with much greater nuance than Käsemann while also showing that Paul attributes significance to Genesis 3 that exceeds the role of this text in other Jewish sources; cf. also, idem, 'Röm 7: Adam oder Eva?', pp. 145-47.

22. Busch, 'The Figure of Eve in Romans 7.5-25', p. 12.

23. Dochhorn, 'Röm 7,7 und das zehnte Gebot', p. 63.

24. Thus Cranfield, *Romans*, pp. 343-44.

25. M.D. Johnson (*Life of Adam and Eve*, in *The Old Testament Pseudepigrapha*, vol. 2 [ed, J.H. Charlesworth; New York: Doubleday, 1985], p. 252) envisions a Hebrew document originating between 100 BCE and 200 CE, most likely 'toward the end for the first

ing of the story in Genesis, the serpent is explicitly identified as Satan in disguise (ApMos 17.1-5). When the serpent speaks, therefore, it is actually Satan who is doing the talking.[26]

> The devil answered through the mouth of the serpent, 'Ye do well but ye do not eat of every plant'. And I (Eve) said, 'Yea, we eat of all, save one only, which is in the midst of paradise, concerning which, God charged us not to eat of it. For, He said to us, on the day on which ye eat of it, ye shall die the death' (ApMos 17.4-5).

> Then the serpent saith to me, 'May God live! but I am grieved on your account, for I would not have you ignorant. But arise, (come) hither, hearken to me and eat and mind the value of that tree.' But I said to him, 'I fear lest God be wroth with me as he told us'. And he saith to me, 'Fear not, for as soon as thou eatest of it, ye too shall be as God, in that ye shall know good and evil. But God perceived this that ye would be like Him, so he envied you and said, "Ye shall not eat of it". Nay, do thou give heed to the plant and thou wilt see its great glory.' Yet I feared to take of the fruit. And he saith to me, 'Come hither, and I will give it thee. Follow me' (ApMos 18.1-6).

Second, having enticed Eve with the promise that a great good has been withheld from her that can now be hers, Satan on oath wrings from Eve the promise that she will give of the fruit to Adam as a reward for getting to eat of the forbidden tree herself (ApMos 19.1-2). Third, there is no need to infer the notion of desire because the word 'desire' (*epithymia*) is explicit in the account, distilling the character and etiology of sin in ways that is similar to what Paul does in Romans (Rom. 7.7). In Eve's words,

> And when he (the serpent) had received the oath from me, he came and entered and placed upon the fruit the poison of his wickedness—*which is (the sense of) desire, for it (desire) is the beginning of every sin*—and he bent the branch on the earth and I took of the fruit and I ate (ApMos 19.3).

Fourth, while deception precedes desire, it is only when Eve has eaten of the fruit that she realizes that her desire was aroused and energized by deception. Hindsight is now 20/20, deception writ large in what the serpent did to her and what she did to Adam. Again, in the words of Eve,

> Then Adam remembered the word which I spoke to him when I wished to deceive him, 'I will make you secure before God'; and he turned and said to me. 'Why have you done this?' And I said, 'The serpent deceived me' (ApMos 23.4-5).

Christian century'. J. Dochhorn (*Die Apokalypse des Mose: Text, Übersetzung, Kommentar* [TSAJ, 106; Tübingen: Mohr Siebeck, 2006], pp. 75-101) acknowledges that dating is difficult but leans toward a First Century CE date.

26. As Dochhorn notes ('Röm 7,7 und das zehnte Gebot', pp. 65-66), the serpent is only the medium for Satan, the actual agent and tempter in the story.

The narrative that is emerging in Romans is in this construct far more than Paul's personal experience even though, as we shall explore separately, the primeval story is to some extent recapitulated in every human being (Rom. 5.12). What we have, as noted already, is not primarily an account of stages in Paul's spiritual journey. Instead, and above all, it is the human story in Genesis that is recounted and, within that story, the *history* of the law. The law is not at this stage explicitly the Ten Commandments, but this distinction is a moot point because the commandment that is the focus in Paul's account is the summary and bridge to everything that follows.[27] J. Louis Martyn does not overstate the case when he says that the law of God has a history.[28] Paul knows what that history is. Echoing Eve, in fact, representing Eve as much as the narrative voice in *The Apocalypse of Moses*, Paul can say that 'if it had not been for the law, I would not have known sin' (Rom. 7.7). This sentence captures the law's existence and the most pivotal event in the law's history.[29] The law was taken captive before she (Eve) was: 'sin, seizing an opportunity in the commandment, deceived me and through it killed me' (7.11).

'Eve' Story: Key Elements		
	Eve story	**Usual view**
Construct	narrative	introspection
Dilemma	character of the divine command	transgression, guilt
Plot	deception	violation
Turning point	distrust and desire	disobedience

> Several statements linking sin to the coming of the commandment or law directly precede Rom. 7.11, the verse containing the clearest echo of the story of Eve's temptation. 'I would not have come to know sin unless through law' (7.7); 'Having taken an opportunity in the commandment, sin worked in me every desire' (7.8a); 'Apart from law, sin is dead' (7.8b); 'After the commandment came, sin came to life' (7.9). These statements all must be understood within the context of Paul's interpretive allusions to Genesis 3, culminating, as they do, in the clear echo of Gen. 3.13 ('Sin, finding opportunity in the law, deceived me').[30]

What happened to the law in this compressed retelling of the law's history? Unlike Galatians, where Paul alludes to the promulgation of the law at

27. Dochhorn ('Röm 7,7 und das zehnte Gebot', pp. 71-72) concludes that when Paul makes the Tenth Commandment represent the law, it is not evidence of a theological fantasy resorting to desperate measures but rather in line with the Hebrew Bible and an exegetical tradition based thereon.

28. Martyn, 'The History of God's Law', pp. 575-87.

29. Thus Krauter ('Eva in Röm 7', p. 15), the commandment was the necessary condition and occasion for the serpent to spring into action in the first place as well as the means by which to achieve his intention. Moreover, as Krauter perceptively notes, 'that the law is (the cause of) sin, is also—in a double sense—a "deception"'.

30. Busch, 'The Figure of Eve in Romans 7.5-25', p. 19.

Sinai, saying that the law 'was ordained through angels by a mediator' (Gal. 3.19),[31] it is the *perception* of the law and not its *origin* that is the focus in Romans. Two verities are in view in Paul's representation. First, as he notes, the commandment God gave 'was for life (*hē entolē hē eis zōēn*)' (Rom. 7.10). That is to say, the commandment had a life-protecting, life-affirming, and life-enhancing intent. How did it turn out to be 'for death for me' (7.10)? Indeed, how did a commandment that 'was for life' get transformed into 'the law of sin and of death (*ho nomos tēs hamartias kai tou thanatou*)' and a veritable instrument for evil (7.10; 8.2)? The answer, focused equally in Genesis, *The Apocalypse of Moses,* and Romans, is *deception.* All three accounts make 'deceive' the crucial verbal element (Gen. 3.13; Rom. 7.11; ApMos 23.4-5). 'For sin, seizing an opportunity in the commandment, *deceived* me and through it killed me', Paul says in Romans (Rom. 7.11). The terminology is distinctive for attributing to *sin* the role that in Genesis is played by the *serpent,* but the difference is less than the words make it appear. Paul compensates for the apparent absence of the serpent by personifying sin.[32] He could therefore have said that 'the *serpent,* seizing an opportunity in the commandment, *deceived* me', which is essentially what Eve says in Genesis (Gen. 3.13). Moreover, the serpent is not absent in Paul's allusive retelling, given that he recapitulates the key steps in Genesis.[33] Surveying the account once more, God gave a commandment that in Paul's retrospective 'was for life': a positive, pro-life commandment (Rom. 7.10; Gen. 2.16-17). Second, sin, *alias* the serpent, seized 'an opportunity in the commandment' (Rom. 7.11), spotting in it a chance to make it to be seen as something other than life-enhancing (Gen. 3.1; Rom. 7.10). Third, deception went to work, and the deception was spectacularly successful: it seized 'an opportunity in the commandment, deceived me and through it killed me', Paul says in first person singular (Rom. 7.11). The serpent poisoned the well, so to speak, putting a spin on the commandment to make it into the exact opposite of what was intended. This is the 'Eve story' in Romans, conveyed by the use of speech-in-character that is strikingly similar to elements in *The Apocalypse of Moses*. Once deception had done its work, the law would no longer be seen as a law that was 'for life'. Instead, it became an agent of, and facilitator for, sin. 'But sin', Paul says, 'seizing an opportunity in the commandment,

31. Martyn (*Galatians*, p. 357) notes that the argument in Galatians has the function of putting distance between God and the law as though the angels ordained the law in God's absence.

32. Dochhorn, 'Röm 7,7 und das zehnte Gebot', pp. 67, 69. 'Sin' resembles 'the serpent'. who, in turn, represents Satan. The parallel between Rom. 7.7-25 and ApMos 15-30 is so striking in content and time of origin as to see both accounts set within a cosmic conflict framework.

33. Thus Dochhorn ('Röm 7,7 und das zehnte Gebot', p. 68), that the account assumes a 'satanologic' or 'demonologic' view of reality.

produced in me all kinds of covetousness' (7.8). '*Seizing opportunity*' is the critical element in the chain reaction, the first move in order to damage the perception of the commandment (7.8, 11).[34]

How was it done, looking back to the original story? In Genesis,

> the Lord God commanded (*ṣāwâ*) the man, 'You may freely eat of every tree of the garden; but of the tree of the knowledge of good and evil you shall not eat, for in the day that you eat of it you shall die' (Gen. 2.16-17).

This is the commandment concerning which the serpent 'seized the opportunity' (Rom. 7.8). A commandment that was at face value 'for life' and a generous ordinance, was represented as an all-out prohibition. 'Did God say', intones the serpent, 'You shall not eat from any tree in the garden'? (Gen. 3.1).

This is certainly as brazen a *mis*-representation of the divine command as can be imagined, and the insinuation will be even more cutting if we add tone of voice. For tone of voice, sarcasm or feigned sincerity will both be effective, but pretend sincerity, well done, would be the hardest to unmask. 'God's words had emphasized freedom', says R.W.L. Moberly,[35] precisely the opposite of the serpent's valuation. A good-will interpretation of the commandment invites readings that include *permission*,[36] *promotion*,[37] and *protection*,[38] the latter in view of the fact that the serpent is itself proof of a hostile reality against which protection was needed. In the Garden they 'are provided for and at the same time protected from danger', says Claus Westermann.[39] A prohibition meant to give protection is not a negative even if it is formulated as though it is taking something away. Indeed, if what God 'takes away' is to circumscribe danger, the protection is good. 'God is good in giving this commandment, for they are free to eat from any tree in the Garden, including the tree of life, with one exception', says Sidney Greidanus.[40] He adds that the prohibition is not meant as a limitation. 'This one prohibition is also good because God treats man as a free moral agent'.[41]

34. Cranfield (*Romans*, p. 350) notes that the meaning of *aformē* is 'starting-point' with a semantic range that includes 'origin', 'occasion', 'pretext', 'base of operations', and 'bridgehead'.

35. Moberly, 'Did the Serpent Get It Right?', p. 6.

36. Walter Brueggemann, *Genesis* (Interpretation; Atlanta: John Knox Press, 1982), p. 46.

37. William N. Wilder, 'Illumination and Investiture: The Royal Significance of the Tree of Wisdom in Genesis 3', *WTJ* 68 (2006), p. 52.

38. Jerome Walsh, 'Genesis 2.4b–3.24: A Synchronic Approach', *JBL* 96 (1977), p. 173.

39. Claus Westermann, *Genesis 1–11* (trans. John J. Scullion; London: SPCK, 1984), p. 239.

40. Sidney Greidanus, 'Preaching Christ from the Narrative of the Fall', *BSac* 161 (2004), p. 266.

41. Greidanus, 'Preaching Christ from the Narrative of the Fall', p. 266.

The serpent's representation of the commandment has a devastating theological bite. What matters here, says Moberly, 'is not that the serpent's words are obviously false, but that they imply that a total prohibition is the sort of unreasonable prohibition that one might expect from God'.[42]

This gets to the heart of the crisis now bearing down on the law and the Lawgiver alike—and on the person coming to see both in a different light. With regard to the commandment, what was 'for life' now looks like a commandment for death! The relationship between the commandment and death, however, does not here arise from the prospect that death will be the *result* of violating the commandment. In the serpent's version, the commandment was not 'for life (*eis zōēn*)' at all; it was a commandment 'for death (*eis thanaton*)' before it had been violated (Rom. 7.10). As seen through the serpent's eyes, the commandment prescribed intolerable terms of existence.[43] A command represented and perceived as an all-out prohibition cannot leave the reputation of the Commander unscathed. In Genesis, the serpent's misrepresentation of the command is thus intended to bring about distrust. The relational avalanche that follows the deception is shattering. Misperception leads to distrust, distrust to alienation, and alienation leads to fear. Phyllis Trible calls it 'a love story gone awry'.[44] When God appears in the Garden 'at the time of the evening breeze', says the narrator in Genesis, 'the man and his wife hid themselves from the presence of the LORD God among the trees of the garden' (Gen. 3.8) 'Where are you?' God calls out (Gen. 3.9). The answer reflects the transformed perception, now bursting at the seams with distance and alienation, 'I heard the sound of you in the garden, and I was afraid...and I hid myself' (Gen. 3.10).

A paraphrase of the story told from the point of view of Eve in the aftermath of the deception, might run like this.

> I once lived happily as though in the absence of law. Honestly, the thought that there was a law did not occur to me. As Paul tells my story, 'once upon a time I lived apart from the law (*chōris nomou*)' (Rom. 7.9). But then the commandment *came*, not in the sense that there had not been any commandment but it came in the sense of raising awareness of its existence and doubts concerning its intent (7.9). The new awareness and the doubts transformed my outlook. Suspicion sprang up where there had been trust. As Paul says on my behalf, 'the sin sprang to life, and I died' (7.10, translation mine). If you wonder how it happened, it was not merely a process in my own head. 'The serpent deceived me, and I ate' (Gen. 3.13, NASB), or, in

42. Moberly, 'Did the Serpent Get It Right?', p. 6.

43. Thus Busch ('The Figure of Eve in Romans 7.5-25', p. 24), 'The serpent suggests that the commandment aims to keep Eve from something she should have, and that therefore she ought not to obey it (a suggestion the serpent makes explicit in 3.4-5)'.

44. Phyllis Trible, *God and the Rhetoric of Sexuality* (OBT; Philadelphia: Fortress Press, 1978), pp. 72-143.

> Paul's compassionate retelling of my story, 'sin, seizing an opportunity in the commandment, deceived me and through it killed me' (Rom. 7.11). In hindsight, I realize that the commandment was pro-life and pro-happiness, but the serpent represented it as a life-denying and restrictive commandment. I lost my respect for the command, and I lost trust in the Commander. You know the rest of my story. I took from the fruit and ate, and I also gave it to my husband with me, and he ate (Gen. 3.6). At that point, my eyes were opened, and I became aware that I was naked (Gen. 3.7). As our existence fell apart, we panicked. The most telling measure of the change was Adam's answer to God later that day, 'I heard the sound of you in the garden, and I was afraid, because I was naked; and I hid myself' (Gen. 3.10).[45]

What opens up in this reading of Romans 7 is quite astounding. Beverly Roberts Gaventa, sensitized to the cosmic power of sin in Romans, calls for a 'widescreen edition' to replace the introspective, individualized emphasis that has dominated readings of this chapter.[46] Her reading recognizes the need for a larger view, 'larger' applying as much to depth as to width. The reality of 'power' and 'combat' set apocalyptic bells ringing, and '[t]his apocalyptic context is...essential for understanding Paul', she says.[47] To this general observation we must add the specific parameters of the 'Eve story' reviewed above. 'Power' and 'combat' are certainly in view, the cosmos now opened up to reveal a hostile, opposing power, but the element that captures the conflict better and more precisely than 'power' and 'combat' is *deception*. This is the key word in Genesis as well as in Romans (Gen. 3.13; Rom. 7.11; cf. ApMos 23.4-5).

Hearing the voice of Eve in Paul's story has the consequence of breaking open the one-dimensional representation of sin in Christian theology, seeing the sinner mostly as culprit and, too, the *sole* culprit. In Paul's account, as in Genesis and *The Apocalypse of Moses*, the 'sinner' is not only a villain. He or she is also a victim. This discovery redefines and expands the redemptive task. As villain, and Paul's opponents take great interest in the villain aspect (Rom. 1.18-32), the sinner risks being seen foremost as a person who deserves punishment (1.32). A victim, on the other hand, is more likely to be seen as a person who needs compassion and help. Paul will not negate human agency and responsibility (7.13-25),[48] but when he traces the reality

45. Dunn (*Romans 1–8*, p. 381) hears a like-sounding story in Romans although he mutes the retelling.

46. Gaventa, 'The Cosmic Power of Sin', pp. 229-40; see also, idem, 'Neither Height nor Depth: Discerning the Cosmology of Romans', *SJT* 64 (2011), pp. 265-78.

47. Gaventa, 'The Cosmic Power of Sin', p. 239.

48. Busch ('The Figure of Eve in Romans 7.5-25', p. 18) notes the tension between activity and passivity in the account, 'activity' meaning human agency and responsibility, 'passivity' referring to a third party that victimizes; cf. also Dochorn, 'Röm 7,7 und das zehnte Gebot', p. 67.

of sin back to its narratival point of origin he stresses deception and powerlessness more. His ultimate depiction of human plight sees a captive crying out for liberation (7.24).

This takes us back to one of J. Louis Martyn's seminal insights. I have already made a note of his claim that *the law of God has a history*.[49] The first pivotal event in the law's history came to pass when the law fell into hostile hands. When Paul speaks of 'the law of sin (*ho nomos tēs hamartias*)' (7.23), as Martyn notes, 'he refers to the Law of God as it has fallen into the hands of Sin'.[50] This law, now in the wrong hands, does not only bring 'the knowledge of sin' in a diagnostic sense (3.20; cf. 4.15; 5.13; 7.7). It also makes sin increase beyond all measure and computation (5.20; 7.5, 8, 23).

In Paul's biography, sin realized its most triumphant scoop when the zealous believer, thinking he was in the line of duty, persecuted believers in Jesus to their death.[51] The sin that comes to light in this perspective is not deception expressing itself in ordinary desire but sin as the 'corruption of *devout* desire'.[52] What remedy is there, Gerald Janzen asks, not for the problem of failing to live up to the highest ideal but for the problem of sinning against the divine author precisely when being hell bent on living up to the will of God?[53] Paul W. Meyer has called this predicament 'the Worm at the Core of the Apple'. The worm, he says, 'is the realization that one has been deceived by a much more sinister power, capable of making the *best* and the most genuine devotion to the one true God produce, as in the case of God's own commandments in the Decalogue, the very thing it is supposed to vanquish'.[54]

If, along lines pursued in the present interpretation, the denunciatory voice that is heard in Rom. 1.18-32 is the voice of teachers that promote circumcision and the remedial powers of the law while also threatening the vile 'other' that is vividly described as fully deserving of the retribution that it sees coming (1.32), this could be an example of what the law is capable of doing when in the hands of sin.[55] In their representation of human plight, there is turning away from God and idolatry for which there is no excuse, sin depicted essentially as violation of the divine command (1.18-20); there is divine wrath (1.18); there are images of sexual desire and excess designed

49. Martyn, 'The History of God's Law', p. 581.

50. Martyn, 'The History of God's Law', p. 581.

51. Acts and the letters of Paul are in complete agreement in their depiction of Paul as a persecutor in the service of God, expressing on his part the wish to be faithful to the law; cf. Gal. 1.13-14, 23; 1 Cor. 15.9; Phil. 3.6; 1 Tit. 1.13; Acts 8.1, 3; 9.1; 22.3-4; 26.9-10.

52. Janzen, 'Sin and the Deception of Devout Desire', pp. 29-61.

53. Janzen, 'Sin and the Deception of Devout Desire', p. 53.

54. Meyer, 'The Worm at the Core of the Apple', p. 74.

55. Cf. Meyer, 'The Worm at the Core of the Apple', p. 74.

to create visceral revulsion (1.24-28); there is the notion of God giving them up and little evidence of compassion (1.24, 26, 28); there is no admission of need on the part of the people represented in the passage or on the part of the people doing the representing (1.18-32); and there is ironclad logic leading from sin to the threat of coming retribution (1.32). In Paul's representation of the human plight in Romans 7, a larger story emerges. Adam and Eve turn away from God because the serpent and sin conspire against them. This representation of sin does not let all the weight fall on human agency, showing instead the human side to be vulnerable to a threat from without (Rom. 7.8, 11; Gen. 3.1). The emphasis is on victimhood and not only on villainy (Rom. 7.7-25); there is admission of need and ownership of the problem on the part of the person represented and the one doing the representing (7.7-24); the overall tenor elicits empathy; and there is ironclad logic, now, however, running from human need to divine right-making and redemption (7.7–8.4).

'So the law is holy, and the commandment is holy and just and good' (7.12). This statement can be seen as a preliminary conclusion to Paul's apology for the law and a forerunner to the law's complete rehabilitation that is yet to come (8.2). The logic of the preliminary conclusion is easily found in the 'Eve story'. According to that story, misrepresentation of the divine command marks a critical moment in the history of the divine command and not only a pivotal event in the human story. For a predicament that sees misrepresentation of God's command as the core problem, cognizant that misrepresentation preceded violation, the solution will have to address more than the problem of violation. Autobiography has not been absent in Paul's account in the sense that his 'I' excludes him (7.7-12), but the self has been partly hidden in the larger 'I' of Eve. In Paul's life story, it was Christ and not the law that created awareness of need (Gal. 1.12-24). Even when the 'I' in Romans 7 inches closer to 'biography' (7.13-25), the problem continues to be framed as captivity, and the message of liberation plays out against the background of Eve's story and not only within a narrowly conceived existential predicament in the life of Paul.[56]

To see the 'Eve story' behind the 'I' in Romans 7 represents a huge shift away from the human-centered, individualistic, and introspective reading that has been usual for this passage. Actually, the 'Eve story' is *extrospective* more than it is introspective. In the emerging widescreen edition, we have a large story along an axis of time and also a vast expansion in spatial terms. There is disruption in the divine-human realm and a rupture in the non-human realm (Gen. 3.10, 14), dislocation in the form of pain and

56. Günther Bornkamm, 'Sin, Law and Death: An Exegetical Study of Romans 7', in *Early Christian Experience* (trans. Paul L. Hammer; New York: Harper and Row, 1969), p. 91.

the prospect of inequality in the human realm (Gen. 3.16), and a curse on the earth suggesting an adversarial relationship between humanity and the earth where before there was harmony (Gen. 3.17-19). This means the the widescreen reading of Romans 7 is ecologically attuned, if at this stage only implicit. More is to come, but my preliminary sounding ensures that Paul's explicit ecological affirmations will not come as an intrusion or a surprise (8.18-23).

Chapter 11

'The Law of the Spirit of Life in Christ Jesus' (Rom. 8.2)

The law receives a clean bill of health in Romans 7 (Rom. 7.12), but the winding path that leads to this conclusion is not a detour. If the first big event in the law's history centers on how it became an instrument of sin (7.8, 11), the second big event is yet to come (8.2). In anticipation of what the second event might be, for now it will suffice to say that Paul is on his way to showing that God has taken action to wrest the law away from its alliance with sin. In the meantime, he has more to say about sin-infested existence that connects Eve's story to present human reality (7.13-25). While Paul's depiction of the divided 'I' makes his exposé a go-to text on anthropology, his overriding aim is to lead the subject down an alley from which there will only be one way out. His 'I' tells the story of sin's origin and current reign but is also 'a performer Paul called out to the stage', the role of whom is to highlight the goodness as well as the impotence of the law.[1]

> Did what is good, then, bring death to me? By no means! It was sin, working death in me through what is good, in order that sin might be shown to be sin, and through the commandment might become sinful beyond measure. For we know that the law is spiritual; but I am of the flesh, sold into slavery under sin. I do not understand my own actions. For I do not do what I want, but I do the very thing I hate. Now if I do what I do not want, I agree that the law is good. But in fact it is no longer I that do it, but sin that dwells within me. For I know that nothing good dwells within me, that is, in my flesh. I can will what is right, but I cannot do it. For I do not do the good I want, but the evil I do not want is what I do. Now if I do what I do not want, it is no longer I that do it, but sin that dwells within me. So I find it to be a law that when I want to do what is good, evil lies close at hand. For I delight in the law of God in my inmost self (*ho esō anthrōpos*), but I see in my members another law at war with the law of my mind (*tō nomō tou noos*), making me captive to the law of sin (*tō nomō tēs hamartias*) that dwells in my members. Wretched man that I am! Who will rescue me from this body of death? Thanks be to God through Jesus Christ our Lord! So then, with my mind I am a slave to the law of God, but with my flesh I am a slave to the law of sin (Rom. 7.13-24).

1. Hae-Kyung Chang, 'The Christian Life in a Dialectical Tension? Romans 7.7-25 Reconsidered', *NovT* 49 (2007), p. 272.

'It was sin' (7.13)

'*It was sin!*' This statement needs to stand alone, and it is wise to pause before proceeding. 'Sin' is in this representation not only something human beings do that they should not or something they do for which they will be called to account. Sin's ontology and narrative are more complex. One import of Paul's exclamation is the suggestion that sin is external to humans, a reality plotting the demise of humanity and all that is good from without. Once again he lets it be known that it is wrong to pin the blame on the law even though he has shown the law to be complicit in sin (7.11). The law is good, and what is good cannot be the cause of death. But sin has made the law its instrument, 'working death in me through what is good' (7.13). This is yet another statement to show that the law in the hands of sin has lost whatever life-enhancing properties it was meant to have. Good is hard to come by in this alliance. If there is a flicker of good, it comes in the form of revelation: 'in order that sin might be shown (*fanē*) to be sin, and through the commandment (*dia tēs entolēs*) might become sinful beyond measure (*kath' hyperbolēn hamartōlos hē hamartia*)' (7.13; cf. 7.11). While it is fine to say that Paul makes sin of all kinds a serious matter, he has thrown the door wide open toward a widescreen representation of sin (7.7-12). In the widescreen edition, sin turns out to be 'sinful beyond measure' by its ability to turn the commandment (*hē entolē*) into the exact opposite of what it was meant to be (7.11, 13). What is essentially a divine provision was represented as a prohibition (Gen. 3.1; Rom. 7.11).[2] 'Beyond measure', moreover, must also be sought in the religious repertoire of sin in present reality. Religion and piety ought to be a safe refuge from sin's inroads. And yet here, too, in Paul's representation, sin refuses to take no for an answer. It shows its colors by what it was able to do to the commandment in the 'Eve story' and by the way it makes the commandment advance the interests of sin even in the religious experience of human beings.

Sin in Multiple Dimensions

- Sin is not only deeds fraught with moral accountability but also a window to human vulnerability.
- Sin's most impressive feat is its knack for turning the good into bad.
- Sin's subversive ability is most clearly perceived at the level of narrative, beginning with the serpent's misrepresentation of the divine command in Genesis.

'For we know that the law is spiritual (*pneumatikos*); but I am of the flesh (*sarkikos*), sold into slavery under sin' (7.14). As Dunn notes, Paul's 'I' now 'broadens out…to that of everyman in the present'.[3] 'Spiritual'

2. This feature of sin's capacity, rarely grasped, is highlighted well by Krauter ('Eva in Röm 7', p. 16).

3. Dunn, *Romans 1–8*, p. 387; cf. Meyer, 'The Worm at the Core of the Apple', p. 64.

(*pneumatikos*) and 'fleshly' (*sarkikos*) are telling contrasts, the former stressing the good material out of which the law is made, the latter pointing to the hopeless material that will surely defeat the law's spiritual aspiration.[4] However, the contrast is not between 'immaterial' and 'material', as though 'spiritual' represents an immaterial entity while 'fleshly' is morally inferior and unpromising because it is materially constituted. Emma Wasserman finds sufficient conceptual and rhetorical overlap between Paul's description of the human plight and Platonic conceptions to make Romans 6–8 an exhibit of 'Paul among the philosophers',[5] but important caveats remain. Paul's conceptions are distinctive in at least five respects. First, he embeds sin in the biblical story, meaning that 'sin' is anchored in narrative rather than in a philosophical conception (Rom. 5.12, 19).[6] Second, Paul's story of sin runs on parallel tracks with the law's history, and his counter-intuitive account of the law as a sin-arousing power is more prominent and far more developed in Romans than in Platonic conceptions. Indeed, whatever sin-stirring properties Plato might attribute to the law have been sought and found because this view of the law looms large in Romans and not because it is a key element in a Platonic framework.[7] Third, Paul's argument does not play out in a vacuum or mainly to fulfill a descriptive errand. The churches in Rome are exposed to an alternative vision of plight that Paul seeks to curtail for pressing theological and pastoral reasons. Fourth, Paul's stress on how sin 'deceived me' (7.11) is so tightly reasoned as to leave it without parallel in the Platonic tradition.[8] The deception that is in view

Cranfield (*Romans*, pp. 344-45) lists seven options for the speaking 'I' in Rom. 7.14-25. (i) Paul's autobiography from the point of view of present experience, (ii) Paul's past experience, (iii) Paul's pre-conversion past seen from the perspective of Christian faith, (iv) the experience of the non-Christian Jew as seen by himself, (v) the experience of the non-Christian Jew, as seen through Christian eyes, (vi) the experience of the Christian who fights the battle in his own strength, (vii) the experience of even mature Christians. He inclines toward (i) and (vii), which are essentially 'Augustinian' readings.

4. Jewett (*Romans*, p. 460) says that as far as he can tell never did Paul or anyone else 'ever connect the word "law" with the adjective "spiritual"'.

5. Emma Wasserman, 'Paul among the Philosophers: The Case of Sin in Romans 6–8', *JSNT* 30 (2008), pp. 387-415.

6. Wasserman's claim ('The Case of Sin in Romans 6–8', p. 405) that Adam's sin 'is not made to be central to Jewish and Christian discussions of the origins of evil until well after Paul's time' must be rejected because (1) Paul makes it prominent in Romans (5.12, 19; 7.7-12); (2) Paul might be more the starting-point of a tradition than a mediator of it; (3) the evidence is more diverse than Wasserman allows.

7. Wasserman ('The Case of Sin in Romans 6–8', p. 408) points to examples of how restraint is seen to inflame passion in Platonic thought, but these concepts are occasional and not central to Platonic conceptions of sin.

8. Martha Nussbaum (*The Therapy of Desire: Theory and Practice in Hellenistic Ethics* [Princeton, NJ: Princeton University Press, 1994], pp. 102-39) shows that

gives sin a non-human, cosmic, and apocalyptic dimension that exceeds Platonic conceptions of how sin deceives, and it comes with the added subtlety that sin also knows how to make what is good serve its end (7.8, 10). Fifth, conceptions concerning the body differ signally and decisively. Paul decries sin. Unlike the Platonists, however, he does not decry materiality.[9]

This does not mean that there is no overlap between Platonic conceptions and the predicament that Paul describes in Romans,[10] and it means even less that such overlap negates the distinctives in Paul's depiction. His portrayal of human plight has resonated across the centuries because it has descriptive verisimilitude. '*That's me*', people say across a broad spectrum of backgrounds when listening to Paul describing the discrepancy between intention and action in the life of his 'I' (7.15-21). '*That's me*', the smoker will say, trying to break the spell of nicotine addiction and sincerely wanting to, and yet finding 'another law' in his or her body that defeats the intention. '*That's me*', I hear the young person suffering from anorexia nervosa say, knowing that he or she should and *must* eat, and yet finding the intention upstaged by a distorted self-image and biological signals that overrule the goal. Indeed, as Beverly Roberts Gaventa shows, '*that's me*' also extends to 'the person of the archetypal "I" who delights in God's Law, producing not simply disobedience but despair'.[11] For this person, too, corroborated by the representation of believers in the Psalms, we recognize voices 'contorted by the inability to do what is desired, an inability produced by Sin'.[12]

'I do not understand my own actions. For I do not do what I want, but I do the very thing I hate', Paul writes (7.15). Readers of many kinds nod knowingly. Even readers who are committed to faith in Christ and faithfulness to God join in, making it difficult for interpreters to tell whether Paul is describing the faith- or the pre-faith-experience, more examples of lived

Epicurean philosophy had an understanding of self-deception and false belief, but Paul's conception is more sharply formulated, and his proposed remedy is of a different order.

9. Hans Dieter Betz, 'The Concept of "Inner Human Being" (ὁ ἔσω ἄνθρωπος) in the Anthropology of Paul', *NTS* 46 (2000), pp. 332-34.

10. Betz ('The Concept of "Inner Human Being"', p. 327) shows how the concept 'inner human being' (*ho esō anthrōpos*) (7.22) carries over into Romans from the Corinthian correspondence (2 Cor. 4.16), finding in 1 Corinthians 'a new level of intense reflection about anthropological problems' (p. 320). He notes that Paul's arguments 'do not consist of simply defending fixed apostolic decrees against opposition' in what is essentially a static stance toward the surrounding environment (p. 320). Instead, the arguments 'show signs of a process of learning and development' (p. 320). If opponents are the negative 'partner' in the process of development and clarification, there is a plus side in the form of discussions with engaged and caring collaborators and interaction with the world.

11. Beverly Roberts Gaventa, 'The Shape of the "I": The Psalter, the Gospel, and the Speaker in Romans 7', in *Apocalyptic Paul*, p. 90.

12. Gaventa, 'The Shape of the "I"', p. 90.

reality included than can be excluded.[13] 'So I find it to be a law that when I want to do what is good, evil lies close at hand', he continues (7.21). Again, readers stand ready to make his admission their own whatever their profession and regardless of whether they are on the same page as Paul's 'I'.[14] It is not an exaggeration to say that Paul in Romans 7 hits an existential nerve. Readers not present or envisioned in the original audience have flocked to the passage for the way it gives voice to their experience even if the experience might differ from what Paul had in mind.

Philosophical conceptions or influence cannot be seen as a threat to the integrity of Paul's exposé. He is not the inventor of the language he uses, and he has already shown Gentile reality to be able to distinguish between what is and what ought to be (2.14-15). Thus, as Wasserman notes, when Paul describes sin, he makes use of metaphor and personification along lines that are similar to Platonic conceptions. Nothing is lost by acknowledging common ground between philosophical depictions of the conflict between reason and passion and Paul's description of the divided self.[15] On the contrary, this could be seen as one area where Paul and the philosophers meet among the people, the feet of both planted in human reality.

Similarities aside, Paul's dissection of the divided self circumscribes and externalizes the sinning self while also internalizing it. Sin is at the same time 'me' and 'not me'. While the division in the self captures the struggle of reason against passion of which most human beings are aware, as noted already, it does not pit a material body against an immaterial soul or matter against immateriality.[16]

> For I do not do what I want, but I do the very thing I hate (7.15).
>
> For I do not do the good I want, but the evil I do not want is what I do (7.19).

The discrepancy between intention and execution is stark in this representation, and it is gloomier still when we include 'the deception of devout desire', that is, the evil committed while meaning to do good.[17] The problem is not just that the good intention fails to translate into action but that the good is subverted by 'the very thing I hate' and by 'the evil I do not want'

13. Gaventa, 'The Shape of the "I"', p. 90.

14. Meyer ('The Worm at the Core of the Apple', pp. 62-84) argues that Paul's 'I' is best understood in an epic sense, where the self functions as a representative for others, and that the distinction between 'godly' and 'ungodly' forces a dichotomy upon the text that is false existentially and historically.

15. Wasserman, 'The Case of Sin in Romans 6-8', p. 403.

16. Thus Dunn (*Romans 1–8*, p. 408), that Paul 'does not...opt for a dualism which understands the "I" as an element of a higher world incarcerated within the lower world of matter'.

17. Janzen, 'Sin and the Deception of Devout Desire', pp. 29-61.

(7.15, 19). Thus, as Jewett notes, the problem in Paul's formulation 'is the objective reversal of good and evil, namely, that the very good one aims to accomplish turns out to be evil in the enactment thereof'.[18] Paul's participation in the stoning of Stephen would be an unsubtle case in point (Acts 8.1), as will be his self-acknowledged zeal (Gal. 1.13-14), and the zeal of his Jewish kin, who show zeal that is 'not enlightened' (Rom. 10.1-3).

> But in fact it is no longer I that do it, but sin that dwells within me (7.17).
>
> Now if I do what I do not want, it is no longer I that do it, but sin that dwells within me (7.20).

Paul repeats himself almost verbatim (7.15, 19; 7.17, 20), as if struggling to come to terms with human experience and how to express it. Sin is an alien resident separate from the self, and yet the self cannot escape responsibility for the resident. 'I delight in the law of God in *my inmost self* (*kata ton esō anthrōpon*)', he says (7.22), but this does not add up to a solution because he has already admitted that 'good does not dwell in me' (7.18, translation mine). 'A kind of cosponsorship of evil is evidently in view, in which human action is at the same time performed by sin as an alien power, so that no evasion of responsibility is possible', Jewett says aptly.[19] Similarly, the self

> watches its own actions and ascribes them to sin, with an 'I, yet not I' agency. The self operates in tandem with a lethal partner, sin, and the partner is stronger. This is a participatory, noncompetitive account of the human self as constituted in relationship to sin, yet not completely conflated with it: the self is still a responsible agent, still the subject of verbs. It also is separated from the results of its actions—the language drives a wedge between what this I wants and what it accomplishes—or rather, indwelling sin accomplishes through it.[20]

Moreover, while Paul's depiction is not strict autobiography, Romans is peerless for its ability to perceive how sin makes what is good serve its end (7.11, 13), and Paul's experience, as noted, proves the point (Gal. 1.13-14, 23; 1 Cor. 15.9; 1 Tim. 1.13). Three things, at least, should be kept in mind when we read this. First, the plight of the divided self in Romans 7

18. Jewett, *Romans*, p. 468.

19. Jewett, *Romans*, p. 462.

20. Susan Eastman, 'Double Participation and the Responsible Self in Romans 5–8', in *Apocalyptic Paul*, p. 101. Marilyn McCord Adams (*Horrendous Evils and the Goodness of God* [Ithaca, NY: Cornell University Press, 1999], p. 191) sketches a similar scenario in her attempt to describe horrendous evil. 'For in my effort to make vivid how bad horrors are, I have stressed their disproportion to human agency—how our power to produce them exceeds our capacity to shoulder responsibility for them; how they prima facie stump our imaginations and stalemate our attempts to defeat or even to balance them off.'

> **Depth Perspective on Human Plight**
> - split self
> - sin as self and non-self
> - predicament of noble intention vs. botched execution

extends to everyday experiences of moral incapacity so as to give Paul's message traction in lived experience. Second, the conflict between competing visions in Romans must not be forgotten. Paul's depiction of human plight is oriented in a different direction than that of his opponents, whose interest is the plight of others more than their own (1.18-32), whose stance is condescending and triumphalist (2.23; 3.27), and whose remedy includes circumcision (2.25-29). Paul's depiction of plight in Romans 7 is oriented toward the self, is devoid of triumphalism, and envisions a different remedy. Third, as Susan Eastman notes, by spelling out the deceptive and lethal power of sin, Paul 'dramatizes the situation of the self...in order to bring home to his Roman auditors, empirically and personally, both that power and the even-greater power of God's deliverance through Christ'.[21]

> Wretched man that I am! Who will rescue me from this body of death? (7.24).

If we pause again for a moment to read this exclamation in the context of Romans as a whole, we have come a long way from the indictment of sinful Gentiles that starts off the letter body (1.18-32).[22] The 'wretched man' in the initial indictment has little in common with Paul's 'I'; he or she in that representation is another person and on the whole a crassly constructed 'other'. In form, there is movement from the third person plural in Rom. 1.18-32 to the first person singular in Rom. 7.7-25, the 'they'-address in the former adapted to the denunciatory tone of the indictment while the 'I'-form in Romans 7 takes human plight closer to home. In content, the shift in pronouns is accompanied by corresponding movement from the awful things 'they' do (1.18-32) to the dreadful plight of what 'I' am (7.7-25). How do these representations of human sin stand in relation to each other? Are they depictions of the same reality, described from different angles? Are they mostly complementary and compatible? Or are they, as seems increasingly likely, competing and contrasting representations in the moving picture that is Romans? Is it now possible to introduce neglected but much-needed nuance to the storied readings of Romans 7 and to the letter as a whole? The 'wretched Gentiles' have in the course of the letter vanished into the background to give way to the 'wretched I' in Romans 7. The vision of wrath and retribution in the initial indictment (1.18-32), wrath and retribution pronounced and proclaimed from without, has yielded the spotlight to a larger

21. Eastman, 'Double Participation and the Responsible Self in Romans 5–8', p. 100.
22. Gaventa ('The Shape of the "I"', pp. 88-90) seems aware of the different and possibly conflicting representations but does not spell out the implications.

and very different representation of human plight, the latter representation arising from the 'Eve story' and from the self-disclosure of Paul's earnest 'I'. Where wrath and retribution loom large in the initial indictment, conveyed in diction that alternates between thunderous and shrill (1.18-32), the 'I' in Romans 7 reads less as an indictment than as a self-aware plea for help.[23] If we should at all be prepared to see these representations as contrasting visions and approaches to human reality, the prospect that the contrasting visions also reflect competing missions will not be far behind. In short, in a bird's eye view of the letter, the indictment in Rom. 1.18-32 can now more confidently be assigned to the counter-missionaries that appear from time to time in the letter, and Rom. 7.7-25 is Paul's take on human plight, the story of the split and sinking 'I' over against pious outrage over the godlessness and depravity of 'they'.

	Representation of plight in Romans 1.18-32	**Representation of plight in Romans 7.7-25**
Perspective	Human and societal	Cosmic and personal
Theological problem	Idolatry	Misrepresentation and misperception of God
View of human condition	Recalcitrant Depraved Sexually inflamed Villain Wretched 'they'	Needy Helpless 'Desire' left unspecified Victim Wretched 'I'
Apocalyptic tenor	Apparent	Real
Biblical narrative	Shallow or absent	Profound and crucial
Perceived divine stance	Wrath	Compassion
Perceived divine response	Giving up Retributive	Right-making Remedial

'Who will rescue me from this body of death?' No one can do justice to Paul's exclamation without hearing tone of voice, and tone requires that the text be read aloud. The emotional tenor has been building along with increasingly charged imagery of war and imprisonment, the self in the end held as a 'prisoner of the law of sin' (7.23). The 'I'-form and the tenor of self-disclosure have been possible because Paul assumes a friendly audience, and it has also elicited buy-in and participation on their part. By now Paul's 'wretched man' is every person, all feeling the predicament of death-in-life reality and ready to make the exclamation their own. A performed

23. While tone of voice has to be imagined, it is impossible to do 'thunderous' or 'shrill' for the depiction in Rom. 7.7-25.

text, therefore, and Romans asks to be performed, at this point swells into the collective outcry, 'Who will rescue me from this body of death?' (7.24)

Jewett hears the cry well. 'The rhetorical question about who can deliver such a miserable person is posed in such a way as to require the answer, "Nobody can!"'[24]

The Law of the Spirit of Life in Christ Jesus

The thought that Paul ends his excruciating exposé of the division in the human self by conferring permanence on the split and then celebrating it, cannot be embraced without qualification. 'Thanks be to God through Jesus Christ our Lord!' he exclaims. 'So then, with my mind I am a slave to the law of God (*tō nomō theou*), but with my flesh I am a slave to the law of sin (*nomō hamartias*)' (Rom. 7.25). There is certainly celebration in this statement, but what is he celebrating? The statement confirms the split, in anthropological terms a contrast between 'mind' (*nous*) and 'flesh' (*sarx*), but we cannot ignore the two elements that cling tenaciously to 'mind' and 'flesh'. One is 'law' in a genitival construct, either as 'the law of God (*ho nomos theou*)' or as 'the law of sin (*ho nomos hamartias*)'. Given that 'a major use of the genitive case is simply to indicate possession', as Martyn notes,[25] who is in possession of the law? We have, on the one hand, the law in God's possession or in the hands of God, and, on the other hand, the law in the hands of sin. 'Law' alone is not precise enough to capture the dynamic of these conceptions. We also have to pay attention to the one or the 'what' in whose hands the law is found.

Just as the law belongs on both sides of the contrast, so does 'slavery'. 'I serve as a *slave*' either 'the law in the hands of God' or 'the law in the hands of sin', no other option offered (7.25). 'Mind' and 'flesh', representing the split in the self in anthropological terms, are captive to realities that intensify the split. Paul's representation suggests that the split and the warring parties on either side have fought to a stalemate. Why, then, the celebration?

Paul has already given an answer (6.17-18), and he will shortly elaborate (8.1-4). His earlier answer, also given in the context of the death-in-life predicament, acknowledges the split but not the stalemate.[26] 'But thanks be to

24. Jewett, *Romans*, pp. 471-72.

25. Martyn, '*Nomos* Plus Genitive Noun in Paul', p. 581.

26. We are now in the textual territory that led Martin Luther to coin the expression *simul justus et peccator*, 'simultaneously righteous and sinner'. Luther's foremost substrate is Romans, but Paul's letter does not conform to the stringent legal framework that Luther imposed on it nor to his demand that Scripture be constituted strictly as either 'law' or 'gospel'. Moreover, as noted by Stendahl and others, Paul's spiritual biography differs from Luther's. Nevertheless, even if we take exception to elements in Luther's exposition of Romans, his contribution remains hugely important, and his representation

God that you, having once been slaves of sin, have become obedient from the heart to the form of teaching to which you were entrusted, and that you, having been set free from sin, have become slaves of righteousness' (6.17-18). In this text, too, the split is evident, but the two sides of the split are not in permanent deadlock. If the forward movement in his representation ('you were once' vs. 'you have become') has not done away with the split, it has opened the door to let one prevail over the other and to allow the good side to have the upper hand. Paul now returns to this representation, to celebration, and to a stunning reversal in the history of the law.

> There is therefore now no condemnation (*katakrima*) for those who are in Christ Jesus. For the law of the Spirit of life in Christ Jesus (*ho nomos tou pneumatos tēs zoēs en Christō Iēsou*) has set you free from the law of sin and of death (*tou nomou tēs hamartias kai tou thanatou*). For God has done what the law, weakened by the flesh (*dia tēs sarkos*), could not do: by sending his own Son in the likeness of sinful flesh (*en homoiōmai sarkos hamartias*), and to deal with sin (*kai peri hamartias*), he condemned (*katekrinen*) sin in the flesh, so that the just requirement of the law (*to dikaiōma tou nomou*) might be fulfilled in us, who walk not according to the flesh but according to the Spirit (Rom. 8.1-4).

Cranfield finds the transition from the description of the split self (7.7-25) to what now follows (8.1-4) awkward, proposing to ameliorate the awkwardness by linking the first verses in Romans 8 to the earlier statement about 'being discharged from the law' (7.6).[27] Dunn is also perplexed by the transition, saying that 'Paul most likely intended a pause between 7.25 and 8.1, an indication of the flow of thought easily signaled both in dictation and in reading the letter to the Roman congregations; once again we must recall that the letter was written more to be *heard* than read'.[28] A pause in the reading is well advised but not because Paul interrupts the train of thought or reverts to an earlier point in the argument. Once we acknowledge that Paul works from a widescreen representation of sin that includes the most important event in the law's history and, too, that he aims to bring resolution to the death-in-life predicament, there is not the slightest hitch in the argument.

The announcement that there is now 'no condemnation (*katakrima*) for those who are in Christ Jesus' (8.1) means, as Jewett notes, that '[t]he era of condemnation and doom is over'.[29] The notion of a new era is also a theme in Galatians (Gal. 1.4). 'No condemnation' implies not only that the believer's legal prospects in the judgment have improved. In the context

of human experience is compelling on its own terms; cf. Eduard Lohse, 'Martin Luther und der Römerbrief des Apostels Paulus—Biblische Entdeckungen', *KD* 52 (2006), pp. 106-25.

27. Cranfield, *Romans*, p. 373.
28. Dunn, *Romans 1–8*, p. 415.
29. Jewett, *Romans*, pp. 479-80.

of the death-in-life predicament, 'no condemnation' also means that there is relief from the unrelenting *sense of doom* and hopelessness of the split self.[30] Paul's depiction of the human plight has reference not only to the past or to the future but also to present reality. Given that he has just taken the predicament of the split self in the hands of the law to its most severe expression (7.24), his presentation of the resolution follows hot on its heels.

'For the law of the Spirit of life in Christ Jesus (*ho nomos tou pneumatos tēs zoēs en Christō Iēsou*) has set you free from the law of sin and of death (*tou nomou tēs hamartias kai tou thanatou*)' (8.2). Why does Paul say 'the law of the Spirit of life in Christ Jesus' and not simply the 'Spirit of life in Christ Jesus'? Why must he include the law? The convoluted phrases in the sentence are initially perplexing.[31] They cease to baffle, however, when we hear it in the widescreen edition. Once we step back to see the context, the appearance of redundancy is not redundancy at all.[32] The history of the law must be included in the larger version. Paul is describing the second critical event in the history of the law, that is, Christ's reclamation and liberation of the law to make it again 'the law of the Spirit of life'. When we let the genitive constructs denote simple possession, we read in this verse that 'the law in the hands of the Spirit of life in Christ Jesus has set you free from the law in the hands of (the) sin and (the) death' (8.2, translation mine). Unexpected luster restored to the law! In Martyn's words, 'Paul coins that expression in order to speak of the Law as it has been taken in hand by Christ, thus being delivered from its lethal alliance with Sin and made pertinent to the church's daily life'.[33]

> The Law of God—the Torah—has a history; and there are in that history two decisive events, its falling under the power of Sin, so that it leads to death, and its being taken in hand by the Spirit in Christ, so that it leads to life. Thinking of both of these events, and especially the second, Paul can even allow the word *nomos* to be the subject of the verb *ēleutherōsen* ('has liberated'), thus qualifying his denial in Gal. 3.21 that there has ever been a Law that has the power to make alive. In short, the restorative effect of Christ on the Law is so profound as to cause that restored Law—*ho nomos tou pneumatos tēs zōēs en Christō Iēsou*—to be God's appointed means for liberating the human race from the Law in the hands of Sin and Death.[34]

30. Jewett (*Romans*, pp. 479-80) notes that 'sense of doom' belongs to the semantic range of *katakrima*.

31. Jewett (*Romans*, p. 481) calls it a 'lumbering phrase'.

32. Dunn (*Romans 1–8*, p. 417) is puzzled by the fact that *nomos* is the subject of the sentence, thinking that this has a rhetorical and not a substantive reason. Cranfield (*Romans*, p. 376) is also thrown off by the role Paul assigns to the law, preferring instead to emphasize the Holy Spirit.

33. Martyn, '*Nomos* Plus Genitive Noun in Paul', p. 583.

34. Martyn, '*Nomos* Plus Genitive Noun in Paul', pp. 583-84. I have transliterated the Greek words in Martyn's essay.

What is now coming to light in Paul's dramatic widescreen story? The law that fell into the hands of sin and death makes a spectacular comeback! For this to be seen clearly, however, requires a wide canvas. According to the 'Eve story' that Paul has reviewed (7.7-12), sin sought and found an opening. The command that was 'for life' was misrepresented to become a commandment of death (7.10, 11). Locating the devil in the detail, sin's primary makeup and *modus operandi* is *deception* with respect to the divine command and not simply *violation* of the command. Only when deception had worked the command over did Eve proceed to violate it (Gen. 3.1, 6). This is what happened to the command in the hands of sin, and now to the command in the hands of the Spirit of life in Christ Jesus: the deception has been unmasked. When the accent falls on *revelation*, the pieces move into place. God revealed in Jesus is a giving God (Rom. 5.8; 8.32), and the law taken in hand by Jesus returns the law to the column of life in the divine economy of abundance (8.2).

There is more to commend this reading because Paul elaborates that 'God has done what the law, weakened by the flesh, could not do: by sending his own Son in the likeness of sinful flesh (*en homoiōmai sarkos hamartias*), and to deal with sin (*kai peri hamartias*), he condemned sin in the flesh' (8.3). This is yet another packed sentence,[35] the law again in the picture, described as weakened and sickly because of human incapacity.[36] God took action 'by sending his own Son', the ontological status of the son that of a pre-existent, heavenly being already designated as 'the Son of God' (cf. 1.3-4). 'In the likeness of sinful flesh' opens the door to many interpretative temptations,[37] but the term is best seen as a return to the 'Adam story' he has told earlier: 'just as sin came into the world through one man' (5.12), the new 'one man' has come to undo the damage as a full participant in the human condition (5.18). Moreover, God sent his own son 'concerning (the matter) of sin' (*kai peri hamartias*), or, as in the NRSV, 'to deal

'The Law of the Spirit of Life in Christ Jesus'

- A strange, convoluted phrase!
- Critical events in the history of the law:
  1. The Law falling into the hands of sin.
  2. The Law wrested from the hands of sin and restored to become the Law of the Spirit of Life in the hands of Christ Jesus.

35. Commentators blame it for awkwardness and 'lack of syntactical coherence'; cf. Jewett, *Romans*, p. 482.

36. Jonathan F. Bayes ('The Translation of Romans 8.3', *ExpTim* 111 [1999], pp. 14-16) captures this aspect well in his proposed translation, 'for this being the law's disability while it used to be weak in the sphere of the flesh'.

37. Whether the phrase denotes total identity or similarity without complete identity has been subject to debate; cf. Florence Morgan Gillman, 'Another Look at Romans 8:3: "In the Likeness of Sinful Flesh"', *CBQ* 49 (1987), pp. 597-604.

with sin'. Jewett calls this an 'oddly appended phrase',[38] but it is not odd or redundant in widescreen. Cranfield notes that the context does not support the sacrificial interpretation that is often invoked, arguing instead that the phrase conveys the Son's mission.[39] Again, therefore, Jesus will deal with sin not only as violation of the command but also as deception and misrepresentation of the command. The phrase should be read within its narratival framework rather than as a dogmatic concept. As narrative, it includes God *sending* his son (8.3), the son born of a woman (Gal. 4.4), and coming as a liberator in the likeness of sinful flesh (Rom. 8.3). He comes in order to 'deal with sin' fully and comprehensively, whether sin as *deception, violation,* or *consequence.* The idea that Jesus 'condemned sin in the flesh' puts fresh demands on the imagination, but it must include notions of unmasking, repudiation, and banishment. Jesus relegates sin to oblivion. The novelty in the widescreen, narratival conception, or rather, the neglected element, is the cosmic aspect within which sin 'exercised dominion' by means of deception, power, and death (5.14, 17, 21). Paul's depiction of what 'the one man' did to bring death, contrasting it with what 'the one man' did to take death away (5.15), recounts contrasting narratives by means of allusions.

Just as Paul assumes knowledge of the 'Adam story' on the part of his Roman audience, he also assumes knowledge of 'the one who was to come' (5.14) and of his accomplishments. Albert Schweitzer's assertion that Paul's letters lack an underlying narrative is misguided and should be dismissed,[40] given that the letters abound with narrative assumptions. It is not far-fetched to assume that Paul and his Roman audience, who know the 'Adam story' well, also have excellent command of the Christ story, including the temptation narratives in the Synoptic Gospels in its depiction of what Christ did in order to 'deal with sin' (Mk 1.11-13; Mt. 4.1-12; Lk. 4.1-12). Moreover, before Paul says that God sent his son 'to deal with sin' (Rom. 8.3), he has already flashed the most riveting image in the 'Christ story' on the screen. Christ 'was handed over (*paredothē*) for our trespasses and was raised to set us right (*dia tēn dikaiōsin*)' (4.25, translation mine). This is the zenith of the story in the widescreen edition, and the zenith, too, of sin: Christ handed over into the hands of the powers.[41]

All this happened, says Paul, 'so that the just requirement of the law (*to dikaiōma tou nomou*) might be fulfilled in us, who walk not according to the

38. Jewett, *Romans*, p. 484.

39. Cranfield, *Romans*, p. 382.

40. Schweitzer, *The Mysticism of Paul the Apostle*, p. 173.

41. Although Gaventa ('The Cosmic Power of Sin', p. 235) sees the contrast between God 'handing over' idolatrous Gentiles to lives of sexual profligacy (1.24, 26, 28) and God 'handing over Jesus' as contrasts playing out within the teachings of Paul, the contrast is telling and will be even greater if the former 'handing over' refers to what happens in the representation of Paul's opponents.

flesh but according to the Spirit' (8.4). Given that death-in-life and not only death has been the immediate antecedent in Paul's line of thought (7.13-25), there is now light at the end of the tunnel. The believer is 'set right' comprehensively and experientially and not only according to a legal conception. In the light of Romans as a whole, Jewett sees the resolution in terms of 'the fatherly will of God for his children', and he points out that 'Paul speaks not of our fulfilling the just requirements of the law, but of its being fulfilled in us'.[42] To get to this point, Paul has drawn on elements that include *revelation*, *participation*, and *justification*. If one of these terms should be preferred above the others, it must be the one that captures the misrepresentation that is sin's bait at the point of origin (7.8, 11; Gen. 3.1) and the image that best represents the result of God's right-making at the point of destination (Rom. 8.15). This comes down to the aspect in Paul's story that has been most overlooked: *revelation*.

In order to do justice to the scenario that appears at the 'point of destination' in Paul's widescreen story, I will move to fast forward. Suffice it to say that Paul's recognition of the split in the human self must be seen as a call to live on the hopeful side of the split: it is not a concession to stalemate and status quo. Against opponents' charge that his script makes it acceptable to continue in sin (3.8; 6.1, 15), Paul has said the exact opposite (6.2, 15). Above all, he has laid out his case by drilling the furrow of human plight deeper than his opponents, by representing human reality in different terms, and by a solution that is distinctive from what his opponents have in mind. In the home stretch of this argument, the pastoral yearning dominates more than theological exposition.

> For those who live according to the flesh set their minds on the things of the flesh, but those who live according to the Spirit set their minds on the things of the Spirit. To set the mind on the flesh is death, but to set the mind on the Spirit is life and peace. For this reason the mind that is set on the flesh is hostile to God; it does not submit to God's law— indeed it cannot, and those who are in the flesh cannot please God. But you are not in the flesh; you are in the Spirit, since the Spirit of God dwells in you. Anyone who does not have the Spirit of Christ does not belong to him. But if Christ is in you, though the body is dead because of sin, the Spirit is life because of righteousness. If the Spirit of him who raised Jesus from the dead dwells in you, he who raised Christ from the dead will give life to your mortal bodies also through his Spirit that dwells in you (Rom. 8.5-11).

Paul does not forget or ignore the split, but we have already seen that he envisions and prescribes more than a stalemate (6.1-23; 8.1-4). The split self has a corollary in different spheres of living, Paul urging the Romans to live on the Spirit side and 'set their minds on the things of the Spirit' (8.5).

42. Jewett, *Romans*, p. 485.

The prescription in Romans unfolds along the exact same lines as in Galatians, not as an opposition between law and sin or sin and righteousness, but as opposition between flesh and the Spirit (Gal. 5.16-17).[43] This is a crucial point because Paul's prescription is not of the kind that crowds the self-help shelves. As Martyn notes in the Galatian context,

> Sin remains a genuine *power* that must be opposed. Its potent opposite, however, is not the Law, but rather the Spirit of the crucified (Gal. 5.16). Indeed, the Spirit of Christ has invaded the realm of Sin in order to commence the war of liberation by calling into its army of freedom fighters precisely those who belong to Christ (Gal. 5.22–6.2). Here is the army whose rations consist of the fruit borne by the Spirit—love, joy, peace, patience, kindness, generosity, faith, gentleness, self-control—and here alone is the battle in which *Non nobis* ('not us') can be truly sung.[44]

One scene still remains in the telling of the story, this scene again bringing into view the close parallels between Galatians and Romans, and, in my view, representing the view from the top of the mountain in Paul's theology.

> So then, brothers and sisters, we are debtors, not to the flesh, to live according to the flesh—for if you live according to the flesh, you will die; but if by the Spirit you put to death the deeds of the body, you will live. For all who are led by the Spirit of God are children of God. For you did not receive a spirit of slavery to fall back into fear, but you have received a spirit of adoption. When we cry, 'Abba! Father!' it is that very Spirit bearing witness with our spirit that we are children of God (Rom. 8.12-16).

Albert Schweitzer designated Paul as 'the patron saint of thought',[45] but he was keenly aware of the 'mystical' aspect in Paul's experience and message. In this passage (8.12-16) thought and experience go hand in hand. The connection between the cry 'Abba! Father!' and baptism is more explicit in Galatians than in Romans (Gal. 3.27-4.6), but baptism is only slightly off center in Romans and just as integral to Paul's line of thought (Rom. 6.3-14). In short, there is convincing evidence that the cry 'Abba! Father!' was central to, if not limited to, the baptismal experience.[46] The parallels between Galatians and Romans on this point represent common ground between believers in Asia Minor who had come to faith through the ministry of Paul and believers in Rome who did not trace their conversion to him. In both cases, Paul could make use of the baptismal memory, drawing

43. John M.G. Barclay, *Obeying the Truth: A Study of Paul's Ethics in Galatians* (Edinburgh: T. & T. Clark, 2005), p. 110.

44. Martyn, 'Apocalyptic Gospel', p. 259.

45. Schweitzer, *Mysticism of Paul*, p. 377.

46. Robinson, 'The One Baptism', pp. 262-63; T.M. Taylor, '"Abba, Father" and Baptism', *SJT* 11 (1958), p. 70; Obeng, 'Abba, Father', pp. 364-65; Betz, *Galatians*, p. 210; Martyn, *Galatians*, p. 391.

a vivid and expressive argument from the mouths of the people he sought to convince. The use of the baptismal memory in Romans makes it a fitting conclusion to the widescreen narrative of sin and redemption. In the 'Eve story' featured earlier in the argument, sin deceptively turned the divine command to its advantage (7.8, 11). The woman, now deceived, 'took of [the] fruit and ate; and she also gave some to her husband, who was with her, and he ate' (Gen. 3.6). In the aftermath, when 'they heard the sound of the LORD God walking in the garden…the man and his wife hid themselves from the presence of the LORD God among the trees in the garden' (Gen. 3.8). With the divine-human relationship now in tatters, the sparse narrative draws a picture drenched in alienation. 'I heard the sound of you in the garden, and I was afraid (*efobēthēn*)' (Gen. 3.10).

Paul's composite retelling gathers up images used previously: of slavery (to sin),[47] of adoption (Abraham),[48] and of fear (of the divine presence) and now the removal of fear,[49] the reversal dealing squarely with the fear-factor. 'For you did not receive a spirit of slavery *to fall back into fear* (*eis fobon*), but you have received a spirit of adoption', Paul writes (Rom. 8.15). 'Abba! Father!' follows, itself a multi-layered exclamation carrying untapped revisionary potential.[50] There is in this image trust, understanding, and emotion, all owing to the revelation of God in Jesus and now brought home to believers through the agency of the Spirit. Nothing in Romans captures more poignantly the reversal of what happened when sin sneaked in to deceive at

47. Rom. 7.14.

48. Gal. 3.29; 4.5, the context and flow of argument similar to Romans.

49. Gen. 3.8, 10.

50. See Tonstad, 'The Revisionary Potential of "Abba! Father!"', pp. 5-18. As to layers, the expression combines allusions to the prayer of Jesus in Gethsemane (Mk 14.36) and to the story of the binding of Isaac in Genesis (Gen. 22.7-8). As to facets, the expression is Spirit-generated, revelatory ('apocalyptic'), participatory and exclamatory, simple and intelligible, and squarely theo-centric. Dunn (*Romans 1–8*, p. 453) considers it likely that 'we cry out' (8.15) intimates an intense, loud cry.

Ground Zero in the story, and nothing proves more definitively that the believers have been *un*-deceived (8.15-16; cf. 7.8, 11). 'Abba! Father!' is the quintessential expression of homecoming.

When we hear this cry against the background of Paul's widescreen representation, we understand better why he turns to give voice to non-human creation (8.19-22), and why we hear non-human creation, believers, and the Spirit speaking the same language of hope (8.22, 23, 26).

Chapter 12

'The Whole Creation Groans' (Rom. 8.22)

Paul surprises readers of Romans when he, as even seasoned interpreters read the letter, suddenly and without apparent warning turns the pulpit over to nature. Not only does he let non-human creation speak as subject in the text. He adds urgency and weight to the voice by depicting what nature says as the cry of a woman in labor (Rom. 8.22), thereby harnessing the strength of a loud voice and the prestige of a powerful Old Testament image.[1] The figure is arresting by any standard because labor pain is excruciating to a degree that most men will never experience anything like it. Conrad Gempf breaks down the pain associated with labor into helpful categories by describing it as (1) 'intense and total pain'; (2) 'helpless pain'; (3) 'productive pain', and (4) 'pain that must run its course'.[2] In Paul's usage there is a preference for 'productive' or 'hopeful' pain (8.19, 20, 21), but the horizon of hope will not mute the reality and intensity of the pain. A startling sight appears in this passage, and a sound is heard that will not be ignored (8.18-23).

> I consider that the sufferings of this present time are not worth comparing with the glory about to be revealed to us (*apokalypthēnai eis hēmas*). For the creation (*ktisis*) waits with eager longing for the revealing (*tēn apokalypsin*) of the children of God (*tōn huiōn tou theou*); for the creation (*hē ktisis*) was subjected to futility (*mataiotēti*), not of its own will but by the will of the one who subjected it, in hope that the creation (*hē ktisis*) itself will be set free from its bondage to decay and will obtain the freedom of the glory of the children of God. We know that the whole creation (*pasa hē ktisis*) has been groaning in labor pains (*systenazei kai synōdinei*) until now; and not only the creation, but we ourselves, who have the first fruits of the Spirit, groan (*stenazomen*) inwardly while we wait for adoption, the redemption of our bodies (Rom. 8.18-23).

1. Isa. 13.4-8; 26.17-18; 42.13-14; 66.6-9; Jer. 4.31; 30.6; 48.41; Mic. 4.10; 5.3-4; Ps. 48.4; cf. New Testament examples in 1 Thess. 5.3; Mk 13.8; Jn 16.21; Rev. 12.2.
2. Conrad Gempf, 'The Imagery of Birth Pangs in the New Testament', *TynB* 45 (1994), pp. 119-35.

Twice in these verses groans are heard, the first the groaning of non-human creation as though coming from a woman in labor (8.22), and then, as though speaking the same language and expressing it the same way, 'we ourselves...groan inwardly' (8.23). At this point in our exposition the sound—and the noise level—will be the cause for attention. Groans are heard, even loud and uncontrollable groans. These sounds expand and amplify the loud exclamations heard in the immediate antecedent to the passage (8.15).

> For you did not receive a spirit of slavery to fall back into fear, but you have received a spirit of adoption. When we cry (*krazomen*), 'Abba! Father!' it is that very Spirit bearing witness with our spirit that we are children of God, and if children, then heirs, heirs of God and joint heirs with Christ—if, in fact, we suffer with him so that we may also be glorified with him (Rom. 8.15-17).

The NRSV may have broken up the passage in the wrong place, focusing on the Spirit behind the exclamation more than on the exclamation itself, but the 'loud cry' will be preserved either way. Attention shifts from the loud cry of the believers (8.15) to the groans of the whole creation (8.22), then back to the believers (8.23), who groan as much as they cry out (8.15), these two 'groups' joined by the Spirit (8.26). The Spirit is decisively on the side of the groaners with a voice that does nothing to hush the intensity because the Spirit joins in with '*inexpressible* groans' (8.26). An ontological threesome are therefore in view, non-human reality (8.22), human reality (8.23), and divine reality (8.26), all three on the same page and all expressing themselves in the verbal currency of groaning.

Making Noise in Romans

- Creation groans (8.22)
- We groan (8.23)
- The Spirit groans (8.26)

> the whole creation groans together (*systenazei*) (8.22).
>
> we ourselves...groan (*stenazomen*) (8.23).
>
> [the] Spirit intercedes with inexpressible groans (*stenagmois alalētois*) (8.26).

A 'noise analysis' of this passage has rarely been attempted, perhaps with Jacob Taubes as the exception. He hears the believing congregation at prayer in the text. 'You must imagine prayer as something other than the singing in the Christian church; instead there is screaming, groaning, and the heavens are stormy when people pray. These are descriptions, these are experiences... This is how Paul experiences the praying congregation.'[3] If we pursue the noise analysis a step further,

3. Taubes, *The Political Theology of Paul*, pp. 72-73.

two movements will be notable. First, there is inwardness and its outward expression, the inward reality a blend of suffering and hope and the outward expression in all spheres captured as 'groaning'. 'Groaning', in turn, is able to work both ends of the field as the authentic language of suffering and as the language of hope. That is to say, when hope lets show its deepest longing, it comes to expression as groaning. Second, however, when the groaning texts are heard in context (8.18-26), the context now including what immediately precedes it (8.15-17) as well as what immediately follows (8.31-39), the auditory image is overwhelming. Noting that we are hearing exclamations at high decibel already at the point of entry (8.15), the noise does not let up when joined by the groans of a woman in labor pain (8.22). The pitch will cover the whole range of the scale, from highest to lowest and back. The symphonic complexity is immense because music that is played in major key (8.15, 31-39) blends with musical scores played in minor key (8.22, 23, 26)—but not in the sense that all things are equal. Hope is an element of music played in minor key, too (8.22, 23, 26), and hope takes full command of the musical score played in major key (8.15, 31-39). Exclamation at the point of entry (8.15), reinforced by the triumphant and exclamatory character of the closing movements (8.31-39), means that the major key and the hope to which it bears witness dominate the auditory image without silencing other voices. If we in this composition hear sounds expressing suffering and plight (8.18, 22, 23), hope (8.19-21), and assurance (8.15-17; 31-39), the dominant score is assurance.

Why, then, the surprise on the part of interpreters that Paul brings non-human creation on stage? Why the impression that it seems to happen out of order and context? And why the apparent need to mute or minimize the impact? John Bolt writes that the passage 'is at risk of becoming little more than a mantra for Christian environmentalism',[4] ostensibly on the logic that it is a rarity that, in view of its rarity, creates the risk of over-use and over-interpretation. Others, seeking to be measured and circumspect, more than hint that 'ecologically-minded interpreters' find in the text what is not there or at least more than the text should be asked to carry.[5] Yet others mute the impact of the passage with parsimonious praise, Brendan Byrne worrying that too much is asked of a small passage and claiming that 'Paul would

4. John Bolt, 'The Relation between Creation and Redemption in Romans 8:18-27', *CTJ* 30 (1995), p. 34.

5. Cherryl Hunt, David G. Horrell, and Christopher Southgate, 'An Environmental Mantra? Ecological Interest in Romans 8.19-23 and a Modest Proposal for Its Narrative Interpretation', *JTS* 58 (2008), pp. 546-47; see also David G. Horrell, Cherryl Hunt and Christopher Southgate, *Greening Paul: Rereading the Apostle in a Time of Ecological Crisis* (Waco, TX: Baylor University Press, 2010), pp. 63-85.

doubtless be startled to discover all that has been wrung out of the tortured sentences and mysterious allusions in this text'.[6]

The compositional features reviewed above and the 'noise analysis' that goes with it contradict the minimalist tendency of these sentiments. What we have, first, are resounding affirmations of a kind that are possible only when the person who leads the way has reason to be confident that his message is clearly understood. A message that is barely intelligible cannot rise to the level of a resounding exclamation. Byrne says that Paul's reference to the hope and the plight of nature is unique, perhaps the first and 'only time in his extant letters Paul considers human beings in relation to the non-human created world'.[7] While this may be true for the letters in quantitative terms, the letters are only a window to Paul's ministry as a whole, and there are clues within the letters as to whether Paul is breaking new ground. In this passage, the blending of voices from the human (8.15, 23), the non-human (8.22), and the divine realm (8.26) suggests much more than an *ad hoc* composition. This is one instance where it is advisable to see Pauline theology as a co-operative and communal enterprise, Paul developing 'his theology in conversation with his collaborators, before he formulated his written statements'.[8] This opens up the possibility that to Paul and his friends in Rome, the appearance of non-human creation in the midst of plight and hope was neither an intrusion nor a novelty, and the compositional features reviewed above confirm as much. Over-use and over-interpretation are not the problem. Byrne is to the point when he admits that interpreters in the traditional paradigm 'were engaged in a virtually exclusive preoccupation with relations between human beings and God'.[9]

Allusions to the Old Testament abound in Romans,[10] key components of this foundation made up of 'Israel's sacred texts'.[11] This part of the letter, too, rests on a narrative foundation. Moreover, Paul is harnessing 'a widespread knowledge and use of Jewish apocalyptic traditions within the earliest Christian congregations', as Dunn notes.[12] Nature's voice is not alien to the apocalyptic perception and witness. These elements are evident in

6. Brendan Byrne, 'An Ecological Reading of Rom. 8.19-22: Possibilities and Hesitations', in *Ecological Hermeneutics: Biblical, Historical and Theological Perspectives* (ed. David G. Horrell, Cherryl Hunt, Christopher Southgate and Francesca Stravrakopoulou; London: T. & T. Clark, 2010), p. 83.

7. Brendan J. Byrne, *Reckoning with Romans: A Contemporary Reading of Paul's Gospel* (GNS, 18; Wilmington, DE: Michael Glazier, 1986), p. 165.

8. Betz, 'The Concept of "Inner Human Being"', p. 320.

9. Byrne, 'Creation Groaning', p. 194.

10. Hays, *The Faith of Jesus Christ*, pp. 33-117.

11. Hays, *Echoes of Scripture*, p. 34.

12. Dunn, *Romans 1–8*, p. 410.

the widescreen representation that has been developed in the wider context of the passage (5.12-21; 7.7-12), and the apocalyptic tenor will not be missed in the language of groaning—especially when an apocalyptic reality is explicit in the passage (8.18, 19). Given that two key passages in Romans are part of the groundwork Paul has laid before he allows non-human creation to speak (5.12-21; 7.7-12), it is unthinkable that the influence of the Genesis story of the fall has worn off by the time non-human creation gets to say what is on its mind. It is equally implausible that we cannot know precisely what Paul had in mind when he talks about creation's subjection to futility.[13] While most interpreters hear the allusions to Genesis very well even without the help of the 'Eve story' that we have explored earlier (7.7-12),[14] there is no other viable candidate than Genesis for the starting point of creation's plight or even one that is thinkable.[15]

Verse by Verse

> For the creation (*hē ktisis*) waits with eager longing for the revealing of the children of God (*tēn apokalypsin tōn huiōn tou theou*) (Rom. 8.19).

'The creation (*hē ktisis*)' in this sentence has been subjected to careful scrutiny. Do we really hear *non-human* creation speaking? Can we be sure that Paul enlists the help of non-human creation in a theological and eco-theological cause? Our answer can be unequivocal, as it now mostly is among interpreters: the speaking voice belongs to non-human creation.[16] Of the possible meanings of *ktisis* in the passage, says Edward Adams 'only non-human creation is possible in 8.19-22'.[17]

13. Hunt, 'An Environmental Mantra?', p. 562.

14. Cranfield, *Romans*, p. 413; Dunn, *Romans 1–8*, p. 470; Joseph A. Fitzmyer, *Romans: A New Translation with Introduction and Commentary* (AB; London: Geoffrey Chapman, 1993), p. 505; Grieb, *The Story of Romans*, p. 80; Adams, 'Paul's Story of God and Creation', pp. 28-29.

15. Thus Edward Adams (*Constructing the World: A Study of Paul's Cosmological Language* [Edinburgh: T. & T. Clark, 2000], p. 178) that the curse of Gen. 3.17-19 'is of course in view'. Cf. also Harry Alan Hahne, *The Corruption and Redemption of Creation: Nature in Romans 8.19-22 and Jewish Apocalyptic Literature* (LNTS; London and New York: T. & T. Clark, 2006), pp. 171-93.

16. Cranfield (*Romans*, p. 411), after surveying eight alternatives, concludes that '[t]he only interpretation of κτίσις in these verses which is really probable seems to be that which understands the reference to be the sum-total of sub-human nature, both animate and inanimate'. See also Dunn, *Romans 1–8*, p. 470; Jewett, *Romans*, p. 511; Bolt, 'The Relation between Creation and Redemption', p. 39; Jonathan Moo, 'Romans 8.19-22 and Isaiah's Cosmic Covenant', *NTS* 54 (2008), p. 75.

17. Adams, *Constructing the World*, p. 176.

Indeed, raising the prestige of non-human creation even higher, Richard Bauckham notes that non-human creation is the speaking voice and subject throughout.

> Creation is the subject of all the important verbs in verses 19-22: the creation waits with eager longing, was subjected to futility, will be set free, has been groaning, has been in travail. God seems to be behind the scenes, concealed by the two divine passives ('was subjected' [v. 20], 'will be set free' [v. 21]) and the cryptic anonymity of 'the one who subjected' (v. 20). God's action is certainly decisive in the story, but Paul keeps God in the background perhaps because he wishes to focus on the solidarity of the other two characters. For just as creation waits, so do believers; just as creation is to be set free, so will believers; just as creation groans, so do believers.[18]

On the whole, non-human creation is subject, not object, speaking as a sentient being that is capable of experiencing suffering and expressing hope. The personification is not a residue of animism but a way to raise the standing of non-human creation. Moreover, eyeing greater precision, Cherryl Hunt, David G. Horrell, and Christopher Southgate suggest that 'Paul has primarily in mind non-human *living* things, rather than the inanimate features of the creation'.[19] Convergence, common interest, and even a shared language of groaning create a strong bond of reciprocity between human and non-human reality, the latter not simply tagging along as a passive partner. On the contrary, as Laurie Braaten notes, in a telling sense non-human creation is leading the way. 'The groaning of the children of God', he says, 'is likened to the groaning of creation, and not the other way around, as the reader might expect'.[20]

'All Creation Groans' Vocabulary

- *ktisis* refers to non-human creation and especially to *living* non-human creation
- *groans* suffering and hope *both* expressed in the form of groaning
- *hope* anchored in promise and not only in need

The wording that 'non-human creation waits with eager longing' (8.19, translation mine) smoothens out a compact genitival phrase, 'the eager longing of the non-human creation (*hē apokaradokia tēs ktiseōs*)'. 'Eager longing' is also the import of the verb in the sentence, thus 'the eager longing of the non-human creation waits with eager longing (*apekdechetai*)'.

18. Richard Bauckham, 'The Story of the Earth According to Paul: Romans 8.18-23', *RevExp* 108 (2011), p. 93.

19. Hunt, 'An Environmental Mantra?', p. 558 (italics added). This seems more plausible than Jewett's generic reference to 'nonhuman components' (*Romans*, p. 511).

20. Laurie Braaten, 'All Creation Groans: Romans 8.22 in Light of the Biblical Sources', *HBT* 28 (2006), pp. 131-32.

The 'eager longing' of the phrase is reinforced along a temporal axis later in the passage when Paul says that 'the whole non-human creation has been groaning...*until now* (*achri tou nun*)' (8.22, translation mine). Temporality is an important feature of apocalyptic conceptions in the form of imminence and intensity. 'Groaning...*until now*' and 'eager longing' speak of a hope that has been burnished by a very long wait. If '*until now*' denotes the point on the axis of time that equals the 'now' of Paul and the Roman believers, where shall we locate the critical point at the other end of the timeline, and what shall we call it? We need not settle this question yet, but we are advised to prepare for it. '*Until now*' at the terminal end corresponds to '*from when*' at the opposite end. 'From when' brings to view how long the entire non-human creation has been groaning (8.22) and how long there has been 'eager longing' (8.19), the eagerness of non-human creation now intensified by the prospect that the end is in sight.

In a more general venue, the expectation and longing that are in view cannot be based on a felt need only. It is crucial to catch the nuance of 'the longing (*hē apokaradokia*)' and to see it not as 'eager *longing*' only but more as 'confident expectation'. Here, too, there is common ground between the hope that applies in the human realm and the hope of non-human creation, given that Paul uses the same word in Philippians (Phil. 1.20), clearly with the connotation 'confident expectation'.[21] Need, even a deeply felt need, cannot itself create expectation and certainly not 'confident expectation'. Promises, however, create expectations, and a promise that is in the process of fulfillment leads to increased confidence. Both elements are in view in the passage.

I made a note above that the groaning of non-human creation in Romans precedes the groaning taking place in the human realm (8.22, 23).[22] The sequence might be incidental, but there is a similar sequence in the creation account in Genesis: blessing in the non-human realm *precedes* and *patterns* the blessing in the human domain (Gen. 1.22, 28). While humanity receives a blessing and a commission to flourish on the *sixth* day of creation (Gen. 1.28), the blessing conferred on humanity is worded almost identically to the blessing that is pronounced on the birds and the creatures of the sea on the *fifth* day (Gen. 1.22). Of the three explicit blessings in the Genesis account, the human mandate on the sixth day and the blessing of the seventh day attract attention (Gen 1.28; 2.1-3), but the equally weighty and similarly worded blessing on non-human creation is rarely noted (Gen. 1.22). Genesis shows that there is a purpose for nature and non-human creatures that is not marginal in the story. Non-human beings, as Fretheim notes,

21. Jewett, *Romans*, p. 511. Hahne (*The Corruption and Redemption of Creation*, p. 182) notes that the word is 'always associated with the idea of eschatological hope'.

22. Braaten, 'All Creation Groans', pp. 131-32.

receive a 'word of empowerment',[23] and the spectacular scenes of creation correspond eloquently to what Westermann calls 'a silent advance of the power of life in all realms'.[24]

'The eager longing' of non-human creation, therefore, has a blessing and a promise stored in the memory bank. Longing is secured at the point of origin in the divine blessing so as to turn the longing into expectation, and the expectation is upheld by the conviction that God has not rescinded the blessing. The paradigm of divine faithfulness that applies to the entire message of Romans is now seen to extend to non-human creation, as well.

Expectation based on promise also has a prophetic anchoring point. When Isaiah gets the upper hand among the Old Testament voices in the closing part of Romans, Paul writes that 'Isaiah says', and then invokes the passage in Isaiah where an all-inclusive hope for human beings meets with the most expansive vision of what awaits non-human creation in the entire Old Testament. 'The root of Jesse shall come, the one who rises to rule the Gentiles; in him the Gentiles shall hope', says Paul (Rom. 15.12; cf. Isa. 11.1, 10). By then, as we have seen, he has already sketched a horizon of hope that makes hope in the non-human realm arise from the same cloth as human hope (Rom. 8.19-23). Allusive networks are by nature elusive, but it is well established that Paul enlists the Old Testament in general and Isaiah in particular in support of his message.[25]

> The wolf shall live with the lamb, the leopard shall lie down with the kid, the calf and the lion and the fatling together, and a little child shall lead them. The cow and the bear shall graze, their young shall lie down together; and the lion shall eat straw like the ox. The nursing child shall play over the hole of the asp, and the weaned child shall put its hand on the adder's den. They will not hurt or destroy on all my holy mountain; for the earth will be full of the knowledge of the LORD as the waters cover the sea (Isa. 11.6-9).

What counts at this point is that Romans has non-human creation speaking the same language of hope as human creation (Rom. 8.18-23), empowered by specific and explicit visions and promises to non-human creation in the Old Testament (Gen. 1.22; Isa. 11.6-9; 65.25).[26] No passage in the

23. Fretheim, *God and the World in the Old Testament*, p. 50.

24. Westermann, 'Creation and History in the Old Testament', p. 30.

25. Hays, *Echoes of Scripture*, pp. 35, 53; J. Ross Wagner, 'The Heralds of Isaiah and the Mission of Paul', in *Jesus and the Suffering Servant: Isaiah 53 and Christian Origins* (ed. W.H. Bellinger and W.R. Farmer; Harrisburg, PA: Trinity Press International, 1998), pp. 193-222. See also Evans and Sanders (eds.), *The Gospels and the Scriptures of Israel*.

26. Isaiah 65.25 repeats the vision of ecotopia in Isa. 11.6-9 but with the twist that one creature is excluded from the harmony: 'but the serpent—its food shall be dust!' The allusion to Genesis strengthens the impression that for Isaiah as a whole the 'root of Jesse' comes on a mission of *revelation*, the goal of which is *restoration* (Isa. 11.1-10).

Old Testament kindles hope in the non-human realm more than Isaiah's depiction of what will happen when the root of Jesse comes.

What non-human creation waits for, now in a posture of 'confident expectation', is 'the apocalypse of the children of God (*tēn apokalypsin tōn huiōn tou theou*)' (Rom. 8.19). Expectation does not run in a straight line directly to God but by way of '*the children of God*'.

'The children of God' have been in view earlier, Paul writing that 'as many as are led by the Spirit of God these are the children of God (*houtoi huioi theou eisin*)' (8.14). Being possessed by the Spirit is the critical element that moves a person from a state of slavery into a state of son- and daughter-ship (8.1-15). In order to become 'the children of God', therefore, the enslaved person must be liberated (8.14-16). Liberation, however, is precisely what non-human creation is longing to experience (8.19), its plight specifically described as '*slavery* to decay' (8.21). This does not openly set up a sequence that leads from the liberation of human beings to the liberation of non-human creatures *by way of* liberated human beings, but there is a suggestion to that effect.

Given that 'the children of God' are in the line of waiting and to some extent the reason for it, in what sense must non-human creation wait *for them to be revealed*? (8.19). Is there ambiguity as to what it means to be 'children of God', the criteria needing to be established or discovered? Are the criteria known, but 'the children of God' have still not come into existence, that is, the liberation has not begun in earnest? Have they come into existence, but they are not yet manifested and therefore not *revealed*? Does the 'not yet' that is implied have something to do with God's plan to bring in Jews and Gentiles into one family? Should we understand the eager waiting on the part of non-human creation as though non-human creation pins its hope on 'the children of God' for its liberation?

Considered answers have been offered to most of these questions. Dunn imagines a scenario within which the children of God 'will take part in that final curtain call, and that the audience's eagerness is to see who these are and what is this transformation they have undergone'.[27] In this scenario, revelation operates chiefly by bringing a hidden but existing reality to the light.[28] Cranfield sees a similar dynamic at work, sonship in the realm of faith at last 'made manifest in their true glory, a public and open proclamation of their adoption'.[29] While the mindset of non-human creation is not fully expressed

The pointed mention of the serpent, singling it out for exclusion, suggests that the prophet is informed by the same narrative canvas as Paul in Romans.

27. Dunn, *Romans 1–8*, p. 470.

28. Thus also Hahne, *The Corruption and Redemption of Creation*, pp. 183-84.

29. C.E.B. Cranfield, 'Some Observations on Romans 8:19-21', in *Reconciliation and Hope: New Testament Essays on Atonement and Eschatology Presented to L.L. Morris* (ed. Robert Banks; Grand Rapids: Eerdmans, 1974), p. 226.

in these sentiments, they invite further thought as to what it might be. Cranfield notes that Paul refers to the eager longing of non-human creation 'as support for the statement made in v. 18'.[30] In this verse Paul compares present suffering in the human realm to future glory. 'I consider that our present sufferings are not worth comparing with the glory that will be revealed in us' (Rom. 8.18, NIV). He backs this up by adding, in a motivating and explanatory sense, how non-human creation 'waits in eager expectation for the sons of God to be revealed' (8.19, NIV). This suggests that non-human creation is not in a state of eager expectation for its own sake only. What comes into view is *selfless* expectation. The body language shows non-human creation craning the neck to get a better look at what is coming (8.19), like 'spectators straining forward over the ropes to catch the first glimpse of some triumphal pageant'.[31] The imagery suggests that non-human creation takes a redemptive interest in human plight, eager to see *human* suffering give way to relief and future glory (8.18, 19). This means that non-human creation expresses solidarity with human plight. Like spectators in the stands, non-human creation stands at-the-ready to encourage suffering believers not to give up.

Jewett, by contrast, focuses squarely on the benefit that awaits non-human creation upon 'the revelation of the children of God'.

> Paul implies that the entire creation waits with baited breath for the emergence and empowerment of those who will take responsibility for its restoration… As the children of God are redeemed by the gospel, they begin to regain a rightful dominion over the created world (Gen. 1.28-30; Ps. 8.5-8); in more modern terms, their altered lifestyle and revised ethics begin to restore the ecological system that had been thrown out of balance by wrongdoing (1.18-32) and sin (Rom. 5–7). In contrast to the civic cult, Paul does not have a magical transformation of nature in view.[32]

This takes the revelation into the realm of practicality, 'the children of God' the designated agent that will bring relief to non-human creation.

Susan Eastman seeks out clues in Romans to the effect that non-human creation must be kept in a state of waiting until the full number of Jews and Gentiles are brought in.[33] The revelation of 'the children of God' runs on parallel tracks with the revelation of 'the righteousness of God' (Rom. 8.19; 1.17; 3.21), and the full revelation 'consists of the salvation of "all Israel" together with the "full number" of the Gentiles (11.25-26)'.[34] In contrast to

30. Cranfield, *Romans*, p. 410.

31. William Sanday and Arthur C. Headlam, *A Critial and Exegetical Commentary on the Epistle to the Romans* (Edinburgh: T. & T. Clark, 5th edn, 1992), pp. 204-205.

32. Jewett, *Romans*, pp. 512-13. The statement should say that the creation waits 'with bated breath' rather than 'baited breath'.

33. Susan Eastman, 'Whose Apocalypse? The Identity of the Sons of God in Romans 8.19', *JBL* 121 (2002), pp. 263-77.

34. Eastman, 'The Identity of the Sons of God in Romans 8.19', p. 277.

Dunn's suggestion above, she envisions a movement 'not from a "hidden" to a "revealed status", but from partial to full redemption, to the salvation of "all who believe" as promised in 1.16'.[35] If 'the righteousness of God' is virtually synonymous with 'the faithfulness of God' along the lines we have explored earlier, God's right-making enterprise includes an ambitious and still unfinished mission. The wide net that Eastman casts with respect to the identity of 'the children of God' does not explore directly the consequences to non-human creation but its logic is the logic of inclusion and completion. God's right-making includes Gentiles *and* Jews, and it also encompasses the non-human realm.

When Jewett emphasizes that the responsibility and obligation of 'the children of God' begin in the present, he has not misread Paul, but after two thousand years of 'Christian' impact it may seem odd to think that 'the entire creation waits with bated breath for the emergence and empowerment of those who will take responsibility for its restoration'.[36] Any caveat in this regard does not mean that non-human creation should cease to have expectations as to what 'the children of God' will do to bring relief, but this view of 'the children of God' is wishful and one-sided. To believe that the forces of exploitation and oppression will at last be tamed by the action of 'the children of God' in the sense that 'their altered lifestyle and revised ethics begin to restore the ecological system'[37] seems to overestimate their impact whether in light of biblical or historical evidence. On this point it is more prudent to say that if non-human creation persists in a state of hope, the apocalyptic intervention cannot depend entirely on mediation through human channels. Marie Turner has shown that the faith in view is resurrection faith,[38] resurrection requiring direct divine agency.

> for the creation (*hē ktisis*) was subjected (*hypetagē*) to futility (*mataiotēti*), not of its own will but by the will of the one who subjected (*hypotaxanta*) it, in hope (*ef' elpidi*) (Rom. 8.20).

Non-human creation is still the subject of the verb, but the verb is in the passive voice. If we revert the verb into the active voice, an acting subject will emerge that is not non-human creation. Moreover, the acting subject that is veiled in the passive voice may now declare itself. Just as Paul locates the origin of problems in the human realm to Adam and Eve's encounter

35. Eastman, 'The Identity of the Sons of God in Romans 8.19', p. 277.

36. Robert Jewett, 'The Corruption and Redemption of Creation', in *Paul and the Roman Imperial Order* (ed. Richard A. Horsley; New York: Trinity Press, 2004), p. 35.

37. Jewett, 'The Corruption and Redemption of Creation', p. 35.

38. Marie Turner, 'God's Design: The Death of Creation? An Ecojustice Reading of Romans 8.18-30 in the Light of Wisdom 1–2', in *The Earth Story in Wisdom Traditions* (ed. Norman C. Habel and Shirley Wurst; Sheffield: Sheffield Academic Press, 2001), pp. 168-78.

with the serpent in Genesis (Rom. 5.12-21; 7.7-12; Gen. 3.1-6), plight in the non-human realm can be traced to the same point of origin.

> And to the man he said, 'Because you have listened to the voice of your wife, and have eaten of the tree about which I commanded you, 'You shall not eat of it', cursed is the ground because of you; in toil you shall eat of it all the days of your life; thorns and thistles it shall bring forth for you; and you shall eat the plants of the field' (Gen. 3.17-18).

Whether in Genesis or in Romans, nature and non-human are passively in the line of traffic. Non-human creation is not at fault for the altered state. Paul does not use the word 'cursed', but he says that non-human creation 'was subjected to futility' (Rom. 8.20), and he infers that a specific event is in view. Cranfield speaks for the scholarly consensus when he says that 'Paul had in mind the judgment related in Gen. 3.17-19'.[39] As to who did what when non-human creation fell victim to futility, there is wide agreement that the passive voice 'veils a reference to God'.[40] As we shall see in a moment, there is real risk of over-projecting and simplifying the notion of divine agency in the Genesis story, but the 'futility' that Paul finds in the non-human realm points to the disruption that Genesis graphically depicts as 'toil', 'thorns', and 'thistles' (Rom. 8.20; Gen. 3.17-19). What has previously been whole and harmonious is now fractured and adversarial.

Old Testament scholars do better work on the text in Genesis than what many New Testament exegetes take away from it. Nahum Sarna says of the 'curse' that

> the punishment is related to the offense. The sin of eating forbidden food results in complicating the production of goods. The man himself is not cursed, only the soil. The matter from which he sprang turns against him. His pristine harmony with nature is disturbed by his transgression. This notion of moral ecology is a major biblical theme; it is explicitly formulated in Lev. 18.24-28 and 20.22, and it underlies the great exhortations of Leviticus 26 and Deuteronomy 28.[41]

'Moral ecology' is a wonderfully descriptive term for a very old subject and proof that theology and eco-theology are linked at the base in the Bible. Eugene Combs has put the Genesis 'curse' in perspective by placing it in the broader context of ever worsening representations of the divine command, on the one hand, and by simplistic depictions of divine agency, on the other.[42]

39. Cranfield, *Romans*, p. 413.

40. Cranfield, *Romans*, p. 413. So also Jewett (*Romans*, p. 513), that 'the divine passive, ὑπετάγη ('was subjected'), points to God's action in response to Adam's fall'. Adams (*Constructing the World*, p. 178) is even more emphatic, saying that 'God is obviously the implied agent of the passive *hypetagē*'.

41. Sarna, *Genesis*, p. 28.

42. Eugene Combs, 'Has God Cursed the Ground? Perplexity of Interpretation in

'Curse' vs. 'Futility'

- Note the voices within and without the Bible that make 'curse' a key word in ever-worsening depictions of God's benevolence.
- 'Moral ecology' is a category of interdependence and not an element of divine retribution.

This is more than a distant analogy to the situation in Romans where, as we saw in the 'Eve story' (Rom. 7.7-12), misrepresentation and misperception of the divine command set the ball rolling. Combs shows that the serpent's interpretation attributes severity to God 'where none is intended'.[43] Worsening depictions of God's benevolence follow in the story of Cain, and it climaxes in Lamech's allegation that God actively 'cursed the ground' (Gen. 5.29). Neither Cain nor Lamech should be trusted in their depictions of God's character. Sin's accelerating momentum in the biblical narrative parallels interpreters' tendency to see increasing severity and divine agency at work. With respect to the original 'curse', significant caveats are therefore in order.

> The verb (curse), in the form of a *Qal* passive participle, serves as a noun which denotes a condition brought about by an external agent, which in this case is not stated or which is at the very least ambiguous. The text, strictly speaking, does not support an interpretation that Yhwh Elohim has cursed the serpent; the text rather suggests that Yhwh Elohim observes that the serpent is in a condition of cursedness by virtue of its action.[44]

While it is true that the passive voice may veil or anonymize the acting subject in a sentence and that many 'passives' in the Bible are 'divine passives', this cannot be the rule wherever God and a verb in the passive voice occur in close proximity to each other. Some passives are not meant to have God as the acting subject; they are passives for reasons that apply to the situation they describe and not for the purpose of hiding or defining agency. Combs' view of the curses in Genesis are examples of the latter use of the passive voice. So, when 'the ground is cursed because of you' (Gen. 3.17), human agency is primary with respect to the disruption, and God's role is descriptive and confirmatory, but the verb centers on what happens to the earth more than on agency. 'As in the case of the serpent's cursedness the text does not support saying that Yhwh Elohim has cursed the ground (Gen. 3.17)', says Combs. 'The passive participle form of the verb denotes that the ground is in a condition of cursedness which may be the consequence of the man's action, not necessarily Yhwh Elohim's punishment'.[45]

Genesis 1–5', in *Ascribe to the Lord: Biblical and Other Studies in Memory of Peter C. Craigie* (ed. Lyle Eslinger and Glen Taylor; JSOTSup; Sheffield: Sheffield Academic, 1988), pp. 265-87.

43. Combs, 'Has God Cursed the Ground?', p. 268.
44. Combs, 'Has God Cursed the Ground?', p. 276.
45. Combs, 'Has God Cursed the Ground?', p. 276.

By way of summary, the disruption 'results from man's actions, not from Yhwh Elohim's punishment... Yhwh Elohim does not impose the curse, strictly speaking; rather, He recognizes and states a condition that has come to be. Yhwh Elohim is not strictly speaking the agent of the cursing.'[46] Again, as the thread that tracks the downward spiral in Genesis in the form of ever worse representations of God's command, interpretations of these texts tend to be dragged along.[47] Paul's allusion to Genesis is in that regard circumspect: there is disruption but no curse. Divine confirmation is in view when non-human creation gets subjected to futility, but the divine disposition cannot help itself. It does not speak the language of curse but of hope (Rom. 8.20).[48]

Being 'subjected to futility' (8.20), in turn, comes with the weight of the Greek word *mataiotēs*, a word that carries the distant drumbeat of Ecclesiastes, the 'vanity of vanities' that the wisdom seeker pronounced on human existence (Eccl. 1.2-14).[49] The *Good News Bible* says that 'creation was condemned to lose its purpose' (Rom. 8.20).[50] On the terms explored above, it would be better to say that non-human creation 'was *consigned* to lose its purpose', and it was likewise *resigned* to the unenviable state that came to exist 'not of its own will'. A sense of purposelessness and flailing pervades Ecclesiastes, now carrying over into Paul's depiction of non-human reality. That Genesis and Ecclesiastes appear in the same sentence in Romans is no coincidence because the source of the preacher's dismay and despair in Ecclesiastes is precisely death's dominion 'from Adam to Moses' and beyond (cf. Rom. 5.12-14).[51]

46. Combs, 'Has God Cursed the Ground?', pp. 278, 285. K.A. Mathews (*Genesis 1-11:26* [Nashville: Broadman & Holman, 1996], p. 252), likewise, says that human sin is the cause of the 'curse'.

47. Combs, 'Has God Cursed the Ground?', p. 286. Hahne's notion (*The Corruption and Redemption of Creation*, p. 188) that the curse 'was God's judicial response to Adam's sin' is an example of interpretations caught in the undertow of increasingly severe representations of the divine action.

48. Dunn (*Romans 1–8*, p. 470) notes a jumbled sentence: 'The phrasing is awkward and suggests a dictation where Paul's thought became slightly tangled but where he decided to press on'.

49. Sanday and Headlam, *Romans*, p. 205.

50. Byrne, *Romans*, p. 260; Jewett, *Romans*, p. 513. Michel (*Der Brief an die Römer*, p. 267) sees Paul referring to 'the transitoriness, the emptiness, and the nothingness, perhaps also the perversion and the disorder of the world'. See also Steve Moyise, 'Intertextuality and the Study of the Old Testament in the New Testament', in *The Old Testament in the New Testament: Essays in Honour of J.L North* (ed. Steve Moyise; JSNTSup, 189; Sheffield: Sheffield Academic, 2000), p. 20.

51. William H.U. Anderson, 'The Curse of Work in Qoheleth: An Exposé of Genesis 3.17-19 in Ecclesiastes', *EQ* 70 (1998), pp. 90-113.

Genesis:	you shall eat bread until you return to the ground, for out of it you were taken; you are dust, and to dust you shall return (3.19)
Ecclesiastes:	All came from the dust and all return to the dust (3.20) the dust will return to the earth as it was (12.7).

'Dust to dust' clouds the human prospect in Genesis and is the reason for Qohelet's pronouncement of vanity and hopelessness. Romans, however, makes this scenario apply to non-human reality, interjecting hope in the place of hopelessness (Rom. 8.20). Death itself now looms as the main reason why non-human creation, too, lives with 'the frustration of not being able properly to fulfill the purpose of its existence'.[52]

The somewhat strained sentence that ends on the note of hope[53] now proceeds to spell out what the hope is and to whom it applies. Paul explains

> that the creation itself (*autē hē ktisis*) will be set free from its bondage to decay (*tēs douleias tēs fthoras*) and will obtain the freedom of the glory of the children of God (*eis eleutherian tēs doxes tēs tōn teknōn tou theou*) (Rom. 8.21).

As to what or who is included, the subject is still and without a doubt 'non-human creation *itself* (*autē hē ktisis*)' (8.21). Hope consists in being freed from 'slavery to dissolution'. Paul puts to use a term that refers precisely to 'breakdown of organic matter...in the world of nature'.[54] His gospel is opposed to death in the human realm. He has invested heavily in making this clear by describing the alliance between sin and death as the root of the problem of existence (5.12-14), by making the death of Jesus the measure of the love of God and the solution to the problem of death (5.6-9), and by claiming for the latter that it represents a hope that 'does not disappoint', that is, a hope that does not put the one who hopes to shame (5.5). The many allusions to Genesis in this part of Romans show an underlying and coherent narrative foundation, here reinforced by a pointed allusion to Ecclesiastes (8.20).

Now the time has come to read hope for the non-human realm off the same page. Just as Paul does not like death in the human realm and, elsewhere, declares death to be 'the last enemy' (1 Cor. 15.26; cf. also vv. 54-57), he makes death in the non-human realm to be a problem, too. Here, he unequivocally holds before non-human creation the prospect of freedom from death (8.21).[55] 'Freedom', in turn, is a key word in his depiction: non-

52. Cranfield, 'Some Observations on Romans 8.19-21', p. 227.

53. Dunn, *Romans 1–8*, p. 470.

54. *Shorter Lexicon of the Greek New Testament* (ed. F. Wilbur Gingrich and Frederick William Danker; Chicago: University of Chicago Press, 1965), art. φθορά.

55. Hahne (*The Corruption and Redemption of Creation*, p. 196) points out the

human creation 'will be *set free...into the freedom*'. Human and non-human reality are walking in step because the freedom that is in view is no less than 'the freedom of the glory of the children of God' (8.21). Moreover, in both realms 'freedom' stands in opposition to 'slavery' so as to make *liberation* the most telling term for what God has set out to do for human and non-human reality alike (8.21; cf. 6.18, 22; 8.2).

The warm, emotive tenor is striking, reflective of a person who is emotionally attuned to his subject matter, and the composition is not lacking in thought. The judicious reflection is yet again suggestive of a perspective that is a collaborative effort and not a curious thought experiment by someone who is at his best when he gets to work solo and alone.[56] A shared outlook becomes explicit when Paul gets to the point in his argument that is at once the most evocative in an emotional sense, the loudest in an auditory sense, and the most sweeping and inclusive in a philosophical and historical sense.

> We know (*oidamen*) that the whole creation (*pasa hē ktisis*) has been groaning in labor pains until now (*achri tou nun*) (Rom. 8.22).

'*We* know', with the emphasis on 'we', ensures for Paul's argument that it has a prior history, that is to say, Paul is not introducing a perspective that is new to his fellow believers. Shared attunement to the plight of non-human creation, however, is not simply the consequence of a natural insight held in common by all decent human beings. Paul speaks on the basis of a revealed, apocalyptic insight, eyes and ears having been opened by prior revelation and now by the Spirit.[57] These verses, says Cranfield, 'are certainly not to be understood as merely an inference from the observable and generally recognized fact of the prevalence of suffering in nature'.[58]

All the verbs in the sentence have either the force of the present active indicative (*oida*) or are in the present tense (*systenazei* and *synōdinei*). A suitable translation is therefore, 'we know that the entire non-human creation groans together and suffers agony together (in labor pains) until now' (8.22, translation mine). The present tense conveys present reality through verbs that make it *urgent* present reality, but the sentence as a whole displays non-human suffering along a very long timeline: 'non-human creation...suffers agony together *until now*'. This brings us back to the origin and end point of the timeline, 'from when' at one end and 'until now' at

connection between 'the eschatological redemption of the material world' and 'the final glorification of believers'.

56. Cf. Betz, 'The Concept of 'Inner Human Being', p. 320.

57. Michel, *Der Brief an die Römer*, p. 269; Moo, 'Romans 8.19-22 and Isaiah's Cosmic Covenant', p. 82.

58. Cranfield, *Romans*, p. 410.

the terminal end. Non-human suffering is depicted as a wall-to-wall reality because the point of origin must be located at the very beginning of the biblical narrative in Genesis, and the long duration of suffering intensifies the thrust of the 'groaning' verbs in the present tense. Otto Michel highlights the eschatological tenor of the verse, a situation of need rising to the level of the most extreme magnitude in the present.[59]

While 'the entire non-human creation' depicts a single entity by means of a noun in the singular, the term is inclusive and all-encompassing. Many voices are coming to expression; indeed, every single voice in the non-human realm groans. The verbs have the prefix *sys-* that conveys coordinated voices crying out in unison. Braaten points out that the verb 'to groan' (*stenazō*) and its cognates often occur in mourning contexts in the Old Testament.[60] He highlights two specific aspects of mourning in the Old Testament that add depth and perspective to the text in Romans. First, the mourning is intensified and made worse if 'no one joins in mourning, or worse yet, if others ridicule the mourner's plight'.[61] For the mourner, then, the mourning gets worse if no one cares. Conversely, communal participation lightens the grief, making it more bearable. In Romans, there is threefold 'communal participation' in the sense that (1) 'all of non-human creation groans *together*', (2) humans who have the Spirit groan, too, (3) and the Spirit joins in with 'inexpressible groans' (8.22, 23, 26). The unison character of the groaning that takes place in non-human creation, together with the human groaning and the groaning of the Spirit, serve to amplify the voice but also to diffuse the pain.

Second, in the Old Testament non-human mourning is often occasioned by human sin along the lines of the 'moral ecology' equation that was mentioned earlier.[62] Human sin has not been left out in Romans, but the causal nexus is to some extent assumed, to some extent blurred, and to some extent nuanced. Paul has dissected 'sin' so as to make it not only violation of the divine command only but also deception and misperception (7.7-13). The link to Genesis that floods this part of Romans (5.1-8.39) is not weakened by the fact, as Braaten notes, that Gen. 3.16 is the only passage that deploys

59. Michel, *Der Brief an die Römer*, p. 269.

60. Braaten, 'All Creation Groans', p. 137.

61. Braaten, 'All Creation Groans', p. 139.

62. Relevant texts are Hos. 4.1-3; Isa. 24.1-20; Jer. 4.15-38; 23.9-12; Joel 1.5-20; cf. Braaten, 'All Creation Groans', pp. 142, 146; also Douglas J. Moo, 'Nature in the New Creation: New Testament Eschatology and the Environment', *JETS* 49 (2006), pp. 461-63. Katherine M. Hayes (*'The Earth Mourns': Prophetic Metaphor and Oral Aesthetic* [Atlanta: Society of Biblical Literature, 2002], p. 196) says that even in Joel (1.5-20) where there is no specific mention of wrongdoing, 'textual and extratextual factors lead the reader (or hearer) to understand the crisis of the community as a consequence of or punishment for unspecified failings'.

'groaning' in connection with 'birth pangs'.[63] According to the LXX, God tells Eve that 'I will greatly multiply your pains and your groaning (*stenagmon*); in pain you shall give birth to children' (Gen. 3.16, LXX, translation mine). Given that the word translated 'pain' (*lypē*) can also mean 'grief', we have the option of a grief-centered reading. 'I will greatly multiply your griefs and your groaning, in grief you shall give birth to children' (Gen. 3.16, LXX, translation mine). 'Pain' and 'grief' and 'groaning' are certainly evident in Romans, as are 'birth pangs' (Rom. 8.22), 'the entire creation' now speaking the language and assuming the role assigned to Eve in Genesis. It follows that Eve has more than a walk-on role in Romans (7.7-12; 8.22). In the experience of giving birth and the pain and groaning that go with it, however, the tenor is moving from grief to hope. 'Groaning' intensifies the emotional note struck earlier (8.21). If we are now seeing the face of Eve in the midst of non-human creation 'groaning in labor pains', the visual image adds to the already overwhelming auditory impact.

What, then, about the suffering inflicted on non-human creation directly and specifically, rather than as a generic fact of the ripple effect of human wrongdoing on the rest of creation? Bauckham says that the passage in Romans 'cannot mandate human activity for the relief of creation from the burden of human mistreatment now, in the present age'.[64] He nuances this sentiment somewhat by adding that 'those who are concerned to live according to God's will for his world must be concerned to avoid and to repair damage to God's creation as far as possible'.[65] Is this as far as Paul's text will go with regard to contemporary ethical and ecological atrocities committed by human beings against non-human creatures?

Paul has made it his priority to show the mutual awareness and reciprocity that exist between the suffering of believers (8.18, 23) and the suffering and hope of non-human creation (8.19-22), counting on the suffering-and-hope in non-human creation to inspire and fortify human hope. If this is the basic structure of the relation between human and non-human reality, and if Paul specifically relates the suffering of believers in the present to non-human suffering (8.18, 19), what can it mean other than awareness, reciprocity, and empathy on the part of believing humans toward egregious animal suffering? Robin Lane Fox says in *The Classical World* that Augustus in 2 BCE in the course of less than five months hosted twenty-six shows that killed off 3,500 wild animals and that Trajan a little over 100 years later oversaw twenty weeks of bloody sports that killed off more than 11,000 animals. Hadrian, Trajan's successor, 'celebrated his own birthday with six days of slaughter which "hunted" to death 1000 animals (including 200

63. Braaten, 'All Creation Groans', p. 140.
64. Bauckham, 'The Story of the Earth According to Paul', p. 96.
65. Bauckham, 'The Story of the Earth According to Paul', p. 96.

lions)'.[66] In 55 CE, just a year before Paul wrote Romans by our reckoning, 'Nero presented a spectacle with men hunting bulls from horseback, while the cavalry of his bodyguard slew 400 bears and 300 lions with javelins'.[67] This was not a novelty to the Romans because Pompey had seen to the slaughter of 500 lions over five days at the Circus in 55 BCE.[68] Non-human suffering was not an abstract matter in the empire, and Paul's imagery in Romans had daily and ever-present referents across Roman society.

In a deep and fundamental sense, therefore, Paul did not need to prescribe action because his description is intrinsic to, and sufficient for, prescription. Indeed, his *de*scription is in itself the most eloquent *pre*scription and might be less than that if he had tried to go beyond it. Likewise, believers and others who listen in to Paul in the twenty-first century cannot be dismissive toward his depiction of the plight of non-human creation 'until now' (8.22). Let the utterly joyless phenomenon of 'concentrated animal feeding operations' that dot the land on more than one continent be a case in point,[69] wails and groaning of non-human creatures now audible even to the ear that is unfamiliar with apocalyptic. Nero's abuse of 300 lions in 55 CE is easily outdone by Matthew Scully's depiction of the reality facing pigs in modern day factory farm in the United States.

> About 80 million of the 95 million hogs slaughtered each year in America...are intensively reared in mass-confinement farms, never once in their time on earth feeling soil or sunshine. Genetically designed by machines, inseminated by machines, fed by machines, monitored, herded, electrocuted, stabbed, cleaned, cut, and packaged by machines—themselves treated like machines 'from birth to bacon'—these creatures, when eaten, have hardly ever been touched by human hands.[70]

Scully, having seen sentient beings crowded together indoors under conditions that can only be described as predatory, abusive, and utterly repugnant, says that '[f]actory farming isn't just killing. It is negation, a complete denial of the animal as a living being with his or her needs and nature.'[71] Human treatment of non-human creatures has more than tangential interest to those who are attuned to the fervency and time-turning sentiments of Paul's vision in the first century.

66. Robin Lane Fox, *The Classical World: An Epic History from Homer to Hadrian* (New York: Allen Lane, 2005), pp. 456-57.

67. Champlin, *Nero*, p. 68.

68. Champlin, *Nero*, p. 62.

69. Daniel Imhoff, ed., *CAFO (Concentrated Animal Feeding Operation): The Tragedy of Industrial Animal Factories* (San Rafael, CA: Earth Aware, 2010); idem, *The CAFO Reader (Concentrated Animal Feeding Operation): The Tragedy of Industrial Animal Factories* (Watershed Media, 2010).

70. Scully, *Dominion*, p. 29.

71. Scully, *Dominion*, p. 289.

Human and non-human creation are linked in suffering and in hope. It is 'not only the creation', Paul says,

> but we ourselves, who have the first fruits of the Spirit, groan inwardly while we wait for adoption, the redemption of our bodies (Rom. 8.23).

Substantive and verbal elements that apply in the non-human realm apply in the human domain, too, whether suffering (8.18), groaning, liberation, or hope (8.23). Hope is not that the immortal soul will be delivered from the prison of the body or even for the soul to be united with the body. Humans and non-humans are earthlings and materially constituted, and the believer's hope is for 'the redemption of our body' (8.23). Sheila E. McGinn captures well what is increasingly the consensus as to what Paul had in mind.

> It is not disembodied 'spiritual' humanity that celebrates this freedom and glory, but an embodied humanity enlivened and transformed by the spirit of God (8.11). Adoption by God entails a physical liberation, 'the redemption of our bodies' (8.23). Life 'according to Spirit' is not some non-corporeal reality, but a glorious freedom *in the body*, a life in harmony with God and nature—truly a new creation.[72]

But this radical hope is not easily sustained even if non-human creation swells the ranks of the believers because it is 'aligned with, and supportive of, the tiny minority constituting the Christ-movement'.[73] God, too, must join in.

God Groaning

And God joins in (8.26). In fact, the terminology that links non-human, human, and divine reality perceives suffering and hope in the divine realm to be similar to but more intense than what we have seen in the non-human and human spheres.

> For in hope we were saved. Now hope that is seen is not hope. For who hopes for what is seen? But if we hope for what we do not see, we wait for it with patience. Likewise the Spirit helps us in our weakness; for we do not know how to pray as we ought, but that very Spirit intercedes with sighs too deep for words (*stenagmois alalētois*). And God, who searches the heart, knows what is the mind of the Spirit, because the Spirit intercedes for the saints according to the will of God. We know that all things work together

72. Sheila E. McGinn, 'All Creation Groans in Labor: Paul's Theology of Creation in Romans 8.18-23', in *Earth, Wind & Fire: Biblical and Theological Perspectives on Creation* (ed. Carol J. Dempsey and Mary Margaret Pazdan; Collegeville, MN: Liturgical Press, 2004), p. 119. See also N.T. Wright, *Surprised by Hope* (London: SPCK, 2007), p. 175.

73. Esler, *Conflict and Identity in Romans*, p. 262.

> for good for those who love God, who are called according to his purpose (Rom. 8.24-28).

This passage projects hope in large letters, but it also speaks of suffering. The NRSV has 'sighs' instead of 'groans', unnecessarily diluting the semantic connection, but the link persists. Hope must be preserved and will be. The Spirit is the foremost enabler of hope, but the language also opens up to seeing the Spirit *suffering*.[74] If suffering in the human and non-human realms increases the urgency of finding relief, what must be true for suffering in the divine realm? Terence Fretheim has explored Old Testament imagery for the idea of *divine* suffering that resonates with Paul's depiction in Romans.[75] While God may suffer *because* God faces people's rejection or suffer *for* the people, God also suffers *with* the people who are suffering and, by extension, God suffers *with* non-human creation that is suffering.[76] In a text that cannot be overlooked from the vantage point of Romans, the prophet Isaiah sees God crying out in labor pains. 'For a long time I have held my peace, I have kept still and restrained myself; now I will cry out like a woman in labor, I will gasp and pant' (Isa. 42.14). Fretheim calls this a 'passage which takes us about as far as we can go along this path in the OT'.[77]

> Just as God birthed Israel at the beginning of its life (Deut. 32.18), God will do so again. But, as we have seen, the period of restraint is a time of ever-intensifying labor pains for God, which finally burst forth in the travail of the emergence of a new creation. The birth-event, however, will entail not simply the emergence of a new people of God; the act of re-creation will affect the whole world (vv. 15-16). God, crying out, gasping, and panting, gives birth to a new order. The new creation *necessitates* the suffering of God.[78]

The reality of death that afflicts human and non-human creation alike can be reversed neither by the birth-pangs of non-human creation nor by humans giving birth. 'Any birthing of a new order can come about only through what God does, and God can accomplish such a creative act only by way of a *via dolorosa*', says Fretheim.[79] This preserves a central place in the story for the *via dolorosa* of Jesus, and it places God at the center of the suffering and hoping threesome that Paul indissolubly links together in Romans (8.17-28).

74. Jewett (*Romans*, p. 478) says that 'groaning' (*stenagmos*) in v. 26 clearly intends to link back to 'groans' in vv. 22 and 23.

75. Terence Fretheim, *The Suffering of God: An Old Testament Perspective* (OBT; Philadelphia: Fortress Press, 1984).

76. Fretheim, *The Suffering of God*, p. 108.

77. Fretheim, *The Suffering of God*, p. 147.

78. Fretheim, *The Suffering of God*, p. 147.

79. Fretheim, *The Suffering of God*, p. 147.

Closing Liturgical Dialogue

I will not let go of Paul's train of thought until I have followed it to its conclusion although we have been there already, in Chapter 8. By way of reminder, the passage I have explored through five long chapters is framed at the beginning and end by resonant assertions regarding the love of God and the death of Jesus (5.1-11; 8.31-39). Edward Adams says perceptively that in these verses (8.31-39), 'Paul celebrates in hymnic style the ultimate triumph of believers over every threat, affliction and foe: nothing can wrest them from the love of God manifested in Christ'.[80] I will now invite the reader to imagine with me how this passage most likely inspired and electrified vulnerable believers when Paul's letter was first read aloud in house churches in Rome. To get this right, we shall imagine that the letter is read by its likely carrier, Phoebe. We shall further imagine that Paul's message is catching on to the extent that the believers find their hearts 'strangely warmed', unable to stay silent when Phoebe reads aloud the most poignant rhetorical questions. Again, raising the stakes still higher, we shall try to get used to the thought that we are reading a letter that resonates like the Gettysburg Address and Martin Luther King, Jr's 'I have a dream' speech. As to the theology at the point of conclusion, it is important to keep in mind that key terms must be not be understood narrowly, as a message about individual salvation only or even as a call to remain faithful in the face of Roman imperial threats. Paul's message projects in widescreen, with a cosmic perspective and within a comprehensive biblical narrative. Finally, before we start, we shall make a note of the fact that the link that we often find in the Old Testament between sin and suffering, or between sin and retribution, does not intrude. We are now ready to hear Phoebe and to participate as she reads (8.31-37).

> **Phoebe**: He who did not withhold his own Son, but gave him up for all of us, will he not with him also give us everything else?
>
> **Congregation**: He will! Everything!
>
> **Phoebe**: Who will bring any charge against God's elect?
>
> **Congregation**: We know who, the one who brought charges against God! We know who, but the charges are null and void! We know who, but the charges are false and baseless.
>
> **Phoebe**: God is the right-maker, who consigns to destruction and doom?[81]
>
> **Congregation**: Right on, sister! Right on! God is the right-maker! And we know who consigns to destruction because we have been un-deceived by the revelation of God in Jesus.

80. Adams, *Constructing the World*, p. 184.

81. This translation of *katakrinein* captures better the cosmic, widescreen perspective that frames Paul's message; cf. BDAG, art. κατακρίνω.

Phoebe: Who will separate us from the love of Christ?

Congregation: Nothing! No-one!

Phoebe: Will hardship, or distress, or persecution, or famine, or nakedness, or peril, or sword?

Congregation: No! No! No! None of the above!

Phoebe: In all these things we are more than victors through him who loved us.

Congregation: Yes, overwhelming victors—supervictors—through him who loved us![82]

* * *

If we still wonder why Paul brings up the subject of non-human creation, the best answer is that Paul was not the kind of thinker tradition made him out to be. His widescreen gospel is bigger, more earthy, and far more inclusive. In all and for all, including non-human reality, hope is ascendant. The night of plight is receding before the light of the revelation of the faithfulness of God. In this hope the entire non-human creation 'has been groaning in labor pains until now' (8.22).

82. Jewett (*Romans*, pp. 548-49), respecting that Paul's message throughout plays out against a horizon of conflict and battle, translates this 'supervictors'.

Chapter 13

'Out of Zion Will Come the Deliverer' (Rom. 11.26)

Scholars have long acknowledged a suture line at Romans 9,[1] but it is important not to make it more than a thin line. The theme that is announced in the letter introduction reappears in this section in the form of an extensive elaboration (Rom. 1.16-17; 10.1-13), here, too, amid a concentration of correctives and rejoinders (9.14, 19-20; 11.1, 11). One of the rejoinders is sharp enough to call to mind the first question in Romans that I have billed as the critical pivot in the letter.

> You have no excuse for your audacity, O 'virtuous' person (*ō anthrōpe*), passing judgment upon another... Do you really imagine, O 'virtuous' person (*ō anthrōpe*), when you judge those who do such things and yet do them yourself, you will escape the judgment of God? (2.1, 3 translation mine)
>
> But who indeed do you think you are, O 'virtuous' person (*ō anthrōpe*), to argue with God? What is formed will not say to the one who forms it, 'Why did you make me like this?' (9.20, translation mine).

Paul is not particularly polite in either of these instances, and this is precisely the point.[2] At these junctures the speech has a haranguing tone, as was duly noted with regard to the first instance of Paul's use of the blunt, direct address (2.1, 3).[3] Bluntness bordering on rude is the import of the

1. Susannah Ticciati ('The Nondivisive Difference of Election: A Reading of Romans 9–11', *JTI* 6 [2012], p. 258) calls the zigzags in Romans 9–11 'twists and turns', aware that some see disconnections and contradictions. Dunn, *Romans 9–16*, p. 518; Shiu-Lun Shum, *Paul's Use of Isaiah in Romans* (WUNT; Tübingen: Mohr Siebeck, 2002), p. 203. Wayne Meeks ('On Trusting an Unpredictable God: A Hermeneutical Meditation on Romans 9–11', in *Faith and History: Essays in Honor of Paul W. Meyer* (ed. John T Carroll, Charles H. Cosgrove and E. Elizabeth Johnson [Atlanta: Scholars Press, 1990], pp. 105-24) sees a sharp break between 8.39 and 9.1 and the contours of stylistic as well as theological discontinuity.

2. I have continued 'O "virtuous" person' as the preferred translation of *ō anthrōpe*, hoping to preserve the tenor of blunt, down-putting address.

3. Dunn, *Romans 1–8*, p. 79.

second occurrence of this address, too (9.20).[4] The contentious tone of the rhetorical exchange in Romans 9 suggests that Paul's diction has reference not only to a point of view but to individuals who do not belong to the Roman churches (9.14-33). These people maintain a rhetorical presence even if they are not actually in the audience. Campbell argues that many difficulties in Romans 9–11 'can be resolved in large measure if we consider this text as part of an ongoing debate with the Teacher, who is, it should be recalled, a learned Jewish Christian still committed in some sense to circumcision and law observance by any converts to Christ'.[5] Questions arising in consequence of Paul's mission are formidable in themselves, but the problem is aggravated by the fact that some people are deliberately misrepresenting his position (3.8; 16.17-20). Underlying the criticism might be the suspicion that Paul formulates the message in a way that solidifies Jewish opposition. On this logic, the circumcision-based message of his opponents, construed as a corrective to Paul, might brighten the prospects for acceptance of the message among Jews.[6] Before we proceed, it will be useful to revisit a modified representation of the zig-zagging story in Romans.

God's Faithfulness and Jewish Unbelief

'I am speaking the truth in Christ—I am not lying; my conscience confirms it by the Holy Spirit' (Rom. 9.1)—everything in the sentence that starts off the part of Romans that deals head-on with the 'Jewish' question suggests that Paul's credentials with regard to Jews are in doubt. This can be taken as proof that his efforts on behalf of the Gentile mission has had a price: distrust toward him to the point of making him seem like a treasonous messenger. Either Paul has written off Israel or he is less concerned about Israel than he ought to be or at least less concerned than his opponents. It would be unnecessary for him to make the threefold claim that 'I am speaking the truth… I am not lying…my conscience confirms it', with Christ at one end of the sentence and the Holy Spirit at the other end unless somebody portrayed his work as though Israel was of little concern to him (9.1). 'In view of these broad missionary dynamics', says Campbell, 'Paul's advocacy of a law-free mission to the pagans makes him vulnerable to the criticism that he is a traitor to his own people, abandoning them and their heritage, and

4. Cranfield, *Romans*, p. 490.

5. Campbell, *Deliverance of God*, p. 771.

6. Campbell (*Deliverance of God*, pp. 771-72) does not say explicitly that this could be the reason, but the effort Paul makes to show that his version of the gospel is not indifferent to the fate of Israel is easier to understand against a background where concern for Israel is the strong card in the opponents' portfolio.

Pivots in Romans

I. Introduction: 1.1-17
Thesis statement: God's right-making revealed: 1.16-17

II. First Pivot: 1.18.32
Indictment of Gentiles by unnamed interlocutor: 1.18-32

III. Second and Decisive Pivot: 2.1-29
Harsh push-back and put-down of unnamed interlocutor: 2.1-3
Alternative representation of Gentile reality: 2.4-29

IV. Third Pivot: 3.1-4.25
Jewish unfaithfulness vs. divine faithfulness: 3.1-8
Alternative representation of sin: 3.9-19
God's right-making by the faithfulness of Jesus: 3.20-31
Abraham as believing Gentile: 4.1-25

V. Fourth Pivot: 5.1-8.39
Love of God and the death of Jesus: 5.6-11
Sin, death, and restoration: 5.12-8.30
Love of God and the death of Jesus: 8.31-39

VI. Fifth Pivot: 9.1-11.36
God's faithfulness and Israel's alienation: 9.1-11.12
Hard push-back and put-down of unnamed interlocutor: 9.20
The Redeemer will come from Zion: 11.13-36

VII. Sixth Pivot: 12.1-15.7
Alternative community: 12.1-21
Relation to governing authorities: 13.1-14
Mediating between the 'weak' and the 'strong': 14.1-15.7

VIII. Seventh Pivot: 15.8-33
Summary of message and warrant for Gentile mission: 15.8-21
Desire to go to Rome—and to Spain: 15.22-33

IX. Final Pivot: 16.1-27
Paul and his friends in Rome: 16.1-16
Beware of the troublemakers—avoid them: 16.17-20

advocating the same to whoever will listen to him'.[7] There is a term in English for a person who transfers his loyalty from his own group to another. If this is how some people have come to see Paul, he is 'that most despicable of all people—a quisling'.[8] Doubts with regard to Paul's Jewish *bona fides* go a long way toward explaining

7. Campbell, *Deliverance of God*, p. 773.
8. Campbell, *Deliverance of God*, p. 773.

> the unprecedented presence of Paul himself in the argumentation of Romans 9–11. Paul inserts biographical fragments into this discussion no fewer than three times—in 9.1-3; 10.1; and 11.1b. His first such insertion is characterized by very strong truth claims—the assertion of truthfulness, the repudiation of lying, the witness of conscience, *and* the attestation of the Holy Spirit.[9]

Paul is no quisling, but he acknowledges that there is a problem with regard to the Jews. The problem, however, is not that he, in his tireless outreach to Gentiles, is unconcerned about the Jews.

> I have great sorrow and unceasing anguish in my heart. For I could wish that I myself were accursed and cut off from Christ for the sake of my own people, my kindred according to the flesh. They are Israelites, and to them belong the adoption, the glory, the covenants, the giving of the law, the worship, and the promises; to them belong the patriarchs, and from them, according to the flesh, comes the Messiah, who is over all, God blessed forever. Amen (Rom. 9.2-5).

Romans 9–11 lays out his answer to this concern—and to those who contend that the circumcision-free Gentile mission proves Paul's version of the gospel to be a mistake and a failure. The shape of his answer has many layers and is at times quite bewildering. But the gist of what is to come can be anticipated from the way Paul formulates the problem, including the emotional tenor and his existential anguish. 'I have great sorrow and unceasing anguish in my heart', he says. 'For I could wish that I myself were accursed and cut off from Christ for the sake of my own people, my kindred according to the flesh' (Rom. 9.2-3). What is this, if not a disclosure that throbs with compassion? What is this if not a heartfelt yearning to include those not already included? These two elements, compassion and longing, give the framework for what follows. Compassion will not rest until every stone has been turned that might alleviate the reasons for his sorrow and anguish. Yearning for the inclusion of those now seeming to be cut off is grounded in a view of real human beings in an individual sense and not only humans as groups or ethnic categories. Our expectation that compassion and a radical vision of inclusion set terms that must be met—and will be met—is confirmed at the close of Paul's zigzagging argument. 'And so all Israel will be saved', Paul says, 'as it is written, "Out of Zion will come the Deliverer; he will banish ungodliness from Jacob"' (Rom. 11.26). Compassion will not suffer a letdown by the Deliverer who is to come out of Zion, and the numbers will be there (11.26). Moreover, the Deliverer coming from Zion ensures that the Person who holds the key to the inclusion of the Jews vindicates the Jewish side of the equation at the deepest level possible. Paul is not turning his back on the Jews whether with

9. Campbell, *Deliverance of God*, p. 773.

regard to means or results. Rather, he is *deep-Judaizing* the Roman world by making the God of the Jews and the Son of the God of the Jews the Deliverer of all human beings.[10] There can hardly be a greater tribute to the Jews than this affirmation, and the gain to the Gentiles comes with no loss to the Jews because the Deliverer that will come from Zion has not set his heart on the Gentiles at the expense of the Jews (11.11-12).[11]

While Paul is harnessing the Old Testament in support of his understanding of the way forward for Israel, offering up a profusion of texts,[12] exegesis alone will not account for everything he says. Some constructs in the argument are better explained by the polemical subtext, and there are also elements of vision and imagination. The text at hand could be a case in point. 'It is written', Paul says, but he does not repeat verbatim what is written. 'And a Redeemer (Hebr. *goel*, Gr. *ho hryomenos*) will come to (*heneken*) Zion, and to those who turn from transgression in Jacob', is Isaiah's wording (Isa 59.20). Where the Old Testament appears to say that the Redeemer will come *to* Zion, Paul says that the Redeemer will come *from* (*ek*) Zion' (Rom 11.26). The benefit to Israel is indisputable in either version, but the Redeemer that comes *from* Zion will not be restricted to a mission that is meant to benefit one group to the exclusion of others.

Why is this important? And why is it important to catch the drift of Paul's conclusion in regard to Jews and Gentiles? Why, too, is it critical to let Isaiah carry the melody of Paul's argument rather than allow rhetorical exchanges and occasional hyperbole made in the course of the argument to dominate?

First, the theological tradition from Augustine onward turned a message whose overall tenor is inclusion of people previously excluded—a message of mercy where mercy was not thought to apply—into a message that prioritized an austere doctrine of divine sovereignty over a lavish vision of inclusion.[13] Second, taking compassion and inclusion to be the thrust

10. Fredriksen, *Augustine and the Jews*, p. 27.

11. Ticciati ('A Reading of Romans 9–11', p. 271) sees Paul altering '*the grammar of human jealousy*' in such a way that 'Israel is set apart from its allegiance to a God who is also the God of others, such that what separates Israel from others (its God) is also what unites it with others (God is Israel's God only *as* the God of others). Israel's difference is a difference that unites—an inclusive difference'.

12. The profusion of Old Testament citations and allusions in Romans includes 9.7, 9, 12, 13, 15, 17, 19, 20, 25, 26, 27, 28, 29, 33; 10.5, 6, 8, 11, 13, 15, 16, 18, 19, 20, 21; 11.3, 4, 8, 9, 26, 33, 34, 35.

13. B.J. Oropeza ('Paul and Theodicy: Intertextual Thoughts on God's Justice and Faithfulness in Romans 9–11', *NTS* 53 [2007], p. 62) argues plausibly that Paul's view of election rests on an aspect of Genesis 'that he assumed his readers knew. God chooses to show mercy on the weak instead of the strong.' Eleonore Stump ('Augustine on Free Will', p. 142) concludes that Augustine's emphasis on divine agency is so firm that it amounts to 'theological determinism'.

of Paul's mission and message, the Augustinian tradition calibrated divine mercy to mean that God sends many more to damnation than to salvation.[14] While Paul in the first eight chapters of Romans declares 'the confidence in God that is the very substance of faith',[15] will he undo his own work by presenting a capricious God who defies comprehension and stress *exclusion* more than *inclusion*? Must compassion surrender to the doctrine of divine sovereignty, suspension of compassion also necessitating the suspension of comprehension? Will the compassion and yearning that Paul expresses at the beginning of these chapters be forced to settle for the kind of percentage Augustine and others took the stage to defend?

We should expect 'no' to be the answer to these questions. Paul formulates his concern in such a way that nothing will upstage compassion (9.2-3). The argument in Romans 9-11 presupposes the message in the first eight chapters in Romans and does not, as has been suggested, 'disrupt the smooth assurances of confidence that have capped the whole argument of chaps. 1-8'.[16] Paul is not promoting a doctrine of arbitrary election of *some* Jews and *some* Gentiles in the context of a letter that claims that 'God shows no partiality' (2.11).[17] His concession to incomprehension at the end of Romans 9–11 is predicated on God's infinite resourcefulness and creativity to bring about God's intent (11.33-36), not on acceptance of divine unpredictability and capriciousness.

14. Augustine (*The City of God*, 21.12, translation here by Paula Fredriksen, *Augustine and the Jews*, p. 351, italics hers) says that 'the whole of mankind is a condemned lump... The result is that there is no escape for anyone from this justly deserved punishment, except by merciful and undeserved grace. Humanity is divided between those in whom the power of merciful grace is demonstrated, and those in whom is shown the might of just retribution. Neither of these could be displayed in respect of all mankind, for if all had remained condemned...then God's merciful grace would not have been seen...and if all had been transferred from darkness to light, then the truth of God's vengeance would not have been made evident. *Many more are condemned by vengeance than are released by mercy*.'

15. Meeks, 'On Trusting an Unpredictable God', p. 107.

16. Meeks, 'On Trusting an Unpredictable God', p. 108. Ultimately, Meeks does not settle for the notion of disruption, but he allows that the rhetoric of Romans 9–11 at face value seems to suggest discontinuity and reversal of the previous argument.

17. Joette M. Bassler (*Divine Impartiality: Paul and a Theological Axiom* [SBLDS; Chico, CA: Scholars Press, 1982], pp. 121-70) gives the theme of divine impartiality in Rom. 2.11 the status of a theological axiom that cannot be undone by subsequent and subsidiary arguments. E. Elizabeth Johnson ('Romans 9–11: The Faithfulness and Impartiality of God', in *Pauline Theology*, vol. III [ed. David Hay and E. Elizabeth Johnson; Minneapolis: Fortress Press, 1995], pp. 211-39) sees in these chapters a complex interplay between partiality and faithfulness within which God's faithfulness to Israel puts the notion of impartiality somewhat at risk. Her conclusion is that Paul affirms both.

Third, therefore, I agree with readers who recognize Isaiah as the dominant Old Testament voice in this part of Romans, especially at the point where Paul moves to its conclusion. As J. Ross Wagner notes,

> at a number of points in the letter the prophet Isaiah virtually takes on a life of his own and becomes a second voice, speaking in concert with the apostle concerning God's plan to redeem Israel and the nations. Isaiah '*cries out* on behalf of Israel', affirming God's unremitting faithfulness even in the midst of judgment (Rom. 9.27-29; Isa. 10.20-23; 1.9). Isaiah '*boldly dares to speak*' of God's astonishing embrace of Gentiles, while God's own people stand off at a distance, estranged and unresponsive (Rom. 10.20-21; Isa. 65.1-2). Isaiah *sings* of the root of Jesse who comes to unite Jew and Gentile into a single community of worship and praise (Rom. 15.12; Isa. 11.1, 10; 66.19).[18]

Prioritizing Isaiah is the right thing to do for more than quantitative reasons.[19] Isaiah's visions of inclusion are as transformative as Paul's message in Romans, creating synergy between two voices that draws compassion and inclusion to a new scale while keeping ecological concerns squarely in the field of vision (Isa. 11.1-10; 65.17-25; 66.22, 23).

Visions of Inclusion in Isaiah

If Paul and Isaiah are voices 'speaking in concert', as Wagner suggests,[20] like Simon and Garfunkel singing harmonies and knowing exactly how to make the most of each other's strengths, how does Isaiah sound when we allow his voice to be heard one step removed from Paul, singing solo? I intend to pursue the implications of this question on the logic that Paul is not producing radical new meaning when he quotes or alludes to Isaiah.[21] Sometimes he does no more than add a new harmony to Isaiah's melody. Hays' contention that Paul has salted his letter with Old Testament allusions,

18. J. Ross Wagner, *Heralds of the Good News: Isaiah and Paul in Concert in the Letter to the Romans* (Leiden: Brill, 2003), p. 2, emphasis added.

19. Nearly half of the Old Testament citations and allusions in Romans come from Isaiah; cf. Wagner, *Isaiah and Paul in Concert*, p. 1.

20. Wagner, *Isaiah and Paul in Concert*, p. 2.

21. Hays (*Echoes of Scripture*, pp. 29-32) delineates specific criteria for identifying echoes and allusions to the Old Testament: *availability, volume, recurrence, thematic coherence, historical plausibility, history of interpretation,* and *satisfaction*. These methodological constraints are circumspect and well-considered. When applied to Isaiah, however, and to the role of Isaiah in Romans, they risk sundering the whole cloth of Isaiah in the sense that we do not get to see how Isaiah—fully and in his own voice—makes the points Paul will argue later. Among Hays' proposed criteria, my inquiry is best seen under the rubric 'thematic coherence'.

that he 'hints and whispers all around Isaiah 53',[22] is well argued, as is the notion that the incompleteness of Paul's allusions is intentional, assigning to the reader the task of finishing the sentence. This leads to a reading that is more dynamic, poetic, and dramatic than what has hitherto been the norm. But sometimes less is more, as an unfettered reading of Isaiah might show. I will anchor the unfettered reading at one end in Isaiah's seminal vision (Isa. 11.1-10), specifically the promise that 'on that day the root of Jesse shall stand as a signal to the peoples; the nations shall inquire of him, and his dwelling shall be glorious' (Isa. 11.10). This text echoes explicitly in Paul's concluding argument for the inclusion of the Gentiles, an in-depth exploration of this left for the last chapter in this commentary (Rom. 15.12). My unencumbered reading will be anchored at the other end in the image of the Redeemer coming to Zion, or, as Paul puts it, 'out of Zion will come the Deliverer', concluding with the claim, 'and so all Israel will be saved' (Isa. 59.20; Rom. 11.26).

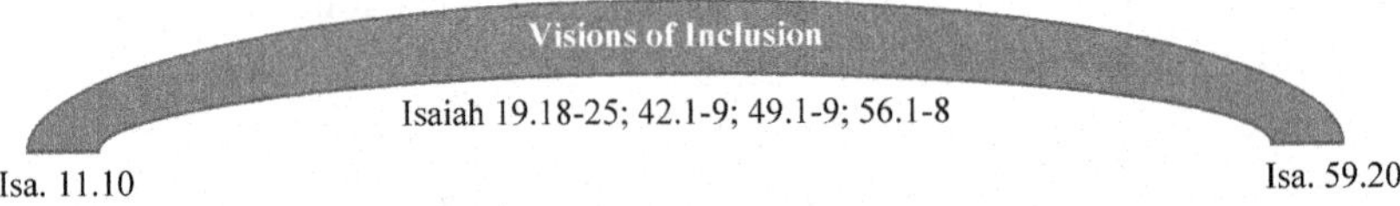

Three tableaus will be explored, the recalibration of the chosen people in what is generally regarded as First Isaiah (Isa. 19.18-25); the character and scope of the mission of the Suffering Servant in the so-called Second Isaiah (Isa. 42.1-4; 49.1-6); and the vision of inclusion in 'Third' Isaiah (Isa. 56.1-8). Mention of the divisions is important only for the purpose of showing that the entire book is dedicated to the proposition of universality and radical inclusion; it is not here a source critical perspective.[23]

From the opening vision that '*on that day* the root of Jesse shall stand as a signal to the peoples' (Isa. 11.10), Isaiah moves to specify in impressive detail what will happen *on that day* (19.18-25).[24]

22. Hays, *Echoes of Scripture*, p. 63.

23. R.E. Clements ('The Unity of the Book of Isaiah', *Int* 36 [1982], pp. 117-29) disputes the notion of a 'school of Isaiah' but not the notion of thematic unity in the book. Rolf Rendtorff ('Zur Komposition des Buches Jesaja', *VT* 34 [1984], pp. 295-320) also highlights striking indicators of thematic unity. While stopping short of dismissing the traditional critical position on sources, Rendtorff finds the notion of an independent 'third Isaiah' quite inconceivable (p. 320). John N. Oswalt (*The Book of Isaiah: Chapters 40–66* [NICOT; Grand Rapids: Eerdmans, 1998], pp. 3-6), argues that the three-source hypothesis is unconvincing.

24. Jacob Strombert ('The "Root of Jesse" in Isaiah 11:10: Postexilic Judah, or Postexilic Davidic King?', *JBL* 127 [2008], pp. 655-69) accepts the idea that Isa. 11.10

> *On that day* there will be five cities in the land of Egypt that speak the language of Canaan and swear allegiance to the LORD of hosts. One of these will be called the City of the Sun.
>
> *On that day* there will be an altar to the LORD in the center of the land of Egypt, and a pillar to the LORD at its border. It will be a sign and a witness to the LORD of hosts in the land of Egypt; when they cry to the LORD because of oppressors, he will send them a savior, and will defend and deliver them.
>
> The LORD will make himself known to the Egyptians; and the Egyptians will know the LORD *on that day*, and will worship with sacrifice and burnt offering, and they will make vows to the Lord and perform them. The LORD will strike Egypt, striking and healing; they will return to the LORD, and he will listen to their supplications and heal them.
>
> *On that day* there will be a highway from Egypt to Assyria, and the Assyrian will come into Egypt, and the Egyptian into Assyria, and the Egyptians will worship with the Assyrians.
>
> *On that day* Israel will be the third with Egypt and Assyria, a blessing in the midst of the earth, whom the LORD of hosts has blessed, saying, 'Blessed be Egypt my people, and Assyria the work of my hands, and Israel my heritage (Isa. 19.18-25).

Commentators have been in want of superlatives when trying to capture the meaning of this passage. André Feuillet calls it 'the summit of religion'.[25] 'Will you believe me when I tell you that no more astounding words than these have ever been spoken or written?' says J. Wilson.[26] While scholars differ widely with respect many things in the text, they agree on one point: the text offers a perspective of reconciliation and inclusion that is unequalled in the Old Testament.[27]

The text deconstructs fixtures of alienation and enmity, culminating in a sweeping vision of reconciliation. It offers a hitherto unimaginable prospect: the arch-enemy and arch-oppressor uniting with wayward Israel in worship of the one God, united, indeed, precisely on the point where division has been most insurmountable.

may be post-exilic and redactional, but he argues that the text 'stands as an important clue for how the book was to be read as a whole'.

25. André Feuillet, 'Un Sommet Religieux de l'Ancien Testament: L'oracle d'Isaïe, XIX (vv. 16-25) sur la conversion de l'Égypte', *RSR* 39 (1951), pp. 65-87.

26. J. Wilson, '"In That Day": From Text to Sermon on Isaiah 19,23-25', *Int* 21 (1967), p. 66.

27. W. Vogels, 'L'Égypte mon people—L'Universalisme d'Is 19,16-25', *Bib* 57 (1976), p. 494.

Five times in this passage we find the phrase 'on that day'. This phrase, as well as many specifics in the text, puts a damper on interpretations that seek to anchor the content in emerging political realities contemporary to the author. The repeated use of this phrase, heralding ever more surprising reconfigurations, conforms better to a scenario where 'the prophet sees these events as occurring in the end times, or at least at the point where God takes decisive action in world events'.[28] Not only is the perspective future-oriented and eschatological. It draws up a vision so contrary to convention and expectation that it presupposes a dramatic, supernatural intervention. 'On that day' is 'the Day of God';[29] the day when God's purpose is revealed and made a reality.

Isaiah Singing Solo	
Passage	**Perspective**
Isa. 11.1-10	Universal Inclusion of the Gentiles Restoration in the non-human realm
Isa. 19.18-25	Eschatological Egyptians as God's chosen people Exodus for the Egyptians
Isa. 42.1-4; 49.3-6	Suffering Servant Inclusion of the Gentiles Restoration in the non-human realm
Isa. 56.1-8	Gathering and inclusion, specifically of people previously *excluded* Membership by *confession* rather than *ethnicity* 'house of prayer for *all* people'

Strange things are said to happen in Egypt 'on that day': 'five cities in the land of Egypt...speak the language of Canaan and swear allegiance to the LORD of hosts' (Isa. 19.18); 'there will be an altar to the LORD in the center of the land of Egypt' (19.19); 'the Lord will make himself known to the Egyptians' (19.21); the Egyptians 'will return to the LORD, and he will listen to their supplications and heal them' (19.22).

This scenario stretches anyone's mental capacity to the limit. Historically, Egypt is the oppressor of Israel, the prototype enemy and the epitome of oppression and arrogance (cf. Exod. 5.2). In Jewish self-understanding, existence centers on the original deliverance from Egypt. 'I am the LORD your God, who brought you out of the land of Egypt, out of the house of slavery', God says at the founding occasion at Sinai (Exod. 20.2). Again and again in the Old Testament, mention of Egypt comes with the qualification that Egypt is known as 'the house of slavery'.[30] It is thus a reliable reference point as Israel's polar opposite, the perennial enemy of God and the good. This view of Egypt does not only relate to the past. In Isaiah, too,

28. John Oswalt, *The Book of Isaiah: Chapters 1–39* (NICOT; Grand Rapids: Eerdmans, 1986), p. 374.

29. Wilson, 'In That Day', p. 69.

30. Exod. 13.3, 14; 20.2; Deut. 5.6; 6.12; 7.8; 8.14; 13.5, 10; Josh. 24.17; Judg. 6.8; Jer. 34.13; Mic. 6.4.

Egypt is a present menace and nowhere more so than in the verses immediately preceding the text we are considering here (Isa. 19.1-15). Hostility to Egypt is such a characteristic feature in Isaiah that Hans Wildberger takes the dramatic turn of heart toward Egypt as evidence that Isaiah cannot have been the author.[31]

And yet, from the very first intimation, cracks appear in notions forged by injury and fortified by memory: 'there will be five cities in Egypt that speak the language of Canaan' (Isa. 19.18). These five cities are not Israeli settlements, *diaspora* Jews, as many commentators believed, reflecting presuppositions as to the time when this passage was written.[32] For the five cities to speak 'the language of Canaan' would not be much of a feat if their inhabitants are Jewish in the first place. If, however, the cities are genuine Egyptian cities and the people speaking the language of Canaan are Egyptians, something unprecedented is stirring in the land.[33] Coming together on the level of language, speaking the same language, as it were, signals a giant leap forward toward reconciliation and mutual understanding. Add to this that the language spoken is the cultic language of Israel, and the sense of a new bond is further deepened. John Calvin took this as proof that 'by such a language must be meant agreement in religion'.[34] Still more amazing, the expression 'the lip of Canaan' 'reflects the beginning of a return to the state where "the whole earth was one lip"' (Gen. 11.1).[35]

Sensing a paradigm shift, it does not matter whether the number five is a small number, a significant number, or a symbolic number. Even the smallest number means that the impasse is broken and something extraordinary happening. Weighing the options more carefully, it is likely that the leading city in Egypt is part of the five because,[36] in the very next verse, Isaiah says that 'there will be an altar to the LORD in the center of the land of Egypt' (19.19). If five is a small number, a mere five 'is able

31. Hans Wildberger, *Jesaja 13–27* (BKAT 10/2; Neukirchen–Vluyn: Neukirchener Verlag, 1978), pp. 730-31.

32. Cf. Kaiser, *Isaiah 13–39*, p. 105; Blenkinsopp, *Isaiah 1–39*, p. 317.

33. Vogels, 'L'Egypte mon people', p. 500; Sawyer, 'Blessed be My People Egypt', p. 59; Oswalt, *Isaiah 1–39*, pp. 376-78.

34. John Calvin, *Commentary on the Book of the Prophet Isaiah* (trans. William Pringle; Edinburgh: Calvin Translation Society, 1850; repr. Grand Rapids: Baker Books, 2003), p. 69.

35. J. Alec Motyer, *The Prophecy of Isaiah* (Downers Grove, IL: InterVarsity Press, 1993), p. 168.

36. The textual *Vorlage* is divided as to whether the named city is *ir ha-heres*, 'city of destruction', or *ir ha-cheres*, 'city of the sun'. 1QIs has *ha-cheres*, 'city of the sun', and this is one example where the Qumran discoveries show their influence on modern translations of the Bible.

to accomplish great things',[37] and if it is symbolic, it conveys 'the radical nature of the turn'.[38]

The text becomes even stranger when we tune our ears to scriptural antecedents in Isaiah's vision. Israel's exodus experience recapitulated.[39] Only this time Egypt, the erstwhile oppressor, *is cast in the role of the oppressed.* When the *Egyptians* 'cry to the LORD because of oppressors, he will send *them* a savior, and will defend and deliver *them*' (Isa. 19.20c; cf. Exod. 6.6; 3.8, emphasis added). A new Moses arrives on the scene, but this time he is commissioned to lead the *Egyptians* to freedom. 'Just as Israel was saved through a mediator, Moses'. says Vogels, 'so he will likewise send to Egypt a liberator, a kind of new Moses'.[40] Brevard Childs notes 'that now the God of Israel will respond to Egypt's cry of deliverance and will send a savior to rescue as he once had done for the oppressed Israelite slaves'.[41]

The Egyptians have also been oppressed, and they, too, need deliverance. To Egypt comes the promise that 'the LORD will make himself known to the Egyptians; and the Egyptians will know the LORD on that day' (Isa. 19.21a) just as it was said to Israel that 'you shall know the LORD' at the time of the original exodus (Exod. 6.7). As a result, the Egyptians 'will worship with sacrifice and burnt offering' (Isa. 19.21b), recalling that Israel's exodus, too, centered on the right to worship and offer sacrifices (Exod. 3.18). The reconfiguration with respect to Egypt unfolds according to the pattern of the chosen people. Isaiah predicts an exodus experience for the Egyptians that equals the exodus of Israel.[42]

And the vision has not yet reached its zenith. 'On that day there will be a highway from Egypt to Assyria, and the Assyrian will come into Egypt, and the Egyptian into Assyria, and the Egyptians will worship with the Assyrians' (Isa. 19.23). Assyria has not been mentioned until now, but its mention adds quantity to what is already qualitatively in place. Assyria, too, the other great enemy of Israel in the Old Testament, is included in the vision. Perhaps the most frightening and cruel of all the conquerors ravaging the Near East,[43] Assyria belongs as a full partner in the new worshiping fellowship. The highway in view drives the point home because a highway 'is a

37. Vogels, 'L'Egypte mon people', p. 501.

38. Oswalt, *Isaiah 1–39*, p. 377.

39. Feuillet, 'Un Sommet Religieux de l'Ancien Testament', p. 65-87.

40. Vogels, 'L'Égypte mon people', p. 506.

41. Brevard Childs, *Isaiah* (OTL; Louisville, KY: Westminster/John Knox Press, 2001), p. 144.

42. Vogels, 'L'Égypte mon people', p. 506.

43. Joseph Blenkinsopp, *Isaiah 1–39: A New Translation with Introduction and Commentary* (AB; New York: Doubleday, 2000), p. 320.

favorite metaphor in the book for the removal of alienation and separation (Isa. 11.16; 33.8; 35.8; 40.3; 49.11; 62.10)'.[44]

Remarkably, language that used to be exclusive for Israel, the chosen people, is now extended to Israel's sworn enemies. 'On that day Israel will be the third with Egypt and Assyria, a blessing in the midst of the earth, whom the LORD of hosts has blessed, saying, "Blessed be Egypt my people, and Assyria the work of my hands, and Israel my heritage"' (Isa. 19.24, 25). Egypt, the enemy of the people of God, is now designated as 'my people'. God's people, reconfigured and reunited along the prophetic highway, 'a blessing in the midst of the earth' (Isa. 19.24)! The other nations have the same status as Israel in a trinity of equals. Importantly, therefore, the other nations 'are not to be subjects of Israel, and in virtue of so being, objects of Yahweh's regard', writes George Buchanan Gray, 'they are to be as directly related to Yahweh as Israel itself'.[45] This is no loss to Israel because recognition of Israel was never the main point. Israel was meant to a blessing in the earth (Gen. 12.2). This goal has been achieved in a spectacular manner even though Israel must acknowledge that Egypt and Assyria, the former enemies, are partners in her vocation. If this seems unsettling to one accustomed to occupy the limelight alone, there is comfort in the thought that God is not eclipsed. 'For although from this time forward there is to be no essential differences between the nations in their relation to God, it is still the God of Israel who obtains this universal recognition'.[46]

This message is so contrary to expectations that it was bound to run into obstacles. If Augustine had prevailed in his discussion with Jerome as to which version of the Old Testament should be the Bible of the church, Augustine defending the Greek version, Jerome the Hebrew text, the most amazing part of the text might have been lost. The translators of the Septuagint could not swallow the idea that the enemies of Israel were to be included in God's mercy on a level indistinguishable from the elect people of God. For this reason, the translators reduced Egypt and Assyria to mere geographic locations housing a smattering of *diaspora* Jews. That is, they made all the three parts of the threesome into ethnic Israelites. 'In that day shall Israel be a third among the Assyrians and among the Egyptians, blessed in the land which the Lord of hosts (hath) blessed, saying, "Blessed is my people that is in Egypt, and among the Assyrians, and the land of mine inheritance, Israel"' (Isa. 19.24, 25, LXX). *With* Egypt and *with* Assyria in

44. Oswalt, *Isaiah 1–39*, p. 380. Note that the term is used throughout Isaiah.

45. George Buchanan Gray, *A Critical and Exegetical Commentary on the Book of Isaiah*, I–XXVII (ICC; Edinburgh: T. & T. Clark, 1912), p. 341.

46. Franz Delitzsch, *The Prophecies of Isaiah*, 2 vols. (trans. James Martin; Grand Rapids: Eerdmans, 1950), p. 368.

the Hebrew text have become *among* the Assyrians and *among* the Egyptians in the Septuagint, and the blessing rests only on the Israelites that are *in* Egypt and *among* the Assyrians.[47] The Septuagint text certainly deserves to be seen as a 'tendentious revision',[48] more likely intentional than accidental and probably justified on the assumption that Isaiah cannot have meant what he actually says.

The take-home message of this passage in Isaiah is (1) inclusion in God's redemptive purpose of erstwhile enemies; (2) a reconfiguration of the chosen people that makes the Egyptians, too, belong to the elect; (3) exodus-like deliverance for erstwhile oppressors now counted among the oppressed; and (4) a notion of being united to the point of speaking the same language.

The Servant Songs in Isaiah project a similar message in a slightly different idiom.[49]

> Here is my servant, whom I uphold, my chosen, in whom my soul delights; I have put my spirit upon him; he will bring forth justice (*mišpāt*) to the nations. He will not cry or lift up his voice, or make it heard in the street; a bruised reed he will not break, and a dimly burning wick he will not quench; he will faithfully (*le'emeth*—'with faithfulness') bring forth justice (*mišpāt*). He will not grow faint or be crushed until he has established justice (*mišpāt*) in the earth; and the coastlands wait for his teaching (*tôrâtohu*) (Isa. 42.1-4).

> And he said to me, 'You are my servant, Israel, in whom I will be glorified'. But I said, 'I have labored in vain, I have spent my strength for nothing and vanity; yet surely my cause is with the LORD, and my reward with my God'. And now the LORD says, who formed me in the womb to be his servant, to bring Jacob back to him, and that Israel might be gathered to him, for I am honored in the sight of the LORD, and my God has become my strength—he says, 'It is too light a thing that you should be my servant to raise up the tribes of Jacob and to restore the survivors of Israel; I will give you as a light to the nations, that my salvation (*j*ᵉ*šuati*) may reach to the end of the earth' (Isa. 49.3-6).

These texts are less specific than the previous passage, but they are no less sweeping with regard to the inclusive, universalistic scope and

47. See Arie van der Kooij, '"The Servant of the Lord": A Particular Group of Jews in Egypt According to the Old Greek of Isaiah', in *Studies in the Book of Isaiah: Festschrift in Honor of Willem A.M. Beuken* (ed. J. van Ruiten and M. Vervenne; Leuven: Leuven University Press, 1997), pp. 390-96.

48. Wilson, 'In That Day', p. 83.

49. The 'Servant Songs' are generally thought to include Isa. 42.1-9; 49.1-9; 50.4-9, and 52.13–53.12. The designation was originally proposed by Bernhard Duhm (*Die Theologie der Propheten as Grundlage für die innere Entwicklungsgeschichte der israelitischen Religion* [Bonn: Marcus, 1875], pp. 288-89).

sentiment.[50] Moreover, they include terminology that holds tremendous interest beyond the original context, and they specify means and agency in a way that go beyond what has been said earlier in Isaiah.

First, the Servant in Isaiah is going to 'bring forth justice (*mišpāt*)' (Isa. 42.1). Paul D. Hanson notes that the concept *mišpāt* 'lies at the heart of Second Isaiah's message'.[51] 'Justice' as here conceived is not merely a judicial notion that ensures accountability in a legal sense.

> *Mišpāt* is the order of compassionate justice that God has created and upon which the wholeness of the universe depends. In Israel, God revealed *mišpāt* in the form of the *tôrāh* (note that in 42.4 *mišpāt* and *tôrāh* form a synonymous parallel). Those who repudiate God's *mišpāt* introduce evil into the world. *God acts through God's servants to nullify the power of evildoers and to restore the harmony* that arises where God's *mišpāt* is acknowledged and observed.[52]

'Justice' or 'righteousness' thus conceived is not a static or a 'parochial concept' but is better understood as active *right-making*. Hanson adds that it 'affects the entire universe, inclusive of human history and natural phenomena alike' and has 'universal connotations'.[53] The entire mission has the undertone of *deliverance*, as in the passage that promises an exodus-like deliverance to the Egyptians (Isa. 19.18-25), 'patterned after Yahweh's care for the Hebrews as they fled from the Pharaoh toward the heritage that God had given them'.[54]

The non-parochial character is spelled out more fully when the agent that is to bring this about is instructed concerning the universal aspiration precisely at the point of experiencing a sense of futility with regard to his mission on home turf (Isa. 49.4-6). Discouragement is unwarranted because God has a bigger plan in mind for the Servant. 'The entire world is to become his territory!' says Hanson.[55] Intriguingly, the stated rationale for

50. The LXX of Isa. 42.4 echoes Isa. 11.10, or *vice versa*.

51. Paul D. Hanson, *Isaiah 40–66* (Int; Louisville, KY: John Knox Press, 1995), p. 42.

52. Hanson, *Isaiah 40–66*, pp. 42-43, emphasis added. Thus also Oswalt (*Isaiah 40–66*, p. 110), '[w]e are not merely speaking of a privatistic forgiveness of sins, or of the imposition of a humanly designed system for redistribution of goods. This is that life-giving order which exists when the creation is functioning in accordance with the design of the Lord.'

53. Hanson, *Isaiah 40–66*, p. 43.

54. Hanson, *Isaiah 40–66*, pp. 132-33. The 'broken reed' that the Servant will not break might even have reference to Egypt, described as a 'broken reed' in Isa. 36.6; cf. John Goldingay and David Payne, *Isaiah 40–55*, 2 vol. (ICC; New York and London: T. & T. Clark, 2006), p. 218.

55. Hanson, *Isaiah 40–66*, p. 130. See also G. Smith, *Isaiah 40–66* (Nashville, TN: Broadman & Holman, 2009), p. 349.

the global mission is not only universal need but the worthiness and stature of the designated agent.[56] For an agent of that kind, nothing short of a universal mission will do.[57]

Second, there is an emphasis on 'how' that brings into view means contrary to expectation, convention, and—to the naked eye—unlikely to bring success (Isa. 42.2-3; 49.4). 'The style of witness of the Servant stands so starkly in contrast to the ways of the nations and their leaders that it must be regarded either as foolishness or as an intriguing alternative to a failed strategy', says Hanson.[58] If the means deployed by the Servant is an 'alternative to a failed strategy', as suggested, it is itself a strategy that seems doomed to collapse even in the eyes of the one charged with carrying it out (Isa. 49.4; cf. 52.13-15). Failure, however, is not an option and will not be the result because the Servant 'will not grow faint of be crushed until he has established justice in the earth' (Isa. 42.4). This means that the Servant 'will not merely present (justice) or offer it as a possibility; he will put it in place'.[59] If, too, 'justice' is the end, 'faithfulness' (*'emet*) is the means (Isa. 42.3). For a person who reads Isaiah after first reading Romans, the linkage between 'justice' and 'faithfulness' will not be missed.

Third, it is difficult to remain indifferent to the identity of the agent as the story of the Servant unfolds in Isaiah.[60] Eventually, personification works better than a corporate construct. '*You* are my servant, Israel, in whom I will be glorified', the second person singular not incidental (Isa. 49.3). As Brevard Child notes, the being in question 'has not only been designated as servant, but he has been designated as Israel. In place of the corporate nation Israel, which up to this point has always born the title, "my servant" (Isa. 41.9; 42.1, 19; 44.1; 45.4), a *single figure* now carries the title and even office.'[61] The stupendous task of this figure is such that it justifies the translation, '[t]o restore Israel is the least part of thy vocation as my servant' (Isa. 49.6).[62] This means that inclusion of the Gentiles is not an afterthought or an add-on.

56. John Skinner, *The Book of the Prophet Isaiah 40–66: With Introduction and Notes* (Cambridge: Cambridge University Press, 1898), pp. 90-91; Oswalt, *Isaiah 40–66*, pp. 293-94.

57. Childs, *Isaiah*, p. 384.

58. Hanson, *Isaiah 40–66*, p. 45. He contrasts the witness of 'quiet, patient gentleness' and 'embodied compassion' with a notion of justice that relies on 'human force' (p. 46).

59. Oswalt, *Isaiah 40–66*, p. 112.

60. Even though David J.A. Clines (*I, He, We, and They: A Literary Approach to Isaiah 53* (JSOTSup; Sheffield: JSOT Press, 1976) counsels that Isaiah 53 be seen in isolation from the other 'Servant Songs' and that it should be seen as a 'language event' rather than as 'a carrier of information', notions of universality and ultimacy persist.

61. Childs, *Isaiah*, p. 384 (italics added).

62. Skinner, *Isaiah 40–66*, pp. 90-91.

The momentum toward a universal, all-inclusive mission is not slowed in the last part of Isaiah (Isa. 56.1-8). The prophetic voice now urges the audience to persevere despite the discouraging outlook of the present situation.

> Thus says the LORD, Maintain justice (*mišpāt*), and do what is right, for soon my salvation (*j^e^šuati*) will come, and my deliverance (*ṣidkāti*) be revealed... And the foreigners (Gr. *tois allogenesi*) who join themselves to the LORD...these I will bring to my holy mountain, and make them joyful in my house of prayer; their burnt offerings and their sacrifices will be accepted on my altar; for my house shall be called a house of prayer for all peoples (Isa. 56.1, 6, 7).

This, too, is a future- and end-oriented perspective. The content and language reinforce the sense of finality, Joseph Blenkinsopp noting that 'everything in 56-66 is decisively oriented to the future'.[63] The future in view, however, does not flow smoothly from dear and familiar ways in the present. Quite the contrary, the predicted future comes 'in the sense of the expectation of a discontinuity in the historical process, a "singularity"', which, in turn, is meant to determine life in the present.[64] Inclusion is writ large and particularized because it specifies the inclusion of eunuchs and foreigners (Isa. 56.4, 6), groups previously and explicitly said to be excluded (Deut. 23.1, 8).[65] At a later point the foreigners are ordained to priestly ministry, a function normally the exclusive preserve of Jews of Levitical descent (Isa. 66.21).[66] Just as there is a new conception as to who constitutes 'my people' in Isa. 19.18-25, and just as there is ambiguity as to the identity of 'Israel' in the Servant Songs (Isa. 42.1-9; 49.1-6), belonging is anchored in confession and not in ethnicity (Isa. 56.4-6). The ascendant verbs in the passage 'make it perfectly plain that membership of the community which worships Yahweh is now based upon resolve, a free affirmation of this God and of his worship', says Claus Westermann. Henceforth, the chosen people 'has turned into the confessing community'.[67] Grace L. Emmerson writes that '[t]hese chapters begin and end with an open-hearted generosity towards foreigners which is unmatched by anything else in the Old Testament'.[68] As we have seen, these chapters face strong competition for that honor from the

63. Joseph Blenkinsopp, *Isaiah 56–66: A New Translation with Introduction and Commentary* (AB; New York: Doubleday, 2003), p. 89.

64. Blenkinsopp, *Isaiah 56–66*, p. 89.

65. Walther Eichrodt (*Theology of the Old Testament*, 2 vols. [trans. John Baker; OTL; London: SCM Press, 1961], p. I.55) notes that the legacy of Deuteronomy tended toward exclusion and 'did in practice set the nations outside the covenant and taught that this should be regarded as a specifically Israelite privilege'.

66. Grace L. Emmerson, *Isaiah 56–66* (OTG; Sheffield: JSOT Press, 1992), p. 55.

67. Claus Westermann, *Isaiah 40–66* (trans. David M.G. Stalker; OTL; London: SCM Press, 1969), p. 313.

68. Emmerson, *Isaiah 56–66*, p. 55.

earlier passage about Israel, Egypt, and Assyria as God's chosen threesome in the midst of the earth (Isa. 19.18-25).

Above all, however, the driving force behind the paradigm-shattering reconfigurations in all these passages is theological. God is redrawing the boundary to the specifications of God's character, saying to those previously stigmatized, excluded, or dispossessed: I welcome you.[69] God aims to embrace everybody, in boundless compassion, with a special note of hope to individuals and groups previously disenfranchised and ignored. God is represented as the insistent and persistent gatherer (Isa. 56.8), so much so that the verb denoting gathering is said to be 'Yahweh's most defining verb, Yahweh's most characteristic activity'.[70] Nothing conveys better the universal intention than the statement, 'For my house shall be called a house of prayer *for all peoples*' (Isa. 56.7). It is not to be a house of prayer for ethnic Israelites only.

All along in these tableaus, faith in the human realm is predicated on God's compassion and faithfulness. In our first tableau, 'the LORD will make himself known to the Egyptians; and the Egyptians will know the LORD on that day', unexpected favor now bestowed on an enemy people (Isa. 19.21). The second tableau 'identifies *God* as the source of all that the Servant is and is called to do' (Isa. 42.1-9), blessing coming to the coastland that long was thought to be reserved for the heartland.[71] In the third tableau (Isa. 56.1-8), and now carrying over at rising decibel to be the central affirmation of the closing chapters of Isaiah and the tenor of the book, God's faithfulness is the central theme.[72]

> Then whoever invokes a blessing in the land shall bless by the God of faithfulness (*'elohei 'āmēn*), and whoever takes an oath in the land shall swear by the God of faithfulness; because the former troubles are forgotten and are hidden from my sight (Isa. 65.16).

This affirmation cannot be read as a message of God's faithfulness to ethnic Israel only. A larger canvas is necessary, inclusive and universal, the message of God's faithfulness now proclaimed from the lips of Jews and Gentiles alike. Richard Hays' way of framing the message of Romans may therefore need to be revised. He says that '[t]he driving question in Romans is not "How can I find a gracious God?" but "How can I trust in this allegedly gracious God if he abandons his promises to Israel?"'[73] In light of Isaiah's visions of inclusion, however, there is already parity between Jews and

69. Walter Brueggemann, *Isaiah 40–66* (Louisville, KY: Westminster/John Knox Press, 1998), p. 165.

70. Brueggemann, *Isaiah 40–66*, p. 173.

71. Hanson, *Isaiah 40–66*, p. 44.

72. Rendtorff, 'Zur Komposition des Buches Jesaja', p. 313.

73. Hays, *Echoes of Scripture*, p. 53.

Gentiles, on one occasion to the point of suggesting that the Gentile mission is primary (Isa. 49.6). Failure to reach out to the Gentiles would by Isaiah's criterion be no less serious than letting Israel down. As it is, God lets down neither of the two.

When we return to Romans 9-11 with Isaiah's visions in mind, the latter's vision is not inferior to Paul's with respect to inclusion, and Isaiah adds clarifying content to many of Paul's key terms. 'Or is God the God of Jews only? Is he not the God of Gentiles also?' Paul asks in Romans (Rom. 3.29), his question already answered in Isaiah (Isa. 11.10; 19.18-25; 42.1-9; 56.7). On the question of agency, the messianic figure in Isaiah is in Romans embodied in Jesus.[74] Tightly linked to the question of agency is the question of means. On this point, as well, Paul walks in lockstep with Isaiah on two counts that are at the heart of Romans. Moreover, when we let Isaiah weigh in as to how the faith-language of Paul should be understood, the ways of God's appointed rectifier is contrary to expectations (Isa. 11.1-5; 42.1-4; 52.13-15), and the stance of the rectifier is best described as *faithfulness* (Isa. 11.5; 42.4; 49.7; 65.16). Second, 'faithfulness' is so closely aligned with 'righteousness' as to make them almost synonymous (Isa. 11.4-5; 42.4, 6; 49.7, 8; 53.11)—as they are in Romans, too (Rom. 1.16-17; 3.22-26).[75] 'Righteousness', in turn, is a transforming, right-making enterprise and not simply a judicial category (Isa. 11.4-5; 42.1-4; 49.1-6). Lastly, Isaiah redraws the landscape of who will constitute the people of God by projecting a vision that includes the Gentiles and by blurring the terminology so as to make the chosen-ness of the Gentiles harness the vocabulary of the chosen-ness of Israel (Isa. 19.18-25; 56.1-8).

Isaiah and Paul in Concert

In light of the foregoing, Isaiah now carrying the tune in concert with Paul, it will be easier to navigate the part of Romans on which Augustine and Calvin built their theology of 'double predestination' (Rom. 9.6-33). In the course of the rhetorical exchange that begins with Paul's deep anguish for his own people, 'my kindred according to the flesh' (9.1-5),[76] he will say that '*not all* Israelites truly belong to Israel...and *not all* of Abraham's children are his true descendants' (9.6; cf. 2.13, 28-29). That is, 'Israel' must be con-

74. Isa. 11.1, 10; 28.16; 53.1; 59.20; cf. Rom. 9.33; 10.11, 16; 11.26; 15.12.

75. Williams ('The Righteousness of God in Romans', p. 289) points out that Paul makes *hē pistis tou theou, theou dikaiosynē*, and *hē alētheia tou theou* ('the faithfulness of God', 'the right-making of God', and 'the truth of God') virtually synonymous, all serving the purpose of demonstrating what God has done to make things right.

76. The vehemence of Paul's reassurance suggests that he is addressing doubts with regard to his 'Jewish' commitment (9.1-5).

figured according to criteria other than natural birth. This is not a novel idea, strong antecedents already found in Isaiah (Isa. 19.18-25; 56.7). Paul thus lends support to a notion of 'Israel' that is not defined strictly along ethnic lines. He adds that it is 'through Isaac that descendants shall be named for you', sounding the same note in Romans as in Galatians: the true children of God are children of promise and not physical descendants (Rom. 9.7; Gal. 3.16).[77] By adopting this line, he has already come a long way toward neutralizing the suspicion that God's word has failed (Rom 9.6). If 'Israel' is not primarily and essentially a matter of ethnicity, the discovery that many Israelites do not believe in Jesus does not prove anything—it certainly does not prove that God's word has failed.

But Paul is not taking the easy route because his concern for his 'kindred according to the flesh' is heartfelt, and the question does not fully dissolve in a re-definition of Israel along spiritual lines (9.3). Isaiah's role in the ensuing argument is to keep the end-point in the picture in focus, and the end-point is inclusion (11.26, 32). Rhetorical sub-plots in the letter must be circumscribed to serve the overriding errand of the vision of inclusion that Isaiah and Paul hold in common; it must not be the controlling element whether Paul treats the reader to God's apparent lack of love for Esau (Rom. 9.13; cf. Mal. 1.2-3) or God hardening Pharaoh's heart (Rom. 9.17, 18).[78] As for Pharaoh's heart, it is a heart already hardened at the outset and not inclined to let God get in the way of anything (Exod. 5.1-2; 7.3, 13; 14.8, 17-18).[79] Paul's examples are not normative, but they serve to set up his conclusions. 'So it depends not on human will or exertion, but on God who shows mercy', he says (Rom. 9.16), and, again, God 'has mercy on whomever he chooses, and he hardens whomever he chooses' (9.18). However, mercy and hardening are not priorities running in parallel or alternatives that God pursues with equal capricious relish.

'You will say to me then', Paul says in anticipation, 'Why then does he still find fault? For who can resist his will?' (9.19) His answer, as noted at

77. J. Louis Martyn, 'Events in Galatia: Modified Covenantal Nomism versus God's Invasion of the Cosmos in the Singular Gospel: A Response to J.D.G. Dunn and B.R. Gaventa', in *Pauline Theology*, vol. 1 (ed. Jouette Bassler; Minneapolis: Fortress Press, 1991), pp. 160-79. Martyn hints that Paul has modified his emphasis on the 'singular seed' somewhat in Romans.

78. To Augustine (*To Simplician—On Various Questions* I.2.16, in *Earlier Writings*, p. 396), grace is not on offer to Esau, whether in persuasive or coercive ways. 'Who would dare to affirm that the omnipotent lacked a method of persuading even Esau to believe?'

79. Oropeza ('Paul and Theodicy', p. 63) wisely sees the use of Esau/Jacob and Israel/Ishmael as attempts to explain 'the current status of corporate Israel', not as an exposition on predestination and not as a statement on 'the eternal destinies of the historical persons he mentions'.

the beginning of the chapter, is curt bordering on rude. 'But who indeed are you, O "virtuous" person, to argue with God? Will what is molded say to the one who molds it, "Why have you made me like this?"' (9.20) Paul seems to be willing to defend apparent capriciousness with a doctrine of inscrutability, but this view should not be embraced uncritically. Paul does not shut up troubling questions on principle (9.14, 19-21), but *he is shutting up some questions in the context that these questions come up in Romans*. Of the speaking voices in the Pauline dialogues, some deserve a long answer, some less than that. Accepting that there is a situational contingency, Paul does not shut down questions of theodicy for the church universal. He is only cutting off that *line* of questioning at certain points in the argument of Romans.[80]

The big questions of theodicy remain firmly in place when they are asked by the right people for the right reasons. It is enough to remember that God did not shut down Habakkuk's agonizing theodicy-question (Hab. 1.2-4). Indeed, God answered his question without delay (Hab. 2.2-4), and Paul's message in Romans is itself an extension of the answer to Habakkuk (Rom. 1.16-17). Abraham, the model believer in Romans (4.16), makes a distinctive contribution to theodicy by asking a question no less forthright than Habakkuk, 'Should not the Judge of all the earth do what is just?' (Gen. 18.25).[81] The charged, situational exchanges in Romans 9–11 should not be used as proof of a generalized muzzling of questions of theodicy.

In fact, there *are* answers to the questions Paul appears to cut off in the broader message of Romans. 'Who can resist his will?' Paul's critic asks (Rom. 9.19). In the immediate context, the question seems to be quashed (9.20-21). In the wider context of Romans, however, the question of God's will and human choice is addressed head-on with a different logic and outcome. 'Who can resist his will?' we hear again, anticipating the answer to be, 'No one'. But the answer elsewhere is clearly that the 'Jews', at least, can resist God's will, and 'they' did. The entire argument about un-faithfulness in the 'Jewish' story breaks down if the story is to be read as divine machination overriding human choice every step of the way.

80. It is not unthinkable that there is common ground if not identity between the 'virtuous person' in Rom. 2.1-3 and the 'virtuous person' in Rom. 9.20. In the former instance, Paul's smack down centers on shallowness and sanctimony. In the latter instance (9.20), he rather rudely silences the 'virtuous person' who may be one reason why there are doubts about Paul's 'Jewish' commitment (9.1-5) and who poses as a theological teacher and expert but is mostly a troublemaker (cf. 16.17-20).

81. Thomas L. Pangle, *Political Philosophy and the God of Abraham* (Baltimore: Johns Hopkins University Press, 2003).

> Or do you despise the riches of his kindness and forbearance and patience? Do you not realize that God's kindness is meant to lead you to repentance? (Rom. 2.4)
>
> But by your hard and impenitent heart you are storing up wrath for yourself on the day of wrath, when God's righteous judgment will be revealed (Rom. 2.5).

In these texts someone is resisting God's will by taking God's forbearance as a reason *not* to repent, instead making God's patience an occasion to *harden* the heart like Pharaoh.[82] Paul's argument implies culpability for resisting God's will. Lack of repentance on the part of the people in view is not described as a state brought about by God's sovereign, overruling power. In Romans 9–11, Paul softens the notion of divine hardening with respect to the Jews by describing it as an action without an acting subject: 'a hardening (*pōrōsis*) has come upon part of Israel, until the full number of the Gentiles has come in' (11.25). We should note that the hardening only applies to 'part of Israel', that it is temporary, and that it has a redemptive consequence. In the case of the Jews, the hardened heart cannot be that they are excluded from the elect as is alleged to be the case with Esau and Pharaoh. B.J. Oropeza cuts the knot in these passages by showing that Romans 9 'was never intended to be read by itself; one must read on to chap. 11 to gain the full perspective of what Paul is attempting to argue and why he uses the sources he does'.[83] To the question whether God's word has failed (9.6), the answer is that God's word has not failed because God has not rejected his people (9.6; 11.1, 2). There is more coming than meets the eye in the present because the climax is yet to arrive, culminating in a sweeping vision of completion and inclusion (Rom. 11.25-32).[84]

Before we get to that point, however, there is more about God's right-making (10.5-13). N.T. Wright demonstrates plausibly that the determinative text of Romans 9–11 is Christ-centered and therefore neither Gentile- nor Israel-centered (10.5-13; 10.9).[85] The passage in Rom. 10.5-13 turns 'the righteousness of faith' into a person, making that 'person' recount

82. Wright, *Paul and the Faithfulness of God*, pp. 1226-228; see also Claire Mathews McGinnis, 'The Hardening of Pharaoh's Heart in Christian and Jewish Interpretations', *JTI* 6 (2012), pp. 43-64; Dorian G. Coover Cox, 'The Hardening of Pharaoh's Heart in Its Literary and Cultural Contexts', *BSac* 163 (2006), pp. 292-311.

83. Oropeza, 'Paul and Theodicy', p. 73.

84. Oropeza, 'Paul and Theodicy', p. 76.

85. Wright, *The Faithfulness of God*, p. 1163; Hays, *Echoes of Scripture*, pp. 73-83. Christ-centeredness is also the key in Barth's exposition of election in Romans (*Romans*, pp. 340-61). Meeks ('On Trusting and Unpredictable God', pp. 113-14) makes Romans 9.30-10.21 the centerpiece of chaps. 9-11.

the entire story of God's right-making intervention so as to justify the translation 'right-making by faithfulness (*ek pisteōs dikaiosynē*)'.[86]

> But the Right-making by Faithfulness (*de ek pisteōs dikaiosynē*) says, 'Do not say in your heart, "Who will ascend into heaven?"' (that is, to bring Christ down) 'or "Who will descend into the abyss?"' (that is, to bring Christ up from the dead). But what does it say? 'The word is near you, on your lips and in your heart' (that is, the proclamation of faithfulness (*to rhēma tēs pisteōs*) that we preach); because if you confess with your lips that Jesus is Lord and believe in your heart that God raised him from the dead, you will be saved (Rom. 10.6-9, translation mine).

Problems abound in the human condition, but—thank God—no one needs to ascend into heaven to bring Christ down because that has already happened. No one needs to descend into the abyss to bring Christ up from the dead because that, too, has already happened, as the 'Right-making by Faithfulness' tells the story. No one needs to yearn for a far-away solution in time or space because the message of God's intervention 'is near you, on your lips and in your heart' in *present* human reality (10.8). In this message, 'there is no distinction between Jew and Greek; the same Lord is Lord of all and is generous to all who call on him' (10.12).

As asserted earlier, therefore, Paul is not replacing a message of God's arbitrary election of ethnic Jews with a doctrine of the arbitrary election of *some* Jews and *some* Gentiles, and he is not shutting down questions about God's justice in a letter that makes the question of God's justice its point of departure (Rom. 1.16-17; Hab. 2.2-4). Likewise, and of supreme importance to the overall concern in Romans, God's solicitous care for the Gentiles does not mean that the chosen people no longer count in God's reckoning. 'I ask, then, God has not rejected His people, has He?' Paul queries (11.1, NASB). 'So I ask, have they stumbled so as to fall?' he queries again (11.11).

86. Williams, 'The Righteousness of God in Romans', p. 289. For the oral character of Paul's diction, see Arthur J. Dewey, 'Acoustics of the Spirit: A Hearing of Romans 10', *Proceedings* 9 (1989), pp. 212-30; idem, 'A Re-Hearing of Romans 10:1-15', *Semeia* 65 (1994), pp. 109-127. In the latter essay, Dewey argues that 'Romans 10 needs to be performed orally to be truly understood, for Paul apparently wants an interplay between the performer of the letter and the audience' (p. 120). Immediacy and participation are also explored by Akito Ito, 'The Written Torah and the Oral Gospel: Romans 10.5-13 in the Dynamic Tension between Orality and Literacy', *NovT* 48 (2006), pp. 234-60. Meeks' interpretation ('On Trusting an Unpredictable God', pp. 115-17) is distinctive for pointing out Paul's theo-centric emphasis. We should hear Paul say, 'Everyone who puts his trust *in God* will be vindicated'. Torah is vindicated, too, by the fact that 'the Torah genuinely did promise God's righteousness, and because God sent his Son 'that the *dikaiōma tou nomou* be fulfilled among us' (8:3-4)'. This means that Paul is not twisting Deut. 30.12-13 to make it say the exact opposite of what the text appears to say in the original context. Rather, we need to 'revise our understanding of Paul's antitheses', here with the understanding that the law, taken in hand by Christ, is no longer antithetical to Paul's gospel.

By now we know Paul well enough to anticipate his answer, 'By no means!' (11.1, 11). The way forward, daunting from a human point of view, will not be by way of fatalism, or determinism, or an arbitrary orchestration of history (10.14-15). There will be equal treatment (10.12; cf. 2.11). Above all, there will be compassion. Given that compassion trumps other categories, rhetoric runs only a small step ahead of reality when Paul says that 'God has imprisoned all in disobedience so that he may be merciful to all' (11.32).

Paul, more than his opponents, is attuned to the boundaries of the prophetic map of 'Israel' in the Old Testament.[87] Isaiah leads the way because 'Isaiah is so bold as to say, "I have been found by those who did not seek me; I have shown myself to those who did not ask for me"' (Rom. 10.20; Isa. 65.1-2). But ethnic Israel has not been abandoned or forgotten even though the boundaries between Jews and Gentiles are beginning to blur. Whether we hear Paul say, 'and in this *way* (*kai houtōs*) all Israel will be saved' along an axis of *means* (11.26),[88] or '*so* shall all Israel be saved' along an axis of *time* (11.26, NRSV),[89] he speaks of the fullness (*plērōma*) of the one Israel of Jews and Gentiles (11.25; cf. 2.28-29). When we hear Isaiah and Paul in con-

Isaiah and Paul in Concert
Romans 9–11

- Paul is not indifferent to the 'Jewish' question (9.1-5) and neither is God (9.6; 11.1, 2).
- Message of inclusion—not arbitrary exclusion
- Exposition of God's mercy and generosity
- Proof of infinite resourcefulness (God) and theological imagination (Paul)

87. Christopher Zoccali ('"And so all Israel will be saved": Competing Interpretations of Romans 11.26 in Pauline Scholarship', *JSNT* 30 [2008], pp. 289-318) describes and evaluates five alternatives for 'all Israel' being saved. (1) historical Israel as 'eschatological miracle' after the ingathering of the Gentiles; (2) 'ecclesiological' interpretation where 'all Israel' represents Jew and Gentile; (3) a 'Roman mission' interpretation that relates to Jews in Rome who will respond to the gospel when they see the success of Paul's mission among Gentiles; (4) a 'two-covenant' approach that sees the historical nation of Israel saved apart from faith in Christ; (5) a 'total national elect' interpretation that is limited to the 'complete number of elect from the historical/empirical nation'. Zoccali finds option (5) most plausible. Jason A. Staples ('What Do the Gentiles Have to Do with "All Israel"? A Fresh Look at Romans 11:25-27', *JBL* 130 [2011], p. 390) concludes that Paul in Rom. 11.25-27, and in Romans 9-11 as a whole, 'has turned the question of God's rejection of Israel on its head by reminding the reader that "all Israel" is a larger entity than just the Jews… In fact, God desired to save all Israel so much that he is even incorporating the Gentiles to do it. God's faithfulness to Israel is so great that he has provided to save all—even Gentiles—in "Israel".'

88. Jewett (*Romans*, p. 701) appears to favor the modal sense while not excluding the temporal or holding the two options to be mutually exclusive.

89. Niels Hyldahl, 'καὶ οὕτως in Rom 11,26', *DTT* 37 (1974), pp. 231-34; Pieter W. van der Horst, '"Only Then Will All Israel Be Saved": A Short Note on the Meaning of καὶ οὕτως in Romans 11:26', *JBL* 119 (2000), pp. 521-25.

cert, gathering in general and gathering outcasts in particular are God's way (Isa. 56.8; cf. Rom. 10.15; Isa. 52.7), not some version of divinely calibrated exclusion. Inclusion in the human realm has a corollary in inclusion and mercy toward non-human creation and the earth (Isa. 11.1-10; 65.17-25).

'O the depth of the riches and wisdom and knowledge of God! How unsearchable are his judgments and how inscrutable his ways!' Paul exclaims at the close of his joint concert with the Old Testament prophet (Rom. 11.33). The way forward assumes infinite resourcefulness on the part of God and theological imagination on the part of Paul, Paul's imagination and confidence greatly helped by his fellow poet Isaiah in this part of Romans (Romans 9–11). The compassion Paul expresses at the beginning of the argument (9.2-3), has not been eclipsed or sidelined by other priorities or concerns. Here, as in the rest of Romans, compassion shows no sign of letting up.

Chapter 14

The Mercies of God in an Ecological Perspective (Rom. 12.1-21)

The twists and turns of Romans 9–11 are so demanding that the reader is hard pressed to emerge at the far end with a sense of momentum. But there is undeniable momentum going into the section, as shown by the exclamatory affirmations preceding it (Rom. 8.31-39), and there is—at least from the point of view of Paul—no less momentum when he concludes his exposition of God's plan with respect to Israel. Here, too, he resorts to exclamations, his confidence in God's mercy and ingenuity undiminished (11.33-36).[1] Before Paul gets to the exclamation, he provides a summary for the benefit of readers who may wonder what the take-home message is (11.30-32). This is important for the reader looking back, still trying to decide whether Paul has presented a message of selective mercy that is subordinate to a doctrine of arbitrary sovereignty, as the Augustinian tradition reads this part, or whether he has laid out a vision of compassion, equality, and inclusion that is reflected in his concluding summary.[2] It is also important for the reader going forward, now heading into a section of admonition dealing with the situation of believers in Rome (12.1–15.7). Four times in the pre-exclamation summary, we find the word 'mercy' in one form or another (11.30-32).

Points of Exclamation

- Rom. 8.31-39 Exclamations at the conclusion of 5.1–8.39
- Rom. 11.33-36 Exclamations at the conclusion of 9.1–11.36

> Just as you were once disobedient to God but have now received *mercy* (*ēleēthēte*) because of their disobedience, so they have now been disobedient in order that, by the *mercy* (*eleei*) shown to you, they too may now

1. Taubes (*The Political Theology of Paul*, pp. 51-2) hears a 'great jubilation' at the end of chap. 11.

2. Recall that Paula Fredriksen (*Augustine and the Jews*, p. 334) sees a new era in the Augustinian reading. Formerly, as in Origen, God was seen to be simultaneously just and merciful to all. From Augustine onward, the divine attributes of justice and mercy are applied serially and selectively. God is 'just' to all human begins, but he is not merciful to all.

> receive *mercy* (*eleēthōsin*). For God has imprisoned all in disobedience so that he may be *merciful* (*eleēsē*) to all (Rom. 11.30-32).

Disobedience is a problem for Jews and Gentiles alike, but God has found a way to make disobedience advance the interest of mercy. Indeed, 'disobedience' is here no longer the toxic state that one would normally take it to be. 'Mercy' or 'compassion' is the key word in the conclusion, in every way and facet matched to human need. If the ending is meant to capture the content and character of the preceding argument (9.1–11.29), as I believe it is, we have been treated to an exposition of the ingenuity of divine mercy. Unfortunately, English lacks the versatility of the Greek original for this part of the argument. A warm and vigorous Greek verb has to be rendered by a tepid noun in English. If we create the verb we need in English, we have the sequence, 'You (Gentiles) *have been mercied*...they (Jews) *may be mercied*...all *may be mercied*' (11.30-32). Human beings need to be 'mercied', and God's willingness to 'mercy' humans, Jew or Gentile, is more than adequate for the need. Moreover, the notion that '*all may be mercied*' extends beyond human creation.[3] We run no risk by saying that Paul goes into the rugged terrain of Romans 9–11 on the momentum of God's mercy (5.1–8.39), emerging on the other side with additional proof that God's mercy does not come up short (9.1–11.36).

Shape of Embodied Mercy
- An alternative community (12.1-21)
- Community and government (13.1-14)
- The 'weak' and the 'strong' (14.1–15.7)

Compassion in Action

Paul now begins to share his thoughts on how compassion is to find embodiment in the believing community in Rome.

> I appeal to you therefore, brothers and sisters, by the mercies of God (*dia tōn oiktirmōn tou theou*), to present your bodies as a living sacrifice, holy and acceptable to God, which is your spiritual worship (*logikēn latreian*) (Rom. 12.1).

We have come from 'mercy' (11.30-32), and to 'mercy' we go (12.1).[4] Or, in a slightly different idiom, we have come from 'compassion' (11.30-32),

3. Thus Marianne Meye Thompson ('"*Mercy upon All*": God as Father in the Epistle to the Romans', in *Romans and the People of God: Essays in Honor of Gordon D. Fee* [ed. Sven K. Soderlund and N.T. Wright; Grand Rapids: Eerdmans, 1999], p. 214), 'Human beings will and do participate in God's liberation of *all* creation, of which the adoption of the children of God is but one facet'.

4. Cranfield (*Romans*, pp. 595-96) notes that Paul's exhortation looks over its shoulder to the passage just finished (Romans 9–11) while acknowledging that 'the whole of

and to 'compassion' we are headed (12.1). Paul's surpassing vision of divine compassion is the foundation on which he prescribes how to live in Rome as an alternative community (12.1-21), how to relate to the governing authorities (13.1-14), and how to find a way forward for a community consisting of people that Paul categorizes as the 'weak' and the 'strong' (14.1–15.7).

Compassion has more legs to stand on than Paul's prior exposition. Nijay K. Gupta shows how Paul's specific word for 'compassion' (*oiktirmōs*) belongs to a tapestry of important texts in the Septuagint.[5] In response to Moses' request to see God's glory (Exod. 33.18), God answers that 'I will make all my goodness (Hebr. *tovi*; Gr. *doxē*) pass before you, and will proclaim before you the name, "The LORD"; and I will be gracious to whom I will be gracious, and will show mercy on whom I will show mercy (*kai oiktirēsō hon an oiktirō*)' (Exod. 33.19). This text, to be sure, has been part of Paul's prior exposition in Romans (Rom. 9.15). In Exodus, God descends in the cloud and then, in close proximity to Moses, proclaims the divine name by naming specific attributes, 'The LORD, the LORD, a God merciful (*oiktirmōn*) and gracious (*eleēmon*), slow to anger, and abounding in steadfast love and faithfulness' (Exod. 34.6). God is in this representation a Person who accelerates and magnifies the momentum of good in the world and, conversely, slows and minimizes the momentum of evil (Exod. 34.7).[6]

As yet another leg, perhaps best seen as the deepest layer in Paul's understanding of God's character, he starts off 2 Corinthians with a note on divine compassion. 'Blessed be the God and Father of our Lord Jesus Christ, the Father of mercies (*ho patēr tōn oiktirmōn*) and the God of all consolation (*paraklēseōs*)' (2 Cor. 1.3). This expression conveys more than God as 'merciful Father': 'it characterizes what God is in himself, the fountain of mercy' and 'the creator and original source of mercy'.[7] Better still, the term believes God to be the epitome of compassion, meaning compassion that is of a higher order and cannot be outdone. 'Compassion (*oiktirmos*)' is paired with 'consolation (*paraklēsis*)', the latter term having 'encouragement' in its range of meanings. God is

Encouragement as Bookends

'I urge and encourage (*parakalō*) you, by the compassions of God' (12.1)

'God of steadfastness and encouragement (*paraklēseōs*)' (15.5)

1.18–11.36 is concerned with the action of the merciful God'. Jewett (*Romans*, p. 727) agrees that Paul's ethical prescription is based primarily on Romans 9–11.

5. Nijay K. Gupta, 'What "*Mercies of God*"? Oiktirmos in Romans 12.1 against Its Septuagintal Background', *BBR* 22 (2012), pp. 81-96.

6. Gupta ('*Mercies of God*', p. 83) says that 'when God invokes his own name, mercy echoes throughout the world'.

7. Ralph P. Martin, *2 Corinthians* (WBC; Dallas: Word, 1998), pp. 8-9; for the latter part of the sentence attribution to Hans Windisch, *Der zweite Korintherbrief* (Göttingen: Vandenhoeck & Ruprecht, 1924), p. 38.

here the bedrock of compassion and encouragement. In Romans, Paul ends the section that explains 'how to live' on the same note. 'May the God of steadfastness (*hypomonēs*) and encouragement (*paraklēseōs*) grant you to live in harmony with one another, in accordance with Christ Jesus' (Rom. 15.5). Encouragement and compassion at the beginning (12.1), reliability and encouragement at the end (15.5) serve as bookends to this section (12.1–15.7). For a community that cannot count on uniformity of background for its make-up, whether ethnic, socioeconomic, religious, or with regard to gender, compassion is singled out as the value that will enable a new reality in the realm of practice and communal life.

Paul calls this 'logical service' (12.1). Translators have balked at the notion 'logical', not because Paul's argument runs contrary to what is rational or logical but because 'spiritual' is felt to be a better representation of what Paul had in mind. His term, however, is 'logical'. In this regard his ethical vision could well lie close to that of the Stoics, as Cranfield notes.[8] A person should be doing what is consistent with what that person is meant to be, the ideal here defined by 'the mercies of God' in the sense that description leads seamlessly to prescription (12.1). Barrett's idea that Paul has in mind 'worship consisting not in outward rites but in the movement of man's inward being' might work if we take 'outward rites' to be a reference to circumcision.[9] Otherwise, the contrast between 'outward rites' and inwardness creates a false dichotomy: it is precisely in the real world of bodies and materiality that the mercies of God are to find outward expression.

> Do not be conformed to this world (*tō aiōni toutō*), but be transformed by the renewing (*anakainōsei*) of your minds, so that you may discern what is the will of God—what is good and acceptable and perfect (Rom. 12.2).

'This world' or 'this age' is implicitly in Romans what it is explicitly in Galatians, 'the present *evil* age' (Gal. 1.4). Paul's view of present reality is in this respect apocalyptic to the core, setting his prescription within a framework that distinguishes Pauline thought from that of Stoic moralists like Plutarch.[10] He creates a resonant antithesis between business as usual and newness, the former by being *con*-formed to the present world and the latter by being *trans*-formed to a different way of life. Conformity is possible without much effort or reflection, but transformation requires thought. Paul describes it as 'renewal (*anakainōsis*) of the mind', using a word that is not found in ancient Greek outside the New Testament. He also strikes a fine balance between active and passive aspects of the *forming* that will happen

8. Cranfield, *Romans*, p. 602.
9. Barrett, *Romans*, p. 231.
10. Jewett, *Romans*, p. 732.

one way or another. Whether *con*-formed or *trans*-formed, outside influences are at work, the world or God as forming agents. Paul's verbal forms signify to 'stop allowing yourselves to be conformed...continue to let yourselves be transformed', as Cranfield notes.[11] This captures the *formation* as an ongoing process and as the result of being subject to outside influences.

Whatever specific counsel Paul will give with regard to behavior, he has signaled that the new values cannot simply be imposed from without. Transformation is anchored in 'the *renewing of the mind*' (12.2); it must resonate within so as to become the will of the believer.[12] 'Renewal' thus suggests profound change, a new way of seeing the self and the world. 'So that you may discern what is the will of God' means, on the one hand, that the renewed mind is the prerequisite for knowing what to do in a given situation: there will not be a specific prescription for each situation. On the other hand, it also means that knowledge of God's will must work itself out at the level of experience, and the proof of the pudding will be in the eating. The conceptions are broad and open-ended, but there is no need to worry because actions will rise from a mind restored to sanity. In this sense the notion of 'logical' or 'rational' worship should not be dismissed. The idea that discernment has 'the will of God' as its point of reference indicates that God is the judge of 'what is good and acceptable and perfect' (12.2), but the terms are inclusive and common and likely to resonate widely in Paul's Roman audience and beyond.

Compassion in Human Terms

If preservation of biodiversity in the ecosphere is one of the main ecological concerns, Paul has an analogous concern for diversity in human relationships. This is not a contrived analogy because ecology is fundamentally 'the science of relationships', as we have seen earlier.[13] When Paul urges a transformed outlook that will lead to discernment of the will of God (12.2), it involves the recognition that we are 'enmeshed in a harmonious web of relationships, infinitely complex in their intersections, that have in God their origin and their point of cohesion'.[14] His exhortation in Romans includes a

11. Cranfield, *Romans*, p. 607.

12. Cranfield, *Romans*, p. 606.

13. Leopold ('Natural History', pp. 209-10) writes observantly that 'modern natural history deals only incidentally with the identity of plants and animals and only incidentally with their habits and behaviors. It deals principally with their relation to each other, their relation to the soil and water in which they grew, and their relation to the human beings who sing about "my country" but see little or nothing of its inner workings. This science of relationships is called ecology, but what we call it matters nothing. The question is, does the educated citizen know he is only a cog in an ecological mechanism?'

14. Davis, *Scripture, Culture, and Agriculture*, p. 57.

vision of human diversity that is respectful of difference, mindful of varieties of gifts and mutual interdependence, and conscious that wholeness is possible only in community.

> For by the grace given to me I say to everyone among you not to think of yourself more highly than you ought to think, but to think with sober judgment, each according to the measure of faith that God has assigned. For as in one body we have many members, and not all the members have the same function, so we, who are many, are one body in Christ, and individually we are members one of another. We have gifts that differ according to the grace given to us: prophecy, in proportion to faith; ministry, in ministering; the teacher, in teaching; the exhorter, in exhortation; the giver, in generosity; the leader, in diligence; the compassionate, in cheerfulness (Rom. 12.3-8).

Jewett notes that Paul's exhortation is formal and declarative, now addressing himself to the house churches in Rome on the strength of his apostolic authority, and perhaps also intending to curtail charismatic influences lacking in restraint and sobriety.[15] His use of the body metaphor is telling not only for pointing out that the body has many members but also for the claim that 'individually we are members one of another' (12.5). This is similar to the Johannine concept of mutual indwelling ('perichoresis'), reflected in Jesus' prayer 'that they may all be one. As you, Father, are in me and I am in you, may they also be in us, so that the world may believe that you have sent me' (Jn 17.21). The Gospel of John spells out how the oneness and mutual indwelling in the divine realm is to be reflected in the body of believers in a way Paul does not, but the notion of being 'members one of another' is conceptually as demanding as John's ideal. For Paul, too, the reputation and standing of the church is a critical concern (Rom. 13.1-8), sober-mindedness singled out as the disposition that will characterize the body of believers internally and in relation to the wider community (12.3). Among the named spiritual gifts, terms that constitute the foundation of Paul's exhortation to the Romans reappear as gifts that are to flourish within the church. Thus, 'the encourager (*ho parakalōn*) is to exercise his or her gift in the giving of encouragement (*en tē parakalēsei*)' ...and the compassionate (*ho eleōn*) do likewise 'in gladness and wholeheartedness (*en hilarotēti*)' (12.8, translation mine).[16]

15. Jewett, *Romans*, p. 738. Dunn (*Romans 9–16*, p. 735) points out that Paul's list of spiritual gifts does not include speaking in tongues that had turned out to be a vexing issue in Corinth.

16. Jewett (*Romans*, p. 753) notes that mercy here describes the ministry of the church to outsiders and not only to insiders. Dunn (*Romans 9–16*, p. 731) notes that '[t]his is the only occasion in the Pauline literature in which ἐλεέω is used of human rather than divine mercy'.

> Let love (*hē agapē*) be genuine; hate what is evil, hold fast to what is good; love one another with mutual affection; outdo one another in showing honor. Do not lag in zeal, be ardent in spirit, serve the Lord. Rejoice in hope, be patient in suffering, persevere in prayer. Contribute to the needs of the saints; extend hospitality to strangers. Bless those who persecute you; bless and do not curse them. Rejoice with those who rejoice, weep with those who weep. Live in harmony with one another; do not be haughty, but associate with the lowly; do not claim to be wiser than you are. Do not repay anyone evil for evil, but take thought for what is noble in the sight of all. If it is possible, so far as it depends on you, live peaceably with all. Beloved, never avenge yourselves, but leave room for the wrath of God; for it is written, 'Vengeance is mine, I will repay, says the Lord'. No, 'if your enemies are hungry, feed them; if they are thirsty, give them something to drink; for by doing this you will heap burning coals on their heads'. Do not be overcome by evil, but overcome evil with good (Rom. 12.9-21).

The NRSV begins Paul's exposition on love (*agapē*) by casting it as an exhortation, but the sentence is in the indicative. It states what love is and not what love ought to be. Thus, 'the love [is] without pretense', and this 'serves as the thesis statement for the pericope', as Jewett notes.[17] Love without pretense might be clarifying and liberating in any context, but it would certainly resonate in Rome, given the memory that the first emperor, Julius Caesar, was murdered by people pretending to be his friends. Cranfield points out that Paul up to this point has used *agapē* only with reference to God's love (Rom. 5.5, 8; 8.35, 39), but he now applies it to believers' relationship to each other and even to non-believers.[18] Love as *agapē* is emerging as a word that will be defined by the message of God revealed in Christ and not by antecedent usage in Greek religion or philosophy.[19] Here, as Jewett notes, the definite article 'indicates that it is not love in general but specifically Christian love already manifest in the Roman churches that now comes under discussion'.[20]

Three general elements are evident in Paul's exhortation. First, the specific attitudes, values, and conduct that he describes, are the outflowing of 'the mercies of God' (12.1), that is, divine mercy made real in relationships. Second, the use of '*the* love (*hē agapē*)' as a second heading (12.9; cf. 12.1) reinforces a life-orientation that is self-giving, dedicated to the good of others and to the building up of the community. Third, while Paul lists many specifics, his 'program' can be actualized only by 'the renewing

17. Jewett, *Romans*, p. 756.

18. Cranfield, *Romans*, pp. 629-30.

19. While J.H. Moulton and G. Milligan (*The Vocabulary of the Greek Testament* [London: Hodder and Stoughton, 1930], p. 2) do not fully endorse the idea that *agapē* is a word 'born within the bosom of revealed religion', the comment itself is suggestive of the distinctive use of this word for 'love' in the New Testament.

20. Jewett, *Romans*, p. 758.

of the mind' (12.2), and the specifics are in that sense mere excerpts of a reality that cannot be represented by specifics. If it could, it would require a much longer list. Nevertheless, Paul's 'list' is fluent and has poetic eloquence, suggesting that this is familiar territory, a subject of which he has exquisite command by virtue of reflection, practice, and teaching. Among the specifics, the most memorable lines are contrasts to what humans would normally do and contrasts to what is prescribed in the Roman code of honor.

> Do not repay anyone evil for evil, but take thought for what is noble in the sight of all (12.17).
>
> If it is possible, so far as it depends on you, live peaceably with all (12.18).
>
> Do not be overcome by evil, but overcome evil with good (12.21).

On this list, there is progression from passive to active virtues in responding to wrong, from not repaying anyone 'evil for evil' to overcoming evil 'with good' (12.17, 21). Paul's concern for the success of the mission cannot be left out, calling for conduct that is 'noble in the sight of all' (12.17). Indeed, in line with the idea that Paul is describing 'logical worship' that requires thought and sober-mindedness (12.1, 3), the short list above urges the Romans to exercise *pro-noeō*, 'to think about something beforehand', that is, to think ahead and be proactive. His list of specifics include a mix of affirmations and negations, what to do and what not to do (e.g. 12.17 and 21), but the affirmations loom larger than the negations. If the believing community in Rome lives out Paul's communal vision, it will stand apart by what the believers do more than by what they don't do.

Compassion in Ecological Terms

Perhaps no chapter in Romans invites an ecologic hermeneutic as much as this one. As noted above, ecology is fundamentally 'the science of relationships',[21] compassion now the sentiment that is most needed and most lacking with respect to critical ecological concerns. Jacques Derrida has articulated what is at stake with regard to animal suffering, drawing on Jeremy Bentham's formulation two centuries ago. To Bentham, the question 'is not to know whether the animal can think, reason, or speak… The *first* and *decisive* question would rather be whether animals *can suffer*.'[22]

> War is waged over the matter of pity. This war is probably ageless…but it is passing through a critical phase. We are passing through that phase, and it passes through us. To think that the war we find ourselves waging is not

21. Davis, *Scripture, Culture, and Agriculture*, p. 57.

22. Jacques Derrida, *The Animal That Therefore I Am* (trans. David Wills; PCP; New York: Fordham University Press, 2008), p. 27.

> only a duty, a responsibility, an obligation, it is also a necessity, a constraint that, like it or not, directly or indirectly, no one can escape… The animal looks at us, and we are naked before it.[23]

A war waged 'over the matter of pity', as Derrida perceives it, will not be a matter of indifference to the message of Romans. Paul, as we have seen above, makes it his task to inscribe an ethic of compassion on the believing community in Rome. Divine compassion, the grounding element of his vision (12.1), is inclusive and not only for the benefit of human beings (8.19-22). Moreover, Paul is aware that a vision of divine compassion entails values that are contrary to the established culture, requiring non-conformity to the world and the establishment of an alternative community (12.2). Given that Paul's ethical take-home message rests on the theological foundation of the entire letter up to this point,[24] we need to read this part, too, in the widescreen edition. While Paul describes God's mercy as the cornerstone of redemption (11.30-32), compassion is not a novelty in the character of God or a trait brought into existence by human need. Compassion is original and eternal, thus Paul's phrase that God is 'the Father of mercies (*ho patēr tōn oiktirmōn*) and the God of all consolation (*paraklēseōs*)' (2 Cor. 1.3).[25] The compassionate God is not absent in creation or at creation. When God confers a blessing on non-human creatures in the Genesis story of creation, we see a God who cares for, and takes delight in, the well-being and flourishing of all sentient beings (Gen. 1.20-22).

Two aspects of Paul's creation retrospective make it possible to make this more than an assumption. In Rom. 5.12-20, Paul looks back to the first chapters of Genesis, recalling how 'sin came into the world through one man, and death came through sin' (Rom. 5.12). The verb depicts sin *coming* or *entering in*, intruding into a space where it did not exists previously. Death piggy-backed on sin, the new reality described as the Reign of Death (5.14, 17). In the ensuing state, death is everywhere, the logic and reality of death felt throughout the created order. The groaning of non-human creation obligates not only because non-human creatures suffer but because the groaning happens in the presence of a God who cares (8.22). Likewise, with respect to groaning, human and non-human creatures speak the same language (8.22, 23), and they are joined by the groaning of the Holy Spirit, the groaning of the Spirit so intense that it is 'too deep for words' (8.26). All of this is testimony to divine awareness, first, and compassion, second.

In the 'Eve story' in Romans 7 (7.7-13), 'Eve' is led to insights that place divine compassion in a broader context. The first insight is 'Eve's' realization

23. Derrida, *The Animal That Therefore I Am*, p. 29.

24. Thus Cranfield (*Romans*, pp. 595-96), that 'the whole of 1.18–11.36 is concerned with the action of the merciful God'.

25. Martin, *2 Corinthians*, pp. 8-9.

that 'the commandment…was for life' (7.11). God set up an economy of life and plenitude and not an economy of lack, deprivation, or rivalry. Second, as we have seen earlier, the commandment was misrepresented to appear as the exact opposite of what God intended (Gen. 3.1). 'Sin, seizing an opportunity in the commandment, *deceived* me', says 'Eve' (Rom. 7.11; cf. 7.8). Third, the misperceived commandment opened the floodgate to desire and death (7.7-11), the momentum of death all the worse because 'the very commandment that promised life proved to be death to me' (7.10). Where is compassion in this landscape? 'Compassion' and 'mercy' are easier to spot in a landscape littered with death, but they are here, too, submerged in a God-ordained economy of generosity and abundance. While compassion may be reckoned as compassion only when vulnerability and need have been defined, it belongs within the continuum of generosity and care that come to view in 'the commandment that was for life' (7.11).

Paul's injunctions are set against a horizon of need that is different from the twenty-first century, but his framework is not outdated. Along the narrative axis, the flashbacks to Genesis are hugely empowering for the earth and the rights of non-human creatures. The 'Father of mercy' in Paul's letters is the Father of mercy not only as a fact of the first century but as the Creator of all that exists. An ethic of compassion had much to keep it busy in Paul's time, but the ecological concerns of the twenty-first century call for redeployment of compassion of a different order. Likewise, the world to which the believer is asked not to conform has taken ecological strides in the wrong direction unimaginable in Paul's time. These changes define areas of non-conformity for our time that are as much in need of thoughtful, pro-active, compassionate living as what Paul urges in Romans (Rom. 12.9-21).

I will specify three such areas, the first regarding the divine economy of *seed*, the second with respect to the economy of *land*, and the third with regard to the suffering of *animals*. The contemporary economy of seeds will serve as a contrast to God's economy of open-ended generosity, the economy of land as a contrast to an economy of acquisition and exploitation, and the suffering of animals as our window to an economy bereft of compassion. All three expose realities that transform Paul's general ethic of compassion into an urgent call for mercy.

'Seeds' of Compassion at Creation: Ecology and Theology

• Seeds	Generosity
• Land	Sustainability
• Animals	Mercy

The Divine Economy of Seeds

Why *seeds*, in *Romans*? I have suggested an answer above, but it bears repetition and elaboration. Seed is the ecological marvel in God's original economy of abundance, corroborating, metaphorically speaking, that the divine command 'was for life' (Rom. 7.11). The prominence of 'seed' in the creation account means that the pro-life character of the divine command has an unrecognized and under-appreciated ecological expression at the point of origin. Ecology is not a late-comer in the biblical narrative, and it does not come theologically empty-handed to the table. The divine economy of seed at creation and the human economy of seed in the twenty-first century are such dramatic contrasts that they become representative images, ecologically and theologically.

> Then God said, 'Let the earth put forth vegetation: plants yielding seed, and fruit trees of every kind on earth that bear fruit with the seed in it'. And it was so. The earth brought forth vegetation: plants yielding seed of every kind, and trees of every kind bearing fruit with the seed in it. And God saw that it was good (Gen. 1.11-12).

The word 'seed' occur six times in these two verses even though translations reduce it to four times to diminish the impression of redundancy. This is unfortunate because the repetition signifies importance. Before the first chapter in Genesis is over, the word has appeared four more times, two more of which fall victim to pruning by the translator's knife (Gen. 1.29). In all, 'seed' occurs ten times in the first chapter of Genesis (Gen. 1.10-11, 29). God is not creating plants only but 'plants yielding *seed*'; God is not making fruit trees grow but 'fruit with the *seed* in it' (Gen. 1.11).[26] Intention turns into actualization: we see the earth bringing forth 'plants yielding seed of every kind', and we see 'trees of every kind bearing fruit with the seed in it' (Gen. 1.12). It is not all about seed, but the seed dominate as the element of priority.

What, then, is the biology and theology of seed? What are the existential ramifications? Are not seeds an ingenious invention for which God can justly be proud? Is there not a theological message in the creation of seed, a message that puts provision and generosity front and center? Are not seed an element of existence that reverberates with renewal, diversity, sustainability, predictability, and abundance? The saying that you cannot have your cake and eat it, too, is true until you apply it to the reality of seeds. Seeds ensure that a new plant will spring up when the mother plant is eaten, and the seeds of the mother plant are often too numerous to count. Another saying holds that there is no such a thing as a free lunch. This saying is also evidence-based, but it is contradicted by the existence of seeds. Given the reality of seeds, especially as seeds are introduced in Genesis, there

26. Ellen Bernstein (*The Splendor of Creation: A Biblical Ecology* [Cleveland: The Pilgrim Press, 2005], p. 37) shows awareness of 'seed' as the element to which the narrator draws attention.

is such a thing as a free lunch. The excitement surrounding the introduction of plants and fruit trees with seeds has the connotation not only of abundance and renewal but also of security and effortlessness. Originally, it takes little effort to earn a seat at God's table of abundance, but a contrast may be implied. Umberto Cassuto intimates that the emphasis on plants having seeds in Genesis 1 stands in contrast to plants requiring effort and labor later in the account (Gen. 3.17-19).[27] In the post-fall representation, the yield of the land will not come without strenuous effort, and humans will do battle with soil that grows thorns and thistles and not only deal with 'plants yielding seed' (Gen. 1.11).

What is most remarkable, perhaps, is how little attention commentators pay to this feature of creation and how little interest it has attracted, whether with regard to biology, ecology, or theology.[28] It is as though God springs a surprise so early in the creation account that readers are not yet ready to look and listen. The theological message, at a minimum, is divine generosity, and the theological message is delivered in an ecological currency. Generosity finds a biological expression. This should be seen as a broad conception that includes compassion, and it refutes the contention of the serpent that God set up an economy of deprivation (Gen. 3.1; cf. Rom. 7.8, 11). Ecology is here the eloquent and evocative handmaid of theology.

We are expected to hear excitement and enthusiasm in God's voice when God brings the phenomenon of plants yielding seed to the attention of human beings on day six in the creation story. God's short statement is formulated exclusively with reference to permission and provision and not with reference to prohibition.

> God said, 'See, I have given you every plant yielding seed that is upon the face of all the earth, and every tree with seed in its fruit; you shall have them for food. And to every beast of the earth, and to every bird of the air, and to everything that creeps on the earth, everything that has the breath of life, I have given every green plant for food.' And it was so (Gen. 1.29-30).

Again, theology and ecology walk hand in hand, theology revealing a generous and giving God and ecology driving home that existence is ecological. Ellen Davis captures both aspects as contrasts to Canaanite fertility religions. Fertility in Genesis is a built-in feature of the created order and not a result of insemination by the fertility gods. Human beings are not 'created to provide food for the gods—a divine commission that was fulfilled through an integrated and state-sponsored food system of irrigated agriculture and cultic sacrifice. The Genesis account claims the reverse: the

27. Umberto Cassuto, *A Commentary on the Book of Genesis: Part I, From Adam to Noah* (trans. I. Abrahams; Jerusalem: The Magnes Press, 1998), pp. 40-41.

28. Major commentaries on Genesis have nothing or next to nothing to say about the theology of seeds, or anything at all on the subject, for that matter.

Creator of heaven and earth is the generous One who provides food for every living creature.'[29]

If seed in the creation account is the currency of life, generosity, and the ticket to a free breakfast, lunch, and dinner, what have seeds become in the twenty-first century? Even seeds, we must say, even *seeds*, the earliest expression of divine generosity in the biblical narrative, have been made a commodity and subjected to commercial interest. No civilization prior to ours had the audacity to patent and claim ownership of seeds, and no civilization prior to ours aspired to make *seeds*, not only *crops*, a commercial commodity to the extent that is happening in the twenty-first century.[30]

'I have given you every plant yielding seed', we read in the creation account (Gen. 1.29). And yet seeds are now held hostage of a commercial mediator in a centralized economy of seeds that that is threatening to become a virtual seed monopoly. As Davis notes, the industrialized food system is eclipsing the vision of self-perpetuating fruitfulness in the Bible 'with the profit strategies of corporations aiming to control the global seed market'.[31] Seeds are a hot button item on in a market that is sacrificing diversity to the hope of short term yield. As of 2007, a mere ten corporations 'sell an astonishing 55 percent of the seeds that produce the world's food crops'.[32] The allure of genetically modified seeds have been hugely facilitated by scientists' efforts to equip seed with chemical resistant properties, the most famous of which are Roundup Resistant seeds. 'Roundup' is the trade name for glyphosate, developed and sold by the giant agribusiness company Monsanto. Glyphosate tolerant crops now include corn, soybeans, canola, cotton, sugarbeets, and alfalfa.[33] The logic of glyphosate use is convenience: it is possible to sow fields with glyphosate tolerant seeds that can subsequently be drenched repeatedly with glyphosate to kill the weeds. This logic means the unleashing of death on a grand scale, counting on a chemical to kill or subdue everything else that grows in the field, hoping that the downside of such massive use of chemicals will be tolerable. Agriculture is now experiencing the phenomenon that is well known in medicine with regard to bacterial resistance to antibiotics. Glyphosate resistance has been reported for horseweed, Giant Ragweed, Common Ragweed, Common

29. Davis, *Scripture, Culture, and Agriculture*, p. 51.

30. Vandana Shiva (*Biopiracy: The Plunder of Nature and Knowledge* [Boston: South End Press, 1997], pp. 43-64) notes the disruption between seeds and the earth in the modern seed economy.

31. Davis, *Scripture, Culture, and Agriculture*, p. 52.

32. John Seabrook, 'Sowing for Apocalypse: The Quest for a Global Seed Bank', *The New Yorker*, August 27, 2007, p. 69. This essay is an excellent introduction to the ecology and history of seeds and modern seed engineering. See also, Davis, *Scripture, Culture, and Agriculture*, p. 52.

33. http://www.sourcewatch.org/index.php/Roundup_Ready_Crops

Waterhemp, and Johnsongrass.[34] A seed economy that counts on selective killing of weeds by chemical means is courting the risk of 'monster weeds', the agricultural counterpart to 'superbugs' in medicine.

In order to ensure patent protection of genetically modified seeds, the technology exists with which to produce 'sterile seeds'. This is the ultimate negation of the ecology and theology of seeds in the creation account in Genesis. It is, at least metaphorically, the ecological poster example of the logic and 'Reign of Death' (Rom. 5.12-21). 'Sterile seeds' are genetically modified seeds that can be sown normally and will grow normally in the first generation.[35] However, the seeds of the mature plant will not grow because they have been equipped with 'terminator genes'.[36] Where Genesis advertises with enthusiasm not only 'plants' but 'plants yielding seed' (Gen. 1.11), commercial interests in the twenty-first century have neutered by rendering impotent the defining property of seeds. The owners of the 'sterile seed' patent have for the time being agreed to observe a self-imposed moratorium on its deployment, but the symbolism is telling.

'That humans now dominate the planet, and do so in a way that would have been unimaginable to any inhabitant of the ancient world, is a fact beyond dispute', says Davis in the context of a discussion of the modification and commodification of seeds in the twenty-first century.[37] For a believing reader of Romans now, the ecological challenge of these realities will be the same as for anyone else although the sense of loss and motivation may be different. Ecological action, however, may not be the first thing that comes to mind. Perhaps the fevered economy of seeds provides an opportunity for theological reflection and witness. When Paul instructs believers not to be 'conformed to this world' (Rom. 12.2), it can be taken as an invitation to reflect on the character of 'this world' and the mind-numbing contrasts between the tight-fisted, commerce-driven logic of 'this world' and the generous logic of 'the Father of mercies' (2 Cor. 1.3; Rom. 12.1). The contrasting economies of seeds will be the ecologic contribution to such a reflection, an opportunity for witness regarding the open-ended divine economy that is for life and an economy of control, profit, and disregard for consequences.

34. http://www.sourcewatch.org/index.php/Roundup_Ready_Crops

35. Robert F. Service, 'Seed-Sterilizing "Terminator Technology" Sows Discord', *Science* 282 (1998), pp. 850-1; Fraser Los, 'The Terminator', *Alternatives Journal* 32 (2006), pp. 24-6; cf. Davis, *Scripture, Culture, and Agriculture*, p. 52.

36. http://www.vintageveggies.com/news/terminator_gene.html

37. Davis, *Scripture, Culture, and Agriculture*, p. 53. Thus also David W. Orr ('The Uses of Prophecy', in *The Essential Agrarian Reader: The Future of Culture, Community, and the Land* [ed. Norman Wirzba; Washington, DC: Shoemaker & Hoard, 2003], p. 181), 'we are witness to death on the largest scale imaginable—that of life on the earth itself'.

The Economy of Land

In Genesis 2, we are brought face to face with an economy of land that is as explicit and tantalizing as the economy of seeds in Genesis 1. In the second, complementary account of creation (Gen. 2.4-25), the story begins with the land.

> In the day that the LORD God made the earth and the heavens, when no plant of the field was yet in the earth and no herb of the field had yet sprung up—for the LORD God had not caused it to rain upon the earth, and there was no one to till (*'ābad*) the ground...then the LORD God formed man from the dust of the ground, and breathed into his nostrils the breath of life; and the man became a living being (Gen. 2.4-7).

The sequence in this story is remarkable, as is the implied rationale guiding it. First, the scene is described in terms of negations or absences.

> no plant was yet in the earth (2.5).
>
> no herb of the field had yet sprung up (2.5).
>
> no one to till (*'ābad*) the ground (2.7).

A plan is implied that will include plants and herbs, and it will also include humans, but the plan seems to be written from the point of view of the earth. Second, therefore, a notion of vocation seems to guide the sequence in creation, the implied commission now becoming the reason for human existence. The translation of the NRSV legitimately hints at a causal relationship between the creation of human beings and the prior observation that 'there was no one to till the earth' (Gen. 2.5). Humans are created with an eye to the task at hand to the point of suggesting that the humans exist for the sake of the earth as much as the earth exists for the sake of humans.[38] Third, God 'formed (*'ādām*) from the dust of the ground (*'ădāmâ*), and breathed into his nostrils the breath of life; and the man (*'ādām*) became a living being' (Gen. 2.7). The person thus formed shares, in the most literal sense, *common ground* with the earth.[39] Adam is an earthling. When death intrudes, he will return to the earth (Gen. 3.19). As humans take up the task of caring for the earth, they will be caring for the matter of which they are made. Fourth, the terms describing the vocational commission are agrarian in the narrow sense but comprehensive for ministry and service in the broad sense.[40]

38. This logic has been grasped and developed by contemporary agrarians (see Jackson *et al.*, *Meeting the Expectations of the Land*). Marty Strange ('The Economic Structure of Sustainable Agriculture', pp. 115-25, above) argues on behalf of farms that are *family centered, owner operated*, and *internally financed.*

39. Newsom, 'An Ecological Reading of Genesis 2–3', p. 63.

40. Swenson, 'Care and Keeping East of Eden', pp. 373-84.

> There was no one to till (*'ābad*) the ground (Gen. 2.5).

> The LORD God took the man and put him in the garden of Eden to till it (*'ābad*) and keep it (*shāmar*) (Gen. 2.15).

> Therefore the LORD God sent him forth from the garden of Eden, to till (*'ābad*) the ground from which he was taken (Gen. 3.23).

The dual commission 'to till it (*'ābad*) and keep it (*shāmar*)' is the earliest statement of God's purpose for human beings (Gen. 2.15),[41] complementing the notion of 'dominion' in the first creation account (Gen. 1.26-28). Men and women will 'till' (*'ābad*), meaning that they will serve, minister to, and preserve the earth.[42] They will 'keep' (*shāmar*), meaning that they will guard, protect, and shield the earth from harm.[43] The narrow occupational connotation of 'tilling' and 'keeping' must not be allowed to eclipse the broad vocational scope of these terms. 'Tilling and keeping' have the sense of 'ministering and protecting'. They inculcate an ethic of care and, as an extension of care, compassion.

There is confirmation of this later in the Genesis narrative, at the point when Cain is confronted with the murder of his brother, Abel.

> Then the Lord said to Cain, 'Where is your brother Abel?' (Gen. 4.9).

> He said, 'I do not know; am I my brother's keeper (*hashomer aḥi*)?' (Gen. 4.9).

The question and the answer in this exchange echo the encounter between God and Adam and Eve in the Garden of Eden after eating of the tree of knowledge (Gen. 3.9-13), only now the distance between the questioner and the one questioned is much greater.[44] Here, outside Eden, Cain responds with an outright lie, 'I do not know' (Gen. 4.9). He takes the offensive, implying that God is unreasonable for implying that he has an unmet responsibility on his hands. What Cain has failed to do is described by the word 'keeping' (*shāmar*), primed for action earlier in God's commission to humans (Gen. 2.15). This reference point makes Cain's evasion resound like peals of

41. Robert Alter (*Genesis: Translation and Commentary* [New York: W.W. Norton, 1996], p. 8) has 'till it and watch it'. The terms are part complementary and part synonymous, a Hebrew parallelism.

42. Thus Sarna (*Genesis*, p. 20), the man 'has duties to perform. It is his responsibility to nurture and conserve the pristine perfection of the garden.'

43. von Rad (*Genesis*, p. 78) says that 'work was man's sober destiny even in his original state. That man was transferred to the garden to guard it indicates that he was called to a state of service and had to prove himself in a realm that was not his own possession.' Wenham (*Genesis 1-15*, p. 67) notes similarly that 'even before the fall man was expected to work: paradise was not a life of leisured unemployment'.

44. Kenneth M. Craig, Jr, 'Questions outside Eden (Genesis 4.1-16): Yahweh, Cain and Their Rhetorical Interchange', *JSOT* 86 (1999), p. 121.

thunder. Cain may be a 'tiller' and a 'keeper' in the narrow, literal sense of these words. At the basic level, he will 'till' the soil. But he rejects the vocation to minister, preserve, and protect. His refusal to be his brother's keeper signals the absence of compassion, a narrow, self-centered view of the original commission.[45] Kristin Swenson is too naïve when she allows for the possibility that Cain did not realize that the responsibility of 'tilling' and 'keeping' goes beyond care for the earth, belatedly waking up to the fact that he is also responsible for the well-being of his brother, but this view of the commission does not weaken the ecological import.[46] Cain's defense might have worked in the context of a lesser oversight, but it does not work when the oversight is murder. Swenson is correct, however, that the story pulls the reader into the text. Cain's, 'I do not know', makes the reader want to cry out, 'Liar! You know perfectly well.'[47] And his question, 'Am I my brother's keeper?' makes the reader answer back, 'Yes of course you are'.[48]

What, then, of what will arguably be the lesser obligation of 'tilling' and 'keeping', the ecological responsibility? 'Am I the earth's keeper?' we can now ask, perhaps in the same combative posture as Cain displayed in Genesis.[49] How do we ask this question with his shadow in the background, the first to declare that he did not see himself as a 'keeper'? Davis notes as a point of congruence between the contemporary agrarians and the biblical writers that both assign value to the land. 'There is no record, biblical or inscriptional, of an Israelite voluntarily selling land on the open market, because—in contrast to their neighbors in Egypt and Mesopotamia—Israelites seem to have had no concept of arable land ('ădāmâ) as a commodity, to be bought and sold freely'.[50]

Nothing sets the modern land economy apart from the commission in Genesis and later practice in Israel as much as how land is now treated as a commodity. Land is valued as scenery, to be sure, one of the emphases of the conservation movement, but this is a side show.[51] Above all, land is held

45. It goes without saying that if the commission to 'till' and to 'keep' are terms inculcating care and compassion, they will have a broad reference as to whom or what should benefit.

46. Swenson, 'Care and Keeping East of Eden', p. 378.

47. Swenson, 'Care and Keeping East of Eden', p. 380.

48. Swenson, 'Care and Keeping East of Eden', p. 380.

49. The problem of soil erosion is a telling case in point, referring to soil depletion and actual, irreversible loss of land. Dawen Yang, Shinjiro Kanae, Tajkan Oki, Toshio Koike and Katumi Musia ('Global potential soil erosion with reference to land use and climate changes', *Hydrological Processes* 17 [2003], pp 2913-28) describe soil erosion as a common natural disaster, estimating that one third of the world's arable land has been lost to erosion over the past forty years.

50. Davis, *Scripture, Culture, and Agriculture*, p. 39.

51. Berry, *The Unsettling of America*, pp. 23-26.

in high regard for its monetary value. Acquisition of land drove the colonial enterprise in the fifteenth and sixteenth century, first on the fading medieval logic that property was the 'money' of the Middle Ages,[52] then as the backbone of the emerging capitalist system.[53] Land is in the United States unlovingly but reassuringly referred to as 'real estate', not land for 'tilling' and 'keeping' but for buying and selling, the term 'real estate' serving as an admission that land alone is 'real' value, and the monetized worth of land is only a fiction of perception. In the financial crisis of 2008, one of the driving elements was precisely the growing discrepancy between the alleged monetary value of property and its 'real' value. Concepts like 'subprime mortgages', for instance, must be understood as a measure of the distance from the debt incurred to the land or property meant to underwrite the debt. 'Subprime' means 'less than prime', meaning that there might be little or no land committed in the deal, only a transaction of large amounts of money disembodied from the land, or, conversely, no money down and thus property changing hands on the strength of a poorly secured loan in the belief that the monetary value of property can only go in one direction: up.[54] Land as commodity is the underlying reason why Wendell Berry and other agrarians see the loss of the family farm, the increasing distance between the proprietor and the land, and the dominance of intensive, industrial methods of land management not only as a crisis of agriculture but as a crisis of character.[55] Davis is even more pointed, saying that biblical study and ecological awareness are of mutual benefit to each other, resting 'not only on the

52. Eric Robert Morse, *Juggernaut: Why the System Crushes the Only People Who Can Save It* (New Classic Books, 2010), pp. 17-18.

53. Georges Lefebre (*The French Revolution: From Its Origins to 1793* [trans. Elizabeth Moss Evanson; New York: Columbia University Press, 1962], pp. 24, 25) says that agriculture was the mainstay of the economy well into the eighteenth century. 'Everyone was in one way or another involved with land: the individual, rich or poor, who aspired to become a man of property; the statesman who knew that population increase depended upon more food and hence meant more taxpayers and prospective public servants'. Profit-seeking, however, was the driving force. 'Their attitude, characterized by a hazardous quest for profit, transformed the warring spirit into a ruthless determination to vanquish competitors and made speculation the mainspring of their activity. With them appeared certain characteristics of what we call capitalism—concentration of capital and business concerns so that exploitation could be rationalized, a development that gave this economic technique cardinal importance in the rise of European civilization.' Lefebre shows how manipulation of the grain trade was a factor in the run-up to the French Revolution.

54. Oren Bar-Gill, 'The Law, Economics and Psychology of Subprime Mortgage Contracts', *Cornell L. Rev.* 94 (2009), pp. 1073-1171.

55. Berry, *The Unsettling of America*, pp. 3-79.

land-centeredness of the Bible but also on the nature of the ecological crisis, which is principally moral and theological rather than technological'.[56]

The ecological obligation to 'serve' and 'preserve' the land in Genesis comes off the same page of mercy as Paul's ethic in Romans: both are meant to be embodiments of 'the Father of mercy' (2 Cor. 1.3). The first setback to compassion is seen in Cain's callous repudiation of his vocation (Gen. 4.9), with much more to follow. As with the divine economy of seed, the creation economy of land is yet another opportunity for theological reflection, identity construction, and witness.

Compassion and Animals

It is now time to return to the reality with which my ecological reflection on an ethic of compassion began, Derrida's contention that '[w]ar is waged over the matter of pity'.[57] The war in question relates to the pitiless treatment of non-human creatures in the twenty-first century. What 'mercies of God' will there be for animal creation, carrying over from the Genesis account of creation to Paul's day and from his time to ours? For animal creation, the outlook is even better than for the seed and the land because it is more explicit.

> Then God said, 'Let the waters abound with an abundance of living creatures, and let birds fly above the earth across the face of the firmament of the heavens'. So God created great sea creatures and every living thing that moves, with which the waters abounded, according to their kind, and every winged bird according to its kind. And God saw that it was good (Gen. 1.20-21, NKJV).

Here, too, abundance is key; there will not merely be 'living creatures' but 'an *abundance* of living creatures' (Gen. 1.20). And then, for the first time in the Bible, we hear God talking to what God has created. 'And God blessed them, saying, "Be fruitful and multiply, and fill the waters in the seas, and let birds multiply on the earth"' (Gen. 1.22, NKJV). Here, God speaks *to* Creation, and God's first word is a blessing. Two more blessings appear in Genesis, as we have seen earlier, one on human creation and one on all creation (Gen. 1.28; 2.1-3), but they follow the pattern of the blessing on non-human creation almost word for word. Non-human creatures are first in line to receive a blessing that has mercy and generosity written all over it.[58]

56. Davis, *Scripture, Culture, and Agriculture*, p. 9.

57. Derrida, *The Animal That Therefore I Am*, p. 29.

58. Fretheim (*God and the World in the Old Testament*, p. 50), as we have seen, sees the blessing as the 'word of empowerment', and Westermann ('Creation and History in the Old Testament', p. 30) calls it 'a silent advance of the power of life in all realms'.

The eagerness to turn seeds and land into commodities reveals a profit-seeking economy that contrasts sharply with the generous economy of creation. The contrasts in these two realms, nevertheless, pales in comparison with the relationship between human and non-human creation in the twenty-first century.

> It is all too evident that in the course of the last two centuries the traditional forms for treatment of the animals have been turned upside down by the joint developments of zoological, ethological, biological, and genetic forms of *knowledge*, which remains inseparable from *techniques* of intervention *into* their object, from the transformation of the actual object, and from the milieu and world of their object, namely, the living animal.[59]

Derrida's account covers the new reality in sweeping but difficult-to-visualize terms, but he has carefully singled out absence of mercy as the main thing. Jonathan Safran Foer describes the problem from a different angle, but 'war' is the common denominator. 'We have waged war, or rather let a war be waged, against all the animals we eat. This war is new and has a name: factory farming,' he says.[60] Matthew Scully, quoted earlier in connection with the groaning of non-creation (Rom. 8.19-22), has tried to combine the concentration of animals in a factory farm and the absence of mercy into one single picture. As to the reality of large scale factory farms in the first decade of the twenty-first century, a mere four companies 'produce 81 percent of the cows brought to the market, 73 percent of sheep, half our chickens, and some 60 percent of hogs'.[61] As to mercy, from 'the 355,000 pigs slaughtered every day in America, even the smallest mercies have been withdrawn'.[62] These animals have been genetically manipulated in order to reduce the time from artificial insemination to slaughter and from slaughter to the consumer's table; they have been deprived of the opportunity to live out their instincts of mating and nesting; they are largely immobilized in order to reduce caloric waste; and they are tightly confined in buildings that, were the fans that circulate air to ensure survival turned off even for a short time, the animals would suffocate. Foer takes stock of the results of the genetic manipulation and industrialized breeding by saying that we have 'focused the awesome power of modern genetic knowledge to bring into being animals that suffer *more*'.[63]

Timothy Pachirat has concentrated on the industrialized slaughter that follows on the heels of industrialized breeding practices. As of 2009, nine

59. Derrida, *The Animal That Therefore I Am*, p. 25.
60. Jonathan Safran Foer, *Eating Animals* (New York: Little, Brown, 2009), p. 33.
61. Scully, *Dominion*, p. 29.
62. Scully, *Dominion*, p. 29.
63. Foer, *Eating Animals*, p. 159.

billion animals were killed for food every year in the United States alone.[64] Of these, there were some 8,500 billion chickens, 246 million turkeys, 114 million pigs, 33 million cattle, 23 million ducks, three million sheep and lambs, and one million calves.[65] These animals, says Pachirat, are killed 'without respect or recognition, demonstrating the horrific efficiency of an industrialized food-production system that reduces sentient beings to raw material'.[66] I am here interrupting Pachirat in mid-sentence, having noted the death-making aspect of reality that he carefully describes. However, along the lines that we find in Romans (Rom. 3.10-17), a narrative must be written that obscures this cruel reality. Pachirat describes this narrative as 'the power of distance and concealment to make the unacceptable acceptable and the extraordinary ordinary'.[67] As proof of the need for concealment, he points to the bill that was voted into law in the state of Iowa in 2011, HF 589, 'A Bill for the Act Relating to Offenses Involving Agricultural Operations, and Providing Penalties and Remedies', making it a felony to report without authorization from a slaughterhouse or animal-production facility.[68]

Pachirat went to work at a large slaughterhouse in Omaha, Nebraska, intending to use his findings in a doctoral thesis at Yale University on the politics of mass slaughter of animals and the policy of concealment. There, although carefully sequestered from other workers at the facility, he witnessed a cow or an ox killed every twelve seconds day in and day out, detailing the penetration of the cow's scull by the large steel bolt at the hands of the designated 'knocker', the gushing forth of brain matter and blood upon the bolt's retraction from the cow's head, the death throes of the animal, the not infrequent need to shoot it again, and then the passage of the animal on the conveyor belt into other specialized and sequestered venues in the facility before appearing on the shelves of supermarkets with little remaining evidence of the sentient being the cow once was.[69] A sentient being going from life to death in seconds—every twelve seconds—deprived of the dignity of creature-hood and the ontological and theological recognition as a creature of value. To Pachirat, the industrialized slaughter of untold billions of sentient animals

> enacts a politics of sight, seeking to subvert particular physical, social, linguistic, and methodological distances separating the reader from the slaughterhouse. At the same time, it is also an account, from the perspective of lived experience, of how concealment and visibility are at work within

64. Timothy Pachirat, *Every Twelve Seconds: Industrialized Slaughter and the Politics of Sight* (New Haven: Yale University Press, 2011), p. 54.

65. Timothy Pachirat, *Every Twelve Seconds*, p. 3.

66. Pachirat, *Every Twelve Seconds*, p. ix.

67. Pachirat, *Every Twelve Seconds*, p. ix.

68. https://coolice.legis.iowa.gov/linc/84/external/hf589_Reprinted.pdf

69. Pachirat, *Every Twelve Seconds*, p. 54.

> the slaughterhouse, demonstrating that hierarchical surveillance and control are not incompatible with the compartmentalization and hiding from view of repulsive practices, even at the very site of killing. Where distance and concealment continue to operate as mechanisms of domination, a politics of sight that breaches zones of confinement may indeed be a critically important catalyst for political transformation. This politics of sight, however, must acknowledge the possibility that sequestration will continue even under conditions of total visibility.[70]

The prospect that the killing would continue even if the slaughterhouses had glass walls or the killing carried out in full view of the world is more than a remote possibility. In the Roman Empire, the slow killing of human beings on crosses near the Esquiline Gate, as noted earlier, is proof that sight, too, fails as a deterrent, or that the sight may be so revolting that no one dares to name it. Derrida notes how displacement and concealment with respect to the cruelty inflicted on animals, physical and rhetorical, show that 'men do all they can in order to dissimulate this cruelty or to hide it from themselves in order to organize on a global scale the forgetting or misunderstanding of this violence'.[71]

Mercy in Ecological Terms

• Seeds	Recognition of seeds as the earliest form of eco-theology—as gift and generosity.
• Land	Recognition of land as gift and shared space, not commodity.
• Animals	Recognition of animals as sentient creatures with God-given rights.

The sentience of animals and human compassion are at the heart of Isaac Bashevis Singer's short story, 'The Slaughterer'. In this story, Yoineh Meir is forced to accede to the villagers' demand that he be their slaughterer, but he cannot stand it because he quickly discovers that the animals are not willing victims.

> His ears were beset by the gawking of hens, the crowing of roosters, the gobbling of geese, the lowing of oxen, the mooing and bleating of calves and goats; wings fluttered, claws tapped on the floor. The bodies refused to know any justification or excuse—every body resisted in its own fashion, tried to escape, and seemed to argue with the Creator to its last breath.[72]

Yoineh Meir's revulsion is so terrifying that it leads him to end his life. For Franz Kafka, a similar but more hopeful ending comes on a visit to the Berlin Aquarium. 'Suddenly he began to speak to the fish in their illuminated tanks. "Now at last I can look at you in peace, I don't eat you

70. Pachirat, *Every Twelve Seconds*, p. 255.

71. Derrida, *The Animal That Therefore I Am*, pp. 25-26.

72. Isaac Bashevis Singer, 'The Slaughterer', in *The Collected Stories of Isaac Bashevis Singer* (trans. Mirra Ginsburg; New York: Farrar, Straus, and Giroux, 1996), p. 209.

any more",' says Max Brod of the experience.[73] It could be more than a moot point that the voices expressing compassion for animal suffering more often than not are 'secular' voices. If we try to put this into perspective for Romans as a whole, these voices are due Paul's commendation earlier in the letter. 'So, if those who are uncircumcised keep the requirements of the law, will not their uncircumcision be regarded as circumcision?' (Rom. 2.26).

Paul prescribes ideals and conduct in Romans that are mostly concerned with human ecology, ecology still understood as the science of relationships. His appeal is based on 'the mercies of God' (12.1), however, and the mercies of God are expressed in seed, land, and the love of non-human creation. Likewise, 'by the mercies of God', a believer's ethic of mercy must in the twenty-first century extend to seed, to land, and to the suffering of non-human creatures as a matter of utmost urgency.

73. Max Brod, *Franz Kafka: A Biography* (trans. G. Humphreys Roberts; New York: Da Capo Press, 1995), p. 74. A similar observant and compassionate account of animal sentience is found in Jeffrey Mousaieff Masson, *The Pig Who Sang to the Moon: The Emotional World of Farm Animals* (New York: Ballantine Books, 2003).

Chapter 15

GOVERNING AUTHORITIES (ROM. 13.1)

The reception history of Paul's exhortation on how to relate to governing authorities can be distilled into three main options, the most radical of which is that Paul did not write it (Rom. 13.1-7). Counting it as a later interpolation, J.C. O'Neill says that the teaching in the passage 'is neither Jewish nor Christian in origin'.[1] A less drastic opinion does not deny Pauline authorship, but it studiously withholds praise. Cranfield says that 'it is still difficult to understand why Paul could write *quite* so positively about the authorities'.[2] Ron Cassidy is more forthright and explicit, writing that '[t]hese words have caused more unhappiness and misery in the Christian East and West than any other 7 verses in the New Testament by the license they have given to tyrants'.[3] Given that tyrants have found support in Romans 13 that Paul had no intention of giving them, the third option is that the passage does not mean what it seems to be saying, or at least not what history has understood Paul to be saying. The passage 'remains a conundrum, an *aporia* through which standard exegetical techniques will not cut, a shoal around which the charts of antiquity formed during the period of European colonialism form no sure guide'.[4] These words of John W. Marshall count as a fair summary of how things now stand.

Views on Paul and 'Governing Authorities' in Romans 13.1-7

1. 'Paul did not write it'.
2. 'I wish Paul had not written it'.
3. Paul wrote it, but what did he write?

Paul's call poses a challenge not only in light of alleged misuse of the passage. The challenge is magnified by the role readings increasingly allot to the Roman Empire in Paul's letters. Adolf Deissmann wrote in 1908 that readers of Paul must not be so gullible as to believe 'that St. Paul and his

1. J.C. O'Neill, *Paul's Letter to the Romans* (London: Penguin, 1975), pp. 207-209. O'Neill argues that the content is Stoic. The interpolation hypothesis also points to lack of references to this passage in extrabiblical sources until 150 or even 180 CE.

2. Cranfield, *Romans*, p. 653.

3. Canon Dr Ron Cassidy, 'The Politicization of Paul: Romans 13.1-7 in Recent Discussion', *ExpTim* 121 (2010), p. 383.

4. John W. Marshall, 'Hybridity and Reading Romans 13', *JSNT* 31 (2008), p. 162.

fellow-believers went through the world blindfolded, unaffected by what was then moving in the minds of men in the great cities'.[5] By this he meant that Paul was aware of the religious claims of the imperial rule, knowing full well that the imperial admixture of religion and politics competed with Paul for the same vocabulary with respect to delivering justice, peace, and salvation.[6] Before we look directly at Paul's explicit counsel regarding believers' duty toward the governing authorities (13.1-7), we need to assess more closely to what extent there is an anti-imperial message in the letter. My terminology in the previous sentence outlines the nature of the assignment and the caveats that will apply. In Romans 13, Paul speaks directly and explicitly about the relationship between the faith community and the government. If he speaks about the subject elsewhere, it must be implicit, perhaps in the sense that there is a 'hidden transcript'.[7]

Jacob Taubes, commenting on Rom. 1.1-7, puts into words the 'political Paul' that in his view is meant to be seen in the opening verses.

> I want to stress that this is a political declaration of war, when a letter introduced using these words, and not others, is sent to the congregation in Rome to be read aloud. One doesn't know into whose hands it will fall, and the sensors aren't idiots. One could, after all, have introduced it pietistically, quietistically, neutrally, or however else; but there is none of that

5. Adolf Deissmann, *Light from the Ancient Near East: The New Testament Illustrated by Recently Discovered Texts of the Graeco-Roman World* (trans. Lionel Strachan; Grand Rapids: Baker, 1978 [orig. 1908]), p. 340.

6. To Deissmann (*Light from the Ancient Near East*, p. 340) 'there arises a polemical parallelism between the cult of the emperor and the cult of Christ, which makes itself felt where ancient words derived by Christianity from the treasury of the Septuagint and the Gospels happen to coincide with solemn concepts of the Imperial cult which sounded the same or similar'. Giorgi (*Theocracy in Paul's Praxis and Theology*, pp. 79-104) has taken these hints much further. Neil Elliott (*Liberating Paul: The Justice of God and the Politics of the Apostle* [Maryknoll, NY: Orbis Books, 1994], pp. 217-26) sets the call for submission in Rom. 13.1 in the context of martyrdom at the hands of the Romans. The flip side of this, Rome being the executioner, will not be praise for the empire. See also, Richard Horsley, 'Introduction', in *Paul and the Roman Imperial Order* (ed. Richard Horsley; Harrisburg, PA: Trinity Press International, 2004), pp. 1-23; Stegemann, 'Coexistence and Transformation', pp. 3-23.

7. James C. Scott (*Domination and the Arts of Resistance: Hidden Transcripts* [New Haven: Yale University Press, 1990], p. 25) distinguishes between *hidden* and *public* transcript, the former 'the privileged site for nonhegemonic, contrapuntal, dissident, subversive discourse'. Neil Elliott ('Strategies of Resistance and Hidden Transcripts in the Pauline Communities', in *Hidden Transcripts and the Arts of Resistance: Applying the Work of James C. Scott to Jesus and Paul* [ed. Richard Horsley; Atlanta: Society of Biblical Literature, 2004], pp. 119-22) argues cogently that there is *hidden* transcript in Rom. 13.1-7 in the form of 'a peculiarly grudging compliance', but he seems too willing to take for granted that much of the *public* transcript is a reliable or valid point of reference.

> here. This is why my thesis is that in this sense the Epistle to the Romans is a political theology, a *political* declaration of war on the Caesar.[8]

Taubes was a Jewish political philosopher on whose work the imprint of the Holocaust is never distant, but there is no reason to attribute his 'political' reading of Romans to matters other than what he believed to be evident in the letter itself. Simply put, the Roman imperial claims are intentionally and not accidentally in the line of fire of Paul's message. N.T. Wright comes to a similar conclusion, admitting that he came to it late. Thus, he says,

> we open the first page of Paul's letters as they stand in the New Testament, and what do we find? We find Paul, writing a letter to the church in Rome itself, introducing himself as the accredited messenger of the one true God. He brings the gospel, the *euangelion*, of the son of God, the Davidic Messiah, whose messiahship and divine sonship are validated by his resurrection, and who, as the Psalms insist, is the Lord, the *kyrios*, of the whole world. Paul's task is to bring the world, all the nations, into loyal *allegiance—hypakoē pisteos*, the obedience of faith—to this universal Lord. He is eager to announce this *euangelion* in Rome, without shame, because this message is the power of God which creates salvation for all who as loyal to it, Jew and Greek alike. Why is this? Because in this message (this 'gospel of the son of God'), the justice of God, the *dikaiosynē theou*, is unveiled. Those of us who have read Romans, written essays on Romans, lectured on Romans, preached on Romans, written books about Romans for many years, may be excused if we rub our eyes in disbelief. Most commentators on Romans 1.1-17 insist that it forms the thematic introduction to the whole letter. None that I know of (myself included) have suggested that it must have been heard in Rome, and that Paul must have intended it, as a parody of the imperial cult.[9]

How does this view fit with the message in Romans 13? Here, Paul exhorts fellow believers not only to submit to governing authorities but to recognize that the governing authority is instituted by God (13.1). Believers are duty bound to submit to it not for reasons strategy or necessity but for reasons of conscience (13.5). The notion that Paul's gospel in subtle and not so subtle ways subverts imperial claims seems, at face value, at least, to be at odds with the idea that the government at hand is divinely ordained.[10]

8. Taubes, *The Political Theology of Paul*, p. 16.

9. N.T. Wright, 'Paul and Caesar: A New Reading of Romans' (2002), in *Pauline Perspectives: Essays on Paul, 1978–2013* (ed. N.T. Wright; Minneapolis: Fortress Press, 2013), p. 240.

10. Wright (*Paul and the Faithfulness of God*, pp. 1290-91) sees 2 Thessalonians as a letter that magnifies and crystallizes the God-defying imperial reality, making Paul's take-down a virtual *exposé* of the Roman Empire as the ultimate adversary. 'Paul is reminding the Thessalonians that for evil finally to be eradicated from God's world it must be brought to full height, must be concentrated at one point and must be dealt with there. In the world of the first century, to speak of someone who insists on his own superiority to other gods and cult objects, installs himself in their place in temples, and

> Let every person be subject to the governing authorities; for there is no authority except from God, and those authorities that exist have been instituted by God. Therefore whoever resists authority resists what God has appointed, and those who resist will incur judgment. For rulers are not a terror to good conduct, but to bad. Do you wish to have no fear of the authority? Then do what is good, and you will receive its approval; for it is God's servant for your good. But if you do what is wrong, you should be afraid, for the authority does not bear the sword in vain! It is the servant of God to execute wrath on the wrongdoer. Therefore one must be subject, not only because of wrath but also because of conscience. For the same reason you also pay taxes, for the authorities are God's servants, busy with this very thing. Pay to all what is due them—taxes to whom taxes are due, revenue to whom revenue is due, respect to whom respect is due, honor to whom honor is due (Rom. 13.1-7).

It is not easy to find an anti-imperial message in this passage, at least not on the surface.[11] While no one can deny that Paul and the Roman imperial cult make use of the same vocabulary with regard to matters like *good news*, *justice*, *salvation* and *peace*, this does not mean that the terms play off each other in consciously different visions of salvation or that Paul dignifies the Roman claims by engaging them directly. John Barclay argues to the contrary that the contrasting and conflicting claims are real, but they are not important and have relatively little explanatory power. Indeed, he says, to the extent that Paul engages with the Roman Empire at all, he renders it theologically insignificant.[12]

In support of this view, Barclay adduces negative as well as positive evidence. Negative evidence is mostly the absence of serious textual evidence that Paul has a Roman imperial referent in mind. He is especially critical of the claim that Paul's references to the Roman Empire are similar to his allusions to the Old Testament. While allusions to, and quotations from, the Old Testament cannot be contested, there is very little in the letters by which to make a similar claim with regard to the Roman Empire. 'Wright is working from nothing explicit in the text, from thin air to even thinner', says Barclay.[13] The evidential base for 'imperial' readings is by this logic scant.[14]

particularly in the Temple in Jerusalem, and gives himself out to be a god, is clearly to refer to the Roman emperor.' For a contrary, apocalyptic view, see Tonstad, 'The Restrainer Removed', pp. 133-51. In the latter view, the shoe-size of evil is far larger than the Roman Empire: the empire is not evil at 'full height'.

11. Giorgi (*Theocracy in Paul's Practice and Theology*, p. 102) finds what one might call 'anti-imperialism light', suggesting that Paul envisions loyalty to local magistrates but remains silent on the subject of the *princeps* or Rome, that is, 'he urges decentralization and undermines the ideology that supports the majesty of the state'.

12. John Barclay, 'Why the Roman Empire Was Insignificant to Paul', in *Pauline Churches and Diaspora Jews* (Tübingen: Mohr Siebeck, 2011), p. 387.

13. Barclay, 'Why the Roman Empire Was Insignificant', p. 380.

14. James R. Harrison ('Paul among the Romans', in *All Things to All Cultures*,

On the positive side—but also with the effect to diminishing the importance of the Roman Empire—is the frankness of Paul's style. He should be tiptoeing in order to avoid getting into trouble with the authorities, but he does not tiptoe, and he gets into trouble again and again (1 Cor. 4.11-13; 2 Cor. 4.8-11; 11.24-27). Caution is not a trait easily associated with him, and avoidance of persecution does not seem to have been a priority. On the contrary, the expectation of persecution is taken to be intrinsic to godly living (2 Tim. 3.12; cf. Gal. 5.11; 6.12).[15] Remembrance of time spent in prison is explicitly mentioned in Romans (Rom. 16.7). A hidden code, if there is one, has little to add to what is not hidden. As Barclay notes, 'Paul's greatest religious offence to Rome—his denial of the gods who were believed to shield and support the emperors and the empire—is perfectly explicit on the surface of his letters'.[16] Beyond this, there is a more ominous element in the fact that Paul preaches belief in a Jewish Messiah who on Roman terms had been designated a political troublemaker. This Messiah is now proclaimed throughout the Empire among the Gentiles. The dissemination of this message, as Paula Fredriksen theorizes, 'put the entire Jewish community at risk'.[17] And yet this aspect of the message is not toned down either, despite the trouble to which it might lead for the Jewish communities and for Gentiles believers that lacked the legal status accorded to the Jews.[18] If there is awareness of the communal risks in the letter, and if caution plays a role, the place could be Rom. 13.1-7.[19]

S.R.F. Price documents extensively the blend of religion and politics in the Roman Empire, especially with reference to the imperial cult in Asia Minor.[20] The posthumous divinization of the emperor by Paul's time is not in question, honors bestowed on the emperor more than sought by him or his family. We cannot claim that the cult of the emperor was imposed from the center.[21] Permission to build temples to the emperor was initiated in the provinces, not in Rome. This created a network of reciprocal fealty between

pp. 143-76) voices agreement with Barclay but is willing to accept the idea of an anti-imperial 'code' in Rom. 13.1-13; 1 Thess. 4.14–5.11; 2 Thess. 2.1-12.

15. Barclay, 'Why the Roman Empire Was Insignificant', p. 381.

16. Barclay, 'Why the Roman Empire Was Insignificant', p. 381. This aspect was also part and parcel of Jewish monotheism.

17. Fredriksen, 'Judaism, the Circumcision of the Gentiles, and Apocalyptic Hope', p. 556.

18. Taubes (*The Political Theology of Paul*, pp. 17-18, 54) points to the risk to the Jewish communities as a *religio licita* and the lack of status for believing Gentiles.

19. Barclay ('Did Paul Found of New Concept of State?' p. 313) finds support for the notion of a 'hidden transcript' with regard to this problem.

20. Price, *Rituals and Power*.

21. Paul Zanker, 'The Power of Images', in *Paul and Empire: Religion and Power in Roman Imperial Society* (ed. Richard Horsley; Harrisburg, PA: Trinity Press International, 1997), pp. 72-86.

the center and the periphery. The ubiquity, imposing character, and busy calendar of the imperial cult, the cult of the emperor edging close to the traditional cult of the Greek and Roman pantheon, projected legitimacy, power, and respect. Indeed, says Price, the symbolism of the religious choreography 'evoked a picture of the relationship between the emperor and the gods...it imposed a definition of the world'.[22]

And yet the cracks in this imposing physical and symbolic edifice are not minor. At times they expose black holes of conspicuous unworthiness on the part of the deceased ruler. Wright says that Paul must have intended Romans to be 'parody of the imperial cult',[23] but a better parody is there already, in Roman literature, written as parody in a way that fits the genre much better than Paul's letter to the Romans. When the emperor Claudius died in 54 CE, two years before Paul wrote his famous letter, the Senate dutifully accorded to Claudius the honor of divinization. It was an embarrassing and loathsome task because the emperor's track record of capricious rule, lawlessness, and the murder of many senators was not of the kind to qualify him for divinization or a place in some emperors' Hall of Fame. The Senate went through the motions, however, giving Claudius divine status on October 13, in 54 CE. This event became the occasion for Seneca's strangest writing, a ruthless parody on the emperor's alleged ascent to heaven, in a book known in English as the *Pumpkinification of the Deified Claudius*.[24] To heap scorn on the departed to the extent that Seneca does cannot have been without risk. That he did it, nevertheless, and that *he* did it, as a prominent member of the Senate, is proof that emperors sometimes were deemed ridiculously unworthy of the honors that religious and political convention bestowed on them. Claudius' elevation is made to be so ludicrous that the notion of *divi filius* cannot have escaped unscathed. Seneca's *Pumpkinification* erodes divinization at its foundation.

A few samples must suffice as evidence.[25] Seneca purports to report from an event that happened in heaven 'on the third day before the ides of October'. On taking leave of this world, Claudius is said to have farted before uttering his parting, undignified words, 'Oh Lord, I think I've shit myself'. The narrator admits ignorance as to what actually happened to Claudius at the moment of death, but he adds that Claudius 'certainly shit all over everything else'. Heaven is not enthusiastic about the palsied, limping, deformed monster presenting himself for divinization, ending deliberations by send-

22. Price, *Rituals and Power*, p. 248.

23. Wright, *Pauline Perspectives*, p. 240.

24. Romm, *Dying Every Day*, pp. 60-64. The Latin title, *Apocolocyntosis Divi Claudii*, has a made-up word that plays on the notion of apotheosis.

25. The excerpts follow Romm's version (*Dying Every Day*, pp. 60-65); see also Seneca, *Apocolocyntosis* (trans. W.H.D. Rouse, 1920), http.//www.gutenberg.org/cache/epub/10001/pg10001.txt

ing Claudius to the underworld to shuffle papers for one of Caligula's freedmen, the mere mention of Caligula doing little to raise the prestige of the imperial office. 'Together they could have a laugh kicking dirt on Claudius' corpse', says Romm.[26]

This is parody in a way Paul's letter to the Romans is not and in a way that throws doubt on Romans as parody.[27] Spectacular unworthiness, however, well known and widely seen to be that, gives some plausibility to T.L. Carter's view that Paul's exhortation in Romans 13 must be understood as irony.

> There is an element of irony in these verses, since Paul's words are pregnant with a significance of which he was unaware. The emperor at the time of writing was Nero, who came to power in AD 54, approximately two years before the most likely date for Romans. Yet within ten years Nero, the very emperor whose authority Paul commended, would unleash a terrible persecution against the church. When much of Rome was destroyed by fire in AD 64, many suspected that Nero was responsible, but he pinned the blame on the Christians, and an immense number were thrown to the dogs, nailed to crosses, or set alight as human torches to illuminate Nero's gardens at night.[28]

Carter's view looks forward to Nero, the emperor during whose reign Paul (most likely) died a martyr in Rome around 65 CE. Nero's maniacal ways would not make him a stronger candidate for divinization than Claudius, but there is enough in the legacy of Claudius to assume that the stagecraft of the imperial cult vastly exceeded the honor due to him. In Nero's case, his victims are daddy, mommy, his brother, his wife, and countless others. 'Daddy' in this case was Nero's adoptive father Claudius, and his murdered brother Britannicus was Claudius' son by natural descent. Romm portrays Seneca as a torn enabler of Nero's lawlessness, having initially introduced Nero to the Roman world as a trustworthy improvement on Claudi-

Approaches to Romans 13.1-7

• Parody	Coded message: Paul does not mean what he seems to say but the opposite.
• Irony	Coded message similar to parody but less pronounced.
• Hybrid speech	Limited options in the sense that the oppressed has to make do with the language of the oppressor.
• Plain language	Paul means what he says, but it must be qualified by the situation and the context.

26. Romm, *Dying Every Day*, p. 65.

27. To Wright (*Paul and the Faithfulness of God*, pp. 1301-1302), the parody of the Roman Empire that he sees in Romans is not found in Rom. 13.1-7 but in the imperial claims of bringing 'good news' and 'salvation'. He takes Rom. 13.1-7 to be 'a classic piece of Jewish writing about how to live wisely under alien rule'.

28. T.L. Carter, 'The Irony of Romans 13', *NovT* 46 (2004), p. 210.

us.[29] Whether we look to the past to Claudius' disregard for law and due process, therefore, or to the present, Nero's villainy already well under way, there could be weighty reasons for regarding Paul's comment on the governing authorities as irony. Carter expands the catalogue of known imperial abuses in the form of people being evicted from their homes, loss of property, and injustice experienced by Paul in person.[30] This, in his view, adds up to making Romans 13 a text replete with irony: a chasm between the straightforward meaning of a text and reality.[31]

> When read against the social context of the original readers of Paul's letter, it is apparent that the way in which political power was exercised in Rome would not have predisposed Paul's readers simply to accept what the apostle wrote at face value. The lack of correspondence between his words and the reality to which they referred was too great. This points in the direction of the rhetorical use of verbal irony, where the tension between the words and the reality they denote can be enough to reverse the plain meaning of the text. In Rom. 13.1-7, Paul's commendation of the authorities is sufficiently overstated for his readers to understand it as a covert exposure of the shortcomings of Roman rule, the apostle adopts the ironic policy of 'blaming through apparent praise'.[32]

According to this view, those who first heard the message of Romans would have understood the code. While Paul on the surface tells believers to accept the governing authorities as divinely ordained, below the surface he counts on the recipients to discern the discrepancy between his description and reality for the purpose of conveying the exact opposite message.

John W. Marshall offers an alternative hypothesis that is ironic, too, of sorts, but not in the overt sense discussed above. Drawing on insights from post-colonial studies, the relationship between the colonizer and the colonized is complex. Survival on the part of the colonized depends on 'content buy-in' as a matter of necessity.[33]

> Much of Paul's communicative tool box is begged, borrowed, stolen and earned from the elites of the Roman Empire's cities. Much of it has also been modified to fit the particular form of Hellenism that is his, namely Judaism. In the mixture that characterizes a colonial situation, multiple constructions of agency—satire, mockery, mimicry, slowness, borrowing, repurposing, reframing language, memory true and false, vilification and blessing, boasting and demurring—all work in partial

29. Romm (*Dying Every Day*, pp. 89-92) describes Seneca's *De Clementia*, 'On Mercy', as his attempt to introduce Nero as a worthy ruler, attributing to the newly minted emperor virtues that he must have known full well that Nero did not have.

30. Carter, 'The Irony of Romans 13', pp. 211-12.

31. Carter, 'The Irony of Romans 13', p. 213.

32. Carter, 'The Irony of Romans 13', p. 226.

33. Marshall, 'Hybridity and Reading Romans 13', pp. 169-70.

> partnership with, which is the same as saying partial independence from, the colonizers.[34]

On this logic, Paul is not simply parodying or acquiescing to Roman imperial rule. The colonized has limited maneuvering space in real and rhetorical terms, in real terms because he or she has no power, and in rhetorical terms because he or she is a captive to communicative limitations: the language given to the colonized is the language of the colonizer. 'Knowing or choosing when to affiliate and when or how to resist are part and parcel of negotiating life and power in a colonial situation', says Marshall. 'Paul's choices in this context are not discrete sets of false and genuine choices, but a continuum of affiliation and resistance that he organizes to suit his purposes'.[35] It is up to the reader sitting outside the text to understand this situation, to grasp the power differential, and to make the right judgment. All-out resistance and all-out submission are in this scenario false options.

Is there a third way that is not strictly anti-imperial, overtly or as parody, or even hybrid? The 'third way' will be more in line with a positive assessment of 'governing authorities' without thereby giving license to tyranny. General and situational aspects concerning government can both be in view. When Paul says that 'there is no authority except from God, those authorities that exist have been instituted by God' (13.1), he is espousing a point of view that has biblical as well as philosophical support. Old Testament wisdom literature claims that 'by [God] kings reign, and rulers decree what is just, by [God] rulers rule…all who govern rightly' (Prov. 8.15, 16); that God 'deposes kings and sets up kings' (Dan. 2.21; cf. 2.37); and that 'the Most High has sovereignty over the kingdom of mortals, and gives it to whom he will' (Dan. 4.25, 32).[36] This perspective establishes a role for God in the secular sphere in the sense that all secular power is derived and subject to conditions. In the texts noted above, the conditions are mostly spelled out for the ruler toward the ruled, on the one hand, and for the ruler toward God, on the other. The main point, however, is to note Old Testament support for Paul's claim that 'those authorities that exist have been instituted

34. Marshall, 'Hybridity and Reading Romans 13', pp. 167-68.

35. To Marshall ('Hybridity and Reading Romans 13', p. 170), '[t]he man thrice "beaten with rods" (a punishment meted out by Roman municipal *lictors*) and bearing the "marks of Christ on his body" (scars, punitive tattoos? 2 Cor. 11.25, Gal. 6.17) is not simply a partisan of empire'.

36. Stefan Krauter ('"Es ist keine Gewalt ausser von Gott": Röm 13,1 im Kontext des politischen Diskurses der neronischen Zeit', in *The Letter to the Romans* [ed. Udo Schnelle; Louvain: Peeters, 2009], pp. 371-401) finds no straight line from prophetic texts to Rom. 13.1, significant differences between Paul and apocalyptic texts, similarities with wisdom texts and also to Josephus and even to Seneca. With regard to an apocalyptic perspective, Paul and Daniel have in common that they envision the end of imperial rule and sudden rise of a different kingdom; cf. Rom. 13.11-12.

by God' (Rom. 13.1). For the reader who allows the Old Testament texts to echo in this verse, it follows that the background texts are aimed not only at establishing the legitimacy of government but also to spell out accountability that applies to tyranny, capricious rule, and hubris.

In philosophical terms, at one end of which is Thomas Hobbes, government is instituted to prevent the natural antagonisms and impulses of human beings from running riot, in acknowledgment of the fact that the human capacity for self-government is not impressive.[37] The tenor of Paul's exposition as to what government is meant to do is in some respects similar to Hobbes.

Closer to Paul and his exhortation in Romans, the things he does not say are as important as what he says, and there are important situational caveats. In contrast to the going standard for tributes to the rulers in Graeco-Roman times, Paul's accolades are sparing or absent. Conduct, not the status of the ruler, is the main point.[38]

What he affirms, moreover, even at face value, may not be irrelevant to the community in Rome. Two general areas of concern can be identified. The Roman believers are told not to stir up trouble (13.2-5), and they are instructed to pay taxes (13.6-7). When we take a closer look at these concerns, Paul is not talking about hypothetical problems only. He argues that 'whoever *resists* authority (*ho antitassomenos tē exousia*) *resists* what God has appointed' (13.2); he says that 'rulers are not a terror to *good* conduct, but to *bad*' (13.3); he tells them to 'do what is *good*, and you will receive its approval' (13.3). He says that 'if you do what is *wrong*, you should be afraid' (13.4), and he concludes that 'one must be subject, not only because of wrath but also because of *conscience*' (13.5). In all the stances and behaviors that are explicit in this passage, there is the possibility that believers might in fact be guilty of *bad* conduct and actual wrongdoing that is seen as such by the governing authorities (13.3, 4). This could be a 'hidden transcript' in Romans in the sense that Paul does not mention a specific incident but knows of at least one. Suetonius' remark that 'the Jews constantly made disturbances at the instigation of Chrestus', leading to their expulsion from Rome in 49 CE, can be taken as evidence that Paul was not urging submission in the abstract.[39] Mention of the authorities' use of the

37. Although humans left to themselves are selfish brutes, Thomas Hobbes (*Leviathan* [London: Penguin, 1985, orig. 1651], pp. 185-88, 232) believed that humans are capable of submitting to a Commonwealth (government) if only for reasons of self-interest. He predicted that humans would self-destruct in the absence of a strong, central authority. *Leviathan* is not the monster many take it to be but the image for the ordering power. Surrender to *Leviathan*, 'that Mortal God', is the way to ensure security and protection.

38. Barclay, 'Did Paul Found of New Concept of State?', p. 310.

39. Suetonius, *Claudius* 25.4; Barclay, 'Did Paul Found of New Concept of State?',

sword would in that case merely indicate that it is the prerogative and duty of the authority to restore order. Further along in the path of violence and resistance, the Jewish War chronicled by Josephus lies only a little over ten years into the future from the time of Paul's writing of Romans.[40] Paul could therefore also be 'thinking of contumacious defiance of the Empire such as was advocated by Jewish fanatics', as Ray Barraclough suggests.[41] He takes this as evidence that 'for Paul the way of redemption for Israel is not to be found in a war of liberation... Instead the fulfilment of Israel's hope is to be found through faith in Christ.'[42] Here, recalling that the meaning of *pistis Christou* in Romans is better understood as *the faithfulness of Christ* than as *faith in Christ* (3.22, 25, 26), Paul remains on topic by inculcating among believers a stance that is imitative of Jesus.

While Romans 13 ranges from the 'lofty' to the 'lowly' in the sense of mixing the highest ideals with behavior that conforms to ordinary notions of goodness, the exhortation in Rom. 13.1-7 might therefore belong in the 'lowly' category. Dorothea Bertschmann sees Paul carving out an area of 'good' that overlaps with society's idea of what is good but only as a piece of the greater love that must guide the believer's conduct.

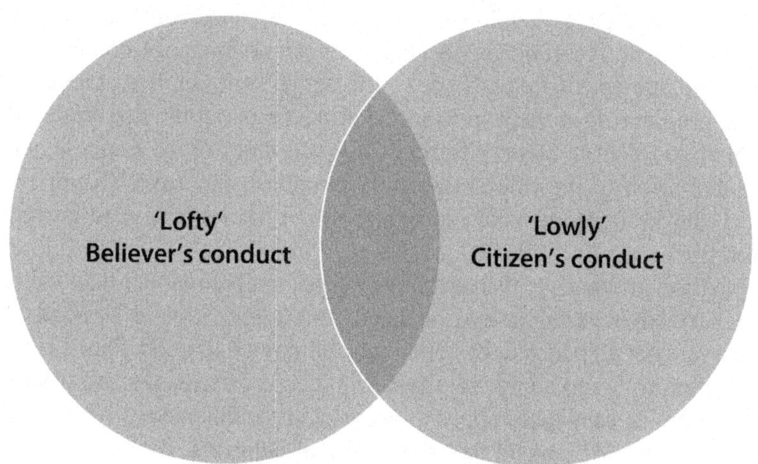

p. 313; cf. Troels Engberg-Pedersen, 'Paul's Stoicizing Politics in Romans 12-13: The Role of 13.1-10 in the Argument', *JSNT* 29 (2006), p. 168.

40. Violent Jewish uprisings in response to repression took place in Alexandria in 38–41 CE, and Claudius' expulsion of Jews from Rome in 49 CE is probably best seen as an instance of unrest in this community and not, as Neil Elliott argues, simply unprovoked repression by the Romans; cf. *The Arrogance of the Nations: Reading Romans in the Shadow of Empire* (Minneapolis: Fortress, 2008), pp. 91-99.

41. Ray Barraclough, 'Romans 13:1-7: Application in Context', *Colloquium* 17 (1985), p. 20.

42. Barraclough, 'Romans 13:1-7', p. 20.

> The Christian paradigm of love, then, is the greater reality which encloses almost as a 'by-product' good and generally approved behaviour in the civic and political world. In other words, the 'good' and 'bad' as perceived by the political authorities are subsets of the Christian good, which is lived out in love. Paul creates and emphasises a shared space between the eschatological people of God on the one hand and the present structures of the world on the other. This is the big achievement of this text.[43]

Submission 'for the sake of conscience' (13.5), moreover, is a two-edged sword. With respect to the believer's obligation, obedience rooted in conscience is of one piece with the earlier notion that 'the love is without hypocrisy' (12.9). What obligates the believer in this scenario is the will of God and not the demands of the emperor. Violent resistance is ruled out as an option not primarily because it represents disobedience to the empire but as disobedience to God. Curiously, Paul's ethic offers the Roman Empire a better citizen than the empire could hope to raise by other means, whether by fear or flattery. On the flip side, however, 'the last thing a totalitarian regime wants is a population with a conscience: conscience gets in the way of unquestioning obedience; conscience submits to the authority of God rather than of the state'.[44] F.J. Leenhardt adds to this that 'if obedience is a matter of conscience, then it is no longer servile; when conscience is introduced as the motive of obedience, the latter can no longer be counted on!'[45]

On the subject of taxes (13.6-7), the same logic applies. There is an actual problem right there in Rome, a protest against the tax burden that led Nero to relent in 58 CE.[46] Barclay, in a summary of the issue, says that 'in submission to the rulers, the Christian are to pay taxes (Rom. 13.7), direct and indirect, at which other groups in the empire were currently balking'.[47]

The third alternative, then, requires a less creative reading than the previous two. We have suggestive evidence from the situation in Rome that the rulers were not all bad and the believing community all good. Paul's closing admonition to 'keep an eye on those who cause dissensions and offenses' (16.17) might reasonably apply to noise- and troublemakers whose influence would be felt beyond the community of believers. In this alternative, in my view the most persuasive, Paul prioritizes the integrity of the believer's witness over the abuses of Roman imperial rule. He is aware of reasons to be concerned. Is there more?

43. Dorothea H. Bertschmann, 'The Good, the Bad and the State—Rom 13.1–7 and the Dynamics of Love', *NTS* 60 (2014), p. 248.

44. Carter, 'The Irony of Romans 13', p. 223.

45. F.J. Leenhardt, *The Epistle to the Romans* (London: Lutterworth, 1961), p. 335.

46. Wengst, *Pax Romana*, p. 82.

47. Barclay, 'Did Paul Found of New Concept of State?', p. 316.

There are at least two additional matters. First, the mission must not be jeopardized or compromised.[48] 'Paul is discouraging anything that would bring the Church into disrepute in the eyes of the authorities and thereby make the fulfilment of the Gospel mission more difficult', says Philip Towner.[49] Second, Paul writes that 'the night is far gone, the day is near' (13.12).[50] Neither the mission nor the time element is as important as submission for reasons of conscience, but they belong in the picture. The temporal aspect must not be collapsed into chronological time only, certainly not as much as Taubes seems to do, but a sense of imminence is undeniable. Taubes' comment bears quoting in full.

> This means: under this time pressure, if tomorrow the whole palaver, the entire swindle were going to be over—in that sense there's no point in any revolution! That's absolutely right, I would give the same advice. Demonstrate obedience to state authority, pay taxes, don't do anything bad, don't get involved in conflicts, because otherwise it'll get confused with some revolutionary movement, which, of course, is how it happened. Because, after all, these people have no legitimation, as, for instance, the Jews do, as a *religio licita*—weird as they were, they were nevertheless recognized and didn't have to participate in the cult of the emperor. But now here comes a subterranean society, a little bit Jewish, a little bit Gentile, nobody knows, what sort of lowlifes are these anyway—for heaven's sake, don't stand out![51]

From the options and the evidence reviewed above, Paul's exhortation in regard to believers and their relationship to governing authorities is best seen as real and necessary advice to a community that was at risk not only from without but also with respect to its own attitudes and choices. Even if there may be parody and irony elsewhere in Romans, and even though much in the Roman Empire would be deserving of parody when the letter was written, Paul's interests and pastoral concerns lie elsewhere. His stance in this passage is neither reactionary nor revolutionary (13.1-7). If it tilts toward one of these options more than the other, it does not tilt toward revolution.[52]

48. Philip H. Towner, 'Romans 13:1-7 and Paul's Missiological Perspective: A Call to Political Quietism or Transformation?', in *Romans and the People of God: Essays in Honor of Gordon Fee on the Occasion of His 65th Birthday* (ed. Barbara Aland; Grand Rapids: Eerdmans, 1999), p. 159.

49. Cassidy, 'The Politicization of Paul', p. 388; cf. Jewett, *Romans*, pp. 794, 803.

50. Jewett, *Romans*, pp. 786-87.

51. Taubes, *The Political Theology of Paul*, p. 54; cf. Dunn, *Romans 9–16*, p. 769. Barclay ('Did Paul Found of New Concept of State?', p. 317) avoids Taubes' rhetorical flourish and has less emphasis on time in a chronological sense; 'Jesus has exposed the hollowness of the boast about the eternity of the Roman Empire and its self-centred culture'.

52. Barth, *Romans*, pp. 477-81.

Love Does No Wrong to a Neighbor

Karl Barth connects passage on the governing authorities to the verse immediately preceding it with salutary effects (12.21–13.7).[53] If we omit the intervening verses, aware that some interpreters regard them as an interpolation,[54] the flow and train of thought are impeccable.

> Do not be overcome by evil, but overcome evil with good (12.21).
>
> Owe no one anything, except to love one another (13.8).

By the logic of these verses, whatever believers do as citizens, they are obligated by an ethic that does not divorce the end from the means. Barth says that the theocratic dream comes to an end 'when we discover that it is the Devil who approaches Jesus and offers him the kingdoms of the world'.[55] For a secular voice saying the same thing, perhaps unexpectedly, Nietzsche writes that 'whoever fights monsters should see to it that in the process he does not become a monster'.[56] If we relate this to Paul's concerns, he prioritizes not becoming a monster over defeating the monsters that are at large. To the extent that he envisions triumph over the monsters, the means available to the believer is of one kind only. He or she must 'overcome evil with good' (12.21). This vision is specified and taken to a higher level right after the appeal regarding governing authorities.

> Owe no one anything, except to love one another; for the one who loves another has fulfilled the law. The commandments, 'You shall not commit adultery; You shall not murder; You shall not steal; You shall not covet'; and any other commandment, are summed up in this word, 'Love your neighbor as yourself'. Love does no wrong to a neighbor; therefore, love is the fulfilling of the law (Rom. 13.8-10).

The commandments are here fully rehabilitated after the put-down they received earlier in Romans, serving now as the means to further a goal that

53. Barth, *Romans*, pp. 475-92. Barth holds it to be improbable that anyone will become reactionary by reading Romans.

54. O'Neill, *Romans*, pp. 207-209; James Kallas, 'Romans XIII.1-7: an Interpolation', *NTS* 11 (1965), pp. 365-74.

55. Barth, *Romans*, p. 479.

56. Friedrich Nietzsche, *Beyond Good and Evil* (trans. Walter Kaufmann; New York: Vintage Books, 1966), p. 89. The maxim is quoted with a cautionary intent by Tracy B. Strong in 'The Sovereign and the Exception: Carl Schmitt, Politics, Theology, and Leadership', foreword to Carl Schmitt, *Political Theology: Four Chapters on the Concept of Sovereignty* (trans. George Schwab; Chicago: University of Chicago Press, 2005), p. vii. Schmitt (1888–1985) was a lawyer and Germany's leading political scientist in the twentieth century but had his reputation diminished after he came out in support of Hitler in 1933.

previously seemed to be out of reach.[57] Granted, the specific commandments are subservient to the one commandment underlying all, but the specific commandments have not dissolved. In Paul's conception, the commandments are 'summed up' or 'joined at the head' in one word, 'Love your neighbor as yourself' (Rom. 13.9; Lev. 19.18, 34). 'No dual commandment, but rather *one* commandment. I regard this as an absolutely revolutionary act,' Taubes says of Paul's apparent contraction.[58] While his *one* commandment is unprecedented in formal terms, however, it is not a novelty substantively. In Galatians, Paul is even more pointed, writing that 'the entire law is summed up in a *single* command: "Love your neighbor as yourself"' (Gal. 5.14). The variant from Jesus's answer in the Synoptic Gospels is remarkable in that, in Mark and Matthew, 'the greatest and first commandment' is the premise for the second commandment (Mk 12.28-34; Mt. 22.36-40), but the difference is only on the surface. In the Gospels, too, a person's true devotion shows itself by that person's relationship to the 'second' commandment, and the entire discussion in Mark and Matthew lays bare the fallacy that it is possible to love God while remaining indifferent to the neighbor. In Paul's argument, the first commandment is subsumed in the second but not negated by it.

The idea that believers must take care not to *owe* anyone anything (Rom. 13.8) has a special ring in our debt-ridden, over-consuming society, where borrowing against tomorrow is a way of life, and easy credit encourages us to live beyond our means. Monetary debt produces vulnerability of many kinds, as individuals, local governments, and nations are discovering the hard way again and again. Paul may not have thought primarily in terms of financial sobriety, but the notion of not owing anyone anything other than love is liberating. As to the reason for the four commandments that are specified in the passage, Jewett suggests that they 'would have been particularly relevant for life in the urban environment of Rome, where interpersonal relations, especially in the slums where most of the Christian cells were located, were tense, volatile, and full of temptations and provocations'.[59]

There is nothing *ho-hum* or marginal about the injunctions Paul lays out in these few verses (13.8-10). Immanuel Kant's 'categorical imperative' to act '*only on that maxim through which you can at the same time will that it should become a universal law*' and to '*act in such a way that you always treat humanity, whether in your own person or in the person of any other, never simply as a means, but always at the same time as an end*' shares common

57. Martyn ('*Nomos* Plus Genitive Noun in Paul', pp. 583-84), as noted earlier, sees the law taken in hand by Christ in Rom. 8.1-4.

58. Taubes, *The Political Theology of Paul*, p. 53; cf. Jewett, *Romans*, p. 813.

59. Jewett, *Romans*, p. 810.

ground with Paul's 'categorical imperative' in Romans.[60] Universality is certainly implied in Paul's ethical vision, and he, too, formulates it with respect to how we should treat another person. Not even small fishes slip through the net of Paul's claim that 'love does no wrong to a neighbor' (13.10). The negative formulation might seem inferior to a similar, positive formulation of the golden rule (Mt. 7.12), but the negative formulation does not accomplish less. Indeed, in a reflection on a lived life, perhaps it accomplishes more.

Details in this passage show that the generalizing tendency is enhanced by particularizing elements that are largely lost in English translations. Cranfield notes the definite article before 'other' (13.8), thus, 'for the one who loves *the* other' (*ton heteron*)'. This is specific *and* inclusive. 'The "neighbor" in the NT sense is not someone arbitrarily chosen by us: he is given to us by God'.[61] Similarly, Paul speaks about '*the* love' just as he speaks about '*the* other'. '*The* love (*hē agapē*) does no wrong to *the* neighbor; therefore, the love (*hē agapē*) is the fulfilling of law' (13.10, translation mine). 'The love', as Jewett notes, appears as the first and the last words in this sentence, each time with the article. 'Love' has in Paul's vision come to ultimate expression when Christ died for the ungodly (5.6-8; cf. 8.31-39). *This* love, love of this kind, is now seeking embodiment in the believing community. Paul thus 'makes clear that the specific and distinctive form of love as experienced by early house and tenement churches is the topic'.[62]

We are still in territory where Paul spells out the meaning of living by, from, and within 'the mercies of God' (12.1). The theological foundation has not changed, and the ethical implication is in principle no different than what he has spelled out earlier (6.1-22). If there is a difference, the word for it is simplicity. There is no fancy theological footwork here; the lines are clear and straight; even the commandments have reclaimed a positive ring that was momentarily in doubt (13.8-10). To be more specific, his 'behavioral' argument is simpler than the previous message of being dead to sin through baptism (6.1-14) or becoming a slave to righteousness (6.15-22). There is 'the neighbor', says Paul, a person to whom he has an unpaid debt (1.14), and 'the love does no wrong to the neighbor' (13.10). We do not over-read what Paul has in mind if we hear him say that the debt to be paid and doing no wrong to the neighbor see communal conduct and completion of the mission as whole cloth.[63]

60. Immanuel Kant, *Groundwork of the Metaphysic of Morals* (trans. H.J. Paton; New York: Harper Torchbook, 1964), pp. 88, 96. Kant calls the first of these maxims the 'categorical' imperative and the second the 'practical' imperative that is derived from the former. See also John Silber, *Kant's Ethics: The Good, Freedom, and the Will* (Boston and Berlin: de Gruyter, 2012), pp. 231-46.

61. Cranfield, *Romans*, p. 676.

62. Jewett, *Romans*, pp. 813-14.

63. In the introduction, Paul describes himself as 'a debtor (*ofeiletēs*) to Greeks and

'You Know What Time It Is'

The completion of Paul's appeal is notable on at least two counts. First, when he draws a contrast between 'pious' and 'impious' behavior, the named criteria for 'impious' are conventional and unexceptional. The result of drawing the contrast, by implication, is indirectly to define 'pious', too, along lines that will seem conventional. Second, the tone seems somewhat less affirming than in the wider passage so far (12.1–13.10), hinting more overtly that there is a discrepancy in the believing community between what is and what ought to be, 'what is' lying too close to the way things are in Rome otherwise. The call to 'wake up from sleep' may be the least flattering statement in the entire letter (13.11). Overall, the tenor and content appear better matched to jaded, affluent Westerners in the twenty-first century than to what one might think appropriate for believers in Jesus, many of them slaves and people of low socioeconomic status, living in Rome within twenty-five years of the death and resurrection of Christ.

> Besides this, you know what time it is, how it is now the moment for you to wake from sleep. For salvation is nearer to us now than when we became believers; the night is far gone, the day is near. Let us then lay aside the works of darkness and put on the armor of light; let us live honorably as in the day, not in reveling and drunkenness, not in debauchery and licentiousness, not in quarreling and jealousy. Instead, put on the Lord Jesus Christ, and make no provision for the flesh, to gratify its desires (Rom. 13.11-14).

Knowing 'what time it is' (13.11), actually 'knowing the time (*ton kairon*)', is crucial, of course, and the bivalent character of the expression must not be missed. There is time *passing* and time *turning*, the passing of time reinforced in the thought that 'salvation is *nearer* to us than when we became believers' (13.11). But there is also an apocalyptic sense because time has turned from 'the present evil age' (Gal. 1.4) to a new era. Knowing 'what time it is' means to read the time signs correctly not only with respect to chronology but also with regard to the deeper

'Knowing' Time

• time passing	eschatological meaning—'the end is nearing'
• time turning	apocalyptic meaning—the old order overturned

to barbarians' (1.14). Being a 'debtor' returns again later; 'we are debtors (*ofeiletai esmen*)', but 'not to the flesh, to live according to the flesh' (8.12). *Not* being a debtor, however, *not* owing anyone anything, is the ideal; thus 'owe (*ofeilete*) no one anything' (13.8). The double negative is striking, as 'no one' and 'nothing' at the beginning of the sentence (13.8). But then the one exception to debt-free living: 'owe no one anything, except to love one another' (13.8). For Paul, debt-free living is possible in all respects except one. Love is the debt owed to all, for Paul a debt the paying of which necessitates his mission to the Gentiles (Rom. 1.14; 1 Cor. 9.16).

convulsions in time and to know that the shelf-life of the old age has expired. Paul captures both aspects strikingly in the next sentence, time passing in the sense of counting down the time and time turning from one reality to another. It is hard to surpass the evocative power of the saying, 'the night is far gone, the day is near' (Rom. 13.12). If, next, he will veer toward the conventional in his depiction of immorality (13.13), the colors going in are not in doubt. The colors are black and white, night and day, darkness and light. 'Let us then lay aside the works of darkness and put on the armor of light', he says (13.12), the image of *laying off* old clothing and *putting on* new suggesting an irreversible movement befitting one who knows what time it is.[64] Believers are to live 'honorably as in the day, not in reveling and drunkenness, not in debauchery and licentiousness, not in quarreling and jealousy' (13.13). The proscribed behaviors are nicely paired, but they are hardly uniquely 'Christian'. 'Instead, put on the Lord Jesus Christ', he says, 'and make no provision for the flesh, to gratify its desires (*epithymias*)' (13.14; cf. 6.12). The first part of this sentence is distinctive enough, but it is mystical, to be followed by a somewhat cryptic proscription to 'make no provision for the flesh' (13.14). This proscription has a sexual connotation, or, since the days of Augustine, the sexual connotation has been inescapable.[65] Jewett casts a wider net, 'the desires of the flesh' expressing themselves in plural ways in pursuits to 'gain dominance, pleasure, and prestige, to act in self-centered ways that demonstrate superior honor'.[66] We cannot read these verses without contemplating their incalculable impact in and through the life of Augustine,[67] however, or without noticing that Paul concludes his exhortation by honing in once more on 'desire'. 'Desire', at least misguided and misdirected desire, is at the heart of human plight (7.7, 8), whether we see it as theology or biology.

64. Martin F. Connell ('Clothing the Body of Christ: An Inquiry about the Letters of Paul', *Worship* 85 [2011], pp. 128-46) shows that the 'clothing' passages in Paul's letters have the connotation of an initiation that is renewable. If so, the likely initiation would be baptism. Dunn (*Romans 9–16*, p. 783) casts doubt on the baptismal association and on whether that association helps the intended message. Friedrich Wilhelm Horn ('Putting on Christ: On the Relation of Sacramental and Ethical Language in the Pauline Epistles', in *Moral Language in the New Testament: The Interrelatedness of Language and Ethics in Early Christian Writings* [ed. Ruben Zimmermann and Jan G. van der Watt; Tübingen: Mohr Siebeck, 2010], pp. 232-44) notes the 'ethical-eschatological' context. 'Putting on Christ' is not performed once only but should be 'performed consistently'. Paul's language suggests 'a participatory Christology encompassing the complete Christian life'.

65. Augustine, *Confessions*, pp. 152-53.

66. Jewett, *Romans*, p. 828.

67. Brown, *The Body and Society*, p. 404.

'You know what time it is', Paul writes to the Romans in 56 CE (13.11). What time is it for the reader of Romans today? What time is it, aware as we must be of the millions who have drawn strength from Paul's assertion that 'salvation is nearer to us now than when we became believers' (13.11)? Dunn's comment is poignant and devoid of cynicism.

> The twentieth-century scholar, nineteen and a half centuries later, and still the darkness of the old age lingers on, cannot help wondering whether the force of the moral imperative is critically weakened by this delay. But it need not be so. The sensitivity to the problem caused by the delay for moral earnestness has only emerged in relatively recent times. Even in the nineteenth century, before infant mortality was so dramatically reduced and life expectancy so dramatically increased, a passage like this could be readily interpreted in the light of the ever-present threat of a life cut short in its prime. A society for whom the finality of death has been pushed back to the margins of concern and largely ignored as a factor influencing lifestyle and conduct can easily sneer at the improving pieties of Victorian sentimentality about death. Such an attitude invites a fearful rejoinder in terms of new and unlooked-for viruses or nuclear catastrophe. Ironically, in a modern nuclear age, it becomes possible to believe more realistically in the imminence of the end, without the passing of the decades reducing the foreboding or expectation, but rather intensifying it for each new generation. The words which resulted in Augustine's conversion (13.13-14) may not yet have lost their power to correct the still too casual and selfish readers of a much later age.[68]

We do not know what Paul had in mind in chronological terms when he wrote of the foreshortening of time (1 Cor. 7.29-31), but we know that within ten years of the writing of Romans, he would be dead and buried. Even so, he left a legacy of hope resilient enough to hold up under the weight of his death and the passage of time till now and beyond.

Governing Authorities and Ecology

Jewett has the support of the majority of interpreters when he says that 'Romans 13.1-7 was not intended to create the foundation of a political ethic for all times and places in succeeding generations'.[69] Nevertheless, it is not contrived to make Romans 13 a point of departure for a reflection on the role of government, good citizenship, and the relationship between the nations of the world. Three premises from the text can serve as the basis of my reflection. First, from a narrow reading of the text, the governing authority is 'God's servant for your good' (13.4). While this is written to enhance the status of the governing authority in the eyes of the believer, it

68. Dunn, *Romans 9–16*, pp. 792-93.
69. Jewett, *Romans*, pp. 786-87.

is implicitly a job-description for the task of the government. It is designed to ensure the safety and well-being of the citizens. Second, now drawing on a wider reading of Paul's admonition, the good citizen is not looking out merely for his or her own good (13.8, 10). In this regard, Paul outlines an ideal that will be distinctly above average. Third, Paul inserts individual *conscience* into the picture (13.5), thereby introducing an element that is deeper, on the one hand, and circumscribed, on the other: the obligation of the citizen runs deep, but it has limits.

In ecological terms, these ideals are put to the test not only with respect to the citizen and the government within a given nation in the twenty-first century. In a globalized world of shared air and water, desertification, melting icecaps, loss of biodiversity, and rising ocean levels, the truly acute test comes in the relationship among nations. Ecological realities require cooperation and consensus among nations and not only the good will of citizens within a certain country.

This could well be the Hobbesian dilemma in the twenty-first century. 'If the modern era can be defined by a single question', says Eric Robert Morse,

> it would be whether or not man is capable of self-government. Of all the ages in history, the question of self-rule has never been asked more often and more sincerely than during the last five hundred years… As Alexander Hamilton stated at the opening of 'Federalist No. 1', the creation of the new nation was a process 'to decide whether societies of men are really capable or not of establishing good government from reflection and choice, or whether they are forever destined to depend for their political constitutions on accident and force'.[70]

Perhaps this question has been answered in the affirmative with respect to the government of a given nation, but it has not been answered in a convincing manner with respect to the relationship of the nations of the world to one another. A solution to this problem is elusive because, philosophically and historically, the concept of the commonwealth or nation has always centered on how the commonwealth can provide protection for its members *against* threats from other commonwealths. This is intrinsic to how societies are defined and understand themselves. Thomas Hobbes insisted that the obligation of the subject to the sovereign was in force as long as the sovereign was able to provide protection for the subject. Conversely, protection was the end and purpose of obedience.[71] Bridges between nations are tenuous at best, and the duty of the citizen is defined in relation to the state of which he or she is a citizen, not in relation to other states.

70. Morse, *Juggernaut*, p. 15.
71. Hobbes, *Leviathan*, p. 272.

Carl Schmitt, acknowledging indebtedness to Hobbes, takes this problem a step further. First, he says, the concept of the political is in itself an expression of one entity defining itself against the other and the interest of another entity. 'The specific political distinction to which political actions and motives can be reduced is that between friend and enemy', says Schmitt.[72] Second, with credit to Hobbes, Schmitt says that

> Hobbes was the first to state precisely that in international law states face one another 'in a state of nature'. In Hobbes' theory of state this is conceptually significant, for it illuminates the distinction between the legal state and the extralegal state of nature. Although covenants are concluded in the state of nature, they always reflect great existential reservations that prevent a rational and legal security from emerging in place of a state of insecurity. Security exists only in the state.[73]

Being 'in a state of nature' is the basic human problem. Chaos is kept at bay when subjects voluntarily surrender to be governed by a sovereign within a state or commonwealth.[74] There is no similar remedy or prescription for governing the affairs between nations, however. These remain 'in a state of nature', inevitably subject to conflicting and belligerent interests. On these grounds there is little ground for optimism if, in the community of nations, a problem arises that requires cooperation and consensus among the nations of the world. Being 'in a state of nature', as Hobbes expressed it, finds support in Reinhold Niebuhr's observation that 'the selfishness of nations is proverbial'.[75] Indeed, a citizen's loyalty to his or her country may in fact aggravate the meaning of being 'in a state of nature'.

> The paradox is that patriotism transmutes individual unselfishness into national egoism. Loyalty to the nation is a high form of altruism when compared to lesser loyalties and more parochial interests. It therefore becomes the vehicle of all the altruistic impulses and expresses itself, on occasion, with such fervor that the critical attitude of the individual toward the nation

72. Carl Schmitt, *The Concept of the Political: Expanded Edition* (trans. G. Schwab; Chicago: University of Chicago Press, 2007), p. 60.

73. Carl Schmitt, *The Leviathan in the State Theory of Thomas Hobbes: Meaning and Failure of a Political Symbol* (trans. George Schwab and Erna Hilfstein; Chicago: University of Chicago Press, 2008), p. 48.

74. Hobbes' *Leviathan* has been understood to be similar to 'the Restrainer' (*ho katechōn*)' in 2 Thessalonians (2 Thess. 2.6, 7) by Carl Schmitt (*The Nomos of the Earth in the International Law of the Jus Publicum Europaeum* [trans. G.L. Ulmen; New York: Telos, 2003], pp. 59-60), Taubes (*Political Theology*, p. 103), and Agamben (*The Time That Remains*, p. 109). When 'the Restrainer' is removed, chaos and lawlessness follow. Paul's contribution to Schmitt's political thought—as Schmitt understood Paul—is substantial.

75. Reinhold Niebuhr, *Moral Man and Immoral Society: A Study in Ethics and Politics* (Louisville, KY: Westminster/John Knox Press, 2001 [orig. 1932]), p. 84.

> and its enterprises is almost completely destroyed. The unqualified character of this devotion is the very basis for the nation's power and the freedom to use the power without moral restraint. Thus the unselfishness of individuals makes for the selfishness of nations. That is why the hope of solving the larger social problems of mankind, merely by extending the social sympathies of individuals, is so vain. Altruistic passion is sluiced into the reservoirs of nationalism with great ease, and is made to flow beyond them with great difficulty. What lies beyond the nation, the community of mankind, is too vague to inspire devotion.[76]

Niebuhr's measured analysis is compelling for the way it describes the problem and for its realism, and it has support from one of the most astute political philosophers of all time (Hobbes). What is the world community to do about national selfishness and self-interest? What is the remedy if the unselfishness of the individual is inversely proportional to the selfishness of the nation? If national unselfishness is out of the question, and if the prospect of bringing about restraint among nations is much less achievable than equilibrium on behalf of the common good within a nation, what is next?[77] Niebuhr does not let up with regard to this problem, writing that 'a combination of unselfishness and vicarious selfishness in the individual thus gives a tremendous force to national egoism, which neither religious nor rational idealism can ever completely check'.[78] Nationalism or patriotism will not solve a problem that calls for unselfishness on the part of the nations,[79] and solidarity is a long shot if, as Niebuhr avers, 'the most significant moral characteristic of a nation is its hypocrisy'.[80] Hypocrisy, in turn, serves policy by allowing the nation to speak as though it embodies universal values and ideals while pursuing policies of self-interest.[81] The bottom line in this scenario is foreboding.

> Since the class character of national governments is a primary, though not the only cause of their greed, present international anarchy may continue until the fear of catastrophe amends, or catastrophe itself destroys,

76. Niebuhr, *Moral Man and Immoral Society*, p. 91.

77. The European Union may to some extent be seen as an attempt to overcome national selfishness in the interest of the common good, but the Union draws new boundaries and zones of exclusion. Alan Paul Fimister (*Robert Schuman: Neo-Scholastic Humanism and the Reunification of Europe* [PP; Brussels: Peter Lang, 2008] traces the generative influences for the European Union to the Neo-Thomist philosophers Etienne Gilson and Jacques Maritain. The religious element in the Union's paternity may not be as significant or clear-cut as Fimister avers. See also François Duchêne, *Jean Monnet: The First Statesman of Interdependence* (New York: W.W. Norton, 1994).

78. Niebuhr, *Moral Man and Immoral Society*, p. 94.

79. To Niebuhr (*Moral Man and Immoral Society*, p. 107), 'a perennial weakness in the moral life of individuals is simply raised to the *n*th degree in the national life'.

80. Niebuhr, *Moral Man and Immoral Society*, p. 95.

81. Niebuhr, *Moral Man and Immoral Society*, 95.

> the present social system and builds more co-operative national societies. There may not be enough intelligence in modern society to prevent catastrophe.[82]

Inability to exercise restraint in the face of the threat of ecological collapse returns a pessimistic answer to the problems raised by thinkers as diverse as Hobbes and Niebuhr.[83] Returning to the three premises that introduced this reflection, there is little choice but to acknowledge that the governing authority that is 'God's servant for your good' (13.4) can no longer be a servant for good unless it starts to think ecologically and unless the nations of the world come together in joint action for the common good. Second, Paul does not advise the *nations* what to do, but he offers the Roman world a citizen that is not looking out merely for his or her own good (13.8-10). He speaks of love without hypocrisy in a world where hypocrisy is rampant (12.9), of overcoming evil with good (12.21, and of doing no harm to the neighbor (13.10), in our time descriptive of a citizen who is ecologically attuned and aware that the neighbor is not limited to people within one's own commonwealth only. This citizen should not be seen as the 'universal man' that some claim to discover in Paul, but he or she is a good person.[84]

Third, obedience from the point of view of *conscience* (13.5) touches on what may well be the most critical element in Paul's admonition with regard to believers, God, and government. Lord Acton says that 'the vice of the classic State was that it was both Church and State in one. Morality was undistinguished from religion and politics from morals; and in religion, morality, and politics there was only one legislator and one authority.'[85] Carl Schmitt, by contrast, did not share the view that it is a vice to mix religion and politics. He faults Hobbes precisely for allowing religion and politics to be separated: Hobbes obligates the believer to obey the state, but he does not authorize the state to interfere with the faith of the believer.[86] This

82. Niebuhr, *Moral Man and Immoral Society*, p. 111.

83. Whether or not Paul shares this pessimism with respect to short-term outlook, the ultimate outlook in Romans is optimistic. 'The root of Jesse shall come…in him the Gentiles shall hope' (Rom. 15.12).

84. Cf. Alain Badiou, 'St. Paul, Founder of the Universal Subject', in *St. Paul among the Philosophers*, pp. 27-38; Boyarin, *Paul and the Politics of Identity*, pp. 13-38.

85. Lord (Sir John) Acton, 'The History of Freedom in Antiquity', in *Essays on Freedom and Power*, p. 45.

86. Hobbes, *Leviathan*, pp. 512-21. Schmitt's critique of Hobbes (*The Leviathan in the State Theory of Thomas Hobbes*, p. 61) centers squarely on the necessity of *not* allowing a distinction between the inner and outer aspects of human existence, that is, between conscience and obedience. 'But when public power wants to be only public, when state and confession drive inner belief into the private domain, then the soul of a people betakes itself on the "secret road" that leads inward. Then grows the counterforce

is a fracturing element that Schmitt does not allow, spotting in it a crack that will inexorably erode the power of the state and ultimately reduce it to a mere mechanical structure, a soulless body.[87] To Schmitt, this is the fatal flaw in Hobbes' *Leviathan*.[88]

We need to get back to Paul although he has been there all along, unseen, as more than an occasional voice at the table. In conclusion, I will let Jacob Taubes weigh in with a final word on how he reads the political theology of Paul, speaking precisely to the issue of a person's conscience and a person's duty to the state that concerned thinkers like Hobbes and Schmitt. 'You see now what I want from Schmitt—I want to show him that the separation of powers between worldly and spiritual is *absolutely necessary*', says Taubes.[89] This is well said and in my view a fitting conclusion to the

of silence and stillness. At precisely the moment when the distinction between inner and outer is recognized, the superiority of the inner over the outer and thereby that of the private over the public is resolved. Public power and force may be ever so completely and emphatically recognized and ever so loyally respected, but only as a public and only an external power, it is hollow and already dead from within. Such an earthly god has only the appearance and the simulacra of divinity on his side. Nothing divine lets itself be externally enforced.' See also Strong, 'Carl Schmitt and Thomas Hobbes', pp. ix-xiv; Steve Ostovich, 'Carl Schmitt, Political Theology, and Eschatology', *KronoScope* 7 (2007), pp. 49-66.

87. Schmitt, *The Leviathan in the State Theory of Thomas Hobbes*, pp. 31-39, 65-77.

88. Clifford B. Anderson ('The Unexceptional Church: An Exploration of Carl Schmitt, Giorgio Agamben and Karl Barth', *ZDTSup* 5 [2011], pp. 8-26) brings the problem of church and state close to home in his discussion of Schmitt's maxim that 'sovereign is he who decides on the exception' (Schmitt, *Political Theology*, p. 5). Agamben's discussion (*The Time That Remains*, pp. 99-111) is part of his exposition of Romans. Schmitt sees the *exception* as the generative source of political sovereignty, taking the exception paradoxically to be the essence of the law (with Agamben). These are risky moves because the Third Reich claimed legitimacy for its lawlessness precisely by appealing to the exception. Barth, by contrast, says that 'the state of exception' is the permanent state of the church. Thus, with the rise of the Third Reich, there was no real exception beyond the exception already in force. Barth's task and that of the church boiled down 'to carry on theology, and only theology, now as previously, and as if nothing had happened' (Karl Barth, *Theological Existence Today* [trans. R. Birch Hoyle; London Hodder & Stoughton, 1933], p. 9). Neither of these options seem tenable, the former because it endorses a notion of arbitrary rule that is rhetorically enticing but potentially calamitous in practice, the latter (Barth) because, even accepting the idea that the church is permanently in a state of exception, the Third Reich must be seen as an exception to whatever exception is otherwise thought to exist.

89. Taubes, *The Political Theology of Paul*, p. 103. Julia Hell ('*Katechon*: Carl Schmitt's Imperial Theology and the Ruins of the Future', *The Germanic Review* 84 [2009], pp.283-326) exposes the imperialist concern underlying Schmitt's conceptions and—ultimately—that Schmitt's 'solution' is worse than the problem it seeks to resolve.

way Paul structures the relationship between the believer and the governing authorities (13.1-7). Obedience for the sake of conscience means a citizen of impeccable integrity (13.5), but it also means a citizen who will not be fooled when the call for unselfish service to the nation is harnessed for the purpose of enabling the nation's selfish conduct in the world. Paul's good citizen may, when conscience dictates, decide on martyrdom over obedience to the state.

The ecological outlook in all of this is bleak despite the luster of Paul's ethic of mercy, but the eschatological horizon that concludes Paul's admonition, by contrast, is as bright as it is necessary. Hope is meant to stir the believers into action, not to lull him or her into a state of fatalistic detachment. 'For salvation is nearer to us now than when we became believers', he says, 'the night is far gone, the day is near' (13.11-12).

Chapter 16

'The Weak Eat Only Vegetables' (Rom. 14.2)

'Some believe in eating anything, while the weak eat only vegetables', Paul writes as he nears the end of Romans (Rom. 14.2). This opens a can of worms just before the finishing line to his exposition of what it means to live 'by the mercies of God' (12.1). Food is now the subject, at face value a choice between 'eating anything' and eating 'only vegetables' and evidently a fraught issue in the Roman community (14.2). To the extent that these options are treated as equally commendable, Paul's adjudication will elicit furrows of worry on the brow of ecologists who are convinced that a drastic change in the world food economy and patterns of consumption are essential in order to save the planet, and it is likely to etch similar furrows of dismay on the forehead of nutritionists and public health experts who are at a loss what to do about the tsunami of metabolic disease that is engulfing the world.[1] Both of these groups will in the twenty-first century hope that 'the weak' who eat vegetables in Paul's text get more favorable mention on the strength of overwhelming evidence that the health of individuals and the health of the planet are profoundly impacted by what we eat.[2]

1. IDF diabetes atlas update 2013 (http./www.idf.org/diabetesatlas/introduction) predicts a rise in the global prevalence of diabetes mellitus from 382 million people in 2013 to 592 million in 2035. See also Yuanka Shi and Frank B. Hu, 'The Global Implications of Diabetes and Cancer', *Lancet* 383 (2014), p. 1947. Y. Xu, L. Wang, J. He, *et al.* ('Prevalence and Control of Diabetes in Chinese Adults', *JAMA* 310 [2013], pp. 948-59) show that the number of diabetics in China already exceeds 100 million, as many as half of whom are not diagnosed.

2. According to Henning Steinfeld, then Chief of FAO's Livestock Information and Policy Branch and senior author of the 2006 report (http.//www.fao.org/newsroom/en/News/2006/1000448/index.html), 'Livestock are one of the most significant contributors to today's most serious environmental problems. Urgent action is required to remedy the situation.' The contribution of livestock to greenhouse gases is greater than the contribution of all the cars and transportation in the world, chiefly through (1) methane, (2) nitrous dioxide, and (3) carbon dioxide. See also Michael Pollan, *The Omnivore's Dilemma: A Natural History of Four Meals* (New York: Penguin, 2006); Raj Patel, *Stuffed & Starved: The Hidden Battle for the World Food System* (New York: Melville House, 2007); Jeremy Rifkin, *Beyond Beef: The Rise and Fall of the Cattle Culture* (New York: Dutton, 1992); Margaret Mellon, Charles Benbrook and Karen Lutz

The apparent nihilism of Paul's statement about food could therefore be a cause for alarm, and there is more to strengthen this concern. 'Those who eat must not despise those who abstain, and those who abstain must not pass judgment on those who eat; for God has welcomed them', says Paul (14.3), again with seeming indifference to the more eco-friendly dietary option that is available in the text.

How to sort this out is the task of this chapter. I will begin by assuming that food has always been an important subject in human society; that it sometimes has religious implications; and that food is today an ecological subject in ways that differs by orders of magnitude from what was the case at the time when Paul wrote his letter.[3] The last of these points requires from the outset a broadening of the options available to the interpreter. Recalling, again, that Paul's letters are situational,[4] this could be an instance where the situation that gave rise to the letter two thousand years ago differs so drastically from our situation that his counsel is poorly matched to our need: need and counsel may be to each other like ships passing in the night. We might be faced with the possibility that what he said will not help us, and what he says, if problematic with respect to our need, could even deter us from doing what is necessary. This does not have to be an insult to Paul if we take the situation and particularity of his letters into account. Romans is a visionary letter, but it did not reckon with factory farming or with the destruction of the rain forests in Brazil, the decimation of which is directly and primarily related to global trends in food consumption.[5]

Then and Now:
Reframing 'Food' and 'Days'

- **Then** communal concern
  mission
- **Now** ecological concern
  communal concern
  mission

Benbrook, *Hogging It: Estimates of Antimicrobial Use in Livestock* (Union of Concerned Scientists, 2001); *Putting Meat on the Table: Industrial Farm Animal Production in America.* A Report of the Pew Commission on Industrial Farm Animal Production, 2008, at www.ncifap.org/bin/e/j/PCIFAPFin.pdf; *Livestock Report 2006.* FOOD AND AGRICULTURE ORGANIZATION OF THE UNITED NATIONS, Rome, 2006 at www.fao.org/docrep/009/a0255e/a0255e00.HTM.

3. Important book-length treatments featured earlier in this commentary are Matthew Scully, *Dominion*; Jonathan Safran Foer, *Eating Animals*; and Timothy Pachirat, *Every Twelve Seconds*; Daniel Imhoff, *The Tragedy of Industrial Animal Factories.*

4. Thus Beker (*Paul the Apostle*, p. 25), that 'Paul's thought is geared to a specific situation and that his arguments cannot be divorced from the need of the moment'.

5. Between 1970 and 2014 about 19% of the Brazilian rain forest has been lost, mostly to cattle ranching and cultivation of soy for export to meat raising industry in Europe; cf. Rhett Butler, July 13, 2014, at http.//rainforests.mongabay.com/20brazil.htm. This affects the climate parameters by increasing the output of greenhouse gases and decreasing carbon dioxide removal by the 'CO2 sink' that the forest represents. In

An ecological hermeneutic will be tempted to strengthen this caveat, looking to a hermeneutic of suspicion for help.[6] In general terms, suspicion may be limited to showing that interpretations of texts have been overwhelmingly anthropocentric, betraying a bias that is inadequate for the world's ecological needs. If a text seems indifferent to how non-human creatures are treated, or if it condones nihilism with respect to ecological concerns, a hermeneutic of suspicion might apply. Indifference to the earth and marginalization of women have in common that Bible texts are often quoted to justify attitudes that consolidate the status quo. As Elisabeth Schüssler Fiorenza notes, it may at times be legitimate to place 'a warning label on all biblical texts: *Caution! Could be dangerous to your health and survival.*'[7] Health and survival are precisely what are at stake when we turn to the subject of food and ecology in the twenty-first century. Will Paul be a help or a hindrance in this quest?

One more preliminary matter is in order. Is it true, factually, socially, and psychologically, that 'some believe in eating anything', as Paul appears to say (14.2)? Are 'the weak' in Romans people who have not yet manned up to shed the culinary inhibitions that hold them back so as to become the omnivores that in the eyes of many interpreters are idealized in the text? Jonathan Safran Foer serves more than the interest of animals when he frames the subject of eating animals in terms of perceptual and cultural constraints that are still in force. 'Despite the fact that it's perfectly legal in forty-four states, eating "man's best friend" is as taboo as a man eating his best friend', says Foer of societal constraints with regard to eating dogs in the United States.[8] Would Paul wish to remove this boundary if he could? Ecologically, it might be a good idea. 'Three to four million dogs and cats are euthanized annually. This amounts to millions of pounds of meat now being thrown away every year. The simple disposal of these euthanized dogs is an enormous ecological and economic problem,' says Foer.[9] Even so, he continues, 'no reader of this book would tolerate someone swinging a pickax at a dog's face'.[10] What holds us back is not that killing a pig is less cruel or less painful to the animal than killing a dog. We are held back

addition, loss of biodiversity is a major concern. See also Rifkin, *Beyond Beef*, pp. 148-49, 194-96, 224-25.

6. Habel, *Readings from the Perspective of the Earth*, p. 33; see also Elisabeth Schüssler Fiorenza, 'The Will to Choose or to Reject: Continuing Our Critical Work', in *Feminist Interpretation of the Bible* (ed. Letty Russell; Philadelphia: Westminster Press, 1985), pp. 125-36; idem, *The Power of the Word: Scripture and the Rhetoric of Empire* (Minneapolis: Fortress Press, 2007), pp. 82-109.

7. Schüssler Fiorenza, 'The Will to Choose or to Reject', p. 130.

8. Foer, *Eating Animals*, p. 24.

9. Foer, *Eating Animals*, p. 27.

10. Foer, *Eating Animals*, p. 31.

by conventions of habit and notions of mercy that do not apply to other animals. 'Is the suffering of a drawn-out death something that is cruel to inflict on any animal that can experience it, or just some animals?' Foer asks.[11] Two thousand years after Paul wrote of the person who 'believes in eating everything' (14.2, translation mine), millions who might profess that they 'eat anything' do not believe in killing dogs for food.

The foregoing reflections arise from the assumption that there are difficulties in the text that bear on the concerns I have mentioned. It is possible, of course, that the stumbling blocks will disappear once we take a closer look at what Paul is actually saying. Should this turn out to be the case, we will be less in need of the hermeneutic of suspicion referred to above. At least we do not need to direct our suspicion at Paul. It will be enough to concentrate our doubts on a theological tradition that has been of little benefit to non-human creation and the earth. Perhaps, too, the notion of 'eating everything' in the original context means less than everything, and the notion of eating 'only vegetables' includes more.

What to Eat

Some interpreters see a clear line of demarcation between the topic in chaps. 12-13 and the topic of food in chaps. 14–15. However, as Stowers points out, all these chapters 'concern the principle of adapting to the needs of others'.[12] Seeing reality from the point of view of others certainly looms large when Paul turns to the subject of food.

> Welcome those who are weak in faith (*ton asthenounta tē pistei*), but not for the purpose of quarreling over opinions. Some believe in eating anything, while the weak eat only vegetables. Those who eat must not despise those who abstain, and those who abstain must not pass judgment on those who eat; for God has welcomed them. Who are you to pass judgment on servants of another? It is before their own lord that they stand or fall. And they will be upheld, for the Lord is able to make them stand (Rom. 14.1-4).

Before looking at the details, it seems clear that Paul seeks to ensure unity in diversity whether the diversity in question relates to opinions or practice. He expressly tells those who are in a position of strength that they are *not* free to persuade the others until the latter see the error of their ways. Indeed, the hope of persuading the other side is precisely what Paul does *not* have in mind as the solution to the problem (14.1b). He therefore maps a difficult path by envisioning diversity in thought and practice that will not divide the community or make one side seem inferior to the other.

11. Foer, *Eating Animals*, p. 31.
12. Stowers, *A Rereading of Romans*, p. 320.

Interpreters are in fairly wide agreement that the two groups in the text break down mostly along ethnic and ethno-religious lines. According to this logic, 'the weak' are by and large Jewish, and they are weak because their dietary scruples have not submitted to the enlightenment and trust that the other group have embraced. The other side, later to be identified as 'the strong' (15.1), has done just that. Speaking for how the majority of interpreters see this passage, John Barclay says that

> [t]here is also now almost universal consensus that the topics addressed in these chapters concern the practice of the Jewish Torah, especially the rules of *kashrut* (kosher food) concerning 'clean' and 'unclean' food (14.1–2.14, 20), the honouring of the Sabbath (and Jewish feasts/fasts… (14.5-6), and (perhaps) Jewish anxieties concerning idol-dedicated wine (14.21).[13]

In major commentaries on Romans, James Dunn is representative of this view. Paul is addressing a problem between a conservative non-eating Jewish minority ('the weak') and a liberal 'eating' Gentile majority ('the strong'). Taking stock of Paul's terminology, Dunn observes that '"the one who is weak in faith", is of course a somewhat pejorative description—a nickname given by others, rather than by the individuals in view'.[14] He goes on to explain the characteristics of the two sides in terms of greater and lesser degrees of trust in God.

> What he means by that is already clear from 4.19: to be 'weak in faith' is to fail to trust God completely and without qualification. In this case the weakness is trust in God *plus* dietary and festival laws, trust in God *dependent* on observance of such practices, a trust in God which leans on the crutches of particular customs and not on God alone, as though they were an integral part of that trust.[15]

'Weak' and 'strong' are by this criterion laden with a value judgment: it is better to be 'strong' because 'the strong' do not need crutches, and a similar value judgment is in force when the two sides are said to represent 'adaptable' and 'rigid'. Again, the Jewish side fits the stereotype in the sense that they are deficient in their trust, and they are rigid. Given that much of the letter is preoccupied with issues related to Jews and Gentiles, Dunn's representation of the majority view is that this division must apply here, too. The concerns seem Jewish, and dietary purity took on increased significance to Jewish self-definition in the wake of the Maccabean revolt.[16] As to caveats, there are at least two. Dunn notes that the food laws in question are not

13. John M.G. Barclay, 'Faith and Self-Detachment from Cultural Norms: A Study in Romans 14–15', *ZNW* 104 (2013), p. 192.

14. Dunn, *Romans 9–16*, p. 797.

15. Dunn, *Romans 9–16*, p. 798.

16. Dunn, *Romans 9–16*, p. 800.

stated, admitting that the Jewish laws of clean and unclean foods nowhere demand complete abstinence from meat.[17] As a second caveat, he notes that 'a straightforward identification of "the weak" as Jewish Christians, and "the strong" as Gentile Christians may not be assumed'.[18] Gentile believers may be included among 'the weak', especially if they had come into the fellowship by way of the synagogue. Although Paul earlier in the letter has been perfectly able to call Jews for what they are—Jews—and identify the Gentiles as Gentiles (especially in Romans 9–11), the elusive labels here should not be taken to mean that there is reason to doubt the ethnic and religious identity of the two sides. Thus, Dunn notes, Paul is expressing himself in a way that is at the same time concise and imprecise 'because his readers would know well what he was referring to'.[19] He implies that by this logic we ought to know, too.

Identity of 'the Weak' and 'the Strong'		
Proponents	**'the weak'**	**'the strong'**
Majority view (Dunn, Barclay)	Jewish 'rigid' believers	Gentile 'liberal' believers
Nanos	Jews who have not accepted Jesus as the Messiah	mixed ethnic identity
Karris	'types': not specifically Jewish or Gentile	'types': not specifically Jewish or Gentile
Reasoner	foreign born Romans with cosmopolitan outlook	native born Romans with patriotic outlook
Bolton	Torah-observant ultra-traditionalists	Torah-observant traditionalists

Barclay sees less need for these caveats for a plausible reconstruction of who are represented by the terms 'the weak' and 'the strong'. He is certain that the issues are 'Jewish issues', as noted, and he is dismissive toward alternative reconstructions. Where Dunn finds a mix of specificity and imprecision in Paul's formulation, Barclay detects clarity. 'The certainty and candour with which Paul here expresses his freedom from the law is thus quite breathtaking. In principle, it appears, he could see no objection to eating shellfish, hare or pork.'[20] Shellfish, hare, and pork are not mentioned among the food preferences of those who 'believe in eating anything', Barclay gratuitously making up for Paul's imprecision. A slight

17. Dunn, *Romans 9–16*, p. 801. By this logic, complete abstinence from meat would be a way to play it safe.

18. Dunn, *Romans 9–16*, p. 802.

19. Dunn, *Romans 9–16*, pp. 804-805.

20. Barclay, 'Do We Undermine the Law?' p. 51.

doubt is registered as to what Paul actually practiced. 'Do we have reason to doubt that his diet was sometimes as scandalously "free" as his principles?' he asks.[21]

Carl N. Toney attempts to carve out distance between his view and the majority view as it is represented by Barclay and Dunn, arguing that there is an overlooked missionary priority in Paul's counsel. Paul is concerned not only about the outreach to the Gentiles but also about a mission to Jews, and he seeks to enlist the Romans in communal practices that will not place unnecessary obstacles in the way of the Jewish mission.[22] This caveat, however, is grounded in reasons of strategy rather than principle. In Toney's view, too, there is a spiritual and theological defect in the attitude of 'the weak'.

> Ultimately, Paul hopes that the weak can be empowered by the Holy Spirit in order to gain their identity from God's Spirit rather than relying upon these Jewish identity markers (this may or may not entail giving up these practices). Paul is especially aware of the need for Jews and Gentiles to be unified in light of his upcoming trip to Jerusalem as well as being aware of the tensions in Rome that caused the expulsion of some Jews under Claudius.[23]

In Barclay's delineation of Paul's theological and pastoral mediation, there is a similar belief that with time and practice 'the weak' will learn from 'the strong' even though 'the strong' are not authorized to persuade 'the weak' up front (14.1-4). Given that 'the weak' are captives to a faith-defect, they cannot permanently remain in that state. Barclay's communal projection is that the influence of 'the weak', the retarding Jewish influence, is on the wane and will at some point vanish. He notes that 'the tone in which Paul grants this permission (to the weak) is somewhat condescending', patronizing the weak and tipping 'the theological balance in favour of the strong, even while attempting to make the scales even'.[24] I will move somewhat prematurely to Barclay's conclusion, his suggestion that '*on the surface* and *in the short term*, Paul protects the Law-observant Christians, in the long term and at a deeper level he seriously undermines their social and cultural integrity'.[25] On this logic, a community divided into 'the weak' and 'the strong' lacks long term viability. These terms are ciphers for Jews vs. Gentile believers, conservative vs. liberal, rigid vs. adaptable, non-trusting vs. trusting, these the respective characteristics of those who do not eat

21. Barclay, 'Do We Undermine the Law?', p. 51.
22. Carl L. Toney, *Paul's Inclusive Ethic: Resolving Community Conflicts and Promoting Mission in Romans 14–15* (WUNT; Tübingen: Mohr Siebeck, 2008), pp. 29, 37.
23. Toney, *Paul's Inclusive Ethic*, pp. 204-205.
24. Barclay, 'Do We Undermine the Law?', p. 54.
25. Barclay, 'Do We Undermine the Law?', p. 56.

certain things and those who do. The scales will in the long run tilt inexorably toward 'the strong'. Paul, says Barclay, 'regards key aspects of the law as wholly dispensable for Christian believers and, more subtly, his theology introduces into the Roman Christian community a Trojan horse which threatens the integrity of those who sought to live according to the law'.[26] Just like the beleaguered defenders of Troy, therefore, 'Jewish Christians were right to fear Paul *and those bearing gifts*'.[27]

Whether or not this is a correct representation of 'the weak' and 'the strong' in Romans, Barclay's conclusion reads like a preview of the history of the Christian community in Rome and beyond, perhaps a conclusion formulated with awareness of the history. There is ample evidence that the Roman church originated within the Jewish community,[28] but there is also evidence that the Church of Rome early on lost its sense of the Jewish origin and connection. In *1 Clement*, a Christian document originating in Rome no later than very early in the second century, there is no sense of indebtedness to, or even conflict with, 'Judaism'. According to Reidar Hvalvik, '*1 Clement* seems to reflect a situation in the Roman church when there was no living memory of a conflict with the Jewish community (almost 50 years earlier), and probably no direct contact with the synagogues. The heritage from the synagogues had been "domesticated" and taken for granted, but its source seems to have been forgotten.'[29] Thus, in *1 Clement*, Jewish elements and awareness of Jewish roots are obliterated. 'So directly is the Old Testament applied to the Church that the author betrays no awareness of a radical new beginning, a new covenant established by Christ; no awareness of the deep disruption between the Christian community and Jewish people', says Oskar Skarsaune of the sentiments expressed in *1 Clement*.[30] Did Paul's letter to the Romans set the stage for this course of events? Barclay maps

26. Barclay, 'Do We Undermine the Law?', p. 59. I have translated the Latin phrase used by Barclay.

27. Barclay, 'Do We Undermine the Law?', p. 59. Gary Steven Shogren ('"Is the Kingdom of God about Eating and Drinking or Isn't It?" (Romans 14.17)', *NovT* 42 [2000], pp. 238-56) takes a position quite similar to Barclay. As to setting, the Jewish element in the Roman church is weakened after the expulsion; 'the weak' are deficient in faith but can otherwise be understood as examples of the 'Conscientious Hero'; 'the weak 'should have known better', but they are still to be accepted by 'the strong'.

28. Hvalvik, 'Jewish Believers and Jewish Influence in the Roman Church', pp. 179-87.

29. Hvalvik, 'Jewish Believers and Jewish Influence in the Roman Church', p. 211; cf. also Gerard Rouwhorst, 'Continuity and Discontinuity between Jewish and Christian Liturgy', *Bijdragen, tijdschrift voor filosofie en theologie* 54 (1993), p. 75.

30. Oskar Skarsaune, 'The Development of Scriptural Interpretation in the Second and Third Centuries—except Clement and Origen', in *Hebrew Bible/Old Testament: The History of Its Interpretation*, vol 1.1, *From the Beginnings to the Middle Ages (Until 1300)* (ed. Magne Sæbø; Göttingen: Vandenhoeck & Ruprecht, 1996), pp. 381-82.

the future for 'the weak' and 'the strong' on exegetical grounds without muddying the water with the historical trajectory, but his map should not be accepted without reservations.

The dominance of the majority view notwithstanding, there are a number of caveats. 'The weak' are not explicitly identified as Jews even though Romans knows full well how to do it. The dietary preference of 'the weak', as noted, are by no means typical of food prescribed or proscribed in the Old Testament (14.2). When Paul speaks of those 'who judge one day to be preferable to another' (14.5), he does not say that the day in question is the Sabbath even though it would have been perfectly possible to do so if that were the case. The fact that he is writing Romans just as he is about to embark on a trip to Jerusalem (15.25-32) casts doubt on the idea that Paul has weighed in on eating pork and shellfish in the context of the fraught situation.[31] These reservations arise from the ambiguity of Paul's terminology, and they are strengthened by the emerging stereotype that being weak in the faith for reasons of dietary commitments is a typical Jewish affliction. Moreover, alternative constructs with regard to the identity of 'the weak' and 'the strong' should not be dismissed as cursorily as Barclay and others seem to do.

Mark Nanos faults interpreters for falling into the 'Luther's trap'. This refers to the long-held notion that Judaism is a religion of works, among the 'works' food laws that do not apply to Christians. In Luther's words,

> When the Apostle here speaks of the 'weak', he has in mind those who were of the opinion that they were obligated to certain laws, *to which in reality they were not obligated*. His words, however, are directed above all against *the Jewish error*, which some false prophets taught, distinguishing between certain kinds of food... *Against this (Christian) liberty*, for which the Apostle contends, many false apostles raised their voice *to mislead the people to do certain things as though these were necessary*. Against such *errorists* the Apostle took the offensive with amazing zeal.[32]

The possibility that the actual Roman referents for 'the weak' and 'the strong' break along different lines than Jewish legalism and Christian liberty is all but ruled out in this statement. Even though Dunn has been the torchbearer for the 'New Perspective' on Paul, arguing that Judaism is *not* a religion of works, his interpretation of this passage conforms to the traditional view, as Nanos points out.

31. It is not necessary to accept Jervell's proposal ('The Letter to Jerusalem', pp. 53-64) that Romans is composed mostly with an eye to concerns in the Jerusalem church about Paul's gospel in order to appreciate the touchiness of the situation.

32. Luther, *Romans*, pp. 194-95, emphasis added; Nanos, *The Mystery of Romans*, p. 92. In his *Lectures on Romans* in 1515–16, Luther says nothing about Jews or Jewish food laws in his comments on this chapter.

> To assume that the 'weak' were Christian Jews who were unwilling or unable to give up the practice of the Law and Jewish customs because they were *deficient in their faith*, in that they 'fail to trust God completely and without qualification' (Dunn, p. 798), or further: 'In this case the weakness is trust in God *plus* dietary and festival laws, trust in God *dependent* on observance of such practices, a trust in God which *leans on the crutches* of particular customs and *not* on God alone, *as though* they were an integral part of that trust' (Dunn, p. 798) is indeed to fall into *Luther's trap*.[33]

If one accepts that 'the weak' are Jewish believers in Jesus who have yet to overcome their dietary hang-ups, we arrive at the ironic situation that Gentiles who accept the gospel do not need to adopt Jewish practices, but Jews who become believers in Jesus ought to give up theirs if they wish to avoid the stigma of being seen as weak in the faith.[34] Paul, who fights a Judaizing approach to the Gentiles will by this criterion be guilty of 'gentilizing' the Jews.[35] To Nanos, therefore, the issue with the Jews is not what they *eat*; the problem is not *food* but *faith*;[36] 'the weak' are not yet on board with respect to accepting Jesus as the Messiah. 'Simply put, the "weak/stumbling in faith" are those Jews who do not yet believe in Jesus as the Christ of Israel or Savior of the nations: they are the non-Christian Jews in Rome.'[37]

Nanos' critique of the majority opinion is merited even if his own proposal is inconclusive. Other options nuance the 'Jewish' question in the text along lines very different from the idea that they are weak in the faith and that it will be incumbent on them to grow up. Rather than implying that the Jews in the Roman communities would be better off theologically and communally by abandoning their dietary inhibitions, Paul's argument is sensitive to the plight of diaspora Jews and eager to reach out to a vulnerable minority. Neil Elliott notes that 'there is abundant evidence that, within an indifferent or hostile Gentile environment, observance of *kashrut* often required Jews to practice de facto vegetarianism'.[38] Roman citizens on the whole regarded the Jewish stance as 'weakness'. Paul, Elliott notes,

33. Nanos, *The Mystery of Romans*, p. 115.

34. David J. Bolton, 'Who Are You Calling "Weak"? A Short Critique of James Dunn's Reading of Rom 14.1–15.6', in *The Letter to the Romans* (ed. Udo Schnelle; Leuven: Peeters, 2009), pp. 616-29. Bolton notes the *sola fide* premise that grounds Dunn's interpretation of 'the weak'.

35. Nanos, *The Mystery of Romans*, pp. 33, 119.

36. Neil Elliott ('Asceticism among the "Weak" and "Strong" in Romans 14–15', in *Asceticism in the New Testament* [ed. Leif E. Vaage and Vincent L. Wimbush; New York: Routledge, 1999], pp. 231-51) supports many of Nanos' arguments, particularly the point that 'weakness in faith' has to do with abstemiousness.

37. Nanos, *The Mystery of Romans*, p. 143.

38. Elliott, 'Asceticism among the "Weak" and "Strong" in Romans 14–15', p. 233.

has warned against Gentile haughtiness toward Jews earlier in the letter (11.17-21). Contrary to the majority view, he concludes that 'Paul calls on the Christians of Rome to honor the diligent observance of a beleaguered Jewish community, injured by imperial edict and insulted by an intellectual elite, as genuine faithfulness to God'.[39]

Given the pluralism within the Roman Empire with regard to religion and dietary concerns, it is possible that the problem in the Christian community does not break along ethnic and ethno-religious lines. Accordingly, 'the weak' are not simply Jews, and 'the strong' are not simply believing Gentiles. To Robert Karris, for instance, Paul's terms refer to *types* or *characters* and not to groups, parties, or ethnic identities.[40] Mark Reasoner constructs a scenario in Rome where 'the strong' 'are Romans citizens or foreign-born residents who display a proclivity towards things Roman' while 'the weak' are people 'of foreign extraction who sympathize with foreign religions and cultures'.[41] The Jews will by this criterion belong to 'the weak', but this entity is not limited to Jews, and the dietary commitment of 'the weak' must be understood in light of syncretism and asceticism. David J. Bolton argues cogently that the issue is much less sweeping than envisioned by the majority of interpreters, and it does not fit the stereotype of works-oriented Jews and faith-leaning Gentiles. Thus, he says,

> the situation in Rom. 14.1–15.6 is about late Second Temple halakhically observant Gentiles and Jews who struggle and divide among themselves over the issue of whether halakhically clean meat should be avoided since it has (potentially) been involved in idolatrous practices before being sold in the market place. The split in the group is not therefore along ethnic lines (*contra* Dunn), but rather along halakhic lines.[42]

More will be said about this, but two other perspectives must be included before we move on. Jewett makes a number of observations about Paul's rhetoric that have consequences for interpretation. First, no one is likely to call themselves 'weak in the faith' voluntarily, especially in a culture that used stigmatizing labels liberally. For this reason it is likely that the epithet 'weak in the faith' is imposed by the dominant group.[43] Second, Paul being

39. Elliott, 'Asceticism among the "Weak" and "Strong" in Romans 14–15', p. 245.

40. Robert J. Karris, 'Rom 14:1–15:13 and the Occasion of Romans', *CBQ* 34 (1973), pp. 155-78. He concludes that Rom 14.1–15.13 has no specific referent, and the exhortation is merely summing up Paul's theology and behavioral counsel.

41. Mark Reasoner, *The Strong and the Weak: Romans 14.1–15.13 in Context* (Cambridge: Cambridge University Press, 1999), pp. 61-63.

42. Bolton's construct ('Who Are You Calling "Weak"?', pp. 620, 621) does not see 'Torah-free "liberals" versus Torah-observant "traditionalists" but Torah-observant traditionalists versus Torah-observant ultra-traditionalists'.

43. Jewett, *Romans*, pp. 834-85.

aware of their precarious situation, 'it must have been apparent to Paul's audience that he intended to reverse the shameful status of the "weak"'.[44] If this is correct, we are headed for a conclusion that that is not condescending toward 'the weak' and not, consciously or unconsciously, introducing a Trojan horse into the Roman churches that will eventually undermine the Jewish believers, as we saw in Barclay's view earlier. Third, Jewett notes that the formulation of eating everything (14.2) 'is broadly drawn, including everything edible, which probably extended considerably past actual practices in Rome'.[45]

> Consistent with the requirements of demonstrative rhetoric, and matching the requirements of the oblique style, Paul creates abstractions that are recognizable by his audience, but that not precisely match any of the groups in Rome. The use of *panta* ('all') may well have evoked smiles among the hearers of Romans, not only at the thought of eating obscure foods but also at the reduction of the concept of faith, which had received so profound a development in the earlier chapters of the letter, into mere license for uncritical consumption.[46]

These observations relate to rhetorical, psychological, and social aspects of speech conventions. People who are said to eat 'everything' actually do not. Conversely, 'the weak' in Rome may not be as restrictive in their food choices as suggested by the word translated 'vegetables' (*lachana*) (14.2). Jewett produces evidence that the term does not function as a description of actual food choices but more likely represents a caricature. The exaggeration may be captured by translating it, 'the weak only eat lettuce'.[47] These insights broaden the options greatly, Paul's terms now wide and general enough to include everything between 'the uncritical omnivores and the leaf mongers', ethnicity now a lesser point and a less defining aspect.[48]

Fourth, therefore, it is possible to see Paul's admonition as a countercultural attempt to break the entrenched habit of shaming nonconformists in Roman culture. 'The disdainful smile of social and theological contempt is no longer to remain in the repertoire of Christian group life', says Jewett.[49] The overall effect is redress of the power imbalance in favor of 'the weak'.

Power and power dynamics are also the concern of Beverly Roberts Gaventa in a study leading to a similar conclusion.[50] She does not chal-

44. Jewett, *Romans*, p. 836.
45. Jewett, *Romans*, p. 837.
46. Jewett, *Romans*, p. 837.
47. Jewett, *Romans*, pp. 837-38.
48. Jewett, *Romans*, p. 838.
49. Jewett, *Romans*, p. 839.
50. Beverly Roberts Gaventa, 'Reading for the Subject: The Paradox of Power in Romans 14:1–15:6', *JTI* 5 (2011), pp. 1-12.

lenge the view that 'the strong' may be Gentiles and 'the weak' Jews, but this is not the most important distinction. Instead, she chooses to recalibrate the power equation so as to expose 'an astonishing power to destroy' on the part of the 'faith-havers', and, in turn, 'the fearful underside to faith itself'.[51] In this scenario, too, 'the weak' are the main concern. Paul is not as evenhanded as some interpreters like to see him because he is addressing a situation where things are not 'even'. 'The weak' and 'the strong' do not have a level playing field. For this reason his instruction is directed at the 'faith-havers', this term now at least as unflattering as naming the others 'the weak'. Why be concerned about the latter group, Gaventa queries. 'Those who eat only lettuce may be an annoyance, they could conceivably prompt impatience and even rudeness on the part of others, but it is hard to imagine a situation in which their limited diet would cause others to fall—to fall into what?'[52] Causing others to fall, however, is precisely what the 'faith-havers' have it in their power to do (14.13, 20-22). This means that the 'faith-havers' in Rome are at risk of placing a stumbling block before another person, causing that person to fall. 'Paul imputes to them the power to destroy'.[53] The stakes are now much higher, even a matter of life and death, and it is the risk to 'the weak' that controls the argument and sets the terms for what to do. 'It is these "faith-havers" who pose the problem, and the problem is not only that their behavior may cause the "weak" to encounter difficulties socially or culturally', says Gaventa. 'Their behavior, as Paul presents it, has soteriological consequences'.[54]

Contrasts:
John Barclay and Beverly Roberts Gaventa on 'the Weak' and 'the Strong'

	Barclay	**Gaventa**
Problem group	'the weak'	'the strong'
Characterization	'faith-deficit'	'faith-haver'
Defect	lack of faith ('the weak')	lack of concern ('the strong')
Key concern	subjective	social and soteriological
Prognosis	'the weak' to vanish	'the weak' to remain
Adjudication	preference for 'the strong'	preference for 'the weak'

The foregoing does not lead to a conclusive view as to the identity of 'the weak' and 'the strong', but it puts a dent in the majority view that the problem breaks along ethnic lines. Even if we allow the dominant 'ethnic' view to stand, the overall import of Paul's argument is not to hamstring the

51. Gaventa, 'Reading for the Subject', p. 6.
52. Gaventa, 'Reading for the Subject', p. 7.
53. Gaventa, 'Reading for the Subject', p. 8.
54. Gaventa, 'Reading for the Subject', p. 8.

dietary commitment of 'the weak' but to strengthen their hand. To the extent that the dietary reservations are anchored in the Old Testament, Paul lets Scripture arbitrate in a way that strengthens their position. 'For whatever was written in former days was written for our instruction, so that by steadfastness and by the encouragement of the scriptures we might have hope', he says (15.3).

On the whole, however, *judging* looms larger in the argument than *eating* or *not eating* (14.3-5, 10, 13). Paul's priority in this regard is striking because the matter of judging, or rather, *not judging*, now becomes the topic that frames the letter, as bookends, at least in a formal sense.

> Therefore you have no excuse, O 'virtuous' person (*ō anthrōpe*), you and all who judge (*ho krinōn*) others; for in passing judgment (*krineis*) on another you condemn yourself (Rom. 2.1, translation mine).
>
> Who are you to be judge (*ho krinōn*) of servants of another? (14.4, translation mine)
>
> Why are you judging (*krineis*) your brother? (14.10, translation mine)
>
> Let us therefore no longer judge (*krinōmen*) one another (14.13, translation mine)

The sin of judging and the call to refrain from judging mark the point of Paul's vociferous and defining push-back at the beginning of the letter (2.1-3). I have argued earlier that the implied recipient of the no-nonsense rebuke are real people who do not have their spiritual priorities in the right order. This person (or persons) is a countermissionary who stands *outside* the believing community, representing a threat to it and its mission. Here, toward the end of the letter, the subject of judging returns from a different angle (14.3-5, 10, 13), this time as a problem *within* the congregation. The judging that is disallowed at the beginning of Romans refers to a misguided assessment of the world (1.18-32) and a shallow conception of the self (2.1-3), but the judging at the end of the letter concerns the commitments of the believing community (14.1–15.7). Curtailment of the disposition to judge is common to Paul's response to both of these problems (2.1-3; 14.3-5, 10, 13). If this is more than a freak coincidence in the overall message of the letter, it means that *judging* the other is not the way of the good news, whether at the point of establishing the community or at the point of building and maintaining it. The stance that Paul takes to task in severe language when speaking of the threat from *without* (2.1-3), he corrects in a measured, pastoral tone when delineating the problems *within* (14.1-15.7). In both cases, Paul's emphasis falls on divine

Judging—and the Good News

• Judging those without	No—see Rom. 2.1-3
• Judging those within	No—see Rom. 14.3-5; 14.10, 13

right-making (1.16-17; 15.3). 'For Christ did not please himself; but, as it is written, "The insults of those who insult you have fallen on me"' (15.3). Thinking back to the reason why Paul sent the letter to Rome in the first place, the threat from without appears more urgent than the problem within, this observation one more reason to conclude that Paul primarily wrote the letter in order to protect the Roman churches from the threat from without.

Judging Days

Paul is not done addressing differences of opinion and practice in the house churches in Rome, now turning to observance and non-observance of 'days'.

> Some judge one day to be better than another, while others judge all days to be alike. Let all be fully convinced in their own minds. Those who observe the day, observe it in honor of the Lord. Also those who eat, eat in honor of the Lord, since they give thanks to God; while those who abstain, abstain in honor of the Lord and give thanks to God. We do not live to ourselves, and we do not die to ourselves. If we live, we live to the Lord, and if we die, we die to the Lord; so then, whether we live or whether we die, we are the Lord's. For to this end Christ died and lived again, so that he might be Lord of both the dead and the living (Rom. 14.5-9).

It comes as no surprise that interpreters' view of 'judging days' conforms to how the food question has been understood. Barclay takes the observance of days to arise from the same scruples as the dietary matters, and the Sabbath is the primary candidate for judging 'one day to be better than another' (14.5). 'While Jewish feasts and fasts may enter into the equation as well, that "days" are the subject of significant controversy suggests that they are a *regular* problem, which the Sabbath could most obviously become'.[55] So also Dunn, laying out the subject in somewhat greater detail.

> From this we may deduce that the problem arose because many Jewish Christians (and Gentile Christians influenced by Jewish tradition) regarded the continued observance of the special feast days of Judaism (particularly the sabbath) as of continuing importance… This is just as we might expect, since observance of the feast days, particularly of the sabbath, was a sensitive issue within Judaism at this time, and since the sabbath in particular was widely recognized as one of the distinctive features or boundary markers of diaspora Judaism. The sabbath, after all, was part of the decalogue and rooted in creation itself… More important, it was bound up with Israel's self-understanding as the elect people of God… Acceptance of the sabbath was to be a mark of proselytes and of their participation in the covenant (Isa. 56.6).[56]

55. Barclay, 'Do We Undermine the Law?', p. 42.
56. Dunn, *Romans 9–16*, p. 805.

Dunn's review of Sabbath texts in the Old Testament invests the Sabbath with theological prestige beyond that of the boundary marker that he deems it to be, but even on his terms the issue will not be a 'slight or casual' but 'a crisis of identity'.[57] Does Paul's treatment of an issue thus understood rise to the requisite level of seriousness? Paul says surprisingly little even if we were to conclude that the 'days' in question refer to the Sabbath. By pastoral criteria alone, a more extensive and empathic instruction might be expected. Yet, 'Paul's counsel was clear', as Dunn perceives it, again casting the groups that do not see eye to eye as 'adaptable' vs. 'rigid' and 'liberal' vs. 'conservative'. 'The more liberally minded should not take advantage of their position (both their majority numbers and their so far less exposed position as non-Jews). They should not exploit their own readiness to discuss their differences as a way of making the more inhibited newer members feel inferior.'[58]

This interpretation commands wide support, but the arguments are not conclusive. Bolton faults this view for being too eager to invoke the Jew vs. Gentile paradigm and for being too quick to assume that Paul's ambiguous and non-specific terminology cannot have other and less fraught referents. 'Despite the Sabbath's clear importance, Dunn is convinced that Paul's gospel relativises it to being of no more value than any other non-festival day and thus strongly moves in the direction of rendering Torah-observance redundant'.[59] This calls for less certainty than the majority of interpreters have allowed. Bolton, by contrast, is appropriately impressed by it.

> Yet the word *sabbaton* is never once used in this pericope, only *hēmera*. Paul is not therefore dealing directly with Sabbath observance as an issue per se despite the significance Dunn gives it as a key identity marker that Paul is undermining. Which 'day/s' then did Paul have in mind? It is simply not stated, though a majority of scholars assume it is a reference to the Mosaic holy days in general, which would of course include, but not be limited to, the Sabbath.[60]

Why, indeed, does Paul not simply write, 'Some judge the Sabbath a day to be observed, while others judge all days to be alike'? Why does he not more clearly adjudicate an issue that, in the history of Christianity, will be settled as a matter of course to the disadvantage of the Sabbath? This is perplexing. Even if Paul had the Sabbath in mind, he is not consigning it to obsolescence. Bolton, as noted, thinks the issue is less fraught and better understood along lines of halakhic practice. The division is not between 'rigid' Jews, who believe that the Sabbath is important, and 'liberated'

57. Dunn, *Romans 9–16*, p. 811.
58. Dunn, *Romans 9–16*, p. 813.
59. Bolton, 'Who Are You Calling "Weak"?', pp. 621-2.
60. Bolton, 'Who Are You Calling "Weak"?', 624.

Gentile believers, who see no benefit in the Sabbath institution. 'Paul is not at any point arguing for non-observance, rather he is taking observance of the day/s for granted', says Bolton. 'His halakhic ruling here, as for the food issue, is that both practices are in fact acceptable and therefore one ought not to judge or scorn the other (14.10) while being fully assured in one's own mind about one's own possession on the matter (14.5)'.[61]

Crucially, if we accept that the Sabbath is thinly veiled in Paul's elusive terminology, he is not 'gentilizing' the Jews, who will be the ones judging 'one day to be better than another' (14.5). He is not even telling the non-observers to be careful not to follow the example of 'the Jews', as John Chrysostom did three centuries later, warning Gentile believers in Antioch that their regard for the synagogue and Jewish practices was fraught with eternal peril.[62] In a historical perspective, it gets worse and worse for those said to 'judge one day to be better than another' (14.5), one example of which must suffice. Many Jewish *conversos*, meaning Jews who had converted to Christianity, were in the heyday of the Spanish Inquisition suspected of secretly practicing the forbidden faith. Did they light candles Friday night? Did they avoid eating pork? Perhaps their conversion was less than genuine? For this possibility the fury of the Inquisition was unleased on them until they, under torture and as the final act of expiation, confessed to the Inquisitor that their conversion had been hollow.[63]

There is no warrant for this course of events in Romans. Throughout in this letter, Paul creates an exquisite balance between theological depth and communal unity. 'Those who observe the day, observe it in honor of the Lord', he says (14.6), putting God into the equation whether with respect to observance of days (14.6), eating or not eating (14.6), and living or dying (14.7-8). Communal unity is in this line of thinking a consequence of each group's (if that is what they were) sincere intent toward God and the frailty of a community living on the knife's edge, secure only because of Christ who 'died and lived again' (14.9).

61. Bolton, 'Who Are You Calling "Weak"?', p. 624.

62. *Saint John Chrysostom: Discourses against Judaizing Christians*, in *The Fathers of the Church: A New Translation* 68 (trans. Paul W. Harkins; Washington, DC: The Catholic University of America Press, 1979), pp. 3-4. John preached a series of sermons full of anti-Jewish invective in Antioch in 386 CE. See also Robert L. Wilken, *John Chrysostom and the Jews: Rhetoric and Reality in the Late 4th Century* (Berkeley: University of California Press, 1983).

63. James Reston, Jr, *Dogs of God: Columbus, the Inquisition, and the Defeat of the Moors* (New York: Anchor Books, 2006), pp. 3-79; Cullen Murphy, *God's Jury: The Inquisition and the Making of the Modern World* (New York: Penguin, 2011), pp. 68-69, 94-99, 152-53.

Judging

Paul believes in accountability (14.10-11; cf. 12.19), but he does not put trust in a human structure to enforce it.[64]

> Why do you pass judgment on your brother or sister? Or you, why do you despise your brother or sister? For we will all stand before the judgment seat of God. For it is written, 'As I live, says the Lord, every knee shall bow to me, and every tongue shall give praise to God'. So then, each of us will be accountable to God. Let us therefore no longer pass judgment on one another, but resolve instead never to put a stumbling block or hindrance in the way of another (Rom. 14.10-13).

Paul does not say who despises whom in this passage, but in most reconstructions 'the weak' are most vulnerable and most at risk to be the ones looked down upon, especially if the strength of 'the strong' entails numerical superiority. The charge 'never to put a stumbling block or hindrance in the way of another' (14.13) makes it more likely that Paul has the plight of 'the weak' in view, as the subsequent elaboration bears out.[65]

> I know and am persuaded in the Lord Jesus that nothing is unclean (*koinon*) in itself; but it is unclean (*koinon*) for anyone who thinks it unclean (*koinon*). If your brother or sister is being injured by what you eat, you are no longer walking in love. Do not let what you eat cause the ruin of one for whom Christ died. So do not let your good be spoken of as evil. For the kingdom of God is not food and drink but righteousness and peace and joy in the Holy Spirit. The one who thus serves Christ is acceptable to God and has human approval. Let us then pursue what makes for peace and for mutual upbuilding. Do not, for the sake of food, destroy the work of God. Everything is indeed clean (*kathara*), but it is wrong for you to make others fall by what you eat; it is good not to eat meat or drink wine or do anything that makes your brother or sister stumble. The faith that you have, have as your own conviction before God. Blessed are those who have no reason to condemn themselves because of what they approve. But those who have doubts are condemned if they eat, because they do not act from faith; for whatever does not proceed from faith is sin (Rom. 14.14-23).

Paul writes *koinos*, translated 'unclean', but it has been argued that a distinction between 'unclean' and 'contaminated' is warranted, *koinos* here best translated 'contaminated'.[66] Paul's discussion in 1 Corinthians covers

64. Thus Gaventa ('Reading for the Subject', p. 6), 'God is the only rightful arbiter of behavior'.

65. Gaventa, 'Reading for the Subject', pp. 6-7.

66. Bolton, 'Who Are You Calling "Weak"?', pp. 621-22. Halakhically proscribed foods are in the LXX exclusively termed *akathartos* (Lev. 11.31; Deut. 14.4). In Bolton's construct, *koinos* appears for the first time in 1 Macc. 1.47, 62), in his view to be understood as Torah-clean food that has been contaminated.

similar ground in the sense that the subject there, too, is food—to eat or not to eat—the problem being food that has been sacrificed to idols (1 Cor. 8.7-13; 10.23-32). As in Romans, the overriding concern is not to place a stumbling block in the way of the brother (1 Cor. 8.9; Rom. 14.13, 21) and not to do anything that puts the brother or sister at risk (1 Cor. 8.10-13; Rom. 14.20-21). As Gaventa notes, the ones designated as powerful 'are *not* eating and drinking to the downfall of others', choosing instead to set aside one's own conviction for the other person's good.[67]

Faith and an alleged 'faith-deficiency' now appear to have a counterpoint in 'faith-havers', believers who may have an excess of faith in the sense that their faith is inconsiderate of others. Instead of saying, with the NRSV, that 'the faith that you have, have as your own conviction before God' (14.22), Gaventa suggests that Paul has in mind a faith-orientation turned outwards. 'As for the faith you have *kata seauton* (that is, turned in on yourself), have that faith instead in the presence of God'.[68] A certain course of conduct is not certified by subjective criteria only, by 'having faith'. Paul may be thinking of 'the strong' when he deems blessed those 'who have no reason to condemn themselves because of what they approve' (14.22). 'Acting from faith' will by this logic not be a matter of a subjective conviction but have an objective point of reference in God's faithfulness (*pistis*). If, as Paul will say, 'whatever does not proceed from faith is sin' (14.23), 'sin' is defined not primarily as the counterpoint to faith, understood introspectively, but as the counterpoint to divine faithfulness. Whatever does not proceed from that, is sin. This direction of Paul's argument is confirmed in his conclusion.

> We who are strong ought to put up with the failings of the weak, and not to please ourselves. Each of us must please our neighbor for the good purpose of building up the neighbor. For Christ did not please himself; but, as it is written, 'The insults of those who insult you have fallen on me'. For whatever was written in former days was written for our instruction, so that by steadfastness (*tēs hypomonēs*) and by the encouragement (*tēs paraklēseōs*) of the scriptures we might have hope. May the God of steadfastness (*tēs hypomonēs*) and encouragement (*tēs paraklēseōs*) grant you to live in harmony with one another, in accordance with Christ Jesus, so that together you may with one voice glorify the God and Father of our Lord Jesus Christ. Welcome one another, therefore, just as Christ has welcomed you, for the glory of God (Rom. 15.1-7).

Interpreters in general tend to believe that Paul counts himself among 'the strong' and thus, as to factual matters and practice, Paul takes the side of 'the strong' in the conflict.[69] This assumption becomes less certain if 'the strong'

67. Gaventa, 'Reading for the Subject', p. 9.
68. Gaventa, 'Reading for the Subject', p. 10.
69. Cf. Barclay, 'Do We Undermine the Law?', p. 38.

hold the key to solving the communal problem in Rome. In that case Paul identifies with 'the strong' for a pastoral reason and is determined to lead by example, just as he proposed to do in the Corinthian conflict over what to eat (1 Cor. 8.13).[70] Paul's approach is not to fix blame but to fix the problem, and he will fix the problem by the logic of the faithfulness of Christ. It is at this point in the argument that he invokes a notion of *substitution*. 'The insults of those who insult you have fallen on me' (Rom. 15.3; cf. Ps. 69.9, 20). That is to say, Christ is the solution to a problem of which he is not the cause. Justice or righteousness are here in behavioral terms what it is theologically throughout Romans: it is not only what *is* right that counts but what *makes* right. 'Righteousness', again, is by this criterion a dynamic action best understood as right-making. This is whole cloth with Paul's appeal at the conclusion of his mediation between 'the weak' and 'the strong', his appeal at the end echoing the vision at the beginning of his exposition of what it means to live 'by the mercies of God' (Rom. 14.4-5; cf. 12.1-2).

At the point of conclusion, the message of the Old Testament scriptures and the character of God speak to the same reality with no daylight between them.

> For whatever was written in former days was written for our instruction, so that by steadfastness (*tēs hypomonēs*) and by the encouragement (*tēs paraklēseōs*) of the scriptures we might have hope (15.4).
>
> May the God of steadfastness (*tēs hypomonēs*) and encouragement (*tēs paraklēseōs*) grant you to live in harmony with one another, in accordance with Christ Jesus (15.5).

God and scripture are not far apart in this representation, the parallels and attributes of both striking. Paul appeals again to God's reliability and trustworthiness (15.5), adding yet another reason to see this as the theme of Romans, and he says nothing that will diminish the relevance of, and reverence for, 'whatever was written in former days' (15.4). If the dietary scruples of 'the weak' in Romans are inspired by the Old Testament, Paul's closing appeal does not encourage the believers in Rome to discount the Old Testament as a source of guidance, illumination, and hope.

Food and Sabbath in an Ecological Perspective

For what 'was written in former days' to disclose its ecological potential in the twenty-first century, it will be necessary to go beyond the widely held idea that stipulations regarding food and the Sabbath in the Old Testament are mainly boundary markers mapping out Jewish identity.[71] Readers of Romans must restore to these topics the possibility that they have enduring

70. Dunn (*Romans 9–16*, pp. 841-42) hints at this possibility.
71. See e.g. Dunn, *Romans 9–16*, pp. 805, 819-20.

theological meaning and testable existential, practical, and ecological benefits.[72] From an ecological point of view, the Old Testament distinctions between clean and unclean animals (Lev. 11.1-8) are less consequential than arguments for a plant-based rather than a meat based-diet (Gen. 1.29-30). The creation perspective takes priority over Israel and Israel's food laws, and universal concerns loom larger than strictly Jewish matters. Romans does not speak directly to these issues, but the Old Testament does, and Paul is not trying to mute the Old Testament voice (Rom. 15.4). The animal-based food economy of the twenty-first century is ethically untenable and ecologically unsustainable, in ecological terms contributing more to greenhouse gases and global warming than transportation.[73] In ethical and eco-theological terms, factory farming represents bone-chilling, unprecedented cruelty to non-human creatures. This assessment follows from the fact that 'ninety-nine percent of all land animals eaten or used to produce milk and eggs in the United States are factory farmed',[74] the statistic only slightly different in other industrialized countries. The distinction between 'the weak' and 'the strong', if relevant at all, will need to be redefined in ways that are ethically and ecologically meaningful with respect to present reality. On such a logic, this will not be the time to scoff at the food preferences of 'the weak' if we see them as people who promote an eco-friendly diet (14.2). If abstaining from pork in the ancient world was a signifier of Jewish identity, the violation of which meant ritual contamination and a troubled conscience,[75] the question confronting conscience today might begin with the realization that pigs are among the most genetically manipulated and intensively farmed animals.[76] Will the person who is sensitized 'by the mercies of God' be insensitive to the suffering of pigs, choosing to abstain not for reasons of ritual impurity but for reasons of compassion? A contemporary delineation of 'the weak' and 'the strong' might on this logic lead to the surprising conclusion that 'the weak' who do not eat are no longer identifiable as 'rigid' believers

72. I have explored neglected ecological implications of the Sabbath in *The Lost Meaning of the Seventh Day* (Berrien Springs, MI: Andrews University Press, 2009), pp. 375-86, 387-401, in chapters entitled, respectively, 'From Creation Time to Clock Time' and 'The Lost Voice of the Earth'.

73. FAO Newsroom, 'Livestock a Major Threat to Environment', www.fao.org/newsroom/en/News/2006/1000448/index.html.

74. Foer, *Eating Animals*, p. 34. Brian G. Henning ('Standing in Livestock's "Long Shaddow": The Ethics of Eating Meat on a Small Planet', *Ethics & the Environment* 16 [2011], pp. 63-94) catalogues the ecological cost of livestock and meat consumption, highlighting a system of economic efficiency at the cost of 'dramatic ecological inefficiency'.

75. Barclay, 'Do We Undermine the Law?', p. 54.

76. Scully, *Dominion*, pp. 28-36, 247-86. Scully urges that questions with regard to the care of animals are less about economics, ecology, or science and primarily 'questions of conscience' (*Dominion*, p. xi).

inclined to Jewish traditions, and 'the strong' who 'believe in eating anything' are not Gentiles. Ethical and ecological realities have eradicated these characterizations as meaningful distinctions. 'The weak', instead, in a sensitized ecological hermeneutic carried out within sight and sound of the modern factory farm, are the animals that are abused before they are eaten, and food preferences are better characterized with reference to health, ecological accounting, and compassion.

And now to those who 'judge one day to be better than another' (14.5). If we go along with the majority of interpreters, the text will be referring to Jewish Sabbath observance carrying over into the Roman community of believers in Jesus. I have reviewed evidence above that the majority reading is not based on iron-clad evidence. In an eco-theological perspective, however, the Sabbath will be more than a Jewish boundary marker, and it will not be held hostage to the law vs. grace polarity that has dominated Protestant theology. Instead, it will be a feature of the biblical narrative bursting at the seams with untapped theological, existential, and practical benefits—and this more so in a society that is bent on productivity and consumption rather than plenitude and conviviality. The ecological working principle of the Sabbath is *cessation*, meaning that the Sabbath speaks the native language of ecology: it is aware of the need to cease and desist (Gen. 2.1-3). 'Many of our ecological sins consist of denying creation the necessary periods of *menuha*', says Susan Power Bratton, picking up the notion of *cessation* and *rest* that lies deep in the theology of the Old Testament.[77]

When I look across the centuries to Paul and his letter to the Romans, seeing him as an anguished man trying to bring to completion the Gentile mission without losing his own kin, I am struck not only with the disappearance of the Jews from the communities of faith that Paul brought into existence but also with the vanishing of the Sabbath.[78] Perhaps this is the time for both to return—or for the believing community to return to them? For this to happen, the Sabbath must be seen as a mediator of grace, and Sabbath-observance cannot be regarded as an expression of deficient faith.[79] Changes in perception of this magnitude, though presently a long

77. Susan Power Bratton, 'Sea Sabbaths for Sea Stewards: Rest and Restoration for Marine Ecosystems', in *Environmental Stewardship: Critical Perspectives—Past and Present* (ed. R.J. Berry; New York: T. & T. Clark, 2006), p. 210. Bratton discusses the urgency of periodic rest for overtaxed marine ecosystems, envisioning eco-systemic time-scales that correspond to the Sabbath Year and the Jubilee. She urges rest for marine ecosystems apart from the threat of extinction.

78. Kenneth A. Strand ('The Sabbath Fast in Early Christianity', in *The Early Christian Sabbath* [ed. Kenneth A. Strand; Worthington, OH: Ann Arbor Publishers, 1976], pp. 9-15) notes that in the Christian community in Rome, the Sabbath was degraded to an anti-Jewish day of fasting.

79. Pinchas Peli, *The Jewish Sabbath: A Renewed Encounter* (New York: Schocken

shot, will not need to transform the food stipulations in the creation account or the Sabbath into mediators of meaning and grace as though they were originally lacking in this regard (Gen. 1.29-30; 2.1-3). Jürgen Moltmann sees the Sabbath as more than a dispensable boundary marker between Jews and the Gentile world, now speaking to the subject in a time of ecological crisis. 'In the Sabbath stillness men and women no longer intervene in the environment through their labour', he says; he, too, keenly attuned to the need to restore *cessation* to its rightful place.[80] 'Without the Sabbath quiet, history becomes the self-destruction of humanity', Moltmann adds, casting the Sabbath as a substantial spiritual and ecological remedy.[81] William H. Willimon hails the Sabbath as 'an act of prophetic resistance' in a culture dedicated to ceaseless and ecologically exhausting productivity, a theme that has also been picked up by Walter Brueggemann.[82] The theological and ethical rationale behind these visions are not only the threat of ecological collapse; it is equally a yearning to reset life's priorities away from self-importance and myopic self-interest.[83] Marva Dawn urges perceptively that

> [t]o return to the Sabbath keeping is not nostalgia. Rather, it is a return to the spiritual dimension that haunts us. In an age that has lost its soul, Sabbath keeping offers the possibility of gaining it back… In contrast to the technological society, in which the sole criterion of value is the measure of efficiency, those who keep the Sabbath find their criteria in the character of God, in whose image they celebrate life.[84]

Books, 1988), pp. 38-43; Bernard Dupuy, 'The Sabbath: Call to Justice and Freedom', in *The Jewish Roots of Christian Liturgy* (ed. Eugene J. Fisher; Mahwah, NJ: Paulist Press, 1990), pp. 153-54.

80. Moltmann, *God in Creation*, p. 277.

81. Moltmann, *God in Creation*, p. 139.

82. William H. Willimon, 'Lord of the Sabbath', *Christian Century* 108 (1991), p. 515; cf. also Barbara Brown Taylor, 'Sabbath Resistance', *Christian Century* 122 (2005), p. 35; Darby Kathleen Ray, 'It's about Time: Reflections on a Theology of Rest', in *Theology That Matters: Ecology, Economy, and God* (ed. Darby Kathleen Ray; Minneapolis: Fortress Press, 2006), pp. 154-71; Walter Brueggemann, *Sabbath as Resistance: Saying No to the Culture of Now* (Louisville, KY: Westminster/John Knox Press, 2014).

83. Dupuy ('The Sabbath', pp. 148-50) shows that the Sabbath in Jewish thought is (1) not a rite but 'a fact *in the order of existence*' and (2) freedom from work in awareness of the inescapable *incompleteness* of all human activity and thus an antidote to self-importance.

84. Marva J. Dawn, *Keeping the Sabbath Wholly* (Grand Rapids: Eerdmans, 1989), p. 50; idem, 'Sabbath Keeping and Social Justice', in *Sunday, Sabbath, and the Weekend: Managing Time in a Global Culture* (ed. Edward O'Flaherty and Rodney L. Petersen; Grand Rapids: Eerdmans, 2010), pp. 23-40.

Seeing the character of God reflected in the Sabbath restores to the Sabbath lost prestige that is both theological and ecological.[85] The tenor of the voices quoted above is similar to Paul's appeal to pay attention to what 'was written in former days', and to find in these writings a message of 'steadfastness' and 'encouragement' (15.4) and a path to 'the God of steadfastness and encouragement' (15.5). In a bird's eye view, Paul's mediation between 'the weak' and 'the strong' in Romans begins by an appeal to let 'the mercies of God' find embodiment in the believing community (12.1-2), and it ends by an appeal to the Old Testament scriptures and its witness to 'the God of steadfastness and encouragement' (15.4-5). Personal and communal commitments that are made under the influence of this vision of mercy and faithfulness—this God-centered and God-sensitized vision—will not stop at harmony within the human community only but also heed its summons to harmony with non-human creation and the earth.

85. I argue elsewhere (*The Lost Meaning of the Seventh Day*, pp. 501-15) that the meaning of the Sabbath is best reflected in a theology of divine commitment rather than a theology of divine commandment. The ecological import of the Sabbath, however, will not be realized apart from some kind of observance and actual cessation.

Chapter 17

'The Root of Jesse Shall Come' (Rom. 15.12)

In material terms, the ending of the book or a letter is found at the point where the writer puts the last period and, at least figuratively, lays down his or her pen. But this commonplace observation must be qualified in connection with many kinds of literature, and the need for nuance is critical with respect to a letter like Romans. The last verse or sentence will be the ending in formal terms, but Paul brings Romans to a close with a panorama of horizons, each one competing for the honor of being seen as the ending. By this criterion, which horizon is the ultimate one in Romans? Is it the doxology at the very end that recapitulates some of the key themes in the letter (Rom. 16.25-27)? I will say 'no' to this option because it is mostly a retrospective summary. Should the greetings at the end be seen as the final horizon, whether the greetings from Paul to his network of cherished friends, co-workers, and fellow-believers (16.1-16) or the greetings from Paul's fellow workers in Corinth to the same network in Rome (16.21-22)? I will say 'no' to these candidates, too, because Paul takes his readers to a horizon beyond Rome temporally and geographically. He is going to Rome on his way to somewhere else (15.24), meaning that the imperial capital is not the final destination. Is the ultimate horizon, then, Paul's missionary map, leading from Corinth to Jerusalem (15.25-32), then to Rome (15.20-24, 32), and then, as the third leg in the far-flung enterprise, on to Spain (15.23-24, 28)? Or, taking a general approach to the same question, should we see Paul's missionary map as open-ended and un-ending, Paul propelled to ever new destinations on the logic, 'Those who have never been told of him shall see, and those who have never heard of him shall understand' (Rom. 15.21; cf. Isa. 52.15)?

This option will be a strong candidate, but it does not rise to the top of the list. My vote goes to the text in the letter-ending that captures the completion of the *divine* mission in the world. 'And again Isaiah says', Paul writes, 'The root of Jesse shall come, the one who rises to rule the Gentiles; in him the Gentiles shall hope' (Rom. 15.12; Isa. 11.10). This text is not centered on Paul's letter, human network, travel plans, or mission but on the person whose messenger Paul understood himself to be (Rom. 1.1-6). Mission is in view, to be sure, but the text is distinctive for describing the completion of *God's* mission.

Characteristically, Paul quotes the Old Testament, the prestige of this text enhanced by coming from Isaiah, Paul's favorite prophet.[1] As Richard Hays notes, Paul 'has saved his clinchers for the end',[2] and the text has the added advantage of being part of what many scholars see as the *peroratio*, or conclusion, of Romans (15.7-13).[3] If we pay attention to 'the loci from which the quotations originate' so as not to miss important intertextual echoes,[4] the clincher saved for the end depicts the ending in an absolute sense (Isa. 11.1-10). This ending, in turn, marks the beginning of a vision of life without an ending.

1. Dunn, *Romans 9–16*, p. 850; Jewett, *Romans*, p. 895.
2. Hays, *Echoes of Scripture*, p. 71.
3. Hays, *Echoes of Scripture*, p. 71. Katherine Grieb ('The Root of Jesse Who Rises to Rule the Gentiles: Paul's Use of the Story of Jesus in Romans 15:7-13', *Proceedings* 13 [1993], p. 73) sees Rom. 15.7-13 as 'the exegetical climax of Paul's argument'. See also J. Ross Wagner, 'The Christ, Servant of Jew and Gentile: A Fresh Approach to Romans 15:8-9', *JBL* 116 (1997), pp. 473-85. Jewett (*Romans*, pp. 886, 901-902) may be correct that the letter's *peroratio* (conclusion) on formal grounds begins at 15.14, but the thematic climax may be legitimately located to 15.7-13.
4. Hays, *Echoes of Scripture*, p. 71.

'The root of Jesse shall come' (Rom. 15.12a). In this chapter I intend to explore this text in detail in its context in Romans and its Old Testament background. A preliminary glance will set the tone. First, the vision is future-oriented and eschatological, straining to portray the ultimate destiny of human beings, non-human beings, and the earth.[5] Second, the text has an apocalyptic tenor in two important senses. On the one hand, it blends continuity and discontinuity, but the accent falls strikingly on an unprecedented, never-before-seen reality.[6] On the other hand, 'the root of Jesse' comes on stage as a mediator of *revelation*, and revelation is the means by which he makes right what is wrong in the world (Isa. 11.9b). The unprecedented reality brought to view and the focus on revelation are features of apocalyptic. Third, Isaiah allows no dissonance or disconnect between the means of the revealer and the end (Isa. 11.2-4). Indeed, the bulk of his vision is devoted to the character of the right-maker and the means at his disposal. In short, 'the root of Jesse' is a non-violent peace-maker who succeeds in establishing peace by non-violent means. Fourth, the entire vision unfolds under the banner of divine faithfulness (Isa. 11.5), using words to this effect that are key terms in Romans. Fifth, Isaiah projects a vision of inclusion, the inclusion of the Gentiles explicit at the point of the vision's culmination (Isa. 11.10) and also the theme of the other Old Testament quotations in the passage (Rom. 15.9-11). Sixth, inclusion is not only a fact in the *human* realm. Right-making extends to animal creation and to the earth, making the vision authentically and profoundly ecological (Isa. 11.6-9). This aspect occupies a large portion of the vision and is not a mere afterthought. Seventh, to the extent that the vision speaks in terms that are disputed in contemporary readings of Paul and Romans, it aligns itself resolutely on the side of 'new' perspectives.

Vision of Inclusion—and Vision of God

Paul's reference to Isaiah's vision—Isaiah by name—belongs in the context of what Hays calls a 'florilegium',[7] a 'collection of literary extracts' or an 'anthology'.

5. Willem A.M. Beuken ('The Emergence of the Shoot of Jesse: An Eschatological or a Now Event?', *CTJ* 39 [2004], pp. 88-108) shows that Isaiah's poem (Isa. 11.1-10) has a historical context suggestive of a 'now' event, but the content of the vision is not accommodated within any conception of a 'now' occurence, this fact so obvious that the messianic texture of the passage is a given.

6. H.H. Rowley (*The Relevance of Apocalyptic* [London: Lutterworth Press, 1944], p. 38) made the distinction between prophecy and apocalyptic hinge on continuity vs. discontinuity. 'The prophets foretold the future that should arise out of the present, while the apocalyptists foretold the future that should break into the present… The apocalyptists had little faith in the present to beget the future.' By this criterion Isaiah's vision of 'the root of Jesse' belongs in the apocalyptic category. Thus also Terrien, *The Elusive Presence*, p. 303.

7. Hays, *Echoes of Scripture*, p. 71.

> For I tell you that Christ has become a servant of the circumcised on behalf of the truth of God (*alētheias theou*) in order that he might confirm the promises given to the patriarchs, and in order that the Gentiles might glorify God for his mercy (*eleous* [*ton theon*]). As it is written, 'Therefore I will confess you among the Gentiles, and sing praises to your name'; and again he says, 'Rejoice, O Gentiles, with his people'; and again, 'Praise the Lord, all you Gentiles, and let all the peoples praise him'; and again Isaiah says, 'The root of Jesse shall come, the one who rises to rule the Gentiles; in him the Gentiles shall hope' (Rom. 15.8-12).

It has been said that this passage is not only the conclusion of the ethical instruction in Romans but 'the climax of the entire epistle'.[8] The first sentence is awkward and difficult to translate (15.8-9). Most interpreters agree that there is an *ellipsis* of some kin, a word or a phrase left out that we can infer from the context, but there is no agreement on what the missing part is. I find J. Ross Wagner's careful analysis and translation the most persuasive (15.8-9). He works from the reasonable assumption that the two parts of the sentence should have the same subject, that is, we should not expect the subject to change in mid-stream.[9] Christ is the subject of the first part of the sentence (15.8); indeed, Christ is the subject in an argument that is rising to a crescendo on the momentum of preceding verses.

> Christ did not please himself (15.3).
>
> Christ has welcomed you (15.7).
>
> Christ has become a servant of the circumcised (15.8).

If Christ is the subject throughout the last of these sentences, modifying Wagner slightly, the complete sentence reads as follows.

> For I declare that[10]
> Christ has become a servant
>   of the circumcision on behalf of the truthfulness of God,
>   in order to confirm the promises made to the patriarchs,
> and (a servant)

8. Wagner, 'Servant of Jew and Gentile', p. 473; Scott Hafemann, 'Eschatology and Ethics: The Future of Israel and the Nations in Romans 15.1-13', *TynB* 51 (2000), p. 161.

9. Wagner, 'Servant of Jew and Gentile', p. 482. Andrew Das ('"Praise the Lord, All you Gentiles": The Encoded Audience of Romans 15.7-13', *JSNT* 34 [2011], pp. 90-110) critiques Wagner's translation but does not significantly weaken it. However, he argues plausibly that the line of demarcation between 'the weak' and 'the strong' in this part of Romans need not be ethnic. 'When Paul's "weak" observe days and abstain from meat, they are doing precisely what gentile sympathizers of Judaism were widely recognized as doing' (p. 102).

10. Cranfield (*Romans, p.* 740) notes the declarative force of *legō*.

with respect to the Gentiles
on behalf of the mercy (of God)
in order to glorify God (Rom. 15.8-9a).[11]

As noted above, the ellipsis—the word or phrase left out—is in this representation Christ as servant. This is the phrase that is most easily inferred without changing the subject of the two parts of the sentence. The ensuing parallels align in a striking and purposeful manner: 'the circumcision' and Gentiles; God's 'truthfulness' and God's 'mercy'; and Christ as 'a servant in order to confirm the promises made to the patriarchs' (15.8) and 'in order to glorify God' (15.9a).[12] Christ, not Paul, is the subject in the letter-ending just as at the beginning of Romans (1.1-7; 15.7-12). A less noted feature is also consistent: God, not Christ, is the source and ultimate subject of the good news (1.1; 15.8-9, 16).

Several important conclusions follow from this, the first of which is theological. Scott Hafemann shows perceptively that Paul argues for his ethics with reference to eschatology (15.1-13),[13] and he puts *God* at the center. Thus, when urging that 'each of us must please our neighbor for the good purpose of building up the neighbor' (15.2), Paul adds the motivating clause that 'Christ did not please himself; but, as it is written, "The insults of those who insult you have fallen on me"' (15.3). This is contrary to expectations, as Hafemann notes. 'Instead of grounding his command in v. 2 by referring to Christ's regard for others, as we might expect, Paul pointed to *Christ's regard for God*'.[14] 'Regard for God' and for the truth about God are precisely the concern that is made to stand front and center in the closing argument. 'Christ has become a servant of the circumcision on behalf of the truth of God (*alētheias theou*)' (15.8, translation mine), and he has become '(a servant)...on behalf of the mercy (of God) *in order to glorify God*' (15.9a). 'The truth of God' at the beginning and 'the glory of God' at the end of this sentence are equally in Christ's line of service, and they are objectives taken from the same page with regard to the cause for which Christ is the servant. Along the same line of thought, with Christ as the speaker, the theological errand remains in the foreground in the first of the four Old Testament quotations to which Paul appeals in his conclusion. 'Therefore I will confess you among the Gentiles, and sing praises to your name', we read (Rom. 15.9b; Ps. 18.49). This adds up to a conspicuous series of affirmations about

11. Wagner, 'Servant of Jew and Gentile', pp. 481-82.

12. Wagner, 'Servant of Jew and Gentile', pp. 482-83. Jewett (*Romans*, pp. 891-93) argues unpersuasively that the *hyper* phrases, 'for the sake of the truth of God' and 'for the sake of mercy', are in antithesis to each other.

13. Hafemann, 'The Future of Israel and the Nations in Romans 15.1-13', pp. 161-92.

14. Hafemann, 'The Future of Israel and the Nations in Romans 15.1-13', p. 168 (italics added).

God leading into the climax of Romans: 'the truth of God', 'the mercy of God', 'the glory of God' (lit. 'in order to glorify God'), and 'praises to (God's) name' (Rom. 15.8-9). These affirmations all belong in the context of a mission to 'the circumcision' (v. 8) and, in particular, to the Gentiles (v. 9). But the point is not simply to state that the Gentiles are included along with the Jews. Christ appears in the world in order to set right what has gone wrong. The worst thing that has gone wrong centers on the way God is represented and perceived. The 'truth of God', 'mercy of God', 'glory of God', and 'name of God' stand as a cluster of virtual synonyms for what is at stake. Something has been amiss in the world's view of God, and this has now been set right. When Christ is represented as saying, 'The insults of those who insult you have fallen on me' (15.3), the content of the statement is precise and to the point. God has been at the receiving end of misrepresentations and insults, and these insults have been shown up for what they are in Christ's witness to the kind of person God is.

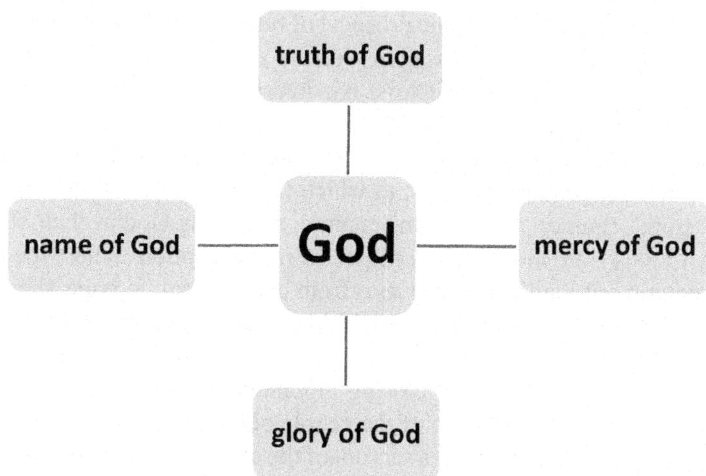

This view of Christ's mission fits well with the widescreen reading of Romans that I have explored in this commentary. It is a key element in the account that sin debuts as *misrepresentation* and *deception* and not only as violation of the divine command (7.7-13).[15] When the 'truth of God', 'mercy of God', 'glory of God', and 'name of God' are allowed to project against the horizon of misrepresentation and deception (Gen. 3.1, 13; Rom. 7.11), their corrective impact expands immensely. As Paul brings the letter to a close, it is clear that he has not left out the element of deception at the point of describing the problem, and he does not leave it out in his portrayal of the solution.

15. See Chapter 10.

This, the widescreen version of the story, is generally missing in commentaries on Romans and in the theological tradition. Hafemann's representation is no exception in this respect: it, too, is anchored in a tradition that regards sin primarily as violation of the divine command. Within such a conception, violation of the divine command triggers divine wrath. The obligation to honor God is essentially no different *before* the coming of Christ than after even though the result after his coming is different. 'From Paul's perspective, the goal of history is the glorification of God in the new creation as the reversal of unrighteous mankind's refusal to honour God (cf. 1.18-21, 23 and 3.23 with 8.18-25, 11.33-36, and 15.5-6)', he says.[16] Glorifying God is an '*eschatological obligation*' and the prudent thing to do in view of the 'coming, eschatological *judgment*'.[17] Paul's mission is essentially 'a call for the nations to repent of their own idolatry in order to escape the *wrath to come*, while they still have the opportunity'.[18] Thus, too, referring to the second quotation in Paul's closing argument (Rom. 15.11; Ps. 117.1 [LXX 116.1], the Old Testament text 'specifically *commands* the nations to praise the Lord'.[19] The prospect of future wrath looms large in this representation, and Paul's message is seen as a stern command for humans to bring their house in order. Christ has intervened chiefly to remedy the problem that runs from violation of the command to the wrath that is certain to follow. In the alternative, widescreen representation, living in a state of deception is the primary problem to which Christ is the solution. The cluster of 'truth', 'mercy', 'glory', and 'name', all having God as their subject (Rom. 15.8-11), are mobilized to dispel the misperception. Where the usual representation of Paul's message runs from divine wrath to hope, the widescreen edition projects a movement from misperception and hopelessness to hope (15.12-13).

A second feature in Paul's closing argument relates to the way theology, mission, and the make-up of the people of God are tightly linked. The notion that 'Christ has become a servant of the circumcision on behalf of the truth of God…and (a servant) with respect to the Gentiles on behalf of the mercy (of God)' (15.8-9a) should not be seen as different objectives that are actualized sequentially even though Paul has argued earlier for a sequential implementation of his vision of inclusion (11.11-29).[20] The two parts of the sentence relate to each other as *one* objective, and the terms used are

16. Hafemann, 'The Future of Israel and the Nations in Romans 15.1-13', p. 168.

17. Hafemann, 'The Future of Israel and the Nations in Romans 15.1-13', p. 168, cf. Reasoner, *The Strong and the Weak*, p. 25.

18. Hafemann, 'The Future of Israel and the Nations in Romans 15.1-13', p. 180.

19. Hafemann, 'The Future of Israel and the Nations in Romans 15.1-13', p. 183 (italics mine).

20. There is more than a hint of a dual, 'both-and' texture rather than one single and indivisible intent in the expositions of Dunn (*Romans 9–16*, p. 848), Wagner ('Servant of

virtually interchangeable. Can we not say, turning the sentence around, that 'Christ has become a servant of the *Gentiles* on behalf of the truth of God in order in order to confirm the promises made to the patriarchs', remembering that the promise to the patriarchs was intended to bring a benefit to all nations (Gen. 12.1-3; 18.18; 22.18)? Does not Paul make Abraham the spiritual progenitor of all believers while in a state of *un-circumcision* (Rom. 4.9-12, 16-18)? Are we not on orthodox ground if we say that 'Christ has become (a servant) with respect to the *Jews* on behalf of the mercy (of God)', mercy the reason for their hope as much as mercy grounds 'the promises made to the patriarchs'? Are not 'the truth of God' and 'the mercy (of God)' two sides of the same reality rather than two realities, as though the first ('truth') is for the benefit of the Jews and the second ('mercy') for the good of the Gentiles? Were not the Gentiles, too, included in 'the promises made to the patriarchs', and is not 'mercy' extended to Jews and Gentiles alike, an excellent way to depict 'the truth about God' and the reason for God's outreach to all humans?

The foregoing prepares for the conclusion to Paul's message. Before embarking on the last leg, it is important to appreciate that the conclusion reads as an acclamation rather than an argument. The argument has been made earlier: nothing new is argued here. Acclamation is possible only when the matter that is acclaimed is already established. Here, in turn, acclamation is reflected in a tone that shifts from exhortation to doxology.[21] Occasions of exclamation are not a novelty in Romans (7.24; 8.15, 31-39), and this acclamation will be second to none in terms of scope, depth, thought, and emotional intensity (15.8-13).

> As it is written, 'Therefore I will confess you among the Gentiles, and sing praises to your name' (Rom. 15.9; Ps. 18.49).

This is the first of four rapid-fire references to the Old Testament, this one from the Psalms (Ps. 18.49). P.C. Craigie acknowledges Paul's use of the Psalm, but he claims that Paul stops short of drawing out its significance in a messianic sense.[22] This reservation is unnecessary and is valid only if we demand that the identity of the implied speaker in the Psalm be made explicit. Paul, however, leaves the identity of the speaker implicit without thereby sowing doubt as to who the speaker is.[23] The royal figure in the Psalm is the object of God's solicitous care. As Steven Shnider notes, the

Jew and Gentile', p. 483), Hafemann ('The Future of Israel and the Nations in Romans 15.1-13', pp. 170-72), and Jewett (*Romans*, p. 893).

21. Käsemann, *Romans*, p. 384.

22. P.C. Craigie, *Psalms 1–50* (WBC; Nashville: Nelson Reference & Electronic, 2nd edn, 2004), p. 177.

23. Richard B. Hays, 'Christ Prays the Psalms: Paul's Use of an Early Christian Exegetical Convention', in *The Future of Christology: Essays in Honor of Leander Keck*

Psalm is distinctive in that 'God does not come to save his people Israel; He comes to save an individual, his anointed one, David'.[24] The entire Psalm can be read as 'the thanksgiving of a king who speaks throughout'.[25] The speaking 'I', however, has qualities that vastly exceed the virtues of 'David' (Ps. 18.20-24). Specifically, although the speaker in the Psalm is grateful for God's intervention and deliverance (Ps. 18.4-19), he does not count it as an undeserved mercy.

> The LORD rewarded me
> according to my righteousness (*kata tēn diakaiosynēn mou*);
> according to the cleanness of my hands
> he recompensed me.
>
> Therefore the LORD has recompensed me
> according to my righteousness (*kata tēn diakaiosynēn mou*),
> according to the cleanness of my hands in his sight (Ps. 18.20, 24).

In the context of Romans, Christ is the one singing God's praise among the Gentiles in a case of 'christological ventriloquism', as Hays puts it (Rom. 15.9; Ps. 18.49).[26] But our interest should not be the Gentile audience only. Steven Shnider finds in the Psalm *theophany*, *epiphany*, and *empowerment*.[27] In Pauline terms, Christ is singing God's praise among the Gentiles because of God's faithfulness, and the one singing God's praise has himself faithfulness and righteousness as his insignia (Ps. 18.20-24). In bullet point terms, God is faithful, and so is the one who is here singing God's praise. God intervenes spectacularly on behalf of the one singing, a person who is threatened with extinction. The telling response from the highest heaven to one who occupies the lowest point in the cosmos shows that God is neither absent nor indifferent to the supplicant's plight.[28] At the same time, the

(ed. Abraham J. Malherbe and Wayne A. Meeks; Minneapolis: Fortress Press, 1993), pp. 122-36.

24. Steven Shnider, 'Psalm XVIII: Theophany, Epiphany, Empowerment', *VT* 56 (2006), p. 386.

25. J. Kenneth Kuntz, 'Psalm 18: a Rhetorical-Critical Analysis', *JSOT* 26 (1983), p. 3.

26. Hays, 'Christ Prays the Psalms', p. 125. Hays notes that Christ is also the implied speaker in Rom. 15.3 and that Paul takes the legitimacy of the Christological use for granted. Hafemann ('The Future of Israel and the Nations in Romans 15.1-13', p. 178) calls for care with respect to who is doing what in the Psalm—and in Romans. 'Psalm 17.50 LXX is about David's praise of God in the midst of the nations—it is not about the salvation of or praise from the nations themselves. And this holds true for its eschatological application to the Christ as well.'

27. Shnider, 'Psalm XVIII', pp. 386-98.

28. H.-J. Kraus, *Psalms 1–59* (trans. Hilton C. Oswalt; CC; Minneapolis: Fortress Press, 1999), p. 260.

royal figure in the Psalm is empowered to become 'head of the nations' (Ps. 18.44). This perspective vastly expands the reach of the Davidic monarchy, projecting it against a universal, eschatological horizon.

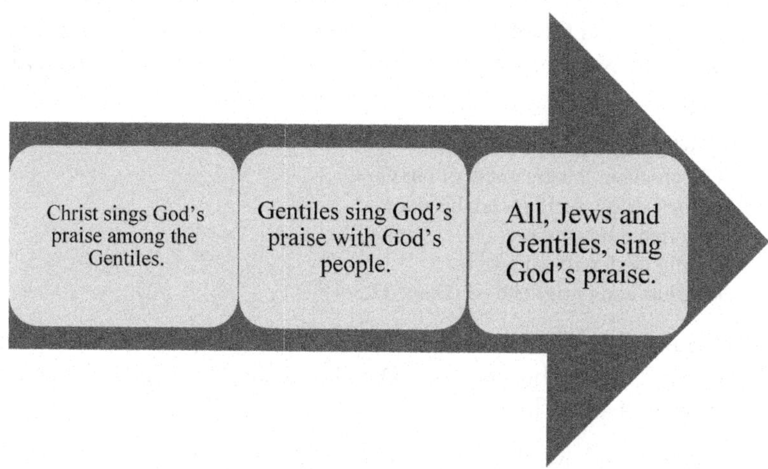

Paul's second Old Testament echo is taken from Deuteronomy (Deut. 32.43). This text shifts the focus from the one who is singing God's praise among the Gentiles to the Gentile response to God's initiative. The NRSV personifies the speaker, saying, 'and again *he* says' (Rom. 15.10). For this to work, Christ remains the implied speaker, calling out to the Gentiles to acknowledge the privilege extended to them.

> 'Rejoice, O Gentiles, with his people' (Rom. 15.10; Deut. 32.43).

Alternatively, Paul's bridge to Deuteronomy can be translated, 'and again *it* says', meaning that the Old Testament or 'Moses' is the speaker. Dunn points out that the quotation 'is verbatim from the LXX of Deut. 32.43, the last verse of the song of Moses', noting also that the LXX has a much longer passage than the Masoretic text.[29] Gentile inclusion is now given by the fact of Christ singing God's praise among the Gentiles (Rom. 15.9; Ps. 18.49) *and* by the Gentiles rejoicing in unison with God's people (Rom. 15.10; Deut. 32.43). *Singing* is the mode of expression in both sources so

29. Dunn, *Romans 9–16*, p. 849. The Greek 'addition' calls for heaven and heavenly beings to rejoice along with the praise ascending from the Gentiles 'with his people'. See also Jewett, *Romans*, p. 895. The MT has four cola, the LXX eight. Qumran manuscripts attest a Hebrew version with six cola that is closer to the LXX; cf. Arie van der Kooij, 'The Ending of the Song of Moses: On the Pre-Masoretic Version of Deut. 32.4', in *Studies in Deuteronomy: In Honour of C.J. Labuschagne on the Occasion of His 65th Birthday* (ed. F. Garcia Martinez, A. Hilhorst, J.T.A.G.M. van Rutten and A.S. van der Woude; Leiden: E.J. Brill, 1994), pp. 93-100.

far, in Deuteronomy no less than in the Psalm (Deut. 32.3; Ps. 18.1-3, 49), and *singing* is now also heard at the receiving end of proclamations that have Christ and Moses as the implied speakers (Deut. 32.43).[30] As to content, the lead singers are on the same page despite the fact that one speaks from the Psalms and the other from Deuteronomy.[31] In Patrick W. Skehan's rendition of 'the Song of Moses', we hear this affirmation at the beginning of the song.

> For I will sing the LORD's renown.
>   Oh, proclaim the greatness of our God!
> The Rock—how faultless are his deeds,
>   how right all his ways!
> A faithful God, without deceit,
>   how just and upright he is! (Deut. 32.3-4)[32]

What is the theme, the central emphasis, of this song? What, as Thomas A. Keiser asks, is 'the big picture'? Details and subplots aside, the central emphasis is not hard to find.

> From the perspective of the 'big picture' of the song, the incomparability of Yahweh is such that, in spite of the gross failure of his people, he will deliver them for his own name's sake. Thus, in the Song of Moses the Lord is referred to as the 'Rock' in a context which declares his incomparability expressed primarily in his deliverance of his people even in spite of their failure.[33]

A message is proclaimed in the world, and 'the Song of Moses' serves as a summary and bottom line. Jews and Gentiles are the intended target of the message, but the subject matter is God. Moses' song in the LXX features nouns describing God's *work* (*erga*), God's *ways* (*hodoi*), and God's *judgments* (*kriseis*), qualified by adjectives that show God to be trustworthy (*alēthinos*), faithful (*pistos*), righteous (*dikaios*), and whole (*hosios*) (Deut. 32.3-4). These attributes are not proclaimed and acclaimed in a vacuum: they are the reasons why there is hope despite human failure.

30. Despite the personal, 'biographical' features in the text (esp. Deut. 32.49), the notion that the Song of Moses is a teaching poem for Israel rather than the confession of Moses prevails; cf. Eckart Otto, 'Singing Moses: His Farewell Song in Deuteronomy 32', in *Psalmody and Poetry in Old Testament Ethics* (ed. Dirk J. Human; New York: T. & T. Clark, 2012), pp. 169-80. To Otto, the song is a bridge between Torah, Prophets, and Writings.

31. Otto ('Singing Moses', pp. 178-80) demonstrates parallels between Deut. 32 and Pss. 90 and 92.

32. Patrick W. Skehan, 'Structure of the Song of Moses in Deuteronomy (Deut 32:1-43)', *CBQ* 13 (1951), p. 157.

33. Thomas A. Keiser, 'The Song of Moses a Basis for Isaiah's Prophecy', *VT* 55 (2005), p. 488.

The vocabulary of the Song of Moses overlaps conspicuously with the vocabulary of Romans with respect to describing God's character. In Romans, however, the affirmations of the song are not only playing out against a background of *human* failure. Recalling the echoes of Habakkuk in the programmatic statement in Romans (Rom. 1.16-17; Hab. 1.2-4; 2.2-4), Paul's message also speaks to the subject of *divine* absence and the terrifying prospect of *divine* failure. In the widescreen edition that does not leave out sin's opening gambit (Rom. 5.12-21; 7.7-13), Paul reinforces the right-setting character of the message whether we define the problem as misrepresentation of God in the story of Adam and Eve (Rom. 5.12-21; 7.7-13), divine absence or inaction in the cry of Habakkuk (Hab. 1.2-4; 2.2-4), or human failure (Deut. 32.15-25; Rom. 3.3-7). As Keiser notes in the context of the Song of Moses, 'the primary theme of Deuteronomy xxxii is the proclamation of the name of the Lord. It is to praise his greatness, specifically his perfect work, his righteous ways, his faithful, true, just, and upright character.'[34]

Paul is not done. His next exhibit is drawn from the shortest Psalm. 'And again', he says, echoing the Psalm,

> Praise the Lord, all you Gentiles, and let all the peoples praise him (Rom. 15.11; Ps. 117.1).

Gentile inclusion and universality have another Old Testament pillar on which to stand, but what is the reason for praising God? Here, too, it turns out, the Psalm centers on God and the faithfulness of God.

> For great is his steadfast love (Hebr. *ḥesed*, Gr. *eleos*) toward us,
> and the faithfulness (Hebr. *'ĕmet*, Gr. *alētheia*) of the LORD
> endures forever (Ps. 117.2).[35]

The three Old Testament texts featured so far in Paul's closing acclamation have in common that they affirm the inclusion of the Gentiles and the oneness of the believing community, Jew and Gentile. But they also have in common—often overlooked—that *God* is the subject of the songs, and they speak with one voice about the praiseworthy character of God: they are texts of *vindication* and *acclamation* for a *theological* reason and not only for reasons of mission or ecclesiology. Anticipating the premier text that is yet to come, from Isaiah (Rom. 15.12; Isa. 11.10), it is already resoundingly confirmed that Paul has the right-making of God as his theme. But this—the

Acclamations
- God is the subject
- Right-making
- Vindication

34. Keiser, 'The Song of Moses a Basis for Isaiah's Prophecy', p. 491.

35. The LXX has variant readings of this text, but the alternatives do not change the basic affirmation.

right-making of God—is actually right-making *about* God and the way God has been perceived in the world. This message 'is attested by the law and the prophets' (Rom. 1.16-17; 3.21), to be sure, 'the law and the prophets' testifying of God plans to intervene to set right what has gone wrong. 'Paul has offered here one quotation from the Pentateuch, one from the Prophets, and two from the Writings, all strung together by the catchword *ethnē*, all pointing to the eschatological consummation in which Gentiles join in the worship of Israel's God: truly the Law and the Prophets are brought forward here as witnesses,' says Hays.[36] Likewise, in the words of Käsemann, 'The Old Testament foreshadowed this message. The recipients of the letter must recognize this agreement with Scripture. An apology could hardly have a more magnificent conclusion.'[37]

The acknowledged 'magnificent conclusion' lets Isaiah have the last word (Rom. 15.12; Isa. 11.10). 'And again Isaiah says', Paul writes, counting on the voice of his prophetic forerunner to make the case.

> The root of Jesse shall come, the one who rises to rule the Gentiles; in him the Gentiles shall hope (Rom. 15.12; Isa. 11.10).

It remains to explore this text in its original context. I will do it in three steps, using Hans Wildberger's careful translation of this 'pearl of Hebrew poetry' as the basis for the exposition.[38]

> *Part 1*
> A shoot will come forth from the stump of Jesse
>   And a sprig will 'sprout forth' from his roots.
> And the Spirit of Yahweh will rest upon him,
>   Spirit of wisdom and insight,
> Spirit of planning and a hero's power,
>   Spirit of knowledge and of fear of Yahweh,
> [And he will have, as his pleasure, the fear of Yahweh].
> And he does not judge according to appearances
>   and does not decide simply on the basis of mere rumor;
> rather, with righteousness, he helps the lightly esteemed to get justice
>   and will intervene with equity for 'the poor' in the land
> and he strikes the 'violent ones' with the staff of his mouth
>   and kills the malicious one with the breath from his lips.
> And righteousness is the girdle of his hips
>   and faithfulness is the loincloth of his loins (Isa. 11.1-5).

We note, first, that 'the stump of Jesse' at the beginning and 'the root of Jesse' at the end frame the passage as a whole (Isa. 11.1, 10). If the inclusion

36. Hays, *Echoes of Scripture*, p. 71.
37. Käsemann, *Romans*, p. 387; cf. Jewett, *Romans*, p. 897.
38. Hans Wildberger, *Isaiah 1–12* (trans. Thomas H. Trapp; CC; Minneapolis: Fortress, 1991), pp. 460-61, 465.

of the Gentiles is the featured achievement of this figure at the end of the passage, no reading—in Romans no more than in Isaiah—will be indifferent to how 'the root of Jesse' comes to be seen as the 'signal for the nations' to whom 'the nations will all turn inquisitively' (Isa. 11.10).[39] Second, from the very first the passage strikes the note of surprise and hope. As to surprise, a shoot coming from 'the stump of Jesse' suggests unexpected newness and renewal coming from a tree stump that has been all but written off. Samuel Terrien hails the poem as 'a manifesto for sane government', stressing that the one who will set things right is represented as 'a shoot from the (cut-off) tree of Jesse'.[40] By this Isaiah signals 'historical discontinuity from the dynasty but ideological continuity from the Davidic model', the surprise described as 'theological disruption of wonder'.[41] Hope, therefore, is not a feature of business as usual or found in a return to Davidic rule as in the good, old days, as though 'the Davidic model' ever delivered the reality depicted in the poem. Apart from the unprecedented surprise there will be no hope.

Third, therefore, if there is such a thing as a 'Davidic model' that can be reclaimed and deployed for future use under the label 'ideological continuity', it must refer to a quality that does not depend on David's genes or genealogy. In Isaiah, the qualifying element is 'the Spirit of the LORD' (Isa. 11.2). This, as Rolf Rendtorff notes, 'was said of David immediately after his anointing by Samuel (1 Sam. 16.13; cf. also 2 Sam. 23.2)',[42] and it will now come to pass in a way that never happened at any previous point in the dynasty of David. Brueggemann says aptly that 'the "spirit" is a self-starter who generates new historical possibility where none was available'.[43] It is impossible to make too much of 'the Spirit of the LORD', yet the shoot that is to come 'from the stump of Jesse' is not a mere instrument of the Spirit. There appears to be synergy between the two: what the Spirit will do in and through the life of this figure could not be done by random selection among the human options available to the Spirit. Moreover, too, there would be no point to mentioning the tribe of Jesse unless there was an important relation. The figure who is to come forth has genuine human credentials, and yet he seems to be ontologically distinct. There is a reason why the Spirit alights on him. In Wildberger's conception, Isaiah does not expect salvation to come from the monarchy as such. The person who is 'prepared to serve as the monarch is dependent upon the outpouring of the Spirit'.[44]

39. Wildberger, *Isaiah 1–12*, p. 461.
40. Terrien, *The Elusive Presence*, p. 303.
41. Terrien, *The Elusive Presence*, p. 303.
42. Rendtorff, *A Theology of the Old Testament*, p. 177.
43. Walter Brueggemann, *Isaiah 1–39* (WBC; Louisville, KY: Westminster/John Knox Press, 1998), p. 99.
44. Wildberger, *Isaiah 1–12*, p. 466.

Three paired qualities are said to characterize the Spirit that is at work in this figure.

> Spirit of wisdom and insight,
> Spirit of planning and a hero's power,
> Spirit of knowledge and of fear of Yahweh (Isa. 11.2).

In the first pair, the Spirit 'gives the king the abilities necessary to carry out the demands of his office', but the two words are not exact synonyms.[45] 'Wisdom' (*hokhmah*) can be understood as 'the type of wisdom which can handle problems in daily living', and 'insight' (*binah*) refers to 'intellectual abilities which are necessary for one to see beyond the details of a particular situation, make the appropriate assessment, and come to conclusions about necessary decisions'.[46] In the second pair, 'a hero's power' has a military connotation, but Wildberger points out that 'counsel' and 'planning' are paired with 'a hero's power' in a way that suggests exceptional foresight. Contrary to traditional representations of heroic figures, the qualities of this person are mobilized for a peace-making mission.[47] The third pair, 'knowledge' (*da'at*) and 'fear of the Lord' (*jir'ât Yahweh*) 'is the decisive terminology for him', says Wildberger.[48] This pair stands apart by the fact that the two terms belong to the realm of faith and faithfulness more than to kingship. The person's character rather than his office stands at the center, and both terms suggest a relational commitment. 'Knowledge' will in this connection not just be any kind of knowledge, but it certainly means knowledge of God. The bottom line is that a person who 'rules in the fear of God is a ruler who has concern for righteousness'.[49]

> (And he will have, as his pleasure, the fear of Yahweh).[50]

> His delight shall be in the fear of the LORD (Isa. 11.3a, NRSV).

This sentence is notoriously difficult to translate, thus the two options above.[51] 'Fear of the LORD' is still the topic, and the NRSV is correct to make 'the fear of the LORD' a delight to the person in question. The stumbling block in the verse has to do with a word the essential meaning of which is 'smell' (*rēaḥ*) without losing its suggestive nuance. On conceptual and stylistic terms, the inclusion of the sense of 'smell' shows the prophet

45. Wildberger, *Isaiah 1–12*, p. 471.
46. Wildberger, *Isaiah 1–12*, p. 472.
47. Wildberger, *Isaiah 1–12*, p. 472.
48. Wildberger, *Isaiah 1–12*, p. 473.
49. Wildberger, *Isaiah 1–12*, p. 473.
50. Wildberger's translation.
51. Arie Shifman, '"A Scent" of the Spirit: Exegesis of an Enigmatic Verse (Isaiah 11:3)', *JBL* 131 (2012), pp. 241-49.

describing the person in question in terms of the three senses smell, sight, and hearing (Isa. 11.3), but with priority for the olfactory sense. On a deeper level, smell is a primeval sense in biological terms, and it reflects the notion of 'essence'. Arie Shifman notes that in English, speaking of a perfume, 'scent/smell' and 'essence' are synonymous.[52] Translating the phrase 'and essence in fear of God will fill him' makes the subject reflect 'the ultimate or elemental nature of a thing or being'.[53] 'Thus', says Shifman, 'the intrinsic meaning of such a translation would be 'and his elemental nature in fear of God will fill him'.[54] This is not a straightforward sentence, a simple concept, or good English, but it suggests a figure who is unique ontologically *and* in his disposition. In colloquial terms, the person has a 'fine nose': his sense of smell reflects exquisite discernment and incorruptible commitment.[55] On this rationale, W.H. Auden's poem is to the point.

Senses of the Right-Maker (Isa. 11.3)

Organ	Sense	Meaning
Nose	smell	affinity, disposition
Ears	hearing	integrity
Eyes	sight	discernment

> The nose and palate never doubt
> Their verdicts on the world without,
> But instantaneously condemn
> Or praise each fact that reaches them.[56]

With the sense of smell listed first, the other two senses also relate to discernment and incorruptibility.

> And he does not judge according to appearances
> and does not decide simply on the basis of mere rumor;
> rather, with righteousness (Hebr. *ṣedek*, Gr. *krisis*),
> he helps the lightly esteemed to get justice (Hebr. *mîshôr*)
> and will intervene with equity for 'the poor' in the land (Isa. 11.3-4).[57]

Just as Israel was constantly tempted to sell out to accommodation and opportunism, religion easily gravitates toward sacramental operations and the quest for personal salvation to the exclusion of social and economic

52. Shifman, '"A Scent" of the Spirit', p. 242.
53. Shifman, '"A Scent" of the Spirit', p. 242.
54. Shifman, '"A Scent" of the Spirit', p. 242.
55. Shifman, '"A Scent" of the Spirit', p. 249.
56. W.H. Auden, 'Smelt and Tasted', in *W.H. Auden Collected Poems* (ed. Edward Mendelson; London: Faber & Faber, 1976), p. 629; cf. Shifman, '"A Scent" of the Spirit', p. 249.
57. Wildberger, *Isaiah 1–12*, p. 461. 'Scent' or 'fragrance' is not a stranger to Paul's theological vocabulary. It is precisely as a 'fragrance' that the good news will go forth into the world, spreading 'in every place the fragrance that comes from knowing him' (2 Cor. 2.14-16).

justice for the vulnerable. Not so for the figure in Isaiah's poem. He 'is to practice righteousness and equity that are not based on surface appearances or on what is said, because a discerning ruler is not to be influenced by the gestures of the wealthy or swayed by the manipulations of the powerful'.[58]

> And he strikes the 'violent ones' with the staff of his mouth
> and kills the malicious one with the breath from his lips.
> And righteousness (Hebr. *ṣedek*, Gr. *dikaiosynē*) is the girdle of his hips
> and faithfulness (Hebr. *'ĕmûnâ*, Gr. *alētheia*) is the loincloth of his loins
> (Isa. 11.4-5).

Three things should here be noted. First, the suggestion of violent action must not be allowed to negate the way Isaiah has carefully stressed the role of the Spirit of Yahweh and the qualities that define the Spirit. When this feature is pondered and respected, consistency comes by way of recognizing that the *word*, not the *sword*, is the weapon and source of authority of the figure in the poem.[59] Second, having detailed the means by which the figure pursues his God-appointed goals (Isa. 11.2-3), the means are now highlighted by the words 'righteousness' (*dikaiosynē*) and 'faithfulness' (*alētheia*). These terms sum up his character and the right-making thrust of his task. A contrast is implied between the coming ruler and rulers preceding him, none of whom could be described this way. Isaiah will later detail that the Messianic figure practices 'righteousness' and 'faithfulness' in a way that not only leads to exceptional results but that also are costly commitments to the one who is thus committed (Isa. 42.1-9; 49.1-9; 50.4-9; 52.13–53.12). Third, again, we have a concentration of terms that will recur in Romans without letting go of the right-making flavor they have in Isaiah. Brueggemann says that 'the clothing of the coming king, that is, his visible political platform, has slogans written all over it: righteousness, justice (v. 5)',[60] terms that signal a concern for economic viability for the poor as well as ecological healing. This figure 'is more than the first among equals; he stands in a relationship with the people as God's proxy, has responsibilities connected with an incomparable task, and acts in unquestioned authority'.[61]

The foregoing does not exhaust the elements that are required in order to describe this person's identity and explain his mission, but it prepares for what follows. Specifically, it prepares for a vision of ecological healing that is without peer in the entire Bible, presented as whole cloth with the rest of the vision.

58. Brueggemann, *Isaiah 1-39*, pp. 100, 101.

59. The Book of Revelation appropriates Isa. 11.1-10 in its description of what is arguably the pivotal scene in the book, 'the root of Jesse' appearing in the crucial *middle* of the heavenly council as a victim of violence (Rev. 5.1-6).

60. Brueggemann, *Isaiah 1–39*, p. 101.

61. Wildberger, *Isaiah 1-12*, pp. 473-74.

Part 2
Then the wolf will be a visitor of the lamb
and the leopard will lie down with the kid.
Then the calf and young lion 'will get fattened' together,
and a little lad will tend them.
Then the cow and the bear will 'be friends with one another',
and their young will lie down with one another.
Then the lion will eat chopped straw like the cow,
and the suckling will play near the hole of a viper.
And toward a young viper
a (weaned) child will stretch out his hand.
No one shall do anything evil or anything destructive
upon my entire holy mountain.
For the land will be as full of the knowledge of Yahweh
as waters cover the sea (Isa. 11.6-9).[62]

Enchantment with the serenity of this scene is certainly in order, but it must not eclipse the theological achievement that has created the new *ecological* reality. What has made the difference? 'The Spirit of Yahweh' rests upon the Right-maker; he has the 'Spirit of knowledge and of fear of Yahweh', we have read (Isa. 11.2). And now, in the wake of his mission, 'the land will be as full of the knowledge of Yahweh as waters cover the sea' (Isa. 11.9). 'Knowledge' describes the person in a decisive way, as noted,[63] and knowledge of this kind signifies *revelation*. The figure in the poem imparts what he is and has, and the concluding statement signals the success and sufficiency of the revelation: a land 'full of the knowledge of Yahweh' (Isa. 11.9). The rest is not commentary, but the key is right-making by revelation.

The biblical imagery pertaining to the right-maker can only be appreciated in light of the losses and dislocations described in Genesis. In this sense, 'the Davidic king to come is a cosmic player', David now 'the "Adam" of Genesis 1, given dominion over the earth and all its creatures; of Genesis 2, summoned to "till and keep" the earth and all its creatures; of Genesis 3 as the agent of primal disorder'.[64] These are huge and far-reaching claims, and they need a wide screen to project clearly. Otto Kaiser notes that in this world, a lion that eats straw would be an unnatural and even sick phenomenon, the lion merely obeying its instincts when attacking another animal. Isaiah's poem, by contrast, creates a new normal even for predatory animals. Predation as such will cease. 'And if suckling and little child play with the most poisonous snakes, the old enmity between the seed of the woman and the seed of the snake has been removed (Gen. 3.15). Thus

62. Wildberger, *Isaiah 1–12*, pp. 460-61.
63. Wildberger, *Isaiah 1–12*, p. 473.
64. Brueggemann, *Isaiah 1–39*, p. 102.

the text probably says less than it knows,' he writes.[65] This keen impression imposes on the reader the duty to grasp what the text knows and not only what it says.

As for the ecological vision itself, it blends seamlessly and organically with its inclusive theology. Nature and non-human creatures are not left out of the right-making. In fact, the 'ecological' scene is essential to describing what the right-maker has been up to all along. Wildberger's comment captures it well.

> The variety, aptness, and spontaneity of the imagery is astounding: the root out of the stump, the rod of the mouth, the breath from the lips, righteousness as girdle and faithfulness as loincloth. Above all, one observes that the description of the pastoral scene—that is, the description of the relationship of the animals—is very animated: wolf, panther, young lion, bear, lion, viper, and young viper are juxtaposed with lamb, kid, calf, little lad, cow, cattle, suckling, and child. In this way, every schematization is avoided; every word-pair testifies in its own way that peace has entered upon the scene.[66]

There is no reason to postulate that Isaiah's poem awkwardly brings together two separate ideas, one theological (Isa. 11.1-5) and one ecological (Isa. 11.6-9).[67] The striking and startling eco-theology in the poem is native and utterly authentic, the composer not missing a beat when he matches 'knowledge' at the point of origin with 'knowledge' at the point of conclusion (Isa. 11.2, 9). The persistence and resilience of the underlying narrative is equally startling, the prophet's horizon now extending not only to the cut-off stump of Jesse but all the way to Adam and the disruption in the Garden of Eden. The ease with which the poet calls up this perspective testifies to its importance and to familiarity on the part of his audience. It should now be less of a surprise why Paul sees all creation included in the restoration (Rom. 8.19-22), that he reads redemption and healing in the non-human realm as inseparable from human redemption, and, too, that we are not wringing an ecological message from Paul where none was intended.

65. Otto Kaiser, *Isaiah 1–12* (trans. John Bowden; OTL; Philadelphia: Westminster Press, 2nd edn, 1983), p. 260. For the 'more' that the text knows, Isaiah offers a sequel. We read in Isa. 65.25 of the lion eating straw like the ox (rather than eating the ox), 'but the serpent—its food shall be dust!' The emphatic *exclusion* of the serpent recalls its role in the misrepresentation of God (Gen. 3.15), this to be seen as the problem that is rectified.

66. Wildberger, *Isaiah 1–12*, p. 465.

67. Hilary Marlow, 'The Spirit of Yahweh in Isaiah 11:1-9', in *Presence, Power, and Promise: The Role of the Spirit of God in the Old Testament* (ed. David G. Firth and Paul D. Wegner; Downers Grove, IL: IVP Academic, 2011), p. 229.

> *Part 3*
> And it will happen on that day: Toward the root of Jesse, which stands there like a signal for the nations, the nations will all turn inquisitively, and its resting place shall be glory (Isa. 11.10; cf. Rom. 15.12).[68]

Paul's explicit reference to Isaiah comes from the transition point at the end of the poem. Dunn notes that the 'quotation is verbatim from the LXX of Isa. 11.10',[69] but the importance of 'the shoot of Jesse' and his role in inspiring hope among the Gentiles depend on everything that has been said about him up to that point in the poem. The original Hebrew in Wildberger's translation contains distinctives with respect to time, scope, tenor, and sense of finality that further unite theology, mission, and ecology.

'That day', as we have seen earlier, has an eschatological ring (chap. 13). 'The root of Jesse' now operates on a global and even cosmic stage,[70] and he attracts attention for reasons of spectacular merit and not reasons of coercion, obligation, or wrath (cf. Rom. 1.18). Need, not obligation, captures the state of the world at the point when the root of Jesse stands up. The idea that 'the nations will all turn to him' is clarified and enhanced by the addition of the adverb 'inquisitively'. This brings out the tenor of what is taking place. The nations, trapped in a state of bewilderment and hopelessness, are turning to 'the root of Jesse' because he represents hope. The hope, in turn, combines illumination and liberation (Isa. 11.2-4); thus the notion that the nations approach him 'inquisitively'. For the last of the four phrases in this verse, Wildberger offers the translation, 'and its resting place (Hebr. *m*ᵉ*nûḥâ*; Gr. *anapausis*) shall be glory' (Isa. 11.10d). He calls this 'a strange-sounding clause',[71] perhaps made less strange-sounding by switching from a neuter to a masculine pronoun, as in the NRSV: 'and *his* dwelling shall be glorious' (Isa. 11.10). Pulling together these options, we read that 'the nations shall turn inquisitively *to him*, and *his* resting place shall be full of glory' (Isa. 11.10, translation mine). The figure at the center of the poem is the subject throughout: there is no *it*. Completion and finality are heralded by the notion of 'resting place' (Hebr. *m*ᵉ*nûḥâ*; Gr. *anapausis*). Nothing defined the yearning 'of the wandering people of Israel as that they might come to such a place of rest' (1 Kgs 8.56; Isa. 32.18; Ps. 95.11 and Isa. 28.12).[72] 'Resting place', however, also comes with shattering theological import. Psalm 132 calls out to God as though *God* is the wandering exile yearning for permanence and rest.

68. Wildberger, *Isaiah 1–12*, p. 461.
69. Dunn, *Romans 9–16*, p. 850.
70. Brueggemann, *Isaiah 1–39*, p. 102.
71. Wildberger, *Isaiah 1–12*, p. 482.
72. Wildberger, *Isaiah 1–12*, p. 482.

Rise up, O LORD,
 and go to your resting place,
 you and the ark of your might.
Let your priests be clothed with righteousness,
 and let your faithful shout for joy.
For your servant David's sake
 do not turn away the face of your anointed one.
The LORD swore to David a sure oath
 from which he will not turn back.
'One of the sons of your body
 I will set on your throne.
If your sons keep my covenant
 and my decrees that I shall teach them,
 their sons also, forevermore, shall sit on your throne.'
For the LORD has chosen Zion;
 he has desired it for his habitation.
'This is my resting place forever;
 here I will reside,
 for I have desired it.
I will abundantly bless its provisions;
 I will satisfy its poor with bread.
Its priests I will clothe with salvation,
 and its faithful will shout for joy' (Ps. 132.8-16; cf. Isa. 66.1-2).

Perhaps this text fills in the most important background for Isaiah's vision and, by extension, Paul's vision. We have here a picture not of the end of Israel's wandering only or of human exile but the end of *God's* wandering (Ps. 132.8). God's rest, in turn, comes at the point when the revelation of God has completed its mission. The vocabulary of the Psalm overlaps with Isa. 11.1-10 in conspicuous ways. Here, too, deliverance for the poor is explicit (Ps. 132.15; Isa. 11.4). The divine 'resting place' is the place where people will find rest, and God's rest will be among people.[73] 'Resting place' also has an ecological connotation because *m*^e^*nûḥâ* 'is the place of rest for herds' (Gen. 49.14-15).[74]

'Glory' or 'glorious' (Hebr. *kābôd*, Gr. *timē*) is the last term in Isaiah's vision of what 'the root of Jesse' will achieve. It is easy to assume that the 'glory' in view refers to what God is and is seen to be, but the entire poem suggests a more complex story line. The 'shoot that shall come from the stump of Jesse' is equipped to perform a right-making mission that plays out

73. 'Rest' as *m*^e^*nûḥâ* represents in Jewish thought the repose of God with creation and is integral to the theology and meaning of the Sabbath; cf. Norman Wirzba, *Living the Sabbath: Discovering the Rhythms of Rest and Delight* (Grand Rapids: Brazos Press, 2006), pp. 32-34; see also Moltmann, *The Coming of God*, pp. 261-7; John Polkinghorne, *The God of Hope and the End of the World* (New Haven: Yale University Press, 2002), pp. 113-23.

74. Wildberger, *Isaiah 1–12*, p. 482.

> **'The Root of Jesse': Reading the Fine Print**
> - 'the nations will turn to him *inquisitively*'—looking for *answers* and *relief*
> - 'Resting place' means that God, too, is presently a *wanderer*.
> - 'Resting place' has an ecological connotation, the shepherd and the herd together at rest.

against the horizon of misperception, ignorance, and loss. Healing comes to the world in the wake of revelation, the earth filling with the 'knowledge of God as the waters cover the sea' (Isa. 11.9).

I conclude that all the four references to the Old Testament in the letter ending affirm the inclusion of the Gentiles, this fact lying on the surface. On closer examination, however, the texts have a theological core that undergirds Paul's mission at the deepest level in the revelation of the right-making of God (Rom. 1.16-17). Theology is now the undisputed center, revelation is the medium, Gentiles and Jews are all included, and the earth and non-human creation are not forgotten or left out (Isa. 11.1-10).

Matters of Mission

I shall return to what in my view should be seen as Paul's ultimate horizon in Romans (Rom. 15.8-13), but important matters of mission recur in the letter-ending. I say 'recur' on purpose because the letter-ending revisits many of the key concepts in the opening passage of the letter (1.1-7) to the point of creating striking symmetry.[75]

> I myself feel confident about you, my brothers and sisters, that you yourselves are full of goodness, filled with all knowledge, and able to instruct one another. Nevertheless on some points I have written to you rather boldly by way of reminder, because of the grace given me by God to be a minister of Christ Jesus to the Gentiles in the priestly service of the gospel of God, so that the offering of the Gentiles may be acceptable, sanctified by the Holy Spirit. In Christ Jesus, then, I have reason to boast of my work for God. For I will not venture to speak of anything except what Christ has accomplished through me to win obedience from the Gentiles, by word and deed, by the power of signs and wonders, by the power of the Spirit of God, so that from Jerusalem and as far around as Illyricum I have fully proclaimed the good news of Christ. Thus I make it my ambition to proclaim the good news, not where Christ has already been named, so that I do not build on someone else's foundation, but as it is written, 'Those who have never been told of him shall see, and those who have never heard of him shall understand' (Rom. 15.14-21; Isa. 52.15).

75. Richard J. Dillon, 'The "Priesthood" of St Paul, Romans 15:15-16', *Worship* 74 (2000), p. 159; Jeffrey A.D. Weima, 'The Reason for Romans: The Evidence of Its Epistolary Framework (1:1-15; 15:14–16:27)', *RevExp* 100 (2003), pp. 17-33; Jewett, *Romans*, pp. 901-902.

Paul commends the Romans for being 'full of goodness, filled with all knowledge, and able to instruct one another' (Rom. 15.14). This commendation need not be insincere, but it is definitely diplomatic. The thought that he has written to them 'rather boldly by way of reminder' is further proof of tact (15.15), but it understates the reasons that led him to write the letter in the first place. The 'reminder' implies that he has told them nothing that was not obvious to begin with when in fact there have been serious problems as reflected in the urgency and fervency that mark most of the letter. We should not be fooled at the modesty expressed, and the next sentence proves as much.[76] Paul has not written because he had nothing better to do that day but 'because of the grace given me by God to be a minister of Christ Jesus to the Gentiles in the priestly service of the gospel of God, so that the offering of the Gentiles may be acceptable, sanctified by the Holy Spirit' (15.15-16; cf. 1.1, 5).[77] This self-designation would be stupendously immodest if not for the fact that Paul really believed it and had his work and ministry to back it up (15.18-19). The priestly character of his mission has already been hinted in the notion of being 'set apart' in the very first sentence of the letter (1.1), and it is now explicit (15.16).[78] His clothing is not the priestly robe, and his arena is not the sacred precincts of the Temple, but he is, as Richard Dillon notes, engaged in a work described by means of verbs 'expressing the transfer between profane and sacred spheres' that resembles the consecration of the Levitical priests (Num. 8.11; 15.20-21; Exod. 13.12; Ezek. 45.1,13; 48.9,20).[79] By this logic, God 'has "requisitioned" Paul as his instrument in taking possession of those very pagan hoards from whose influence the Levitical code aimed to protect the Chosen People'.[80] A cynic might regard it as supreme irony to abolish lines of separation that have been drawn for such compelling reasons, but God's right-making in the gospel works no less wonder than this.

76. Daniel Patte ('Thinking Mission with Paul and the Romans: Romans 15:1-33', *Mission Studies*, 23 [2006], p. 83) highlights nicely features of two-way, reciprocal exchange between Paul and the Romans (1.11-12; 15.14-15) as a feature of good mission strategy, but the reciprocity notwithstanding will not quite make it a relationship of equals.

77. An offering of Gentiles to God that is *acceptable* to God finds a parallel in the gift from the Gentiles that Paul will carry to the saints in Jerusalem, hoping that it will be *acceptable* to the saints (15.16, 31), 'acceptance' in both realms aspects of Paul's priestly ministry.

78. Paul is 'acting as priest' (*hierourgounta*), bringing converted Gentiles an 'offering' (*prosphora*) that is 'acceptable' (*euprosdektos*) in God's eyes because it has been 'sanctified' (*hēgiasmenē*) (Rom. 15.16).

79. Dillon, 'The "Priesthood" of St Paul', p. 160.

80. Dillon, 'The "Priesthood" of St Paul', p. 161.

Here, Dillon is right in saying that Paul's use of Jewish symbols conveys the character of his mission while his mission at the same time exceeds what the symbols are able to convey: this feature amounts to 'much more than a tissue of playful metaphors'.[81] Paul's appropriation of the vocabulary of the priesthood establishes his mandate on the scaffolding of the priestly ministry but then turns the tables so as to claim definition rights on behalf of the ministry he is doing. This makes Paul's unfettered and indiscriminate ministry in the Mediterranean basin what priestly ministry is meant to be (2 Cor. 2.14.16).[82] His ambition 'to win obedience from the Gentiles, by word and deed' (15.18) assumes that 'word and deed' are the means describing his work while also making the obedience of the Gentiles an obedience in 'word and deed'. Above all, 'obedience' (*hypakoē*) is shorthand for 'obedience of faith' (*hypakoē pisteōs*) (1.5; 16.26), and this phrase, as we have seen earlier, is most in harmony with Paul's message when we see it as obedience that is the response to, and the fruit of, God's faithfulness (*pistis*).

It is hardly a coincidence that Isaiah is the last Old Testament voice to be heard in Romans or that the focus is again *revelation*. 'As it is written', Paul says one last time, 'Those who have never been told of him shall see, and those who have never heard of him shall understand' (Rom. 15.21; Isa. 52.15), his wording only slightly different than in the LXX.[83] This text speaks not only of those who shall see but also of the one who is seen. The inclusion of the Gentiles in Paul's mission cannot be separated from the message that makes the Gentiles want to be included. Klaus Baltzer explains that the setting within which Isaiah predicts success is 'a court of law, where a dispute about the view to be taken of a certain person is under consideration. Those present are: the judge, the person in question, witnesses brought by the disputing parties, and listeners.'[84] This thickens the plot to its actual density because 'the person in question' in the text is the Suffering Servant, who is, in turn, God's representative and revealer (Isa. 53.1). Paul will take the monetary gifts of the Gentiles to the needy saints in Jerusalem and then go to Rome before he continues on to Spain (Rom. 15.22-33), but he makes clear once more that he is an apostle and a minister on behalf of 'the gospel of God' (1.1; 15.16). *Good news about God* is the express reason for his mission. At the end of the revelation, there will be *seeing* and *understanding* (Rom. 15.21; Isa. 52.15). This means *mission accomplished*.

81. Dillon, 'The "Priesthood" of St Paul', p. 167.

82. John Knox ('Romans 15:14-33 and Paul's Conception of His Apostolic Mission', *JBL* 83 [1964], pp. 1-11) argues persuasively that when Paul describes himself as an apostle *eis ta ethnē* (Rom. 15.16), *ethnē* does not always refer to 'Gentiles'. It is equally legitimate and sometimes more correct to read it as 'nations'.

83. Jewett, *Romans*, pp. 916-17.

84. Klaus Baltzer, *Deutero-Isaiah: A Commentary on Isaiah* (trans. Margaret Kohl; Hermeneia; Minneapolis: Fortress Press, 2001), p. 398.

The letter-ending allays doubts regarding the most contentious areas in Paul's theology and the message of Romans. Read in widescreen, Paul's longest letter maps the story of human plight from the point of origin in the form of deception and misrepresentation of the divine command (Rom. 5.12-14; 7.7-13; Gen. 3.1-6), to the terrifying sense of God's absence in Habakkuk (Hab. 1.2-4; 2.2-4; Rom. 1.16-17), and to the reality of human unfaithfulness (Rom. 3.3-4). For all of the above, Paul falls back on 'the right-making of God by the faithfulness of Jesus Christ' (Rom. 3.22, translation mine).

Hope

A reader sensitized to the threat of nuclear holocaust and ecological catastrophe in the twenty-first century can hardly afford to ignore Paul's arsenal for bringing about transformation of thought, embodiment of mercy, and faithful discipleship (Rom. 12.1-2). But the same reader will be wise to gather up the texts that speak of hope. In Romans, hope rests not only on a world set right by concerted human action. It also refers to the eschatological hope that lights up the letter throughout. This, the eschatological hope, is the ultimate remedy for the Reign of Death that Paul describes in Romans. For Abraham, this means a stance of 'hoping against hope' (4.18). For the present-day believer, it means to boast 'in our hope of sharing the glory of God' (5.2) and to say that 'hope does not disappoint us, because God's love has been poured into our hearts through the Holy Spirit that has been given to us' (5.5). Hope entails an unseen reality (8.24), says Paul, but the hope is nevertheless 'seeable' because non-human creation sees it and waits for it to be fulfilled, swelling the ranks of those who live in hope (8.20).

Hope is the theme-word in the letter-ending. 'For whatever was written in former days was written for our instruction, so that by steadfastness and by the encouragement of the scriptures we might have hope', says Paul (15.4). And then, as the reason for having hope, for 'again Isaiah says, "The root of Jesse shall come, the one who rises to rule the Gentiles; in him the Gentiles shall hope"' (Rom. 15.12; Isa. 11.10). Hope is set loose in the world, anchored at one end in the faithfulness of the root of Jesse, who *came*, and in the other end in the hope that 'the root of Jesse *shall come*' in a sense that is still future. This train of thought, pointing to the ultimate horizon of hope for human and non-human creation, comes to a climax in language that is ecstatic, 'reaching far beyond the bounds of human capacity either to produce or to describe'.[85] Paul, whether among Jews and Gentiles, prophets or philosophers, persecutors or people—and now among ecologists—is

85. Jewett, *Romans*, p. 898.

a bearer of hope. Hope may well serve as his last word in Romans and the word most needed today. 'May the God of hope fill you with all joy and peace in believing, so that you may abound in hope by the power of the Holy Spirit' (Rom. 15.13).

APPENDIX
'WRATH' IN ROMANS

'The wrath of God' (*orgē theou*) is a topic early on in Romans (Rom. 1.18) and is by most interpreters seen as a key premise for what follows. Salvation, ultimately, means salvation from 'the wrath of God', and the divine wrath works itself out as retribution. In the most severe version of divine retribution—although no longer as dominant in the theological tradition as it used to be—retribution means that the reprobate will suffer torment for all eternity.[1] In this commentary I question the central role allotted to 'wrath' and 'retribution' in traditional interpretations of Romans. Instead, I privilege a reading that runs straight from human need to divine right-making. Here, in what will be no more than an outline, I will explore textual and rhetorical caveats that call into question the traditional understanding of 'the wrath of God'. In the order that they are considered here, I shall look at caveats that are (1) conceptual or terminological, (2) interpretative, (3) rhetorical and thematic, and (4) contextual, the latter in the sense that we must be careful not to constrain or collapse the cosmic, widescreen framework of Paul's outlook.

Conceptual Caveats

Toward the conclusion of the vigorous rhetorical exchange that begins at Rom. 1.18, Paul mixes an assertion and a problem that follows from the assertion, both by way of questions. 'But if our injustice (*adikia*) serves to confirm the justice of God (*theou dikaiosynēn*), what should we say? That God is unjust to inflict (the) wrath (*tēn orgēn*) on us? (I speak in a human way' [*kata anthrōpon*]) (Rom. 3.5). My interest is the caveat, '*I speak in a human way*' (3.5). Strictly speaking, Paul says '*according to human*'—full stop. He is here—gratuitously—acknowledging that he is putting to use

1. Thus Pierre Bayle (1647–1706), in *Historical and Critical Dictionary: Selections* (trans. Richard H. Popkin; New York: Bobbs-Merrill Company, 1965), p. 171, 'Christian theology invincibly confirms this, in that it tells us that the torments of the damned will be eternal and continuous, and as strong at the end of one hundred thousand years as they were the first day'. This is Christian theology according to the Augustinian tradition. See also Augustine, *The City of God*, pp. 257, 522.

concepts and terms that are 'according to *human norms* (*kata anthrōpon*)' and that caution will be in order.[2] The human convention regarding the meaning of 'the wrath' does not necessarily reflect his view of the matter. This caveat is hugely consequential. First, Paul is marking distance between himself and 'the wrath' even as he finds the term serviceable to his argument without the need to explain it further. Second, he implies that the statement needs to be nuanced, indicating that it represents a figure of speech 'according to human ways' and not a concept that has been defined and developed from the ground up in Paul's system. Speech *kata anthrōpon* is in this verse only a 'human conception', and 'wrath'-speech must for this reason be qualified and taken with a grain of salt. Third, the verbal element in the question will now be open to interpretation in much the same way as is 'the wrath'. In what sense does God 'bring' or 'inflict' (*epipherō*) 'the wrath' when Paul adds the caveat that he is expressing himself by way of concepts and conventions of speech that are 'according to human norms'? Paul adopts language and terminology that are not his, strictly speaking, in order to advance the argument that is his through and through: his opponents will not succeed in proving that God is unfaithful even though they imply that Paul's story line leads to that conclusion (Rom. 3.3). In sum, while Paul's caveat does not explain how Paul envisions 'the wrath', his interjection, in the NRSV appropriately placed in brackets, serves notice that a caveat is in order.

Interpretative Caveats

In his study of wrath-language in the New Testament, A.T. Hanson finds in Romans more references to 'the wrath' than in all the rest of Paul's letters put together, and he takes Rom. 1.18-32 to be 'what we might almost

2. The term *kata anthrōpon* is not uncommon in Paul's letters (Rom. 3.5; 1 Cor. 3.3; 9.8; 15.32; Gal. 1.11; 3.15), sometimes merely referring to 'common human practice' without any value judgment. Of the texts noted here, the one that holds the most interest for how to understanding *kata anthrōpon* in Rom. 3.5 is Gal. 1.11 (NRSV): 'the gospel that was proclaimed by me is not of human origin' (*kata anthrōpon*). Martyn (*Galatians*, p. 142) argues perceptively that *kata anthrōpon* in Galatians is not only a matter of source but also of content. The gospel Paul preaches '*is not what human beings normally have in mind when they speak of "good news"*'. He adds that *kata anthrōpon* in the Galatian context very likely has a specific referent: it refers to the gospel construct of his opponents. A specific referent for *kata anthrōpon* may also be in view in Romans. Whether general or specific, we have a gospel in Galatians that is *not* 'what human beings normally have in mind' as to gospel, and we have in Romans 'wrath'-speech that is *kata anthrōpon* and thus, roughly, 'what human beings normally have in mind' when they speak of wrath. Looking in both directions, to 'the gospel' and to 'the wrath', speech that is *kata anthrōpon* is inadequate for the subject at hand.

call a handbook to the working of the wrath'.[3] He argues that a face value interpretation of 'the wrath' runs the risk of missing that Paul is 'using language which suggests that he viewed the wrath essentially, not as something directly inflicted by God, but as something which men bring upon themselves'.[4] On this logic, 'God allows the wrath; he does not inflict it'.[5] Hanson's conception is distinctive for seeing the wrath as impersonal: it 'does not describe an attitude of God but a condition of men'.[6] Distinctive, too, is his view that even where 'the wrath' has an eschatological import, it 'is as much a revealing as an execution'.[7] To Hanson, therefore, 'consequences' describe the sin-problem better than 'retribution'.

Steven H. Travis agrees that 'the wrath' refers to sin working itself out as 'intrinsic punishment', but he takes issue with other features in Hanson's interpretation.[8] Specifically, he recognizes that 'wrath' that refers to observable realities in everyday life endangers the notion of 'revelation'. How can 'revelation' apply to a commonplace reality when the term is chiefly language for the exceptional event that will not otherwise happen or be knowable? To neutralize this problem, Travis argues that it is only to *faith* that these everyday occurrences are known to be the workings of God's wrath. 'The believer looks at the same phenomena as unbelievers, but puts a theological interpretation on them'.[9] Travis also faults Hanson for seeing 'the wrath' in impersonal terms only. In his view, Rom. 1.18-32 describes sin as 'a personal affront to God which is met by his personal reaction'.[10] God's response is 'fitting' but not 'retributive'. The dynamic is personal because sin 'is *against God*'; it is God who 'gave them up' (1.24, 26, 28); and the wrath 'comes from heaven' (1.18).[11] Nevertheless, Travis agrees with Barth that 'the enterprise of setting up the "No-God" is avenged by its success... Our conduct becomes governed precisely by what we desire.'[12] There is a Barthian texture to the idea that the key to Paul's use of retributive terms is 'to safeguard the essentially God-ward relation to humanity... God, not

3. Hanson, *The Wrath of the Lamb*, p. 83.
4. Hanson, *The Wrath of the Lamb*, p. 85.
5. Hanson, *The Wrath of the Lamb*, p. 85.
6. Hanson, *The Wrath of the Lamb*, p. 110.
7. Hanson, *The Wrath of the Lamb*, p. 110.
8. Steven H. Travis, *Christ and the Judgement of God: The Limits of Divine Retribution in New Testament Thought* (Peabody, MA: Hendrickson, 2008), pp. 60-70. 'Intrinsic punishment' means that people 'experience the consequences of their refusal to live in relationship to him' (p. 62).
9. Travis, *Christ and the Judgement of God*, p. 60.
10. Travis, *Christ and the Judgement of God*, p. 61.
11. Travis, *Christ and the Judgement of God*, p. 61.
12. Barth, *Romans*, p. 51; Travis, *Christ and the Judgement of God*, p. 61.

humanity, has the last word.'[13] Protection of divine sovereignty is an important element in this conception.

Rhetorical and Thematic Caveats

Rhetorical and thematic caveats are related but not identical. The rhetorical question refers chiefly to whether we hear another voice than Paul's in the leading wrath passage in Romans (1.18-32), discussed in Chapter 5. The thematic question, on the other hand, centers on the relationship between 'the right-making of God' ('righteousness of God') in Rom. 1.16-17 and 'the wrath of God' in Rom. 1.18 without assuming that there is speech-in-character in the passage. Reinhard von Bendemann's observations are mostly in the 'thematic' category.[14] He wonders why Paul, ostensibly, speaks at length about 'the wrath' in Romans while omitting the subject entirely in Galatians, the letter most closely resembling Romans by way of theme and content. He answers that Paul does it for reasons that are conscious and intentional to the point that 'the wrath (of God) represents a leading motif in the letter to the Romans',[15] but he is quick to add a series of caveats. He notes that Rom. 1.16-17 is in itself 'a linguistically and self-sufficient passage' as to the letter theme; that the semantics favor a suture line between 1.17 and 1.18 and, perhaps most important, that 'wrath' and 'gospel' are antonyms.[16] He argues further that the revelation of wrath is 'not meant to be integrated in the gospel in 1.16-17' and that the three wrath-statements in 2.5, 8 do not represent the key to subsequent wrath-statements in Romans or determinants of the sense of Rom. 1.18'.[17] This sets up a sequence in Paul's logic that begins with divine right-making (1.16-17) that does *not* have 'the wrath' as the reference point. In other words, the reality of 'the wrath of God' is not the main reference point for 'the right-making of God' even in constructs where 'the wrath' is accepted as a concept brought into the discussion by Paul himself. According to Bendemann, the reference point for 'the wrath' that has the most explanatory power has to do with 'a non-theological use with an eye to managing the punitive practices of the state', the topic of Rom. 13.1-7.[18]

13. Travis, *Christ and the Judgement of God*, p. 62.

14. Reinhard von Bendemann, '"Zorn" und "Zorn Gottes" im Römerbrief', in *Paulus und Johannes: Exegetische Studien zur paulinischen und johanneischen Theologie und Literatur* (ed. Dieter Sänger and Ulrich Mell; Tübingen: Mohr Siebeck, 2006), pp. 179-215.

15. Bendemann, '"Zorn" und "Zorn Gottes" im Römerbrief', p. 182.

16. Bendemann, '"Zorn" und "Zorn Gottes" im Römerbrief', p. 183.

17. Bendemann, '"Zorn" und "Zorn Gottes" im Römerbrief', pp. 183, 185.

18. Bendemann, '"Zorn" und "Zorn Gottes" im Römerbrief', pp. 190-91.

If, however, the leading passage about 'the wrath of God' (1.18-32) looms large in Romans because it is a key tenet in the message of counter missionaries along the lines suggested by Douglas Campbell,[19] the rhetorical dynamics of the letter are far more fluid and complex. This possibility does not mean that Paul is unfazed by what goes on in the Gentile world, but it means that conceptions of 'the wrath of God' appear in the letter for reasons that have more to do with the message and activity of hostile opponents than with the core convictions in Paul's proclamation. Subsequent references to 'the wrath' (e.g. 2.5, 8) must be seen in light of the initial rhetorical give-and-take until we encounter the explicit caveat in Rom. 3.5, 'I speak in a human way'. The 'human way' in this conception will be not be indeterminate, referring to the way of Paul's opponents. It follows that so far in the letter, he has to some extent argued with reference to premises of his opponents more than his own.

Contextual and Theological Caveats

What, nevertheless, of the warning to the implied speaker in Rom. 1.18-32 that 'by your hard and impenitent heart you are storing up wrath for yourself on the day of wrath, when God's righteous judgment will be revealed... while for those who are self-seeking and who obey not the truth but wickedness, there will be wrath and fury'? (Rom. 2.5, 8) The notion of 'the day of wrath' seems distinctly eschatological. 'God's righteous judgment' suggests divine agency when the day of reckoning for the impenitent arrives, and an element of retribution might be inferred from the warning that 'there will be wrath and fury'. Caveats arising from the immediate context include some of the points that have been outlined above, among which are concepts and language that are *kata anthrōpon* (3.5), wrath working itself out in history, and the possibility that Paul is engaged in an argument with opponents who have 'the wrath' (1.18) as a competitor and not merely as a complement to Paul's 'right-making' good news (1.16-17).

In my view, the most important caveats will be drawn from the widescreen version of Paul's message. The widescreen perspective has a cosmic frame of reference. It sees God engaged in a struggle of revelation and liberation on behalf of humans who are victims of deception and helpless in the face of overwhelming hostile forces (7.7-12; 8.31-39). The existence of supra- and super-human forces is not in doubt in Paul's letters, as seen in the statement that 'the god of this world has blinded the minds of the unbelievers, to keep them from seeing the light of the gospel of the glory of Christ' (2 Cor. 4.4); in the fact that 'even Satan disguises himself as an angel of light' (2 Cor. 11.14); and in Romans in the reality of hostile 'angels',

19. Campbell, *Deliverance of God*, p. 495.

'rulers', and 'powers' (Rom. 8.38). These forces or powers, in turn, are not only metaphors or the sum total of Roman imperial reality, and their ontological status is not reducible to *human* powers only.

The *story*-character of this aspect in Paul's outlook is most evident in 2 Thess. 2.1-12, a text that has not been given the attention it deserves.[20] Here, Paul speak of a 'lawless' entity that 'opposes and exalts himself above every so-called god or object of worship, so that he takes his seat in the temple of God, declaring himself to be God' (2 Thess. 2.4). He echoes texts taken from the Old Testament story of cosmic rebellion that features the most audacious examples of overreaching (cf. Isa. 14.13-14; Ezek. 28.2, 12-19). The evil power in view traces its roots to a primordial point of origin and to a non-human 'person' as to cause. Now, in Paul's view of the eschaton, evil will be unmasked and defeated for good, the unmasking described in a series of the passive form of *apokalyphtein*, 'to be revealed', or, as in Louw-Nida, 'to uncover', 'to take out of hiding', 'to make fully known'.[21]

> and the lawless one is <u>revealed</u> (*kai apokalyphthē ho anthrōpos tēs anomias*) (2.3).
>
> so that he may be <u>revealed</u> (*eis to apokalyphthēnai auton*) (2.6).
>
> then the lawless one will be <u>revealed</u> (*tote apokalyphthēsetai ho anomos*) (2.8).

The verb charged with the task of making evil emerge from hiding is *apokalyptō*, the same verb that has the disclosure of God's faithfulness in its portfolio. These *revelations* are *not* everyday occurrences, and the definitive unmasking cannot happen until 'what is now *restraining* (*to katechon*) him' or 'until the one who now restrains (*ho katechōn*) it is removed' (2 Thess. 2.6-7). In the short version of this drama, *God* is the one who *restrains*. This is the great theological stumbling block because the text suggests a divine disappearing act 'from the middle' that enables the lawless reality to set up house in the location from which God has 'disappeared'. These matters belong to 'the day of the LORD' or 'the day' (2 Thess. 2.2, 3), and 'the day' in question corresponds to 'the day of wrath' that we encounter in Romans (Rom. 2.5, 16; cf. 1 Cor. 3.13). Now, however, we have a far more complex picture because 'the day of wrath' is not only a showdown between God and human beings—the day of divine retribution. It is also—and primarily—the

20. For background, see Sigve K. Tonstad, 'The Restrainer Removed: A Truly Alarming Thought (2 Thess. 2:1-12)', *HBT* 29 (2007), pp. 133-51; idem, 'Theodicy and the Theme of Cosmic Conflict in the Early Church', *AUSS* 42 (2004), pp. 169-202; idem, *God of Sense and Traditions of Non-Sense*, chapter entitled 'Lost Sense in the Letters of Paul' (Eugene, OR: Wipf & Stock, forthcoming).

21. *Louw-Nida Greek English Lexicon of the New Testament* (ed. J.P. Louw and E.A. Nida; New York: United Bible Societies, 1988), art. ἀποκαλύπτω.

day for the ultimate showdown between God and the cosmic opponent. This showdown has the character of an unmasking in a sense that supports Hanson's contention that 'the wrath', even in its eschatological dimension, '*is as much a revealing as an execution*'.[22] When the unmasking is accomplished, the lawless reality will have been shown up for what it really is.

The depiction of a final unmasking in 2 Thessalonians circumscribes the divine agency with respect to 'the wrath' in several ways. First, this conception of 'the day of wrath' has a cosmic texture and is not only the divine judgment on human beings. Second, God's role is portrayed in terms of loosening of restraint and then, finally, *absence* (2 Thess. 2.6-7). Execution of 'the wrath' happens with God one step removed, as though God stands outside the picture on the day when 'there will be wrath and fury' (Rom. 2.8). Third, the unmasking and undoing of evil has a revelatory character all the way through till the end: the Lord Jesus will destroy 'the lawless one with the breath of his mouth, bringing him to naught by the epiphany of his coming' (2 Thess. 2.8, translation mine). 'Breath of his mouth' is an allusion to the reality and right-making ways of 'the shoot from the stump of Jesse' (Isa. 11.1, 4), and 'epiphany' means that the divine reality is revealed.

Caveats of this kind and magnitude are in order when we ponder the meaning of 'the wrath' in Romans, seeking to compose a picture that is not *kata anthrōpon*, that is, not a *human* conception only (Rom. 3.5).

22. Hanson, *The Wrath of the Lamb*, p. 110 (italics added).

Bibliography

Acton, Lord (Sir John), 'The History of Freedom in Antiquity', in *Lord Acton: Essays on Freedom and Power* (ed. Gertrude Himmelfarb; Boston: Beacon Press, 1949 [orig. essay 1877], pp. 30-57.

—'The Protestant Theory of Persecution', in *Lord Acton: Essays on Freedom and Power* (ed. Gertrude Himmelfarb; Boston: Beacon Press, 1949), pp. 88-127.

Adams, Edward, *Constructing the World: A Study of Paul's Cosmological Language* (Edinburgh: T. & T. Clark, 2000).

—'Paul's Story of God and Creation: The Story of How God Fulfils His Purposes in Creation', in *Narrative Dynamics in Paul: A Critical Assessment* (ed. Bruce W. Longenecker; Louisville, KY: Westminster/John Knox Press, 2002), pp. 19-43.

Adams, Marilyn McCord, *Horrendous Evils and the Goodness of God* (Ithaca, NY: Cornell University Press, 1991).

Aernie, Jeffrey W., *Is Paul also among the Prophets? An Examination of the Relationship between Paul and the Old Testament Prophetic Tradition in 2 Corinthians* (LNTS; New York: T. & T. Clark, 2014).

Agamben, Giorgio, *The Time That Remains: A Commentary on the Letter to the Romans* (trans. Patricia Dailey; Stanford, CA: Stanford University Press, 2005).

Albertz, Rainer, 'The Social Setting of the Aramaic and Hebrew Book of Daniel', in *The Book of Daniel: Composition and Reception* (2 vols.; ed. John J. Collins and Peter W. Flint; Leiden: Brill, 2002), pp. 171-204.

Alcoff, Linda Martin, and John D. Caputo (eds.), *St. Paul among the Philosophers* (Bloomington, IN: Indiana University Press, 2009).

Alter, Robert, *Genesis: Translation and Commentary* (New York: W.W. Norton, 1996).

Andersen, Francis I., *Habakkuk: A New Translation with Introduction and Commentary* (AB; New York: Doubleday, 2001).

Anderson, Clifford B., 'The Unexceptional Church: An Exploration of Carl Schmitt, Giorgio Agamben and Karl Barth', *ZDTSup* 5 (2011), pp. 8-26.

Anderson, William H.U., 'The Curse of Work in Qoheleth: An Exposé of Genesis 3.17-19 in Ecclesiastes', *EQ* 70 (1998), pp. 90-113.

Auden, W.H., 'Smelt and Tasted', in *W.H. Auden Collected Poems* (ed. Edward Mendelson; London: Faber & Faber, 1976).

Badiou, Alain, *Saint Paul: The Foundation of Universalism* (trans. Ray Brassier; Stanford, CA: Stanford University Press, 2003).

—'St. Paul, Founder of the Universal Subject', in *St. Paul among the Philosophers* (ed. Linda Martin Alcoff and John D. Caputo; Bloomington, IN: Indiana University Press, 2009), pp. 27-38.

Bailey, Wilma Ann, 'The Way the World Is Meant to Be: an Interpretation of Genesis 1.26-29', *Vision* 9 (2008), pp. 46-52.

Baltzer, Klaus, *Deutero-Isaiah: A Commentary on Isaiah* (trans. Margaret Kohl; Hermeneia; Minneapolis: Fortress Press, 2001).

Baptist, Edward E., *The Half Has Never Been Told: Slavery and the Making of American Capitalism* (New York: Basic Books, 2014).

Barclay, John M.G., *Obeying the Truth: A Study of Paul's Ethics in Galatians* (Edinburgh: T. & T. Clark, 2005).

—'Paul and Philo on Circumcision: Romans 2.25-29 in Social and Cultural Context', in *Pauline Churches and Diaspora Jews* (ed. John Barclay; WUNT; Tübingen: Mohr Siebeck, 2011), pp. 61-79.

—'Why the Roman Empire Was Insignificant to Paul', in *Pauline Churches and Diaspora Jews* (ed. John Barclay; WUNT; Tübingen: Mohr Siebeck, 2011), pp. 363-88.

—'Faith and Self-Detachment from Cultural Norms: A Study in Romans 14–15', *ZNW* 104 (2013), pp. 192-208.

Bar-Gill, Oren, 'The Law, Economics and Psychology of Subprime Mortgage Contracts', *Cornell L. Rev.* 94 (2009), pp. 1073-1171.

Barr, James, 'Man and Nature: The Ecological Controversy and the Old Testament', in *Ecology and Religion in History* (ed. David Spring and Eileen Spring; New York: Harper & Row, 1974), pp. 48-75.

Barraclough, Ray, 'Romans 13:1-7: Application in Context', *Colloquium* 17 (1985), pp. 16-21.

Barrett, C.K., *The Epistle to the Romans* (BNCT; Peabody, MA: Hendrickson, 1991).

Barth, Karl, *Theological Existence Today* (trans. R. Birch Hoyle; London: Hodder & Stoughton, 1933).

—*The Epistle to the Romans* (trans. Edwyn C. Hoskyns; London: Oxford University Press, 6th edn, 1968).

—*Church Dogmatics* III.2 (trans. Harold Knight, G.W. Bromiley, J.K.S. Reid and R.H. Fuller; Edinburgh: T. & T. Clark, 1986).

Bassler, Joette M., *Divine Impartiality: Paul and a Theological Axiom* (SBLDS; Chico, CA: Scholars Press, 1982).

Bauckham, Richard, 'The Story of the Earth According to Paul: Romans 8.18-23', *RevExp* 108 (2011), pp. 91-97.

—*Living with Other Creatures: Green Exegesis and Theology* (Waco, TX: Baylor University Press, 2011).

Bauer, Walter, F.W. Danker, W.F. Arndt and F.W. Gingrich, *Greek-English Lexicon of the New Testament and Other Early Christian Literature* (Chicago: University of Chicago Press, 3rd edn, 2000.

Bayes, Jonathan F. 'The Translation of Romans 8.3', *ExpTim* 111 (1999), pp. 14-16.

Bayle, Pierre, *Historical and Critical Dictionary: Selections* (trans. Richard H. Popkin; New York: Bobbs-Merrill, 1965).

Beker, J. Christiaan, *Paul the Apostle: The Triumph of God in Life and Thought* (Philadelphia: Fortress Press, 1980).

—'The Relationship Between Sin and Death in Romans', in *The Conversation Continues: Studies in Paul and John in Honor of J. Louis Martyn* (ed. Robert T. Fortna and Beverly R. Gaventa; Nashville: Abingdon Press, 1990), pp. 55-61.

Bernstein, Ellen, *The Splendor of Creation: A Biblical Ecology* (Cleveland, OH: The Pilgrim Press, 2005).

Berry, Wendell, *The Unsettling of America: Culture and Agriculture* (New York: Avon Books, 2nd edn, 1996).

Berthelot, Katell, 'The Biblical Conquest of the Promised Land and the Hasmonean Wars according to 1 and 2 Maccabees', in *The Books of the Maccabees: History, Theology, Ideology. Papers of the Second International Conference on the*

Deuterocanonical Books (ed. Géza G. Xeravits and Jósef Zsengellér; Leiden: Brill, 2007), pp. 45-60.

Bertschmann, Dorothea H., 'The Good, the Bad and the State—Rom 13.1–7 and the Dynamics of Love', *NTS* 60 (2014), pp. 232-49.

Betz, Hans Dieter, *Galatians* (Hermeneia; Philadelphia: Fortress Press, 1979).

—'The Concept of "Inner Human Being" (ὁ ἔσω ἄνθρωπος) in the Anthropology of Paul', *NTS* 46 (2000), pp. 315-41.

Beuken, Willem A.M., 'The Emergence of the Shoot of Jesse: An Eschatological or a Now Event?', *CTJ* 39 (2004), pp. 88-108.

Bickerman, Elias, *The God of the Maccabees: Studies in the Meaning and Origin of the Maccabean Revolt* (Leiden: E.J. Brill, 1979).

Bird, Michael, and Preston M. Sprinkle (eds.), *The Faith of Jesus Christ: Exegetical, Biblical, and Theological Studies* (Peabody, MA: Hendrickson, 2009).

Black, C. Clifton, 'Pauline Perspectives on Death in Romans 5–8', *JBL* 103 (1984), pp. 413-33.

Blenkinsopp, Joseph, *Isaiah 1–39: A New Translation with Introduction and Commentary* (AB; New York: Doubleday, 2000).

—*Isaiah 56–66: A New Translation with Introduction and Commentary* (AB; New York: Doubleday, 2003).

Bolt, John, 'The Relation between Creation and Redemption in Romans 8:18-27', *CTJ* 30 (1995), pp. 34-51.

Bolton, David J., 'Who Are You Calling "Weak"? A Short Critique of James Dunn's Reading of Rom 14.1–15.6', in *The Letter to the Romans* (ed. Udo Schnelle; Leuven: Peeters, 2009), pp. 616-29.

Bolyki, János, '"As soon as the Signal Was Given" (2 Macc. 4.14): Gymnasia in the Service of Hellenism', in *The Books of the Maccabees: History, Theology, Ideology. Papers of the Second International Conference on the Deuterocanonical Books* (ed. Géza G. Xeravits and Jósef Zsengellér; Leiden: Brill, 2007), pp. 131-39.

Bonhoeffer, Dietrich, *Creation and Fall: A Theological Interpretation of Genesis 1–3* (trans. John C. Fletcher; London: SCM Press, 1959).

Bornkamm, Günther, *Early Christian Experience* (trans. Paul L. Hammer; New York: Harper and Row, 1969).

Boyarin, Daniel, *A Radical Jew: Paul and the Politics of Identity* (Berkeley: University of California Press, 1994).

Braaten, Laurie, 'All Creation Groans: Romans 8.22 in Light of the Biblical Sources', *HBT* 28 (2006), pp. 131-59.

Bratton, Susan Power, 'Sea Sabbaths for Sea Stewards: Rest and Restoration for Marine Ecosystems', in *Environmental Stewardship: Critical Perspectives—Past and Present* (ed. R.J. Berry; New York: T. & T. Clark, 2006), pp. 208-12.

Brod, Max, *Franz Kafka: A Biography* (trans. G. Humphreys Roberts; New York: Da Capo Press, 1995).

Brown, Peter, *The World of Late Antiquity AD 150–750* (London: Thames and Hudson, 1971).

—*Augustine of Hippo: New Edition with an Epilogue* (Berkeley and Los Angeles: University of California Press, 2000).

—*The Body and Society: Men, Women and Sexual Renunciation in Early Christianity* (New York: Columbia University Press, 2008).

—*Through the Eye of a Needle: Wealth, the Fall of Rome, and the Making of Christianity in the West, 350–550 AD* (Princeton, NJ: Princeton University Press, 2012).

Bruce, F.F., *Paul, Apostle of the Heart Set Free* (Grand Rapids: Eerdmans, 1978).

Brueggemann, Walter, *Genesis* (Interpretation; Atlanta: John Knox Press, 1982).
—*Isaiah 1–39* (WBC; Louisville, KY: Westminster/John Knox Press, 1998).
—*Isaiah 40–66* (Louisville, KY: Westminster/John Knox Press, 1998).
—*The Land: Place as Gift, Promise, and Challenge in Biblical Faith* (OBT; Minneapolis: Fortress Press, 2002).
—*Sabbath as Resistance: Saying No to the Culture of Now* (Louisville, KY: Westminster/John Knox Press, 2014).
Bruno, Christopher, '*God Is One': The Function of Eis Ho Theos as a Ground for Gentile Inclusion in Paul's Letters* (LNTS; London: Bloomsbury, 2013).
Bultmann, Rudolf, *Der Stil der paulinischen Predigt und die Kynischstoische Diatribe* (FRLANT; Göttingen: Vandenhoeck & Ruprecht, 1910).
Burleigh, Michael, *Earthly Powers: Religion and Politics in Europe from the French Revolution to the Great War* (London: HarperCollins, 2005).
Busch, Austin, 'The Figure of Eve in Romans 7.5-25', *Bib Int* 12 (2004), pp. 1-36.
Butler, Rhett, on Brazilian Rain Forest, July 13, 2014, at http.//rainforests.mongabay.com/20brazil.htm.
Byrne, Brendan J., *Reckoning with Romans: A Contemporary Reading of Paul's Gospel* (GNS, 18; Wilmington, DE: Michael Glazier, 1986).
—*Romans* (SP; Collegeville, MN: Liturgical Press, 1996).
—'An Ecological Reading of Rom. 8.19-22: Possibilities and Hesitations', in *Ecological Hermeneutics: Biblical, Historical and Theological Perspectives* (ed. David G. Horrell, Cherryl Hunt, Christopher Southgate and Francesca Stravrakopoulou; London: T. & T. Clark, 2010), pp. 83-93.
Calvin, John, *Commentary on the Book of the Prophet Isaiah* (trans. William Pringle; Edinburgh: Calvin Translation Society, 1850. Reprinted Grand Rapids: Baker Books, 2003).
Campbell, Douglas A., *The Rhetoric of Righteousness in Romans 3.21-26* (JSNTSup, 65; Sheffield: Sheffield Academic Press, 1992).
—'The Meaning of ΠΙΣΤΙΣ and ΝΟΜΟΣ in Paul: A Linguistic and Structural Perspective', *JBL* 111 (1992), pp. 91-103.
—'An Echo of Scripture in Paul, and Its Implications', in *The Word Leaps the Gap: Essays on Scripture and Theology in Honor of Richard B. Hays* (ed. J. Ross Wagner, C. Kavin Rowe and A. Katherine Grieb; Grand Rapids: Eerdmans, 2008), pp. 367-91.
—*The Deliverance of God: An Apocalyptic Rereading of Justification in Paul* (Grand Rapids: Eerdmans, 2009).
—'An Apocalyptic Rereading of "Justification" in Paul: Or, an Overview of the Argument of Douglas Campbell's *The Deliverance of God*', *ExpTim* 123 (2012), pp. 382-93.
—*Framing Paul: An Epistolary Biography* (Grand Rapids: Eerdmans, 2014).
Campbell, William S., *Paul's Gospel in an Intercultural Context: Jew and Gentile in the Letter to the Romans* (Frankfurt: Peter Lang, 1991).
Carroll, James, *Constantine's Sword: The Church and the Jews* (New York: Mariner Books, 2002).
Carter, T.L., 'The Irony of Romans 13', *NovT* 46 (2004), pp. 209-28.
Cassidy, Canon Dr Ron, 'The Politicization of Paul: Romans 13.1-7 in Recent Discussion', *ExpTim* 121 (2010), pp. 383-89.
Cassuto, Umberto, *A Commentary on the Book of Genesis: Part I, From Adam to Noah* (trans. I. Abrahams; Jerusalem: The Magnes Press, 1998).

Chadwick, Henry, 'Envoi: On Taking Leave of Antiquity', in *The Roman World* (ed. John Boardman, Jasper Griffin and Oswyn Murray; New York: Oxford University Press, 1986), pp. 401-23.

Champlin, Edward, *Nero* (Cambridge: Belknap Press, 2003).

Chaney, Marvin L., 'You Shall Not Covet Your Neighbor's House', *PTR* 15 (1982), pp. 3-13.

Chang, Hae-Kyung, 'The Christian Life in a Dialectical Tension? Romans 7.7-25 Reconsidered', *NovT* 49 (2007), pp. 257-80.

Childs, Brevard, *Isaiah* (OTL; Louisville, KY: Westminster/John Knox Press, 2001).

Clark, Christopher, *The Sleepwalkers: How Europe Went to War in 1914* (London: Penguin, 2013).

Clements, R.E., 'The Unity of the Book of Isaiah', *Int* 36 (1982), pp. 117-29.

Clines, David J.A., *I, He, We, and They: A Literary Approach to Isaiah 53* (JSOTSup; Sheffield: JSOT Press, 1976).

Collins, John J., 'Daniel and His Social World', *Int* 39 (1985), pp. 131-43.

—*Daniel: A Commentary on the Book of Daniel* (Hermeneia; Minneapolis: Fortress Press, 1993).

—*The Apocalyptic Imagination* (Grand Rapids: Eerdmans, 2nd edn, 1998).

Combs, Eugene, 'Has God Cursed the Ground? Perplexity of Interpretation in Genesis 1–5', in *Ascribe to the Lord: Biblical and Other Studies in Memory of Peter C. Craigie* (ed. Lyle Eslinger and Glen Taylor; JSOTSup; Sheffield: Sheffield Academic, 1988), pp. 265-87.

Connell, Martin F., 'Clothing the Body of Christ: An Inquiry about the Letters of Paul', *Worship* 85 (2011), pp. 128-46.

Conzelmann, Hans, *1 Corinthians: A Commentary on the First Epistle to the Corinthians* (trans. James W. Leitch; Hermeneia; Philadelphia: Fortress Press, 1975).

Cortez, Marc, 'Body, Soul, and (Holy) Spirit: Karl Barth's Theological Framework for Understanding Human Ontology', *IJST* 10 (2008), pp. 328-45.

Cousar, Charles B., *A Theology of the Cross: The Death of Jesus in the Pauline Letters* (Minneapolis: Fortress Press, 1990).

Cox, Dorian G. Coover, 'The Hardening of Pharaoh's Heart in Its Literary and Cultural Contexts', *BSac* 163 (2006), pp. 292-311.

Craig, Jr, Kenneth M., 'Questions outside Eden (Genesis 4.1-16): Yahweh, Cain and Their Rhetorical Interchange', *JSOT* 86 (1999), pp. 107-28.

Craigie, P.C., *Psalms 1–50* (WBC; Nashville: Nelson Reference & Electronic, 2nd edn, 2004).

Cranfield, C.E.B., 'Some Observations on Romans 8:19-21', in *Reconciliation and Hope: New Testament Essays on Atonement and Eschatology Presented to L.L. Morris* (ed. Robert Banks; Grand Rapids: Eerdmans, 1974), pp. 224-30.

—*A Critical and Exegetical Commentary on the Epistle to the Romans* (2 vols.; ICC; Edinburgh: T. & T. Clark, 1975–79).

Crouzel, Henri, *Origen* (trans. A.S. Worrall; Edinburgh: T. & T. Clark, 1989).

Dahl, Nils Alstrup, 'The Atonement—an Adequate Reward for the Akedah (Rom. 8.32)', in *Neotestamentica et Semitica: Studies in Honour of Matthew Black* (ed. E. Earle Ellis and Max E. Wilcox; Edinburgh: T. & T. Clark, 1969), pp. 15-29.

Das, Andrew, '"Praise the Lord, All you Gentiles": The Encoded Audience of Romans 15.7-13', *JSNT* 34 (2011), pp. 90-110.

Davis, Ellen F., 'Learning Our Place: The Agrarian Perspective of the Bible', *WW* 29 (2009), pp. 109-20.

—*Scripture, Culture, and Agriculture: An Agrarian Reading of the Bible* (New York: Cambridge University Press, 2009).

Davis, Joshua B., and Douglas Harink (eds.), *Apocalyptic and the Future of Theology: With and Beyond J. Louis Martyn* (Eugene, OR: Cascade Books, 2012).

Dawn, Marva J., *Keeping the Sabbath Wholly* (Grand Rapids: Eerdmans, 1989).

—'Sabbath Keeping and Social Justice', in *Sunday, Sabbath, and the Weekend: Managing Time in a Global Culture* (ed. Edward O'Flaherty and Rodney L. Petersen; Grand Rapids: Eerdmans, 2010), pp. 23-40.

de Boer, Martinus C., *Galatians: A Commentary* (NTL; Louisville, KY: Westminster/ John Knox Press, 2011).

Deissmann, Adolf, *Bible Studies* (trans. Alexander Grieve; Edinburgh: T. & T. Clark, 1901).

—*Light from the Ancient Near East: The New Testament Illustrated by Recently Discovered Texts of the Graeco-Roman World* (trans. Lionel Strachan; Grand Rapids: Baker, 1978 [orig. 1908]).

Delitzsch, Franz, *The Prophecies of Isaiah* (2 vols.; trans. James Martin; Grand Rapids: Eerdmans, 1950).

Denniston, J.D., *The Greek Particles* (London: Oxford University Press, 2nd edn, 1950).

Derrida, Jacques, *The Animal That Therefore I Am* (trans. David Wills; PCP; New York: Fordham University Press, 2008).

Descartes, René, 'Meditations on First Philosophy', in *The European Philosophers from Descartes to Nietzsche* (ed. Monroe C. Beardsley; New York: Random House, 1960).

Dewey, Arthur J., 'Acoustics of the Spirit: A Hearing of Romans 10', *Proceedings* 9 (1989), pp. 212-30.

—'A Re-Hearing of Romans 10:1-15', *Semeia* 65 (1994), pp. 109-27.

Dillon, John, *The Middle Platonists 80 B.C. to A.D. 220* (New York: Cornell University Press, 1996).

Dillon, Richard J., 'The "Priesthood" of St Paul, Romans 15:15-16', *Worship* 74 (2000), pp. 156-68.

Dochhorn, J., *Die Apokalypse des Mose: Text, Übersetzung, Kommentar* (TSAJ, 106; Tübingen: Mohr Siebeck 2006).

—'Röm 7,7 und das zehnte Gebot: Ein Beitrag zur Schriftauslegung und zur jüdischen Vorgeschichte des Paulus', *ZNW* 100 (2009), pp. 59-77.

Dodd, C.H., *The Epistle of Paul to the Romans* (MNTC; London: Hodder and Stoughton, 1932).

Donaldson, Terence L., 'The Juridical, the Participatory and the "New Perspective" on Paul', in *Reading Paul in Context: Explorations in Identity Formation. Essays in Honour of William S. Campbell* (ed. Kathy Ehrensperger and Brian J. Tucker; London: T. & T. Clark, 2010), pp. 229-41.

Donfried, Karl (ed.), *The Romans Debate* (Grand Rapids: Baker Academic, rev. edn, 2011).

Duchêne, François, *Jean Monnet: The First Statesman of Interdependence* (New York: W.W. Norton, 1994).

Duhm, Bernhard, *Die Theologie der Propheten als Grundlage für die innere Entwicklungsgeschichte der israelitischen Religion* (Bonn: Marcus, 1875).

Dumbrell, William J., 'Genesis 1–3, Ecology, and the Dominion of Man', *Crux* 21 (1985), pp. 16-26.

Dunn, James D.G., *The Epistle to the Galatians* (BNTC; London: A. & C. Black, 1993).

—*Romans* (2 vols.; WBC; Dallas: Word, 1998).
—*The Theology of Paul the Apostle* (Grand Rapids: Eerdmans, 1998).
—*The New Perspective on Paul* (Grand Rapids: Eerdmans, rev. edn, 2005).
Dupuy, Bernard, 'The Sabbath: Call to Justice and Freedom', in *The Jewish Roots of Christian Liturgy* (ed. Eugene J. Fisher; Mahwah, NJ: Paulist Press, 1990), pp. 148-57.
Eastman, Susan, 'Whose Apocalypse? The Identity of the Sons of God in Romans 8.19', *JBL* 121 (2002), pp. 263-77.
—'Double Participation and the Responsible Self in Romans 5–8', in *Apocalyptic Paul: Cosmos and Anthropos in Romans 5–8* (ed. Beverly Roberts Gaventa; Waco, TX: Baylor University Press, 2013), pp. 93-110.
Ebeling, Gerhard, *Luther: An Introduction to His Thought* (trans. R.A. Wilson; London: Collins, 1970).
Ehrensberger, Kathy, *Paul at the Crossroads of Cultures: Theologizing in the Space-Between* (New York: Bloomsbury, 2013).
Eichrodt, Walther, *Theology of the Old Testament* (2 vols.; trans. John Baker; OTL; London: SCM Press, 1961).
Eisenbaum, Pamela, *Paul Was Not a Christian: The Original Message of a Misunderstood Apostle* (New York: HarperOne, 2009).
Elliott, Neil, *Liberating Paul: The Justice of God and the Politics of the Apostle* (Maryknoll, NY: Orbis Books, 1994).
—'Asceticism among the "Weak" and "Strong" in Romans 14–15', in *Asceticism in the New Testament* (ed. Leif E. Vaage and Vincent L. Wimbush; New York: Routledge, 1999), pp. 231-51.
—'Strategies of Resistance and Hidden Transcripts in the Pauline Communities', in *Hidden Transcripts and the Arts of Resistance: Applying the Work of James C. Scott to Jesus and Paul* (ed. Richard Horsley; Atlanta: Society of Biblical Literature, 2004), pp. 97-122.
—'The Apostle Paul's Self-Presentation as Anti-imperial Performance', in *Paul and the Roman Imperial Order* (ed. Richard A. Horsley; London: Trinity Press, 2004), pp. 67-88.
—*The Arrogance of the Nations: Reading Romans in the Shadow of Empire* (Minneapolis: Fortress Press, 2008).
Emmerson, Grace L., *Isaiah 56–66* (OTG; Sheffield: JSOT Press, 1992).
Emmrich, Martin, 'The Temptation Narrative of Genesis 3:1-6: A Prelude to the Pentateuch and the History of Israel', *EQ* 73 (2001), pp. 3-20.
Engberg-Pedersen, Troels, 'Paul's Stoicizing Politics in Romans 12–13: The Role of 13.1-10 in the Argument', *JSNT* 29 (2006), pp. 163-72.
Epp, Eldon Jay, *Junia: The First Woman Apostle* (Minneapolis: Fortress Press, 2005).
Epstein, Isidore, *Judaism: A Historical Presentation* (Baltimore: Penguin, 1959).
Esler, Philip, *Conflict and Identity in Romans: The Social Setting of Paul's Letter* (Minneapolis: Fortress Press, 2003).
—'The Sodom Tradition in Romans 1:18-32', *BTB* 34 (2004), pp. 4-16.
Eusebius, *The History of the Church* (trans. G.A. Williamson; London: Penguin, 1989).
Evans, C.A., and J.A. Sanders (eds.), *The Gospels and the Scriptures of Israel* (JSNTSup, 104; Sheffield: Sheffield Academic Press, 1994).
FAO Newsroom, 'Livestock a Major Threat to Environment', www.fao.org/newsroom/en/News/2006/1000448/index.html
Farmer, William R., *Maccabees, Zealots, and Josephus: An Inquiry into Jewish Nationalism in the Greco-Roman Period* (Westport, CT: Greenwood Press, 1956).

Fee, Gordon D., 'Who Are Abraham's True Children? The Role of Abraham in Pauline Argumentation', in *Perspectives on Our Father Abraham: Essays in Honor of Marvin R. Wilson* (ed. Steven A. Hunt; Grand Rapids: Eerdmans, 2010), pp. 126-37.

Felleman, Laura Bartels, 'A Necessary Relationship: John Wesley and the Body-Soul Connection', in *'Inward and Outward Health': John Wesley's Holistic Concept of Medical Science, the Environment and Holy Living* (ed. Deborah Madden; Eugene, OR: Wipf and Stock, 2008), pp. 148-67.

Feuerbach, Ludwig, *The Essence of Christianity* (trans. George Eliot; New York: Harper & Row, 1957).

Feuillet, André, 'Un Sommet Religieux de l'Ancien Testament: L'oracle d'Isaïe, XIX (vv. 16-25) sur la conversion de l'Égypte', *RSR* 39 (1951), pp. 65-87.

Fiedler, Peter, 'Röm 8.31-39 as Brennpunkt paulinischer Frohbotschaft', *ZNW* 68 (1977), pp. 23-34.

Fimister, Alan Paul, *Robert Schuman: Neo-Scholastic Humanism and the Reunification of Europe* (PP; Brussels: Peter Lang, 2008).

Fiorenza, Elisabeth Schüssler, 'The Will to Choose or to Reject: Continuing Our Critical Work', in *Feminist Interpretation of the Bible* (ed. Letty Russell; Philadelphia: Westminster Press, 1985), pp. 125-36.

—*The Power of the Word: Scripture and the Rhetoric of Empire* (Minneapolis: Fortress Press, 2007).

Fitzmyer, Joseph A., *Romans: A New Translation with Introduction and Commentary* (AB; London: Geoffrey Chapman, 1993).

Flowers, Margaret, 'A Wesleyan Theology of Environmental Stewardship', in *'Inward and Outward Health': John Wesley's Holistic Concept of Medical Science, the Environment and Holy Living* (ed. Deborah Madden; Eugene, OR: Wipf and Stock, 2008), pp. 51-93.

Foer, Jonathan Safran, *Eating Animals* (New York: Little, Brown, 2009).

Fox, Robin Lane, *The Classical World: An Epic History from Homer to Hadrian* (New York: Allen Lane, 2005).

Frankfurt, Harry G., *On Bullshit* (Princeton, NJ: Princeton University Press, 2005).

Fredriksen, Paula, 'Judaism, the Circumcision of the Gentiles, and Apocalyptic Hope: Another Look at Galatians 1 and 2', *JTS* 42 (1991), pp. 532-64.

—'Judaizing the Nations: The Ritual Demands of Paul's Gospel', *NTS* 56 (2010), pp. 232-52.

—*Augustine and the Jews: A Christian Defense of Jews and Judaism* (New Haven: Yale University Press, 2010).

—*Sin: The Early History of an Idea* (Princeton, NJ: Princeton University Press, 2012).

Frend, W.H.C., *The Rise of Christianity* (Philadelphia: Fortress Press, 1984).

Fretheim, Terence, *The Suffering of God: An Old Testament Perspective* (OBT; Philadelphia: Fortress Press, 1984).

—*God and the World in the Old Testament: A Relational Theology of Creation* (Nashville: Abingdon Press, 2005).

Friedländer, Saul, *The Years of Persecution: Nazi Germany and the Jews 1933–1939* (London: Phoenix, 1999).

Gaca, Kathy, 'Paul's Uncommon Declaration in Romans 1:18-32 and Its Problematic Legacy for Pagan and Christian Relations', *HTR* 92 (1999), pp. 165-98.

Garlington, D.B., 'The Obedience of Faith in the Letter to the Romans', *WJT* 52 (1990), pp. 201-24.

Gathercole, Simon, 'Romans 1–5 and the "Weak" and the "Strong"', *RevExp* 100 (2003), pp. 35-51.

Gaventa, Beverly Roberts, 'Galatians 1 and 2: Autobiography as Paradigm', *NovT* 28 (1986), pp. 309-26.

—'The Cosmic Power of Sin in Paul's Letter to the Romans: Toward a Widescreen Edition', *Int* 58 (2004), pp. 229-40.

—'God Handed Them Over: Reading Romans 1:18-32 Apocalyptically', *ABR* 53 (2005), pp. 42-53.

—'Interpreting the Death of Jesus Apocalyptically: Reconsidering Romans 8.32', in *Jesus and Paul Reconnected: Fresh Pathways into an Old Debate*' (ed. Todd D. Still; Grand Rapids: Eerdmans, 2007), pp. 125-45.

—'From Toxic Speech to the Redemption of Doxology', in *The Word Leaps the Gap: Essays on Scripture and Theology in Honor of Richard B. Hays* (ed. J. Ross Wagner, C. Kavin Rowe and A. Katherine Grieb; Grand Rapids: Eerdmans, 2008), pp. 392-408.

—'Neither Height nor Depth: Discerning the Cosmology of Romans', *SJT* 64 (2011), pp. 265-78.

—'Reading for the Subject: The Paradox of Power in Romans 14:1–15:6', *JTI* 5 (2011), pp. 1-12.

—'The Shape of the "I": The Psalter, the Gospel, and the Speaker in Romans 7', in *Apocalyptic Paul: Cosmos and Anthropos in Romans 5–8* (ed. Beverly Roberts Gaventa; Waco, TX: Baylor University Press, 2013), pp. 77-92.

Gempf, Conrad, 'The Imagery of Birth Pangs in the New Testament', *TynB* 45 (1994), pp. 119-35.

Gillman, Florence Morgan, 'Another Look at Romans 8:3: "In the Likeness of Sinful Flesh"', *CBQ* 49 (1987), pp. 597-604.

Gingrich, F. Wilbur, and Frederick William Danker (eds.), *Shorter Lexicon of the Greek New Testament* (Chicago: University of Chicago Press, 1965).

Giorgi, Dieter, *Theocracy in Paul's Praxis and Theology* (ET; Minneapolis. Fortress Press, 1991).

Gnuse, Robert, 'Jubilee Legislation in Leviticus: Israel's Vision of Social Reform', *BTB* 15 (1985), pp, 43-48.

Goldingay, John, and David Payne, *Isaiah 40–55* (2 vols.; ICC; New York and London: T. & T. Clark, 2006).

Gorman, Michael J., *Reading Paul* (Eugene, OR: Cascade Books, 2008).

Gray, George Buchanan, *A Critical and Exegetical Commentary on the Book of Isaiah*, I-XXVII (ICC; Edinburgh: T. & T. Clark, 1912).

Green, Joel B., *Body, Soul, and Human Life: The Nature of Humanity in the Bible* (Grand Rapids: Baker Academic, 2008).

Greene-McCreight, Kathryn, 'Restless Until We Rest in God: The Fourth Commandment as Test Case in Christian "Plain Sense" Interpretation', in *The Ten Commandments: The Reciprocity of Faithfulness* (ed. William P. Brown; Louisville, KY: Westminster/John Knox Press, 2004), pp. 223-36.

Greidanus, Sidney, 'Preaching Christ from the Narrative of the Fall', *BSac* 161 (2004), pp. 259-73.

Grieb, Katherine, 'The Root of Jesse Who Rises to Rule the Gentiles: Paul's Use of the Story of Jesus in Romans 15:7-13', *Proceedings* 13 (1993), pp. 71-88.

—*The Story of Romans: A Narrative Defense of God's Righteousness* (Louisville, KY: Westminster/John Knox Press, 2002).

Griffith-Jones, Robin, 'Beyond Reasonable Hope of Recognition? Prosōpopoeia *in Romans 1:18-38*', in *Beyond Old and New Perspectives in Paul: Reflections on the Work of Douglas Campbell* (ed. Chris Tilling; Eugene, OR: Cascade Books, 2014), pp. 161-81.

Gupta, Nijay K., 'What *"Mercies of God"?* Oiktirmos in Romans 12.1 against Its Septuagintal Background', *BBR* 22 (2012), pp. 81-96.

Habel, Norman C., *The Land Is Mine* (OBT; Minneapolis: Fortress Press, 1995).

Habel, Norman C. (ed.), *Readings from the Perspective of the Earth* (Sheffield: Sheffield Academic Press, 2000), pp. 24-37.

Habel, Norman C., and Vicky Balabanski (eds.), 'Ecojustice Hermeneutics: Reflections and Challenges', the Earth Bible Team, in *The Earth Story in the New Testament* (London: Sheffield Academic Press, 2002), pp. 1-15.

Hafemann, Scott, 'Eschatology and Ethics: The Future of Israel and the Nations in Romans 15.1-13', *TynB* 51 (2000), pp. 161-92.

Hahne, Harry Alan, *The Corruption and Redemption of Creation: Nature in Romans 8.19-22 and Jewish Apocalyptic Literature* (LNTS; London and New York: T. & T. Clark, 2006).

Hanson, A.T., *The Wrath of the Lamb* (London: SPCK, 1957).

Hanson, Paul D., *Isaiah 40–66* (Interpretation; Louisville, KY: John Knox Press, 1995).

Harding, Mark, and Alanna Nobs (eds.), *All Things to All Cultures: Paul among Jews, Greeks, and Romans* (Grand Rapids: Eerdmans, 2013).

Harink, Douglas, *Paul among the Postliberals: Pauline Theology Beyond Christendom and Modernity* (Grand Rapids: Brazos Press, 2002).

Harrison, Carol, *Rethinking Augustine's Early Theology: An Argument for Continuity* (Oxford: Oxford University Press, 2006).

Harrison, James R., 'Paul among the Romans', in *All Things to All Cultures: Paul among Jews, Greeks, and Romans* (ed. Mark Harding and Alanna Nobs; Grand Rapids: Eerdmans, 2013), pp. 143-76.

Hattersley, Roy, *John Wesley: A Brand from the Burning* (London: Little, Brown, 2002).

Hayes, Katherine M., *'The Earth Mourns': Prophetic Metaphor and Oral Aesthetic* (Atlanta: Society of Biblical Literature, 2002).

Hays, Richard B., *The Faith of Jesus Christ: An Investigation of the Narrative Substructure of Galatians 3:1–4:11* (*SBLDS*, 56; Chico, CA: Scholars Press, 1983. Reprinted Grand Rapids: Eerdmans, 2002).

—'"Have We Found Abraham to Be Our Forefather according to the Flesh?" A Reconsideration of Romans 4:1', *NovT* 27 (1985), pp. 76-98.

—'"The Righteous One" as Eschatological Deliverer: A Case Study in Paul's Apocalyptic Hermeneutics', in *Apocalyptic and the New Testament: Essays in Honor of J. Louis Martyn* (ed. Joel Marcus and Marion L. Soards; JSNTSup, 24; Sheffield: Sheffield Academic Press, 1989), pp. 191-215.

—*Echoes of Scripture in the Letters of Paul* (New Haven: Yale University Press, 1989).

—'Christ Prays the Psalms: Paul's Use of an Early Christian Exegetical Convention', in *The Future of Christology: Essays in Honor of Leander Keck* (ed. Abraham J. Malherbe and Wayne A. Meeks; Minneapolis: Fortress Press, 1993), pp. 122-36.

—*The Moral Vision of the New Testament: Community, Cross, New Creation* (Edinburgh: T. & T. Clark, 1996).

Heitzenrater, Richard P., *Wesley and the People Called Methodists* (Nashville: Abingdon Press, 2nd edn, 2013).

Heliso, Desta, *Pistis and the Righteous One: A Study of Romans 1:17 against the*

Background of Scripture and Second Temple Jewish Literature (WUNT, 2; Tübingen: Mohr Siebeck, 2007).

Hell, Julia, '*Katechon*: Carl Schmitt's Imperial Theology and the Ruins of the Future', *The Germanic Review* 84 (2009), pp.283-326.

Helyer, Larry R., 'The Separation of Abram and Lot: Its Significance in the Patriarchal Narratives', *JSOT* 26 (1983), pp. 77-88.

Henning, Brian G., 'Standing in Livestock's "Long Shaddow": The Ethics of Eating Meat on a Small Planet', *Ethics & the Environment* 16 (2011), pp. 63-94.

Hiebert, Theodore, 'Rethinking Dominion Theology', *Direction* 25 (1996), pp. 16-25.

Hobbes, Thomas, *Leviathan* (London: Penguin, 1985 [orig. 1651]).

Hochschild, Adam, *To End All Wars: A Story of Loyalty and Rebellion, 1914–1918* (New York: Houghton Mifflin Harcourt, 2011).

Hooker, Morna D., '*Pistis Christou*', *NTS* 35 (1989), pp. 321-42.

Horn, Friedrich Wilhelm, 'Putting on Christ: On the Relation of Sacramental and Ethical Language in the Pauline Epistles', in *Moral Language in the New Testament: The Interrelatedness of Language and Ethics in Early Christian Writings* (ed. Ruben Zimmermann and Jan G. van der Watt; Tübingen: Mohr Siebeck, 2010), pp. 232-44.

Horrell, David G., Cherryl Hunt and Christopher Southgate, *Greening Paul: Rereading the Apostle in a Time of Ecological Crisis* (Waco, TX: Baylor University Press, 2010).

Horsley, Richard A., 'Introduction', in *Paul and the Roman Imperial Order* (ed. Richard Horsley; Harrisburg, PA: Trinity Press International, 2004), pp. 1-23.

Horsley, Richard A. (ed.), *Paul and Politics: Ekklesia, Israel, Imperium, Interpretation. Essays in Honor of Krister Stendahl* (Harrisburg, PA: Trinity Press International, 2000).

Hossfeld, Frank-Lothar, and Erich Zenger, *Psalms 2: A Commentary on Psalms 51–100* (trans. Linda M. Maloney; Hermeneia; Minneapolis: Fortress Press, 2005).

Hossfeld, Frank-Lothar, and Erich Zenger, *Psalms 3: A Commentary on Psalms 101–150* (trans. Linda M. Maloney; Hermeneia; Minneapolis: Fortress Press, 2011).

Hultgren, Arland J., *Paul's Letter to the Romans* (Grand Rapids: Eerdmans, 2011).

Hunt, Cherryl, David G. Horrell and Christopher Southgate, 'An Environmental Mantra? Ecological Interest in Romans 8.19-23 and a Modest Proposal for Its Narrative Interpretation', *JTS* 58 (2008), pp. 546-79.

Hvalvik, Reidar, 'Jewish Believers and Jewish Influence in the Roman Church until the Early Second Century', in *Jewish Believers in Jesus: The Early Centuries* (ed. Oskar Skarsaune and Reidar Hvalvik; Peabody, MA: Hendrickson, 2007), pp. 179-216.

Hyldahl, Niels, 'καὶ οὕτως in Rom 11,26', *DTT* 37 (1974), pp. 231-34.

Idinopulos, Thomas A., 'Religious and National Factors in Israel's War with Rome', in *Jewish Civilization in the Hellenistic-Roman Period* (ed. Shemaryahu Talmon; Philadelphia: Trinity Press, 1991), pp. 50-63.

Imhoff, Daniel (ed.), *CAFO (Concentrated Animal Feeding Operation): The Tragedy of Industrial Animal Factories* (San Rafael, CA: Earth Aware, 2010).

—*The CAFO Reader (Concentrated Animal Feeding Operation): The Tragedy of Industrial Animal Factories* (Watershed Media, 2010).

International Diabetes Federation atlas update 2013; http./www.idf.org/diabetesatlas/introduction.

Ito, Akito, 'The Written Torah and the Oral Gospel: Romans 10.5-13 in the Dynamic Tension between Orality and Literacy', *NovT* 48 (2006), pp. 234-60.

Jackson, Wes, Wendell Berry and Bruce Colman (eds.), *Meeting the Expectations of the Land: Essays in Sustainable Agriculture and Stewardship* (San Francisco: North Point Press, 1984).

Jaeger, Werner, 'The Greek Ideas of Immortality', in *Immortality and Resurrection* (ed. Krister Stendahl; New York: Macmillan, 1965), pp. 97-114.

Janzen, Gerald J., 'Sin and the Deception of Devout Desire: Paul and the Commandment in Romans 7', *Encounter* 70 (2009), pp. 29-61.

Jenkins, Philip, *The Great and Holy War: How World War I Changed Religion For Ever* (Oxford: Lion, 2014).

Jeremias, Joachim, 'Zu Rm 1:22-32', *ZNW* 45 (1954), pp. 119-21.

Jervell, Jacob, 'Romans 14:1–15:13 and the Occasion of Romans', in *The Romans Debate* (ed. Karl P. Donfried; Peabody, MA: Hendrickson, 1991), pp. 53-64.

Jervis, L. Ann, '"The Commandment which is for Life" (Romans 7.10): Sin's Use of the Obedience of Faith', *JSNT* 212 (2004), pp. 193-216.

Jewett, Robert, *Romans: A Commentary on the Book of Romans* (Hermeneia; Minneapolis: Fortress Press, 2006).

—'The Corruption and Redemption of Creation: Reading Rom 8:18-23 within the Imperial Context', in *Paul and the Roman Imperial Order* (ed. Richard A. Horsley; New York: Trinity Press, 2004), pp. 25-46.

Johnson, E. Elizabeth, 'Romans 9–11: The Faithfulness and Impartiality of God', in *Pauline Theology*, vol. III (ed. David Hay and E. Elizabeth Johnson; Minneapolis: Fortress Press, 1995), pp. 211-39.

Johnson, M.D., *Life of Adam and Eve*, in *The Old Testament Pseudepigrapha*, vol. 2 (ed. J.H. Charlesworth; New York: Doubleday, 1985).

Jones, A.H.M., *Constantine and the Conversion of Europe* (Toronto: University of Toronto Press, 1978).

Josephus, Flavius, *The Antiquities of the Jews* (trans. William Whiston; Project Gutenberg; E-book #2848; www.gutenberg.org.

Judge, E.A., 'St. Paul and Classical Society', *JbAC* 15 (1972), pp. 19-36.

Kaiser, Otto, *Isaiah 1–12* (trans. John Bowden; OTL; Philadelphia: Westminster Press, 2nd edn, 1983).

Kallas, James, 'Romans XIII.1-7: an Interpolation', *NTS* 11 (1965), pp. 365-74.

Kant, Immanuel, *Groundwork of the Metaphysic of Morals* (trans. H.J. Paton; New York: Harper Torchbook, 1964).

Karris, Robert J., 'Rom 14:1–15:13 and the Occasion of Romans', *CBQ* 34 (1973), pp. 155-78.

Käsemann, Ernst, *Commentary on Romans* (trans. Geoffrey W. Bromiley; Grand Rapids: Eerdmans, 1994).

Keck, Leander, 'What Makes Romans Tick?', in *Pauline Theology*, vol, III (ed. David M. Hay and E. Elizabeth Johnson; Minneapolis: Fortress Press, 1995), pp. 3-29.

Keiser, Thomas A., 'The Song of Moses a Basis for Isaiah's Prophecy', *VT* 55 (2005), pp. 486-500.

Kennan, George, *American Diplomacy, 1900–1950* (Chicago: University of Chicago Press, 1951).

Kirk, J. Daniel, *Unlocking Romans: Resurrection and the Justification of God* (Grand Rapids: Eerdmans, 2008).

Kittel, Gerhard, and Gerhard Friedrich (eds.), *Theological Dictionary of the New Testament* (10 vols.; trans. Geoffrey W. Bromiley; Grand Rapids: Eerdmans, 1964).

Klostermann, Erich, 'Die adäquate Vergeltung im Rm 1:22-31', *ZNW* 32 (1933), pp. 1-6.

Knox, John, 'Romans 15:14-33 and Paul's Conception of His Apostolic Mission', *JBL* 83 (1964), pp. 1-11.

Koch, Klaus, *The Rediscovery of Apocalyptic* (trans. Margaret Kohl; London: SCM Press, 1972).

Kraus, H.-J., *Psalms 1–59* (trans. Hilton C. Oswalt; CC; Minneapolis: Fortress Press, 1999).

Krauter, Stefan, 'Eva in Röm 7', *ZNW* 99 (2008), pp. 1-17.

—'"Es ist keine Gewalt ausser von Gott": Röm 13,1 im Kontext des politischen Diskurses der neronischen Zeit', in *The Letter to the Romans* (ed. Udo Schnelle; Louvain: Peeters, 2009), pp. 371-401.

—'Röm 7: Adam oder Eva?', *ZNW* 101 (2010), pp. 145-47.

Kraybill, J. Nelson, *Apocalypse and Allegiance: Worship, Politics, and Devotion in the Book of Revelation* (Grand Rapids: Brazos Press, 2010).

Kuntz, J. Kenneth, 'Psalm 18: a Rhetorical-Critical Analysis', *JSOT* 26 (1983), pp. 3-31.

Lampe, Peter, 'The Roman Christians of Romans 16', in *The Romans Debate* (ed. Karl Donfried; Grand Rapids: Baker Academic, rev. edn, 2011), pp. 216-30.

Landeen, William M., *Martin Luther's Religious Thought* (Mountain View, CA.: Pacific Press, 1971).

Leenhardt, F.J., *The Epistle to the Romans* (London: Lutterworth, 1961).

Lefebre, Georges, *The French Revolution: From Its Origins to 1793* (trans. Elizabeth Moss Evanson; New York: Columbia University Press, 1962).

Leopold, Aldo, *A Sand County Almanac: With Essays on Conservation from Round River* (New York: Ballantine Books, 1970).

Limburg, James, 'The Responsibility of Royalty: Genesis 1–11 and the Care of the Earth', *WW* 11 (1991), pp. 124-30.

Livestock Report 2006. FOOD AND AGRICULTURE ORGANIZATION OF THE UNITED NATIONS, Rome, 2006 at www.fao.org/docrep/009/a0255e/a0255e00.HTM.

Lohse, Bernard, 'Conscience and Authority in Luther', in *Luther and the Dawn of the Modern Era: Papers for the Fourth International Congress for Luther Research* (trans. Herbert J.A. Bouman; ed. H.A. Oberman; Leiden: E.J. Brill, 1974), pp. 158-83.

Lohse, Eduard, 'Martin Luther und der Römerbrief des Apostels Paulus—Biblische Entdeckungen', *KD* 52 (2006), pp. 106-25.

Longenecker, Bruce W., *Remember the Poor: Paul, Poverty, and the Greco-Roman World* (Grand Rapids: Eerdmans, 2010).

Longenecker, Bruce W. (ed.), *Narrative Dynamics in Paul: A Critical Assessment* (Louisville, KY: Westminster/John Knox Press, 2002).

Longenecker, Bruce W., and Todd D. Still, *Thinking Through Paul: An Introduction to His Life, Letters and Theology* (Grand Rapids: Zondervan, 2014).

Los, Fraser, 'The Terminator', *Alternatives Journal* 32 (2006), pp. 24-26.

Louw, J.P., and E.A. Nida (eds.), *Louw-Nida Greek-English Lexicon of the New Testament Based on Semantic Domains* (New York: United Bible Societies, 2nd edn, 1988).

Lucas, Alec J., 'Unearthing an Intra-Jewish Interpretive Debate? *Romans* 1,18–2,4; *Wisdom of Solomon* 11–19; and *Psalms* 105 (104)-107(106)', *ASE* 27 (2010), pp. 69-91.

—'Reorienting the Structural Paradigm and Social Significance of Romans 1:18-32', *JBL* 131 (2012), pp. 121-41.

Luther, Martin, Sermon preached on March 10, 1522, in *Luther's Works* 51 (ed. J.J. Pelikan, H.C. Oswald and H.T. Lehmann; Philadelphia: Fortress Press, 1959), pp. 71-78.

—*Luther's Works* 25: *Lectures on Romans* (ed. Jaroslav Pelikan; St. Louis: Concordia, 1972).

—*Commentary on the Epistle to the Romans* (trans. J. Theodore Mueller; Grand Rapids: Kregel Publications, 1976).

Madden, Deborah, 'Pastor and Physician: John Wesley's Cures for Consumption', in *'Inward and Outward Health': John Wesley's Holistic Concept of Medical Science, the Environment and Holy Living* (ed. Deborah Madden; Eugene, OR: Wipf and Stock, 2008), pp. 94-139.

Marlow, Hilary, 'The Spirit of Yahweh in Isaiah 11:1-9', in *Presence, Power, and Promise: The Role of the Spirit of God in the Old Testament* (ed. David G. Firth and Paul D. Wegner; Downers Grove, IL: IVP Academic, 2011), p. 220-32.

Marshall, John W., 'Hybridity and Reading Romans 13', *JSNT* 31 (2008), pp. 157-78.

Martin, Dale, 'Heterosexism and the Interpretation of Romans 1:18:32', *BI* 3 (1995), pp. 332-55.

Martin, Ralph P., *2 Corinthians* (WBC; Dallas: Word, 1998).

Martyn, J. Louis, 'Apocalyptic Antinomies in Paul's Letter to the Galatians', *NTS* 31 (1985), pp. 410-24.

—'Events in Galatia: Modified Covenantal Nomism versus God's Invasion of the Cosmos in the Singular Gospel: A Response to J.D.G. Dunn and B.R. Gaventa', in *Pauline Theology*, vol. 1 (ed. Jouette Bassler; Minneapolis: Fortress Press, 1991), pp. 160-79.

—*Galatians: A New Translation with Introduction and Commentary* (AB; New York: Doubleday, 1997).

—'Romans as One of the Earliest Interpretations of Galatians,' in J. Louis Martyn, *Theological Issues in the Letters of Paul* (Nashville: Abingdon Press, 1997), pp. 37-46.

—'The Apocalyptic Gospel in Galatians', *Int* 54 (2000), pp. 246-66.

—'*Nomos* Plus Genitive Noun in Paul: The History of God's Law', in *Early Christianity and Classical Culture: Comparative Studies in Honor of Abraham J. Malherbe* (ed. John T. Fitzgerald, Thomas H. Olbricht and L. Michael White; NovTSup; Atlanta: Society of Biblical Literature, 2003), pp. 575-87.

Masson, Jeffrey Mousaieff, *The Pig Who Sang to the Moon: The Emotional World of Farm Animals* (New York: Ballantine Books, 2003).

Matera, Frank J., *Romans* (Paideia; Grand Rapids: Baker Academic, 2010).

Mathews, K.A., *Genesis 1-11:26* (Nashville: Broadman & Holman, 1996).

Matthew Scully, *Dominion: The Power of Man, the Suffering of Animals, and the Call to Mercy* (New York: St. Martin's Press, 2002).

McCormack, Bruce L., *Karl Barth's Critically Realistic Dialectical Theology: Its Genesis and Development 1909–1936* (Oxford: Clarendon Press, 1995).

McDonald, Patricia M., 'Romans 5.1-11 as a Rhetorical Bridge', *JSNT* 40 (1990), pp. 81-96.

McGinn, Sheila E., 'All Creation Groans in Labor: Paul's Theology of Creation in Romans 8.18-23', in *Earth, Wind & Fire: Biblical and Theological Perspectives on Creation* (ed. Carol J. Dempsey and Mary Margaret Pazdan; Collegeville, MN: Liturgical Press, 2004), pp. 114-23.

McGinnis, Claire Mathews, 'The Hardening of Pharaoh's Heart in Christian and Jewish Interpretations', *JTI* 6 (2012), pp. 43-64.

Meeks, Wayne, 'On Trusting an Unpredictable God: A Hermeneutical Meditation on Romans 9–11', in *Faith and History: Essays in Honor of Paul W. Meyer* (ed. John T Carroll, Charles H. Cosgrove, and E. Elizabeth Johnson (Atlanta: Scholars Press, 1990), pp. 105-24.

Mellon, Margaret, Charles Benbrook and Karen Lutz Benbrook, *Hogging It: Estimates of Antimicrobial Use in Livestock* (Union of Concerned Scientists, 2001).

Meyer, Paul W., 'The Worm at the Core of the Apple: Exegetical Reflections on Romans 7', in *The Conversation Continues: Studies in Paul and John in Honor of J. Louis Martyn* (ed. Robert T. Fortna and Beverly R. Gaventa; Nashville: Abingdon Press, 1990).

Michel, Otto, *Der Brief an die Römer* (KEK; Göttingen: Vandenhoeck & Ruprecht, 1978).

Milgrom, Jacob, 'Leviticus 25 and Some Postulates of the Jubilee', in *The Jubilee Challenge: Utopia or Possibility?* (ed. Hans Ucko; Geneva: WCC Publications, 1997), pp. 28-32.

—*Leviticus: A New Translation with Introduction and Commentary* (3 vols.; AB; New York: Doubleday, 1998–2000).

Minear, Paul S., *The Obedience of Faith: The Purposes of Paul in the Epistle to the Romans* (SBT; London: SCM Press, 1971).

Mitton, C. Leslie, 'Romans 7 Reconsidered—1', *ExpTim* 65 (1953–54), pp. 78-81.

Moberly, R.W.L., 'Did the Serpent Get It Right?', *JTS* 39 (1988), pp. 1-27.

Moltmann, Jürgen, *God in Creation: An Ecological Doctrine of Creation* (trans. Margaret Kohl; London: SCM Press, 1985).

—*The Coming of God: Christian Eschatology* (trans. Margaret Kohl; London: SCM Press, 1996).

Moo, Douglas J., *The Epistle to the Romans* (Grand Rapids: Eerdmans, 1996).

—'Nature in the New Creation: New Testament Eschatology and the Environment', *JETS* 49 (2006), pp. 449-88.

Moo, Jonathan, 'Romans 8.19-22 and Isaiah's Cosmic Covenant', *NTS* 54 (2008), pp. 74-89.

Morse, Eric Robert, *Juggernaut: Why the System Crushes the Only People Who Can Save It* (New Classic Books, 2010).

Motyer, J. Alec, *The Prophecy of Isaiah* (Downers Grove, IL: InterVarsity Press, 1993).

Moulton, J.H., and G. Milligan, *The Vocabulary of the Greek Testament* (London: Hodder and Stoughton, 1930).

Moyise, Steve, 'Intertextuality and the Study of the Old Testament in the New Testament', in *The Old Testament in the New Testament: Essays in Honour of J.L North* (ed. Steve Moyise; JSNTSup; Sheffield: Sheffield Academic, 2000), pp. 14-41.

Murphy, Cullen, *God's Jury: The Inquisition and the Making of the Modern World* (New York: Penguin, 2011).

Murphy, Roland E., *Ecclesiastes* (WBC, Dallas: Word, 1998).

Murray, John, *Romans* (2 vols.; NICNT; Grand Rapids: Eerdmans, 1974).

Murphy-O'Connor, Jeremy, *Paul: A Critical Life* (Oxford: Oxford University Press, 1996).

Myers, Benjamin, 'A Tale of Two Gardens: Augustine's Narrative Interpretation of Romans 5', in *Apocalyptic Paul: Cosmos and Anthropos in Romans 5–8* (ed. Beverly Roberts Gaventa; Waco, TX: Baylor University Press, 2013), pp. 39-58.

Nanos, Mark D., *The Mystery of Romans: The Jewish Context of Paul's Letter* (Minneapolis: Fortress Press, 1996).

Newsom, Carol, 'Common Ground: An Ecological Reading of Genesis 2–3', in *The Earth Story in Genesis* (ed. Norman C. Habel and Shirley Wurst; Sheffield: Sheffield Academic Press, 2000), pp. 60-72.

Niebuhr, Reinhold, *Moral Man and Immoral Society: A Study in Ethics and Politics* (Louisville, KY: Westminster/John Knox Press, 2001 [orig. 1932]).

Nietzsche, Friedrich, *Beyond Good and Evil* (trans. Walter Kaufmann; New York: Vintage Books, 1966).

Nussbaum, Martha C., *The Therapy of Desire: Theory and Practice in Hellenistic Ethics* (Princeton, NJ: Princeton University Press, 1994).

O'Connor, Flannery, 'Revelation', in *Flannery O-Connor: The Complete Stories* (New York: Noonday, 1996), pp. 488-509.

O'Neill, J.C., *Paul's Letter to the Romans* (London: Penguin, 1975).

Obeng, E.A., '"Abba, Father": The Prayer of the Sons of God', *ExpTim* 99 (1988), pp. 363-66.

Odell-Scott, David (ed.), *Reading Romans with Contemporary Philosophers and Theologians* (New York: T. & T. Clark, 2007).

Olivier, Daniel, *The Trial of Luther* (trans. John Tonkin; St. Louis: Concordia, 1978).

Origen, *Contra Celsum* (trans. Henry Chadwick; Cambridge: Cambridge University Press, 1965).

—*Origen on First Principles* (trans. G.W. Butterworth; London: SPCK, 1936. Reprinted Gloucester, MA: Peter Smith, 1973).

—*Commentary on the Epistle to the Romans, Books 1–5* (trans. Thomas P. Scheck; FC, 103; Baltimore: Catholic University of America Press, 2001).

—*Commentary on the Epistle to the Romans, Books 6–10* (trans. Thomas P. Scheck; FC, 104; Baltimore: Catholic University of America Press, 2002).

Oropeza, B.J., 'Paul and Theodicy: Intertextual Thoughts on God's Justice and Faithfulness in Romans 9–11', *NTS* 53 (2007), pp. 57-80.

Orr, David W., 'The Uses of Prophecy', in *The Essential Agrarian Reader: The Future of Culture, Community, and the Land* (ed. Norman Wirzba; Washington, DC: Shoemaker & Hoard, 2003), pp. 171-87.

Orwell, George, 'Politics and the English Language', *Horizon*, April, 1946.

—*1984* (New York: Signet Classics, 1950).

—*Shooting an Elephant and Other Essays* (London: Secker and Warburg, 1950).

Ostovich, Steve, 'Carl Schmitt, Political Theology, and Eschatology', *KronoScope* 7 (2007), pp. 49-66.

Oswalt, John, *The Book of Isaiah: Chapters 1–39* (NICOT; Grand Rapids: Eerdmans, 1986).

—*The Book of Isaiah: Chapters 40–66* (NICOT; Grand Rapids: Eerdmans, 1998).

Otto, Eckart, 'Singing Moses: His Farewell Song in Deuteronomy 32', in *Psalmody and Poetry in Old Testament Ethics* (ed. Dirk J. Human; New York: T. & T. Clark, 2012), pp. 169-80.

Otto, Marc, and Michael Lodahl, '"We Cannot Know Much, But We May Love Much": Mystery and Humility in John Wesley's Narrative Theology', *Wesleyan Theol J* 44 (2009), pp. 118-40.

Outler, Albert C. (ed.), *John Wesley* (LPT; New York: Oxford University Press, 1964).

Pachirat, Timothy, *Every Twelve Seconds: Industrialized Slaughter and the Politics of Sight* (New Haven: Yale University Press, 2011).

Packer, J.I., 'The "Wretched Man" in Romans 7', *SE* 2 (1964), pp. 621-27.

Pangle, Thomas L., *Political Philosophy and the God of Abraham* (Baltimore: Johns Hopkins University Press, 2003).

Patel, Raj, *Stuffed & Starved: The Hidden Battle for the World Food System* (New York: Melville House, 2007).

Patte, Daniel, 'Thinking Mission with Paul and the Romans: Romans 15:1-33', *Mission Studies* 23 (2006), pp. 81-104.

Peli, Pinchas, *The Jewish Sabbath: A Renewed Encounter* (New York: Schocken Books, 1988).

Pew Commission, *Putting Meat on the Table: Industrial Farm Animal Production in America*. A Report of the Pew Commission on Industrial Farm Animal Production, 2008, at www.ncifap.org/bin/e/j/PCIFAPFin.pdf.

Plato, *Euthyphro, Apology, Crito, Phaedo* (trans. Benjamin Jowett; New York: Prometheus Books, 1988).

—*The Last Days of Socrates* (trans. Hugh Tredennick; New York: Penguin Books, 2003).

Polkinghorne, John, *The God of Hope and the End of the World* (New Haven: Yale University Press, 2002).

Pollan, Michael, *The Omnivore's Dilemma: A Natural History of Four Meals* (New York: Penguin, 2006).

Porter, Roy, *Flesh in the Age of Reason: How the Enlightenment Transformed the Way We See Our Bodies and Our Souls* (London: Penguin Books, 2003).

Portier-Young, Anathea E., *Apocalypse against Empire: Theologies of Resistance in Early Judaism* (Grand Rapids: Eerdmans, 2011).

Price, S.R.F., *Rituals and Power: The Roman Imperial Cult in Asia Minor* (New York: Cambridge University Press, 1986).

Pulcini, Theodore, 'In Right Relationship with God: Present Experience and Future Fulfillment. An Exegesis of Romans 5.1-11', *SVTQ* 36 (1992), pp. 61-85.

Purcell, Nicholas, 'The Arts of Government', in *The Roman World* (ed. John Boardman, Jasper Griffin and Oswyn Murray; New York: Oxford University Press, 1986), pp. 150-81.

Rad, Gerhard von, *Genesis* (trans. John H. Marks; London: SCM Press, 2nd edn, 1963).

Ray, Darby Kathleen, 'It's about Time: Reflections on a Theology of Rest', in *Theology That Matters: Ecology, Economy, and God* (ed. Darby Kathleen Ray; Minneapolis: Fortress Press, 2006), pp. 154-71.

Reasoner, Mark, *The Strong and the Weak: Romans 14.1–15.13 in Context* (Cambridge: Cambridge University Press, 1999).

Reis, Pamela Tamarkin, 'Hagar Requited', *JSOT* 87 (2000), pp. 75-109.

Rendtorff, Rolf, 'Zur Komposition des Buches Jesaja', *VT* 34 (1984), pp. 295-320.

—*The Canonical Hebrew Bible: A Theology of the Old Testament* (trans. David E. Orton; Leiden: Deo Publishers, 2005).

Reston, Jr, James, *Dogs of God: Columbus, the Inquisition, and the Defeat of the Moors* (New York: Anchor Books, 2006).

Richardson, William E., *Paul Among Friends & Enemies* (Boise, ID.: Pacific Press, 1992).

Rickett, Dan, 'Rethinking the Place and Purpose of Genesis 13', *JSOT* 36 (2011), pp. 31-53.

Rifkin, Jeremy, *Beyond Beef: The Rise and Fall of the Cattle Culture* (New York: Dutton, 1992).

Robertson, A.T., *A Grammar of the Greek New Testament in the Light of Historical Research* (London: Hodder and Stoughton, 3rd edn, 1919).

Robinson, John A.T., 'The One Baptism as a Category of New Testament Soteriology', *SJT* 6 (1953), pp. 257-74.

Rodriguez, Daniel, 'On *Gar'd*: Dialogue in LXX Isaiah and Romans', paper presented to the Biblical Lexicography section, San Diego, November 22, 2014.

Romm, James, *Dying Every Day: Seneca at the Court of Nero* (New York: Vintage Books, 2014).

Rouwhorst, Gerard, 'Continuity and Discontinuity between Jewish and Christian Liturgy', *Bijdragen, tijdschrift voor filosofie en theologie* 54 (1993), pp. 72-83.

Rowland, Christopher, 'The Visions of God in Apocalyptic Literature', *JSJ* 10 (1979), pp. 137-54.

—*The Open Heaven: A Study of Apocalyptic in Judaism and Early Christianity* (London: SPCK, 1982. Reprinted Eugene, OR: Wipf & Stock, 2002).

Rowley, H.H., *The Relevance of Apocalyptic* (London: Lutterworth Press, 1944).

Ruden, Sarah, *Paul among the People: The Apostle Reinterpreted and Reimagined in His Own Time* (New York: Pantheon Books, 2010).

Runciman, Steven, *A History of the Crusades*. I. *The First Crusade and the Foundation of the Kingdom of Jerusalem* (Harmondsworth: Penguin, 1971).

Runia, David T., 'Philo and Origen: A Preliminary Survey', in *Origeniana Quinta: Papers of the 5th International Origen Congress* (ed. R.J. Daly; Leuven: Leuven University Press, 1992), pp. 333-39.

Russell, Stephen C., 'Abraham's Purchase of Ephron's Land in Anthropological Perspective', *Bib Int* 21 (2013), pp. 153-70.

Saint Augustine, *Augustine on Romans: Propositions from the Epistle to the Romans; Unfinished Commentary on the Epistle to the Romans* (text and translation by Paula Fredriksen Landes; TT, 23; Society of Biblical Literature; Chico, CA: Scholars Press, 1982).

—*Confessions* (trans. Henry Chadwick; Oxford: Oxford University Press, 1991).

—*The Political Writings of St. Augustine* (ed. Henry Paolucci; Washington, DC: Regnery Publishing, 1996).

—*The City of God* (trans. Henry Bettenson; London: Penguin, 2003).

Saint John Chrysostom: Discourses against Judaizing Christians, in *The Fathers of the Church: A New Translation* 68 (trans. Paul W. Harkins; Washington, DC: The Catholic University of America Press, 1979).

Sampley, J. Paul, 'Romans in a Different Light: A Response to Robert Jewett', in *Pauline Theology*, vol. III (ed. David Hay and E. Elizabeth Johnson; Minneapolis: Fortress Press, 1995), pp. 109-29.

Sanday, William, and Arthur C. Headlam, *A Critial and Exegetical Commentary on the Epistle to the Romans* (Edinburgh: T. & T. Clark, 5th edn, 1992).

Sanders, E.P., *Paul and Palestinian Judaism: A Comparison of Patterns of Religion* (Minneapolis: Fortress Press, 1979).

—*Paul, the Law and the Jewish People* (Minneapolis: Fortress Press, 1983).

Sandnes, Karl Olav, 'Abraham, the friend of God, in Rom 5', *ZNW* 99 (2008), pp. 124-28.

Sarna, Nahum, *The JPS Torah Commentary on Genesis* (Philadelphia: The Jewish Publication Society, 1989).

Scheck, Thomas P., *Origen and the History of Justification: The Legacy of Origen's Commentary on Romans* (Notre Dame: University of Notre Dame Press, 2008).

Schell, Jonathan, *The Fate of the Earth* (London: Picador, 1982).

Schellenberg, Ryan S., 'Does Paul Call Adam a "Type of Christ"? An Exegetical Note on Romans 5,14', *ZNW* 105 (2014), pp. 53-61.

Schille, Gottfried, 'Die Liebe Gottes in Christus: Beobachtungen zu Rm 8.31-39', *ZNW* 59 (1968), pp. 230-44.

Schmitt, Carl, *The Nomos of the Earth in the International Law of the Jus Publicum Europaeum* (trans. G.L. Ulmen; New York: Telos, 2003).

—*Political Theology: Four Chapters on the Concept of Sovereignty* (trans. George Schwab; Chicago: University of Chicago Press, 2005).

—*The Concept of the Political: Expanded Edition* (trans. G. Schwab; Chicago: University of Chicago Press, 2007).

—*The Leviathan in the State Theory of Thomas Hobbes: Meaning and Failure of a Political Symbol* (trans. George Schwab and Erna Hilfstein; Chicago: University of Chicago Press, 2008).

Schnelle, Udo, *Apostle Paul: His Life and Theology* (trans. M. Eugene Boring; Grand Rapids: Baker Academic, 2005).

Schottroff, Luise, 'Die Schreckensherrschaft der Sünde und die Befreiung durch Christus nach dem Römerbrief des Paulus', *EvTh* 39 (1979), pp. 497-510.

Schweitzer, Albert, *The Mysticism of Paul the Apostle* (trans. William Montgomery; Baltimore: Johns Hopkins University Press, 1998; orig. London: A. & C. Black, 1931).

Scott, James C., *Domination and the Arts of Resistance: Hidden Transcripts* (New Haven: Yale University Press, 1990).

Seabrook, John, 'Sowing for Apocalypse: The Quest for a Global Seed Bank', *The New Yorker*, August 27, 2007.

Seneca, *Apocolocyntosis Divi Claudii Apocolocyntosis* (trans. W.H.D. Rouse (1920), http.//www.gutenberg.org/cache/epub/10001/pg10001.txt

Service, Robert F., 'Seed-Sterilizing "Terminator Technology" Sows Discord', *Science* 282 (1998), pp. 850-51.

Shi, Yuanka, and Frank B. Hu, 'The Global Implications of Diabetes and Cancer', *Lancet* 383 (2014), p. 1947.

Shifman, Arie, '"A Scent" of the Spirit: Exegesis of an Enigmatic Verse (Isaiah 11:3)', *JBL* 131 (2012), pp. 241-49.

Shiva, Vandana, *Biopiracy: The Plunder of Nature and Knowledge* (Boston: South End Press, 1997).

Shnider, Steven, 'Psalm XVIII: Theophany, Epiphany, Empowerment', *VT* 56 (2006), pp. 386-98.

Shogren, Gary Steven, '"Is the Kingdom of God about Eating and Drinking or Isn't It?" (Romans 14.17)', *NovT* 42 (2000), pp. 238-56.

Shum, Shiu-Lun, *Paul's Use of Isaiah in Romans* (WUNT; Tübingen: Mohr Siebeck, 2002).

Sigal, Philp, 'A Prolegomenon to Paul's Judaic Thought: The Death of Jesus and the Akedah', *Proceedings* 4 (1984), pp. 222-36.

Silber, John, *Kant's Ethics: The Good, Freedom, and the Will* (Boston and Berlin: W. de Gruyter, 2012).

Singer, Isaac Bashevis, 'The Slaughterer', in *The Collected Stories of Isaac Bashevis Singer* (trans. Mirra Ginsburg; New York: Farrar, Straus, and Giroux, 1996), pp. 207-16.

Skarsaune, Oskar, 'The Development of Scriptural Interpretation in the Second and Third Centuries—except Clement and Origen', in *Hebrew Bible/Old Testament:*

The History of Its Interpretation, vol 1.1, *From the Beginnings to the Middle Ages (Until 1300)* (ed. Magne Sæbø; Göttingen: Vandenhoeck & Ruprecht, 1996), pp. 373-442.
Skehan, Patrick W., 'Structure of the Song of Moses in Deuteronomy (Deut 32:1-43)', *CBQ* 13 (1951), pp. 153-63.
Skinner, John, *The Book of the Prophet Isaiah 40–66: With Introduction and Notes* (Cambridge: Cambridge University Press, 1898).
Smiles, Vincent M., 'The Concept of 'Zeal' in Second-Temple Judaism and Paul's Critique of It in Romans 10:2', *CBQ* 64 (2002), pp. 282-99.
Smith, G., *Isaiah 40–66* (Nashville, TN: Broadman & Holman, 2009).
Smyth, Herbert Weir, *Greek Grammar* (Cambridge, MA: Harvard University Press, 1966).
Snyman, A.H., 'Style and Rhetorical Situation of Romans 8.31-39', *NTS* 34 (1988), pp. 218-31.
Sourcewatch, 'Roundup Ready Crops', at www.sourcewatch.org/index.php/Roundup_Ready_Crops.
Speiser, E.A., *Genesis: Introduction, Translation, and Notes* (AB; New Haven: Yale University Press, 2008).
Speiser, Ephraim A., *Genesis* (AB; Garden City, NY: Doubleday, 1964).
Spitaler, Peter, 'Analogical Reasoning in Romans 7.2-4: A Woman and the Believers in Rome', *JBL* 125 (2006), pp. 715-47.
Staples, Jason A., 'What Do the Gentiles Have to Do with "All Israel"? A Fresh Look at Romans 11:25-27', *JBL* 130 (2011), pp. 371-90.
Stegemann, Ekkehard W., 'Coexistence and Transformation: Reading the Politics of Identity in Romans in an Imperial Context', in *Reading Paul in Context: Explorations in Identity Formation: Essays in Honour of William S. Campbell* (ed. Kathy Ehrensberger and J. Brian Tucker; London: T. & T. Clark, 2010), pp. 3-23.
Steinfeld, Henning, FAO's Livestock Information and Policy Report; http.//www.fao.org/newsroom/en/News/2006/1000448/index.html.
Stendahl, Krister, 'The Apostle Paul and the Introspective Conscience of the West', *HTR* 56 (1963), pp. 199-215.
—*Paul among Jews and Gentiles, and Other Essays* (Philadelphia: Fortress Press, 1976).
Stern, Menahem, 'The Jewish Diaspora in the Second Temple Era', in *A History of the Jewish People* (ed. H.H. Ben-Sasson; Cambridge, MA: Harvard University Press, 1976), pp. 277-82.
Stjerna, Kirsi, *Women and the Reformation* (Hoboken, NJ: Wiley-Blackwell, 2009).
Stone, I.F., *The Trial of Socrates* (New York: Anchor Books, 1989).
Stone, Ronald H., *John Wesley's Life and Ethics* (Nashville: Abingdon Press, 2001).
Stowers, Stanley K., *The Diatribe and Paul's Letter to the Romans* (SBLDS, 57; Chico, CA: Scholars Press, 1981).
—*A Rereading of Romans: Justice, Jews, and Gentiles* (New Haven: Yale University Press, 1994).
—'Romans 7:7-25 as a Speech-in-Character (προσωποποιία)', in *Paul in his Hellenistic Context* (ed. T. Engberg-Pedersen; Minneapolis: Fortress Press, 1995), pp. 180-202.
—'Paul's Four Discourses about Sin', in *Celebrating Paul: Festschrift in Honor of Jerome Murphy-O'Connor and Joseph A. Fitzmeyer* (ed. Peter Spitaler; Washington, DC: Catholic Biblical Association of America, 2011), pp. 100-27.

Strand, Kenneth A., 'The Sabbath Fast in Early Christianity', in *The Early Christian Sabbath* (ed. Kenneth A. Strand; Worthington, OH: Ann Arbor Publishers, 1976), pp. 9-15.

Strange, Marty, 'The Economic Structure of Sustainable Agriculture', in *Meeting the Expectations of the Land: Essays in Sustainable Agriculture and Stewardship* (ed. Wes Jackson, Wendell Berry and Bruce Colman; San Francisco: North Point Press, 1984), pp. 115-25.

Strombert, Jacob, 'The "Root of Jesse" in Isaiah 11:10: Postexilic Judah, or Postexilic Davidic King?', *JBL* 127 (2008), pp. 655-69.

Strong, Tracy B., 'The Sovereign and the Exception: Carl Schmitt, Politics, Theology, and Leadership', in Carl Schmitt, *Political Theology: Four Chapters on the Concept of Sovereignty* (trans. George Schwab; Chicago: University of Chicago Press, 2005), pp. vii-xxxvi.

Stuart, Moses, *A Commentary on the Epistle to the Romans* (New York: Wiley and Halsted, 4th edn, 1859).

Stump, Eleonore, 'Augustine on Free Will', in *The Cambridge Companion to Augustine* (ed. Eleonore Stump and Norman Kretzmann; New York: Cambridge University Press, 2001), pp. 134-47.

Suetonius, 'Claudius', in *Lives of the Caesars* (trans. Catharine Edwards; Oxford: Oxford University Press, 2000).

Swenson, Kristin, 'Care and Keeping East of Eden: Gen 4:1-16 in Light of Gen 2–3', *Int* 60 (2006), pp. 373-84.

Taubes, Jacob, *The Political Theology of Paul* (trans. Dana Hollander; Stanford, CA: Stanford University Press, 2004).

Taylor, Barbara Brown, 'Sabbath Resistance', *Christian Century* 122 (2005), p. 35.

Taylor, T.M., '"Abba, Father" and Baptism', *SJT* 11 (1958), pp. 62-71.

Tcherikover, Victor, *Hellenistic Civilization and the Jews* (Peabody, MA: Hendrickson, 1999).

Terrien, Samuel, *The Elusive Presence: Toward A New Biblical Theology* (New York: Harper & Row, 1978. Reprinted Eugene, OR: Wipf and Stock, 2000).

Thayer, Joseph H., *Thayer's Greek-English Lexicon of the New Testament*. Electronic edition generated and owned by International Bible Translators (IBT), Inc., 1998–2000.

Thompson, Marianne Meye, '"*Mercy upon All*": God as Father in the Epistle to the Romans', in *Romans and the People of God: Essays in Honor of Gordon D. Fee* (ed. Sven K. Soderlund and N.T. Wright; Grand Rapids: Eerdmans, 1999), pp. 203-16.

Thorsteinsson, Runar M., *Paul's Interlocutor in Romans 2: Function and Identity in the Context of Ancient Epistolography* (CBNTS; Stockholm: Almquist & Wiksell, 2003).

Ticciati, Susannah, 'The Nondivisive Difference of Election: A Reading of Romans 9–11', *JTI* 6 (2012), pp. 257-77.

Tilling, Chris (ed.), *Beyond Old and New Perspectives in Paul: Reflections on the Work of Douglas Campbell* (Eugene, OR: Cascade Books, 2014).

Tisdale, Leonora Tubbs, 'Romans 8.31-39', *Int* 42 (1988), pp. 68-72.

Tomkins, Stephen, *John Wesley: A Biography* (Oxford: Lion Publishing, 2003).

Toney, Carl L., *Paul's Inclusive Ethic: Resolving Community Conflicts and Promoting Mission in Romans 14–15* (WUNT; Tübingen: Mohr Siebeck, 2008).

Tonstad, Linn Marie, 'Trinity, Hierarchy, and Difference: Mapping the Christian Imaginary', PhD Dissertation, Yale University, 2009.

Tonstad, Sigve K., '*πίστις Χριστοῦ*: Reading Paul in A New Paradigm', *AUSS* 40 (2002), pp. 37-59.

—'Theodicy and the Theme of Cosmic Conflict in the Early Church', *AUSS* 42 (2004), pp. 169-202.

—'The Revisionary Potential of "Abba, Father" in the Letters of Paul', *AUSS* 45 (2007), pp. 5-18.

—'The Restrainer Removed: A Truly Alarming Thought (2 Thess. 2:1-12)', *HBT* 29 (2007), pp. 133-51.

—'Creation Groaning in Labor Pains', in *Exploring Ecological Hermeneutics* (ed. Norman C. Habel and Peter Trudinger; Atlanta: Society of Biblical Literature, 2008), pp. 141-49.

—*The Lost Meaning of the Seventh Day* (Berrien Springs, MI: Andrews University Press, 2009).

—'Inscribing Abraham: Apocalyptic, the Akedah, and "Abba! Father!" in Galatians', in *Galatians as Examined by Diverse Academics* (ed. Heerak Christian Kim; Newark, NJ: Hermit Kingdom Press, 2013), pp. 15-27.

—*God of Sense and Traditions of Non-Sense*, chapter entitled 'Lost Sense in the Letters of Paul' (Eugene, OR: Wipf & Stock, forthcoming).

Torjesen, Karen Jo, *Hermeneutical Procedure and Theological Method in Origen's Exegesis* (Berlin: W. de Gruyter, 1986).

Torrance, Thomas F., *Karl Barth, Biblical and Evangelical Theologian* (Edinburgh: T. & T. Clark, 1990).

Towner, Philip H., 'Romans 13:1-7 and Paul's Missiological Perspective: A Call to Political Quietism or Transformation?', in *Romans and the People of God: Essays in Honor of Gordon Fee on the Occasion of His 65th Birthday* (ed. Barbara Aland; Grand Rapids: Eerdmans, 1999), pp. 149-69.

Townsley, Jeramy, 'Paul, the Goddess Religions and Queer Sects: Romans 1:23-28', *JBL* 130 (2011), pp. 707-28.

Travis, Steven H., *Christ and the Judgement of God: The Limits of Divine Retribution in New Testament Thought* (Peabody, MA: Hendrickson, 2008).

Trible, Phyllis, *God and the Rhetoric of Sexuality* (OBT; Philadelphia: Fortress Press, 1978).

Tsui, Teresa Kuo-Yu, 'Reconsidering Pauline Juxtaposition of Indicative and Imperative (Romans 6:1-14) in Light of Pauline Apocalypticism', *CBQ* 75 (2013), pp. 297-314.

Turner, Marie. 'God's Design: The Death of Creation? An Ecojustice Reading of Romans 8.18-30 in the Light of Wisdom 1–2', in *The Earth Story in Wisdom Traditions* (ed. Norman C. Habel and Shirley Wurst; Sheffield: Sheffield Academic, 2001), pp. 168-78.

van der Horst, Pieter W., '"Only Then Will All Israel Be Saved": A Short Note on the Meaning of καὶ οὕτως in Romans 11:26', *JBL* 119 (2000), pp. 521-25.

van der Kooij, Arie, 'The Ending of the Song of Moses: On the Pre-Masoretic Version of Deut. 32.4', in *Studies in Deuteronomy: In Honour of C.J. Labuschagne on the Occasion of His 65th Birthday* (eds. F. Garcia Martinez, A. Hilhorst, J.T.A.G.M. van Rutten and A.S. van der Woude; Leiden: E.J. Brill, 1994), pp. 93-100.

—'"The Servant of the Lord": A Particular Group of Jews in Egypt According to the Old Greek of Isaiah', in *Studies in the Book of Isaiah: Festschrift in Honor of*

Willem A.M. Beuken (ed. J. van Ruiten and M. Vervenne; Leuven: Leuven University Press, 1997), pp. 390-96.

von Bendemann, Reinhard, '"Zorn" und "Zorn Gottes" im Römerbrief', in *Paulus und Johannes: Exegetische Studien zur paulinischen und johanneischen Theologie und Literatur* (ed. Dieter Sänger and Ulrich Mell; Tübingen: Mohr Siebeck, 2006), pp. 179-215.

Verbrugge, Verlyn D., 'The Grammatical Internal Evidence for 'EXOMEN in Romans 5.1', *JETS* 54 (2011), pp. 559-72.

Vickers, Brian, 'Grammar and Theology in the Interpretation of Rom 5.12', *TrinJ* 27 (2006), pp. 277-88.

Vogels, Walter, 'Abraham et l'offrande de la terre (Gn 13)', *SR* 4 (1974–75), pp. 51-57.

—'L'Égypte mon people—L'Universalisme d'Is 19,16-25', *Bib* 57 (1976), pp. 494-514.

Vögtle, Anton, *Die Tugend- und Lasterkataloge im Neuen Testament* (NTAbh; Münster: Verlag der Aschendorffschen Verlagsbuchhandlung, 1936).

Wagner, J. Ross, 'The Christ, Servant of Jew and Gentile: A Fresh Approach to Romans 15:8-9', *JBL* 116 (1997), pp. 473-85.

—'The Heralds of Isaiah and the Mission of Paul', in *Jesus and the Suffering Servant: Isaiah 53 and Christian Origins* (ed. W.H. Bellinger and W.R. Farmer; Harrisburg, PA: Trinity Press International, 1998), pp. 193-222.

—*Heralds of the Good News; Isaiah and Paul in Concert in the Letter to the Romans* (Leiden: Brill, 2003).

Wallace-Hadrill, A., 'The Golden Age and Sin in Augustan Ideology', *Past & Present* 95 (1982), pp. 19-36.

Wallis, Ian G., *The Faith of Jesus Christ in Early Christian Traditions* (SNTSMS, 84; Cambridge: Cambridge University Press, 1995).

Walsh, Jerome, 'Genesis 2.4b–3.24: A Synchronic Approach', *JBL* 96 (1977), pp. 161-77.

Wasserman, Emma, 'The Death of the Soul in Romans 7: Revisiting Paul's Anthropology in Light of Hellenistic Moral Psychology', *JBL* 126 (2007), pp. 793-816.

—'Paul among the Philosophers: The Case of Sin in Romans 6–8', *JSNT* 30 (2008), pp. 387-415.

Watson, Francis, *Paul and the Hermeneutics of Faith* (London: T. & T. Clark, 2004).

Webster, John, 'Introducing Barth', in *The Cambridge Companion to Karl Barth* (ed. John Webster; Cambridge: Cambridge University Press, 2000), pp. 1-16.

Weima, Jeffrey A.D., 'The Reason for Romans: The Evidence of Its Epistolary Framework (1:1-15; 15:14–16:27)', *RevExp* 100 (2003), pp. 17-33.

Welborn, L.L., '"Extraction from the Mortal Site": Badiou on the Resurrection in Paul', *NTS* 55 (2009), pp. 295-314.

Wengst, Klaus, *Pax Romana and the Peace of Jesus Christ* (trans. John Bowden; London: SCM Press, 1987).

Wenham, G.J., *Genesis 1–15* (WBC; Dallas: Word, 1998).

Wesley, John, *A Survey of the Wisdom of God in Creation: A Compendium of Natural Philosophy* (London: J. Paramore Upper Moorfields, 4th edn, 1784).

—*Primitive Physic: Or, An Easy and Natural Method of Curing Most Diseases* (London: 24th edn, 1792).

—*Sermons on Several Occasions* (London: Epworth Press, 1944).

Westerholm, Stephen, *Perspectives Old and New on Paul: The 'Lutheran' Paul and His Critics* (Grand Rapids: Eerdmans, 2004).

Westermann, Claus, *Isaiah 40–66* (trans. David M.G. Stalker; OTL; London: SCM Press, 1969).

—'Creation and History in the Old Testament', in *The Gospel and Human Destiny* (trans. Donald Dutton; ed. Vilmos Vajta; Minneapolis: Augsburg, 1971), pp. 11-38.

—*Genesis 1–11* (trans. John J. Scullion; London: SPCK, 1984).

—*Genesis 12–36* (trans. John J. Scullion; Minneapolis: Augsburg, 1985).

White, Jr, Lynn, 'The Historical Roots of Our Ecologic Crisis', *Science* 155 (1967), pp. 1203-207.

Whiteley, D.E.H., *The Theology of St. Paul* (Oxford: Basil Blackwell, 1974).

Wildberger, Hans, *Jesaja 13–27* (BKAT, 10/2; Neukirchen–Vluyn: Neukirchener Verlag, 1978).

—*Isaiah 1–12* (trans. Thomas H. Trapp; CC; Minneapolis: Fortress Press, 1991).

Wilder, William N., 'Illumination and Investiture: The Royal Significance of the Tree of Wisdom in Genesis 3', *WTJ* 68 (2006), pp. 51-69.

Wilken, Robert L., *John Chrysostom and the Jews: Rhetoric and Reality in the Late 4th Century* (Berkeley: University of California Press, 1983).

Wilckens, U., *Der Brief an die Römer* (3 vols.; EKKNT; Neukirchen: Neukirchener Verlag, 1978).

Williams, Sam K., 'The "Righteousness of God" in Romans', *JBL* 99 (1980), pp. 241-90.

Willimon, William H., 'Lord of the Sabbath', *Christian Century* 108 (1991), p. 515.

Wilson, Emily, *The Death of Socrates* (Cambridge, MA: Harvard University Press, 2007).

Wilson, J., '"In That Day": From Text to Sermon on Isaiah 19,23-25', *Int* 21 (1967), pp. 66-86.

Windisch, Hans, *Der zweite Korintherbrief* (Göttingen: Vandenhoeck & Ruprecht, 1924).

Wink, Walter, *Naming the Powers: The Language of Power in the New Testament* (Philadelphia: Fortress Press, 1984).

—*Unmasking the Powers: The Invisible Forces that Determine Human Existence* (Philadelphia: Fortress Press, 1986).

Winter, Bruce, *Philo and Paul among the Sophists: Alexandrian and Corinthian Responses to a Julio-Claudian Movement* (Grand Rapids: Eerdmans, 2nd edn, 2002).

Wirzba, Norman, 'Placing the Soul: An Agrarian Philosophical Principle', in *The Essential Agrarian Reader: The Future of Culture, Community, and the Land* (ed. Norman Wirzba; Washington, DC: Shoemaker & Hoard, 2003), pp. 80-97.

—*Living the Sabbath: Discovering the Rhythms of Rest and Delight* (Grand Rapids: Brazos Press, 2006).

Wöhrle, Jakob, '*dominium terrae*: Exegetische un religionsgeschichtliche Überlegungen zum Herrschaftsauftrag in Gen 1,26-28', *ZAW* 121 (2009), pp. 171-88.

Wolter, Michael, *Rechtfertigung and zukünftiges Heil: Undersuchungen zu Röm 5,1-11* (BZNW, 43; Berlin: W. de Gruyter, 1978).

Wright, N.T., *The Letter to the Romans*, in the *New Interpreter's Bible* (ed. Leander Keck; Nashville: Abingdon Press, 1994–2004).

—*Christian Origins and the Question of God*. III. *The Resurrection of the Son of God* (Minneapolis: Fortress Press, 2003).

—*Surprised by Hope* (London: SPCK, 2007).

—*Paul and the Faithfulness of God* (2 vols.; London: SPCK, 2013).

—'Paul and Caesar: A New Reading of Romans', in *Pauline Perspectives: Essays on Paul, 1978–2013* (ed. N.T. Wright; Minneapolis: Fortress Press, 2013), pp. 237-54.

Xu, Y., L. Wang, J. He *et al.*, 'Prevalence and Control of Diabetes in Chinese Adults', *JAMA* 310 (2013), pp. 948-99.

Yang, Dawen, Shinjiro Kanae, Tajkan Oki, Toshio Koike and Katumi Musia, 'Global potential soil erosion with reference to land use and climate changes', *Hydrological Processes* 17 (2003), pp. 2913-28.

Young, Brad H., *Paul the Jewish Theologian: A Pharisee among Christians, Jews, and Gentiles* (Peabody, MA: Hendrickson, 1997).

Young, Stephen L., 'Romans 1.1-5 and Paul's Christological Use of Hab. 2.4 in Rom. 1.17: An Underutilized Consideration in the Debate', *JSNT* 34 (2012), pp. 277-85.

Zanker, Paul, 'The Power of Images', in *Paul and Empire: Religion and Power in Roman Imperial Society* (ed. Richard Horsley; Harrisburg, PA: Trinity Press International, 1997), pp. 72-86.

Zerwick, Maximilian, *Biblical Greek: Illustrated by Examples* (trans. Joseph Smith; Rome: Biblical Institute Press, 1963).

Zhang, Wenxi, *Paul Among Jews: A Study of the Meaning and Significance of Paul's Inaugural Speech in the Synagogue of Antioch* (Eugene, OR: Wipf & Stock, 2011).

Zoccali, Christopher, '"And so all Israel will be saved": Competing Interpretations of Romans 11.26 in Pauline Scholarship', *JSNT* 30 (2008), pp. 289-318.

Indexes

Index of References

Old Testament/Hebrew Bible

New Testament

Other Ancient References

Index of Authors

CPSIA information can be obtained
at www.ICGtesting.com
Printed in the USA
LVOW04*0639090216
474222LV00010B/110/P

9 781910 92802